LEADING LADY

LEADING LADY

The World and Theatre of Katharine Cornell

§ ℓ

TAD MOSEL
with GERTRUDE MACY

with a Foreword by Martha Graham

AN ATLANTIC MONTHLY PRESS BOOK

LITTLE, BROWN AND COMPANY   BOSTON   TORONTO

FIRST EDITION

T11 / 78

The lines from Rose Macauley's "Many Sisters to Many
Brothers" appeared in POEMS OF TO-DAY: An Anthology
published for the English Association by Sidgwick & Jackson, Ltd., reprinted by permission.

The lyrics by Cole Porter are from "Let's Face It." Copy-
right © 1941 by Chappell & Co., Inc. Copyright renewed.
International Copyright Secured ALL RIGHTS RESERVED/
Used by permission.

ATLANTIC—LITTLE, BROWN BOOKS
ARE PUBLISHED BY
LITTLE, BROWN AND COMPANY
IN ASSOCIATION WITH
THE ATLANTIC MONTHLY PRESS

Library of Congress Cataloging in Publication Data

Mosel, Tad.
Leading Lady: the world and theatre of Katharine Cornell.

"An Atlantic Monthly Press book."
Includes index.
1. Cornell, Katharine, 1893–1974. 2. Actors—
United States — Biography. I. Macy, Gertrude,
joint author. II. Title.
PN2287.C62M6   792'.028'0924 [B]   78–16291
ISBN 0–316–58537–8

Designed by Susan Windheim

Published simultaneously in Canada
by Little, Brown & Company (Canada) Limited

PRINTED IN THE UNITED STATES OF AMERICA

Foreword

by MARTHA GRAHAM

This is the biography of a lady of many names — Katharine Cornell, the actress, Mrs. Guthrie McClintic, socially, Katharine to many on Martha's Vineyard, Kit to those of us who worked with her and who loved her.

The special name to me is Kit — it has a gallantry, a daring about it; and as such it rests in many hearts today. Even to us so privileged to work with and to know her as a friend, she had a warm aloofness about her as though she were a Head of State. And to those who could count her as a friend there was found a deep vulnerability about her that made her a very special kind of friend.

The first time that I saw Katharine Cornell the actress, long before I knew Kit the person, I was overwhelmed by her theatricality, her beauty, and her innocence.

Beauty is a thing apart. The face is like an interior landscape. It shows a state of grace achieved by the elements of one's own life; theatricality and innocence are an inseparable unit to me, and so they were with Kit.

I was privileged to behold Kit in many roles, some on stage, some off stage. One unforgettable moment was when she held a meeting of her friends in her home on Beekman Place; the meeting was held for me. It was an attempt to interest people in providing time for me in which to work; as such, it was an appeal for funds. Kit had never appeared in such a role. And she, who lived in a world of words, was terrified of speeches. She stood behind a high wing backed chair, clutching it for support. Gertrude Macy spoke to Kit's husband Guthrie Mc-Clintic; "She is so white I'm afraid she will faint." To which Guthrie the fine director said: "Let her alone, she looks beautiful."

After a time I had the opportunity to offer Kit a gift in return. She was preparing for a performance as Juliet when the call came; I was truly needed. The balcony scene was the problem. It was a matter of the nightgown; the one provided was nondescript and devoid of meaning. A new costume had to be devised quickly. I cannot sew in the traditional sense but with the aid of many safety pins and my ability to drape, sometimes a costume emerges. Juliet's balcony scene demands a special gown, an imagined one, such as might be worn on a soft Italian night; a garment of promise and of adventure. The costume had to compete with a formidable orchestration, a moon, a nightingale, a lark, an image of love, and Shakespeare's lines. Kit was pleased; the costume served.

At still another moment a word of despair reached me from Boston; this time the image of Egypt had to be evoked. A seamstress and I arrived at the Ritz with bolts of fabric, a sewing machine, and millions of pins. It perhaps was not Egypt we achieved, but the costume made Kit feel like a Queen of Egypt and so that is what she became for the public. A woman emerged who perhaps never existed on land or sea, but a memory of a forgotten image evoking a goddess. This was theatricality in its truest sense, made all the more incredible because of Kit's painful shyness and her innate innocence.

One evening Kit spoke of making an exit: "Martha, when you exit take everything with you, even the grand piano if there is one on the stage." That is what Katharine Cornell could do, strip a stage leaving the audience a little forlorn and eager for her return. I feel that now, that Kit has left this stage on which we are still playing, leaving us forlorn, she has this once left something even her exit cannot take away: the innocence of greatness.

Martha Graham
22 January 1978

Contents

Foreword by Martha Graham   v

PART ONE: Buffalo Girl (1893–1916)

1. The Cornells of Delaware Avenue (1893)   3
2. The Cornells of Mariner Street (1893–1909)   18
3. "Hurry and Grow Up . . . !" (1900–1911)   32
4. Stage Wait (1911–1916)   49

PART TWO: Katherine (sic) (1916–1920)

5. Fifth Business (1916–1918)   63
6. Marcelle and Jo (1919)   83
7. Guth (1893–1919)   100
8. Whispering (1920)   113

PART THREE: Mrs. McClintic (1920–1925)

9. *Nice People* on Broadway — and Not So Nice (1921)   127
10. Sydney (1921)   140
11. Passing Plays (1922–1925)   159
12. "From the Cradle of the Human Race" (1924–1925)   179

PART FOUR: *Kath Cornell (1925–1930)*

13. Iris of the Golden Slum (1925–1926)   191
14. Gert (1926–1928)   211
15. The Last of the Tarnished Lady (1928–1930)   222
16. Love and Money (1930)   241

PART FIVE: *Cornelia (1930–1934)*

17. *The Barretts* (1930–1931)   257
18. Disciplined Fury (1931–1932)   274
19. Haus Hirth (1932–1933)   295
20. The Long Tour (1933–1934)   318

PART SIX: *Miss Cornell (1934–1936)*

21. Wanton Juliet (1934–1935)   345
22. Smiling Joan (1935–1936)   365
23. Magnetic Influence (1936)   377

PART SEVEN: *First Lady (1936–1945)*

24. Degrees of Fame (1936–1937)   397
25. Time for Comedy (1937–1939)   412
26. "Kit Cornell Is Shellin' Peas . . . !" (1939–1944) 439
27. The Barracks of Wimpole Street (1944–1945)   456

PART EIGHT: *Cornell (1945–1974)*

28. A Nice Lady from Buffalo (1945–1960)   471
29. "I'm the Captain!" (1945–1961)   495
30. Finishing Out the Week (1961–1974)   513

List of Illustrations

1. Katharine Cornell's mother   10
2. Katharine Cornell in costume for amateur performance   26
3. As Jo in *Little Women*   94
4. As Sydney Fairfield in *A Bill of Divorcement*   141
5. As Mary Fitton in *Will Shakespeare*   164
6. In *The Outsider*   172
7. As Iris March in *The Green Hat*   192
8. With her father at a McClintic opening   208
9. Guthrie McClintic and Katharine Cornell in 1926   208
10. As Ellen Olenska in *The Age of Innocence*   223
11. As Madeleine Cary in *Dishonored Lady*   235
12. With Brian Aherne in *The Barretts of Wimpole Street*   258
13. In the garden of Beekman Place   267
14. As Lucrece   309
15. With James Rennie in *Alien Corn*   314
16. With Basil Rathbone in *Romeo and Juliet*   347
17. Curtain call of last performance of *Romeo and Juliet*   360
18. Katharine Cornell at Garmisch   360
19. As Saint Joan   373

20. With Tyrone Power and Joseph Holland in *Saint Joan*   373

21. With Laurence Olivier in *No Time for Comedy*   425

22. In *The Doctor's Dilemma*, with Raymond Massey   440

23. With Alexander Woollcott and "Illo"   440

24. Two Views of *Candida*   446

    a. Burgess Meredith as Marchbanks   446

    b. Raymond Massey as Morell   446

25. In *The Three Sisters*   449

26. On wartime tour, Italy   459

27. Brian Aherne and Katharine Cornell with busts of the
    Brownings   459

28. In *Antigone*   477

29. As Cleopatra   479

30. At a Laurence Olivier party   496

31. Last production: as Mrs. Patrick Campbell in *Dear Liar*   508

I

Buffalo Girl (1893-1916)

1

The Cornells
of Delaware Avenue (1893)

ON NEW YEAR'S DAY Miss Lydia Cornell of Delaware Avenue, Buffalo, New York, started a diary as if to make it quite clear to herself that the year 1893 was to be the start of a new life. She was twenty-five, just recovering from a broken engagement to a local physician. She writes that she is very low in her mind. A few days later she has had such a small touching letter from her doctor, but she has given it a cold hard answer and he will never know the heartbreak it has caused her.

And we will never know what Dr. DeWitt H. Sherman did to warrant a cold hard answer. He himself has left only his calling card, perhaps surrendered hopefully to a housemaid at the front door of the big house on Delaware Avenue and then later put out of sight, but saved, jammed between the pages of a family scrapbook where it has survived. It gives his address as 666 Main Street, Buffalo. This humble summation of his existence is more tantalizing than a volume of intimate revelations. One holds the card and wonders if Dr. Sherman's very address could have been his undoing. Life was circumscribed in 1893, and after a romantic, even headlong, declaration of love, could the words "Main Street" have eventually proved him ineligible to be Lydia's husband?

Because 484 Delaware Avenue was not only the Cornells' address, it was their credential. According to the rules of social reporting in the Buffalo press, they and their neighbors did not live on Delaware Avenue, they were *of* Delaware Avenue. Furthermore, the Cornells had been among its first residents and may even have helped set its tone of high respectability.

In the 1850s Samuel Garretson Cornell came to Buffalo with his wife, the former Sarah Bates Douglass. Sarah's maternal grandfather was the famous Andrew Ellicott who was employed by President George Washington to survey the boundary of the Federal District of Columbia. He was a member of the survey that continued Mason and Dixon's line; he surveyed the boundary between the United States and Spain in Florida. He was the older brother of Joseph Ellicott, Sarah Cornell's granduncle, the man who platted the site of Buffalo in 1799, laying it out in salable lots.

Andrew Ellicott was also at one time vice-president of the American Philosophical Society in Philadelphia, and had a nodding acquaintance with the society's founder, Benjamin Franklin. In the later years of his life he taught mathematics at West Point, a post that he passed on to his son-in-law, David Bates Douglass, Sarah's father, who later occupied the academy's chair of civil and military engineering and subsequently held a position at the University of the City of New York and designed its principal building. From 1840 to 1844 he was president of Kenyon College in Gambier, Ohio. At his death in 1849, he was professor of mathematics at Hobart College, Geneva, New York, thirty miles east of Buffalo.

Sarah's husband was an energetic figure in the state's industrial development. He invented a process for making lead pipe, which a governmental institute in France deemed worthy of a distinguished medal. In the 1850s, armed with his citation, in French, Samuel Garretson Cornell built the Cornell Lead Works on Virginia Street and then invaded the nearby wilderness of Delaware Avenue, where he built a house. It was an imposing house, and other imposing houses followed, with stables behind and coachmen in white gloves and breeches driving victorias in the afternoon.

Both the lead works and the house were carried on by a son, Samuel Douglas Cornell, who disliked the inherited "Samuel" so much that he reduced it to an initial in his signature and refused to pass it on to either of his sons, naming the elder son Peter, born 1865, and the younger son after himself, minus the Samuel, born 1869. The name Douglas (or Douglass) appears frequently in the Cornell family. Since S. Douglas Cornell was a colonel in the New York State Guards and rather fancied being called Colonel, that is what he will be called here.

A third child, named Lydia Hadfield Cornell for her mother, was born between the two boys, in 1867. It was Lydia whose engagement to Dr. Sherman was terminated in December 1892.

Colonel S. Douglas Cornell conducted himself like a colonel, his wrath inspiring fear and acquiescence, and he came by it naturally. His grandfather, David Bates Douglass, was so strict and unpopular with the students at Kenyon College that he induced a kind of rebellion and followed through with so many instant dismissals for drinking and "grave infractions of decency" that the enrollment fell off alarmingly and he was dismissed as president of the college after only four years. It is quite possible that his grandson would find intolerable the thought of a Cornell of Delaware Avenue being married to a doctor from commercial Main Street and that the grandson's daughter would endure the heartbreak rather than stand up to her father, sending instead a cold hard answer to her lover's small touching letter.

But that would be a fantasy devised to coincide with a twentieth-century view of stern Victorian fathers and gentle lovesick daughters as they have been portrayed, movingly, in such plays as *The Barretts of Wimpole Street*. Actually, along with their autocratic dignity and accomplishment, the Cornells brought to Delaware Avenue an almost festive enjoyment of life and people, independence of spirit and a willingness to tolerate it in others, and above all, a redeeming earthiness.

The Colonel was a graduate, class of 1860, and later a trustee, of Hobart College, where his grandfather had taught mathematics. He was a member of Theta Delta Chi fraternity, and since the Hobart "charge" (as the chapters are called in that fraternity) only came into being in 1857, he must have been one of its founders. Fraternities were then what they are now, groups of young men who band together for conviviality, and in the annals of Theta Delta Chi, the Colonel is referred to affectionately as "our own Douglas Cornell." He was popular. He must have been likable. In Buffalo in the 1890s he may still have carried himself like a colonel, but it was well known that his military bearing was achieved with the help of a corset. He waxed his mustache and loved charity balls. Even when he was in his late sixties, women would desert their younger partners to dance with him. He loved dressing up for amateur theatricals. His autocracy seems to have sprung more from vanity than militancy.

Although he must have been deeply disappointed that neither of his sons chose to take his place in the lead works, he did not stop them when Peter chose to become a physician and Douglas an engineer. It is not really likely that he would raise that much fuss over Lydia's engagement — especially since in less than a year Peter, recently graduated from medical school at the University of Buffalo and now studying at the University of Berlin, Germany, would come home and settle on Mariner Street, an address no more fashionable than Main Street. In fact the Colonel, unless it was out of conscience, seems to have had sympathy for Lydia's low spirits at the beginning of 1893, taking her on a shopping tour to New York City for a few days in January.

A now elderly ex-resident of Buffalo who was a small child at the time vividly remembers her mother telling her that the handsome Dr. Sherman was the one who changed his mind and broke the engagement. This version of the story does not jibe with the tone of Lydia's diary, but it does show that whatever actually happened, the engagement was not secret and its termination was common knowledge to the point of being handed down from generation to generation as the only significant event in Lydia's life. Perhaps that is why the Colonel decided that a brief shopping trip to New York City was not healing enough and that what Lydia needed was an extended time away from Buffalo to forget, be forgotten, and let the whole thing blow over.

Early in February the Colonel and his wife and daughter set out from Buffalo on a railroad excursion trip to California by way of Mexico. Lydia and her mother had a stateroom at the end of the car, and the Colonel had a section. Peter and his new bride were in Berlin, and Douglas was at Rensselaer Polytechnic Institute at Troy, New York.

In her diary Lydia dutifully records the departure from Buffalo and the journey south through Louisville, Atlanta, and down to New Orleans, where they sported themselves at the Mardi Gras. Then on to Texas and down to Mexico, Mexico City, and then they are on their way back north, through Texas again to California where the diary ends.

But two-thirds of the way through the diary's perfectly ordinary one hundred days, Lydia makes an entry that has extraordinary interest; on March 10 she matter-of-factly records an event that was to give a joyful color to the rest of her life, to the lives of all the living Cornells, their children, and to the world. No newspaper clippings survive to commemorate it, no letters. She is its only chronicler.

It was a Friday, and as the train made its way north again from Mexico City Lydia wrote:

News tonight that Alice and Peter had a little daughter born the 16th of February. Felt very anxious for them all in Berlin.

The Barretts of Wimpole Street is an ironic title. By the time the play was written and produced in 1931, it didn't much matter where the Barretts had lived, who they were, or what they had done with their lives. For all their accomplishments, their successes, failures, their affluence, marriages, children, titles, and broken engagements, they survived only as the family of Elizabeth Barrett.

The child born on February 16, 1893, in Berlin, Germany, would grow up to become first a beautiful woman, then a beautiful actress. It would be thirty-eight years before she would assume the role of Elizabeth Barrett, making it her own but giving it to the world, and by then the Cornells of Delaware Avenue would be known as the family of Katharine Cornell.

With Lydia's journalistic exposition of who, what, when and where, it is surprising that she did not add why, discreetly legitimizing the birth by explaining that it was premature. But she probably did not think it necessary, for no baby born into the Cornell family after only seven months and eighteen days of marriage could, after all, be anything but premature.

The events leading up to and including the birth were as dramatic as any play in which Katharine Cornell would later appear and, seen with a little imagination, bore an actual resemblance to the plot line of one of them, George Bernard Shaw's *Candida*.

Peter Cortelyou Cornell and Alice Gardner Plimpton were married at high noon on June 28, 1892, which also happened to be Peter's twenty-seventh birthday. The Cornells were Episcopalian, but the Plimptons were Presbyterian, so the "brilliant wedding," as the *Buffalo Evening Express* described it, was solemnized at the First Presbyterian Church.

Peter Cornell was not small but was short, smoothly rounded at the corners, tightly contained in his skin like a sausage and bounding to get out. In his photographs he managed to look big and impressive, as if quite able to keep the world to his level, as indeed he was. Someone who knew him in later years said, "He always looked you straight in the neck-tie."

He was born to manage, out to win. The *Express* concludes its account of the wedding, "Immediately after the ceremony this afternoon, Dr. and Mrs. Cornell left on an eastern trip. Later they will sail for an extended stay in Europe." If Peter had a hand in the wording, it's a wonder it didn't read, "Later they will sail for Europe where Dr. Cornell will continue his medical studies at the University of Berlin," giving the news the importance of an announcement. But in a way that would have diminished the reader's impression. Married and nearing thirty, he was a little late to be crossing the ocean to go to school. "An extended stay in Europe" was provocative, grandly mysterious and in its vagueness, absolutely true.

Peter Cornell's history as a doctor does not indicate any burning dedication to medicine; as time went on, he developed an indifference to it, then apathy. There is no record of what he studied in Berlin, nor any evidence that it advanced him beyond the level he had achieved by graduating from the University of Buffalo, for he remained a general practitioner to the end of his doctoring days. He was not the kind of man to enjoy the concentration and solitary labors of medical study, although in practice he would be able to outdo all competitors in the social sense of making contacts and bringing in patients. He was the kind they would always call "Doc."

He went to Berlin to study because that was where every young doctor went if he could afford it. It was the prestigious thing to do; therefore he had to do it. It also gave him an admirable excuse to put off settling down to the tedious routine of day-to-day practice for at least another year.

Alice and Peter lived in a pension on Friedrich Strasse, a quarter probably not unlike Candida's corner of London, "blighted by a callously endured monotony of miles and miles of unlovely brick houses." It is unlikely that they set up housekeeping, but instead probably lived in one room or at most a sitting room and bedroom, taking their meals with the other guests in a common dining room.

At first glance it is not an ideal setting for a twenty-two-year-old bride from Buffalo, fresh from the honeymoon and already pregnant, in a day when pregnant women did not step out and mix freely but withdrew into seclusion. The further isolation imposed by an unintelligible language would abandon Alice to the oppressive gloom of a German winter, waiting in solitary silence for her husband to come home from school and for life, such as it was, to begin.

But that was not the case.

As a young man, George Davis Plimpton, Alice's father, could not find his niche in life. When he married Mary Augusta Tifft it was hoped his luck would improve, for his father-in-law, George Washington Tifft, was a progressive and successful man of property and affairs. He was among the founders of the International Bank of Buffalo and served as its first president until the financial crash of 1857. He became president of the New York and Lake Erie Railroad and an extensive builder and landowner. When he died, it was his son-in-law's chance to take over the family affairs and shine, but George Plimpton was not a good businessman, and the family considered it less expensive to let him travel abroad with his wife and children than to set him up in Buffalo businesses which he didn't know how to handle. His daughter Alice practically grew up in Europe. Her father died a year and a half before she married Peter.

As a young women she is said to have had "a shining and abiding faith in life, in people, in the goodness of human nature," but what shows in her photographs — in the funny teased fringe above her forehead, in what surely must have been called at the time "the aristocratic tilt of her head," in the set of her lips, pursed on the verge of a laugh or at least a smile — is a wonderful good humor, as if she will oblige by keeping her mouth shut for the click of the camera but can't wait to tell you an impertinent thought she has just had. The good humor is gone from photographs taken late in her life, or at least turned to gall, barely glimpsed in a handsome, stuffed, almost arrogant mistrust of what she sees.

But in late 1892 and early 1893 Alice must have been a joy to be with. Like Candida, she was "well built, well nourished, likely, one guesses, to become matronly later on, but now quite at her best, with the double charm of youth and motherhood." She was slim with dark hair and hazel eyes, and although only five feet five inches tall, she was at least as tall as Peter, even taller. Wives with short husbands tend to lean toward them, and it's pleasant to think she hugged him a lot. If she didn't always enjoy his expansiveness and pomposities, she could waft them away with sly asides tossed over his head.

Katharine Cornell's mother, Alice Plimpton Cornell.

Before her marriage Alice had rather shocked Buffalo with a display of small silver ashtrays she brought back from Europe. Display was all right in Buffalo, it was even encouraged. What shocked was the fact that the ashtrays had her name engraved on them. Ten years later another far more daring Alice, Theodore Roosevelt's daughter, had to climb out on the roof of the family's Oyster Bay house to smoke her cigarettes, but Alice Plimpton smoked hers in the living room, using her own silver personalized ashtrays.

Europe, even Germany, was where she had grown into a woman and discovered the fun of being alive, of smoking cigarettes and playing the mandolin. She wouldn't mind being taken back there by the man she adored. She wouldn't be shy about it. It would give her fulfillment as a wife to fall in with his plans wholeheartedly. She would feel valuable helping him with the language. She may have felt an ease with life in Europe that she never could or would feel in Buffalo.

If Alice's pregnancy prevented her from going out into the German winter, it did not stop her from making friends with the other guests at the pension, among them a young German officer, Baron von Bülow, presumably handsome, dashing in his uniform, romantic and, as it turned out, certainly dramatic. Alice was so young herself that he can't have been much younger, if at all, but because of her marital status and her pregnancy, he seems to have romanticized her into an older woman and made her his confidante. While Peter was off attending classes, Alice and her young officer would have earnest conversations together, even as the poet Marchbanks spent an intimate evening with Candida while the Reverend Morell was off speaking to the Guild of St. Matthew.

They may have sat together in the public rooms (but the nature of the young officer's confidences indicates something more private — although not improper) or maybe in Alice's sitting room where, as she poured out the tea, he poured out the details of his unhappy love for a lady who loved loving an officer but objected to the tours of duty that constantly snatched him from her side. It is said, as if to allay suspicions, that he once brought his lady to meet Alice, either seeking her approval or hoping she would use her powers of persuasion on his behalf. Some say Alice's sitting room provided a trysting place for the lovers.

A crisis arose in mid-February. The young officer was being called to duty out of the city, he would be away for an extended period of time, and his beloved flatly refused to wait for him. It was all over between them. He was crushed, defeated, desperate.

Or so the story goes. All that is known is what Alice herself chose to tell in later years. Add the interpretations and embellishments and niceties of those who took it from there, and the details become so fuzzy that it is possible, just possible, that what actually happened was something quite different. It is tempting to suggest that the young officer's interest was in Alice herself, that his lady came for a confrontation, that Alice's hand was finally forced in mid-February and she had to put an end to Baron von Bülow's advances, refusing to see him again. She may have had to make a choice between the young officer and her husband, as Candida eventually had to choose between Marchbanks and Morell. Like Candida, Alice would easily choose her husband. But Candida, in making her choice, spoke the famous line, "I give myself to the weaker of the two," whereas Alice would have been choosing the stronger. For unlike Marchbanks, the young officer did not "fly out into the impatient night," ennobled and purified by his rejection.

On the evening of February 15, 1893, as Colonel and Mrs. Cornell and their daughter Lydia headed southwest from the Mardi Gras through Texas into Mexico, Alice walked into a room unexpectedly on the Friedrich Strasse as Baron von Bülow shot himself with his rifle. It was a scene she should not have witnessed. The next night she gave birth to her baby, and leaving her in the hands of German doctors, Peter had to fetch Mrs. Plimpton, who was vacationing in Munich. One month later, Baron von Bülow's lady died, also by her own hand.

Amid intrigue, romance, and tragedy, Katharine Cornell was born.

———

There is a family joke that it was so cold that Peter put the baby in the oven. The first crude incubator, for hatching eggs, had been invented twenty years before, and it would be like Peter to cut through all his practicable knowledge of medicine to seize one impracticable idea and then have the audacity to make it work. But since his audacity was more in the storytelling line, this family joke could be one he made up to entertain them back in Buffalo.

In her autobiography, *I Wanted to Be an Actress*, published in 1939, Katharine Cornell says she weighed three pounds at birth. Her friends today have gotten it down to two. Her father, reminiscing in a letter written to her in 1935 on her forty-second birthday, remembers "that little bit of three and a half pound bunch of humanity," surprisingly conservative since Peter is the one most likely to exaggerate. Whatever her weight, it was crucial, and she was wrapped in cotton batting and made to lie on a wooden board, in the austere Germanic belief that it would strengthen her tenuous hold on life.

Years later when admirers and critics would go on at length about the perfection of her "dark ivory-colored beauty," she would temper their sincere but embarrassing effusions by pointing out her great flaw. When she was born, she would explain, they put her on a board and it flattened the back of her head. She always tossed it off, lightly patting the flat place, and friends scoff at the idea that she was at all self-conscious about it.

Still, she never objected if a role required her to change the shape of her head by doing something drastic to her dark brown hair, and since it was too fine and soft and straight to respond to teasing and puffing and she was afraid the marcel irons and permanent wave machines would burn it up, she actually seemed pleased if she could wear a rat, fall, braid, mantilla, wimple, bonnet, and in at least one instance, Shaw's *Saint Joan*, a helmet.

Her first starring role in 1925 was as Iris March in Michael Arlen's dramatization of his novel *The Green Hat*, in which the green hat itself was a close-fitting felt affair, snugly hugging the back of the neck and pulled low over the brow in the style of the period. It was smart-looking and at the same time covered everything, and she incorporated it into her own wardrobe and continued to wear it after the play closed, even though it was recognizable wherever she went. Passengers crossing the Atlantic on the *Laconia* in the summer of 1926 gasped at her appearance among them striding the deck for her morning walk, in all her smiling good health still evoking the tragic image of Michael Arlen's doomed heroine. They were thrilled by her daring sense of the dramatic. Who knows, maybe she was only thrilled to have a well-shaped head at last.

In Berlin, with all the tension in the air, the wooden board, the rented rooms, gossip, and maybe even a slow bake in the oven, it's no wonder the baby screamed in protest and could not be quieted. Sometimes Peter had to carry her outside and walk the winter streets to give the other guests a respite. Eventually the new family was made to feel unwelcome and forced to move from pension to pension until the end of term at the university. Not only rented rooms, then, but a tour of rented rooms, disorder piled on impermanence. The baby was not ready for the world at its best, let alone a makeshift world. She was not ready to live, and there was constant fear that she wouldn't.

In the 1935 birthday letter to his daughter, Peter writes, "I can just feel you now, lying in the palm of my hand floating in the tub of water and kicking like the devil and splashing the water." Even with his studies to attend to, Peter seems to have taken over much of the baby care, or it devolved upon him. He adds, "How you did love it," so at least things were getting better.

The passenger list for the *Kaiser Wilhelm II* sailing from Bremen to New York on July 8, 1893, lists "Herr Dr. T. C. Cornell, Frau Alice Cornell, *und kind*," and under the p's, "Frau George D. Plimpton, Fraulein Louise Plimpton." Since they got Peter's initial wrong and thought Lucy's name was Louise, even the steamship line seems to have been nervous about these passengers, which may be why the captain came down every day to take a look. Peter writes, "I do not suppose the old gentleman is alive now, he could not be as he was very old then, but how surprised he would be to see what you have grown up to." The old gentleman would have been indeed surprised, since the supply of milk he had stowed on board, enough to last the entire trip, curdled in mid-ocean while Peter unconcernedly "prepared your milk for you and fed you and took care of you." "Und kind" had apparently survived so much that she was now determined to live, no matter what the hazards.

Peter continues:

I also have a very vivid recollection of the awful day I put in traveling from Berlin to Bremen-Harve [sic], where the rest of the family pushed me into a compartment with you, as they were all played out taking care of you, and how you yelled every inch of the way. Fenshell tea and everything I knew except paragoric, failed to allay the outburst. All that night in Bremen-Harve I walked the floor with you, I do not know whether I liked you so much or not that night. I probably did but I would not say so. You kept it up until we arrived on the ship and after we were settled in the stateroom and I took you up on deck, you quieted down and were the most wonderful child one could imagine all the way to Cobourg.

Not once in his "very vivid recollection" does Dr. Cornell recollect Alice, except presumably to include her with "the rest of the family" on their side of the train compartment door.

Cobourg, Ontario, was where the Cornells of Delaware Avenue spent their summers. On the north shore of Lake Ontario, almost directly across from Rochester and seventy miles northeast of Toronto, it is an accessible, picturesque resort town with a fine harbor. But the American occupation of Cobourg came about because it was the jumping-off place for Pittsburgh steel men on their way to the mines, iron or coal, in the northern part of the Canadian province.

Since a rough mining-camp sort of life was considered too rugged for women, these men would bring their wives as far as Cobourg, settle them into the pleasant small hotels there, continue by rail into the hinterland, see to their remote properties, and then collect their wives on the way back to Pittsburgh.

As this practice grew, the number of hotels increased, and eventually the Americans began to build or purchase very elegant homes in Cobourg. Quite a society grew up.

Colonel Cornell's demesne, called Hadfield Hurst to honor his wife's family, centered around an abrupt, rather Gothic house set in a grove of absolutely straight trees. The grounds were so broad and flat and well kept that they have been likened to green marble, but considering the Colonel's inclinations and interests, it might be more fitting to liken them to an autocratic man's billiard table, with corner pockets of stables, cow barns, vegetable gardens and flower beds. There was a tennis court and the shore of Lake Ontario. Inside the house the rooms were hardly more than large closets opening onto a grand central area, rising squarely the full height of the house as in a hotel or public building, with pillars and draped balustrades on each level.

The Cornells may have gone to Cobourg originally seeking the new society of wealthy Pittsburgh steel families, but it is refreshing to learn that they did not acquire Hadfield Hurst in an effort to impress. The story around Cobourg has always been that the Colonel won it in a poker game.

Lydia's diary ends in California on April 10. Then she and her parents recrossed the country to pick up life where they had left off in Buffalo, then on to Cobourg, and by the end of July they were eagerly awaiting the arrival of the Peter Cornells from Germany. It must have been a happy family reunion, for there was much to catch up on and the new baby to be admired. As if to make up for the fact that Peter and Alice had been married in the Presbyterian way, the Colonel's first grandchild, the only one he would live to see, was baptized in St. Peter's Anglican Church, Cobourg.

No middle name, and Katharine with two a's.

To the end of her life this beautiful and distinctive spelling of Katharine would be a small point of pride with her.

Her handwriting was always emotional, impatient, a scrawl beyond reading. It was so bad that her friends would pass her letters around to be deciphered. Once, in June of 1936 when she wrote to her father after accepting an honorary degree at the University of Wisconsin, the first of twelve doctorates she received, he wrote back,

> Your letter written on the train was lovely and I did so appreciate it, as I do all your letters. I really think your writing is a little better, in fact read all of it easily and I was almost willing to try and have some kind of machine built, upon which you could sit while writing letters, some mechanical device that would shake like a train. Or perhaps it was your attendance at the college that improved your penmanship.

But however illegible her writing might be, her signature a large K, a wild random t, an inverted fishhook for a C somewhere in the middle and two parallel lines at the end, one letter was always legible, the second "a" in Katharine.

Still it went unnoticed by many, revealingly by those seeking to ingratiate themselves, surprisingly by some who honored her and should have known better.

On January 10, 1974, a month before her eighty-first birthday and four months before her death, she received the American National Theater and Academy's National Artist Award for "her incomparable acting ability" and for "having elevated the theater throughout the world." She was ill with her last illness, too ill to go out, so the presentation was made in her living room.

The next day the *New York Times* reported:

> Miss Cornell sat in the large elegant room, wearing a long, pale pink gown of Thai silk, and while she was waiting for the little ceremony to begin, she . . . remembered how her celebrated nervousness had over-

come her at another award presentation years ago at the White House.

"Mrs. Roosevelt said one or two words, and I couldn't think of a thing to say, so Mrs. Roosevelt suddenly just put it into my hands and said quickly, 'Here it is' and ended the whole thing."

Then telegrams were read aloud, and David Seawell, board chairman of ANTA, placed the large gold medallion around her neck.

" 'How adorable, how simply wonderful,' Miss Cornell said. Later, she was distinctly annoyed when it was pointed out to her that her name had been misspelled on the award."

It was her last public appearance. Her baptism in St. Peter's Anglican Church, Cobourg, was her first.

2

The Cornells
of Mariner Street (1893-1909)

SHE ALWAYS SAID the house on Mariner Street had a friendly front
porch. It was a small three-story frame house with part of the ground
floor given over to Peter Cornell's consulting rooms, and the porch was
probably low, on a level with the street, not set back behind hedges or
elevated by steps. A porch so close to the sidewalk that passersby
became visitors, a friendly front porch.

That is all she ever said about the house on Mariner Street, her
home for the first twenty-three years of her life. It doesn't betoken
much friendliness inside.

As a child, she wasn't conventionally pretty. Her face was so wide
that it might have been flattened between the jaws of a vise, the great
distance between cheekbones giving her a Slavic or even Oriental cast.
Her mouth was large and undefined, the lips too full to fit into the
space allotted them, bunching up in the middle and pulling down at
the corners. Her straight brown hair was almost black, flattened by two
floppy bows, parted in the middle and skinned back, tightening the
forehead and bulging the eyes into prominence. She looked exposed,
as if some protective covering had been peeled away leaving only the
raw elements of eyes, mouth, and brow. She had no neck, and when at
the age of four she was photographed in a stiff white dress, her head
seems to have arrived late and been placed hurriedly on top of the
shoulders until some more satisfactory arrangement could be worked
out. They might not even be shoulders but a T-frame on which the
dress is hung, hanging open at the back out of sight where it doesn't

count, with a plaster hand pushed through the sleeve. Add a frilly poke bonnet in another pose with her father and the impression of facade is complete. There is her head, pinched through a hole in a photographer's painted backdrop, looking for the rest of herself.

With the eyes of love, Mary Augusta Plimpton insisted she was beautiful, protesting entirely too much for the more clear-eyed Colonel's lady who finally had a sharp word with her co-grandmother. The next time Mrs. Plimpton felt the uncontrollable urge to glorify her granddaughter's incomparable beauty, she also felt the steady eye of Mrs. Cornell upon her and came up with a defiant, "There's nothing repulsive about her!"

It was about the best that could be said.

When she was six or seven, she had scarlet fever and all her hair fell out. If having large eyes meant she couldn't help seeing too much, then even Grandmother Plimpton's last stand of defiant faint praise had to give way, for she certainly saw herself as repulsive. But if her body could not provide a protective covering, her mind could. Accepting unacceptability, she dropped a curtain and behind it carried on outrageously with imaginary friends.

It took an endless year for her hair to grow out, during which time someone she loved, either Alice Cornell or Grandmother Plimpton, her two favorites, started calling her Kit because she looked like a boy.

It stuck. There would always be those who called her Katharine, including her father when he was feeling fatherish or speaking of her to a third person. Actors wanting to be both respectful and affectionate called her Miss Kit. A few unsentimental types leveled her off as K.C. But to those who loved and were loved, she was always Kit.

An old family friend and one-time neighbor tells another story. As she remembers it, she was the one who had scarlet fever, her hair turned white, had to be whacked off, and Alice Cornell was so enchanted with the effect that she went home and sheared her own daughter. If that is what happened, then the year of painful isolation was not accidental but inflicted. It is possible, for pretty Alice's only parental transgression seems to have been one of loving thoughtlessness.

The same cannot be said of Peter.

With the Colonel for a father and David Bates Douglass for an example, it is not surprising that Peter was a disciplinarian. As a boy he attended the Buffalo Classical School whose headmaster, Dr. Horace

Briggs, was something of a martinet, but he was magnetic and later became genial and very understanding of a boy's nature. For instance, he knew that one could not chain a boy in school the day of a circus parade.

Peter, too, was genial, a word that is still applied to him by all who knew him, and like Dr. Briggs, he wouldn't dream of chaining his daughter to the house when the greatest show on earth came to town. He would take her to a performance. He would let her feed the elephants.

It wasn't exactly a circus, it was an extravaganza about a circus or a durbar or something of the kind that was being put on at the Vaudeville Theatre. Kit was about five, so it was even before the crew-cut year, and to her childish mind an elephant was something about the size of a dog, which might, if coaxed, sit up and beg for food. All that week she was like one possessed and went around muttering, "Wanna feed the elephants, wanna feed the elephants." At last the day came and she was taken to the theatre on the streetcar, a bag of buns clutched in her hand. Genial Peter had gotten seats in a box, practically on the stage, and she waited breathlessly through the whole performance The elephants didn't come on until the end, the last act on the bill, and eventually, suddenly, there they were, colossal, swaying, living mountains, towering above her head, seemingly about to trample her.

As she later understated it, "My heart froze in terror. My gala day was in ruins."

At the end of the performance she told her father she had changed her mind about feeding the elephants, that she would rather go home.

But Peter said, "You've been wanting for a week to feed those elephants. Now you are going to do it."

Before the large and, as she remembered it, delighted audience she was dragged, screaming her lungs out, onto and over the longest stage she would ever be made to cross to put one of her buns into a snaky black trunk.

The penalty for crying was to have a leather placard hung around her neck with "Timmy Toodleshanks" stamped on it in gold letters.

Sometimes when a father is afraid of his own father, as Peter was, he can't help instilling the same fear in his own child, which may have been part of Peter's strictness. If Katharine did not eat her vegetables at dinner, they were set before her at breakfast the next morning on the plate as she had left them, as they had been sitting on the kitchen sink overnight, and she was not allowed to begin the new day until she had eaten up the old. At breakfast on the day she started kindergarten she spilled egg on her clean dress, and Peter decreed that when she came home in the afternoon she must practice for one hour "how to eat eggs."

She once poured a bottle of ink over the leather chair in Peter's waiting room and had several good slides down the slippery surface before she was stopped. She said she did it to find out what sort of toboggan ink on leather would make, but it also looks like an angry attempt to get back at Peter for what she considered injustices. She couldn't admit it, of course, because Alice insisted there was no such thing as anger, there was only bad circulation. When her daughter showed signs of losing her temper, becoming moody, sharp or intractable, she was sent out to run around the block to stimulate the blood. By dodging situations and denying unrefined emotions, Alice accidentally became wise, for the child always returned home with her face flushed, her eyes bright, her mind having moved on to other things. Years later in New York City, Katharine Cornell would take a taxi from her house on Beekman Place up to Central Park for a brisk, solitary walk around the reservoir.

She should have had a happy childhood. There were no financial worries, good health (except for scarlet fever), a colorful, energetic family of doting aunts, uncles, and grandparents, servants to make life easy, and glorious summers in Cobourg. But much was missing, simple things other children took for granted. On Christmas Eve she was allowed to pin a stocking to the arm of the sofa in Alice's upstairs sitting room. On Christmas morning she was led into the room, which was stacked high with loving presents. But there was no Christmas tree. It was never explained. It was simply one of Peter's restrictions.

Inexplicable deprivations and punishment piled on punishment gave her a sense of inadequacy, of never being able to please her father. The feeling never went away. Once when he berated her for not writing to him more often, she characteristically apologized for being an unsatisfactory child. He wrote back, "I do not know of any child in the world who is more satisfactory than you; in fact we are so swelled up with pride over you and your achievements that we are ready to burst almost. So don't ever make that remark or think such a thing again."

Genial Peter. His idea of give and take was to give her a sense of inadequacy in the first place so that he could magnanimously take it away later on. Even his affection had a sharp, demanding tone.

She was fifty-two at the time.

———

In her 1933 production of Sidney Howard's *Alien Corn*, Katharine Cornell played a concert pianist, and several times in the course of the action she had to perform like one. It presented a problem. She had a strong feeling for music but had never learned to play.

It wasn't for lack of opportunity. Alice played the piano as well as the mandolin and saw to it that her daughter took lessons. If Peter thought it was a waste of time (unless, of course, she could learn to play "Wait Till the Sun Shines, Nellie"), he went along because if she became proficient it would give him a chance to boast, which he dearly loved to do.

She took her piano lessons at the home of a girl her own age whose mother one day gave the two children twenty cents for ice cream sodas. The minute they were out of the mother's sight, her "friend" ditched her for someone more attractive, and Kit was left standing outside Smither and Thurston's Drug Store, unable to deal with the situation. That would make it hard, next to impossible, to deal with the next lesson.

She much preferred staying at home with a punching bag and trapeze, at first, perhaps, to work off anger — you can run around the block just so many times — but then she discovered the pleasure and satisfaction that physical dexterity could give her, and it became a goal in itself.

With confidence, the piano in *Alien Corn* was angled in such a way that her hands were visible to at least half the audience, and even those who did not know her were impressed by her facility with Bach, Chopin, and Franck. Her friends were openmouthed and mystified. By practicing long hours over a dummy keyboard, painstakingly matching her onstage fingering to the offstage music, she convinced them that she was actually playing. It was her remarkable ability, under any circumstances, to control her body.

When a Fanny Kemble or a Julia Marlowe or an Ethel Barrymore played Juliet, she played in ease, if not luxury. Behind the scenes she had a flight of steps with a handrail leading up to her balcony and a generous platform at the top with a velvety cushion where she could wait in comfort for Romeo's "He jests at scars who never felt a wound," then to reveal herself shyly at her window. When Katharine Cornell played Juliet for the first time, the season after *Alien Corn*, it was in repertory with two other plays on an eighteen-thousand-mile tour of the United States. The sets were built to travel, and there was no room in the baggage car for star indulgences, even if they had been asked for. In performance, the fit of the scenery was so tight that there was nothing but a plain carpenter's ladder leading up to a narrow ledge behind the balcony window. Her only request was not in the interest of personal comfort or even safety but professional perfection. To repair the ravages of the hazardous climb, she asked that a mirror be hung on a nail at the top, that she might check her makeup before showing her face.

One night in Nashville, Tennessee, an able property man, removing the mirror between scenes, lost his balance and fell from the ledge breaking his leg. And yet at every performance Juliet would climb the plain carpenter's ladder in the dark, wearing a white nightdress and satin slippers, perch precariously in midair to adjust her makeup, sigh languorously as Romeo wished to be a glove upon her hand that he might touch her cheek, and then burst into view, a radiant sun from the east, far more fair than the envious moon who is already sick and pale with grief.

She learned very early that her body was hers to command, that it was not subject to the whim or caprice of anyone else, aunt, uncle, father, adult or child, that with care and training it would respond, with practice and hard work it would do whatever she wanted it to.

By the time she was ten she was such an expert gymnast that she was asked to take part in a charity circus, and probably for the first time in her life her assurance was greater than her shyness, and she was able to perform well, even creditably. Success — pleasing people, that is — was a new experience.

On the same program there was a professional acrobat who did a hobo act on a slack wire, and spurred on literally to dizzying heights, Kit at once decided passionately, strenuously, that she had to master that difficult art. The acrobat was the first of countless thousands of strangers who would be moved by her dark intensity, and he succumbed so completely that he made her a grateful present of his own slack wire, probably wondering what on earth had happened when he arrived at his next booking without it.

————

The friendly front porch, that was where Alice sat waiting for passersby to stop and pass the pleasant, empty afternoons with her. At first there were Peter's patients going in and out, but if there was one thing Peter did not like about doctoring, it was patients who chained him to his office. He was probably very good at house calls because it gave him a chance to be out moving through the streets, keeping track of what went on. He was a familiar sight "making his rounds," always ready to stop for a joke or a jaw, calling up to his sedate mother-in-law's bedroom window, "I got that case of whiskey you wanted, Mrs. Plimpton!" and laughing as she called back loudly and distinctly for the neighbors' benefit, "Peter Cornell, you know I don't touch a drop!" He undoubtedly had a restorative bedside manner and was welcome everywhere as much for his jovial funloving ways as for his medical know-how. No one knows when he started having girl friends, but he seems always to have had them and never to have stopped. Their existence was accepted and indulged, if not discussed, by all those who knew, probably even Alice. As a young woman Kit would be walking down the street with a friend and say, "Here comes Father with his girl. I suppose I have to stop and talk to them."

No sooner had Peter built up a healthy practice than he developed an extravagant habit of recommending his patients to other doctors, of generously passing them on to his colleagues. His practice declined, eventually fell off to nothing. He gave up doctoring. And for Alice, sitting on the friendly front porch, the passersby were too few, too predictably on their way somewhere else, too unreal.

For Kit they were the opposite — too real, too many, too predictably present. She retreated to the leafy backyard, fenced in and secluded, where her imaginary friends lingered on long after her hair grew out and she looked like a girl again. The backyard was the place to be, and that was where she strung up the slack wire.

It had to be done in secret, of course, without Peter's knowledge. Her dread of Peter was greater than the dread of falling, and she was learning more than one kind of balancing act in those days. Secretiveness, the risk of being found out, added an extra thrill.

She was too earthbound to try for handsprings against the sky, twirling a parasol the while, although that may have been a far off image at the back of her mind. Here, at this moment, a plain walk was enough to learn, one slow smooth, continuous walk on air, from here to there, that was beautiful enough, majestic enough, and hard enough. With little patience but a lot of practice she developed a skill much admired by her imaginary friends. She added a parasol to the act. Her absorption transformed loneliness into simple solitude, which was manageable, even pleasurable, and then her accomplishment transformed her imaginary friends into real ones.

She became something of a star attraction to neighborhood children, most of them boys, who began trooping into the backyard to watch. At first they were satisfied to be impressed, but then they wanted to learn and goaded her into teaching them. As news of mishaps, falls, scrapes, and sprains traveled from house to house, word soon reached the ubiquitous Peter, who appeared out of nowhere and confiscated the slack wire.

If it was meant as a deterrent, it had the opposite effect. She was now an accepted leader and with the battleground of the backyard laid to waste, it was as if she had been freed from all constraints and vigorously escorted her charges, now all boys, out into the street where it became a contest of valor to keep step with her, to match her exploits deed for deed, feat for feat. "Follow the leader!" was the cry. But one day they ganged up on her in somebody's barn and pinned her down. She had dared to be as daring as a boy and they got even with her by proving she was just a girl.

She returned after that to the backyard world, fenced in and secluded. She always said she could not have survived her childhood had it not been for her imaginary friends. They were not only friends, they were family — her brothers and sisters. They all had the same mother; she did not know who their father was. She conjured them up in ones and twos, and they understood her and listened to her. In return, she entertained them and dressed up for them.

There is a photograph taken in the backyard when she was twelve or thirteen. She wears a man's suit, a wing collar and tie. The sleeves are too long, the trouser cuffs are rolled up, and her left foot in a large shoe is propped up on a wooden crate. Her elbow rests on her knee, a straw hat is clenched in her fingers, turned back over her forearm in the jaunty manner of a chorus gentleman in a "Floradora" musical. Her right arm is crooked against her side, and she sports an unlighted pipe.

Katharine Cornell in costume for an amateur performance, 1906.

Her hair seems to be short, but it may be pinned up at the back. On top it is thick and loose. She smiles quizzically. There is a sly look in her eyes. She is terribly pleased with herself.

There are other childhood photographs, but in this one she looks happy.

———

Colonel Cornell had a passion for amateur theatricals. He was talented, and his young friend John Drew, Charles Frohman's dashing new star in the 1880s, seriously urged him to join the ranks of the professionals. But the Colonel would not, perhaps because he was by then well into his middle years, but more likely because he preferred doing things his own way on his own terms. He wouldn't even join the community groups in Buffalo. He simply liked to get up on a stage and rant and have a good time, and he especially liked directing plays because then he could tell other actors, his neighbors, his cousins, and his children, what to do. When his children were small he turned the attic of the house on Delaware Avenue into a complete theater with a curtain, lights and scenery. In summers, a long gallery at the back of Hadfield Hurst, overlooking the garden, made an excellent outdoor arena, but to insure performances against bad weather and to accommodate growing audiences, either the town hall, known as Victoria Hall, or the Cobourg Opera House was more reliable.

Peter, Lydia, and Douglas grew up being in plays. Peter, of course, loved it from the start and never had to be coaxed. Lydia probably did what she was told simply to be agreeable and then discovered to her delight that she had a very pleasant talent and enjoyed herself. Douglas was quieter, less gregarious, more staid, like his mother, and must have been a reluctant exhibitionist. But he was spared too much participation: he went to work as a state engineer on the barge canal at Amsterdam, on the other side of the state, and simply was not available.

The three acting Cornells perfected certain playlets and sketches to the degree that they developed a repertoire and were often invited to perform at elegant social entertainments and charity benefits, sometimes filling an entire evening with their antics, which seem to have been on the zany side. Lydia and the Colonel were very successful with a curtain-raiser called "A Pair of Lunatics," and they frequently followed it with "The Two Buzzards," in which, according to one surviving program, a benefit at the Twentieth Century Club for St. Paul's Cathedral in 1897, Mr. Benjamin Buzzard was played by Mr. Cornell, Miss Laetitia Buzzard was played by Miss Cornell, and the part of Jonathan Small was played by Dr. Cornell. They were so popular and well known that, in the old theatrical tradition, they did not have to use their first names in the cast list. Sometimes they dived into the classics, but never out of their depth, and one of Peter's best roles was Charon, raucously snapping coins from the mouths of the dead as he ferried them across the River Styx into Elysium. Whenever they performed, they were rapturously reviewed in the local press, and at the end of each summer residents of Cobourg wrote fan letters of gratitude, and in the spring they wrote welcome-back letters of happy anticipation.

Lydia, then, would seem to have been the first "Miss Cornell" to appear on any stage, or at least the first to be billed as such, but her infant niece made an early debut in a baby buggy pushed by a neighbor, John Lord O'Brian, through a scene in the Colonel's own version of *Alice in Wonderland.* Her performance went so unnoticed that in later years it was completely forgotten by everybody, including the actress herself, or it may be that she was never even told about it. In *I Wanted to Be an Actress* she said she never acted in Grandfather Cornell's attic theatre, and Mr. O'Brian's daughter, rather indignant at being forced to perpetuate the lie by selling the autobiography at the Bay Tree Book Store in Buffalo, wrote to clear up that "glaring error." As she put it, "Your father, Peter Cornell, lent you, as a baby, to be wheeled across the stage in a buggy. . . ." Alice, it seems — as usual — had nothing to say in the matter. To everybody's disappointment, Alice didn't like acting, which excluded her from a say in the productions, and it was generous Peter who "lent" his daughter as a stage prop.

In time she was allowed to sit on the stairs and watch rehearsals, and her earliest memories were of that stage, the curve of the proscenium, and the curtain "with something wonderful behind it, which might lift at any moment." The "something wonderful behind it" was, of course, the world of make-believe. But she was not an airy-fairy child: she was active and energetic, with a quick mind, and the kind of make-believe that delighted her was bustling, realistic and tangible — properties, scenery, lights, familiar people in funny clothes they would not dare wear on the street, and probably most delightful of all the sight of her father pretending to be somebody else. If only it could last forever. She did not necessarily relate the whole thing to the secret, inner world of her imaginary friends, nor did the two kinds of make-believe give her the same kind of comfort and sustenance.

—

St. Margaret's School was founded in 1884 "in harmony and compliance with the wishes and convictions of The Right Reverend Arthur Cleveland Coxe, D.D., LL.D., Bishop of the Diocese of Western New York and the Protestant Episcopal Church." A number of girls from elite Buffalo families attended St. Margaret's, among them at least one daughter of John Lord O'Brian (who would later become a trustee), and it was the logical school for Kit to attend after kindergarten. It was as if Alice, having been allowed to say "I do" at a Presbyterian wedding, was heard no more in the land.

If both mother and daughter did not participate in the fun in the attic theatre, when Kit began appearing in routine school pageants and fairy plays at St. Margaret's, the two outsiders found their own closeness, for it was Alice who made her costumes.

From the descriptions of Alice, it is surprising that she did not like acting, that she actually seems to have had a fear of getting up on a stage that gave her the strength to resist all persuasion, even Peter's demanding kind. "There was a childlike quality about her . . . simple and direct . . . had great personality and warmth . . . liked people and they never gave her anything except their best . . . possessed that rare faculty of encouraging and stimulating others." One would expect this exceptional woman to be at the center of all the fun, the generator of it — even with Peter as a husband.

But those are the words, or a distillation of words, spoken by her daughter, to be written down for publication long after Alice's death. Unquestionably there is truth in them, but there is a sadder, deeper truth in their excess. They are the words a strenuously loyal, compassionate woman would use to soften the memory of an alcoholic mother.

It is doubtful that Peter, after the first few years of marriage, went on calling up to his mother-in-law's bedroom window, "I got that case of whiskey you wanted, Mrs. Plimpton!" The joke would have become too painful for them both, even for Peter, because apparently Alice started withdrawing very early, and a silence grew up around her, a silence dating back to the young officer in Berlin, to the violence that induced her daughter's birth, to the homeless months that followed, to her return to socially proper Buffalo as a confused and blushing bride and mother. It may be that she was too young, too childlike, too protected, too inexperienced to assimilate all that happened that first year.

And Peter, to whom the whole experience would simply be a marvelous story to entertain his friends and family, would not be the most gentle and considerate companion and protector. His impatience would only speed her inward journey, which would, in turn, sharpen his impatience into abrasiveness, which would, in turn . . .

If Kit the innocent, whom Peter loved dearly, felt the insensibility of both his attention and neglect, what must have been the feelings of Alice — the guilty? Much of his oppression of the daughter may even have been directed against the mother, and whatever Kit's unhappiness, Alice, the more childlike of the two, must have found life intolerable.

Peter is never known to have referred to Alice's alcoholism. His brother Douglas's son Douglas, Kit's first cousin, born in 1915, the year of Alice's death, "heard she had a drinking problem, but I don't remember if my mother or father ever said anything about it." Kit confided in those closest to her, but today, at the mention of Alice's name, they become uncomfortable and look away, one of them saying with dignity, "I don't want to pass along rumors." Kit's loyalty, like her compassion, was contagious. Only one lifelong friend, an elderly one-time neighbor in Buffalo, had the openness to admit, with impatience, "Alice Cornell drank in secret, so of course everybody knew it." Then she added stiffly, "I don't think Kit would want it put into a book."

As a child and as a young woman, for the length of her mother's life, Kit protected her and tried to help her. She may have covered up for her. And as she herself learned to break through her own shyness to take part in the life that was going on, she probably tried unsuccessfully to draw her mother into the same kind of participation. The Cornells were always into something and getting their names in the newspapers, but Alice's name seems to have appeared in print only once. It must have been at her daughter's instigation, and it was an event worthy of description.

Kit left St. Margaret's at the end of the eighth grade in 1908. Nineteen-o-nine was the school's twenty-fifth anniversary year, and a celebration was "gayly entered into at the June Commencement" and waged relentlessly until December. Robert E. Peary had finally reached the North Pole in April, after five unsuccessful attempts, and using his "discovery" as a theme, St. Margaret's Alumnae Association, of which Kit was now a member, climaxed their celebration by turning Buffalo's Convention Hall into "An Arctic Carnival" the week before Christmas.

According to the program, the main feature was the Esquimaux Village, where the star LIVE SNOWMAN was Crystaletta Eysicle, played by Katherine (*sic*) Cornell. Miss Cornell also graced the Children's Vaudeville, sponsored by the Alumnae Association on Thursday, Friday, and Saturday afternoons at the North Star Theatre, playing the title role in a playlet called "Mr. Kris Kringle."

Not one of the prominent Episcopalian Cornells is listed on the committees that worked hard to make "An Arctic Carnival" a success for their Church and St. Margaret's School. But in Santa Claus' House and Workshop, hard by the Snow Queen's Court, under the protective eye of sixteen-year-old Crystaletta Eysicle, that lost Presbyterian "Mrs. Peter Cornell" is the fifth name on a committee of nine "In Charge of Dolls."

3

"Hurry and Grow Up...!"
(1900-1911)

ABOUT 1900 THE COLONEL RETIRED from the lead works, sold the house on Delaware Avenue, and took his wife to live in Dansville, New York, a small health resort fifty miles southeast of Buffalo. There the elder Cornells settled into the Jackson Sanitarium, which must have been the equivalent of today's exclusive retirement homes. The Colonel continued his amateur theatricals, waxed his mustache, corseted his figure, and swept the ladies around the room in a waltz for the remaining ten years of his life.

Lydia took up residence at the Lenox Hotel when she was in Buffalo, but Hadfield Hurst now became her permanent home, and the entire family still congregated there in the summer.

Douglas Cornell returned from his stint on the barge canal at Amsterdam to become Structural Engineer of the City of Buffalo, a position he held for forty years until his retirement.

And in 1901, Peter Cornell gave up the medical profession for good.

The world at large had to be told why, and he said it was because he suffered from hematophobia. But it is not likely that he suddenly developed a morbid fear of blood at the age of thirty-six, and if he had always had it, why on earth did he choose the medical profession? How did he even get through medical school with hematophobia? The whole thing sounds like one of his jokes — the doctor who couldn't stand the sight of blood.

If so, it was a joke he came to believe, and so did everybody else. In 1901, hematophobia had a nice ring to it. It made it seem that he surrendered his dedication reluctantly, that it was only the irony of fate that prevented him from continuing to serve humanity. With hematophobia, he could retire from the field with honor and a great deal of sympathy.

What Peter wanted to do and now did was to become manager and part owner of the Star Theatre, where the professional touring companies played, the hit shows out of New York and the famous repertory groups.

Brooks Atkinson says in his chronical *Broadway* that theatre at the turn of the century was extravagant and sentimental, and so too was Peter. Audiences only wanted amusement and excitement, the big emotions, "power, passion, sacrifice, romance, salvation," *Way Down East*, *Ben-Hur*, *Sherlock Holmes*, and two completely different dramatizations of *Quo Vadis?* opening on the same night at two different New York theatres (and, as Atkinson points out, "the one adapted by the more cultivated author was the one that failed").

Atkinson also points out the diversity of the theatre that could present Maude Adams as both a girl and a boy in one season in Barrie's *The Little Minister* and Rostand's *L'Aiglon*; two equally startling sides of dramatist Clyde Fitch in *Sappho*, which the police closed until Olga Nethersole could learn to control her love scenes, and *Barbara Frietchie*, with Julia Marlowe firing a real rifle onstage; Mrs. Leslie Carter as David Belasco's *Zaza* competing with Mrs. Fiske as *Becky Sharp*. Stars were so idolized that Richard Mansfield could risk stopping in midscene to rebuke the audience for making too much noise.

Ostentatiously realistic with no relation to real life, weighty with "themes" while avoiding all pertinent subjects, American plays passed themselves off as art, and the predominantly middle-class audience embraced the deception and shelled out their $1.50 or $2.00 for the best seats, delighted that they could elevate themselves and still have a whale of a good time. This ingenuousness on all sides was the great charm of the period. Serious theatre people from abroad deplored it but couldn't resist coming over to reap the benefits. Cultural New York in 1900 gave a lift to the aging Modjeska's declining career, and Sarah Bernhardt made her sixth American tour, offering the great Coquelin as the First Gravedigger to Madame Sarah's own Hamlet.

For all the noble sentiments expressed in American plays, the theatre itself was at the mercy of a syndicate headed by Abraham Lincoln Erlanger. According to Brooks Atkinson, "if a star actor or a producer did not sign an exclusive contract with the Syndicate, it made it difficult for him to get a theatre on Broadway and almost impossible to organize a national tour. It harassed and persecuted actors who tried to remain independent," among them Mrs. Fiske, James O'Neill (Eugene's father), and Sarah Bernhardt, who played in tents to huge sympathetic audiences when denied bookings by Abe Erlanger.

To offset these independents, the Syndicate had in its ranks producers such as the ingratiating Charles Frohman, whose stars included John Drew, Ethel Barrymore, Viola Allen, and William Faversham, names enough to guarantee popularity and profit season after season.

The situation was further complicated in the early 1900s when the Syndicate was challenged by three brothers from Syracuse, New York — Sam, J.J., and Lee Shubert. A struggle for power was on.

It took courage at the age of thirty-six to throw over one career and with no experience plunge into another so unstable and unpredictable that even a younger man with no encumbrances would have been called self-indulgent. But Peter had three things working for him: first, money never seems to have been a worry in the Cornell family; two, no matter who controlled the theatre bookings, Abe Erlanger or the Shuberts, to benefit themselves they would have to benefit the theatre managers; and three and most important, Peter had the golden touch.

He never looked back on doctoring with any regret or, it would seem, with any knowledge, complaining to the end of his long life of perfectly ordinary aches and pains which oddly enough, for all his training, education, degrees, and practice, he had no power whatsoever to diagnose. He enjoyed railing against the ineptitude of all doctors as much as he enjoyed being called "Doctor Cornell" respectfully or "Doc" hobnobbingly by the theatrical greats of the day who came to town to perform in his theatre.

His daughter never could understand how just managing a theatre could satisfy a man who loved acting so much, but Peter loved managing even more, he loved managing above all else, and arranged his life to have the glamour and excitement of show business without the artistic risk, and the prestige of being a doctor without the inconvenience. He made such a success of the Star Theatre that he took on the Majestic, managing both until his retirement in the late 1920s.

By the time Kit was old enough to take an active interest in theatricals, her grandfather's attic theatre was gone from the family, but there was still the back gallery at Hadfield Hurst where she produced and directed plays she either wrote herself or in collaboration with a friend. She also played the leading roles indiscriminately, heroes and heroines, villains and princesses, and to ensure herself and her productions press coverage, she started a four-page sheet called "The Cobourg Sun," written in pencil. From the Editorial Page of Volume I, Number I:

ACTING IS HARD

Katharine Cornell and Jo Pierce wrote an A-1 play called "The Hidden Treasure." The editor played the part of the Duke. In one part where Katharine was on the stage and the curtain man was asleep, she called out "Curtain, curtain," which made the people laugh. We made twenty-cents on the whole thing.

Newspaper publishing was also hard. The first issue of "The Cobourg Sun" was its last.

That was when she was eight years old, the same year Peter went into show business. It would be enormously satisfying to report that by then she knew she was a born actress, that her genius had just been waiting to emerge, and that Peter's capricious change of careers paid off by immediately giving direction to his daughter's life. None of it would be true. Even the slack-wire summer was still two years in the future, and if she seemed to have been born anything, it was an athlete. She wrote plays and acted in them because it was what the adults in her family did and she found she could do it, too, and did it for their much-needed admiration and approval. She would rather climb a tree any day.

At Cobourg she learned to swim and play tennis, and by the time she was fifteen she was amateur swimming champion of Buffalo and runner-up for city championship at tennis. She loved anything to do with water — swan dives, back dives, dives from a standing position on her friends' shoulders, canoeing, camping, portage — and she is said to have run the rapids, but no one is quite sure what rapids or when. At Cobourg she learned to ride horseback as soon as she was old enough, and while still a child was privileged to ride the Colonel's own horse, called Rubber because of his color. She condescended to acknowledge her father's new career by riding a horse from Twothy's stables through the lobby of the Star Theatre, but the lobby, wide and smooth with a little slope, was really better for roller-skating, to the annoyance of playgoers lined up to buy tickets for Sothern and Marlowe, Maxine Elliott, Otis Skinner, and George Arliss.

In June of 1907 the following article appeared in the *Buffalo Commercial:*

FRENCH PLAY AT ST. MARGARET'S

A delightful little French play was given before a very large and enthusiastic audience in the gymnasium of St. Margaret's School yesterday afternoon by the pupils of the seventh grade. It was written by a member of the class, Miss Katharine Cornell, the talented little daughter of Dr. and Mrs. Peter C. Cornell. The play is a comedy in two acts and five scenes and is entitled "Patty en tension". . . . Miss Cornell has displayed wonderful ability as an actress in the amateur performances in which she has appeared and the little sketch written by her and presented under her direction yesterday was worthy of much praise. French recitations and songs were given between the scenes and acts.

She had turned fourteen in February and was just finishing the seventh grade in June, which suggests that she was not a superior student, but to write a play in French and get it onto a stage before a large and enthusiastic audience was certainly a superior accomplishment. Nothing she ever did in her life that turned out to be "worthy of much praise" was achieved without hard work. Nothing ever came easily. So it would seem that the stage or plays or whatever the effort of "Patty en tension" represented meant a great deal to her, probably more than her ordinary schoolwork but not as much as the swimming championship.

Sports and the outdoors gave her an ease with life she lost when she stepped into rooms and tried to be social. At once she became shy to the point of repression. Her voice was already beautiful and mature, but what good was it when she could not form her impassioned and intricate thoughts into words, let alone coherent sentences? Since theatricals meant getting up in front of people and being on display, it is a wonder she was able to get up the courage, let alone sustain an interest. On the other hand, by writing plays she could get thoughts out of her head with no one there to repress them, and acting was a way to be with people and participate without relying on giveaway spontaneity. It is worth noting that when she wrote she chose for a heroine Patty, whose big problem seems to have been tension.

When asked what she wanted to be when she grew up, she forswore both the theatre and sports and said a trained nurse. It may have been an expedient to stop further questioning, or she may have meant it. With such a worthy calling maybe she was seeking approval. Or, with her complete lack of self-esteem, to make up for being so inferior in looks and accomplishment, she may have felt she ought to aspire to noble drudgery rather than something she enjoyed, and of course she did not think herself good enough to aspire too high. Nursing was just dreary enough and elevated enough. Or she may have been truly aware of her growing compassion for people.

But two things are clear, that at the age of fourteen she did not yet associate an acting career with herself, and that had she become a trained nurse, she would have had such sympathy for her patients that she would have been unable to stay in the same room with them.

It is natural that she never let herself think of herself as an actress because at that time it was a rule that all actresses were beautiful. When she took a moment to look at the posters in the lobby of the Star Theatre, she saw the statuesque beauty of Maxine Elliott or the sad beauty of Julia Marlowe or the exotic beauty of Madame Nazimova, and whatever shape or form beauty took, rosebud and be-curled or full-blown and frazzled, it was ultra-feminine. Beauty's eyes were not set too far apart, beauty's mouth was not large and irregular, beauty's shoulders were not wide and strong, beauty's walk was not graceless.

Then at the end of 1905 Charles Frohman produced a play, against the advice of his friends, that made theatre history. After playing a year or more at the Empire Theatre in New York, it took to the road, heading straight for the Star Theatre in Buffalo. At about the time Kit was trying to alleviate her own tensions by exploiting Patty's, Maude Adams flew into town as Peter Pan, and Maude Adams was not beautiful.

Nothing about her, beginning with her name, was beautiful. Already a theatrical legend, offstage she was an insignificant figure in brown clothes. Brooks Atkinson writes that she would be denied credit in stores she could have bought and sold, because clerks couldn't believe she was good for the merchandise she wanted to charge. If she gave her name and they knew the name, they didn't believe her, this mousy plain person of no distinction; a woman so withdrawn, so private, so compulsively shy that she spent thirty thousand dollars on a curtained railroad car to take her from city to city. A woman so lacking in the trappings of feminine beauty that she did not even try to compete but came on the stage dressed as a boy.

Despite her apologetic air on the street and in stores and hotels, Maude Adams did not creep onto the stage, nor did she hide behind scenery or other actors. She flew. She burst through the window exulting in her own difference, reckless in her physical fragility, all the more brave because the wire suspending her glinted in the stage lights. She flew into sight the champion of youth, barely larger and scarcely more robust than the band of worthies she commanded, the lost boys in Never Land. With her pervasive sweetness of personality, she made strength in others seem an essential, a necessity, she made a child like Kit feel her own strength and value it, even revel in it. Maude Adams as Peter Pan was not a mirror image, she was an ideal to be protected and cherished. And yet she embodied each child who loved her from the audience, weak or strong — this very serious thirty-five-year-old woman dressed in the clothes of a boy. She flew in from the wings with all the cathartic force of the deus ex machina in old Greek drama. The cry of "Follow the leader!" was heard again, and this time even leaders followed.

At first, to be in her presence, even as a member of the audience, was too beautiful, and Kit hid her face in the draperies of the stage box. When she finally brought herself to look, to focus on what was happening, her world was irrevocably changed, just as other young worlds would be changed years later by her own Juliet, Joan, and Elizabeth Barrett.

The real and the imaginary in her life came together at last; the slack wire of the leafy backyard became taut and glinted, swinging in the stage lights; and the earthbound child who had dared to walk on air now passionately, strenuously wanted to fly, and to fly meant to act.

———

In those pre-radio, pre-movie, pre-television days, touring road companies out of New York could not begin to meet the audience demands for entertainment all across the country. The gaps were filled in by professional stock companies, some resident, some traveling, most of which never went near Broadway and flourished in the hinterlands with their own hierarchies of leading players and local stars.

The Jessie Bonstelle Company was one of the best of these and divided its summers between Detroit and Buffalo. Miss Bonstelle was in her late thirties, well dressed, with reddish blond hair, more invigorating than she was theatrical, but overpowering in her command of scenes and situations when she had to be. She hired her own company, decided what plays would be done, directed them, and played the leading feminine roles, all without stopping for breath. She was her own executive. If Broadway managers did not accept her on an equal basis, they respected her judgment and taste, often asking her to try out their new plays before they put them into rehearsal for New York productions.

Her manner was more hearty than warm, and she had more ability than talent, more know-how than creativity, but she got the shows on, and good shows they were, week after week. Counting Peter, she was the second in a line of busy managerial types who would be as attracted to Katharine Cornell as Kit was to them, who would always in some way, directly or indirectly, influence her life, and who would to an even greater degree, which they were perfectly willing to acknowledge, be influenced themselves. After Peter, however, more often than not they were women.

The life of a stock company was rigorous, with three plays always in the works — one being performed, one being rehearsed, and a third being planned. For once Kit was undoubtedly glad to be her father's daughter because it meant that at the Star Theatre they were familiar with her and wouldn't notice when she slipped into the auditorium to watch Miss Bonstelle's rehearsals.

Indoors, out of the sun, she was used to being cautious, to walking softly on carpets so as not to intrude, not to be heard, not to be known. With much practice she knew how not to draw attention to herself. Sitting on the balcony stairs in the Star Theatre, she made herself invisible.

Miss Bonstelle was a disciplinarian, and it is a wonder that having spotted Kit, she didn't throw her out on her ear. But "Bonnie," as she like to be called, fell like a ton of bricks for Doc Cornell's shy kid, gave her the run of rehearsals, taught her the stage lingo and superstitions, and one day said to her, "Hurry and grow up so you can play Jo for me."

Kit had reached the point in her life after which she would never again be able to go unnoticed. After that the theatre and everything about it became a realistic part of her life, and although only an observer, she was privileged to see more of it, both behind the scenes and out front, than the average child. She met many of the greats, at least one of whom saw through her awkwardness to hidden grace and signed a copy of her autobiography, "Katharine Cornell, avec sympathie, Sarah Bernhardt." The book was stolen later on at boarding school.

Her new love did not replace the old, but frequently now when the others went out skating or skiing, she would escape to the library and bury herself in plays. On camping expeditions when she and her friends did their own portage, food was severely rationed, and Kit was always in disgrace for having illegally raided the sugar and jam. Now she found a way to make it up to her companions. At sunset after a tiring day, against pines and lake, they in turn against a colored sky, she would do an interpretive dance on the rocks or act a monologue for them and all would be forgiven — until the next time.

She went on being in school plays, but like her grandfather she shunned participation in the local amateur group, run by a woman named Jane Keeler, preferring rather removed private theatricals in the homes on Delaware Avenue with ballrooms large enough to accommodate them — Mrs. Rumsey's house, for one, and especially the Spragues', where another attraction was a good-looking son named Karl.

She continued writing, tending toward the literary rather than the theatrical with such efforts as a dramatization of Robert Browning's "On the Balcony," in which she acted with a young man named Bill Donovan, who would later head the OSS in World War II.

Boys were falling like tons of bricks, too, and old-time Buffaloans who were there at the time say she had numerous affairs, but to them the word "affair" means that Kit and her "lover" may have had hot chocolate together three days running, after a fast afternoon of roller-skating.

With the more ardent ones, roller-skating sometimes led to canoeing, and Bryant Glenny, for one, pursued her so passionately that she actually went on a chaperoned camping trip with him and he got to carry her canoe. Athletic but not physical, love affairs were none the less serious, and later on Anna Glenny, Bryant's sister, asked him why he had not married Kit. He said he knew it wouldn't work out. Anna maintains to this day that Kit would have married Bryant in a minute if he had crooked his little finger. Kit always maintained that she was once engaged to Bryant Glenny and broke it off because she knew it wouldn't work out and that he would have married her in a minute had she crooked her little finger.

There was no interim of prettiness in her looks. She went from plain and homely straight to beautiful with no stops between, a year without spring, winter to dazzling summer. And in the photographs of her at fifteen, sixteen, and seventeen, there is in her face no awareness that this is going to happen, is happening, and has happened, which of course makes her all the more beautiful. She still thought of herself as odd-looking and ill-proportioned and was convinced that she always would be. Since her beauty never was, especially at the beginning, conventional, there were those around her who did not recognize it and thought themselves wise and kind to agree with her about herself, strengthening her self-abnegation. She might have grown into a more assured woman had they been perspicacious enough to disagree, but she might also have lost that careless disregard for her looks which always so enhanced them.

It takes beauty to wear beautiful clothes, and lest it be thought she had any such pretensions, she stuck to self-effacing blouses, wide skirts, low-heeled shoes, roomy coats, deep pockets, and comfort. Maybe it was just easier that way. Maybe she didn't want to bother. From the start she had an eruptive sense of her own dramatic style, which smoldered in indolence unless fired by some element outside herself: a person, a situation, a role, or an emotion, if worthy and deeply enough felt. The resulting display could be stunning or volcanic or sometimes simply a nuisance to her friends.

Anna Glenny was a few years older than Kit, a stylish and talented sculptor. After study in Paris, she returned to Buffalo in 1909 or 1910 and set up a studio, which attracted Kit with its touch of affluent and respectable Bohemianism. It may have been Anna's taste, or maybe Kit's feeling for Bryant was so sentimental that she wanted to win his approval by emulating his sister, but one day she so admired what Anna was wearing, a black suit with a sealskin stand-up collar, that she immediately went out and had it copied for herself. There followed a series of public encounters, with sealskin stand-up collar bumping into sealskin stand-up collar in narrow, conspicuous places. Kit, not always able to recognize a contretemps, not even when in one, beamed in admiration and friendship, and Anna learned a lesson that all of Kit's women friends had to learn sooner or later if they wanted to remain her friends, as they always did: if she admired what you were wearing, you would never again be able to call it your own, so you might as well give it to her and get credit for generosity.

Edward Streeter seems never to have forgotten what she wore to a dinner party at the Manns' home on Bryant Street just off Delaware Avenue. In his "memorandum" of the evening, he does not specify the year, but he was quite young, and she was two years younger. Whenever he was with Kit, he felt they should discuss "deeper things than who loves who in Buffalo — things tending to do with great philosophy, transmutation of ideas, early Egyptian astronomy, or anything else we knew nothing about."

Seated next to her at dinner, he was surprised, therefore, to hear her whisper in a low voice, "Have you seen my snake-dance?"

He said that he had not but was sure he would enjoy it.

"Let's get away from this crowd as soon as dinner is over," Mr. Streeter reports her as saying. "They don't understand us. We will go into the library where we can be alone."

Alone in the library, she suggested he sit on the floor under the piano, apparently to be on a level with her performance. She threw herself on her face on the floor at the other end of the room facing him, and it was then that he fully appreciated her unforgettable low-cut dress. She extended her arms, clasped her hands in front of her and began to wiggle across the room in a sinister manner. Just as she neared him and seemed about to pounce, she veered off to do figure eights around the room, "hissing slightly from time to time and letting her tongue dart in and out temporarily."

He moved farther back under the piano for safety, pleased to have this delightful performance all to himself, when he happened to look at the door of the library, "and to my amazement found that it had been opened a few inches very quietly and that the faces of all the dinner guests were piled up one on top of the other, taking in the entire scene. . . . Katharine came to the climax of her dance, which I fortunately have forgotten. The door burst open and the dinner guests fell forward into the room as if it were a football scrimmage."

Some of Kit's friends have insisted, with earnestly wrinkled brows, that she had a great sense of humor. But in later years she was never one to "do a turn" at a party; she was usually the least theatrical woman in the room, much less actressy than many women who were not even in the theatre. Mr. Streeter's reminiscence, therefore, even allowing for the color a professional humorist might add in transcrib-

ing it into an anecdote, provides a welcome, uncharacteristic picture of
Kit as a young woman, part clown, part siren, and generously unin-
hibited.

On another occasion, Anna Glenny took over the huge Sprague
house on Delaware Avenue for a masked ball, calling it a *bal masque*,
which moved eighteen-year-old Kit to appear in an orange jumper,
black velvet skirt and tam, ostensibly under the impression that she
was dressed as a French artiste, but perhaps because she sensed that
with her odd dark looks she would be a startling sight to see. So startling was she that a young Buffaloan named Conger Goodyear accosted her with, "I don't know you and you don't know me, but will
you dance with me?" and extravagantly told his hostess, she reports
today, that he had met the most fascinating woman in the world and
fallen irrevocably, hopelessly in love.

While Conger Goodyear reeled under the impact and Bryant Glenny
wondered whose little finger should be crooked first, Karl Sprague
stepped in and took Kit home from the *bal masque*. It was about two
o'clock in the morning, much later than Peter allowed her to be out,
and lights were on in the house on Mariner Street, but the front door
was locked. When no amount of knocking and pounding could sum-
mon anyone to open it, Kit slipped around a corner of the house and
managed to peer into a lighted downstairs room where she saw her
mother and father in violent argument, gesticulating wildly. She may
have rapped on the glass for their attention but they couldn't hear her
above themselves, and it was obvious that she was deliberately locked
out. Perhaps her mother was pleading her case while Peter ranted that
girls who stayed out all night must be punished. Or he may have been
threatening to let Kit in to see her mother drunk at 2 A.M. while Alice
begged him to keep the door locked.

In any event, she fled with Karl Sprague, who offered to take her
back to the Sprague mansion for the night; but she knew she could
stay with a friend named Madeline in the next block, no matter how
late, and he took her there.

She never, all her life, could stand the sight of harsh open contention. It almost became a phobia, and if she had to be present, if it
could not be stopped and absolutely had to be witnessed, then she
would always have chosen to see it as she saw it that night — sound-
lessly, wordlessly, through a tightly shut window.

Another version of the lockout has it happening on a Christmas afternoon when Karl Sprague took her to a coming-out party of a friend, and she was told by Peter to the minute when to be home for the holiday meal. At the end of the afternoon and already running late, the young people got stuck in the snow. Kit jumped out and ran the rest of the way home. She arrived at the house on Mariner Street and had to ring the bell because Peter never allowed her to have her own key. A maid opened the door, informed her that Dr. and Mrs. Cornell were at dinner, that she was not to be admitted to the house, and closed the door in her face. Kit ran around the corner of the house and through a window saw her mother and father at the dinner table, gesticulating wildly in violent argument. At this moment Karl Sprague caught up with her and offered to take her back to the Sprague mansion, but she chose to seek the protection of two women who lived across the street, one of whom, Marian de Forest, wrote the dramatization of *Little Women* which in a year or two Jessie Bonstelle would direct on Broadway and in which, less than ten years later, Katharine Cornell would make her London debut as an actress.

The significant thing in both versions is that Kit always said she did not choose to go home with Karl Sprague because if she had she would have married him.

By which she didn't mean that she loved him so much that she was only waiting for the impulse, or that she was feeling adventurous or even reckless. She meant that at that particular moment, peering through the window to see her mother and father in hopeless conflict, she would have done about anything to escape from life in the house on Mariner Street with the friendly front porch.

At the time of the *bal masque* she had been away at school for a year or more, but it was the kind of separation that almost strengthened the ties instead of loosening them. Oaksmere School at Mamaroneck, New York, was at the extreme other end of the state, on Long Island Sound, and while the hundreds of miles from Buffalo gave her an exhilarating sense of freedom, the distance also removed her from what was going on or what she imagined was going on and brought worry and concern, and she found herself hurrying home at every opportunity because no matter what, no matter where she was or what her emotions, she must look after her mother, she must protect her mother, she must not abandon her mother.

But on the night of the *bal masque,* if a legitimate escape from home presented itself, something that would not hurt her father or separate her from her mother — marriage to a fine, upstanding Buffalo boy like Karl Sprague, who would remove her only as far as the next block — if at that moment he should feel a sudden determination to marry her, she knew she would do it.

At the same moment she realized that she knew instinctively how to induce in him such a sudden determination. This became more important than the moment; it was no longer a matter of whether or not she wanted ever to marry Karl Sprague or Bryant Glenny or anyone else. She sensed a power in herself that made her uneasy, a power to influence others.

Better to run for shelter to Madeline in the next block, or to seek comfort on Christmas afternoon with the literary ladies across the street.

What impelled Peter to discipline her so humiliatingly, even into young womanhood? There is no question that he loved her — it may be an answer. From the moment boys started coming around the house after supper to swing on a gate, Peter's attitude toward them can reasonably be put down to jealousy. Often he would find a way to send her to her room from the supper table as a punishment, and then he would tell the boy when he arrived that she had gone to bed. Although he would have denied any such intention, he let the boy think Kit had forgotten him or didn't want to see him.

But now she was grown. If Peter was still jealous, he was also too intelligent to lock her out in the middle of the night and drive her straight to the arms of any Karl who happened to be standing by, as indeed he almost did. His belief in discipline cannot have blinded him to this self-defeating risk.

To understand Peter, it is necessary to look more fully at his letter to her on her forty-second birthday in 1935.

I could write volumes about your early life and our little visits together upon numerous occasions. I remember once when you were quite small, you and I took a trip to Detroit. I had to go on business and I thought it would be nice to have you go with me. You were so glad to go with

me and were so afraid that your mother, who came to see us off, would
get left on the boat that you were almost frantic, and in your wild ges-
ticulations waving good-bye to your mother who stood on the dock, you
bursted all the buttons off your shirt which was buttoned to your waist.
That was a bad start for me, but with the help of the stewardess we got
the buttons back on and I tried to keep your hands down below your
head after that. We did have a good time.

Peter was seventy when he wrote that, and although he begins the
letter by saying, "I am addressing you a little differently this time," the
salutation he refers to, "My Dearest Little Girl," is the way he had always thought of her. It was more than that, it was the way he classified
her in his well-managed life, and it rather angered him that she dared
to step out of character by growing up. In his self-serving and self-
deceiving vision, he was a loving and clumsy old Daddy, and his Dearest Little Girl was so glad to go away with him to Detroit (and leave
Mother on the dock, don't forget) that she did not just burst her buttons, she *bursted* 'em! Despite the archness of these "little visits," the
only way gentle Daddy could keep her there in that world with him
was to waylay suitors and lock her out of the house in the middle of
the night. It wasn't really the suitors whom he waylaid, it was the girl
they pursued, the adult she was becoming against his wishes, and it
wasn't Kit herself that he locked out, it was the creature in the orange
jumper and black velvet skirt who danced and won their hearts at the
bal masque.

When, later, she turned out well, Peter was not only proud of her
but claimed credit. From the distance of 1935, he was somehow able to
believe that his efforts to stop her from growing up had actually created
the magnificent woman then being acclaimed by the world. His mood
is joking, but he longs to be believed:

You know, I will not say how many years ago it was that you arrived in
this world and little did anybody think then that that little bit of a three
and a half pound bunch of humanity was going to sweep the theatrical
world off the board. However, it has been done. Perhaps the baths I gave
you when you were about three or four weeks old, continuing up to the
time you were sixteen, and which I enjoyed giving you and you seemed
to enjoy having, cleaned you up and cleared you up to such a point that

you could achieve this position. I can just feel you now, lying in the palm of my hand floating in the tub of water. . . .

St. Margaret's School, while offering advantages in Art, Music and Sloyd ("a Swedish system of manual training designed for training in the use of tools and materials but emphasizing training in woodcarving as a means to that end"), also claimed with commendable but perhaps rash conviction, "Preperation [sic] for college work is a specialty, and the many honors bestowed on pupils who have entered all the various colleges for women on St. Margaret's diploma testify to the splendid groundwork they have received."

Which may be why in 1908, at the end of the eighth grade, Kit was taken out of St. Margaret's and sent away to Oaksmere, a finishing school which "prepared young women for social life rather than for a vocation or professional career" and fell more in line with Peter's ideas for her future.

Life at Oaksmere was pleasant. Should Long Island Sound prove too rough for swimming, there was a pool as well. There were sweeping lawns for brisk morning walks, gardens and hedgerows for afternoon strolls, and shady spots and summerhouses for ladylike pursuits of knowledge. There were tennis courts, congeniality, and lovely manners. Kit's favorite subject was psychology. She also loved Bible Study and History of the Novel, courses that helped turn her into a voracious reader. No graduate of Oaksmere seems to remember any classrooms or any classes having to do with such ordinary matters as history, geography, or mathematics. The actress Natalie Schafer recalls, "We were taught to drink tea with our little finger sticking out and later on it took years to unlearn it."

Like Jessie Bonstelle the year before, Mrs. Merrill, the owner and headmistress of Oaksmere, was bowled over by fifteen-year-old Kit and encouraged her to develop her theatrical talents, which she did in schoolgirl fashion. For special treats there was Mamaroneck's close proximity to New York City. Kit had been to Broadway only once, a few years before with Peter who insisted on taking her to the biggest extravaganza in town: whatever was playing at the Hippodrome. In small theatre parties from Oaksmere, supervised by Mrs. Merrill, she was able to see plays more to her liking.

Jessie Bonstelle had said, "Hurry and grow up so you can play Jo for me!", practically an assurance that there would be a place waiting for her, and yet here she was, from 1908 to 1911, going along with Peter's plans for her future, preparing for life in Buffalo's polite society and, it has to be admitted, under no protest, in fact enjoying it. She even considered going on to college at Bryn Mawr, although one look at the stiff entrance examination changed her mind.

Becoming an actress was something that would happen only when she had done everything that was expected of her as a dutiful and loving daughter.

4

Stage Wait (1911-1916)

AFTER GRADUATION FROM OAKSMERE in the spring of 1911 she did not go into the theatre, she did not try, she did not even go to New York to stay until more than five years had passed. In 1912 William A. Brady produced Marian de Forest's dramatization of *Little Women*, featuring his nineteen-year-old daughter Alice as Meg, the play staged by Jessie Bonstelle. Kit, too, was nineteen, out of school at last, her duty done to her father, presumably impatient to begin the Great Adventure, certainly grown up enough to play Jo, and yet she made no attempt to call herself to Bonnie's attention, if only to remind her of her old injunction and be turned down. Modesty and shyness cannot account for it all. She simply passed up that chance and did not go to New York to become an actress until the fall of 1916.

Twelve years later, in 1928, when she had been a recognized star for several years, she was still so oblivious to the unwritten laws of stardom that she was more than likely to begin any casual conversation with the confidential admission, "Well, I'm thirty-five years old . . . !" In the era of Flaming Youth that was a bit long in the tooth for the most beautiful woman on the American stage, and her friends, associates, advisers, and protectors openly winced. No amount of exhortation availed. She simply could not remember not to give away her age, and so it was decided, in secret conclave, that her age would have to be changed. On her driver's license renewal application that year, the three in her year of birth, 1893, was easily altered to a nice authoritative eight, and it was drilled into her head that whenever she got to feeling chatty and confessional, please remember that she was thirty. The lie, however, stuck in her throat, and the original end was achieved in that she stopped talking about her age altogether.

But from then on in the annals of the theatre she was born in 1898, and in *I Wanted to Be an Actress* it was said, without specifying dates, that she graduated from Oaksmere and went directly to New York where she made the rounds of the managers' offices and soon found herself playing bit parts. To make her life come out even, chronologically, the years 1911–1916 were the proper, logical five years to elide, since they were waiting years, marking-time years. Why did she mark time? What was she waiting for?

The answer seems to be, simply, that her attention kept being diverted.

First there came her Uncle Douglas's marriage in June of 1911. The wedding was a big, happy, overriding event in the Cornell family, after which Douglas and his new wife, Gwendolyn, planned to go to London for the coronation of King George V.

At the same time Aunt Lydia decided to give Kit a graduation present and take her to England that summer to meet her Hadfield cousins. It worked out, therefore, amid general family merriment, that Aunt Lydia and Kit would accompany Uncle Douglas and Gwendolyn on their honeymoon.

A cousin named Charles Hanson, later to be knighted, was at that time an officer of one of the big insurance companies in London. His offices overlooked the route of the coronation parade, and he arranged for the party from Buffalo to watch it from his windows. After that the foursome split up. All the places where Aunt Lydia took Kit for the rest of the summer are not known, but fifty years later, in 1961, in a letter from the Beau Rivage Hotel in Lausanne, Switzerland, Kit wrote, "This is a fantastic hotel. I stayed here with Aunt Lydia in 1911. It was old then."

Just out of school, with a bid to travel, a chance to see the world, invaluable research experience for a young actress — these were irresistible reasons for deferring personal ambition until fall.

And in the fall Mrs. Merrill had found that she could not let Kit go and begged her to return to Oaksmere as dramatics instructor and athletics coach. Alice Cornell was receding deeper into alcoholic oblivion, beyond needing or being needed, and a call for help from the motherly

Mrs. Merrill filled a vacancy in Kit's life that was stronger and more immediate than the call to Broadway.

Almost as soon as the automobile was invented, Kit seems to have known how to drive, and one of her duties at Oaksmere was to chauffeur a select group of young ladies, usually about five, to a polite luncheon and midweek matinee in the city, with all five young ladies (taking Natalie Schafer as an example) plotting, conniving, and vying with one another to sit next to her in the automobile, the restaurant, and the theatre. That was the only call to Broadway she would answer for the next five years.

She was sidetracked by whatever came up, whatever seemed worthy of her attention, and that included just about every kind of pleasurable experience — provided it had a certain dash to it and managed to be self-improving at the same time. She was drawn to the immediate, to the familiar, even to the safe — if it could be made to offer a challenge. Oaksmere in the fall of 1911 was the known, where she would be elevated by personal popularity to a kind of stardom — with responsibility as the challenge — while Broadway was the unknown, full of uncertainty despite the certainty of her ambition. To someone with Kit's strong self-doubts, as long as the new career was not embarked upon, it could not fail.

Her return to Oaksmere was no more than a kind of reprieve, but she was too conscientious to waste time and worked hard to develop her theatre crafts within the limitations of a dilettante school and a troop of teenage girls. She concocted all the pantomimes and wrote her own productions, including an allegorical play about Vestal Virgins with holy fire and an epic involving Alexander the Great and a captive maiden. She improvised on past experience, especially her campfire recitations, introducing outdoor productions at Oaksmere. She became intensely interested in directing. She did all the sets and of course played Alexander the Great.

Amateurism was a big thing in the American theatre just before World War I. As a reaction against the meretricious professionalism of Broadway where, as Brooks Atkinson puts it, "anything that worked was good enough," the little-theatre movement came into being. The art theatre and the community theatre were springing up across the country far away from New York, with 30,000 members enrolled in drama leagues. It amounted to a revolution, an active determination that the theatre be taken seriously as an art. New York itself began to feel the pressure and the presence of the revolution in 1914 with the emergence of the Neighborhood Playhouse on Grand Street. Next, a group of restless young people, among them Eugene O'Neill, descended on the city from Cape Cod and settled into the Provincetown Playhouse on Macdougal Street in Greenwich Village. In 1915 a small bunch of amateurs leased the Band Box Theatre on East Fifty-seventh Street to produce programs of short plays by such known but unfamiliar European writers Maurice Maeterlinck and Alfred de Musset and such unknown American writers as Lawrence Langner, Zoe Akins, Philip Moeller, and Edward Goodman. They "called themselves the Washington Square Players because their cultural center had been Lawrence Langner's Washington Square Book Shop in Greenwich Village." As Brooks Atkinson goes on to describe their operation, "they played on Friday and Saturday evenings in a tiny theater that seated forty people, and they charged 50 cents admission. The total payroll consisted of one stagehand and one office boy." Robert Edmond Jones helped them bring in their first bill of plays at a cost of thirty-five dollars. Professional showmen expected them to fail, but they did not. They flourished.

Amateur dramatics also flourished at Oaksmere, in a general sense because they had become fashionable, specifically because of the impetus provided by Kit. All her life she gave the impression that the things that interested and consumed her had never before existed on earth, or if they had that she was the first to discover them. Such enthusiasm is contagious, and at Oaksmere she found willing followers. Natalie Schafer, for one, came to school with the idea that she wanted to be a costume designer when she grew up, but soon she was telling Mrs. Merrill that she had changed her mind and wanted to be an actress. If Kit's devoted crew were more lovestruck than stagestruck, that meant an even greater determination to give their lives for her. Soon they were putting on a different play every two weeks.

That was Kit's last year at Oaksmere, and the schedule was so heavy that outside directors were needed. Theresa Helburn, a young Bryn

Mawr graduate who had gone on to Radcliffe and the Sorbonne — and George Pierce Baker's famous 47 Workshop at Harvard — came to direct *Twelfth Night* and ended up playing Sir Toby Belch to Kit's Malvolio. Others who commuted from New York to lend their services were Florence Enright, a leading actress with the Washington Square Players, and Edward Goodman, one of the group's founders. These three, with Kit, took turns coaching the productions, among them Shaw's *Man of Destiny*, in which she played Napoleon.

Brooks Atkinson writes that the Washington Square Players eventually moved to the Comedy Theatre (with a seating capacity of six hundred) on Forty-first Street just east of Broadway where they charged a dollar admission and played seven performances a week, for which the actors received twenty-five dollars each. Succumbing to commercialism, they became a new kind of professional, talented, serious, hardworking, and dedicated. Only slightly older than Kit and already so accomplished, they can only have strengthened her belief in the theatre as an art and in acting as a career worthy of her finest efforts.

In the summer of 1914 an eighteen-year-old Canadian youth with a keen enthusiasm for horses was visiting family friends in Cobourg, and his hostess introduced him to a dark beauty three years his senior who took him in hand and offered to show him the local barns and stables. She strode off and he followed. Getting him alone, she turned on him with penetrating intensity.

"What are you going to be?" she demanded to know. Not "What would you like to be?" or "What are your plans for the future?" but a no-nonsense request for plain information.

She listened while he murmured something about becoming a farmer because his family's business was in farm machines, but she really seemed to have asked the question only so that she could say, when he had finished, "I am going to become a professional actress."

It was a statement, allowing for no doubt or difference of opinion, and the youth fell into such a state of besottedness that he changed all his life plans, or rather he formed them for the first time on the spot, forsaking horses, farms, and family and pledging himself to become a professional actor so that one day he might step onto a stage with this dark goddess. The longings and predilections she inspired were never fleeting, so it is no surprise that it took Raymond Massey twenty-six years to achieve this particular goal and that he has always considered it well worth the effort.

The word "professional" is the new, clear-sighted specific in Kit's ambition. It was as if she were now able to distinguish between what she was and what she was determined to become. As far as she was concerned she had been an actress for some time, and it wasn't much to be an actress — even Aunt Lydia was an actress. She intended to become something more, and the something more was not vague and elusive. She was not going to become anything as amorphous and self-congratulatory as a "great" actress or an "emotional" actress or a "classical" actress or a "tragic" actress. She was going to become a "professional" actress. As she used it, there was a soundness to the word "professsional" as there was beauty in the voice that spoke it and intelligence in the mind that conceived it, and it was almost inevitable that she would become all the things she did not claim she would become — emotional, classical, tragic — sustained by the quality that supported all the others and, in fact, sometimes passed for them: her superb professionalism.

———

Mrs. Merrill's tall, good-looking, and rather nice son had nothing to do with his mother's school, but soon after Kit went there as an instructor he began dropping in with some regularity, and with Mrs. Merrill's blessing and encouragement, he and Kit went out together a few times. But Kit, who could be so easily diverted from her course by someone else's wedding, had no intention of being sidetracked into one of her own. What is puzzling is her continued inaction, why she went on to Oaksmere month after month, now amounting to year after year, when the world of the theatre was out there waiting.

She never lost sight of the dream; her ambition never wavered — but it was ambition without drive or vanity. Looking back on herself fifty years later she said she was indiscriminate, that she drifted, that she slid from one thing to another, and even discounting her strenuous modesty, it is clear that she was always influenced by circumstances and that she drifted until circumstances allowed her to pursue the dream or, more accurately, until circumstances left her no choice.

That seems to be the way it happened. Finally, when there was nothing else to do and no place else to go, she left Oaksmere and went to New York to become a professional actress.

Meanwhile, she kept returning to Buffalo in the belief that her attendance and loving care might still rescue Alice Cornell from complete self-destruction. Sometimes when it seemed that Buffalo itself was to blame for everything, she would take her mother to Atlantic City, but they took the problem with them. Kit had to stay with her mother every minute of the time to make sure she did not get hold of any alcohol, and when she sought a brief and necessary respite, she would lock Alice in her room and go downstairs to the dining room. Invariably when she returned she would unlock the door to find her mother drunk. The obese, arrogant creature who had once been pretty Alice died in Buffalo on June 19, 1915. In October she would have been forty-five.

Probably at once Kit began mythologizing her mother into that childlike, beautiful personage she would remember with such clarity later on, but Peter went silent. In all of his letters that survive, written in the 1930s and 1940s, there is only one reference to Alice; it is not written to his daughter but to a third party, and he does not refer to her as "Alice" or "Mrs. Cornell" or "my wife," but as "Katharine's mother."

Kit inherited enough money from her mother to make her independent of her father, if that had been holding her back, and still she returned to Oaksmere in the fall of 1915.

But circumstances were fast arranging themselves, and it would be her last year there.

———

Back in Buffalo she was of course expected to go into mourning for her mother; it was correct and seemly.

Spontaneous zaniness on the order of the snake-dance does not seem to have been a regular part of the drifting, perhaps restless days of her youth, but it was her way, when she so chose, to take what was expected of her and give it a lift into the dramatic, sometimes with extravagant results. There was her sudden astonishing appearance at Oaksmere in the fall of 1915 wrapped in deepest black, with a black silk blouse recklessly open at the throat and tucked into a circular black skirt reaching almost to the ground, revealing glimpses of black stocking as she strode in solitary grief across the wide lawns and down to the Sound — leading a white Russian wolfhound.

In anyone else it would seem to have been calculated for effect
simply because it is hard to be spontaneous about acquiring a white
Russian wolfhound. Even seeking quick comfort in the derangement
of grief, most of us would be forced to give serious thought first to the
feeding and housing of such an animal, especially if we lived on someone else's premises, our employer's premises at that, in a rather com-
munal atmosphere. To anyone but an exhibitionist, a white Russian
wolfhound would be a damned nuisance at such a time — but Kit was
not an exhibitionist.

She was, however, a mature woman now with an inner life so robust
that at times her external world would be unable to deal with the flow
of feeling. Urgent impulses would pile up and, unable to wait for
adequate expression, would impatiently emerge as ambiguous, sometimes ridiculous, gestures. In the instance of her mother's death, she
would reach out blindly to life — and embrace a big dog. To make the
solace as overpowering as the grief it was alleviating, it had to be a
white Russian wolfhound. The inner grace of spirit which was hers
could not always conceal a certain awkwardness of action. In life, as
on the stage, it gave a moving fallibility to the grandness of her manner.

Wherever the dog was acquired and however it was transported to
the lawns of Oaksmere for dramatic walks down to the Sound, it was
probably done so impulsively. At the school, her adoring pupils were
so struck by the spectacle that they begged to be allowed to look after
the beast she had thrust into their midst and couldn't believe their
good fortune when she graciously granted permission.

Schoolgirl crushes were all the more passionate for being completely
innocent. Two girls were expelled from Oaksmere that year, but they
were the exception, and nobody even thought to question whatever
official reason was given. The resulting new regulation that in the
future girls might only go for walks in three's, never two's, under
threat of severe disciplinary measures, was just another rule and meant
nothing to anybody until years later in hindsight. For girls growing
up in 1915, women in life as on the stage had not progressed much
beyond *Good Gracious, Annabelle*.

But even though the mind could not conceive of anything deeper
than the very kind, sweet and proper teacher-pupil relationship, yet at
least one of her pupils maintains to this day that her feeling was so
strong that she would have done anything in the world "Miss Cornell"
asked her to, whether she understood it or not, that she would have

gone wherever led in whatever direction, emotionally or geographically.

Kit must have been aware of the emotions that she evoked and perhaps she sensed again, as she had with Karl Sprague on the night of the *bal masque,* her own power to influence people in their actions. Perhaps again it made her uneasy, especially with people so young and unformed. Perhaps it was time to leave Oaksmere.

Certainly nobody wanted her to. In fact there suddenly appeared a formidable obstacle. Mrs. Merrill had decided to marry Kit to her son, who appeared ready and willing, and thereby secure her to Oaksmere forever. And if the mother-son alliance was not persuasive enough, they were flanked by two Merrill daughters, teachers and chaperones at the school, who had welcomed Kit as a friend with an eye to acquiring her as a sister-in-law.

Kit began to feel an uncomfortable pressure. And even though she had refused Mrs. Merrill's boy from the start, she knew that in her dread of hurting people sometimes her smiling rebuffs were taken as encouragement. She may have had a growing sense that she owed him something, that she owed the whole family something simply for wanting her so much. She had a tendency to acquiesce to others' wishes if she thought she owed it to them, and sometimes if she thought it would make them happy. Besides, she was undoubtedly attracted to the Merrills, really drawn to this generous, charming family. But if she had wanted to get married and settle for the conventional life, she could have stayed in Buffalo, and if that was what she found she wanted now, why not return to Buffalo where family position and eligible beaux were already established and waiting? Or did she really mean to become a professional actress?

She wrote a play that year, which Edward "Eddie" Goodman came up from the Washington Square Players to direct. With growing theatrical good sense, in this effort she abandoned Alexander the Great to draw on personal observations made during summers in Cobourg and her one visit to England. Its subject was a girl her own age, a French-Canadian girl who marries an Englishman and goes to London where she has a bad time of it among the disdainful British aristocracy. It was a "Ruth amid the alien corn" theme that would always attract her later on as an actress, though there was no clue to it in the title: she called the play "Play." When the performance was over Eddie Goodman said, "If you're thinking of going into the theatre, let me know when you get to New York."

Fortunately circumstances had arranged themselves so that this invitation could be most willingly acted upon. She knew she had to leave Oaksmere, but she never would have hurt the Merrills by walking out on them without giving some reason having nothing to do with them, something too big to be denied, so that they could — in fact would have to! — cheer her on her way.

Eddie Goodman supplied the reason. Circumstances had conditioned her to be able to leave Oaksmere; then circumstances had gone so far as to make it necessary; and now circumstances provided the getaway.

In 1948 Helen E. Hokinson did a drawing for *The New Yorker* of two suburban clubwomen entering the Martin Beck Theatre for a performance (surely a Wednesday matinee) of Katharine Cornell's production of *Antony and Cleopatra*. Portly, hatted, tippeted, and agog, the first hungry culture-seeker whets the other's appetite for the soaring, classic, theatrical joys to come by assuring her, "I just know you'll love her, she's a Buffalo girl, too, you know!"

For Katharine Cornell, life would have many variations, some of them contradictory. She would be led by circumstances to be many people, all extensions, embellishments or modifications of the smiling, intense twenty-three-year-old woman who left Oaksmere for New York in the fall of 1916 to become a professional actress. She did not change from one being to another, she accumulated them. She did not give up being a hoyden to become a distinguished woman of style; she did not give up being a distinguished woman of style to become an A-number-one athlete; she did not stop being an athlete to become an artist and actress; while to stop being an actress would have undermined all her accomplishment in becoming a manager; she did not give up being a manager when she was needed to be a daughter; she did not forsake being a daughter to function as a wife; she was no less a wife for becoming a lover; and she never stopped loving to become a good friend. Each variation only added richness to the others, and the miracle is that she could sustain them all to the end of her life. It took skill to keep all the balls bouncing; it took imagination to be so many things completely and deeply, without ever betraying one for another.

Had Mrs. Hokinson's merry matinee ladies gone backstage after the performance of *Antony and Cleopatra* to have a program signed ("To show them back home!"), they would have found in the warm, knowledgeable exchange of familiar names, places, and recollections that their faith was confirmed, and that without ever stooping to be folksy or familiar, the woman who left Buffalo to become a professional actress had never given up being a Buffalo girl.

With her mother's death in 1915, however, she no longer felt responsible for anyone in Buffalo, and with the economic freedom it gave her she no longer felt responsible *to* anyone in Buffalo. Her father undoubtedly opposed her going to New York and wanted her to come home, but whether he understood it or not, Buffalo had ceased *being* her home. She would keep going back there until there was nobody to go back to; she would always open her plays there; and knowing full well that to fashionable New Yorkers of the day, "upstate" was considered very unfashionable, she delighted in telling the world that that's where she came from.

But in the fall of 1916, New York was the place to be because Eddie Goodman had said to let him know when she got there.

§ II

Katherine (sic) (1916-1920)

5

Fifth Business (1916-1918)

EVERYONE SEEMS TO AGREE that Anne Park came from Montrose, Pennsylvania. Beyond that the information is contradictory, perhaps because Anne Park herself was contradictory. Some say she and Kit were fellow students at Oaksmere, but old Buffaloans maintain she went to Miss Nixon's, a finishing school in Florence, Italy, where socially prominent American families sometimes sent their daughters. There she met a set of Buffalo girls, and through them, Kit.

She arrived in New York in the fall of 1916 to study singing and wanted Kit to join forces with her there. It assuaged the upstate social sense of propriety to know that Kit would not be going it alone. Nevertheless, to be on the safe side, Aunt Lucy Plimpton was dispatched from Buffalo to act as chaperone, and the genial older woman and her charge settled into a Miss Pennypacker's boardinghouse on East Thirty-ninth Street between Fifth and Madison Avenues. Anne Park did not live far off.

In the fall of 1916 the United States was on the verge of entering the Great War. The public was in no mood to be told that war was cruel, ugly, inhumane, or uncivilized. Anything more critical or probing than the bittersweet Sigmund Romberg tunes in the operetta *Her Soldier Boy* was not worth going into a theatre for. By the time Kit joined Anne Park in New York, antiwar sentiments on the stage were actually considered by many to be unpatriotic.

Not only the rash ones, the romantics, or the blood-thirsty, but also quiet intellectuals, even the simple and dutiful young men who would have to do the actual fighting longed for us to get into the scrap. They ached to join up and then, arms linked, to march off to brisk military airs, all fellows together, to that beautiful "somewhere," the front line of battle. There was a derisive theatrical phrase of the day to describe a certain kind of prolonged, overly sentimental stage scene — "death to slow music." A pejorative inside the theatre, it was almost a credo outside.

Thus the atmosphere in late 1916 and early 1917 when the United States finally entered the Great War was as romantically patriotic as the poems of Rupert Brooke. Camaraderie, service, loyalty, high ideals, and courage were in the very air, and sacrifice was a matter of pride. The nature of war divided the sexes, and while most young women had to be content with smilin' through as they kept the home fires burning, the English writer Rose Macauley spoke for others in her "Many Sisters to Many Brothers":

> In the trench you are sitting, while I am knitting
> A hopeless sock that never gets done.
> Well, here's luck, my dear; — and you've got it, no fear;
> But for me . . . a war is poor fun.*

The marching fever was catching to all, but only men were permitted to succumb. It was a compensation, therefore, and great fun for two of Rose Macauley's "sisters" to step off to their own tunes of glory. It was stirring for Kit and Anne to move to the front line, if only the front line of art. In the emotional warmth of this cavalier climate, the friendship of the unawakened young actress and the unsleeping young singer, smiled upon by Aunt Lucy, stabilized Kit's life while at the same time propelling it forward. Anne Park was single-minded, outgoing, artful, and clever — a good balance for her darker, shyer, more ingenuous, and higher-minded opposite. This was the first serious attachment of Kit's life, outside the family, to which she chose to give her deepest feelings, and therefore it may have been a last, somewhat belated step into maturity. So it was with more than her accustomed

---

* From: *Poems of To-Day, An Anthology* (London: Published for the English Association by Sidgwick & Jackson, Ltd., 1932); first issued August 1915; "Many Sisters To Many Brothers" originally published in *The Westminster Gazette*.

ebullience that she set off to let Eddie Goodman of the Washington Square Players know that Katharine Cornell had, at last, come to town.

The Washington Square Players' business offices in the Comedy Theatre were always crowded with actors. Into their midst came Kit. For the first and almost the last time in her life and career, she joined the ranks of the waiting and unemployed.

There have been those since, writers and friends, who seize this brief period and exaggerate it out of all proportion, as though she had to undergo a great struggle to achieve recognition. They say, and she herself never denied it, that she had to wait weeks before anyone paid attention to her. Eddie Goodman, they contend, despite his previous interest in her, literally brushed past her, sometimes seeing her, sometimes not. Had she been thus ignored, had Eddie Goodman refused to see her, she would have been so deeply hurt that she would have gone away and never returned. The chances are that he welcomed her absentmindedly and gave her enough incentive to keep her coming back. It may have seemed like forever but it was in the normal course of events that one day he said some people were to read parts and asked her to join them.

She followed him into the darkened auditorium and experienced for the first time the terror of a casting call.

"Louder, Miss Cornell. We can't hear you."

Another attempt, a dry fear that paralyzes the throat muscles, then the final dismissal, "I'm sorry, you won't do."

Such utter failure at the very beginning is devastating, but there is also something exhilarating about it. One has to be considered before one can be turned down, and having been considered one is, at least, a part of whatever it is. The failure hurts, but there is a glamour to the hurt, a protective need to hug it for a while, to luxuriate in it. Thus, according to the legend, Kit shortly found herself creeping into St. Patrick's Cathedral and slumping into the back pew to weep softly in mourning for her stillborn art.

Apparently the only way to get a part in a play was to answer casting calls with other actors, and after her one experience she knew she could not do that, not even if she knew how to go about it, how to find out where they were and who to see to get in.

Anne Park's imperturbability bucked her up, and her friend's example gave Kit a clue to the next step. Even with her self-assurance, Anne had not plunged into auditions and direct competition with other aspirants in her field as Kit had. She had begun with singing lessons from a talented teacher, Laura Elliot. Kit, deciding perhaps she had skipped a step, went back to the Washington Square Players not to ask for another audition, but to ask Florence Enright to be her acting coach. Florence Enright suggested that she watch rehearsals as an observer, if Eddie Goodman would agree, which he did.

They were rehearsing a one-act Japanese play called *Bushido*, in which the part of Shusai, a Japanese mother, was so small and unimportant that it did not need to be rehearsed, and the actress who was to play it did not even have to come to rehearsals. Eddie Goodman asked Kit to pinch-hit for the time being. It was simple expediency, with nothing depending on it for either one, but it bolstered her confidence to find she was, at least, useful, and it suited her just fine to be no more than a body standing up in a part, because it meant that unobserved, by herself, she was able to become familiar with the play and make it her own. In Japanese, the word "bushido" defines a code of ethics emphasizing loyalty and duty. These were two qualities Kit understood so well that she found her way into the play and fell in love with Shusai who, stripped of all she loved by loyalty and duty, could only murmur four words, "My son, my son." It was what was then called "a heavy-thinking part" and Kit thought heavy. Had Eddie Goodman been looking closely, he would have noticed that the girl from Buffalo was not simply coming to rehearsals, she was entering rehearsals with the glidelike walk of a Samurai woman.

There came the day toward the end of rehearsals when the actress engaged to play Shusai was to take over the role, and Kit, in case there were any subtle vibrations in the air that might disturb anyone, including herself, stayed away. The following day she was back in her old place as an observer. But Helen Westley, a founder of the Washington Square Players and its leading character woman, called her up on the stage, told her that the other actress hadn't showed up the day before, and asked if she would like to try for the role herself in the next run-through.

It was very close to the opening, and all eyes were suddenly on Kit, appraisingly, ready to pass judgment. Prepared and rehearsed though she was, it is probably just as well that the role amounted to only four words; had it been any bigger, with the onset of nerves under the sudden critical pressure, she might very easily have failed this second chance with the Washington Square Players. As it was, the role was just long enough, she was familiar and comfortable with what she had to do, and it was over in a few minutes. Legend has it that after she murmured "My son, my son," the play stopped and everyone applauded. If they did, it was in relief that she had gotten through it and could stay on as one of them. Eddie Goodman may have engineered the whole thing to make it as easy as possible for her. Wherever she went, once she was there, people always wanted her to stay.

In December 1916 when Kit made her New York debut in *Bushido* just half a block off Broadway, on Broadway Charlotte Greenwood was doing the highest kicks and deepest splits in town in *So Long, Letty;* Laurette Taylor, after an almost endless tour in *Peg o' My Heart,* was back in another J. Hartley Manners play, *The Harp of Life,* supported by a new young English actress, Lynn Fontanne; David Belasco, in the face of strong anti-German popular sentiment, had the nerve to revive *The Music Master* and make it a hit despite David Warfield's thick German accent in the title role; that nondescript person, Maude Adams, was typecast as nondescript Miss Thing and, as always, made the character glow in James M. Barrie's *A Kiss for Cinderella;* and William A. Brady was reviving *Little Women,* once again staged by Jessie Bonstelle with a girl playing Jo who was unknown at the time and remained so. Kit's performance as Shusai went by too fast to make more than a momentary impression, and her next appearance that season for the Washington Square Players was not even an appearance but a series of off-stage cries as a mother in childbirth in Leonid Andreyev's symbolic drama, *The Life of Man.*

On March 26, 1917, less than two weeks before the United States finally declared war on Germany, Kit played her first real part in *Plots and Playwrights* by Edward Massey, a prize play from George Pierce Baker's 47 Workshop at Harvard.

Heywood Broun in the *New York Tribune* said she was "extremely effective in a quiet telling manner," and in the *New York Evening Mail* Burns Mantle wrote, "The Washington Square Players have done one thing for which they should be praised, and that is they have brought to the notice of New York theatre-goers a young woman, Katherine [*sic*] Cornell, who is the most promising actress of the present season."

———

Guthrie McClintic, who many years later described himself at that time as "a tender plant," worked in the office of producer Winthrop Ames. As part of his casting duties, he went to every show in town, keeping track of new talents as they arrived on the scene, filing their names in the Ames office for future reference. Scribbling on his program in the dark at a performance of *Plots and Playwrights*, he wrote three words next to the name of his future wife: "Interesting — monotonous — watch."

An impressionable critic who saw Kit in *Plots and Playwrights* was moved to describe her as "a dead-white, young American Duse." But in assessing her performance, Guthrie McClintic was probably more accurate, as he always would be from then on. His word "interesting" is mild and unspecific, but so was her talent at that time. It was still so undeveloped that she undoubtedly lacked variety and fell into monotony without the craft to pull herself out.

The word "watch" simply means "This girl may be going places," but it is also a terse admission of his own fascination. Guthrie was a cautious and superstitious man, and perhaps the word is sharp for he senses he is being influenced in some mysterious way, that his life is being changed, and alerts himself not just to watch but to watch out.

If that seems fanciful and complicated, one might as well get used to the fact right here that Guthrie McClintic was a fanciful and complicated man, and a rambunctious theatrical man. If simplicity is all that's wanted, then his cryptic injunction to himself to "watch" was, in fact, redundant, since from then on he would be unable not to, as a tender plant suddenly set in the sun will feel the warmth and instinctively turn its face in that direction.

———

Frances M. Wolcott, widow of Nevada Senator Ned Wolcott, influential Buffaloan friend to the Cornells of Delaware Avenue, prodigious cosmopolite and Patroness-at-Large, was, as Kit herself put it, "a dynamic war-horse of a woman," the kind who would always feel challenged by the disparity between the intensity of Kit's talent and her amiable and rather aimless ways. She decided that the helpless child didn't know how to push herself properly and needed a leg up.

Mrs. Wolcott's great talent, and it was a valuable one, was introducing people to other people with an eye to the broadening of horizons. Now with Kit in New York and actually on view in *Plots and Playwrights*, Mrs. Wolcott was stirred to specific action. The Americanized English actor William Faversham, for years popular and loved as *The Squaw Man*, was persuaded to invite Mrs. Wolcott and Kit to dinner along with an English playwright, Cyril Harcourt, revered stage designer Robert Edmond Jones, and John Corbin, the brand-new drama critic on the *New York Times*, and his wife.

In a dark green velvet dinner gown, Kit arrived punctually, to get herself off on the best foot she could, and found herself seated in the place of honor beside her host's young and lovely middle wife (overall, he had three), the former Julie Opp. While she counted the minutes before she could with propriety excuse herself and run to the theatre, Kit gained assurance, talked animatedly as if she were having a rattling good time, reached eloquently for a piece of bread and knocked a full glass of Burgundy into Mrs. Faversham's lap. Don Giovanni, of all people, came to her mind at that moment as she wished the floor would open up for her as it had for him and let her "slip into the blessed oblivion of the coal bin." She sopped up Julie Faversham as best she could and turned to chatter brightly to Mrs. Corbin, pretending nothing had happened.

Later on it was said that onstage, when in a grand emotion she threw her arm blindly into the air, she knew without looking exactly where her hand rested in space, to the very inch. If the same was not always true at fashionable dinner tables, her awkwardness nevertheless became a grace rather than a fall from it, endearing her to the spilled-upon. The Favershams were no exception.

When the warm weather came, the Washington Square Players closed their doors, but Kit was invited to come back in the fall for another season (which no one could foresee would be their last). Like a schoolgirl released from class, she fled to Cobourg for the summer, where William Faversham tracked her down with a telegram beseeching her to try out for the leading woman's role in his new play, *The Old Country*. Notwithstanding Mrs. Wolcott's pushing her to push herself, she wired back a refusal, her sense of inadequacy for once standing her in good stead. She was barely getting used to playing bits and pieces and was in no way ready to play a leading role opposite a prominent star. And she must have felt that the offer was suspect since Faversham had never seen her perform. He had sent Ray Henderson, his press representative, to a performance of *Plots and Playwrights* and may have received a good report, but still it would be reasonable for Kit to wonder if his interest was not mere courtesy to her or, more likely, deference to the formidable Mrs. Wolcott.

Still, it takes courage to pass up such an opportunity.

The Old Country opened in October 1917, played fifteen performances, and closed. William Faversham never offered her another part.

Back in New York that fall, Kit and Anne Park shared an apartment on Forty-ninth Street, with Aunt Lucy Plimpton still the resident duenna.

In her second and last season with the Washington Square Players, Kit played Mis' Cary Ellsworth, the childless woman in Zona Gale's *Neighbors*, Mrs. Frank Darrel, the only unintroverted New Englander in *Blind Alleys*, by Grace Latimer Wright, played the drums in a pantomime called *Yum Chapab*, and appeared swathed in yards of gauze in *The Death of Tintagiles*. Of *Blind Alleys* the *New York Tribune* said, "Katherine [*sic*] Cornell, as the sister, exacts admiration for the fine accents of her speech." No more than an acknowledgment that she was in the play, but the *New York Times* reviewer that November wrote, "Katharine [!] Cornell disclosed a personality of distinguished spirits, marked intelligence, and increasing skill." She always claimed that this was her first New York review, probably because it was more prestigious to be noticed first by the *Times* than by the *Tribune*. But the truth is even more impressive: that the *Times* was the first to spell her name correctly.

For her second season with the Washington Square Players Kit received forty dollars, paid in two twenty-dollar installments. Professional at last.

Raymond Massey, a captain in the Canadian Army at that time serving as an instructor for Yale's R.O.T.C., one night found himself sitting through *Yum Chapab*, which was based on a Mayan legend. He was fascinated by the young woman with her hair hanging down around her shoulders and topped by a wild turban with huge polka dots on it. She spoke no lines, beating a drum unremittingly throughout the presentation. To his astonishment, the program listed her as Katharine Cornell. They had supper together at a Child's restaurant near Columbus Square.

In those days of the great stock companies, there were usually five actresses per company: the leading woman, the heavy (villainess), the character woman, the ingenue, and a fifth woman who belonged to none of the other categories and was expected each week to play whatever part was left over, a maid one week (in those days usually French, or at least with a French accent), a beggar the next, then a saucy flirt, followed perhaps by a withered old crone. In companies as affluent and professional as Jessie Bonstelle's, the actress who played these parts was known as "fifth business." The parts were never long and seldom important, and smaller, cheaper companies did away with them completely, cutting them out of the scripts to save money.

In the spring of 1918, while Kit was in *Neighbors*, Jessie Bonstelle at last reappeared in her life and asked her to play fifth business with her company for thirty-two weeks starting immediately, opening the new season at the Star Theatre in Buffalo, later moving on to the Garrick Theatre in Detroit. Eddie Goodman and the others would have liked her to stay on with the Washington Square Players through the season, but even had their days not been numbered and even had they not known it, they would not have been able to compete with Jessie Bonstelle's magnificent on-the-line offer of fifty dollars a week.

In relaying her plans to Dr. Cornell, manager of the Star Theatre, Jessie Bonstelle wrote, "I have engaged a young woman for the season who, I feel sure, has great promise. Her name is Katharine Cornell." Peter had already had other reports of Kit's progress, certainly from Mrs. Wolcott and also from William Faversham's public relations man, Ray Henderson, who as advance man had often visited Buffalo and wrote to Dr. Cornell that in *Plots and Playwrights* his daughter had "conducted herself like a professional." Peter Cornell nevertheless shot back at Jessie Bonstelle, "Have you gone crazy?"

Stock was the hardest, toughest training an actor could have, and the best. Ten performances a week, seven nights and three matinees, a new play every Monday. On matinee days rehearsal for the next play was called at ten in the morning and lasted until twelve-thirty. When there was no matinee, it lasted all day. Between shows and rehearsals, late nights and early mornings, parts had to be studied and learned. The only free time in the entire week was Thursday morning, and then costumes had to be planned, pieced out, and put together. There was no time for temperament, tantrums, or shyness. Kit, for example, was a bad reader and a slow study, but there was no time to indulge herself. You read and got on your feet no matter what. The craft thereby learned was utilitarian, but it formed for the intelligent actor a good foundation, a place to begin.

If stock was the best training, Jessie Bonstelle's was the best stock. Simply watching her, a young actor or actress could learn the basic principles of theatre wisdom. There was little friction in a Bonstelle company because she kept good discipline. If you were ready to fall with exhaustion, you were lifted (or shamed) into going on by seeing her get up at dawn, go to the theatre, see to the sets, see to the painters, the props, set the lights, learn and rehearse her own part, and do a day's work before the day began. She was the kind who pulled everybody up to her level and then, with the awareness of a good teacher and the generosity of a good leader, was able to boost those who deserved it higher than herself. She was a clever and versatile actress, but she was known for the talents that came out of her stock companies rather than for her own. There was one season when forty of her actors were appearing on Broadway, twenty of them doing leads.

In 1939 when *I Wanted to Be an Actress* was published, Kit wanted to call it "Twenty Years of Hard Work" because that was her own impression of how she had managed to become a star. In the spring of 1918 the twenty years of hard work began. That she was able to get up on the stage and be an actress in her father's theatre where ten years before she had ducked behind pillars to avoid notice and had sought obscurity in corners and shadows was not due to sudden, new-found self-confidence. It was her assiduousness, her industry, the one quality she had above all others that could transcend her shyness, or at least nullify it, that could give her a strength far greater than mere self-assurance — her flat-footed sense of the work to be done and her matter-of-fact willingness to do it. She always said that had she decided to become a waitress, she would not have stopped until she had become the best waitress in the land. And when there was a job to be done, she forgot to be afraid.

———

"How's your wardrobe?" was the first question asked an actress being engaged to play stock. Not only did she have to supply all her own clothes for a long season and a wide variety of characters, but she did not dare repeat, for to do so would be to make the entire company look cheap. And although not a contractual stipulation, it was a courtesy, the kind of tradition Kit learned from the start and always believed in, to consult with the leading lady or star, find out what she was wearing and then make sure not to clash with her (unless to clash was part of the play).

There was always a great deal of clothes-trading among the actresses, but it could not be relied on, and even fifth business had to arrive for the season with a trunkload of skirts, blouses, dresses that could be made to pass in the morning, afternoon, evening, as walking, motoring, winter, summer dresses, and an inexhaustible supply of ruffles, fichus, collars, cuffs, shawls, hats, scarves, furs, capes, cloaks, aprons, shoes, feathers, and beads. Some actresses were clever with their hands and could do fast alterations, retrimming, recutting, taking tucks, adding trains, pulling up, letting out, dyeing, shortening, lengthening. Maybe because she had never had to be clever in that way, Kit wasn't. Some actresses could make deals with the local dress shops, wearing their clothes on the stage in return for passes to the show, a mention in the program, or free modeling and publicity. But to the Buffalo dress shops Kit was Doc Cornell's kid who had never cared two cents about clothes all the time she was growing up. They liked her, of course, but they were not eager to have her represent their ideas of fashion and taste.

Stock companies built their audiences by offering them the plays they had heard about, the hot hits in New York, as soon as possible, before national touring companies arrived on the scene and in time to beat out other stock companies within driving distance. Kit's first role with the Jessie Bonstelle Stock Company was Grace Palmer in Marjorie Rambeau's Broadway success of the previous season, *Cheating Cheaters*.

Grace Palmer was a small straight role with no character eccentricities. The impression she made was chiefly visual and thus her clothes were unusually important, an importance given piquancy by the fact that it was Kit's first appearance on the stage in her hometown. Only a new dress, bought with care just for Grace Palmer, would do.

Now that Kit was earning a living as an actress, it would have been sensible and practical to live within her salary, but economy had never been a consideration in whatever whimsical clothes-buying she had gone in for in the past. With the double importance of Grace Palmer's appearance, it was certainly no time to start practicing economy, so she kicked off her career in stock by going into debt for a dress of gray crepe, plain and well cut, undoubtedly from the best shop in Buffalo. She stayed in debt for clothes her entire three seasons with Jessie Bonstelle and didn't clear the slate until years after her stock career had ended.

But that was all right, it was well worth starting off in debt to start off right. If she only gave occasional thought to what she wore offstage, Kit developed a knowledge of what to wear onstage, and this new dress created the kind of impression she wanted to make as Grace Palmer. In fact, the only trouble with the dress was that it was in such good taste. Jessie Bonstelle liked actresses to look like actresses, not fashion plates from Buffalo's upper crust, and as Kit stood in the wings on opening night waiting for her cue to go onstage, Miss Bonstelle stopped to say an encouraging word and pinned a bunch of flaming red satin roses on the gray crepe, plain, and well-cut shoulder. Thus adorned, Kit was sent forth to face her townsfolk, her peers, her critics and her family. (She always said it taught her an invaluable lesson in the theatre, that the stage director's word is absolute law.)

From a dignified local editorial the next morning:

There were many in the audience who came out with a triple purpose, viz, to be entertained, to see Jessie Bonstelle and to view Miss Katharine Cornell, the Buffalo young woman who is a member of the Bonstelle company. Miss Cornell came to Buffalo with success achieved that promised much. And that she made good was self-evident from the applause that wafted up to her. She is indeed accomplished, has a winning way and is of an appealing type of femininity. She is a daughter that Buffalo and Dr. Peter Cornell might well be proud of.

Jessie Bonstelle was generous to new young talents, but she was also a shrewd businesswoman who knew the lay of the land — other openings get reviewed, this one got editorialized.

The fact that Kit's hometown debut was more of a social note than a theatrical event may have helped disguise inexperience and nerves at those early performances. Buffalo loved her as long as she smiled at them a lot and was gracious and humble, which came easily to her but for many actresses under the circumstances would have required more histrionic skill than the roles they were required to play on the stage. After *Cheating Cheaters* she appeared in a David Belasco nothing called *Seven Chances*, playing a part variously described in the press as "a moonstruck maid" and "a sentimental person."

Then in the third week she made a dramatic hit.

The play was *Romance* by Edward Sheldon, and she had one good scene as Signora Vanucci, middle-aged Italian lady-in-waiting to a famous opera singer (Jessie Bonstelle). The placement of the scene, as the curtain went up on the last act, was a young actress's dream. Applause for the set, a high-ceilinged, white and gilt suite in New York's posh Brevoort Hotel where earthy, comic, humble Signora Vanucci, alone, out of keeping with her surroundings, cooks spaghetti in two saucepans over a grate fire, putting in the time between stirrings by telling her own fortune with a pack of greasy cards. Sure-fire stuff good for laughs all the way. Then bands playing offstage, singing, dancing, the final entrance of the star (Doris Keane — Jessie Bonstelle) who with champagne, caviar, and high living behind her must now eat low spaghetti prepared by her faithful Signora Vanucci before going on to the tearful parting with her lover and the play's end. It would have been hard to miss in the part, and Kit didn't.

Everyone in Buffalo was there, ready to claim credit. One reviewer wrote, "Katharine Cornell did a bit of character acting . . . which bears out my prediction made several weeks ago that this young Buffalo girl would develop high-class histrionic ability in the near future. If she never does anything else, her work as Signora Vanucci tonight stamps her as an actress of much ability. . . . Miss Cornell will surely bear watching."

If she began the season certain of special attention, it must be remembered that such attention can work against as well as for. Now, in only her third week, it simply didn't matter anymore. She was being noticed for what she could do rather than who she was.

The week after *Romance* she played a deaf, aging southern spinster in *Pals First*, and a reviewer wrote, "Katharine Cornell won applause for her work in a slight role . . . one of the funniest things in the play." They were all getting on the bandwagon: "This Buffalo girl's work grows better from week to week," said another.

In late April she took on Dora, the cockney girl who "likes her bit of a good time," in *Fanny's First Play*. She again "won much applause" and "added another to her long list of triumphs." Since it was only her fifth fifth business, it is obvious that hyperbole was setting in.

Reviews and box office receipts were very well and good, but the popularity of the season could better be gauged by the sale of Liberty Bonds at each performance. For all her might and strength, Jessie Bonstelle was referred to in the Buffalo press as "this little actress," and when she came out before the curtains to plead for generosity, "sales were immediately numerous." On opening night alone of *Fanny's First Play*, three thousand dollars was subscribed. As one newspaper summed it up, Miss Bonstelle had "a wonderful hold on the hearts of Buffalo."

After fourteen prosperous weeks, Miss Bonstelle marshaled her troupe on to Detroit where they opened at the Garrick Theatre on June 23 with a new play called *The Man Outside*, which appropriately enough, with Miss Bonstelle's usual eye for the main chance, dealt with the motor car industry and was "written in the patois of gasoline that the city has been talking so glibly for more than a decade."

By now it was taken for granted that Kit would be reviewed, no matter how small the part or what she did with it, and the local critic that hot summer had this to say about her in *The Man Outside*: "Miss Cornell was delicious . . . acting much in the saucy, brittle manner of Lynn Fontanne, giving the authors every aid in their creation of a clean-cut character, and capturing first honors among the players."

For one who came in on Katharine Cornell's career at its height, the words "saucy" and "brittle" are inconsistent with memories of Elizabeth Barrett, Juliet, and Joan, the Maid of Orleans. And yet the further, incomprehensible comparison to witty, clever Lynn Fontanne must have been valid at the time, for all of Kit's "long list of triumphs" that first

year in stock were comedy roles, light-hearted, exaggerated, even farcical, which she obviously carried off to everyone's delight.

She was twenty-five. A pleasing small success had released her spirits
from some of the awkwardness and repression of self-doubt, while
practice was teaching her to live with and override self-consciousness.
She was working hard, she was on her way, she loved and was loved,
life was surely as funny as it was beautiful, and sometimes acting
was easy.

In fact, sometimes acting was fun.

The season in Detroit ended the week of October 20, 1918, and Kit
returned to New York, this time to an apartment with faithful Aunt
Lucy Plimpton on Fifty-seventh Street. Anne Park was still very much
in the picture.

The Washington Square Players had closed the spring before never
to reopen, at least not as the Washington Square Players. In a very
few years the group would be reincarnated as the Theatre Guild, but
as yet that was only a gleam in Lawrence Langner's eye.

For the first and almost the last time Kit began making the rounds
of the managers' and agents' offices, leaving her name, photograph,
biography and professional résumé (which was growing) in case a part
came up that she was right for.

One morning Jessie Bonstelle called to say she was directing a play
for Grace George and there was a part in it for Kit.

Except for a brief period two years later, Kit never again would
have to make the rounds.

Not that she got the part with Grace George; she didn't. In fact, that
reading was the worst experience she had yet had as a professional
actress and set her back in spirits and morale. Being an actress stopped
being easy. Acting itself stopped being fun.

It was her problem, already an old one, of being unable to read a
script cold. She went, as instructed by Jessie Bonstelle, to the Playhouse, the theatre owned by Miss George's husband, William A. Brady.
From the accounts of the incident as they have been passed on, it does
not sound like a tryout for the part but an actual reading of scenes
from the play as if Kit were, at least for that morning, definitely cast.
She was handed the script. The play was a "clipped, high-paced com-

edy, opening with a very snappy scene." She was on at the beginning, as luck would have it, the first to speak, the pace-setter.

All her experience vanished, and she was left with nothing but the old terror. Never having seen the lines before, she could only mumble them, which made her so miserable that the words became inaudible. Presently she was aware of a slight cough out front. So absorbed was she, so unaware of what was going on, that the cough had to be repeated several times before she realized that Miss George had come down to the footlights and was trying in her politest stage cough to get her attention.

Grace George was genteel Irish, and in all her delicate, small-boned honey blondness looked up rather reproachfully at Kit's athletic big-boned darkness.

"You don't think you can do this part, do you, Miss Cornell?" she asked, living up gorgeously to her first name.

Kit was suddenly fourteen again, roller-skating through the lobby of the Star Theatre, deliberately not looking at the posters of the beauties of the day. On the stage of the Playhouse, with Miss George shimmering out there on level ground, she was made to feel huge and gauche and did not answer.

Bonnie spoke up (at moments like this one is inclined to use Jessie Bonstelle's own affectionate name for herself), dismissing Miss George's observation, saying that of course Kit could do the part, she had seen her do many, many parts just like it.

It was not much of a tribute to the originality of Miss George's play, and Miss George was unimpressed.

"I can imagine you in a languorous part, but not this sort of thing," she continued with her exquisite smile.

The reading went on to other scenes, and as soon as nobody was looking Kit left the theatre, telling the preoccupied stage manager as she handed him the script, "Miss George doesn't think I will do."

(This the story as it is told in *I Wanted to Be an Actress*. But according to theatrical records, Grace George did not appear on Broadway in the fall of 1918. William A. Brady did produce a play at the Playhouse, called *Home Again* and based on the folk poems of James Whitcomb Riley, directed by Jessie Bonstelle. If that is the play Kit read for, Grace George was not the star and would not have been there, no matter how close her professional association with her husband. Nor is it likely that a play based on the folk poems of James Whitcomb

Riley would be a "clipped, high-paced comedy, opening with a very snappy scene." Perhaps Miss George went into rehearsal with a play so bad that it never opened, which, if this account of her manners is to be believed, served her right.)

Kit said she left the theatre in tears, but instead of heading for a back pew in St. Patrick's Cathedral, she remembered that a friend had a car down in Washington, D.C., that had to be driven up to New York and decided that this would be as good a time as any to do it. She left immediately for Washington and dropped completely out of sight for two days.

She knew herself well enough by now to know that at a difficult time such as this, physical activity, sometimes extravagant and illogical, was more efficacious than self-pity, and her sense of extravagance and illogic often took a heavy, utilitarian turn, but even so this was a peculiar action in 1918 when a socially prominent, struggling young actress of twenty-five would hardly have been anybody's choice to shuttle a cumbersome machine from the Potomac to the Hudson.

She probably had a friend with a car and simply went off for a few days.

She returned to find that Jessie Bonstelle had been searching for her frantically, imagining her at the bottom of the East River, and was justifiably furious. Only a few minutes after Kit had walked out of the rehearsal, Grace George had asked to do her scene again. The stage manager had had to say that Miss Cornell had disappeared, and Grace George had turned her now ineffable smile on Jessie Bonstelle to remark, "There, you see, she hasn't the right stuff in her!" Jessie Bonstelle did not like being told that about one of her protégées and laid down the law to Kit in no uncertain terms about professionalism and never leaving a rehearsal before being dismissed. Kit, who was sometimes quick to feel wounds but never one to pursue them long when it reduced efficiency or impeded progress, took the tongue-lashing to heart and jumped when her mentor ordered her immediately to try out as a replacement for the leading woman's part in the third road company of *The Man Who Came Back*, for William A. Brady.

The original director of the play, whose staging was the model for all subsequent companies, was John Cromwell. As an actor he had played John Brooke in Jessie Bonstelle's first *Little Women* in 1912, which may be why Kit was accorded special grace and favor, being allowed to rehearse for a week with the stage manager before actually auditioning. Then on Wednesday morning, January 1, 1919 (in show business, just another mid-week matinee day), at Loew's Seventh Avenue Theatre where the third road company was at that time playing, aided by a few desultory and probably hung over members of the company whom she had never met before, Kit did her scenes for Cromwell, who at the end went into a prolonged brown study before asking abruptly, "Can you play this afternoon?" All her stock training having returned in a rush, Kit at last tossed modesty to the winds, returned a decisive "Yes!" and telephoned Aunt Lucy to hurry to the theatre with an evening dress and her makeup box.

And so it happened that she graduated to second leads. She would never again play fifth business with any theatrical company. Her twenty years of hard work had just begun, but in little more than two years all the "struggling" part of her career was over, at least the struggle for recognition, and it had passed just about as painlessly as possible. She had simply appeared at the gate and been given permission to enter the kingdom.

———

A number of the original members of the Washington Square Players still clung together, meeting now and then in an effort to build a new structure to be called the Theatre Guild.

In his book of reminiscences, *Me and Kit*, Guthrie McClintic tells of attending one such meeting with an actress friend, Noel Haddon. The meeting took place at Lawrence Langner's apartment off lower Fifth Avenue, and among those present were Maurice Wertheim, Lee Simonson, Philip Moeller, Helen Westley, and Theresa Helburn. Everybody did a lot of talking, and Guthrie writes, "I had nothing to say, so I listened, when suddenly I felt a presence! And there in a dark corner sat my 'interesting' girl from *Plots and Playwrights*, Katharine Cornell. She didn't see me, but as I watched her I realized that off stage she had that mystic aura, too . . . a curious haunting luminosity. Noel talked to her just before we left, but I didn't get to meet her."

In *I Wanted to Be an Actress*, Kit recalls the same evening. "I wasn't asked to join The Guild, but I did go to one of the first meetings at Lawrence Langner's house. Everybody was discussing repertory feverishly and at great length. Then they turned to a young man — a pale, fragile creature he was — and I was astounded at the way he summed the whole thing up in less than a minute. I asked who he was and was told he was Winthrop Ames' casting director, Guthrie McClintic." She says they barely spoke.

That is the complete account of the evening as she remembered it in 1939. Guthrie wrote his version in 1955. Apparently they saw no reason to check with each other, let alone read what each other wrote. He says he had nothing to say all evening and simply listened, while she claims that everyone looked to him to sum up the whole thing, which he then did. She implies that they at least said a few words to each other, he is certain they did not meet at all. So much can be put down to tricks of memory. But in Kit's book she sets the evening firmly in the spring of 1917, while Guthrie just as firmly puts it almost two years later, specifically in January 1919, after she had been engaged to play in *The Man Who Came Back.*

As close as these two people would be for over forty years, to the mystification of some, the jealousy of others, the incredulity of many, and the eventual wonder of all, and as impenetrable and impregnable as their closeness would be, it was obviously not based on factual agreement as to how it began. And since dates and places and who-said-what had nothing to do with what happened between them, dates and places and who-said-what become useless in trying to explain it. The only important thing about that elusive evening at Lawrence Langner's, is that they became aware of each other, as the song goes, "across a crowded room." It would be over a year if you listen to him, or almost three if you listen to her, before they would even become acquainted, but something had been put in motion and was working in the meantime. Inevitability had set in.

As if to answer years of skeptical head-shaking, plain curiosity, and even some exasperation, in their individual accounts of that enchanted evening they settle once and for all the question always asked by outsiders of any lasting twosome, "What do they see in each other?" She saw in him "a pale, fragile creature," and he saw in her a "mystic aura . . . a curious haunting luminosity." At the risk of oversimplifying, but on the basis of what seem to have been their individual needs and temperaments, it is safe to say that those qualities are what they began by loving in each other. And of all the thousands of descriptive words written about them in the years that followed, their own original impressions of each other are still the most telling and true.

Until this point Kit had been playing fifth business off the stage, perhaps, as well as on. Neither heroine, heavy, character woman, nor ingenue, yet essential to the vitality and flow of each scene, she had moved through other people's lives in a random range of contributory roles. Now, just as *The Man Who Came Back* would begin to define her as an actress, so with the entrance of Guthrie McClintic into her life she would begin to find her center as a woman. In fact there was gathering around her at this time a nucleus of people, a cadre it might be called, whose lives she would enrich by gaining from them for herself consistency and stature both as an actress and a woman.

Guthrie first, and always first. But then, surprisingly, William Faver- sham's advance man, Ray Henderson, who would one day become Kit's press representative and remain a loved and honored adviser until his death in the actual line of duty as he planned a world tour for her. And Laura Elliot, Anne Park's singing teacher, would become Kit's teacher, too, and more, a gentle, wise confidante. Another lifelong friend of Kit's says today, "Once you knew her, you just loved her. You just couldn't help it. Whether she was going to encourage you to continue in your friendship was something else again. . . ." But the encouragement having been given, it amounted to a promise and was never broken. Even Mrs. Wolcott was around, like the others, to her dying day saying every time she saw Kit, "Didn't we have a lovely time that night at the Favershams?" and watching wickedly as Kit once again broke into a cold sweat remembering lovely Julie Faversham smiling above a lapful of Burgundy.

Having once loved her, no one is ever known to have stopped, except Anne Park. One day out of the blue Anne married a handsome, elegant architect, gave up her career, and moved to a southern city. Aside from the fact that capriciousness was a trait so alien to Kit's own nature and contrary to the way she believed life should be lived, there is nothing at all amiss in what Anne Park did. The sadness — and it may have intensified the cautiousness Kit had learned as a child with her father and her mother — the sadness is that where Kit first learned to love completely, she also learned to lose.

6

Marcelle and Jo (1919)

THE MAN IN *The Man Who Came Back* (billed as "an American Play by Jules Eckert Based on John Flemyng Wilson's Like-Named Story") is rich, twenty-five-year-old spendthrift Henry Potter, whose "weakness is his evil genius." He starts off at the place he eventually comes back to, the Manhattan breakfast room of his father, Thomas Potter, "the world renowned financial octopus" who, hoping it will either make him or break him, gives his son a one-way ticket to San Francisco and tells him not to come back. Henry leaves, threatening to make the name of Potter a joke all over the world.

But in Act Two nobody is laughing when Potter Sr.'s agents find young Henry drunk and forging his father's name in a San Francisco joint, chloroform him on the old man's orders, and ship him off in disgust to Shanghai.

Before that happens, however, Marcelle, a high-minded but low-living singer in the " 'Frisco resort," falls in love with Henry. He "tears her heart by a thoughtless word at a drunken revel," or as another, less-emotional, reviewer puts it, "breaks her heart with a careless word." Only one reviewer is brave enough to say what the "thoughtless" or "careless" word is — Henry "asks Marcelle to be his unmarried wife."

After that Marcelle cries that she, too, no longer cares what happens. A precedent for this kind of scene was set in 1909 in Eugene Walter's *The Easiest Way*, in which Frances Starr, abandoned by her lover to a life of prostitution, uttered the famous, shocking curtain line, "I'm going to Rector's to make a hit and to hell with the rest!" Marcelle outdoes her prototype by fleeing all the way to China.

In Act Three Henry is discovered pawning his fraternity signet ring (the last shred of respectability) to buy a bottle of rum in the lowest opium den in Shanghai. He calls for someone to join him in a drink, and while a weird phonograph drones out "Dearie," from one of the bunks crawls "a woman in a threadbare kimono and disheveled hair." It is Marcelle, now a hopeless opium fiend, "shattered and seared almost beyond recognition." First Henry tries to cut her to ribbons with a whip, and then he tries to strangle her, all this to save her from becoming "all bad" like himself. But then the sight of the girl he loves "throwing away her soul because of her love for him ... suddenly grips the manhood in him and brings him back to the vision of what he ought to be for her sake."

It is with "an overwhelming passion to save each other" that they agree to climb out of the depths together, which they do in Act Four on a "pinery" (pineapple farm) just outside Honolulu, where Marcelle feels it is time to test his love and loyalty by having him tempted back to his old ways. He is saved from himself once and for all by the strength of her love in time to "come back" in Act Five, prosperous and reclaimed, to his father's breakfast room, there to be welcomed into the family with the long-suffering, noble, wise, battered, and loving Marcelle at his side.

―――

From the synopsis, it is not surprising that among young actresses Marcelle was considered "a swell acting part." Mary Nash played it first at William Brady's Playhouse Theatre for four hundred and sixty-seven performances opposite Henry Hull (an erstwhile roommate of Guthrie McClintic's). Kit was replacing an actress named Laura Walker, and apparently it was a very sudden replacement, for when she opened at the Shubert-Majestic Theatre in Providence, Rhode Island, on January 6, 1919, she was listed in the program as Laura Walker, a circumstance that Kit may have taken as a blessing, removing her as far as possible from her self-conscious self. Surely no other great actress has ever had such a contradictory need for anonymity.

Or perhaps "contrary" is the word. Sometimes her modesty amounted to a blind spot as she made bold, self-deprecatory claims in the face of bold, incompatible evidence. Years after that opening in Providence, she said of it in print, ". . . my first press notices were under the name of Laura Walker — in which she, poor girl, took a good beating." That is nonsense, since Laura Walker, probably never came off as brilliantly either before or after. The *Providence News* proclaimed the next day, "Miss Walker's interpretation of the opium addict in the den in Shanghai . . . and in the scene near Honolulu where she tests the love of her husband . . . are new laurels for this clever star." The reviewer's integrity may be suspect since he claims familiarity with Laura Walker's work without realizing that a substitution has been made, but the core of his comment is for Kit, no matter who he thought she was: "Words [are] vain to depict the realism of her work. It leaves nothing to the imagination. It is the real thing."

Conrad Nagel made a "convincing, altogether likeable, easygoing" Henry Potter that night in Providence and was followed in the course of the next weeks by three more bright young leading men — Frank Morgan, Henry Hull, and Arthur Ashley — none of them too big, apparently, to step in and pinch-hit for a night or two, but too big to send out with the third road company. The tour was further delayed by the flu epidemic which closed theatres, at least in the hinterlands where in some cities only ghostly figures in white gauze masks were permitted through the streets.

The show hovered near home (the Majestic Theatre, Brooklyn) until the danger was past and then with James Dyrenforth in the lead took off to Rochester, New York, where the opening night audience on January 27 was "a particularly genial one . . . made up entirely of the Rochester Consistory, Scottish Rite Masons, and their women friends."

The press the next day compared the play favorably to *The Pilgrim's Progress* and *Everyman* and the parable of the Prodigal Son, the chief honors of the evening "falling to Katherine [sic] Cornell . . . a well known Buffalo girl who with . . . exceptional emotional power and a singular interpretive vividness . . . played with an unerring and telling force and lent a convincing realism to a thoroughly theatrical part."

For as big a New York hit as *The Man Who Came Back*, even the third road company was given a "high-class production" so high class that the audience could all but smell "the stench of the opium den and the sweet, lulling fragrance of the pineapple farm." From Rochester the tour went on to Utica, crossed the Canadian border to Ottawa, London, Ontario, and Montreal, then suddenly swooped south to Richmond, Virginia; Lexington, Kentucky; Charleston, West Virginia; and Newport News, Virginia. Such a heavy production was complicated and time-consuming to set up and strike and very expensive to travel. Therefore the management would have been justified in sticking to these key cities, but the play had been so eagerly awaited for over two years that it was worth the time and money to make one-night stands along the way where simple gratitude filled the auditoriums and the box office cash drawers. In Ogdensburg, New York, a night which fell between Utica and Ottawa, the newspaper review the next day was little more than an expansive public commendation of the local theatre manager for his efforts to "give Ogdensburg the best shows on the road." For William A. Brady and local theatre managers, "the road" was no more than shrewd business practice. Katharine Cornell, when she became a star, would recognize it as a tradition and a trust.

Wherever the play went, it was considered worth the long wait, but enthusiasm was tempered with caution. With its depiction of "Bohemia and general depravity," it was considered by many reviewers to be "about as pleasant as an Armenian massacre." But most of them finally agreed that "the punches of the play considerably outweigh its defects," and the man in Lexington, Kentucky, might have been speaking for them all when he decided it fell safely "within the category of stage stories that we 'rube' reporters customarily refer to as 'strong.' " If it seems charmingly ingenuous of him to refer to himself as rube, there is also a warning in the word, as if to say, "I may be small town, but my morality keeps the theatre filled — or empty — so be careful." "A bit lurid?" asks another, and in answering himself "Of course!" quickly adds the saving grace that "this one has a moral tucked away in its thrills." It is with relief that to a man the reviewers are able to point to the moral or "the lesson behind the story," although none will venture to say exactly what it is except a lone journalist in London, Ontario, who feels quite seriously that "if there is a moral it is that rich men should not pamper their sons too much." For the rest it is enough to assure their readers that the play does have a moral and it is all right to see it.

Which is uplifting and fine in newspaper print, but when it comes to selling tickets, even in 1919, a good moral by itself could empty a theatre faster than it could fill it. Assuming the subject matter of *The Man Who Came Back* to be as shocking outside New York as it seems to have been, there had to be something besides a moral to explain the devotion of the audiences.

It certainly can't have been the presence in the star spot of poor James Dyrenforth, who seems to have been quite strong enough to portray Henry Potter's weaknesses but too weak to portray Henry Potter's strength. "Unequal to the requirements" they say of him, and "fails to measure up."

Kit, on the other hand, was invariably reviewed as if she were the star, no matter how the program read, and at least twice was headlined as such. Her portrait "of an opium addict was . . . graphic and realistic, yet instead of being repulsive, it commanded sympathy." That, in essence, is what they all said, but by no means did they stop there.

She is found to be "charming and intelligent . . . with admirable natural and technical equipment." She may act "with violent ardor and fervent zeal, enticingly languorous or spirited and commanding on occasion," but always "with modulated voice and properly restrained gestures." "Miss Cornell can be seductive and she can be fascinating . . . her love-making is the best part of her performance, very real love-making, romantic and without a shade of mawkishness," and always "her voice is good and her diction well cultivated." She is "a young woman of statuesque proportions with nut brown profusion of hair that goes with romance and eyes that go with novelistic warmth. She is every inch an artist though not far beyond the years of girlhood."

Cultivated, charming, intelligent, modulated, restrained, statuesque, romantic — it was her kind of realism to endow Bohemia and general depravity with just a touch of nobility, another vain word the reviewers inexplicably missed. By this time she was, as they said, "every inch an artist," but in addition to that she made an audience feel that if this "well-known girl from Buffalo" could be trapped in an opium den with her obvious background and breeding, then surely it was all right for everybody else to be trapped there, too, if only to share her "bitter passion" and root for her to get out of there in one piece and back to the shores of Lake Erie where she belonged. A Canadian critic said, "At three different points in this play of deep emotional pathos, she attains the height and depth of emotional acting, strikes celestial sparks from the anvil of histrionic achievement." Maybe the word the others were searching for was "celestial." For the stuffiest, sternest, church-goingest member of the audience, she made it *all right* to enjoy depravity.

In three months of touring she had two detractors, both of whom defended her against their own carpings on the basis of her youth, and since one suggested that she indulged in moments of overplaying and the other hinted that she underplayed, they can be said to cancel each other out. A third reluctant semi-detractor, after calling her "a very handsome girl" and tossing her extravagant bouquets, finally confesses "but to this humble reviewer, the 'real class,' as one might say, of the female roles was Esther Howard as Olive. This young woman is a real actress. True she was not on the stage long enough for one to become very familiar with her mannerisms, but whenever she was there she held the center of things."

It helps to define Kit's effect that these men seem to be conscience-stricken for daring to criticize her. Whether they liked her performing or not, she was the kind of actress they wanted to make gestures to publicly, as if to protect her from being hurt.

Far from being hurt, she had made great strides since her first reading for Eddie Goodman in the fall of 1916 and had brought from the athletic fields into the theatre a kind of honor and sportsmanship. It is not surprising that in spite of good and competitive reviews that would have alienated her from many a leading lady, Esther Howard, who played Marcelle's confidante in the 'Frisco cabaret scene, became Kit's sidekick offstage as well.

Together they braved the rigors of touring. The junk towns and drafty dressing rooms in firetrap theatres; sitting up all night in stifling day coaches or putting up at bad hotels with inedible food; three-thirty calls to catch four o'clock trains on zero mornings in towns without taxis; battling blizzards with suitcases to make the railroad station on time, there to find that all trains are hours late — or cancelled — with a first-act curtain to make in the next town — all for a hundred dollars a week, pay your own expenses.

It was Kit's first experience on the road, and she loved every minute of it. There was something in her that found expression and satisfaction in rising to occasions, bad as well as good. She was never known to have deliberately made things difficult for herself or anybody else — quite the contrary, she spent her life easing situations (even if it sometimes meant pretending they did not exist). But when hardship was inevitable and there was something to be accomplished by enduring it, she somehow had more energy than anybody else, more vigor, more accommodation, more plain stamina. Having come into the world as

one of what is called the "socially privileged," and now with the growing conviction and proof that she was also artistically gifted and therefore privileged all over again, she could relish rough patches as a
balance and a responsibility. When one of the girls in *The Man Who
Came Back* came down with the flu in some out-of-the-way place, it
was Kit who nursed her back to health between performances.

Jimmy Dyrenforth took a lot of rising to. One of his troubles seems
to have been that he was too nice a fellow to play Henry Potter, especially in the opium den scene which was the focal point of the play.
Came the time at each performance to pursue Kit with the whip, she
could see his hands tremble and his face turn white. Sensitiveness and
nerves are fatal at such a moment; the actor simply has to lay on the
whip and know that he is going to strike right. Dyrenforth was so
terrified of hitting Kit that invariably he did, the uncontrolled whip
flicking up to cut her, the blood often spurting through her white
kimono. She undoubtedly "used it" for the reality of the scene, although such a term and such a method of acting were not known to
American actors at that time. In those days the actors still took curtain
calls at the end of each act, and the critics in Ottawa, after noting that
Kit's "strenuous part" demanded "vivid expression and much emotion,"
went on to say that "so deeply did she convey it that one forgave her
seriousness when the house stormed its applause." Her "seriousness"
was probably a good part pain.

Dyrenforth had his champions and defenders, of course, or he could
not have gone on with the tour. Years later Kit referred to him as a
"sweet boy," but at the time it must have been hard for her to know
how to cope with him. The generous instinct of the girl from Buffalo
would be to go along with him, to understand what it was like to be
inadequate, to put up with his shortcomings. But chronologically and
emotionally, if not geographically, she was a long way from Buffalo,
and with her growing sense of professionalism she valued more highly
than anything else the actor who did his job well. Esther Howard's
competence on the stage was one of the reasons why she and Kit were
able to become good friends; her good reviews, rather than being a
threat, were an attraction. On Kit's idealistic, rather romantic, professional side, only such an actor could command her loyalty and patience
and friendship; she would drop a curtain on the Jimmy Dyrenforths in
a company, as if they did not exist. But her realistic, matter-of-fact
professional side, her belief that the play must be gotten through and

that the audience must never be cheated, her earthbound practicality would tell her that an actor of James Dyrenforth's instability, already nervous and apprehensive, must not be further upset or he would be unable to function at all. He needed special sympathy, encouragement, consideration — more than a brilliantly competent actor — if the play was not to be scuttled.

Marcelle redeemed Henry Potter; Katharine Cornell redeemed James Dyrenforth — and the play.

———

With barely a week off at the end of the tour, Kit went right back to the Bonstelle Stock Company, shuttling between Buffalo and Detroit, in second leads that spring and summer at sixty dollars a week. Winifred Lenihan was in the company. One of Kit's first roles of the season was in *Ann's Adventure*, later played in New York as *Ruined Lady* by Grace George, who did not ask Kit to join the New York Company.

———

Nobody ever thought they would do it. Even though Actors' Equity had been in existence since 1913, most actors considered a labor federation beneath their dignity as artists. But their dignity as artists had been diminishing along with their social status ever since the decline of gentleman actor-managers like Augustin Daly and Daniel Frohman. In service to commercial managers (the Shubert Bros., Klaw & Erlanger, and others), they were being given credit for the tastelessness of their masters; chafing at their bondage, they were picking up their old Elizabethan reputation as rogues and vagabonds. Finally pushed to the limit, led by Milton Sills, Frank Gillmore, and others, the actors went on strike in August 1919, not for "more pay, just fair play."

Almost all of Broadway shut down. William A. Brady, like a number of other producers, tried to reopen his current production, *At 9:45*, with understudies and himself in the star role, failing when the musicians and stagehands walked out in sympathy with the actors. The strike was settled in a month, and as Brooks Atkinson puts it, "Everyone knew that the old days were over."

With the signing of the Armistice, it had again become feasible to work abroad, and perhaps reluctant to accept the "new days" on Broadway, Brady decided to send his seven-year-old hit *Little Women* to London, again to be staged by Jessie Bonstelle who this time insisted that Katharine Cornell play the part of Josephine March.

It can be said that Jessie Bonstelle finally kept the promise made to Kit as a child and that in the theatre, where magnanimous promises are easily made and forgotten, her loyalty was something of a marvel and that Kit was fortunate to have learned her professional ethics from a teacher of such integrity. But why did she wait through two previous productions to decide that Kit was "grown" enough to play Jo at a time when Kit, at twenty-six, was perilously close to being too old for it? And why, when it was decided that the cast would be all English, did she jeopardize the consistency of the production by insisting that Kit be the one American exception? Guthrie McClintic always said that Jessie Bonstelle "had one of the keenest noses for acting talent that I have ever encountered," and it seems to have been true, but was it sound professional judgment to cast a fully developed, rather exotic-looking woman in the role of a brash, undeveloped, nineteenth-century New England adolescent? There seems to have been more at stake than simply casting a part. For Jessie Bonstelle there was something obsessive about it.

At first Kit refused the part, not because of her age but because she was tired. Friends had begun telling her she was working too hard, and she was rather ready to believe them. With Jessie Bonstelle's autocratic way of taking over, it was not difficult to feel she was being abused. Besides, she claimed, Jo was practically a starring role, and she still wasn't ready for that, especially not in London, which was regarded by too many as the home of all great acting — Buffalo and Detroit and touring in the U.S. were quite good enough for her. To get around all other arguments, especially the one that no matter what her age she would be perfect as the forthright, coltish Jo, she said flatly that she did not want to play the part. Her reasons for refusing were as valid as Jessie Bonstelle's for insisting that she accept, but Kit had too many of them. Either she hadn't yet emerged from the opium den or she was as usual shying off from the next step in her career. There is a delicate moment when the talent is ready and bursting to go forward while the spirit backs off from the responsibility of success.

Fortunately, she was unable to hold out. Once Jessie Bonstelle made up her mind, she was inflexible, and rather than hurt her feelings or cause any friction between them, Kit gave in quickly and allowed herself to be kidnapped to England.

The day before they were to sail on the *Rochambeau*, Kit was having lunch in a restaurant on Forty-eighth Street, near the Playhouse Theatre in New York. Grace George came in and made a point of stopping at her table to say, "I hope you won't like England so much that you won't come back." Kit's performance in *Ann's Adventure* had registered. It was one of those moments that you wish would last forever.

Joyce Carey, daughter of the beloved actress Lillian Braithwaite, twenty-one years old, fresh from playing Juliet at Stratford-on-Avon and now engaged to play Meg, the ostensible lead in *Little Women*, was only one of the gifted English performers Kit was up against on their home ground. But if she was awed in advance by the richness of their theatrical heritage and their classicism, they, in turn, were braced to meet a cigarette-smoking flapper who would lay claim to the play because it was American and try to tell them all what to do. Joyce Carey still remembers her "joy and relief when this awfully nice rather shy girl in a beautifully cut brown suit buttoned all the way down the front came smiling into rehearsal." As usual with Kit, they loved her on sight and couldn't understand why Jessie Bonstelle, who claimed to love her, too, picked on her all through rehearsals, criticizing her, even ridiculing her, making her go over scenes again and again to the point of pointlessness, supposedly in the cause of a good performance. Years later, with characteristic understatement when speaking of others' shortcomings, Kit said, "How she worked over me!" when it would have been truer to say, "How she worked me over!"

The war was over but not forgotten, its effects being felt in mysterious, calamitous, ridiculous, and not surprising ways. One of the more ridiculous (but not surprising) was a script revision in *Little Women*. Mr. Bhaer, the eccentric German professor who in Louisa May Alcott's book woos and wins Jo, in this postwar version of the play became Mr. Baret, an addled French professor, because, as one newspaper put it, "No one, I'm sure, would wish Jo anything so terrible nowadays as a German husband."

But the most calamitous after effect of the Great War was economic instability, with the threat of a general strike. It didn't materialize until 1926 but it was in the air in 1919 when the railway strike in September all but closed down commerce and travel. *Little Women* was scheduled to open in Manchester early in October, and the scenery and costumes had to be sent up from London by truck. They did not arrive in time for the opening performance, which was therefore cancelled, nor did they arrive the next night. On the third night Jessie Bonstelle decided to open the play anyway, on a bare stage if necessary. Then in the late afternoon the scenery and costumes were discovered waylaid "somewhere in the potteries" nearby and came clattering up to the stage door just at curtain time and "a patient and cordial audience saw the curtain rise an hour late . . . in an exceptionally uncritical mood" (so reported the local press).

The audience and critics loved it all and said so, but the company, trapped in Manchester hotels and rented rooms, had been unnerved by the uncertainty and waiting. Even Kit had fallen into a mood that in a young woman of less refined emotions would have been called sulky. With the extra days the play was dangerously close to being overrehearsed, but even after the opening Jessie Bonstelle continued to badger Kit about her performance until Leslie Faber, the Daudet-like "Professor Baret" who gallantly became Jo's defender offstage as well as on, finally told Miss Bonstelle off one night over dinner in the hotel dining room. Kit and Joyce Carey sat at a nearby table, aware of what was going on and horrified. A not so "Bonnie" Bonstelle went ashy silent and simply kept refilling Faber's wine glass as fast as he emptied it in his effort to find the courage to accuse her first of imagining herself to have given birth to Kit, next of making her more self-conscious than she already was, then of destroying her individuality, and finally of ruining her talent.

By then the two young women had crept out of the dining room to hear no more, but later that night a compulsively generous Kit went to Jessie Bonstelle's room, where she was admitted not by her resilient, redheaded mentor but by a fierce, stony-faced replica, a sagging, thick-waisted, second-rate stock actress facing the fact that she had tried to project her own unfulfilled ambitions onto a brilliant, malleable young talent and had ended up flagellating her Trilby as if she were (as in-

As Jo in Little Women, *1919*.

deed she was) flagellating herself. Kit, of course, would listen to none of this, waving it all away, assuring Miss Bonstelle that these too-gentle well-mannered English people simply didn't understand her ways . . .

Jessie Bonstelle wasn't really daunted, of course, and vigorously snapped back to launch *Little Women* in London and to go on to produce and direct plays for the rest of her life.

Fifty years had passed since the publication of the novel *Little Women*, and 1869's dash of rue was 1919's bowl of treacle. The London press called it "a pretty play," "too obviously sob stuff," in which "the sentiment is spread on with a trowel" and "the pathos is a good deal too buckety." "Gone forever," wrote one offended gentleman, "surely, are the days when the dying maiden (Beth in Act III), dragged from her couch (upstage) can be planted in an armchair just above the footlights (centre) so that the limelight may shed its sickly ray upon her (greasepainted) pallor."

Miss Bonstelle apparently even introduced a singing bird onto the windowsill in Beth's final moments, for another critic said, "One actor in the drama might, I think, be paid off with a loaf of bread or some sultanas in lieu of a week's notice — the 'robin'. And yet I owe him thanks. He dried the tear that threatened to break down my critical detachment. Death to 'slow music' is preferable to hoarse twitterings made by a property-man with a whistle and a glass of water."

With the crowded Christmas holidays approaching in the first full postwar theatre season, *Little Women* found itself caught in the London booking jam and had to open in a series of weekday matinees at the New Theatre (still there in St. Martin's Lane but now called the Albery) on November 10, 1919. As if to protect the unsuspecting public from "this dear little play of dear little souls," it was firmly announced that *Jack o' Jingles*, the regular bill at the New, would continue to give its evening and Saturday matinee performances.

Still, "rarely has there been such floods of tears . . . as at the first performance" when "the reception was extremely cordial and Miss de Forest was loudly cheered in taking the call" and the play was pronounced "a complete success." The matinees would have been thought sufficient to handle the Christmas crowd of young people, but the demand was so great that inside a fortnight *Jack o' Jingles* gave up the ghost and surrendered its evenings to *Little Women*, which settled into a comfortable and prosperous run.

What happened? The situation was the reverse of *The Man Who Came Back*. Instead of Bohemia and general depravity, *Little Women* had to counteract goodness and innocence. What made it *all right* for post-war Londoners in "the matter-of-fact world of King Coin" to wallow in sentiment and "emerge sobbing" from a play it was so easy to make fun of?

One critic refers sarcastically to the character of Jo as "the bold independent spirit of the family," and having had his fun he turns serious: ". . . about the middle of the second act the bold and independent spirit . . . began to be interesting and to emerge from the morass of sugar. She was played with originality and something considerably more than artificial sentiment by Miss Katharine Cornell."

The *Times* says of the play, "as soon as it leaves Jo, it ceases to be human and becomes merely sugar plums," going on to exult, "does the book give us such a Jo as Miss Katharine Cornell? We cannot believe it. The book cannot give us Miss Cornell's face (of which etiquette prevents us saying more than that it is brilliantly expressive), Miss Cornell's frank, broad, eloquent gestures, the humour and downrightness, the exhilarating vitality of this jolly, sensitive tomboy."

A publication called *The Englishwoman* offered the most pertinent observation when it said that Kit as Jo "is so jolly and tomboyish and mischievous that she might be the subject of a volume on human depravity, for, grievous to relate, she, the only person in the play who has the spice of the devil in her, is the only one who wins our wholehearted imagination. London is unanimous in her praise, and London will flock to see her."

And London did.

It was quite a year for Kit. At home she had taken the depravity of Marcelle and given it a redeeming, celestial glow of innocence; abroad she put the devil in Jo, giving her innocence a redeeming touch of depravity.

———

Statistics: Thirty out of thirty-seven English reviewers of *Little Women* spelled her name correctly, while in the United States and Canada during the tour of *The Man Who Came Back* only two (both Canadian) spelled it correctly and twenty-four misspelled it, one myopic gentleman even misreading it in his program as "Catherine."

News of her triumph in *Little Women* moved the Buffalo *Evening News* to print a proud article about their local daughter, of course misspelling her name as did *Vogue* magazine in its caption to a full-page picture of her as Jo. The *Detroit Free Press* also claimed her for their own and got her name right, perhaps because Ed Stair, owner and operator, was a friend of Dr. Cornell's and had inside information.

It was only four days until Christmas, and Jessie Bonstelle was sailing for home. No matter how hard it was to have affection for her or how difficult to be close to her, no matter what the frictions and constraints, of all people in London that Christmas season, Jessie Bonstelle alone was *familiar* — a word only one letter removed from "familial" — not close to Kit, but intimate; not essential to her life but basic to it; worlds apart in years, outlook, and attitude, but tied by loyalty, service, and shared experience. Even at that age Kit was not good at having familiar people go away. It wasn't attention she required, it was proximity. For a woman so shy of crowds and public gatherings, she was also, paradoxically, shy of solitude. She rarely sought it except to read, and even then could not achieve concentration unless there was somebody familiar in the house or hotel, down the corridor, on the floor above, or in the next room.

She went to Southampton with Jessie Bonstelle to see her off. It was a miserable trip with bad weather and a crowded train. Fog delayed the sailing and their good-byes four hours.

Kit always had remarkable success meeting people on trains. In the restaurant car on the way back to London a distinguished-looking white-haired man befriended her because he thought from her looks she was Russian, but he was quite agreeable to her being American and talked with her knowledgeably (and on an equal plane) about music, casually inviting her to "hear some of the Bach chorales at the Abbey some time." He turned out to be Sidney Nicholson, organist at Westminster Abbey, and he epitomized Kit's situation in London. She had no difficulty lining up distinguished old gentlemen to show her Westminster Abbey, but they could hardly be classified as "familiars." She did have one London beau her own age whose family invited her to dine, promising in the midst of postwar rationing and shortages to ease her homesickness with American corn on the cob, which they did

— only they sliced each ear like a cucumber. For this transgression, that young man has come down through the years without a name.

One day a strange woman called to say she was a friend of an American boy, Guthrie McClintic, who had asked her to do something nice for Kit while she was in London.

Guthrie had borrowed money the previous June for his first trip to London, where he holed up in a cheap room in Bloomsbury and saw every play in town. Then, having spent all his money, he borrowed more and stayed on and on to fall in love with Gladys Cooper, Charles Hawtrey, Gerald du Maurier, and Meggie Albanesi. A letter from Noel Haddon informed him that Kit was to do *Little Women* in London, but by the time it reached him she was already down in Manchester sitting out the railway strike and his money had finally run out. One day he stood before Lord Nelson's column in Trafalgar Square and watched a big red penny roll down from the National Gallery and settle at his feet. That and ten dollars and a steerage ticket were his entire fortune, so he put the penny in his left shoe for luck and sailed for home before Kit arrived for her first matinee at the New Theatre in St. Martin's Lane.

Kit recognized his name and thanked his friend for calling her.

She spent most of the winter playing golf.

———

The Englishwoman said that she was "so exactly and wonderfully Jo, I refuse to believe she can be anybody else." It was a warning, and other reviewers expressed the same doubt that she could be effective in any other role. Therefore she was very interested late in February, when the run of *Little Women* was about to end, by a cable from Brady and Bonstelle to ask if she would be willing to stay on and play Marcelle in the London production of *The Man Who Came Back*. It was an attractive suggestion because it would allow her to stay on where she was, even though it was not home; to drift on as she was. But Mary Nash, who had created the part on Broadway, had first refusal and did not refuse; and Kit returned home in time for the stock season in the spring of 1920.

Bonstelle was now operating both companies, Buffalo and Detroit, for the full season and had at last come up against a job she could not handle — that is, she could not play all the leads in both cities. So she settled for playing alternate leads in each, elevating Kit to alternating leads with her in Detroit. She met her at the boat and also told her she had engaged a young director named Guthrie McClintic for Detroit that summer.

———

The entire company met at William A. Brady's office in the Play-house Theatre to sign the stock contracts and get acquainted. Frank Morgan was leading man, Walter Abel the juvenile. Kit gave Guthrie a warm smile when they were introduced in the reception room, and this is how he later described the scene: ". . . when Miss Bonstelle asked us to go into Mr. Brady's private office I lagged behind and watched the company as they filed in. I was fascinated with Kit. I couldn't take my eyes away from her. I watched her as she moved with slow, easy grace across the hall of the outer office, and suddenly I thought: 'That's my wife . . . isn't it funny she doesn't know it, but I am going to marry her.'" Later in the day he confided his discovery to Olive Wyndham.

No matter that he was already married to someone else.

7

Guth (1893-1919)

GUTHRIE McCLINTIC WAS BORN in Seattle, Washington, on August 6, 1893, and unlike Kit, he seems to have been born for the theatre, making an instant connection with it to the total exclusion of everything else in life the minute he discovered there was such a thing. For him it was acting from the start, at the sacrifice of family feeling, school, and — when necessary — honesty. He didn't have to sacrifice friends because as a boy he didn't have many. Had he been destined from birth to play a specific role, it would have been yon Cassius, not alone for his ambition and his deviousness, but for his lean and hungry look. If Kit in her childhood appearance was skinned, Guthrie was boned, rubbery thin with too much uninteresting brown hair detracting from his small amorphous face, and susceptible to every childhood ailment that would keep him from fleshing out.

His father and mother, Edgar Daggs McClintic and Ella Florence McClintic, were third cousins, both born McClintic and descended from a common ancestor, also named McClintic, an illiterate North Irishman who came to the Virginia Colony in 1740 with a land grant from George II.

Ella was raised on a farm outside Staunton, Virginia, and her older brothers fought with the Confederate Army in the Civil War. Edgar came from Marlinton, West Virginia, the son of Mary Mathews McClintic who, as great-grandniece of George Mathews, the second governor of Georgia, brought a considerable sum of money into the family. She was a fanatical Presbyterian and every Christmas and birthday sent

Guthrie five dollars with a note "trusting that you will grow up to be a true Christian."

Edgar was a good-looking six-footer with a strong back and stomach, a low powerful voice, and a talent for using that voice to string profanities together endlessly without ever resorting to obscenities. He had no charm for his son but he must have had for his mother, because while still a youth he was able to talk her out of a great deal of money, renouncing on the spot any claim to a share in her estate at her death. Had he been a poet with such a fine bridge-burning spirit, it would have justified his rashness. But he had no touch of the poet, only bad judgment, and left college to buy a cattle ranch in Texas, which the following winter was wiped out in a blizzard.

He salvaged what he could, and with an apparently obsessive attraction to disaster hied himself northwest to Seattle, which he heard had just been destroyed by fire. It was rebuilding when he got there, and seeing in that, quite rightly, promise for the future, he spent whatever money he had left on as much land as it would buy, went back east to claim his bride, and brought her out to Seattle in 1889 to find that his virgin land had acre by acre slid into the Pacific.

Ella McClintic was little and charming, gentleness personified, with a lovely speaking voice and a picture of Jefferson Davis hanging on the bedroom wall. When the violent pall of failure settled over her husband and the dreadful silence of futility settled over her marriage, she took to switching churches — from Presbyterian to Unitarian to Theosophist to Ethical Culture — and gazing off to the Cascades as if they were prison walls (so her son later claimed), murmuring softly, "East of the mountains, son, it's nicer." But they never could go back to the home Ella dreamed of, not even for a visit, because one of the first facts impressed upon Guthrie's mind was that east of the mountains he and his parents were nothing but poor relations. These were the kind of relations the Cornells of Delaware Avenue didn't even have.

Guthrie's birth and the added responsibility slowed Edgar down still further. But he churned into action one more time, trying to make life happen by striking it rich. When Guthrie was five, at just about the time Kit was shunning her homely reflection in the mirror after scarlet fever and seeking the company of imaginary friends in the backyard, Edgar mortgaged the last negotiable possession he had, the house in which Guthrie had been born, and joined the gold rush to the Klondike.

When he returned empty-handed eighteen months later, the house was sold for its mortgage to the husband of the woman who had in the past done Ella's washing. At just about the time Peter Cornell was forsaking the medical profession to become rich and fat doing exactly what he wanted to do with his life, Ed McClintic, with a resentful glance at his wife and an accusing glare at his oddity of a son, gave up and submerged his hurt in a common job so ignominious that his son would never say what it was. He was forty.

Guthrie once said of his father, "God knows, while I never tried to please him I never tried to offend him either," and this on-the-fence remembrance offered fifty years later is evidence that he never stopped being evasive and noncommittal, at least outwardly. It helped to hide which way he was jumping, inwardly. Edgar was harsh with Guthrie, and the rigidly evasive child, with no hope of developing aggressive toughness, accepted second best for himself and became impervious. Thus he was somehow able to go his own way.

Kit took to the automobile so instinctively that she could undoubtedly have been found out on the road teaching others to drive without ever seeming to have learned herself, whereas Guthrie remained placidly on the front porch throughout that climactic part of the Industrial Revolution, reading *Oliver Twist*, probably for the fifth time, and even in Oliver's pitiful plights finding much to envy in orphanhood. Owning an auto was out of the question for the McClintics, but even when someone else's broke down at their very stoop, creating a sensation in the neighborhood, Guthrie barely looked up from the page, and it only seemed to deepen his concentration when his mother tried to keep his father from hearing a neighbor say you couldn't trust a boy who wasn't interested in mechanics. He rode in automobiles all his life, but he never became sufficiently interested in them to learn how to drive. Even Kit, a patient, gifted teacher, stopped trying to teach him, realizing it was more peaceful and certainly safer to be his driver whenever he wanted to go some place.

While Kit was spending summers swimming and horseback riding at Cobourg, Guthrie was working from 8:45 A.M. to 5:30 P.M., five days a week, as office boy to an attorney's firm. His main job was copying letters on a primitive, makeshift kind of mimeograph machine, a gelatin press. There was not even such a thing as carbon paper, and the letters were first placed in a large book with a damp cloth on the other side of the page they fronted. After as many pages as possible were laid out this way, the book was put in a press and the handle turned down tight for about three minutes. When it was released, the copies had been made and the originals were then put into envelopes and mailed. If the process is difficult to understand, it is because it is offered here practically in Guthrie's own words, and proud he was of his proficiency in describing such a contraption. In his misfittedness he must truly have been an office boy out of comic opera, but the deadening symbolism of constant copying cannot have escaped his notice.

He was twelve, the age when Kit was weeping solemnly into the velvet drapes of the stage box at *Peter Pan*. One day Guthrie spotted two men in an elephant suit chasing a kid dressed as Buster Brown around the corner of Third Avenue and Madison in Seattle. He followed the troop into the stage door of the Third Avenue Theatre, where Charles A. Taylor's New York Company was rehearsing for the opening of the sensational melodrama *Escape from the Harem*, with Taylor's wife, Laurette, the company's soubrette, making the daring escape on elephant back.

Guthrie took one look at the painted trees, the rock flats, the rows of lights overhead; he smelled the filthy glue; he watched the actors learning lines; he thrilled to a raw rehearsal. He had never seen a performance, and at the Saturday matinee he paid ten cents for a rush seat at the back of the balcony where the play was obscured by pompadours and hats; for subsequent matinees he hocked stamps he swiped from his father's Confederate collection, ignorantly accepting one four-hundredth of their worth to get reserved seats at the front of the balcony. He lied at home. He hung around the backstage door waiting for someone to leave it open so that he could enter.

Charles A. Taylor's leading woman, Ailleen May, was lured over to a rival company, and Guthrie had his life enriched by seeing the much less popular Laurette Taylor take over her roles.

With no knowledge or experience and without Kit's privileged access to professional rehearsals in her father's theatre; simply by seeing two actresses attack the same roles, one a popular star, the other a genius, and by recognizing the difference — by "crying like a fool" at Laurette Taylor's performance and trusting his instincts — Guthrie stopped being a dilettante.

When he went on to high school, he was terribly impressed to be called "Mr. McClintic." Although it was only a convention in that more formal day, it was a consideration for his existence that he was not used to, and he felt he might be rising in the social scale. He found a friend in Harold Harshman, a blond, Teutonic-looking boy who vowed passionately to write plays for Guthrie when he became a famous actor, and he found a confidante in Rose Glass, his history teacher. Together, the three of them saw all the shows at the Third Avenue Theatre, the more dignified Moore Theatre, and the newer and flossier Lois Theatre — Grace George in *Divorcons*, Mrs. Leslie Carter as *Zaza*, William Faversham as *The Squaw Man*, E. H. Sothern as Hamlet, and Blanche Bates in *The Fighting Hope*.

Guthrie was delighted to get the job as office boy because the five-dollar gold piece he received each Saturday morning supported his new habit in style. His father misinterpreted his industry as a predilection for the study of law, which was the first heartening sign he had seen in his son. He was certain that if Guthrie applied himself in school, his uncle George, a successful lawyer back in Charleston, West Virginia, would be willing to take him into his office as a gracious act of charity toward a poor relation.

Rose Glass was too gentle and conventional a woman to suggest defiance of family, but she did suggest that if Guthrie was set on becoming an actor, he owed it to his parents to tell them so, and he did. Both Edgar and Ella were shocked that a teacher would conspire with a student against his parents, but at about that time a wealthy woman from Roanoke settled in Seattle and came to call. She had known the McClintics in their younger and better days, and to everyone's surprise was undismayed by Guthrie's theatrical ambitions, explaining that her sister had attended the American Academy of Dramatic Arts in New York and had made quite a lovely career for herself on the stage before deciding to get married.

Edgar was impressed. If it was good enough for the sister of a family connection from back east, it just might be good enough for his son. After careful consideration, he volunteered eight hundred dollars tuition money and living expenses for two terms at the American Academy of Dramatic Arts. It was more than Guthrie had ever hoped for, but his gratitude was limited to admitting later on that having made the decision, which entailed every kind of economy, his parents were stoic. Thus suggesting that his entire future was settled by the sanction of a lady bountiful from Roanoke, Guthrie remained noncommittal toward his father, even toward his memory. There is something revealing in his evasion of the possibility that Edgar cared enough about him to let him have his chance.

In the fall of 1910, as Kit was going into her senior year at Oaksmere, Guthrie enrolled in the American Academy of Dramatic Arts. His father was surprised that he could get in, and in his innocence, so was Guthrie. But this five-foot-ten, one-hundred-and-seventeen-pound poor relation had come to New York to learn more than just acting. He had come to learn sophistication and worldliness in both deed and thought. The mean side of worldliness is easy to grab hold of, and Guthrie decided that, providing he had a bank draft in his hand, he would have been accepted at the Academy had he been "cross-eyed, harelipped and spavined." He kept aloof from his fellow students because he thought they were better than he was, at least better off financially, and where he came from that was the principal way of judging social station.

His courses at the Academy were a disappointment. He studied dramatic reading, voice, makeup, fencing, and dancing. In "pantomime and action" class he was never able to make it clear to anybody whether it was an orange, a lemon, or an apple he was peeling, and he never developed any respect for such exercises. In the same class he turned against sophistication and resented being made to learn for stage purposes how a gentleman stands in the presence of ladies (with his right knee bent) and how a gentleman behaves in restaurants (he does not talk to waiters).

But as contemptuous as he was of his courses he ate them up and became wildly defensive of them when he went home for summer vacation. With no report card to go on, the only thing his father could understand or grasp to be proud of was Guthrie's new knowledge of makeup "formulas," and he would invite neighbors over for the evening to see him make up Chinese, Italian, Irish, Jewish, and hobo. Guthrie gritted his teeth and probably noted vengefully that his father did not know enough to bend his right knee when standing in the presence of ladies.

As a kind of final exam at the end of the second year, Guthrie's class appeared in a play on the stage of Charles Frohman's aristocrat of theatres, the Empire, where even the lobby was all red velvet, red leather, and polished brass, with larger-than-life paintings of Margaret Anglin, Maude Adams, Ethel Barrymore, Billie Burke, John Drew, and

William Gillette. He was then given a diploma from the same stage and officially pronounced an actor. He was terribly impressed when *Theatre* magazine covered the class's graduation production and labeled him "an actor with a future."

For a time the future seemed to be rising directly out of the past. Laurette Taylor, now a star, long deserted by Charles A. Taylor and about to marry J. Hartley Manners, saw Guthrie's graduation performance and thought he would be just right to play her son in a new play Mr. Manners was writing for her, but first she had to do another of his plays in which there was no part for Guthrie, so would he please keep in touch. He was then sent to see Ailleen May who was about to go on tour as Nancy in *Oliver Twist*, and she saw to it that he got the part of the Artful Dodger. The tour was a flop, and the company was abandoned by the management in an obscure Canadian town, not an unusual occurrence in those days — it would be seven years before the great strike would give strength to Actors' Equity Association and protection to actors. Ailleen May, who turned out to be a grand gal despite her phony acting, assumed a star's responsibility for the company and moved them to Wilmington, Delaware, for a season of stock, which also failed. The grand gal went broke paying them all off, and then, through the efforts of his friend and sometime roommate Henry Hull, Guthrie found himself plunged into five-a-day vaudeville, which, in those days, mixed one-act dramas with songs and dances and funny sayings.

Guthrie probably had an affinity for the part of the Artful Dodger, not only because of his afternoons on the front porch in Seattle reading *Oliver Twist*, but because of a certain artful dodgery in his own nature, and he undoubtedly played it well. But from his vaudeville assignment he was fired, let go after one day for incompetence. He was then denounced by the agent who had gotten him the job. Guthrie explained it all away, pointing out quite truthfully that the whole thing was "show business at its cheapest and dirtiest," but the fact remains that no matter how reluctant he was to admit it, ever, he was not a very good actor.

There were other failures in other companies, and if he had private misgivings, wondering if he would be like his father, doomed to miss every time, publicly he blamed his shortcomings on his directors, starting back in his Academy days, complaining that he could not understand what they wanted and that if they would only leave him alone he would do just fine. It sounds like the protestations of a young actor refining his ego, but it was more than that. What he didn't understand then, and even looking back on himself years later still did not see, was that at that time he was an incipient director, unable not to criticize an established director for not knowing how to get what he wanted out of an actor, even a green actor like Guthrie McClintic.

It is fortunate for Guthrie and for the general health of the American theatre that Laurette Taylor's interim play turned out to be *Peg o' My Heart*, which she played for two years in New York and then two years in London. *The Harp of Life* was the play in which she wanted Guthrie to play her son, but she didn't get around to it until the fall of 1916. By that time Guthrie had long since gone to work for Winthrop Ames in casting and stage managing, on the other side of the fence from acting, and his sights were shifting.

———

Winthrop Ames, with his aristocratic New England background, was known as the First Gentleman of Broadway and guided graceful plays by Clyde Fitch and Arnold Bennett into his tasteful Little Theatre on West Forty-fourth Street, space now occupied by the *New York Times*. He was such a professional gentleman that when Laurette Taylor was still out in the sticks, touring *Stolen by Gypsies*, he went to see her work and decided not to include her in a repertory company he was forming because she was not a lady like Janet Beecher and her sister Olive Wyndham.

Guthrie described him as "a Velásquez cardinal in mufti" and felt a kind of religious reverence for his grace and manners, his breeding and refinement. It was a signal day in his life when he was finally able to call him "W.A."

But that was a long way off in June of 1913 when he walked into the Little Theatre looking for an acting job, dizzied by the scent of living box trees on either side of the Georgian entrance. Awkward, cautious, and awed, he probably longed to be nonchalant, in some way to be at ease with elegance, unruffled by splendor. But when the Negro doorman, towering over him in his high silk hat and cockade, imposing in his long black coat with silver buttons, saluted smartly and snapped the door open for him, Guthrie, everybody's poor relation from west of the Cascades, cringed past him as though he were a policeman.

It is not surprising that having come unannounced off the street, in fact from Bryant Park where he had been sitting with his shoes off, he did not find Mr. Ames in his office and was instead received by an associate; and it is not surprising that Guthrie immediately felt he had been fobbed off on an underling. It mattered not that the associate was a distinguished director (George Foster Platt) — in fact with Guthrie's resentment of directors that only made it worse — nor that this distinguished associate was, like W.A., a recognizable gentleman, "the kind of gentleman," Guthrie wrote later on, "that makes you acutely aware of it and puts a tender plant like myself completely ill-at-ease."

It is not surprising that to puff himself up in front of such a personage Guthrie lied about his experience, nor that the personage spotted the lies and treated Guthrie with icy suspicion; it is certainly not surprising that it infuriated Guthrie to be thought a liar (especially since he was), and that in his agitation he knocked over an inkwell and when he tried to mop up the desk was ordered rather sharply to leave. Unlike Kit's social gaucheries, Guthrie's did not endear him to the spilled-upon.

Who could blame him for feeling bruised and put upon, snubbed, insulted, to say nothing of badly treated, all at the hands of this band of gentlemen? A part of himself so secret that even he didn't know it was there had constructed a situation in which he could feel justified in resenting and reviling where he longed to belong and could not.

Out on the street, he resolved to put W.A. himself to the ultimate test of gentlemanly fair play by writing him a letter telling him everything that had passed, describing the ignominy of his treatment, describing himself honestly and without prejudice as having "wit, intelligence, sensitivity and an unplumbed capacity for work," asserting his right to another chance, demanding "the right to be seen . . . and not tossed into the discard." In challenging W.A.'s credentials as First Gentleman of Broadway, his letter had to reflect his own gentlemanly dignity, honesty, and impeccable good taste down to the very paper it was written on. He rushed to the mezzanine of the Astor Hotel and swiped some stationery marked "for the special use of patrons only."

By simply writing the letter he was purged of the need to send it. But he liked what he had said about himself, and since no one else was likely to come to his defense at that particular time in his life, he sealed the envelope and stowed it away in his trunk as a reminder of his worth.

A few weeks later his landlady, who dabbled in things other-worldly, got to tipping tables with a cousin one night and called Guthrie from his room to say the table had a message for him. Rapping once for "no" and three times for "yes," the table tediously spelled out "Mail that which you have written. Your entire future depends on it." Guthrie sent the letter and was engaged (with a less-gentlemanly producer he would have been "hired") as stage manager for Winthrop Ames's first production that fall, directed, ironically, by George Foster Platt.

W.A. turned out to be a sympathetic man with quiet persuasive ways, who never compromised his theatrical standards of excellence. Guthrie was so gratified to be wanted by such a cultivated man that he signed a contract, even though it was not for acting. He always loved acting and actors and never surrendered his claim to be called one, but before he knew it, encouraged by W.A., he decided he wanted to become a director. By obeying the spirit world and mailing the letter, his life had suddenly changed for the better. Is it any wonder that from then on he believed in all signs, portents, and oracles?

———

In *Me and Kit* Guthrie says, "All my life no one has been more aware of my own shortcomings than myself and, odd as it may appear, few have been as conscious of my good points." He was certainly right about himself when he said he had "an unplumbed capacity for work." Once he learned to saunter past the cockaded doorman, he grabbed at every bit of experience inside the Little Theatre as if hoping some of W.A.'s bearing and manner of thinking and personal taste would rub off on him, which it did. He was also right in claiming for himself wit and intelligence, for all the ladies and gentlemen in W.A.'s various companies, even those paragons Janet Beecher and Olive Wyndham, who became his friends, found him amusing and resourceful. And he was so fired with love for the English actors W.A. kept importing that he married one of them, Estelle Winwood, or as he put it in an unattractive Wall Street analogy, "I took a matrimonial flyer."

Estelle Winwood, with her wide globular eyes and brittle stillness, was ten years Guthrie's senior and came over from the Liverpool Repertory Company to be in a play the title of which could have served as a watchword for their entire relationship — *Hush*. The marriage was so clandestine that forty years later, writing about it in *Me and Kit*, Guthrie would not reveal her name and referred to her as "the lady," a revealing epithet.

After *Hush* closed, "the lady" stayed on to do other plays. Guthrie courted her through *A Successful Calamity*, and while she was appearing in the first Pulitzer Prize play, *Why Marry?*, they were married. With his superstitious nature, it is a wonder that he did not see ominous signs in the titles of her plays.

Winthrop Ames was the first manager to think of sending entertainment to the American troops overseas, and while he was abroad on that patriotic and philanthropic mission, Guthrie got married with the sassy furtiveness of a Booth Tarkington adolescent (*Penrod* was popular that year) who waits until nobody is looking to steal the piece of pie from the kitchen windowsill.

He was correct in his anticipation of his employer's disfavor, for when W.A. returned from Over There, Guthrie reports he "disapproved of the marriage. He frowned on the lady. I was in the doghouse." No explanation for the disapproval, just a peculiar, rather smirky "I knew it would happen!" from Guthrie. If he knew beforehand that he was entering into a calamitous misalliance, then indeed "Why marry?"

To go back. Earlier that year, in the spring of 1917, just a few months after Estelle Winwood came to this country and, to keep the chronology straight, at about the time Guthrie saw Kit for the first time in *Plots and Playwrights*, he was stricken with patriotic fever and tried to enlist. He was turned down and sent on his way with a jovial parting shot from his examiner, "We want to win this war, fella!"

Poor Guth. It was bad enough that spring for a young man to be ineligible for military service because he had the responsibility of a wife and children and other dependents. To be twenty-four, unattached, with good vision (no glasses), apparently fit, obviously able, and still to be in civilian clothes came close to being a disgrace. It did little good to mutter that he had tried and the doctors said this or thought that; it added up to one thing, that he was physically inadequate — "too weak" would be the dreaded way of putting it. What a severe blow to his self-esteem, just when it was being encouraged in other ways. On top of this outward disgrace there was an inner one, the hidden shame that he was actually glad he did not have to do military service, that he was intimidated by the awful hearty maleness of it all and was secretly relieved to be spared.

Six months later, just when he had learned assorted clever, witty answers to "Why aren't you in uniform?", he was called up in the draft when they were taking just about anybody and rejected again, officially tagged with a degrading 4-F classification. It may have been pure coincidence, but at that precise moment he married Estelle Winwood.

It may be too cynical to say he married so that he could at least point to the saving grace of a personal, living responsibility. The psychology may be too easy to suggest that it was the indiscreet stand of an overnice young man going through a period of doubt about his masculinity and virility and confusing them both with his manhood; it may be too farfetched to say that in a sudden retrogression to hurt immaturity, he reached out to the closeness of an older-wiser-woman-etc., to an older beautiful *lady*. But it is well to remember that Guthrie could be indiscreet, farfetched, and cynical.

Because of the rather sniggering way he remembers the marriage in *Me and Kit*, the last possibility to suggest itself is that he married Estelle Winwood out of a genuine feeling for her, and yet there must have been a genuine feeling for the *idea* of her, a wish to be identified with poise, breeding, class, experience, and Englishness. There is, however, a bizarre story that he made her dress up in all the white lace frills and flowered innocence of a bride when he took her home to meet the elder McClintics. In whatever form it could be made to take, the panoply of marriage was what he wanted.

On the seventy-five dollars a week Winthrop Ames paid him he gave up furnished rooms and established an apartment. Along with his discovery of good antiques, he discovered he had a taste for them and a talent for creating domestic elegance out of silver, gilt, swag, and long candles — a fitting background for his household companion if she could be made to stand still. He took unto himself a Negro maid named Emma Jones, an emotional Christian Scientist who adored him, understood him, and called him "Hon." For eighteen months he put up a big matrimonial front, living way beyond his means and, as he put it, "trying to look like a bigshot when I was anything but."

In June 1919 when the marriage quietly ceased to be, Guthrie did not know if it was necessary to get a divorce since by then he had reason to believe that his bride had never been divorced from a previous husband.

Here was sophistication to challenge the sensibilities of a poor relation from west of the Cascades where they just didn't do such things. But he couldn't press his beleaguered morality without laying his wide-eyed helpmeet open to a bigamy charge. To escape, he borrowed money from his one true friend, the treasurer of W.A.'s new theatre, the Booth, and made his first trip to England where the ladies came from, found a penny in Trafalgar Square, tucked it in his shoe, and came home broke and in debt to begin a new life.

On the day his new life began, the day he saw Kit in William Brady's outer office and confided to Olive Wyndham, "There's the girl I'm going to marry!", Estelle Winwood, with her infallible instinct for choosing just the right vehicle, was delighting audiences in a Somerset Maugham play called *Too Many Husbands*.

———

Guthrie can't have imagined that all this was a secret, especially forty years later, and it must have been gallantry that prompted him not to reveal Estelle Winwood's name when he told their story in *Me and Kit*.

Or maybe it was his love of plots and mystery. To build suspense about his life even further, as the years went by he did not deny rumors that he had been married before Estelle Winwood to a performer at the Hippodrome. After a few drinks he would sometimes confirm the rumor. It may have been after a few drinks that he *started* it. Or it may be absolutely true. One of his oldest friends swears to have been told by a friend of having seen a newspaper clipping about the marriage. How he loved intrigue and drama. He would be delighted to know that this much time and space has been devoted to trying to figure it all out.

8

Whispering (1920)

PROHIBITION THREW A DRY WET BLANKET over the entire country in 1920, but no one was really downhearted, least of all in Detroit, handily situated across the river from Walkerville, Ontario, the home of Hiram Walker. Nights were alive with hushed traffic, boats running without lights, gangs prowling the shores, and distilled whispering in back alleys. Spirits, whether evil, high, damp, blithe, or alcoholic, were irrepressible that spring and summer.

The Great War had made the world safe for democracy, the great strike had made the stage safe for actors, and American theatre was blooming and bustling. The staid, esteemed actor-managers were fading along with their musty preoccupation with the classics, and the younger crowd, the ones who had fought a war for the right to a bright future, were taking over with their zesty loyalty to American ways and American plays. Their love for the theatre was sacramented by a determination to keep themselves pure and untainted by contact with the crazy movies. The word "legitimate" was tacked onto "theatre" to distinguish it from the bastardy of the other medium.

A young actor like Walter Abel, in his first year out of the American Academy of Dramatic Arts, could spend twenty-two weeks doing one-night stands, work the other twelve weeks in and out of New York without ever straying farther than Mount Vernon, begin his second professional year as juvenile with the famous Jessie Bonstelle Stock Company in Detroit, and still have the breath and enthusiasm to be thrilled when Miss Bonstelle's alternate leading woman, fresh from the golf courses of Great Britain, galloped up on horseback to her first rehearsal, at the old Garrick Theatre in downtown Detroit.

She seemed immune to the notorious Bonstelle discipline, perhaps privileged, but she broke no rules with her dramatic stance, disrupted no regimen; in fact, order seemed to be established with her unorthodox entrance. On time to the moment, her lines letter-perfect, she tethered her horse in Grand Circus Park and gave herself up completely to the director Guthrie McClintic, as if turning herself in to the authorities. Katharine Cornell took it all in stride as if every actress began a new season this way. How, Abel wondered, could the other members of the company and Miss Bonstelle herself be so unimaginative as to call her "Kit"? "Katharine" was a name big enough for her, with enough character and substance. To a young actor just a year out of the American Academy of Dramatic Arts, every stock company of course had a leading woman, but here was a heroine.

Guthrie was directing all the plays in which she was appearing, and because of her slogging way with a new part, he found it helpful to coach her privately, saving valuable rehearsal time for the other actors. It was the way they would work all their shared professional lives, and in that first spring and summer in Detroit, it made it easy and logical for them to become inseparable.

The courtship was theatrically conventional. When not performing, rehearsing, or coaching, they went dancing at the Hotel Statler Roof or sat on a bench in Grand Circus Park, talking the nights away in hushed voices. Later on Guthrie always said, "I am married to one of the most beautiful voices in the world." It was indeed a resonant, liquid voice, even a sigh of which could rouse a sleeper in the end seat of the last row in the top balcony. Guthrie himself claimed to have a powerful voice, which he attributed to having practiced long hours in falsetto in closets, bathrooms, and subways, thereby developing a second, amplifying set of vocal cords. It is difficult enough to imagine them whispering on a hot, carrying summer night in a Detroit public park without trying to conjure up what these disparate lovers from opposite ends of the country and incompatible backgrounds would find to say. However they managed to reach each other, theatre was undeniably at the heart of it at first, and then came agreements, declarations, perhaps admissions, secrets, and certainly endearments, for one thing is clear, that from the start it was what at the time would have been called a love match, and no amount of subsequent confounding was ever able to obliterate that fact.

A love match defies logic and needs no explanation. The surface trappings are often a parody that belies the depth of feeling. They had "their bench" and resented anyone else who dared to sit on it. With Guthrie's fear of the law in uniform, there of course had to be a policeman who patrolled the park all night and eventually broke them up, sending him off to the rooming house where he lived with Frank and Alma Morgan, and Kit off to the hotel apartment she shared with Aunt Lucy Plimpton, surely the most noninterventive chaperone ever to come out of Buffalo. The genial cop from central casting, the whispers in the dark, the parting at dawn — Guthrie might have been staging the whole scene for a not very good play.

Several years later Kit told a friend that she came back from England in the spring of 1920 with a big decision to make, whether to marry her English beau or Bryant Glenny, and that Guthrie came along and made the decision for her, all of which sounds like drama-after-the-fact.

If she was thinking of marriage, it was in the general way that any young person does. From all other accounts, she hadn't a serious thought in her head. She was at home in Detroit, at home with the Bonstelle company, at home with her leading man, Frank Morgan, with whom she had played *The Man Who Came Back* briefly the year before — she was at home with herself. With her recent successes, there was nothing especially to be proved, nothing at stake, nothing hanging in the balance. If there is a point when drifting changes character to become riding with the wind, this was it, and with Guthrie to give her direction in both the metaphorical and the literal meanings of the word, she was able to take what came with an equanimity that would have been impossible a few years earlier and would again become impossible a few years later.

When she now avoided taking center stage, it was no longer always out of shyness; sometimes it was burgeoning artistic taste. She found the treacle of the Ruth Chatterton part in *Daddy-Long-Legs* unpalatable and all through rehearsals persisted in making her entrances backwards, standing behind other actors and muttering her lines unintelligibly to get them over with.

On the other hand she adored the unadulterated farce of *Lombardi, Ltd.* Frank Morgan was a musical comedy man, an expert farceur, brilliant at establishing a farcical tone, and Kit was perfectly able to play into whatever he set up. She could not establish the tone herself, but given the lead she could follow. As Lombardi, Morgan talked for half the first act about his Italian girl friend, how gorgeous she was. Kit was perfectly able to live up to the gorgeousness, but when she finally appeared at the top of a long curved flight of stairs, she was a skinny dumb model in a horrible dress that hung on her and didn't seem to move when she did. By the time she reached the stage floor, the audience was so convulsed with laughter that Walter Abel, who waited for her at the bottom of the stairs with the next line, couldn't get it out despite her muttering "Walter, go *on!*" It was the last of the freewheeling, zany performances that her worshippers later on in the 1930s would find it hard to imagine her ever having given.

No drifting for Guthrie, who came to Detroit in search of hard concentrated experience. In January, Winthrop Ames, whom he was at last allowed to call "W.A.," had expressed New Year's faith by offering to put up the money for any play Guthrie might choose to present and direct. Should the play succeed, the money was to be paid back; should the play fail, the whole thing would be forgotten. With that incentive to work, Guthrie took on his first serious directorial assignment with Bonstelle, and the response of everyone in the company convinced him that he was on the right track.

Stock directors in those days, at least the eager ones, also played leftover roles, which was all right with Guthrie. But he must have been taken aback to find himself early in the season directing "the girl he was going to marry" in Estelle Winwood's too recent role in *Too Many Husbands*, with himself as illegal husband number two. It is surprising that he did not take it as an omen of some kind, but undoubtedly he was diverted from a psychic moment by vanity. Fancying himself as an Englishman in an English drawing room comedy, he hunched himself up, set his teeth in what he thought was a British occlusion, and toddled onstage too pleased with himself to be bothered by omens. As for Kit, dismayed as she must have been, she probably told herself that a director's best experience is to be an actor, and if she felt either her artistic tolerance or her personal attraction challenged, she never let on.

Years later his ineptitude as an actor would make her uneasy, but for now she seemed to enjoy it. In a typical postwar play called *Civilian Clothes*, he played her father and never had time to learn his lines. Instead, they were pasted inside his newspaper on the set, and whenever he dried up in a scene, he puffed his cigar and picked up his newspaper — until the performance when his stage daughter deliberately sat on the newspaper and with that damnable smile of hers waited for him to say his next line.

It was the first and only practical joke she ever played onstage. She was always rather proud of it and loved telling about it, but at the time she must have been surprised at herself. She was becoming aware of the dangers of stock acting, of how easy it was to become second rate and settle for it. Three seasons before, Miss Bonstelle had been a shining example, but her red hair no longer shone, it had burned without ever flaming, and here she was, still the feted darling of her audiences, but at fifty-four trying to play a kittenish Ina Claire part with flirtatious ribbons flowing from her shoulders to hide a great ledge of a bust, heavy hips, and a benign but unaesthetically protuberant abdomen. If challenged she would have pointed out with the false logic of the second-rater that Sarah Bernhardt was seventy-six that year and with only one leg to stand on was being acclaimed as a full-bodied thirty-one-year-old man in a fashionable new play.

There was more involved than age and appearance. The Ina Claire play was Walter Abel's debut performance with the company, and when in his opening night nervousness he changed a piece of stage business, the mighty Bonstelle, without ever breaking the flow of action — but for all the audience to hear — reprimanded him impatiently: "You're supposed to do it this way!" she said and showed him how.

Kit had a similar experience herself when she played the lead in an Austin Strong tryout called *Heaven*. There was a scene in which she heard of her lover's death and attempted to jump out an open window, to be stopped in the nick of time by a fellow actor. At one performance the window was not only closed but securely locked by the trustworthy property man, and as Kit turned in her emotional state to make her dramatic dash for oblivion, she was startled to see the fellow actor go to the window, unlock it, throw it open, step back with a courtly bow, apparently urging her on to self-destruction, and then position himself to stop her in the nick of time, all this for the audience's pleasure.

As Kit put it, "He was just a dear person trying to help," but it was becoming increasingly clear how difficult it was to go on in a part with any semblance of character, let alone to sustain it. An actor just went out there and did whatever he had to do to get off again, and it was so easy to stop noticing what went on in between.

Kit, already a "dear person," never showed signs of settling for that, especially not with Guthrie around. During rehearsal one day he accused her of letting out a cry that was dead and wooden, a "stock" cry. No matter how many times she tried, it got no better. In exasperation he leaped onto the stage, accidentally bumping into a heavy table, which turned over and gave her a bad whack on the shins. She let out a yell, and he shouted with glee that it was exactly what he wanted. This story has been told about other directors and actresses, and it even turned up in the movie version of Hecht and MacArthur's play *Twentieth Century*, with the variation that John Barrymore deliberately jabbed Carole Lombard with a long pin to make her scream properly. Guthrie would certainly never have deliberately whacked Kit on the shins, and the whole story may be apocryphal, but it accurately reflects their professional relationship.

But even without Guthrie, Kit would have been saved from becoming no more than a stock actress by her own conviction that she could never be a good one because she was such a slow study. She was not one to stay with something she couldn't be good at. Who can say if she ever articulated it to herself or to Guthrie, but it was time for her to break the habit, for habit it was becoming, of drifting easily back to Jessie Bonstelle each season. She was in her twenty-eighth year. It was time to be on Broadway.

It almost happened with *Heaven*.

———

She got the part of Diane because the English playwright St. John Ervine told his friend Austin Strong that the American girl who played Jo in London would be perfect for it. Strong passed the word along to John Golden, his New York producer, who had never heard of Katharine Cornell. When he found out she was playing leads in Detroit that summer, he let Jessie Bonstelle try out *Heaven* for him so that he could see Kit in the part.

She played a young French prostitute who falls in love with a sewer cleaner in the Paris of 1914, and Golden eventually decided she didn't have enough sex appeal. Then, however, in keeping with his reputation for producing clean plays, he had Strong change Diane from a prostitute to a pickpocket, changed the play's title to *Seventh Heaven*, and cast blond, pale, rather affected Helen Menken in the part that sweet, adorable Janet Gaynor would later play in the movie. It is obvious from this subsequent history that despite what Golden said, Kit had too *much* sex appeal.

Knowing what was at stake, Kit's nerves were so on edge that she almost didn't get through the opening night performance in Detroit, shutting herself in her dressing room while the orchestra played over again several times the overture to the last act. Finally a friend who was a nurse, Jeannette Kimball, was called backstage from the audience to calm her. At the end of the performance, Miss Kimball wrote in a letter many years later, "the audience split their gloves for you. A bouquet of roses came over the footlights, and you came forward with a sweet sort of wistful smile. The house went wild. You tried to say something but couldn't, so you just held out your hands to them — they were yours." Miss Kimball went back to Kit's hotel with her, put her in a hot tub, laid cold towels against her spine, gave her a cologne rub, and stayed with her until she dropped off to sleep.

Frank Morgan was the only one to go on with the play to Broadway, and the entire company were shocked by Golden's rejection of Kit, having seen in her portrayal the first signs of the slashing intensity she would become known for. She was the only one who was not disturbed. She was disappointed, she said, but added that she didn't think she was ready for such a big part.

Perhaps it was simply easier to let Guthrie react for her. Sputtering resentment was more in his line. They were empathizing emotions by this time, catching attitudes from each other. She even had one of Guthrie's psychic moments one hot night when they hired a cruising car to take them for an hour's cool drive around Belle Isle. Later, having scrambled eggs and coffee at Thompson's, near the Statler Hotel, Guthrie suddenly realized he had left next week's script of *Civilian Clothes* in the hired car, which had long since disappeared into the far reaches of Detroit. Rehearsals were to begin at ten in the morning, and it would be forty-eight hours before a new script could be sent from New York. The sense of failing what they both considered a high responsibility was sickening. Suddenly Kit got up and said, "Come, let's go! — *now!*" They dashed out of the coffee shop and down the street to the corner just as the hired car passed and the driver called out, "Want another ride?"

One night two-thirds of the way through the season, Jessie Bonstelle called Guthrie to her dressing room and asked him if he knew what was wrong with Kit, who, she said, was losing her grip and her popularity. Letha Walters, the second woman, was getting a bigger hand on her entrance.

"Do you know what's happened? I hear she is interested in some man and it is taking her mind off her work. Do you know who it is?"

For deviousness, Miss Bonstelle had met her match and got nothing from Guthrie but wit and a shrug.

Civilian Clothes was the last play of the season, and on the day it opened Kit came downstairs in the hotel elevator to see the lobby filled with people gesturing and talking animatedly, all without sound. It was rather anticlimactic to find it was only a deaf-and-dumb convention and not her fevered brain.

The season that had started out in such high spirits had been happy but hellish, too, long and crowded, and now there was the awful void to be faced at the end of the week. For the first time in two years there was no job to fall into, no one trying to lead her into a new project, nothing to go along with. There was only New York to look forward to, and the rounds of the agents' and managers' offices. Whatever confidence was gained could be so easily lost, and the summer heat had been intensified by Miss Bonstelle's open disapproval of Guthrie. Besides, Letha Walters *was* getting a bigger hand on her entrance.

At that point she probably would have welcomed a nice pleasant breakdown, the kind she told Jeannette Kimball she had almost had in London playing Jo in *Little Women*. But illness, as much as she feared it and sometimes courted it, could never provide her with an out because she was just too healthy. She had to escape in other ways, and at the end of the interminable season in Detroit she hurried off to Cobourg to visit Aunt Lydia, who just that year had sold the huge

Hadfield Hurst and moved into a smaller, much more comfortable house diagonally across the way. There Kit swam, rode horseback, and played tennis while Guthrie returned to New York and W.A.'s office where he was now making one hundred and twenty-five dollars a week.

W.A. was casting William Archer's *The Green Goddess* and as a change from his favorite Olive Wyndham he was looking for a new face, a young Ethel Barrymore, to play opposite that most English of all English actors, George Arliss. Guthrie suggested Kit, who was nowhere near being a young Ethel Barrymore, but he would have suggested Kit had W.A. been looking for a young Marie Dressler.

When Kit arrived in New York she had an interview with W.A. and did not get the part. Guthrie reported that after the interview W.A. said she had no emotional power.

"Has Miss Wyndham?" asked Guthrie, personally piqued.

"After all," W.A. replied, "Miss Wyndham is a lady." And Miss Wyndham got the part.

Guthrie told the story that way because it gave him a chance to continue, "It would have been silly to mention that Kit was in the 'Social Register' (and anyway I fixed that, for when she married me she was dropped)." He was beside himself with pride that when it came to picking winners in the Lady Derby, Winthrop Ames, the supposed master hand, didn't know beans, while he, Guthrie, picked the real, true-blue-blooded article without even trying, simply by putting his heart in the right place at the right time. There was something cocky in his announcement that Kit had been pulled down just a peg for marrying him. What he didn't see and maybe never saw was that the reverse was true, that she had pulled him up a peg.

Kit described the interview with W.A. quite differently. He asked her, "If you had your choice, what part would you like to play?"

She couldn't think of an answer. She knew she was supposed to say Juliet, the part every well-bred young actress of the day aspired to, but she didn't want to play Juliet; she would be relieved if she never in her life had to cope with all that poetry. In answering W.A.'s question she replied that all she wanted was any job she could get, and after she was gone, he said to Guthrie, "No ambition."

Her total lack of pretension had become an adult character trait, almost a fault, and all her life she would regard her talent cautiously, carefully, more than a little mistrustfully. Years later when she was persuaded to take on Juliet and coped with all that poetry magnificently, the cast backstage used to while away the time playing a rather unkind game that involved rating themselves and everyone they knew in every endeavor, virtue, and vice, on a scale of ten. When Kit played the game, she gave herself two for acting.

In her recounting of the interview with W.A. there was also a shrewd bit of self-knowledge, an admission that she knew she had no overpowering, all-consuming ambition. One wonders what kept her going; the truth seems to be that up to this point in her life, despite the persistence of her dreams and the time already expended on them, despite her dedication and accomplishments, it is conceivable that she could have been diverted from her course.

But with Guthrie's entrance into her life and emotions there was no longer the slightest doubt of where she was going. He seems to have crystalized her ambition for her and provided the practical drive.

For an outsider, looking at her life until now, moving in sequence from one event to the next, is like looking at Katharine spelled with an *e* instead of an *a*. Something seems to be slightly off — one is not sure what, and it doesn't really matter — and yet there it is. A veering thrust of heart. Absentmindedness of spirit. A striking lassitude. Remembering her the first summer he knew her Guthrie said there was about her "something you find away from the haunts of man, deep in a forest — or in the middle of the ocean at the dead of night." Perhaps that is all it was, a remoteness. Or inertia. A fixed misspelling of her name.

Whatever it was that had been puzzling, from now on was not.

———

On September 8, 1920, Guthrie took her dancing at the Hotel Pennsylvania Roof on Thirty-third Street at Seventh Avenue, now the Statler-Hilton. In the middle of the evening they stepped onto a balcony or terrace, and as they looked down at the bright lights of New York, Guthrie outlined his assets, which took not a moment, dumped his unresolved entanglement with Estelle Winwood in her lap, spoke feelingly of the future, and asked her to share this messy disarray with him as his wife. The importance of the moment — and the drama of it

— elevated him to an ingenuous straightforwardness that was becoming and wise, for the steeper his problems and the more helpless he seemed, the more strongly she was moved to accept. The story goes that the orchestra was playing "Whispering." New York lay prophetically at their feet. Again, Guthrie might have staged it all for a play.

III

Mrs. McClintic (1920-1925)

9

Nice People on Broadway - and Not So Nice (1921)

LEFT TO HIS OWN DEVICES, Guthrie would have been inclined to accept Estelle Winwood's droll disavowal of their marriage, announce cryptically to his friends that he was a free man, and enjoy their puzzlement without explaining further. Pushed instead into action by a sense of responsibility to Kit, he had to seek advice and help — but where? Considering the shabby nature of the situation, he would have been loath to turn to the upright and revered W.A.; with his general fear of authority, it would have been his way to dodge it completely and seek a solution on Broadway, his Street of Chance, where there was always a handy pool of characters who knew how to fix anything from an unwanted baby to a bigamy rap.

With Kit, the stickier the situation, the higher the authority that should be enjoined to resolve it. She had a way of attracting influential people who were always eager to volunteer their services.

William Barnes was a one-time Republican boss, the one who spiked Teddy Roosevelt's nomination at the 1912 convention. Now owner of the *Albany Journal*, he was still a mighty power in the Empire State where divorce, even of the honorable, straightforward kind, was all but impossible to obtain and usually had to be procured through manipulation. Some say he was an old friend of the Cornells of Delaware Avenue; Guthrie claimed Barnes's wife, Maude, had been Kit's

English teacher at Mrs. Merrill's school. However they came into the picture, the older couple took to asking the younger out to their home in Mamaroneck for Sunday lunch, and when they heard there was a problem they asked if they could help. Guthrie was so delighted to have such a Pooh Bah take an interest in his affairs that he forgot to be afraid of him.

Barnes listened to Guthrie's story, told him he had been a goddamned fool, and said he would mull the situation over and see if he could think of a solution that would legally free Guthrie of all ties without endangering the reputation, sensibilities, and legal status of "the lady."

A few days later he called Guthrie back to his office for his instructions. First, he was to pack a suitcase with clothes he did not want. This presented a problem right away since Guthrie had but two suits to his name. He canvassed Third Avenue, then a notorious hutch of hock shops, bars, and second-hand joints huddled in the shadow of the elevated, and managed to find some old clothes he could afford and a cheap wicker suitcase.

Then on the following Sunday he took a train up the Hudson to a town in Greene County, the gateway to the Catskills. There he was met by a John Doe who took him to a house where he rented a room for six months. He never had to go back there; he just had to hang up his clothes and put the suitcase under the bed to establish residence.

After his recent splurge of wedded high-living, Guthrie was trying to economize, but this was no time for pinching pennies, and he did everything Barnes told him to, setting himself back two hundred and twenty dollars. Then, since nothing more could be done until he had been a resident of Greene County for six months, he went to work reading plays, looking for just the right one with which to present himself as a presenter on Broadway. For the last time in her life, Kit was climbing stairs to the managers' and agents' offices.

A friend of Mrs. Wolcott's at her exclusive New York women's club, the Colony, was Rachel Crothers, the amusing, rather preachy and very popular playwright. Miss Crothers's work mainly dramatized the position of women in modern society, especially the society known as "high" that would later become known as "café." When she heard Kit's background from the aggressively informative Mrs. Wolcott, she thought there might be a part for her in her new play, *Nice People*.

The actual hiring was put in the hands of an agent at the Packard Agency whom Kit knew as Miss Humbolt and Guthrie, with the supreme disdain these two had for each other's facts, knew as Miss Humbert. Coincidentally, she was the agent who had denounced Guthrie as an actor nine years earlier for his disgracefully bad performance in vaudeville.

In *Nice People* Miss Crothers was launching the roaring third decade of the twentieth century with an up-to-the-minute look at what nice (i.e., rich) young women were doing with their lives, which turned out to be what upstarts and parvenus had been doing for years — casting off their corsets, taking up cigarettes, drink, and frank language, and in the example of Theodora "Teddy" Gloucester, the play's heroine (played by Francine Larrimore), staying out all night with members of the opposite sex.

Teddy is twenty years old, and her two closest friends of her own age are Hallie Livingston and Eileen Baxter-Jones (played by Tallulah Bankhead and Katharine Cornell, respectively). Miss Bankhead was already a Broadway veteran, this being her second Broadway engagement and her second Rachel Crothers play, and it is worth noting that she was nine years younger than Kit. It is also worth noting that nobody noticed it.

Their roles were small and essentially the same girl, both "finely bred animals of care and health and money — dressed with daring emphasis on the prevailing fashion, startling in their delicate nakedness and sensuous charm." A slight difference in the characters suggests the greater difference in the actresses who played them. Bankhead's Hallie was more chancy, plunging into the fray, risking open warfare to get Teddy's man for herself, while Kit's Eileen Baxter-Jones stood back just a little, not enough to be excluded but just outside the entanglements, better able to see who was hurting whom and trying to prevent it.

Noël Coward made his first visit to these shores in May 1921 "with a bundle of manuscripts, a one-way ticket, and only seventeen pounds to spare," and in *Present Indicative* goes on to describe his first evening in New York:

> I walked up and down several side streets, looking at the pictures outside the theatres, and, finally deciding upon one, went into the Klaw Theatre. The play was *Nice People* by Rachel Crothers, starring Fran-

cine Larrimore, and including among the smaller parts Tallulah Bankhead and Katherine [sic] Cornell. I thought the production and acting good, and the play poor, but what interested me most was the tempo. Bred in the tradition of gentle English comedy with its inevitable maids, butlers, flower vases, and tea-tables, it took me a good ten minutes of the first act to understand what anyone was saying. They all seemed to be talking at once. Presently I began to disentangle the threads, and learnt my first lesson in American acting, which was the technique of realising, first, which lines in the script are superfluous and second, knowing when, and how, to throw them away.

It is ironic that the earnest young Englishman was learning his lesson from actors not all of whom were as sure of what they were doing as he thought they were.

Sam Harris produced the play and Sam Forrest directed it, but Rachel Crothers ran the show. All through rehearsals she kept giving Kit special coaching in three or four sure-fire lines that she said were her favorites, but no matter what Kit did she could never get the sure-fire laughs in performance. Miss Crothers would plead, even give line readings — an unforgivable directorial practice even then — and Kit would try again, twisting the lines and turning them every which way without raising a smile out front. Tallulah never needed such special instruction, never had a moment's trouble with the throwaway delivery Coward admired so much because it was at the heart of the art she brought to the theatre and to life. Kit's way was to ponder and think through, to store up and burnish. A line of dialogue such as Eileen Baxter-Jones's "I like a sort of frank flash of pash once in a while" could not stand up under such studied care, no matter how light the comic spirit that had brought down the house in *Lombardi Ltd.*

Both actresses were products of the affluent American environment Rachel Crothers wrote about (which is probably why they were in the play in the first place), but the young Bankhead fell in with the play's characters both on the stage and off, whereas Kit could do no more than cultivate their acquaintance. The girl from Alabama epitomized the decade; the girl from Buffalo was like a searching traveler who happened to land there for ten years. Tallulah draped the 1920s around her shoulders like a cloak, whereas Kit could assume the style of that decade or any other, but not its faddishness, the fashions but not the crazes. Kit could move an entire audience, even in comedy, with an open burst of passion, but not with a frank flash of pash.

Kit's Broadway debut, then, so late, after such a long apprenticeship, was inauspicious in a day when Broadway debuts were set great store by. Today, *Nice People* is only interesting as the play in which those two extraordinary young actresses met and touched before skyrocketing, each on her own startling career. It is not surprising that they did not become close friends. Kit always recalled that Tallulah was "very beautiful and smoldering with talent," but Guthrie was more Tallulah's speed, and she frankly never could understand his attachment to "that Christer." But something interesting had been set up, a kind of unacknowledged race, and a few years later the difference between the two high-keyed actresses would be played off with surprising results.

Kit almost missed being in *Nice People*. Immediately after she got the part early in 1921 she came down with a sore throat which the doctor diagnosed as diphtheria. The next day he changed his mind to quinsy, but she had to have her tonsils out and withdrew from the cast. She was laid up for five weeks, and although it must have been a painfully uncomfortable illness, it was not entirely unwelcome since it gave her a good legitimate reason for not making the rounds.

While she was convalescing, Guthrie found his dream play, *The Dover Road* by the English (of course) playwright A. A. Milne (also author of the "Pooh" books). Winthrop Ames was as good as his word and immediately gave Guthrie five hundred dollars for the necessary author's advance so that he could get started on casting and other preproduction details.

When she was well again, Kit was delighted to hear that for some reason *Nice People* had not yet gone to rehearsal. She contacted Miss Crothers and got her part back. The play opened March 1 at the Klaw Theatre to a mediocre press but enthusiastic audience response and settled in for a long popular run.

Kit and Guthrie couldn't hurry up the divorce, but they couldn't wait to start looking for a place to live. Frank Morgan's wife, Alma, had told them the summer before about Beekman Place where she had lived as a child, and they started walking over there on Sunday afternoons. Running from Forty-ninth Street to Fifty-first Street between First Avenue and the East River, it was too short to be a street and was quite correctly called a "Place." With a slaughterhouse to the south (with its odors) and a coal yard to the north (exactly where 433 East

Fifty-first Street is now), it was not a fashionable section but a comfortable one, two cobblestoned blocks of old New York brownstone houses, all of them fully occupied, mostly by staunch German-American families.

In May an advertisement appeared in the Sunday *Times* offering for rent three floors and a garden at number twenty-three. The garden overlooking the river traffic as it plowed north to the Queensboro Bridge thrilled Kit, and Guthrie was lost in the grandeur of the high-ceilinged parlors. There was a kitchen on the ground floor, also overlooking the river, and sleeping quarters on the third floor. A Mrs. Schmid owned the house and planned to continue living in the two top floors. She was persuaded to let Guthrie take over the premises immediately and sublet them until he and Kit were able to move in themselves. He also asked for and got a first refusal clause should the property be put up for sale. He signed a three-year lease at one hundred and fifty dollars a month.

It had been decided that Guthrie would be the plaintiff in the divorce action, but the defendant refused to have the papers served on her because she thought the whole thing unnecessary. When a friend succeeded in putting the papers in her hand one afternoon along with a cocktail, she scorned them as in the future she scorned the faithless friend.

William Barnes went to all possible lengths to keep the divorce action not only out of the newspapers but out of the courts as well. On a properly dark and fateful night, Guthrie and Emma Jones, his character witness, boarded the Albany night boat. The next morning they were met by a lawyer who drove them to the courthouse in Greene County where the divorce was scheduled to come up. A murder trial was in progress, and they were made to wait in the judge's chambers until a recess was called and the judge could join them. As Guthrie's housekeeper, Emma Jones testified that he lived alone, that his wife did not even keep her clothes under his roof. Since the housekeeper lived in New York City and Guthrie was supposedly a resident of Greene County, it is not clear how this testimony was made to appear legitimate, but the judge apparently liked it, and in less than fifteen minutes, the length of the recess, he granted Guthrie a divorce on the grounds of desertion, and hurried back to the courtroom where real life was going on. It is a wonder that Guthrie, who was always an avid murder fan, didn't stay on for the other trial, too. From this distance it is hard to guess which would have tickled him more about the whole divorce — his freedom or the ten-twenty-thirty melodrama.

There was no longer any need for "whispering," and the word was officially let out that Kit and Guthrie planned to marry. In Seattle, Ed and Ella McClintic only wanted to be assured that the bride's family was good enough to merge with the McClintics. Dr. Cornell didn't give a rap about the groom's family; knowing the groom himself was more than he could bear. It is said that he burst into tears when he heard the news. Who knows all the things he had stored up against Guthrie; what reports with the smell of officialdom emanated from his friend Ed Stair of the *Detroit Free Press;* what vagaries Jessie Bonstelle innocently confirmed in personal exoneration; what future social oblivion Mrs. Wolcott intuited. Guthrie was more shocked than angry when he heard some of the objections raised by his father-in-law-to-be, calumnies so extensive that they were not repeated or handed down. Dr. Cornell disliked Guthrie because he was divorced; he disliked him even more because he was unimportant, because he was thin and pasty; because of his personal mannerisms, the maddening way he pointed for emphasis with that long damned forefinger curving down at you; because he was in the theatre; because he was arty, by which Dr. Cornell meant effeminate.

If in the past Kit had ever equivocated to placate her father, she did not now. She simply waited. Guthrie had been warned that in New York State three months had to elapse before he could marry again. As far as Kit was concerned, that gave Dr. Cornell until September to come around.

It also gave Kit and Guthrie a lovely anticipatory summer to while away. Twenty-three Beekman Place was sublet and paying for itself. *Nice People* continued to please theatregoers, who in those days loved comedy in hot weather and, since air-conditioning was unheard of, did not know how much they suffered. *The Dover Road* was a simple play, a producer's dream, with one set and ten characters, four of them walking-on servants, but Guthrie was developing its production with the slow, tasteful, painstaking care he always seemed too impatient to waste on other areas of his life. He was mainly waiting for just the right theatre to become available.

His idea of a happy day off was to read plays, any plays, all plays, finding relaxation and escape in their not being *The Dover Road*. Kit's idea of a happy day off was sun and water. And so on Sundays they would pack a picnic basket and go to Mamaroneck where Kit knew a sheltered piece of shore on a deserted estate not far from Oaksmere. After a swim in the Sound, they would cook their dinner over an open fire, and while Kit stretched out in the sun Guthrie would hunch in the shade, pull a play script from his pocket, and read aloud.

One Sunday afternoon he read *A Bill of Divorcement*, a play by Clemence Dane that had already been a success in London with Malcolm Keen, Lillian Braithwaite, and Meggie Albanesi in the leading roles. The American rights had not been sold, and the script had been sent to Guthrie in the hope that he would find it interesting either for himself or for Winthrop Ames.

With its odd title and ingrown winter theme, its Christmas melancholy so unsuited to a Westchester beach, the play was a far cry from *Too Many Husbands* and other popular British drawing-room comedies. It was the story of a man, a shattered relic of war, making his way back from derangement, his emergence into light unexpectedly propelling his daughter down the same road in the opposite direction, her nerves straining the bonds of her own reason; the two meeting but not passing, stopping instead in recognition of a shared imbalance; joining forces and moving on — but in which direction? To madness or sanity? A lovely, lonely, eerie moment set against "the holly and the crackle of the fire"; and Kit said, "I could play that girl."

Until that summer she had played every part because she was told to or because she was the actress who happened to be around or because she was talked into it by someone who said she would be wonderful or because she wanted the job — or in the case of *Nice People* because of influence at the Colony Club. It is true she had never chosen, because she had no choice; actors don't at the beginning. But as Winthrop Ames proved, at least to his own satisfaction, in the casting interview for *The Green Goddess*, even had she been given choice, she had no preference.

There were two quiet changes of attitude that idle waiting summer of 1921. First, Guthrie wanted her for Anne, the girl in his bright, civilized English drawing-room comedy *The Dover Road*, and despite her feeling for him which ordinarily would have inspired acquiescence, she was hedging. And second, had Winthrop Ames walked down the beach on that particular Sunday afternoon and asked her again, "If you had your choice, what part would you like to play?", she would have said Sydney Fairfield in *A Bill of Divorcement*.

She had chosen.

Of course they tell different stories of what happened next.

According to Guthrie, since he had already committed himself to *The Dover Road* and couldn't take on another play, he gave *The Bill*, as he and Kit soon came to call it, to W.A., who read it and enthusiastically cabled London for the rights only to discover they had just been sold to the British actor Allan Pollock, who planned to appear in it himself in New York that fall under Charles Dillingham's management. (Already things were working in Kit's favor — if W.A. had acquired the rights he would never have considered her for the part of Sydney.) There followed several weeks when Kit and Guthrie put *The Bill* out of their thoughts.

As Kit tells it, when Guthrie read the play on the beach he told her Allan Pollock owned the American rights, and at breakfast the next morning she received a postcard from Ada Humbolt/Humbert saying Pollock had cabled the Dillingham office asking if Katharine Cornell would be available in September.

The only other young woman in *The Bill* was a maid, and they would hardly be having a transatlantic cable correspondence about the casting of a walk-on. Kit called Guthrie at the Allerton where he was living, and he brought her down to earth by telling her that Pollock had another unidentified play he planned to produce in New York that fall and he might be thinking of her for something in that.

Humbolt/Humbert cabled London that Kit would be free in September and asked what it was for. After a day and a half of trying not to anticipate, came the one-word answer, "Sydney."

Nobody could figure it out, not Humbolt/Humbert, not Guthrie, certainly not Kit, and especially not Fred Latham, the casting director at the Dillingham office who had been instructed to hire her. He, like most of New York, had been unimpressed with her wise-cracking, blazered, tennis-racketed performance in *Nice People* and did his best to put Pollock off, cabling him to wait until he had met Miss Cornell before making any decisions. Pollock cabled back to hire her. Meggie Albanesi had been a sensation as Sydney in London, and Latham begged Pollock to let her come over at least for the first two weeks of the New York run, but Pollock cabled back, "If Cornell good enough for part, good enough for New York opening." That was precisely the point as far as Latham was concerned; she wasn't good enough for the part. Up to the time Pollock boarded the ship that would take him to New York to begin rehearsals, he was still cabling unexplained and persistent orders to hire her. And Latham had to.

Kit would have been completely demoralized had she known the extent of the Dillingham office's antipathy to her. She knew they wanted Meggie Albanesi (and couldn't blame them), but she assumed that Pollock's preference for her was accepted without question.

She had no idea what salary to ask. The character of the mother would probably be played by a star, but the play belonged to Sydney, and an established actress would have demanded six or seven hundred dollars a week and gotten it. Kit was making one hundred a week in *Nice People* and considered it generous. Probably with some prodding from Guthrie, she decided she would be worth two hundred and fifty dollars in the part and dared to ask for it. By this time Latham was philosophical and shrugged and mumbled, "Quite all right," convinced it was all academic anyway since she couldn't possibly last beyond the first rehearsal.

When Pollock arrived, Latham and Dillingham begged him to attend a performance of *Nice People* and see for himself what he had hired. He wouldn't do it and Kit stayed hired. In August she gave Miss Crothers her two weeks' notice, and on September 3 she played Eileen Baxter-Jones for the last time.

As Guthrie reports this string of events, a few weeks after the play reading on the beach, Ada Humbert called Kit to her office, offered her two hundred and fifty dollars a week to play Sydney, and signed her up. When it came to storytelling, Guthrie was inclined to be bored with theatrical shadings not of his own invention.

————

The only concession Kit made to her father's vigorous disapproval of her marriage was to decide against a big church wedding in favor of a civil ceremony.

If Aunt Lydia Cornell, like her brother, was dismayed by Guthrie, she was even more dismayed by the crossfire of family emotions he caused, perhaps because it all sounded familiar. With lingering memories of the cold hard answer she had once had to send to her lost Dr. Sherman's small touching letter, she favored her niece's defiance of parental authority and was shocked by the thought of a Cornell of Delaware Avenue being married by a justice of the peace. Her own living room was long and generously proportioned, really two parlors thrown into one with tall windows looking out to the garden, and she implored Kit to be married there by a clergyman — if one could be found. The groom being a divorced man, of course, the rector of St. Peter's (where Kit had been baptized) could not preside, nor could any Anglican clergyman, but Cobourg was expanding and surely someone could be found with fewer scruples; a Methodist, perhaps.

Guthrie must have had a superstitious hand in the selection of Thursday, September 8, 1921, for the wedding — exactly one year to the day after he had asked Kit to marry him at the Hotel Pennsylvania Roof.

Dr. Cornell let it be known that he would not attend. Kit wrote to him saying she could accept his attitude because she knew that one day he would regret it, and she wanted to put it in writing now, here at this moment, that she would never hold anything against him, nor would Guthrie. When he was ready, and she was confident that one day he would be, he must come to New York and see them and stay with them in their new home on Beekman Place.

Perhaps Dr. Cornell was only waiting to see who could hold out the longest; perhaps he always intended to relent in time and just wanted to throw his weight around first; perhaps his sense of fair play won out; perhaps he was moved by his daughter's generosity to him (although she had offended him deeply) and unyielding (and completely misguided) allegiance to the individual she was determined to marry. Whatever went through Dr. Cornell's mind, he was not proud enough to miss out on a good party if there was a chance he could be the life of it. He showed up in Cobourg in plenty of time to give the impression that the whole thing had been his idea.

When she saw him, Kit said, "I knew you'd come," and never again referred to his past attitude. It is not surprising that she was as good as her word; it is perhaps more surprising that Guthrie was. He had more cause than anyone to be offended, and it must have been hard for him to like Dr. Cornell, because in addition to everything else he was afraid of him. But once past the difficult beginning, the two men, so completely opposite, came to love each other, and there eventually came a time when Guthrie knew how to get along with the stuffy old doctor almost better than anybody else. Dr. Cornell always boasted about Guthrie's theatrical achievements as if he were his son.

Uncle Douglas Cornell and his wife Gwendolyn were the only other witnesses at the wedding. Kit wore a silk street dress. Guthrie wore a new dark suit. The Methodist preacher showed up in a funereal black Prince Albert and a rusty silk hat. When it was over, the groom gave him ten dollars in gold, a gesture reminiscent of the way they did things out west of the Cascades.

Every time Guthrie looked over his shoulder he caught Dr. Cornell watching him, and at the wedding rehearsal it so rattled him that when the minister instructed him to salute the bride, he raised two fingers to his forehead. He finally got it straight that to salute meant to kiss, but even so when the time came in the actual ceremony he either had to be prompted three times to kiss the bride or he kissed her three times before he was supposed to, depending on whose version one reads, his or hers.

It probably only happened to one of them, but they both claim to have been told beforehand by a fortune-teller that immediately after the ceremony they would cross a great body of water. Kit's version is vague and therefore suspect, while Guthrie's is full of details. His fortune-teller was Olive Wyndham's mother, who saw the water-crossing in tea leaves. As Guthrie boarded the train for Cobourg he dismissed the prediction as preposterous. Kit met him at the station with the news that *The Bill* was to go into rehearsal Friday, September 9, the morning after the wedding. To get there on time she and Guthrie would have to board the Twentieth Century Limited as it went through Rochester, New York, at midnight Thursday. The wedding was scheduled for Thursday noon, and to get to Rochester by midnight they would have to leave Cobourg in midafternoon and take a six-hour ferry ride across Lake Ontario.

And so it happened that immediately after the ceremony they crossed a great body of water and sat up all night on the train; Kit arrived at rehearsal the next morning on time if nothing else and despite weeks of familiarity with the script she gave her usual bad first reading.

Pollock was congratulatory when he heard about her wedding only the day before and solicitous when he heard about the wild trip from Cobourg, and Basil Dean, who had come over from London to direct the play, was effusive in his insistence that she take the weekend off. She and Guthrie were thus able to take advantage of a friend's offer of a shack on a deserted island off Norwalk, Connecticut, for two days' honeymoon.

Kit thought Dean was being generous. Up until now everyone in the theatre had always been generous; not once had she been the victim of anyone's ego, jealousy, or competitiveness. But the brilliant, ubiquitous Basil Dean, whom theatrical annals credit with having already directed six plays in London that year, among them *A Bill of Divorcement*, was determined, along with Charles Dillingham and Fred Latham, to have Meggie Albanesi play Sydney in New York. After Kit's bad first reading, he was confident. In a last-ditch stand over the weekend, he was sure that Pollock could be convinced. By giving Kit two days off, he hoped never to see her again.

Since it didn't happen that way and she was not fired, Kit, of course, was always sure that the story of Basil Dean's perfidy was exaggerated.

10

Sydney (1921)

"A Bill of Divorcement" is set in the future, 1933, and Sydney Fairfield is a war baby, now seventeen, in love with the rector's son and looking forward to marriage and family, her share of the good things in life. Hilary Fairfield, her father, hopelessly crazed by shell shock, has been institutionalized since the war. A new divorce bill, only under discussion in England when the play was written, has become the law of the land. Under its more lenient provisions Margaret Fairfield, Sydney's mother, has been granted a divorce on the grounds of her husband's insanity. On Christmas morning Margaret is within a week of remarrying when she learns that Hilary has suddenly fully recovered his senses and walked out of the sanitarium. Sydney learns what the rest of the family has always known, that shell shock merely contributed to bringing out Hilary's derangement, which at its root is an inherited family disorder. Sydney's own "nervy" ways become clear to her with fierce flashes of insight, and when her father appears, bewildered to find the world changed, she seems to understand him even though she has never seen him before in her life.

Hilary does not know he has been divorced and pathetically expects to take up his marriage where he left off seventeen years ago. Whenever Margaret tries to explain the change that has taken place, he fights it with irrationality, showing signs of reversion to his deranged state, and Sydney is the one who knows how to calm him.

Margaret is in an agony of indecision, torn between her compassion for Hilary and her love for Gray, the man she has promised to marry.

As Sydney Fairfield in A Bill of Divorcement, *1921. (Abbe)*

The rector and the family doctor both appear to position the physical and the spiritual worlds for and against the sins of the fathers, even as they do in Ibsen's *Ghosts*.

Sydney, now finding only horror for herself in the thought of marriage and the good things in life, in passing on to helpless unborn children her appalling "quick-like" ways, falls back on the flippancy expected of youth to dismiss the rector's son from her world and her future. Then she sends her mother off with Gray, assuring her, "Father — he's my job, not yours," and is left with that awkward broken man who puts his arms around her in fatherly protection.

———

Like Hilary Fairfield, Allan Pollock had been shell-shocked in the Great War and worse, so wounded that his face and insides had to be rebuilt before he could be dismissed into civilian life again. Before the war the young Scotsman had been a rising actor, but now he was so fearful of resuming his career that a group of concerned friends at the Players Club, headed by the dramatist A. E. Thomas, got together and bought him the American rights to *A Bill of Divorcement* and persuaded Dillingham to take over the management while they supplied the backing. With the kinship Pollock felt for Hilary Fairfield, it was an inspired gesture, and the only problem from the start had been who would play Sydney.

In the London boardinghouse where Pollock lived there was a little old Scottish lady, an artist named Lillian Wardlaw, who was so devoted to him that he sent her to see *A Bill of Divorcement* for her opinion. She reported that all evening she kept thinking that the American girl who played Jo in *Little Women* two years before would be perfect as Sydney. Pollock remembered her, too, but couldn't think of her name, which he finally got from Leslie Faber. Then, having sent off his cable to America and found that Katharine Cornell was available, he felt the part had been cast to his satisfaction and never saw any reason to change his mind. It was as refreshingly simple as that.

Basil Dean was intent on reproducing a carbon copy of the London production, a pedestrian and inept way for a director to work even then, and at the start mainly railed at Kit for not being Meggie Albanesi. But it soon developed in rehearsal that he had an even more pressing problem in the actress engaged to play Margaret, and Kit was left on her own for a while.

The problem was to keep Sydney within bounds, not to make her unnatural or even unusual, just different enough so that when the audience discovers, with her, that she carries the taint of inherited insanity, they will be dramatically shocked but not incredulous, having intuitively realized it from the start. Working at home with Guthrie, she found her hands doing a great deal of her acting, so that when the old aunt in the Fairfield family says, "We're nervous, all of us . . . look at you now!" she became an extension of her hands rather than the other way around.

Basil Dean finally had to fire the actress playing Margaret. He replaced her with Janet Beecher, who needed as much if not more attention than her predecessor. By the time he got around to Kit she had the part of Sydney well in hand and he could find nothing to criticize. To save face he kept snapping at her, "*Must* you walk like Henry Irving?" to which Guthrie responded when he heard it, "I never saw Irving but I will say if he walked like Kit then he walked real nice."

The play opened in Philadelphia to respectable reviews, but most playgoers, put off by the severity of the title, went elsewhere for their fun. A few, conversely sensing in the word "divorcement" something racy and vaguely French, entered the theatre in titillated anticipation, to emerge two and a half hours later sulky and resentful at what they had been put through. Nobody, not even its defenders, seemed to realize that the title was not a stiff English expression or a legal term but a Biblical one from the twenty-fourth chapter of Deuteronomy.

The New York opening was scheduled for October 10 at the George M. Cohan Theatre on the east side of Broadway between Forty-second and Forty-third Streets, which in today's New York would be equivalent to opening *Ghosts* at the Metropolitan Opera House. Twenty-three Beekman Place was not ready for their occupancy, so Kit and Guthrie were staying at the Chatham Hotel at the top of Vanderbilt Avenue on East Forty-seventh Street.

Monday the tenth was cloudy in the morning, and despite rain in the afternoon, Kit went to the theatre to see to her wardrobe. At the theatre a polite war was being waged among the more famous ladies and gentlemen of the company about the assignment of ground floor dressing rooms, which Kit literally circumvented by walking around it and up the stairs to the top floor where, like any healthy creature glad to be in out of the weather, she established her turf, set out her makeup, and hung up Sydney Fairfield's clothes.

Back to the Chatham for an early dinner which she could not eat, then back to the theatre accompanied by Guthrie who sat uselessly in her dressing room until it was time for him to go out front and watch the audience arrive.

He and Kit were in the process of inheriting friends from each other, and among Dillingham's usual dressy first-nighters he spotted with pride the arrival of Mrs. Wolcott, Laura Elliot, Maude and William Barnes, and Mrs. August Belmont, who, until her retirement in 1910, had been the actress Eleanor Robson.

One could always tell how well a play was going by the number of curtain calls at the end of the second act. That night there were six. It had been seven years since Allan Pollock had appeared before a New York audience, and his wartime ordeal was apparent in his most casual movements. As one critic pointed out later, "The cicatrice of a shrapnel wound shows white upon his neck, the erstwhile crisp brown locks have silvered," and much of the tribute was to him on his courageous return to the stage. But Kit was given one call alone, the first of her career, and there was what a witness described as "an ear-splitting crash of applause." With the heartbreaking third act yet to come.

In *I Wanted to Be an Actress* Kit says Noël Coward was there that night, but in *Me and Kit* Guthrie maintains he didn't come until Thursday, three nights later. (Maybe he came twice.) At the end of the performance he descended with aplomb from his cheap seat at the top of the balcony and with equal aplomb climbed to Kit's third-floor dressing room to say that he had not thought he could like anyone in the part of Sydney after seeing Meggie Albanesi, but that Kit was in her own different way admirable.

Despite the warmth of the audience on opening night, Allan Pollock had lost whatever following he had had seven years before; Clemence Dane, a pseudonym for Winifred Ashton, was so unknown on this side of the Atlantic under either name that almost everybody, including the drama critics, thought she was a man; and there were four other theatrical openings that night. It is not too surprising, then, that of the newspapers publishing in New York City at the time — the *American*, *News*, *World*, *Times*, *Tribune*, *Herald*, and *Telegraph* uptown in the morning; the *Wall Street Journal* and *Journal of Commerce* downtown; and the *Telegram*, *Mail*, *Globe*, *Post*, *Journal*, and *Evening World* in the evening — only three sent their first-string critics, the rest apparently sending whoever was handy.

The arbiter of theatregoing taste was Alexander Woollcott of the *Times*, who chose to bestow his favor that evening on Helen Hayes, opening in the popular Booth Tarkington's new comedy, *The Wren*.

Kit was not feeling well at the time of the opening; in fact, as she put it later, she was "very sick." She and Guthrie did not wait for the newspaper reviews but went back to the Chatham where they read them the next morning in bed.

The three first-strings who saw *The Bill* regretted it. Alan Dale of the *American* was the most articulate when he said Kit "performed flippantly as a flapper." The "flip" and "flap" of his smart-alec alliteration were euphemisms for "flop." The second-, third-, and fourth-string reviews were little more than dreary statements from unimaginative second-, third-, and fourth-raters that the play had opened. That night the box office took in two hundred dollars. The elegant and dressy Charles Dillingham did not have the elegance to come back stage with a word of consolation; he simply released the theatre which he had taken under a four-week guarantee.

Among the first-nighters and among those who took the trouble to climb to Kit's dressing room afterward was Carl Van Vechten, the novelist, essayist, and music critic, whose dedication to the unacknowledged and unappreciated artist was by no means limited to the music world. The day after *The Bill* opened he called Alexander Woollcott and said, "It's a wonderful play but it's going to die right away unless someone does something."

It was the kind of call to arms that always stirred Woollcott, who swept into the Wednesday matinee and rushed out at the end to bring the good news to Heywood Broun, Kenneth McGowan, Burns Mantle, and all his most illustrious confreres, wheedling, begging, and ordering them with tears in voice to the Cohan Theatre (as if to the bedside of Little Nell) before it was too late. With her usual generosity of spirit Tallulah Bankhead climbed the stairs to Kit's dressing room Wednesday night to tell her that Woollcott's Sunday piece in the *Times* was going to be excellent.

It was more than that, proclaiming that

the crier should go through the streets calling out the good news that a vivid, beautiful and deeply moving tragedy has come to town. . . . Four other plays clamored for attention on the night of its New York premiere. *A Bill of Divorcement* is worth more than all of them put to-gether.

It is amusing to study the little vanities of the placards which pro-claim England's Allan Pollock as the star and our own Janet Beecher (in nicely graded smaller type, of course) as the "featured" player and blandly say nothing at all of Katharine Cornell who, as the daughter, has the central and significant role of the play and who gives therein a performance of memorable understanding and beauty.

By no means did Woollcott stand alone. On Friday evening the *Mail* and the *Globe* ran splendid notices, for both the play and Kit, by Burns Mantle and Kenneth McGowan, and over the weekend there was an avalanche of praise from the remaining first-string critics.

On Monday night the box office receipts were twelve hundred dollars, with a healthy advance sale building. By the end of the second week they were playing to standees, and Dillingham, sorry to have released the huge Cohan Theatre the morning after the opening, secured the Times Square Theatre (today an all-night pornography house) to finish out the play's run of one hundred and seventy-three performances. A play was then considered an artistic and financial hit if it achieved one hundred performances.

As part of Guthrie's job with W.A. he was authorized to buy and charge household accessories and even furniture to decorate the stages of W.A.'s theatrical productions. It was too good an opportunity for Guthrie to pass up, and he used the same authorization to decorate a fine Jacobean dining room in the apartment on Beekman Place, trusting to luck that he would be able to cover his tracks before getting caught. The staff from the Ames office sent a wedding present to Kit of a pair of Adam candlesticks (revealing a greater consideration for Guthrie's taste than for hers), and she brought with her some furniture from her last apartment, which they scattered through the living room and bedroom. Guthrie claimed later he was too poor to bring more than his personal effects, his dinner clothes, and his wedding suit. It would have spoiled the story to say that he also brought a Japanese houseman, which he did.

Two weeks after *The Bill* opened, the McClintics moved into the house where they would remain for thirty years.

Frank Gillmore, one of the founders of Actors' Equity Association, lived at 20 Beekman Place, directly across the street. John Barrymore and his second wife, Michael Strange, the poet, lived nearby briefly during the time they fancied dressing alike, and when a ruction broke out in their house one night, Frank Gillmore's daughter Margalo supposed they were fighting about "who gets to wear the dress suit."

Otherwise it was a sedate old-world neighborhood where the German wives in fresh morning aprons sat rocking on their front porches as their husbands went off to work. It was so remote that nobody, not even most taxi drivers, had ever heard of it, and a small bus had to be subsidized by the residents to convey them to the world of inner Manhattan. The most exciting topic of conversation was the love affair between the young bus driver and the daughter in the corner house.

From her upstairs window, Margalo Gillmore, who already knew Guthrie but only knew *of* Kit, watched them move in. She was a popular young actress much in demand, currently in rehearsal for *The Straw*, Eugene O'Neill's play about love among the patients in a tuberculosis sanitarium, which was scheduled to open at the Greenwich Village Theatre instead of on Broadway because its subject matter was considered too grim for uptown audiences. She watched Kit in her exuberant health and success swing her golf clubs in and out of the house on Sunday mornings and longed to trade plays, if not places.

Kit was not only admired and envied by other young actresses, even successful ones such as Miss Gillmore, but from the moment Woollcott's review appeared in the Sunday *Times* she was interviewed, photographed, talked about, and sought after. Acquaintances who had been discreetly silent when the play opened now called to congratulate her and ask if she could possibly get them seats, for which some of them even generously offered to pay.

One night Guthrie dropped into the Booth Theatre where George Arliss, turbaned and bejeweled as the Raja of Rukh in *The Green Goddess*, gave a start at sight of him, narrowed his eyes in a characteristic squint, adjusted his monocle, and turned to the stage manager.

"Who is that young man?" he asked, and then without waiting turned back to Guthrie with malicious charm and said, "Of course! It's Miss Cornell's husband!"

Others — with malice minus charm — wondered just how he came to be "Miss Cornell's husband." It got back to him that one of his own friends said, "What in the world did she ever want to marry *him* for? All he has ever done is buy lampshades for Ames."

It somehow follows that the telephone number on Beekman Place being only one digit removed from that of the Colony Club, every time he picked up the telephone a rich elderly lady mistook him for the club's doorman and ordered him to send a taxicab for her at once.

Whatever may be said of Guthrie's outbursts of temperament through the years, it was not his way, not then or ever, to take his frustrations out on Kit. The put-upon poor relation, the tender plant, the devious lampshade buyer, simply yelled obscenities at the rich old hags on the telephone, had the number changed, and knew it was time to push his own luck for fame and glory.

They had moved into 23 Beekman Place on October 23, and when the new telephone number came up Plaza 123, Guthrie knew a sign when he saw one and grabbed the next number twenty-three that came along, staking his all on it, hanging on for dear life.

It was December 23, the day he chose for the opening of *The Dover Road.*

Cards, fortune-tellers, and astrologers had not helped Guthrie find the right theatre for *The Dover Road,* and he had not been able to get on with the production. Then the day after Thanksgiving Rachel Crothers had a rare failure. Even with her favorite Tallulah Bankhead in the cast along with Henry Hull and Lucile Watson, her play, called *Everyday,* proved to be just that and closed after twenty performances. The producer had taken the Bijou Theatre for eight weeks and was anxious to unload four of them. W.A. had the opportunity of securing the theatre for Guthrie and reminding him that the Christmas season was an excellent time to open and that refusal might mean delay until spring, which gave him one hour to make up his mind. Guthrie accepted without even tossing a coin.

That was Friday, November 26. Working eighteen hours a day he interviewed dozens of actors, spent a whole night trying to convince H. B. Warner to return from the cinema to play the lead, lost him to the English actor's snobbish mistrust of youthful producer-directors, found the delightful Charles Cherry who was delighted to accept the part, arranged for the scenery (i.e., designed it and contracted to have it built), engaged the rest of the cast, including Winifred Lenihan in the part he had first thought of for Kit, and on Sunday eight days later assembled everybody for a calm and smoothly run first rehearsal.

For months he had been reading the play aloud to anyone who would listen and often, as would always be his way, to those who were not willing to listen but unable to escape. As he acted all the parts, characterizing them sharply — male, female, servant, master, and child — his friends and acquaintances were lucky it was not a sad and tragic play or he would have kept reading at them until they wept, all the time weeping himself and mopping his eyes as he made detailed, observant notes on the alchemy of tears. As it was, *The Dover Road* being the brightest and gentlest of comedies in the James M. Barrie tradition, they only had to listen until he made it impossible for them not to smile, and then laugh. He brought to the first rehearsal a sure knowledge of every laugh in the play, where it was hiding and what to do to bring it out.

In his later days when he was a noted raconteur as much as a director, Guthrie loved to waste rehearsal time telling fabulous stories of great rehearsals gone by. But in December 1921 he had no repertoire and the days were spent in creating stories for the future rather than re-creating them from the past. Having watched the impeccable W.A. direct, he knew better than to impose himself and his ideas on the actors, but instead "suggested" choices like the consummate maître d' in an expensive restaurant where there are no menus. The actors, having responded to the play's charm to begin with, were further inspired by Guthrie's authority with it. Before they realized it, it was time to open and they were ready.

Guthrie clung superstitiously to Friday, December 23, for the opening, but an "all-star revival" of *Trilby* was also scheduled to open that night. With the experience of *The Bill* a too recent reminder, he feared he had little chance of attracting the first-string critics. Relying on the advice of a deck of cards, he decided to have the premiere at a matinee performance on the afternoon of the twenty-third and sent carefully hand-written, personal invitations to the first-string critics explaining the reason for the move and expressing his hope that they would be able to attend. He emphasized that he had no way of knowing whether or not anyone would like his first New York presentation, but if no one did, he preferred to hear it from gentlemen of the front rank.

Trilby was not that much of a threat. Thus Guthrie's decision to open at a matinee was a shrewd bit of showmanship allowing him to express an ingenuous and admirable respect for his older, more experienced, and esteemed competition; to impress upon the critics his earnestness and good manners; to personalize his contact with each critic, appealing to both his better nature and his vanity; and to create for his opening a situation intriguingly different — and memorable — without breaking with tradition.

It rained on the twenty-third, which by now Guthrie took to be a good luck sign. Another of his signs almost prevented him from getting to the theatre on time — an endless funeral procession slow-poking up First Avenue, which he would not cross. He arrived in time to give flasks filled with bootleg scotch to the actors in his cast and vanity cases to the actresses. Stationed at the back of the house, he watched George and Mrs. Arliss arrive, W.A. and his wife, Kit and Laura Elliot, and all the first-string critics to a man. Once the play began he couldn't hear the actors and kept swigging his whisky all through the performance, thinking it might brighten the stage, which seemed to be plunged in murk. The audience coughed when it should have laughed, and before the final curtain hit the floor he had disappeared.

Kit found him backstage waiting to be found, rather ostentatiously standing in a corner facing a blank wall. She congratulated him, saying the show was marvelous and other people had thought so, too, only they couldn't find him to say so. On their way home that night, after his evening performance and hers, the first night of their lives that they both had shows running on Broadway, she wouldn't let him buy whatever morning papers were out, feeling they had established a precedent and a ritual with *The Bill* and insisting they wait until morning.

Hare, the Japanese manservant, brought them breakfast in bed and a great stack of newspapers. Kit picked abstractedly at the bedclothes as Guthrie read aloud eight rave reviews (and one bad one from Alan Dale, the same representative of the *American* who had said Kit performed flippantly as a flapper).

Kit began crying at Woollcott's throbbing excesses of praise and burst into fresh tears every time anybody called on the telephone to say, "Isn't it wonderful about Guthrie?" Later in the morning George Arliss, whose approval meant a great deal to Guthrie, said, "I didn't like your play when I read it. I didn't like it when I saw it yesterday, but I am glad to say I seem to be in the minority." W.A. was conservative as usual but beamed with paternal pride when he observed, "You've had a wonderful press, boy." By afternoon the ticket brokers had bought up the entire lower floor of the Bijou for the next sixteen weeks, the phone never stopped ringing in the box office, and the line of patrons stretched to Broadway.

The bit of Woollcott's that made Kit sob focused on the presenter-director himself who, he said, "has risen to the occasion, and as the American theatre's poverty is most conspicuous in the matter of directors, his advent takes on the nature of an occasion. More power to Mr. McClintic, then — more power and a Merry Christmas."

———

Guthrie was six months younger than Kit, from February to August, at a time when it was considered unmanly for a man to marry an "older woman." Kit probably never gave it a thought one way or the other, but Guthrie could be conventional or unconventional about their marriage depending on where and how it hit his vanity. Because he was terribly proud of whom he had managed to marry, he put both their names on the Beekman Place doorplate, in contradiction of conventional doorplates, and was delighted that a neighbor took it as an open admission of an illicit arrangement; it made him feel glamorously wicked. Conversely — and conventionally — he was probably secretly relieved when five years were lopped off Kit's age to conform to the accepted idea of a reigning stage star's youthfulness, because it made him, at last, a comfortable four and a half years her senior.

Perhaps even more irksome to him because it was more obvious to everybody was that in an age when husbands were not only older than their wives but taller, he often gave the impression of being shorter.

He wasn't. He was five feet ten and a half inches tall to her five feet six and three-quarters, but statistics were confounded by essences. Her face was wide, larger, her bones less delicate than his, her legs longer, her body's frame more angular and extended, her presence more undeniable, her manner, even in silence, somehow resonant. She was larger in so many inner, undefinable ways that she seemed to tower outwardly.

Just as wives were supposed to be shorter than husbands, actresses were supposed to be shorter than actors, and all through Kit's years on the stage, young six-foot, statuesque women striving hopelessly for careers would write to her begging to know how she got her start being so unusually tall. The unusual thing was that when and if they presented themselves at the stage door to confront her in person, they were not always put off by her actual height, bending toward her without seeming to notice that she was inches shorter than they had thought.

In her 1947 production of *Antony and Cleopatra,* Charlton Heston played Proculeius, who toward the end of the play surprises Cleopatra in the monument and leaps down a flight of (twenty-one) steps onto the stage to grab her by both arms when she tries to stab herself. It was his first professional job, and he likes to say that Guthrie chose him because only his six feet three inches could make him overwhelming enough, in the audience's eyes, to make the scene believable physically. It is true that Guthrie surrounded Kit with tall actors whenever possible — especially in *Romeo and Juliet* where the point was not to make her shorter but younger — but the astonishing thing is that Heston, having interrupted her suicide and wrestled her for the dagger one hundred and twenty-six times, to this day finds it hard to believe that she was no taller than five feet six and three-quarters inches.

Given the choice of their own senses or the illusion she created, most people chose to accept the illusion. She *seemed* tall, therefore she *was* tall.

———

Poor Guth, with his arms and shoulders folded in on himself against the elements like the leaves of a tender plant, what chance did he stand against her vigorous, perfect proportions? Even when he stood straight, drawing himself up, pointing his forefinger in a huff or waving his cigarette, one shoulder was noticeably lower than the other, which somehow put his hips out of alignment, too, or that may have been the sag of the hip-hugging pants he sometimes affected. Ready-made clothes were not ready enough to accommodate the oddness of his construction, and it was only when he was able to buy his suits in London that the tailors at Anderson, Shepard, presumably with the magic of custom padding, found ways to give him a look of symmetry. Even then, with his scrawny short arms and his short entwined legs, he didn't look his height, not even when standing by himself, let alone next to his lady.

———

One night during the run of *Antony and Cleopatra,* Charlton Heston arrived at the theatre to be told by the stage manager, Jimmy Nielson, that Miss Cornell wanted to see him in her dressing room. It was in a way, at least to him, a royal command, and he wondered what it meant. He had never been late getting to the theatre, nor missed a cue, nor misbehaved on the stage, so he didn't think he was going to be fired. As he walked to her dressing room, he fantasized that maybe she wanted to have an affair with him. He was new to the ways of Broadway, but he had heard stories of such things happening to other tall, handsome young actors and other beautiful leading women. It didn't seem likely, but he wondered what he would do and felt he ought to be ready. He decided that if he was asked into her inner dressing room, there was a possibility; if she was wearing a dressing gown, it was a certainty.

Eveline Drysdale, Kit's theatre maid, opened the door and said that Miss Cornell wanted to see him in the inner dressing room. He went inside, and there she stood in a dressing gown.

"Chuck, I want to show you something," she said, and opened her dressing gown. He was getting his response ready, whatever it was going to be, when she pointed to a huge bruise on her hip and said, "Do you see that? When you grab me to take the dagger away from me, you twist me in such a way that every night I hit my hip against your sword, and this bruise is the result. Do you think you could wear your sword on the other side?"

Heston was young, well put together, and cannot be blamed for thinking, just for a moment, that he might be the kind of man this magnificent woman would set her sights on, if not her heart. He was in no position to guess the fallacy of such a supposition, that his sun-godlike masculinity was as unlikely to attract her at fifty-four as it would have been twenty-five years earlier.

From the moment she settled on Guthrie, she always assured him and everyone else in an offhand way that of course he was six feet tall, but it was no more than a gesture to his conventional vanity; it seems quite clear that had he really been a giant six-footer, had he been endowed with all the great physical attributes of young Charlton Heston, she probably would not have been drawn to him at all. It was his rickety loose-jointedness that she needed to have compassion for; she found completeness in his incompleteness, in the ideal of what she herself described as the "pale, fragile creature" she first set eyes on at Lawrence Langner's.

For many years, in all the places where she was likely to light, to rest, to work, to read, and repose — by her bed in many houses, in countless hotel rooms and various theatres — she always displayed where she could see it, propped up or pinned up, a small photograph of Michelangelo's Pietà. She carried one in her purse. She never failed to be moved by that restrained expression of sorrow, by the wasted, anguished Christ figure splayed across the Virgin's lap, fragile, spent, but blameless, protracted, sinewy. If asked, she said she loved it because it reminded her of Guth.

———

If she romanticized his physical fragility into a spiritual need for her solace and protection, he pragmatized her "mysterious aura, her curious haunting luminosity" into a very practical need for his. For all her elegance and maturity and bigness of spirit, he was fond of calling her "Baby" and treating her as such, shepherding her from place to place through traffic like a desiccated nanny. If they got separated at parties, it was quite usual to hear his voice sounding off above the common babble, "Are you okay, baby?" or "Get out of the draft, baby!" At at least one such party when he saw "Baby" leave the crowd for a few minutes in midevening, he couldn't help himself and followed, and with only the risky and exciting privacy of a closed bathroom door, wanted to make love, which they did.

She was always more deeply emotional than physical in her relationships, but she could respond to urgent physicality and at times initiate it. Once in her middle years circumstances arranged themselves in such a way that she decided on a random physical afternoon with a man because he had loved her so long, so loyally, and so purely that she thought he deserved it. Unfortunately, he was so overcome by the magnanimity of her sudden and dazzling acquiescence that he was unable to rise to it.

Guthrie was so physically demonstrative in the early years of their marriage that it often embarrassed friends and acquaintances, especially the way he had of greeting her in public places, coming at her head on, mouth already open in a greedy, gaping kiss. It bothered everyone but Kit, who didn't even seem to notice, because whatever she accepted she accepted completely — or strenuously, the word used by those who knew her then to describe her intensity.

For the first few years of their marriage, she and Guthrie had a strenuous physical relationship, and sometime during the run of *A Bill of Divorcement* she found that she was pregnant.

Despite all the conscious and conscientious hard work that went into it, acting was so intuitive with Katharine Cornell that she could not always be articulate about it. In the 1920s she liked to say she was so shy that what mattered more than anything was to hide, and that if she could pretend to be somebody else, as she did when she played a role on the stage, it relieved her of the anxiety of being herself. But that is an expression of her shyness, not a delineation of her approach to acting, implying as it does that she could only play roles completely removed from herself. Just the opposite was true. She almost said it in an interview forty years later, at the end of her career, after she had actually played all the roles and could look back at them and perhaps evaluate what went into them — had she wanted to. "Every part I've played," she said instead, rather impatiently lumping them all together, "I've twisted and turned in my mind until I've made it something of my own."

So completely did she make each one her own that the premise, stated earlier, that she was many people in her lifetime — actress, artist, manager, athlete, Buffalo girl, Mrs. McClintic — can be extended to include Elizabeth Barrett, Joan the Maid, Jo March, Juliet, Candida, and all the other stage variations of herself. She probably did not realize — or at least could not articulate — the exact nature and depth of the consanguinity, so it is impossible for anyone else to. But as each role comes along — Sydney Fairfield in *A Bill of Divorcement*, for example — it is interesting to speculate, to look for clues.

Douglas and Gwendolyn Cornell, Kit's aunt and uncle, had two fine healthy sons, John, born December 1, 1913, and Douglas, born April 16, 1915. In December 1920, nine months before Kit married Guthrie and nine months (always a tantalizingly symbolic length of time) before she went into rehearsal for *A Bill of Divorcement*, Gwendolyn gave birth to a third son, christened Peter, who was mongoloid.

The baby almost didn't survive the first terrible year of his life for the simple reason that he could not be made to eat. It was a three-times-a-day fight to keep him alive, as every morsel of food he swallowed his mother had to push down his throat with a spoon while he kicked and screamed. A breakthrough came when it was discovered that the one thing the child would not only eat but enjoy was applesauce, and Augusta, the maid, was put to work stewing endless stores of apples into sweetened puree.

That summer of 1921 when Guthrie first read *A Bill of Divorcement* aloud on the beach at Mamaroneck, Kit's mind must have been full of the struggle for existence then being waged up in Buffalo in her uncle's house, the same house where two bright, normal, happy boys had been conceived and born, the house where this other malformed creature would spend his entire long life. It was the kind of family tragedy, especially in the heretofore regular, undeviating line of Cornells, that would move her deeply. Her compassion for her aunt outweighed her impatience with the older woman's rather complaining letters, and she had special feeling for the infant who bore her father's name, the desperately flawed, helpless being who although of another generation was her first cousin. His welfare would always be her special concern as she sought schools for him and saw to it that he was financially able to attend them.

But that was in the future. As Guthrie read aloud Sydney Fairfield's stark awakening to the shocking reality of her life, Kit, with her strenuous dramatic imagination, could not have been unaware that she herself was experiencing a similar realization of her own.

Perhaps a birth defect is not analogous to the insanity Hilary Fairfield would hand down to Sydney, but mongolism, or Down's syndrome, has always been thought to "run in families," and even today is greatly feared by childbearing women whose brothers, cousins, or, yes, uncles have produced mongoloid babies. In fact, modern geneticists grant there is cause for their concern, having determined that one specific type of mongolism is not a random occurrence but an inherited family trait. Today, a woman can consult a genetics counselor to determine in the early stages of pregnancy whether or not her child will be born with a defect, and if so to take steps toward therapeutic abortion. In 1921 there was no such counseling, no such knowledge, no such legal way out. There was only the fear learned from experience, that if it happened in one place in the family, it was likely to happen in another. For a young woman in love and about to be married, there was either the terrible risk or there was despair and Sydney Fairfield's solution.

Kit's state of mind that summer, then, was quite possibly comparable to Sydney's. She was ten years older but just as in love, about to be married, and she may actually have been as apprehensive of the future. When Guthrie finished reading, it was not an idle observation when she said, "I could play that girl."

She could understand Sydney's resolution to renounce life, but being at the same time of a more robust nature, that was certainly not her way out and she went on to marry Guthrie. It is more than possible that it never entered her mind not to, that she never caught her analogous relationship to Sydney, but it is revealing that during the run of *A Bill of Divorcement* when she found she was pregnant, she chose to have an abortion.

No one knows exactly when it happened, but in later years she made such a point of the fact that she was not well when the play opened, in fact insisting that she was "very sick," that it suggests the possibility that the abortion came that early in the run, only a few weeks after her marriage. If that is the case, it puts the wedding in a different light at that awkward, rushed, inconvenient time, and the tension of rehearsing, opening and playing Sydney must have been all but unendurable.

Who can say what she and Guthrie said to each other in private before deciding not to have the baby, but outwardly she never connected the decision to the birth of her mongoloid cousin or to the influence of Sydney Fairfield and inherited insanity. All that is putting hindsight thoughts into her head, although they may have been there. What she did say was that she had had such a miserable childhood and the world was such a painful place that she thought it a terrible thing to bring new life into it. That seems contradictory to her own tremendous enjoyment of life, and yet she meant what she said so sincerely that to emphasize her conviction she sometimes claimed to have had *two* abortions on the strength of it, and she was almost always openly shocked when friends and friends of friends — with no Down's syndrome in the family — went blindly ahead perpetuating themselves by having children, although she was always willing to play godmother.

More intimately, she sometimes said there were traits in Guthrie and in herself that she did not want — or did not dare — to pass on to another generation. She was never more specific than that, but she must have had something specific in mind, something dark and frightening enough to make her act so decisively.

Guthrie's pool of Broadway characters at last came in handy and put him in touch with someone, some shady doctor, perhaps the notorious, rich, and outwardly respectable man who in the 1920s was known affectionately in theatrical circles as Dr. Sunshine.

———

For those who think the foregoing kind of supposition is pure fantasy and that everything in life happens independently of everything else, for those who think that an actress's character, married life, and family history cannot all be mysteriously mixed up with the roles she plays, for those who believe only in coincidences, there is an ironic one in the text of *A Bill of Divorcement*. The rector's son who loves Sydney, the healthy boy she flippantly sends packing without an explanation, the confused, not-to-be father, is named Kit.

11

Passing Plays (1922-1925)

WITH THE SUCCESS of *The Dover Road* Guthrie was able to leave the Ames office and open his own. He settled all his old debts, paid for the Jacobean dining room he had purchased on W.A.'s credit, and went on to furnish the rest of the house on Beekman Place. Through his efforts and talent the two Victorian rooms on the second floor managed to become both elegant and comfortable, running through from the street to the river with lovely arches connecting them and red Italian brocade draperies at either end. Long mirrors in gilt and white enamel reached to the molded plaster ceilings, contrasting and reflecting the bookshelves and white marble fireplaces.

One Saturday afternoon in the mid-1920s Kit's friend Mildred Oppenheimer dropped in to wait for her to come home between the matinee and evening performances. They were going to have a snack together, and then they would walk across town to the theatre where Mildred could sit in the dressing room if she wanted to until the play began.

"If I wanted to!" she remembers today. "All Kit's friends, male and female — sex had nothing to do with it — wanted nothing more than to be where she was."

Mildred selected a book to pass the time and found an envelope tucked into it, one of those small, narrow envelopes theatre tickets come in, only this one was stuffed full of money, hundreds and hundreds of dollars. When Kit arrived and saw what her friend had found, she flushed and said, "So that's where it was — ?" It was her salary from some weeks back, or even months. "Don't tell Guthrie!" she said, and she wasn't really joking.

Her attitude toward money, since she had never had to do without it, was offhand compared to the intensity of his. *The Dover Road* had cost seventy-five hundred dollars, which was paid back in less than two weeks after the opening, and soon he was depositing in his personal account at the Harriman Bank checks of five thousand dollars or more, his weekly profit. The play ran twenty-eight weeks in that season alone and then ran well into the next. He had never seen, let alone handled, so much money in all his life.

When *A Bill of Divorcement* closed the first week in March 1922, after one hundred and seventy-three performances, Kit went out on a short tour with it. Guthrie planned to meet her at the end of the second week in Montreal and go with her for a visit to Buffalo. The time had come, he decided, to give her a present, a real present that would not only express what she meant to him but impress them in Buffalo as well.

He went to Cartier's, where they tried to put him at ease. When he attempted to pay for a diamond and sapphire bracelet with five wadded-up thousand-dollar bills, they sensed he might be a personage of some sort and tried to coax his name out of him. It may or may not be significant that he always had trouble pronouncing his last name, and on this occasion it came out quite clearly "M'Klenk." But when Cartier's persistent salesmen finally associated him with the stage success *The Dover Road* and with the exciting new actress Katharine Cornell, they smoothed out his thousand-dollar bills nicely for him and handed them back, saying they would be happy to open a charge account.

Square-cut diamonds and a charge account at Cartier's meant to Guthrie that he had arrived. It might be said that he had arrived where Kit had been all along, except that unlike most women of her day who could have diamonds and sapphires if they wanted them, she didn't want them. Guthrie hadn't noticed that as far as jewelry went, she had a diamond and sapphire horseshoe pin of her mother's that she loved, and that was about it. She wore his bracelet in Buffalo, but never afterwards if she could avoid it. She had a careless habit of hiding it in the torn lining of her coat when she went onstage and then forgetting about it. This upset Guthrie, but what could he expect from a woman who used money for a bookmark?

That summer they sailed on the S.S. *Scandinavian* for their first trip abroad together, and Mrs. Wolcott, flushed with Kit's success, went with them. It sounds like an intrusion, but with her respect for age and strength, Kit could never say no to older, redoubtable women who took a shine to her and ordered her about, not even as the years went by and she got older and they got younger. And Guthrie doted on spirited older women and had a distinct way with them, usually preferring them to be actresses on their uppers, but certainly he was not averse to a governor's widow. Therefore, it was probably an equable traveling arrangement. Mrs. Wolcott had her way, Guthrie had a new charge, and if everyone else got along and was happy, Kit was.

They started off in England before moving to the Continent in a kind of grand tour, the kind rich young people used to take as part of their education. How impressive Guthrie must have felt with the currency in Munich so inflated that they had to carry money in a suitcase when they went to a good restaurant for lunch. On to the sights of Vienna and Prague and then back to England for golf, down on the south coast near Plymouth.

Despite the vast differences in age, Mrs. Wolcott proved to be a tireless traveler, eager to keep pace with her ardent young companions. To avoid the always delaying search for comfort stations so often necessary to one of her years, she dispensed with obstructive undergarments, and with the resulting freedom of movement never held the party up for a moment, breasting history through botanical gardens, imperial parks, winter palaces, and fifteenth-century cathedrals, now and then dipping behind a column, sidling around a pillar, curtseying under a tree, ducking beyond a hedgerow, barely stepping clear of the line of march to do what had to be done, practically without breaking stride.

"When everyone is somebodee, then no one's anybody," wrote W. S. Gilbert, and now that movies and television have reduced most actors to stars, superstars, guest stars, and special guest stars, with the rest of the profession "also starring," it is hard to recall the value the word "star" once had in the theatre, the respect and reverence its attainment commanded. To use the word itself in billing, as is done so clamorously in our own time, was unnecessary because stars were identifiable without it. A featured actor's name came after the title of the play in the program, the star's name came before it; a featured player was listed below the title in all advertising, the star above. It was as simple as that. Prepositions told the story — the star was "in" the play "with" the featured and supporting player. This protocol was strictly observed and had great meaning for actors and audience alike, as actors (accumulating a following and encouraged by them) worked their way up from bit player to supporting player to featured player, which was as far as most of them went. A featured player became a star when it was impossible not to, not when he chose to. Sometimes it happened prematurely or mistakenly, sometimes by manipulation or in the push of personal vanity, but in such cases the lack of talent or what Noël Coward called "star quality" eventually manifested itself and the theatregoing public, always the final judges, rectified the error by withholding their acceptance of the upstart.

Some managers prided themselves on being star-makers — Al Woods, for example, who had risen from perpetrator of *Bertha the Sewing Machine Girl* to producer of class-one dramas. A silk-shirted, bighearted man with a huge head and a walleye, he was reputed to have said, when presented to George V during the Great War, "Hello sweetheart, have a cigar." Every man and woman, friend and manager, stranger, king and commoner was "sweetheart" to Al, all except Guthrie, who for some unknown reason was called "Gunthrie." After *A Bill of Divorcement*, Woods wanted to put Kit under a five-year contract and make her a star the following season, but she refused. Fighting off stardom the way other actors fight off failure, she accepted instead in close order over the next three years six featured roles in six passing plays.

Immediately after *A Bill of Divorcement* opened, in its first week, in fact, before it caught on, Winthrop Ames sent his card backstage to Kit with the message, "I think you're damn swell. My homage to you." It was not just a sop to make her feel better; he had completely reversed his opinion of her acting ability. A few months later when he asked her to play Mary Fitton in *Will Shakespeare*, she accepted.

Shakespeare was played by Otto Kruger; Haidee Wright came over to repeat her London success as Queen Elizabeth; Anne Hathaway was played by W.A.'s favorite, Winifred Lenihan; and way down the list, a Maid of Honor was played by Cornelia Otis Skinner, who also understudied Kit. Mary Fitton was the third woman's role, but the length of a part never meant much to Kit if she wanted to play it, and she probably wanted to be in *Will Shakespeare* because Clemence Dane had written it and because she had caught from Guthrie a reverence for Winthrop Ames.

As much as Kit might have wanted to meet Clemence Dane while visiting England in the summer of 1922, she would have hesitated to be so forward if Guthrie had not urged her on, and from their first meeting Winifred Ashton, the woman who took her pen name from Wren's church of St. Clement Danes in the middle of the Strand, assumed a role in Kit's life similar to Laura Elliot's. Only five years Kit's senior, she gave the impression of being of much greater age and wisdom, a wise earth-rock woman with a touch of the heavens in her. In the years to come there would be many lunches together in her flat at 10 Tavistock Street, lunches which she invariably cooked with a great deal too much garlic and just as invariably burnt or forgot to put in the oven, dribbling wine down her front and rattling on with contagious laughter as she enmeshed herself inextricably in themes and subjects and gossip. She was always called Winifred, and yet one always said one was lunching at Clemence Dane's.

That summer she invited Kit and Guthrie down to Tunbridge where she was living and later wrote to her American agent, Curtis Brown, "I like her. She doesn't wear lipstick and travels third." Since Kit would never give a thought one way or the other to which class she was traveling, the third must have been Guthrie's idea. Ordinarily he would have been the first to travel first if he could afford it, as he certainly could that summer, but there was a kind of British snobbery about *not* traveling first which he would have been sure to pick up.

Clemence Dane never saw Kit play Sydney Fairfield but had heard about it, which made Kit more secure in attacking Mary Fitton. She always felt more comfortable working in the company of already established associates rather than new people, perhaps thinking they would be more forbearing of her faults.

But she also wanted to be in *Will Shakespeare* because Mary Fitton, "that alluring, marauding and rampagious baggage," was about as far as an actress could get from Sydney Fairfield. She was a Jo March gone berserk, a "gusty wind" whose big scene came in a tavern brawl involving Shakespeare and Christopher Marlowe, her great love, ending with the death of Marlowe. Jumping on tables, being dragged

As Mary Fitton in Will Shakespeare, *1923. (Kendall Evans)*

across the stage, charging in and out, Kit could call on her growing-up days on Mariner Street, rallying the neighborhood buckos over fences, through ravines and up the walls of the neighborhood church. She had a glorious time, and when a critic said, "If she does not learn to bounce upon the furniture a little more shrewdly she will undoubtedly break a table or something," she was piqued enough to explain that if she had not been very ill just before rehearsals started, her bouncing would have been smoother. It is one of the few instances when she felt called upon to answer a criticism (even though years later and in retrospect), and it is characteristic that what roused her was not an attack on her theatrical talents or emotional power, but an attack on her physical agility.

But there was more to Mary Fitton than gymnastics. Shakespeare, as written by Miss Dane and played by Otto Kruger, was a "poor fish" pushed, pulled, and led by the three women in his life, and of these Mary Fitton was the big romantic influence, the Dark Lady of his sonnets and the profound inspiration for Juliet. The play was poetic and eloquent but had some twists perhaps more suitable to latter-day under-study-to-star-overnight plays and movies, for when the boy playing Juliet sprained his ankle on opening night, it was Mary Fitton who stepped into the part, going out there a hoyden and coming back a star, thereby saving the play for Ethel Barrymore, Jane Cowl, and Katharine Cornell.

In his newspaper column, "The Conning Tower," Franklin P. Adams composed a sonnet to Kit as Mary Fitton, made up of one line each from fourteen of Shakespeare's sonnets, ending "For who so dumb that cannot write of thee?"

———

Will Shakespeare closed after eighty performances on March 11, 1923, and only training in Jessie Bonstelle's stock company could have given Kit the facility and fortitude to open as Laura Pennington twenty days later, on March 31, in *The Enchanted Cottage* by Sir Arthur Wing Pinero.

Shy and unattractive, Laura befriends Oliver Blashforth, late lieutenant, 8th Bengal Regiment, who has brought back from the war a twisted leg, wryneck, shell-shocked nerves, and seeks only seclusion from the world. They marry and immediately the spell of the cottage in which they spend their honeymoon falls on them and each becomes beautiful in the eyes of the other.

The previous summer when she met Clemence Dane in England, Kit also met Pinero who, over a single luncheon, with the magic of his words and manner, introduced her to a London that was fast disappearing — Edwardian and gracious. It is possible that Kit, enchanted with the man, thought she was enchanted with his play, which was also Edwardian and gracious, with the kind of fanciful theme that a sentimentalist like Sir James M. Barrie would have delighted in. The play was a failure. Woollcott, as usual, summed up for the critics: "The reviews of *The Enchanted Cottage* when compared and collated will prove to be the best notices Barrie has ever wrung from the New York press."

The momentum that carried Kit from *Will Shakespeare* to *The Enchanted Cottage*, with no time between and less than three weeks' rehearsal, was stimulated not alone by Jessie Bonstelle's training but by Jessie Bonstelle herself, who was back on the scene directing the Pinero play for William A. Brady's son, William A., Jr.

It was the last time Jessie Bonstelle would appear professionally in Kit's life. Kit sometimes saw her when she played in Detroit, and when Miss Bonstelle came to New York or attended one of Kit's performances, she was treated like a visiting dignitary with the best seats in the house and a ceremonial visit backstage. When a book was written about her, Kit contributed a gracious foreword saying everything that was expected and dutifully ending with "Thank you, Bonnie." In her own book, Kit said, "I owe her more than any other one person except my husband." Kit was loyal, but even she could not express affection where she did not feel it.

Jessie Bonstelle died in 1932 at the age of sixty-six.

———

Guthrie also had two flops simultaneously with Kit's: *Gringo* by Sophie Treadwell in December 1922 and *The Square Peg* by Lewis Beach in March 1923, both of which he directed and produced with money from his personal account at the Harriman Bank. It was the accepted practice at the time for a theatre to be taken on a four-week guarantee at three thousand dollars a week, automatically adding twelve thousand dollars to the production cost, and since its home was paid for in advance, a flop did not always close after its first performance, as it is likely to today, but hung on looking for an audience until there was no more money to pay the actors. As Kit recalled later, she worked only sixteen weeks that season (although arithmetic, perhaps more reliable than her memory, adds it up to eighteen), and she and Guthrie together rattled the change at the bottom of their cash drawers and kept the two flops going for thirty-five and forty-one performances respectively.

There is no record of what became of Hare, the Japanese houseman at 23 Beekman Place, but Guthrie's faithful character witness, Emma Jones, had been coming in now and then to help out with the housekeeping. If she originally came for "Hon," she stayed on for "Shug," short for "Sugar," her pet name for Kit, and when the money ran so low with all the flops that Shug had to take over the cooking, even though she was "not well" (a phrase that occurs with great regularity in Kit's reminiscences), Emma Jones laid down the law.

"You can't do all this, Shug," she said. "I'm coming in regular whether you can pay me or not."

And so she moved in and the kitchen overlooking the East River became her watchtower as she permeated the neighborhood with a rigorous concord. Merchants were made to see how privileged they were to be the ones chosen to give Miss Cornell credit and how crass they were to accept money from her at all. Believing firmly in a rightly tuned spirit, she would clasp Kit to her bosom when she left for an opening night and then stand in the door and shout for all the German burghers to hear, "Harmony, Sugar, harmony!" But she was nobody's fool and could size up Shug and Hon when she wanted to, often with humor. When Guthrie had to be hospitalized for a hernia, it was Emma Jones who said, "He must've got it from lifting his voice."

When the financial picture was at its worst, Mrs. Schmid announced from the top floor that she had decided to sell 23 Beekman Place and gave Kit and Guthrie the chance to buy it, as stipulated in their lease. Between the two of them they managed to come up with ten thousand dollars, half the purchase price, and took a mortgage for the rest.

Or so Kit says in I Wanted to Be an Actress. In Guthrie's book he puts the purchase of the house back a year in the spring of 1922, at the prosperous height of both The Dover Road and A Bill of Divorcement when there could not possibly have been any difficulty raising the cash. He describes with relish the élan with which he signed a check for twelve thousand five hundred dollars (they don't even agree on the purchase price) with an agreement to pay the remaining half in three years (but it wasn't paid off until 1930). And then, as he puts it, "Presto! I owned a house in New York!" A great deal of Guthrie's presto was always in his head.

As if to hang on to his gentleman status and flout rumors that he was lowborn enough to work for a living as a New York theatrical producer, Winthrop Ames maintained his home in Boston. He and his wife also had a summer place on Cape Cod and a pied-à-terre in a New York hotel. It was probably when Mrs. Schmid moved out of 23 Beekman Place and Kit and Guthrie became lords of the manor that they (Guthrie) expansively invited the Ameses to come live with them. It cannot be imagined that Guthrie would ask his idol to climb to quarters on the top two floors, so it is more than likely that Kit and Guthrie moved up and the Ameses wedged themselves in below.

No one is quite sure when or how long this arrangement lasted, one winter, two winters, probably something less than a full year, but it sounds so awkward that it may explain why, in the summer of 1923, the McClintics, with no money to squander on travel, fled to Canada on a fishing trip, dignifying the economy measure by calling it a belated honeymoon. Nothing less extreme than flight can explain Guthrie's participation in camp living and hobo existence. Kit taught him to swim that summer and went on teaching him to swim for the next twenty years, or at least as long as there was hope that he would learn. (He finally managed to fake a dog paddle so that she would leave him alone.) They also canoed, with Kit, of course, manning the paddles while Guthrie huddled low in the boat, using her shadow for shade, reading manuscripts.

In 1919 the Washington Square Players established themselves as the Theatre Guild with the first American production of St. John Ervine's *John Ferguson*. When Actors' Equity went on strike and closed every play in town, it did not close *John Ferguson* because the profit-sharing arrangement the Guild had with its actors was in line with Equity goals. *John Ferguson*, therefore, became the only hit in town because it was the only play in town, and the Guild was on its way. In 1920 with Shaw still in disgrace for his antiwar views and actually considered a traitor by many in England, the Guild was the only producing organization in the world willing to give a production to his antiwar play, *Heartbreak House*. There had always been a cult that expressed contempt for Broadway by hero-worshipping Shaw, and now they were robbed of their thunder because he became the hottest ticket in town. The American theatre had been changed. Brooks Atkinson writes in *Broadway* that by making art vastly more entertaining and profitable than commerce, the Guild "led Broadway into the modern world."

In the fall of 1923 the Theatre Guild was planning the world premiere of another Shaw play, *Saint Joan,* and all of Broadway took an active interest in casting the title role. As a result of his own personal poll, Woollcott listed the leading candidates: Laurette Taylor, Frances Starr, Margalo Gillmore, Peggy Wood, Katharine Cornell — "and if we might have only one, it would probably be Miss Cornell." But Kit couldn't even "try out for it," she said — as if it were a high school senior play — because she had already committed herself to *Casanova*. With so much unconscious stalling and bad timing, it is a wonder her career was ever able to burst forth, even considering the inevitability of it. Which wouldn't be worth mentioning again at this point had the gain in any way compensated for the loss, but *Casanova* was a trashy affair, a bad translation of a Spanish play dealing with the great seducer's brief liaison with one Henriette, with whom he unexpectedly falls in love.

The role of Henriette was the shortest Kit had played since *Nice People,* only eighteen sides (pages), and she said she wanted to play it because of the interesting dramatic contrast between Henriette in the first act and her daughter in the last, which she also played.

Having begun his career eighteen years before as the Rider of the Pony Express in *The Girl of the Golden West,* Lowell Sherman was somewhat surprised to find himself playing Giacomo Casanova. Never having played "a high-class costume romance," as it was called by one critic, he was leery of it, and it showed. "*Must* I die on those watermelons?" he asked politely when he saw the particularly outrageous period carpeting for the last act.

He adored Kit and called her his "dearie" because he could make her laugh and on opening night sent a crudely printed good-luck message from "Cassie himself" wishing her "dandruff, sunburn, the screaming 'mimis,' hangnails, ginger snaps, that old Kentucky home feeling, Broadway's future — and success and some horse's hoofs and just a few bananas to prove we have them." But he still had no illusions about the outcome of that evening. In the first act when Henriette decides to have the affair with him and stops briefly on the threshold to ponder, "Three little steps. Where will these steps lead me?", he took her hands, bending over her passionately, and whispered, "To Cain's, dearie, to Cain's!", Cain's Warehouse being the place where scenery went when bad plays closed.

The next day's press assured him and everyone else that as he had feared, yes, they had no bananas, but he took it in good cheer, haling Kit into his dressing room the second night with, "Weren't they *wonderful* to you and weren't they *rotten* to me?"

Casanova was Kit's first appearance at the Empire Theatre and established lasting professional associations with Gilbert Miller, Al Woods's urbane co-producer, Deems Taylor, who composed the incidental music, and Sidney Howard, who did the bad translation but who would one day write *Alien Corn* for her. The play included a Fokine ballet that featured a young dancer who would eventually become the designer Valentina and create some of Kit's most beautiful theatre clothes.

The watermelon carpet was shipped off to Cain's Warehouse on December 2, 1923, after seventy-seven performances. The historic first production of *Saint Joan* was not scheduled to open for almost four weeks, but Winifred Lenihan had been cast in the part of Joan.

Clemence Dane never saw Kit play either Sydney Fairfield or Mary Fitton, but she felt she had found the one American actress able to interpret her plays properly and entrusted her with *The Way Things Happen* even before its London production. Gratitude for such blind faith is the probable explanation for Kit's own blind faith in the role of Shirley Pride, the mousy foster child who loves the son of the house and sacrifices her virtue to keep him from going to prison for "borrowing" securities from his office on the eve of his marriage to another girl. There was one good scene as the boy backs Shirley into an admission of what she has done, which was more exhausting than anything Kit had ever acted. That scene by itself was given twenty-one curtain calls on opening night at the Lyceum Theatre, January 28, 1924. But when the final curtain came down, the women in the audience didn't understand the girl and the men in the audience hated the man, and the play, which had been rapturously received during its tryout in Philadelphia, eked out a bleak twenty-four performances in New York.

Guthrie had had a modest success in November with a thriller-melo-drama called *In the Next Room*, written by Kit's old friend Eleanor Robson (Belmont) and Harriet Ford, and with his confidence thus bolstered he produced *The Way Things Happen* and directed Kit for the first time since the Jessie Bonstelle stock days. Even with the play's failure, it was a bold step forward for both of them thus to join forces.

If *The Way Things Happen* was a step forward for Kit despite its failure, her next choice was a step backward despite its success. An English play, *The Outsider*, had already opened in Baltimore to bad reviews when *The Way Things Happen* suddenly closed, and the producer, William Harris, Jr., asked Kit to rush down to Baltimore and take over the leading role (opposite Lionel Atwill) from an actress named Ann Davis. At that point in her career Kit should have been beyond replacing an unknown actress in a play that was already a failure. She was undoubtedly moved by the fact that Harris had asked her to play the part originally and she had not been able to because of *The Way Things Happen*. She probably felt she was in some way responsible for whatever trouble *The Outsider* was in and that the least she could do was to help Harris out.

First being assured that Ann Davis was going to be replaced no matter what, that her firing was not contingent on Kit's decision, the McClintics went to Baltimore to see a performance and Kit agreed to play the role of Lalage Sturdee, a character-defining name to rival Lydia Languish and the Hardy boys, only in this case it was ironic, for sturdy Lalage was a hopeless cripple. It was the most meretricious of all the plays Kit had appeared in since *A Bill of Divorcement*.

The outsider of the title, played by Lionel Atwill, is Anton Ragatzy, a self-taught, unlicensed physician who wants to serve humanity and is opposed by the organized medical profession. The play pits him against a gaggle of recognized practitioners (who seem to be rejects from an old Shaw play) and focuses on Lalage, the daughter of the greatest surgeon of them all, Jasper Sturdee, a man embittered by the fact that his daughter has been crippled for life by the butchering of a quack. In the course of the action, Ragatzy establishes his superiority and the right to continue his work by curing her.

The entire second act is a depiction of Lalage's life in her father's house as, leaning on her stick, she twists her way from chair to piano

In The Outsider, *1924. (Steichen,* Vanity Fair)

where she sits deluding herself with the notion that in playing music and writing it she finds solace. But when an upholding young man comes to call and with charity caresses her, she is "hungry with the starvation of isolation for the touch of his hands, the warmth of his cheek, the glow of his eyes, the softening of his voice." When he speaks idly of dancing and mountain climbing (he is not the soul of tact), her passion for motion smokes and flames, and she glows with life's deeper ardors. At the end of the act she commits herself, in defiance of her father and his entire profession, to be stretched for a year on what is called in the play "Ragatzy's Rack," in the hope of being made to walk again.

Dorothy Brandon, the author of *The Outsider*, was herself a cripple, and this second act, although as clumsy and jagged as the rest of the play, came directly out of her own experience and had a kind of raw revelation. To externalize this, the director had Kit's predecessor bouncing around the stage as if she were on a pogo stick. Kit felt that a girl obsessed with the fact that her affliction made her unlovely and therefore unlovable would walk as little as possible and insisted on playing the second act almost from one position. When she did struggle to her feet, then, her movements were so ugly and pitiable that the audience, not having had a chance to get used to them, winced.

It was the last act that gave the most trouble to both players and audience. In England, "Ragatzy's Rack" did not work, but that was deemed too harsh for American audiences. As rewritten, the girl who has been lashed to a kind of vibrating ironing board for a solid year is unlashed, and under the stern and accusing eyes of the leaders of the British medical profession, with no limbering-up practice, no preparation, and blessed little encouragement, is expected to get to her feet and all but slip into a time step. When she falters and sinks to the floor, the learned men cry "Quack! Quack!" and feel vindicated by Ragatzy's humiliating defeat. Then as they are all, including Ragatzy, about to depart, Lalage, a mere heap on the floor, cries out to the Ragatzy she now loves, pushes herself to her feet, and totters toward him blindly, stops, straightens up, and walks. Behold the miracle of love.

It was two weeks from the closing of *The Way Things Happen* to the opening of *The Outsider*. Kit had six days' rehearsal, an out-of-town run-through in Stamford, Connecticut, and a Sunday night dress rehearsal in New York to open the following night, March 3, 1924, at the Forty-ninth Street Theatre. During that time the third act was rewritten, restaged, speeded up, slowed down, expanded, cut, and finally put back the way it was when they started.

The Outsider may have been a step backward professionally, but it also turned out to be the most successful, financially and critically, of her plays thus far, and its success, as noted by the critics, some of whom even made pilgrimages from other cities, was entirely due to Kit's performance. H.T.P., the famous critic of the *Boston Transcript*, went home and wrote, "Through years obscure and years in the public eye and the public applause . . . she has become an actress ripened with powers still supple with youth. She has gained technical readiness and variety that make possible the works of insight and imagination." Therefore, with the perversity that is the theatre's most enduring quality, she was right to accept *The Outsider*.

She said Lalage was "one of those gift-of-the-gods parts you can't go wrong on," a statement so untrue that one despairs of the extremes her modesty will lead her to, until one realizes that in this case it was not so much modesty as it was consideration and compassion for crippled Dorothy Brandon, who she knew would read whatever she said in print.

It was this same compassion that enabled Kit to play Lalage in that difficult second act, and it was her playing of the second act that gave believability to the impossible, unactable third act. It was reported that members of the audience actually fainted from grief when it seemed likely that Lalage would fail in her efforts to walk. H.T.P. was right to imply that "technical readiness and variety" can only do so much, that they can only make *possible* "works of insight and imagination" powerful enough to induce such a strong empathic response. The insight and imagination must be there first, in the actress herself, especially if her technical readiness and variety have been learned at the beloved but clayey feet of Jessie Bonstelle.

Early in her career, it might be said, all Kit's roles would fall somewhere between the depraved innocence of Jo and the noble depravity of Marcelle; but in Sydney Fairfield, Laura Pennington, and Lalage Sturdee she established rapport with another dimension of character, an uncanny identification with the crippled, the flawed, the physically weak, the psychologically maimed. It was an insight gained from her own experience, probably starting with her own inward sense of inadequacy coupled with an outgoing nature, and can be seen developing all through her life, at its simplest in her schoolgirl need to help her mother, at its most obvious in her acceptance of her mongoloid cousin, and at its most complex in her relationship with Guthrie. She probably could not have played Sydney Fairfield, Laura Pennington, and Lalage Sturdee successfully ten years before, not until she could see them with the same eyes that enabled her to see Guthrie in Michelangelo's Pietà.

The Outsider, a slow starter, built to a late-season hit. But at the end of thirteen weeks Actors' Equity once again went on strike, this time for a closed shop. It was their last big push for establishment, and the managers were more determined than ever to resist them. Consequently, on May 31 every play in town was closed by the strike. The actors were like a bunch of children suddenly let out of school and seem to have headed merrily, en masse, for Europe. Kit was always quite proud of the gold star on her Equity card, meaning that to support the strike she had walked out of a play while it was doing excellent business.

Not all actors were in favor of the strike. Jeanne Eagels told the press as she boarded the *Berengaria*, "I'm going to Russia or some place where personal liberty isn't just a name or a mockery, and there is no Equity." Gilbert Miller was on board for that madcap voyage, and as soon as they were beyond the three-mile limit Lowell Sherman instructed the bartender to keep lining up the drinks the length of the bar while he invited his friends to drink their way down the row. "You drink up to here," he would say, "and then you drink from here to here . . ."

It was the kind of party Guthrie would have loved, but not with Kit, and they slipped abroad by themselves for a quieter time roaming, resting, play-hunting. Down on the coast of Devon, probably visiting Clemence Dane, they read Michael Arlen's *The Green Hat*. Guthrie said it was all plush and claptrap and, it might be added, he never changed his mind.

A joke advertisement in the *New York Herald* announced: "The Theatre Guild presents 'Indigestion,' a new drama of alimentary passions by Eugene O'Neill, with Helen Westley as Gastritis," and continued: "Guthrie McClintic presents Katharine Cornell in 'The Texas Nightingale' by Zoe Akins Smith, 800th performance Saturday night, Reservoir Theatre." Broadway could make fun of its newfound seriousness which nevertheless was crowding out the old ornate hokum of David Belasco. "The old master," or "the Broadway Rasputin," as George Jean Nathan called him, was coming to the end of his long career. Some of the younger crowd thought it was about time and made no secret of it. Lionel Atwill had come from England a few years before to find himself entrapped in a series of Belasco productions, and when he finally escaped to *The Outsider* he was congratulated in print by the critics — regardless of what they thought of his performance — for having been "happily released from the Belascan yoke." Even Mrs. Leslie Carter, his *Zaza* and his *Du Barry*, had not spoken to "Mr. Dave" for twenty years.

In little more than a year's time he would have one of his biggest hits with Lenore Ulric playing blackface in *Lulu Belle*, but in the fall of 1924 when Kit was beckoned into the presence, he was a white-haired old man from another era, claiming reverence with the reversed collar of a priest, holding his court together in monastic quarters atop the Belasco Theatre where the air was heavy with the scent of joss sticks and in the dim lighting, from his desk on a Ming dais, "The Governor" summoned his minions with chimes rather than buzzers, and when alone kept watch over them through peepholes in the intricate grillwork between rooms.

He had nothing to offer Katharine Cornell in either personal or theatrical style, and she had nothing to offer him, but priding himself on a benevolent interest in rising young actresses, he bestowed upon her the role of Suzanne Chaumont in *Tiger Cats*.

Kit felt at the time (along with the critics later) that Suzanne was a horrible woman, "the most horrible I have ever known," in a very disagreeable play. But Belasco was, after all, a man who had given forty-five years to the theatre; he was a domineering man with mesmeric ways; he was a courtly man; and what Kit would find most persuasive of all, the theatre he loved was beginning to turn against him. It is not surprising that she accepted the role.

The reason she gave was that it would be good discipline.

———

Tiger Cats was an adaptation by Karen Bramson of a French play called *Les Félines* in which Suzanne Chaumont's husband André is so absorbed in his work (neurology), writing books, getting acclaimed, and teaching, that he comes to resent and then loathe his extravagant, voluptuous, incessantly egotistical wife who cries for races, romps, and roadhouses and seeks to have and to own all of him, his work, his life. Infuriated by his rejection of her, she takes a lover and boasts of it until André shoots her. He misses, but in the histrionic aftermath he loses his work and has nothing left but her, and she has all of him at last. It was the feeling of the critics that had André Chaumont been a better marksman, the play would have been more to their liking.

———

Edith Evans had briefly played a strident, dynamic, shrieking Suzanne in London with Robert Loraine, who was repeating André in New York, and Kit was in trouble right away, up against the old Basil Dean–Meggie Albanesi situation, with Loraine insisting she do what Edith Evans did. Just as Kit had sought to keep Lalage Sturdee from loping around the stage like a gazelle, so she thought it a good idea to keep Suzanne's voice down, playing softly and sliding in under her completely unsympathetic viciousness. But that would spoil it for Loraine who had liked Evans's carrying-on because it let him be more dramatic as the quiet one. Kit was getting bolder in standing up for what she wanted, and with each of them refusing to steal the other's thunder, so to speak, they did not get along well. (What is more, for a wonder, Kit admitted they didn't get along well. Usually, if she couldn't say something good, she said nothing at all.)

It probably had no serious connection with their antipathy to each other that at a late rehearsal one day Loraine held the pistol too close to her and the shot burned her arm badly. The truth seems to be that Kit's wish to play Suzanne quietly was not merely a matter of taste and choice, she didn't have the craft to play it loud and clamorous, and when Karen Bramson saw her try it in Baltimore, she was appalled. Kit found herself wishing she would get blood poisoning from the gunshot wound and they would have to cut her arm off.

Instead, she had a private talk with Karen Bramson the next morning, explaining what she wanted to do with the part and got her grudging permission to try. Belasco was directing the play as well as producing it, but he seems to have had no arbitrating or pacifying authority over what was going on, and when Kit arrived at the theatre for the matinee she found Loraine sitting center stage immobile with his head in his hands while Belasco wandered about murmuring "I won't let anybody bother Miss Katharine. No one is going to bother Miss Katharine."

Here Miss Katharine had her first and what she always insisted was her last outburst of temperament. She walked to a chair, put her things down quietly, seated herself, and pounded her thighs with doubled fists.

"Between the two of you I haven't slept a wink on the last three nights!" she shrieked, as if she were Edith Evans playing Suzanne Chaumont. "Now I am going to make up."

Halfway to her dressing room she realized what she had said and it struck her funny. Nobody else ever saw the joke, but she played Suzanne her way at that performance, Karen Bramson admitted it was better, Loraine said it would have to do, and they opened at the Belasco Theatre on October 21, 1924.

Stark Young called her playing remarkable, mordant and secure. "The portrait she created was not always palatable, but the directness with which she was willing to establish the neurotic and the ugly in the character, and the distortion and decadent acid in the theme was a fine proof of her sincerity as an artist and of her promise in the theatre." A generous review, but one senses a slight strain in talking too long for too many years about her sincerity and promise.

Suzanne Chaumont would probably seem rather tame today, but it was all but impossible for Katharine Cornell in 1924 — or later — to be at ease, let alone give credibility to a woman who was all depravity, all neurosis, and all acid with no innocence, no heights, no nobility. Robert Garland in *Theatre Arts* after describing André Chaumont as a literary figure, said that Suzanne "is not constructed for the library, although just what she is constructed for you'll never learn from me. Surely not for Katharine Cornell. . . ."

12

"From the Cradle
of the Human Race" (1924-1925)

TIGER CATS expired after forty-eight performances, and Kit cannot have felt more relief than a chronicler of her career feels in having charted (at last) the six passing, rather impossible plays after *A Bill of Divorcement*. They can be justified: no experience is ever wasted; an actress cannot create her own opportunities as, for example, a playwright can; at that point in her career it was better to be in a play, any play at all, than to disappear from the stage for want of the perfect role. The best that can be said is not surprising but could hardly have been said of any other actress in the same circumstances: not one of the roles was chosen out of vanity.

Unlike the others, her next play was *meant* to be passing. With no regular run and only a few matinees, it wasn't even a commercial production but a kind of intramural activity, an inside exercise. It was actors having fun experimenting with their craft. The irony is that it gave her one of the great roles that will always be associated with her name, Shaw's *Candida*.

Some say the Actors' Theatre came out of the strike of 1924, dreamed up by actors sitting around with nothing to do. A more popular account is that it was founded after the great strike of 1919 by Francis Wilson, an actor so venerable that he received his training with Joseph Jefferson (*Rip Van Winkle*), post Civil War. The concept was an ideal for actors, a sort of sublimated repertory in which all the great of the theatre would play their favorite roles at special matinees for two weeks without remuneration. The trouble was that a few matinees require as much preparation, time, and effort as a full-scale commercial run, and the great of the theatre found it difficult to fit the Actors' Theatre into their schedules.

Eventually it fell into the hands of a few who used it for their own immediate advantage, but in 1924 it seems merely to have democratized its original conception to become a theatre without stars; that is, "the great of the theatre" were welcome to take part but not treated as stars or billed.

Candida was a good choice for such a group because it didn't have a starring role, or until that time was not thought to have. Of its six roles only one, "Lexy" Mill, the Reverend Morell's curate, is too small and slight to be played by a leading actor. Each of the other five is rich in substance and Shavian wit, and if one of them stands out a bit more than the others, it is Eugene Marchbanks, the eighteen-year-old poet who falls in love with Candida Morell. This was the role that most concerned Shaw himself in the play's first production, and it was only after a great search that he entrusted it to Granville-Barker. And it was the role that Arnold Daly, who was responsible for four of the play's five previous American productions, always played, even into his forty-fifth year. Morell was meaty enough for an actor of Holbrook Blinn's stature, and "Prossy" has always been a favorite with the best young character actresses, starting with Louise Closser (Hale) in 1903.

Candida is, of course, the focal character, the provocation for the long Shavian arguments between Marchbanks and Morell with contributive attitudes from Prossy and old Mr. Burgess, Candida's father, but she herself is talked about more than she actually appears. She does no more than pass through the first act with a little chatter about taxi fares and housekeeping and when lunch will be ready. She is "well-aproned" in her second act scene, and in the midst of her characteristic talk of scrubbing brushes, black-leading, and "nasty little red onions," she has the beautiful "shawl" speech which, at its first London presentation, the Lord Chamberlain wanted to cut as offensive: "Ah, James, how little you understand me, to talk of your confidence in my goodness and purity! I would give them both to poor Eugene as willingly as I would give my shawl to a beggar dying of cold, if there were nothing else to restrain me." The third act is hers, of course, starting with "I give myself to the weaker of the two." But throughout the play, until the last fifteen minutes, the character of Candida is in the play what the woman Candida is in life, a buffer.

Dorothy Donnelly was Daly's first Candida in 1903 for one hundred and thirty-three performances. Thereafter, the play had only enough popularity for him to revive it in repertory, with Chrystal Herne in 1905, Margaret Wycherly in 1907, and Hilda Spong in 1915. They were all fine actresses who went on to have long and satisfactory careers, and Chrystal Herne, James A.'s daughter, reached a special height in the mid-1920s in George Kelly's *Craig's Wife*, but it is clear that not only was Candida not considered a starring role, it was not, or never had been until Kit, the kind of role that propelled an actress into the star ranks.

Guthrie headed the Actors' Theatre for two years, but it was his friend Clare Eames, the niece of the great soprano Emma Eames, who suggested *Candida* for production so that she could play Prossy. Dudley Digges, the Theatre Guild's popular character man, was directing, and with a nudge from Woollcott and a prod from Robert Edmond Jones, Kit was chosen to play Candida. In an actors' theatre, actors feel they have a right to grumble, and they did. With Kit's Broadway appearances thus far limited to maladjusted, physically flawed, mentally tainted, sexually boisterous, neurotically driven females, she seemed an odd choice for healthy, smiling, straightforward Candida.

While Kit was playing in *Tiger Cats* at night and rehearsing *Candida* by day, Guthrie was fulfilling a youthful dream. As a boy back in Seattle he had wangled his way in to meet Blanche Bates, pretending to be a reporter from the *Seattle Daily Times*. Now he was presenting her as well as directing her on Broadway in *Mrs. Partridge Presents*. She was such big time and so expensive that Guthrie, who was poor again, had wondered at his own audacity in approaching her, but Miss Bates had appraised him shrewdly and said, "Look here. You are a young man who is going to do things. I am an old star about to retire. I have money. I don't need work and I am not going to hold you up. Suppose we say I'll take two hundred dollars a week expense money and one quarter of the profits, if there are any." Guthrie was quick to agree. He revered the old actresses. He liked their style, the way they conducted themselves, their sometimes impenetrable dignity. He believed in their codes of behavior in the theatre. Also in the cast, just emerging from her Booth Tarkington period and stealing shows right and left with her buzz-saw talent, was Ruth Gordon, who returned twenty minutes late from lunch one day, full of apologies; Miss Bates went to sit by her, saying she thought it might give her courage.

Guthrie was tied up with his own rehearsals and unable to attend the first special matinee of *Candida*, but he sent his stage manager's laconic wife who endangered her life by reporting that the production was fine and Kit was all right, she supposed. Guthrie, who by this time had certainly studied his Shaw thoroughly, was probably more aware than anybody else of the potential involved, because when Kit arrived and gave the same laconic review of herself, he is reported to have screamed, undoubtedly wagging his finger and twisting his legs, "All *right! Candida can't* be *all right!* She must be either magnificent or terrible!"

It is theatre history which Kit was.

———

Shaw once announced to Ellen Terry, "Candida, between you and me, is the Virgin Mary and nobody else." And when Ellen Terry begged him to write a "Mother" play for her, he replied, "I *have* written THE Mother play — *Candida* — and I cannot repeat a masterpiece."

Considering the affinity Kit had to feel for a character before she could make it her own, and considering her antipathy to parenthood professed at the time of her abortion and many times afterward, it is safe to say that Mother plays were not for her, as the list of her successful roles bears out. Still she was able to make her way through to Candida, perhaps starting with the old Cornell family story of the rooming house in Berlin in 1893 and the dashing officer who spent intimate evenings with Alice Cornell while Peter was off at school, even as Marchbanks spent his one intimate evening with Candida while Morell was off preaching to the Guild of St. Matthew. It wasn't necessarily identification with Candida or mothering that Kit found to act; it was the chance to embody the romanticized image of Alice that had been forming in her mind, over the truth, ever since she could remember. It almost seems predestined that Candida should have come along, and it may be an instance in which an artist, by the pure practice of her art, resolves a portion of her life. In Candida, THE mother, she found her own.

Which is another way of saying that what Kit really found was herself. Her wise, dignified, generous and movingly vulnerable Candida was a woman who would have given her love and compassion — as easily as she would have given her shawl to a beggar dying of cold — not only to Marchbanks and Morell, but to Sydney Fairfield, Laura Pennington, Shirley Pride, Lalage Sturdee, and Guthrie McClintic.

It may have helped credibility that the mothering in *Candida* is mostly metaphorical, since the Morell children are mere Shavian dummy props who mercifully never appear. The only play in which children actually appeared on the stage claiming to have been birthed by Kit was *The Wingless Victory*, in the last act of which she slew them.

The special matinees of *Candida* overlapped the short run of *Tiger Cats* by a week, and at the end of three weeks, with two afternoon performances each week, the demand for tickets was so great that the Actors' Theatre decided to risk a regular commercial run at the Forty-eighth Street Theatre. The play officially opened on the evening of December 12, 1924, moving Burns Mantle to say in summing up the season that December was *Candida* month, and although its five months' run seems modest today, it outran the original American production by ten performances.

Kit's Marchbanks was a young English actor over for his first visit, Richard Bird; Pedro De Cordoba was Morell; Ernest Cossart, old Mr. Burgess; a young actor named Gerald Hamer at least got his name in theatre annals as Lexy; and Prossy was, as planned, Clare Eames, whose husband, Sidney Howard, had recovered sufficiently from *Casanova* to write *They Knew What They Wanted*, which had just opened and would win the Pulitzer Prize in the spring. In a season that included other new plays *What Price Glory?* and *Desire under the Elms*, as well as the Lunts' famous revival of Molnar's *The Guardsman*, *Candida* more than held its own. Shaw always patronized his own play and had once said, "There is a sort of snivelling success possible for *Candida*," and yet his most popular play and at the time the one considered to be the most notable, *Caesar and Cleopatra*, was revived by the Theatre Guild for Helen Hayes and Lionel Atwill during the run of *Candida* and was only able to stick it out twenty-eight performances.

The Guild controlled the rights to Shaw's plays, and for decades Kit was the only actress they allowed to play *Candida* in New York City.

Kit never liked the star system, and her antipathy to it, combined with her modesty (or as a result of it), was probably responsible for her stalling and bad timing, her unconscious postponement of her own inevitable elevation. But it wasn't only the artificial limelight she was dodging, the pretentious glamour that she felt had nothing to do with acting; the chances are she was dodging the responsibility.

The Enchanted Cottage had been badly stage-managed. Something drastic went wrong at every performance. It was the first play Kit was in in which there was neither a star nor any older actors of high stage authority and experience. The other actors in the large company therefore appealed to her, asking her to do something about the stage manager.

She kept putting it off, but one night the curtain didn't come down when it was supposed to, the music cues were off, and the lights went wrong, blinking on and off like a lighthouse all through a tricky dream sequence. After the performance, Kit finally worked herself into a rage and accosted the stage manager: "What in blazes happened to those lights tonight?"

"Oh, a *million* things, Miss Cornell," he answered truthfully.

Kit could not cope with a million things either in actuality or concept, and she suddenly felt she had no right to ask him to, and so her effort was lost and the play was badly stage-managed until the end of the run. She told this story on herself charmingly, explaining that she didn't have enough temperament to press the poor stage manager, but it wasn't temperament she lacked, it was authority, and she probably knew it. Blanche Bates and George Arliss would have seen to it, with no temperament, that that stage manager did his job properly. That was what it meant to be a star.

In the days of the great stars, at least the ones Kit and Guthrie admired, members of a company did not run to the management with their problems or to their unions, they went to the star, who enjoyed privilege, prestige, position, eminence, and glory, in return for which he or she ran a tight ship. A conscientious star would not tolerate, could not afford to tolerate, lights blinking like a lighthouse during a tricky dream sequence.

Because of a commitment made during the run of *Tiger Cats* when nobody dreamed that *Candida* would be such a success, Kit had to leave the cast before the end of the run and turned over the role to Peggy Wood, who writes in her book, *How Young You Look*, that Kit, her contemporary, whom she consistently refers to as "Miss Cornell," said to her, "How I envy you. You are going to know what it is to be impatient to get to the theatre every day of the week and to resent Sundays because you can't play Candida that day as well."

Kit was enjoying herself at last, completely, and somewhere in the back of her mind she knew that if and when she ever became a star, she would have to surrender a certain amount of that enjoyment to the responsibility of wielding authority. It would no longer be enough to be "nice" backstage, to be gracious, to smile a lot; she would have to learn to be critical. She did not find the prospect a pleasant one.

But it could not be put off much longer. It is ironic that in the starless, democratic Actors' Theatre, this became apparent. Whatever she did next, good or bad, large or small, her name would have to go above the title.

———

Three letters about her Candida say everything there is to say: one from an old admirer, two from new; one anonymous, two signed; one from a nobody, two from somebodies.

The first, signed, came from an old admirer who was somebody, A. Conger Goodyear, the Buffaloan who had met Kit at Anna Glenny's *bal masque* almost twenty years before. At that time, already in his thirties, married and a father, he had been well established in the lumber business. He went on to have a dynamic military career in the First World War, coming out a colonel. As a major general, 1st Division, N.Y. Guard, he enjoyed being addressed as General Goodyear, just as Kit's grandfather had enjoyed being called Colonel. With a desire to bring art to the public and the public to art, Goodyear became head of the Albright Museum in Buffalo, but after differences with the trustees over his special interest in modern art, he eventually broke with them and went to New York, where in the 1930s he founded the Museum of Modern Art and became its first president.

Although he claimed not to remember dancing with Kit at the *bal masque* and declaring to Anna Glenny that he had "met the most fascinating woman in the world and fallen irrevocably, hopelessly in love," he had followed her career with devoted attention. In his own words, he came away from a matinee of *Candida* "drunk with excitement" and decided that Buffalo needed a portrait of Kit. The directors of the Albright authorized him to make arrangements for such a work with Eugene Speicher, the Buffalo-born artist. In a memoir called *Sidelights*, privately printed in the 1950s, Goodyear recalled:

> I gave Gene what was practically a blueprint for the operation. The portrait was to show Candida standing in her red dress, quite without any encumbering details; like Manet's Woman With a Parrot. It is certainly Speicher's masterpiece, but there was criticism. It didn't have the smoothly ironed out surface that certain of the lower Buffalo brows preferred. So I bought the canvas from the Albright and gave it to Kit. It hung in the lobby of the Empire Theatre for a while. Some years later, at my suggestion, she gave it to the Museum of Modern Art. I still felt it belonged in Buffalo and when the Albright Gallery management announced that it felt so too, it was sold for twenty percent more than the original purchase.

In 1932 the *New York Times* wrote of a showing at the Museum of Modern Art:

> There is in the main gallery one supreme example of the hanging committee's art, which we could not expect to find duplicated. This involves the inspired placing on opposite end walls of Whistler's "White Girl" and Eugene Speicher's portrait of Katharine Cornell in *Candida*. With all its store of technical triumphs and despite its crossroads significance as a document, Whistler's painting need not hope still to hold the eye that has, from afar, caught sight of the masterpiece from Speicher's brush. The portrait of the celebrated actress is vital in every line, in every passage. The modelling is simply superb. Character essentials, like those of form and color, are rendered living and memorable in ratio to the omission of all the cluttering props for verisimilitude deemed urgent by so many lesser artists.

After the *Candida* matinee, Conger Goodyear also wrote a letter to Kit. When he showed it to his wife, she said, "But you can't send that! It is crazy!" He said, "Fine, then it says what I want it to," and mailed it, launching, or relaunching, one of the closest, more persistent relationships of Kit's life, one that in time would influence the actual purpose and direction of her career.

———

The second letter, from a new admirer, anonymous, a nobody, was scribbled inside a program around the play's title sometime during the week beginning Monday, January 12, 1925: "I saw you first in *Will Shakespeare* and thought you very gallant for a woman; then, in *The Enchanted Cottage* your voice came to me very clearly: every sound of it seemed to retell for me the story of creation. And now — now you are so beautiful it is too painful not to say. I am allowing myself, during this second intermission, under the spell of this play, to become a little like Marchbanks, and with an anonymity poor Marchbanks hasn't, a little bolder. I love you, and I hope some day to say it to your living face. I love you. And let the years come, I love you. S.R."

———

The third letter, signed, from a new admirer, a somebody, didn't come until twelve years after her first *Candida* in New York, when she was planning her second and wrote to him concerning the rights. He never saw her play the part or any other, and was reluctant even to visit the United States because he said he would be so popular with the Americans that they would elect him President, and that, he confessed without apology, would bore him. He would have been annoyed to find out that he agreed with the anonymous American, S.R., when it came to Katharine Cornell's part in the creation. He wrote:

Dear Katharine Cornell: I don't think I was ever so astonished by a picture as I was by your photograph. Your success as Candida and something blonde and expansive about your name had created an ideal British Candida in my imagination. Fancy my feelings on seeing the photograph of a gorgeous dark lady from the cradle of the human race ... wherever that was ... Ceylon ... Sumatra ... Hilo ... or the southernmost corner of the Garden of Eden. If you look like that it doesn't matter a rap if you can act or not. Can you? Yours, breath bereaved, Bernard Shaw.

§IV§

Kath Cornell (1925-1930)

13

Iris of
the Golden Slum (1925-1926)

GEORGE JEAN NATHAN WROTE in the *American Mercury* in September 1925, "The two most recent contributions to the art of drama are *The Green Hat* and *The Vortex*. The authors of these great masterpieces are, respectively, Mr. Michael Arlen, a clever young man and a swell dresser, and Mr. Noël Coward, a clever young man and a hot piano player. Both plays have come to us with a loud preliminary beating of drums; both have been vouchsafed an amount of newspaper space unparalleled . . . both are flapdoodle."

The two flapdoodles, which opened within twenty-four hours of each other, both depicted the licentious, disillusioned spirit of the time, Coward's with drugs at the vortex, Arlen's with sex under his hat. It was Coward's Broadway debut as playwright and actor, and Nathan notwithstanding, he was "hugged and kissed and crowned with glory." It was Arlen's Broadway debut as a playwright, and Nathan notwithstanding, his play doubled the dazzling international success the novel on which it was based had been enjoying for over a year, and even Nathan had to admit it was "superbly acted in its leading role by that one young woman who stands head and shoulders above all the other young women of the American theatre, Miss Katharine Cornell."

———

It has occurred to the writer to call this unimportant history "The Green Hat" because a green hat was the first thing about her that he saw: as also it was, in a way, the last thing about her that he saw. It was

As Iris March in The Green Hat, *1926. (New York Public Library, Vandamm Collection)*

bright green, of a sort of felt, and bravely worn: being, no doubt, one of those that women who have many hats affect "pour le sport."

So begins the novel, trying its title on for size and finding it a loose but rather charming fit. The play eschews any reference to the green hat in either dialogue or stage direction. In performance, however, it was "bravely worn" in the second act and at a crucial moment taken off and tossed onto a sofa like caution to the winds. For all its tenuous connection with the story, it became a kind of symbol of the "gallantry of a hungry heart" with which Iris Fenwick, née March, of the "rotten" Marches, bears her "thousand carnal calvaries."

In luxuriant Arlenese Iris takes her long-legged stand early in the play, proclaiming to Napier Harpenden, the one man she loves but cannot have because his father forbids him to marry one of the rotten Marches, "I think I have a body that burns for love. I shall burn it with love, but I shall never say 'I love you' to any man but you."

When she suddenly marries Boy Fenwick she continues, "I married Boy because he loved me and because I wanted love, because my body, this body, was hungry for love and born to love and must love."

On their wedding night in the Hotel Vendome in Deauville, Boy jumps out the window to his death because, as Napier reveals in the last act, "Boy had picked up some beastly woman before Iris suddenly accepted him and caught about the foulest disease a man can have." He grabbed Iris when he had the chance, it seems, hoping to put it right on their honeymoon by asking her to wait till he was better. The disgust on her face was too much for him and he "chucked himself out."

But at the time of the suicide in Act One Iris lets Napier and his father and all the world think that she was the one to be found impure on the wedding night, driving Boy and his "clean ideals" out the window. The only one to know the truth is the doctor who examined the dead body, who asks Iris why she has ruined herself by lying. She answers with a cry, with a sob, with a laugh, "Let's all do one decent thing in life!"

Ten years later, after streams of casual men, Iris comes back, tosses her hat on the sofa and consummates her love for Napier on the eve of his wedding to Venice, who has such "clean eyes" that they frighten Iris even in a photograph in *Tatler*. Since Venice is designed by God and playwright to have children, lots and lots of clean-eyed children, her surname is Pollen.

But before Venice Pollen can have Napier's children, Iris has one in a convent nursing home on one of the outer boulevards of Paris where the playwright manages to assemble almost the entire company in such a way that Woollcott felt, watching it, that he was sitting on the terrasse of the Café de la Paix, and if he sat there long enough he would meet everyone he ever knew. Iris's child has died and she herself may be dying of septic poisoning which Napier, having been summoned from the ends of the earth by the doctor, is somehow able to believe is ptomaine.

Iris is recalled to life by Napier's willingness to run away to South America with her, but in a fourth-act confrontation with his father he must blurt out the truth about Boy Fenwick's death. Iris begs him not to, but he must clear her name with his father. This humiliates her; her pride is greater than her love; she speaks her own requiem: "You have taken from me the only generous thing I have ever done in my life." She sends Napier back to his wife with the lie that Venice is about to have a baby that will continue the Harpenden line. Then, having flung her victory back into the faces of those who withheld it so long, she drives her yellow Hispano-Suiza into eternity against a giant elm tree.

Flapdoodle *The Green Hat* may have been, or to borrow a more polite (and more accurate) phrase from a Coward play, "big romantic stuff," but it still had something powerful to say about the mid-1920s woman — or perhaps it was said to her rather than about her. Iris was rich and English, so it can hardly have been identification that filled the Broadhurst Theatre in New York for twenty-nine weeks, although revolt against the hypocrisy of "decent" society will always be empathically received in all lands at all economic levels. The theatre was more a window than a mirror in those days, and maybe Iris, that lovely desolate lady who loved many men casually because she loved one too intensely, maybe self-sacrificing Iris, noble Iris, Iris the outcast woman, Iris Fenwick, née March, was an ideal.

Whatever she was and whatever she signified, Iris was rooted in the 1920s and certainly was meant to be played by an actress who could epitomize the decade, not by Kit, a mere "searching traveler who seemed to land there for ten years." Tallulah Bankhead would be perfect, of course, but she had become the rage of London and would probably play the part there. That left, in New York, only Jeanne

Eagels. But Jeanne Eagels epitomized the licentious disillusionment of the decade so well, she was so far ahead of the game that she had long since outdistanced Iris March to become unreliable, all but unemployable.

Al Woods offered the part to Kit while she was still playing in *Tiger Cats*. Had he waited to see her finally hit her stride as Iris March's direct opposite, as intelligent, not to say brainy, clean, serene, competent Candida; had he waited to see vegetarian Shaw's comparatively bloodless play officially claimed as her territory, hailed as her strength, her forte, her metier, he might have thought how wrong she was for Iris and never made the offer. Even as it was it was made with a lack of conviction that she couldn't help feeling, as if it came out of his longtime habit of offering her whatever came along. It was offered as if he almost hoped she would refuse — and that Jeanne Eagels would for God's sake straighten up.

But Kit did not refuse. Guthrie hated *The Green Hat* both book and play, and thought she would be terrible in it, and still she did not refuse. She had been badly advised, persuaded and even emotionally blackmailed into doing the six passing plays after *A Bill of Divorcement*; here was a part nobody wanted her to do, and she was determined to do it. It was a new attitude, a rising assertiveness that came at precisely the right moment in her life. She was so determined to play Iris that she did something unprecedented in her theatrical career, she agreed to play to part in violation of a contract she had signed (been coerced into signing) with David Belasco for one more play after *Tiger Cats*. When it was pointed out to him that he did not have a play ready for her, he had to give her permission to do the other. But the minute Al Woods announced a spring tryout of *The Green Hat* with Katharine Cornell as Iris March, Belasco countered with the news that Miss Cornell would immediately start rehearsing *The Doll Master*, to be presented by David Belasco. Had he been younger, he might have been able to come up with, over a long weekend, a concoction called *The Doll Master* and the theatre might have been deprived of Kit's Iris and who knows, all the parts it led to. But *The Doll Master* was only a title, and after harassing her in the press for a while, the Old Master finally let her out of her contract providing the program read, as it had for *Candida*, that Katharine Cornell appeared as Iris "by permission of David Belasco." To which a wit added, "because the rotten Marches are never let off anything."

She got out of her contract with Belasco but didn't ask for one from Woods because of his reservations about her, nor did he offer one. Guthrie reluctantly agreed to direct, more from an unwillingness to abandon her than from any enthusiasm for the project, and on these waves of optimism, while she was still playing in *Candida*, they went into rehearsal. Whenever she saw Woods she asked, "Are you sure you want me?", and when he answered "Absolutely! I think you can do it — don't you?", she reassured him with, "Let's not decide until Arlen comes." But when Arlen arrived, nothing was decided. He was the new kind of hero-celebrity that emerged in the 1920s along with channel swimmers and movie stars, and in town to be feted, wined, and dined, he simply dashed into rehearsal for two or three minutes at a time, pleased with everything, with Guthrie, with Kit, with his own waistcoats, with life, and dashed out again. He probably knew what he was doing; he knew what a difficult job they had and thought it best only to encourage, never interfere.

With Leslie Howard as Napier and Ann Harding as Venice, *The Green Hat* was first given March 29, 1925, in Detroit at the same Garrick Theatre where Kit had tethered her horse five years before, slogged through *Lombardi, Ltd.* et al., and with Guthrie had made plans for a future which certainly did not include having Jeanne Eagels planted in the audience on the opening night of *The Green Hat*, studying the play with an eye to taking it over. When a producer pulls such a trick, he usually tries to be quiet about it, but wherever Jeanne Eagels went, everybody knew it. Michael Arlen also found time to be there, and the press reported the next day that for all his elegance, he got sick.

After that performance, however, Mrs. Al Woods came backstage and confessed that it was she who had doubted Kit's ability to play Iris. All along she had been trying to undermine her husband's faith and had almost succeeded, but now that she had seen what Kit was trying to do, even in this difficult, sketchy, harassed tryout performance, she was sincere in her apologies and her enthusiasm. The next morning Jeanne Eagels decamped and Al Woods asked Kit to play Iris in New York. They still did not have a contract; they never did have a contract. The arrangement, having arisen out of mutual doubt, continued in mutual trust. Guthrie, too, was heartened by the Detroit opening, but still feeling the play needed work sent out for all Michael Arlen's other novels and went through them assiduously cribbing lines to put into *The Green Hat*.

After two weeks in Detroit, they moved on to the Selwyn Theatre in Chicago, which was meant to be no more than a stop for polishing on the way to New York. But here the play caught on and the demand for tickets became so great that it stayed on through the season for fourteen weeks.

Today, with on-the-spot television communication and instant world-wide movie distribution, the expression "international success" sounds quaint and redundant. Today, if a success isn't international it can hardly be counted a success. It is hard, therefore, to imagine the magnetic strength of an international success that could only be read about in newspapers and visualized through black-and-white photographs in magazines, that could only be seen by making a pilgrimage to Chicago, Illinois. Ashton Stevens, the senior drama critic in Chicago, was traveling abroad at the time of the opening, in constant touch with home, and yet he reported that Parisians knew about the sensational new play before he did and extravagantly told him all about it. In London, where Michael Arlen was regarded as their own, the delight with Stevens's ignorance was undoubtedly patronizing; in New York, where "risqué" was a new popular word, he was regarded as a poor drama critic and a disloyal Chicagoan for not being able to quote the lines from the play about syphilis and loose morals.

When he got home and finally wrote his own review beginning "So this is *The Green Hat*," he expressed complete astonishment; by all that was sane and logical the play should die at every performance of its melodramatics, its rouge and rhinestones, its preposterous third act, "instead of which it prospers like the bay tree of similar hue. Already I am beginning to forget its imperfections and remember only its charms." Its chief charm, of course, was Katharine Cornell, who sent tiny bells up and down his "unpurchasable vertebrae." Having seen her so recently as Candida, he knew "what a tribute to her versatility and power of impersonation is this brooding, self-pitying, burning lady of Mr. Arlen's golden slum."

The Green Hat came to New York, then, on Tuesday, September 15, 1925, already an established hit. It had been running so long, in fact, that it was undergoing cast replacements, although Leslie Howard continued on as a tight-jawed, credulous Napier, holding the audience miraculously steady through such posers as, "You have a white body that beats at my mind like a whip." Robert Benchley suggested that Howard was able to make the fellow more than bearable because at heart he was an excellent comedian, and another critic wondered if he would be able to play a like part with such high faith in ten years.

Al Woods had decided, however, to transfer Ann Harding to another of his fall offerings, and Guthrie replaced her with his friend and neighbor Margalo Gillmore, of whom Benchley said, "We can think of no more difficult assignment for a young actress than to play a scene in competition with Miss Cornell, and yet it is done with thrilling success by Margalo Gillmore in a smaller and much less grateful role." As it had been with Esther Howard in *The Man Who Came Back*, Kit felt easier with Margalo because she was talented and took the play and her part seriously, and together they were able to survive the not always generous opinions from outside. On one occasion an important manager bellowed forth to Kit his disapproval of Margalo before she could stop him, and when he had gone, Kit, knowing Margalo had heard every word through the paper-thin dressing-room walls, went to make amends. She opened Margalo's door to see a heartrending tableau — Margalo, white and still, stretched out on an improvised bier, with candles burning at her head and feet and a lily in her hand. She never would reveal how she assembled her props so quickly.

The critical reception was consistent, a rather stunned reaction to the extravagances of the play, a tentative sort of apology for enjoying it, then a big rush to embrace Kit for redeeming one's sense of taste. Benchley, however, having had a glorious time, made the following request: "May we not please some afternoon have a special matinee of *The Green Hat* in which this sensible cast are allowed to broaden their performances one-eighth of an inch, making the whole thing the most delightful burlesque of the season?"

———

Even the physical description of Iris in the novel was against Kit — small and fair with tiger tawny hair and eyes the color of the sea of Capri. Kit felt she had to work all the harder to make up for her lack. Since she was obviously cast against type, she played against type, a technique she was developing with each part. Since she didn't even look like Iris, she did nothing that Iris would do and she did nothing that an audience would expect Iris to do — she never had a cigarette in her hand, or a drink, and she didn't slink in and out being seductive. While everybody else smoked, drank, and slunk, she became quiet, pensive, and still. It was what she called making Iris "unobvious" and was an unusual approach for an actress in those days. It was a great deal technique, but it was also a good part reticence.

———

Others did not always see in her or in the parts she played or, for that matter, in the way she played them what she saw. The gentle critic Percy Hammond described her Iris as a "carnal madcap," and with reason. In her last-act entrance, for example, when Napier's father has surrounded himself with men friends and neighbors to confront Iris and dissuade her from eloping with his son, she comes in and announces gaily, "Messieurs, a lady has called about her morals!" To which one of the gentlemen retorts, "Optimist, Iris! We've just been discussing the fact that you haven't any!" Now that is pretty madcap, but what Kit would have her eye on, the element that would shape the scene for her and perhaps the whole character, comes immediately after from Napier's father who, it must be remembered, has stood between her and Napier from the start. He says it was good of Iris to come, but he knew she would because she had always been a "gallant gentleman."

Michael Arlen wrote, "It is common knowledge that there are very few gentlemen among men; but it is not generally recognized that there are even fewer gentlemen among women. That is why Iris March has seemed so unreal and surprising to many people. That is why she has appealed to so many men as the ideal mistress, the ideal companion. She was a gentleman with all the weaknesses of a woman."

Percy Hammond may have seen her as a carnal madcap, but Kit was playing a gallant gentleman.

———

No one will ever know what Jeanne Eagels's Iris would have been like, but Tallulah Bankhead played the part in London and failed. A critic wrote at the time, "Tallulah Bankhead is almost the most modern actress we have. She belongs to the semi-exclusive set of whom Michael Arlen writes. She has beauty and a shimmering sense of theatre." She also came very close to Arlen's own physical description of Iris, and she identified herself with the character loudly and publicly.

Perhaps that is why she failed. Perhaps the play, regarded as meretricious by the gentlest of critics, simply couldn't stand up under more of the same. Instead of illuminating the play's virtues, perhaps she belabored its faults, compounded its felony. Try to imagine Zelda Fitzgerald consciously playing the part of Zelda Fitzgerald.

On the other hand, Kit must have identified with the role, too. There are those who say that she saw her mother in Iris; that that is what attracted her in the first place; that her mother was her actual acting model. It hardly seems likely. Both Alice Cornell and Iris March were sad, desperate ladies, but Alice's desperation came from an addiction to alcohol, the one twentieth-century affliction that does not seem to have touched Iris. And since it was Kit's way of playing Iris not to have her drink at all, she can hardly have had her mother in mind. There is no indication that Alice Cornell ever indulged in Iris March's licentiousness or took lovers except in the most romantic way that it can be said Candida did. All in all, Candida fits so much more snugly the idealized picture of her mother that Kit liked to believe was the true one.

But it is certainly possible and more than likely that she found in the dark recesses of Iris's nature bits of herself, the parts, say, that she didn't want handed down to another generation when she decided to have her abortion, the parts that with Peter Cornell as a father she learned to hide and discipline and control. And seeing herself in Iris would be a secret identification, certainly an unacknowledged one, the kind that would lead to a denial of its existence along with an indulgence of it, all of which would give a tug to the performance, an introspective excitement, even a vague threat, a sinister quality which some critics noted.

Bankhead's identification was open, laid out, rather pulp magazine confessional. Lee Israel, in her biography *Miss Tallulah Bankhead*, writes that she took to wearing green offstage as well as on, an excess Iris March would have found in bad taste. Kit sometimes wore Iris's hat in public, but with a sense of the dramatic, always as an actress wearing her stage clothes, not as a woman assuming a new identity. When told that according to the new psychology Iris March had a death wish, Bankhead was delighted and decided she had one, too, chattering on about the early and violent end she would soon meet. Kit's only identification with Iris's death was a love of fast, powerful automobiles, but she knew she was too good a driver ever to smash into a tree, even if she wanted to.

What Kit would see reflected most clearly in Iris was her own capacity for obsessive love, a kind of love that seems to have been remote from Tallulah Bankhead's changeable nature, love that persists against and beyond all persuasion, that at its best is called enduring and noble and loyal but when life takes a bad turn wallows in itself, whines, demands, and destroys. And when Iris sank to the latter, Kit, understanding it well, played the former.

It was the quality of the identification, then, that made the difference between the two performances. That and the difference between the two women themselves. Iris Fenwick, née March, was a sophisticate. Tallulah Bankhead was a sophisticate. Katharine Cornell was not.

The Green Hat was famous for being a play about decency. In Act One, after Boy Fenwick's suicide, Napier asks Iris what she wants. She answers: "I want decency. . . . I don't mean your kind of decency. I'm not sure what kind of decency I do mean, but it's not your kind or your father's kind. The decency I mean has nothing to do with the playing fields of Eton, the battle of Waterloo or the Silent Navy . . . it has nothing to do with how to behave when people are watching you, but it has something to do with how to behave when no one is watching you. (With a cry:) That's what I want, Napier! The final, ultimate decency!" In the last scene after Napier has, to vindicate her, exposed her protective, gentlemanly lies about Boy Fenwick's "purity," he says, "Come, Iris, it's time to go." It is then that she delivers her requiem, which is also her resolution as a character: "Yes, it's time to go. You've taken from me the only gracious thing I ever did." Substitute the word "decent" for "gracious" and it becomes clear that her "It's time to go" means it is time to drive her Hispano-Suiza into the elm tree.

When Tallulah Bankhead, with a worldliness in her manner far more probable than Kit's, pleaded for the final, ultimate decency, an audience would understand it and go along with her. An admirable goal for such as she, the lost sophisticate. But they would not hold out much hope of her ever finding decency, and when she failed and died in her failure, an audience would nod and say yes, they had feared that would happen. But when Kit pleaded for decency, something in her as a woman, that quality everyone had been waiting to reach out to, that whatever it was she brought to the stage, would alert an audience to sit up in their seats and exclaim to themselves, "But she's already *got* it! How can she not see it? How can the others not see it! Why do they torture her!" Until the last moment of the play, then, there would be a growing incredulousness as they watched, an urgent hope that Iris and the other people in the play would discover what they, the audience, had known from the beginning, and when that didn't happen, when the world Iris lived in actually allowed her to die, then the hypocrisy and blindness of that world would be made more striking than Michael Arlen ever dreamed of making it with his verdant language, and the play's meaning would be brought home with theatrical impact.

Along with everyone else, Kit clucked over Michael Arlen's language, tolerated its lush excesses, and told funny stories about how it was gotten around. There was that line at the end of Act Two, for instance. It is the eve of Napier's wedding to Venice and Iris has turned up again in his life. After a long scene of verbal fencing, Napier asks his favorite question of Iris, the one he seems to ask at least once every act: "Iris, Iris, what do you want?" As written, Iris answers, "*You, baby!*", tosses her green hat on the sofa, and flicks out the light as the curtain falls. Faced with the danger of getting a big laugh at this tense moment in the play, Kit simply dropped the comma from the line, which then became a motherly "You *baby!*" as she flicked out the light. It is a good story, but in every published version of the play the line has become, "You, darling!" Either Arlen decided when the galleys came that he didn't want anyone else taking credit for saving his dialogue or Kit imagined a specific instance to illustrate a general problem. The censor in Philadelphia, incidentally, objected to having the woman turn out the light, and there followed a moralistic dialogue on who is put in a worse position by doing what. Kit, the ultimate authority on gentlemanly gallantry, won the right to throw the switch.

In Act One there is the most famous line of all. It is the morning after Boy Fenwick's death, Iris's first scene in the play, and she is pressed to explain why Boy died. Not wanting to reveal his horrible secret, but not wanting to lie (whatever else she is, Iris is not a liar!), she comes out with "Boy died for purity." Guthrie said it was the "wettest" line he had ever read or heard, but Kit just smiled as she said it, as if to say, "That's the worst nonsense I can think of, a catch-phrase that I know is bunky, and you know that I know and I know that you know — and yet there is God's truth in it."

There are still people around who saw *The Green Hat*, all of them well into middle age and some of them quite elderly — the boy who came in from the Chicago suburbs every Saturday to attend a matinee with his grandfather; the girl who had never seen a play and came to New York for a weekend from Bryn Mawr; the young actor, yet to do more than walk on in a play that lasted three nights, boldly gaining admittance "courtesy of the profession" — with all these and many more, when they remember *The Green Hat* the first image that comes to mind is a dark young woman with a white face and slashing red mouth lounging against a door frame, smiling a smile that bespeaks all living sorrow back to Eden, mouthing the words in a low, fluid voice, "Boy died for purity." They all remember that one wettest of all lines and get it word perfect after fifty years.

Her stories of surmounting the difficulties of these lines are amusing and instructive to young actors — the whole theory of turning disadvantages into advantages — but it is an oversimplification to imply that craft alone can enable an actor to so affect an audience. Clucking over Michael Arlen's garish language was a fashionable pose, and maybe Kit adopted it because she was embarrassed to admit that she liked the way he wrote and responded deeply to it. Only that would explain why she was able to give the words such validity on the stage. She was not an articulate woman when it came to her own strong emotions; she kept them very much to herself, perhaps because she did not want to risk hearing how they would sound. Although she read every book that came her way, she had literary taste — her favorite book that year and for several years to come was *The Magic Mountain*. But perhaps only she knew that if she ever spoke her own thoughts freely or gave utterance to her deepest emotions, they would come out sounding more like Michael Arlen than Thomas Mann.

———

The London production of *The Green Hat* was not scheduled to open until after the New York production, but the New York production stayed so long in Chicago that the two opened almost simultaneously and ran concurrently. Guthrie always adored Bankhead — they liked the same kind of marathon parties — but he was so incensed that another actress would dare play a role of Kit's while she was still playing it that as soon as her Iris was launched on Broadway, he hopped on a boat and crossed the Atlantic to take a look at the other one. After only the barest time necessary, logistically, he shot back a triumphant cablegram: " 'Hat' worse than I hoped."

———

Under the title *A Woman of Affairs*, *The Green Hat* was made into a movie with Greta Garbo in 1929. Perhaps because Garbo was a lone holdout against progress and insisted the film be silent, the producers felt she could pass for a young Britisher.

Michael Arlen was too polished in his ways ever to state an open preference for one or the other of the three actresses who played Iris, but it can be inferred from what his son, Michael J. Arlen, writes that through the years his preference for Kit emerged by the simple process of elimination.

He was smart enough to know that *The Green Hat* was meretricious, but he was also smart enough to know that it was a "hell of a book," and he was smart enough to know that although Iris had all the ear-marks of a slick romantic heroine, there was a great deal more to her, which was how she got written in the first place. Bankhead managed to be less than was written, and the fact that he was never able to care for her in anything else she ever did would indicate that he did not care for her as Iris. The motion picture production got snarled up in studio politics, and he always dismissed it as a cipher, apparently including in that evaluation Garbo's performance.

But he was always open in his gratitude to Kit, or being the kind of man he was, perhaps "honored" is a better word: he was honored by her appearance in the play. He had in a sense made his name with the book just as in a sense she made her name with the play, and he felt a gentlemanly kinship in that coinciding of youthful ambitions. But more than that, she brought the *more* to the part that he knew was there. Perhaps it was one of the sadnesses of his life that he was a man who respected quality.

———

When Kit's first stage green hat wore out, it was ritualistically pre-sented to the Actors' Club as a display relic. During the long run of the play she wore two hats at every performance, which were raffled off when she was through with them. They were cheap felt, a screaming yellow-green that carried perfectly under the stage lights but had to be softened for the more than two hundred thousand commercial copies sold to women in stores across the country. Kit kept the original Riboux model for herself and eventually had it dyed black.

Just before the New York opening of *The Green Hat*, Kit's elegant Jamaican theatre maid, Eveline, married Leslie Howard's dresser, Arthur Drysdale. To honor Kit and Guthrie, they chose September 8 for their wedding day. In the next thirty-four years, Eveline Drysdale served only two other actresses briefly in the 1950s — Ruth Gordon and Kim Stanley. She retired when Kit retired and outlived her by a year.

In Guthrie's romantic pursuit of aging actresses out of the past (Margalo Gillmore still refers to him as "Bring-'em-Back-Alive Mc-Clintic"), he was persuaded by Al Woods, after *The Green Hat* settled into its run, to take on one of David Belasco's old girls, Mrs. Leslie Carter, in a play written for her by John Colton, *The Shanghai Gesture.* When Mrs. C. (as she informed Guthrie Mr. Dave used to call her) turned out to be uncooperative, unmanageable, unpleasant, unpopular, and worst of all, untalented, Guthrie proved himself to be more a director than a romantic by persuading her to leave the company (whereupon she demanded and got a large share of the poor author's royalties); he recast a younger actress, Florence Reed, in the part of Mother Goddam, which made her famous. He then reshaped the play, cut it, tightened it and brought it into New York in February 1926, a colorful, surprise hit. It was a repeat of the *Bill of Divorcement* and *Dover Road* combination — with *The Green Hat* and *The Shanghai Gesture* running simultaneously, Kit and Guthrie were the two most talked-about people in the theatre.

After twenty-nine weeks and two hundred and thirty-one performances, *The Green Hat* went to Boston for eight weeks and then closed down for the summer. In the fall it set out on a cross-country tour, beginning at the Majestic Theatre in Brooklyn, where *The Man Who Came Back* had waited out the flu epidemic of 1919. Here Al Woods starred Katharine Cornell for the first time, billing her name above the title in the program and outside the theatre. The Majestic marquee was too narrow to take her full name, which in a way was fortunate, because the electrician was forced to stop while he was still winning, with "KATH CORNELL IN . . ." If he had been able to fit in the rest of it, he undoubtedly would have misspelled it.

Aunt Lydia Cornell took her two nephews, Douglas's sons John, aged thirteen, and Douglas, aged eleven, to Atlantic City to see Kit on the stage for the first time. Although the play didn't mean much to them, they never forgot seeing their cousin's name spelled out in electric light bulbs over the theatre. And across the country, as far west as Saint

Louis and Kansas City, that name was suddenly recognizable and people bought tickets because of it.

Kit was the only one who was not impressed. Being a star meant responsibility, and responsibility meant work.

Which began immediately. It was the third season for the sets and furniture, and much of it was beginning to show strain. At the end of the play when Napier hears that Iris has driven her car into a tree, he cries, "It must have been an accident!", and sinks into a chair. On one particular night the chair collapsed and he sprawled to the floor. The actors momentarily gave way to laughter and the audience joined them. They quickly got hold of themselves and the audience quieted down to hear Venice's next line, "It wasn't an accident." Her final speech, "The only accident that ever happened to Iris was to be born into this world," and her pleading with Napier that they must be together now, they must not hate each other, all that was barely spoken and completely unheard as the curtain came down to the wildest laughter since *Getting Gertie's Garter*. A leading lady could walk away from it, leave it to someone else, go to her dressing room and wait in haughty indignation to be told what had been done about it. A star had to deal with the stage manager on the spot, and if necessary, the management. It didn't matter that an audience loves to see actors break up and more than anything loves a good pratfall; whether they knew it or not and whether they liked it or not, they had been cheated, and that was not allowed in any Cornell company that ever existed. Not if it meant going onstage herself before each performance and testing all the chairs.

———

When *The Dover Road* closed, a large, cumbersome, overstuffed chair from the set was moved to 23 Beekman Place and a precedent was established. From then on, the house became a sort of domestic museum of two long careers, and the rooms took on a comfortable theatricality that tempered the austerity of high ceilings, ormolu, and symmetrical arches. In prosperous times new and expensive pieces would be added, but before long they would be sent off like theatrical children to work in the stage set of this play or that, returning a little faded and nicked (the degree depending on the success of the show) and exuding frayed professionalism.

The piano in those rooms was selected by Deems Taylor, and on it George Gershwin played his newly composed "Rhapsody in Blue," which had its premier performance at the Aeolian Hall just two weeks after the opening of *The Way Things Happen*. Kit, along with her other gifts, was a talented whistler; she warbled the obbligato to Gershwin's playing of "The Man I Love" before the public knew there was such a song. That hot piano player Noël Coward played and sang his favorite repertoire, always ending with Guthrie's favorite, "Parisien Pierot," and later on Ethel Waters would sing all night to please Dr. Cornell, who was a frequent visitor and participant in his daughter's success.

Sometimes at a party Kit would go into a time step with Clifton Webb, who opened with Marilyn Miller — and Esther Howard, Kit's old sidekick from *The Man Who Came Back*, whom Guthrie came to love as much as Kit did — in *Sunny* a few weeks after *The Green Hat*. Webb was on his way to becoming a darling of both New York and London. Many considered him to be the most graceful of living performers, and since Kit was generally thought to be the shyest, it at first seems odd that she would take him on in dance, his specialty, even in fun. Except that Webb was also as witty as he was graceful, and Kit was never completely at ease with witty people, thinking herself incapable of keeping up with them. She probably danced with Webb because with darlings of the day it was easier to be clownish than clever.

There was always a discomfort in crowds of bright, terribly talented people, and since Guthrie felt no such reticence, more and more Kit sought the company of one friend at a time, a woman usually a little younger and, if of the theatre, not of the quick witty calibre of Clifton Webb or Noël Coward. These friendships could be formed by the unlikeliest of circumstances.

While Kit was playing Iris in Chicago, for example, it happened that Mildred Oppenheimer in New York fell in love with a man who was in the throes of getting divorced from her best friend, and her conventional old New York mother thought she ought to get out of town until things quieted down. It was the kind of situation in which Kit loved to be of use, and Mildred was packed off to Chicago. When the divorce was settled, it was all right for Mildred to return to New York, but by then the newly freed ex-husband had gone to Rochester to open a stock company, and since his feelings toward Mildred were as yet unknown, Kit used all her persuasion to make her friend promise not to stop over in Rochester. Not on moral grounds (although Kit believed

Katharine Cornell with her father at a McClintic opening in the thirties.

Guthrie McClintic and Katharine Cornell in 1926.

in convention), but in common sense. Inclined to strong emotions herself, she understood them and was able, at times, to be unemotional about them in others. Mildred acquiesced and went straight to New York and mother, and it must have been the right thing to do because the next year she married the man of her choice, and in 1976 they celebrated their golden wedding anniversary.

It was the kind of role Kit liked to play in someone else's life, but what she really liked and liked most of all was having someone else in the suite at the Drake Hotel in Chicago, sitting out the long run of the play with her. Sometimes, when all others disappeared, she would have Eveline Drysdale, her theatre maid, come in for meals to sit across the table. Not that she was able to eat that regularly or properly. Mildred Oppenheimer Knopf recalls that during her tenure at the Drake, they would come in from an afternoon of shopping or visiting, and at about five-thirty Kit would say they had better order dinner. She liked things like roast beef or meatballs, custard, baked potato — but by the time dinner arrived at six, she would be lying flat out on the bed, pea green with nerves about the evening's performance, unable to do more than pick at her food. No friend or companion, not Eveline, not Guthrie, not even experience was ever able to cure her pre-performance stage fright.

The Green Hat had such an extended pre-Broadway stay in Chicago that there began to be cast changes as actors became restless and moved on to other jobs. When the lady's maid in Act One departed, Guthrie immediately sent out Anne Tonetti from the New York company of *Mrs. Partridge Presents* in which she held a rather tenuous position anyway, playing a character not written into the script, an offstage French woman talked about onstage at great length and finally greeted by Blanche Bates at the very end, letting loose a flow of French from the wings as the curtain came down. Anne, a 1921 graduate of Miss Chapin's School, made up her own offstage French, which impressed Guthrie enormously, and when the lady's maid left *The Green Hat* in Chicago, he decided no one but Anne could replace her — it was a maid in a French hotel, wasn't it? a hotel in Deauville? and didn't Anne speak French like a native? It mattered not that the maid in the play spoke only English as she gave out opening-scene exposition. What did matter was that Anne Tonetti, who came into their lives through Walter Abel and Lewis Beach when Guthrie produced *A Square Peg* two years before, was a favorite friend of Kit's, who at last had someone to sit across the table and play golf with her at the challenging course in Winnetka. Anne was even loyal enough to take tennis lessons at the Racquet Club, but had to stop for lack of talent.

After the mid-July closing in Chicago, in the weeks before the Broadway opening on September 15, 1925, Kit drove Anne and Guthrie to New York the long way around through Canada, with Guthrie hanging out the car window bestowing obscenities upon the natives much as Marie Antoinette must have called from her carriage, "Let 'em eat cake!" and Nell Gwynn from hers, "I'm the Protestant whore!"

In the New York run of *The Green Hat* Anne played one of the two nuns in the much trafficked third act, the ones who bring Iris from her sickroom to see Napier and then maneuver her back again. The other nun was playing it ethereal and beautiful, and Kit, who could be wily on the behalf of others and protective of those she loved, coached Anne to play her nun old and plain with glasses and sore feet. After the first run-through in which Anne appeared onstage in her makeup, she asked if Kit had recognized her, and Kit said only by the end of her nose.

Anne had a pleasing career as an actress, among other things playing in one of Guthrie's revivals of *Saturday's Children* with Ruth Gordon and Humphrey Bogart, but after a few years she found that her true interests lay in other directions, in real estate and interior decoration, like her mother "providing and making different homes." But she earned a place in theatre history if only for being the one to introduce Katharine Cornell to Mae West. Anne was once in a show with Miss West, who liked the other girls in her cast to be sweet and pretty, and several years later Anne took Kit backstage at another show for the improbable meeting. Kit was open and honest, telling Miss West how much she enjoyed her performance and how much she admired her art, to which Miss West replied, after chewing her thoughts for a moment, "Thanks, honey. Hope I can say the same about you some-time."

After twenty-nine weeks in New York and eight in Boston, *The Green Hat* closed for the summer of 1926 and Kit, Anne and Guthrie sailed on the *Laconia* for Europe early in June. Kit wore Iris March's hat for the embarkation, and since it gave Emma Jones an opportunity of visiting the Mother Church, she came up to Boston to see them off.

14

Gert (1926-1928)

FIVE GIRLS — three Macys, Gertrude (Gert), Louise (Louie), and Mary Lloyd (Min); and two Brookses, Mary and Ruth — leaned over the railing of the *Laconia* in Boston Harbor to see who was getting on board. Ranging in age from sixteen (Min) to almost twenty-two (Gert), they were off for a summer in Europe, the first for each of them, with a chaperone, Miss Gerecke. It was Miss Gerecke's life work, at least in summer, to escort young ladies abroad and expose them to Old World culture for an honorarium of one thousand dollars, in addition to all expenses. The Brooks girls' mother felt it was time her daughters saw something of the world and knew from Miss Gerecke's fine reputation in boarding school circles that she was worth every penny she commanded, but still, five hundred dollars per daughter seemed a little steep. Since Mary Brooks and Louise Macy had been best friends and roommates at Smith, Mrs. Brooks suggested that the Brookses and the Macys band together, bringing Miss Gerecke's fee down to two hundred dollars per girl. The Macys had no parents, so Gert made all their decisions and even at that age knew a good business arrangement when she saw one. She persuaded the trustees at their bank in Pasadena that the trip was educational, bought the tickets, negotiated a passport (one for the three of them), and convoyed her underage charges across the country to join up with the Brookses.

The *Laconia* sailed at five o'clock in the afternoon from New York and stopped to pick up more passengers in Boston. With Miss Gerecke tucked away below, the girls hung over the rail and when Gert nudged

Louie, "There's Iris March!", the word spread along the first-class deck. In the untheatrical glare of the night lights on the pier, there indeed was Iris March, thin and fascinating, her head tilted back just enough to reveal that wide, recognizable face with the well-known deep eyes peering out from under the brim of the famous green hat. She was being clung to and almost prevented from embarking by a colored woman who kept her arms around her with her head on her shoulder, hugging her all the way up the gangplank, crooning "Shug," impeding progress and creating a hazard while "Shug," not wanting to slough her off, persisted in inching herself forward. "Hon" McClintic seemed sedate by comparison as he and a proper Anne Tonetti led the strange procession onto the deck while Emma Jones, invoking harmony for all, returned to land with a wave, and one wonders if the enthralled passengers ever realized that this emotional scene was nothing more than an affectionate farewell between an actress and her cook.

For the girls, the voyage out was a success and they hadn't even left the United States yet. Gert Macy had actually seen *The Green Hat* and could pass on the experience to the others. She had just left Bryn Mawr, a physics major with no special interest in theatre except for significant reactions on several occasions as an audience member. While an undergraduate she had been bowled over by Emily Stevens in *Fata Morgana*, a performance that was surpassed for her when Jeanne Eagels came to Philadelphia in *Rain*. For all her composed, businesslike ways, she was reacting emotionally to the theatre; she was certain that Jeanne Eagels could never be supplanted in her heart. Then she went to New York with a friend one weekend in her senior year. Sitting in the balcony of the Broadhurst Theatre she saw an intense woman with the saddest of all smiles appear in a doorway and say, "Boy died for purity." From then on, for Gert, Katharine Cornell replaced Jeanne Eagels.

The five girls were in their deck chairs early the next morning, but Iris March did not pass by; she did not appear all day, nor did the man she was traveling with, or the young woman. Miss Gerecke insisted that well-brought-up girls went in to the early sitting. As they were leaving the dining room, Iris March and her party were entering for the late sitting, and the girls were disgusted when some people rushed up to say they had seen *The Green Hat* and would Miss Cornell please sign their menus. The girls made a pact that they would not do that; they would be the only passengers on the boat not to make boors of themselves just because she was a famous actress. They could hardly wait for her to show up on deck or in the lounge so that they could prove their restraint, and starting the next morning they had plenty of opportunity as Kit strode around the deck for exercise, sometimes with Guthrie before dinner or with Anne before lunch, and the Macys and the Brookses kept their promise to themselves by not even smiling lest they be thought pushy and forward.

About five days into the ten-day trip Gert felt queasy at dinner and excused herself to sit in the bar with her book while the others finished their dessert. She took a big round wooden table so that there would be room for her friends when they joined her. Then the McClintics and Anne Tonetti were there in the bar for a drink before dinner and Guthrie was asking if they might sit with her, being charming and funny while Kit smiled and Anne Tonetti didn't say much.

When Louie and Min and the Brookses came up from dinner they were shocked to see that Gert had broken their pact and bagged the entire lot for herself; looking the other way in embarrassment, they went to sit as far away as possible at the other end of the bar.

Starting the next day it became part of her routine for Kit to pause in her walk around the deck to sit on the edge of a deck chair and talk to the girls. Guthrie had all the effusive charm but Kit was the one who made friends. She would lend Louie her green hat so that she could go to the ship's masquerade as Iris March, and Louie certainly didn't mention the Pierrot costume she had packed in her trunk for that purpose. On the last day Kit said she and Anne and Guthrie would be staying at Browns' Hotel in London; she hoped the girls would come to tea one afternoon. They blushed to mention the old ladies' Hotel Goring Miss Gerecke had booked them into, and clamored how much they would love to call, which of course they never had the courage to do.

Unwittingly they put poor Guthrie to shame when the boat docked at Liverpool and they were seen to step into the seven-passenger Rolls-Royce Miss Gerecke had engaged to whisk herself and her charges to London. But if they had outdone him in elegance, that only made him all the quicker to spot them some days later in the Tate Gallery. The girls couldn't get over being recognized. Guthrie said they would always be remembered because they were the only passengers on the *Laconia* who had not asked Kit to sign their menus. He insisted on taking them to tea.

But in spite of this effusive beginning, Gert would not see the Mc-

Clintics again until the winter of 1928, when Kit was playing in *The Letter.*

Spithead
Bermuda
July 25, 1927

Dear Miss Cornell,

Your letter reached me here a few days ago. It was particularly gratifying to hear that you and Mr. McClintic thought so well of *Strange Interlude* and I am anxious to have a talk with you both about it . . . because I have not yet lost *all* hope that you may be able to do it. I should hate to relinquish all hope of that because to my mind there is absolutely noone [sic] else who could touch what you would do with "Nina." . . .

Of course I know you are going to do *The Letter* and I am sure you will make a tremendous personal success of it, judging from what I know of the play and the part through English papers and periodicals. Also, because I like Maugham's work and liked him very much the one time I met him. I hope the play will score a hit — than which, under the circumstances, no gent could be more nobly unselfish! But if the Guild do *Strange Interlude* they will not do it until midseason or later, and by that time you might feel you needed to play a new part — and the Guild, I know, are strong for you to do *Interlude* and I am sure, if they thought there was any chance of his having that time off from the directorship of the Actors [Theatre], would be equally eager to have your husband direct it.

So, as I say, I still hope and I'll hope to have a talk with you both soon as I'm coming to town in about a week.

And even if this hope comes to nothing, I'll still hope again that we'll get together on something else of mine before too long.

Mrs. O'Neill joins me in all the best to you both.

Cordially,
Eugene O'Neill

ACT ONE

It is a large square room in a house constructed for life in the tropics . . . across the entire back runs a verandah, separated from the room proper by heavy square posts with railings between. The time is about midnight. The room is softly lighted by the light from the two lamps on the desk and on the table. The lamp on the piano is not lighted, that end of the room being somewhat in shadow. Outside, seen across the verandah, the rattan shades or blinds of which are rolled to the top, is seen the deep blue light of the tropical moon. The direct rays of the moon shine in and glisten on the foliage of the verandah. There is heard the sound of a shot, and a woman's piercing scream, as the curtain rises, and Leslie Crosbie is discovered firing at Geoffrey Hammond who staggers up center and falls prone on the verandah. He clutches his heart, "Oh, my God!" Leslie follows him and fires again as he makes a feeble attempt to rise. As he sinks back she empties her revolver into his body as he lies on the floor, continuing to click the trigger several times before she realizes the gun is empty. She looks at his body for a moment with a look of horror, then staggers uncertainly to the table, and with her other hand almost tears the empty revolver from her grasp and puts it on the table. She tries to pull herself together with suppressed sobs and shudders . . . there is heard the excited jabbering of the Chinese Houseboys as they enter by the steps on the verandah. . . .

So begins *The Letter*, the play Kit chose in preference to *Strange Interlude*. Somerset Maugham suggested her for Leslie Crosbie, although he had never seen her act, saying only, "The lady knows how to shoot." Nobody ever knew what he meant by that, least of all Kit, but apparently it meant something to producer Messmore Kendall who pursued her throughout her 1926–1927 tour of *The Green Hat* until she decided to accept. Such is the quick progression that leads to typecasting: it was but a step from Iris March, the lost lady who took lovers, to Leslie Crosbie, the lost lady who *shot* a lover.

Remembering how Kit's commitment to *Casanova* prevented her from being considered for *Saint Joan*, one could easily shake one's head over her choice of *The Letter*, but it would be unfair. Besides writing a straight, down-the-line actable play, Maugham told a suspenseful theatrical story.

The unfashionable fact is that he was a better craftsman than O'Neill or even Michael Arlen and was certainly more precise and judicious in his use of words than either. Having just come from *The Green Hat* and faced with *Strange Interlude*, it is quite understandable the relief with which an actress would seize *The Letter*.

The press was unfavorable. But by this time Kit had an audience of her own. They kept *The Letter* going for thirteen weeks and actually created a sensation on opening night, blocking traffic outside the Morosco Theatre on Forty-fifth Street until after midnight. It had been so long since such homage had been paid to a star along Broadway that Ward Morehouse reported it as a news item in the *New York Sun*, saying that a full hour passed after the curtain fell before "Miss Cornell came through the stage door and started up the alleyway to the street. The sidewalk was packed, packed with people who had seen the opening and people who hadn't but who stuck to the theatre front determined to get a glimpse, and by necessity a close one, of the troubled lady of Mr. Maugham's drama."

Gert Macy came back from her first trip abroad such a Francophile that she tried unsuccessfully to get a job with Brentano's that would use her knowledge of the French language. Then, not knowing what to do with her life, she drifted back to southern California where she took up real estate and insurance and became her own best customer, selling herself a policy that in ten years would yield her ten thousand dollars with which she intended to buy a Rolls-Royce. Such were her serious plans for the future.

On one of her visits to New York she was invited out for the evening by an old friend of her father's, a doctor from Pasadena. He asked what play she would like to see and she said *The Letter*. At the theatre she scribbled a note on her program and sent it backstage with an usher asking if Miss Cornell remembered her and could she come backstage with her escort to say hello at the second-act intermission. The answer came back that Miss Cornell never saw anyone during intermissions but would be glad to receive Miss Macy and her escort at the end of the performance, just come to the stage door. It was a pleasant reunion and Gert was surprised at how much Kit remembered about the Macys and the Brookses and the good times they had on board ship, claiming they all knew one another far better than Gert would have dared to suggest. The doctor from Pasadena was of course smitten and asked Miss Cornell to go to a nightclub with them, which embarrassed Gert because she knew that serious actresses did not go out to nightclubs with strangers just because they came backstage and asked her to. She jumped into the breach saying she would be in town for a week or so and would Miss Cornell have lunch with her, and Miss Cornell explained that she had strange mealtimes when she was working, a late breakfast and a five o'clock dinner, and Gert suggested tea some afternoon and Miss Cornell said no, she never had tea . . .

Kit's social secretary that winter was a girl from Santa Barbara named Susie Hyde, who had been recommended to her by Anne Tonetti's mother, Marie, a seasonal resident of Santa Barbara. Kit always regarded Mrs. Tonetti as one of the important people in her life — in the theatre and out of it — relying on her, as on Laura Elliot, not so much for specific guidance as for sympathy and an example.

Marie Tonetti owned much of Sneden's Landing, a Palisades community on the west side of the Hudson in New York State, but she lived most of the time in New York City at 134 East Fortieth Street (where Susie Hyde stayed the winter of 1927–1928). One of her daughters had married a man in Santa Barbara, and Mrs. Tonetti was given perpetual use of the caretaker's cottage on his grounds, which she made beautiful with special attention to its garden. She usually traveled west for a visit in the spring.

During Anne Tonetti's years in the theatre, one of her great pleasures was to bring within her mother's sphere the exceptional people she knew and worked with, and Kit's was the happiest joining of them all. She had given the final performance of *The Letter* in Saint Louis in May, and exhausted from a five-month tour, she headed straight to Santa Barbara and Mrs. Tonetti.

Gert Macy, who spent every summer in Santa Barbara with her sisters, knew Susie Hyde. One day she looked up to see Susie coming down the steps to the beach with Anne Tonetti, Kit, and Guthrie. Guthrie said it was the kind of reunion that called for a drink, but Goddamn it, Mrs. Tonetti didn't have anything except medicinal sherry in the house and did Gert know a good bootlegger. Gert said yes. It so happened, however, that they had at their house a barrel of their father's prewar bourbon, which they had brought from their cellar in Pasadena thinking they might entertain this summer. There was mint growing outside the door of their house and cracked ice and why didn't everybody come that afternoon for mint juleps?

It became a daily ritual for which Gert gladly gave up tennis parties with people her own age.

———

Al Woods had wanted "Gunthrie" to direct Kit and Glenn Hunter in *Jealousy* by Louis Verneuil, a two-character melodrama complete with murder in the third act, but Kit was growing wary of plays and parts that demanded pyrotechnical displays of emotion. Besides, *Jeal-*

ousy had another European setting, this time Paris. Kit was so well suited to European plays in America, her voice being what one critic called "the American equivalent of what is the best the English can do with speech," that she had not appeared in a play with an American setting since *Nice People.* Turning down *Jealousy,* she bought Margaret Ayer Barnes's dramatization of Edith Wharton's Pulitzer Prize novel, *The Age of Innocence,* which Gilbert Miller had agreed to produce. Guthrie would direct. At least the character of Ellen Olenska was a native American, despite her European marriage, and the setting was New York. Valerie in *Jealousy* was given to Fay Bainter, and Kit was scheduled to sail for Paris in midsummer to be fitted by Worth for Mme. Olenska's clothes.

Then came word that Glenn Hunter had withdrawn from *Jealousy,* and Woods wanted to know if Guthrie would take over his part as well as the direction. The previous December Guthrie had directed Fay Bainter in Noël Coward's *Fallen Angels* (co-starring Estelle Winwood), and it was Miss Bainter who now wanted him to play opposite her in *Jealousy.* Who could resist? — certainly not Guthrie. The only difficulty was that he would be unable to accompany Kit to Paris and someone else would have to be found. It was becoming an accepted condition of life that she should never travel alone.

One afternoon over mint juleps Gert told them how she had traveled through Europe the year before without so much as a passport, and Guthrie pounced. With that kind of moxie she was just the one to look after Kit! And Gert said, "Give me a chance and I will."

The McClintics left for New York without anything having been settled, and Gert wondered if it had all been mint julep talk. But a telegram sent from the train at Kansas City said if she was serious they hoped to see her at midnight, August 4, aboard the *France.* That was Monday, giving her five days. She headed straight for Pasadena where she talked the trustees out of five hundred dollars for emergencies.

When word arrived that Gert was on her way, Simpson, the butler at 23 Beekman Place, remembers Kit wringing her hands in exasperation saying, "She's coming; — that girl is actually coming!" Perhaps she assumed that Gert wouldn't dream of accepting a casual invitation to go abroad and expected her to be grateful but politely decline. If so, she had not been paying very close attention, which is more likely.

The warmth of her welcome to Gert can be gauged by the caliber of ambassador dispatched to greet her as she got off the train. People were always met at trains in those days, but not always by Stanton Griffis, future United States ambassador to, at various times, Poland, Egypt, Argentina, and Spain, and a beau of Kit's in that he constantly professed love for her (despite a wife of sixteen years' tenure) and as a partner in the Stock Exchange firm of Hemphill, Noyes was trying to persuade her, unlike most beaux, to let him put his money where his heart was by backing her in plays of her own choice. In the meantime he ran errands for her and met trains.

Gert was probably even more impressed by Simpson, who opened the door. The first thing that always impressed visitors to 23 Beekman Place was the beauty and impeccability of the servants; even so, Simpson was something special. Dubbed "The Black Prince" by Emma Jones, he created the illusion that he had been designed by the architect to go with the house, although he had only come there ten months before, during the run of *The Letter*.

Guthrie's secretary, Jimmy Vincent, affected a businesslike air of welcome. He had turned in Guthrie's ticket to the French Line, informing them that a Miss Macy would want a round-trip ticket, but not knowing if she would want the same price ticket as Miss Cornell's (first class) or less, he had made an appointment for her to go there in the morning and make her own arrangements. Gert was rather taken aback, having understood that Guthrie would simply sign over his ticket to her, and here she was being asked to lay out money for her own ticket, which she could not afford.

She never regretted squandering her emergency money on a first-class ticket. In Paris there were meetings at Worth with Gilbert Miller. In London they stayed at Duke's Hotel in St. James's Street. There was lunch with G. B. Stern at her house in Suffolk; an overnight visit with Clemence Dane in Devon. Her house was very like a farm but not a farm, with no amenities, and at Winifred's instigation Gert found herself in the middle of the afternoon lying on her muddy stomach in a creek only inches deep, with her head so placed that she could nibble fresh watercress without using her hands. The twenty-four-year-old Bryn Mawr graduate from the beaches of Santa Barbara had never heard of anybody doing this, but she was learning about high life in theatrical-literary circles. Boarding the ship at Plymouth, they heard a cry from the next-to-top deck, "Kitty Cornell!", and when they sorted out the faces there was Clifton Webb and his mother Mabel and the trip home was an assured success.

They arrived in New York on a Wednesday, and immediately Kit had to dash up to New Haven where Guthrie was opening Thursday night for a split week in *Jealousy*. At 23 Beekman Place there were stacks of mail, telephone messages, accumulated bills, and deliveries, which she distractedly kept picking up and putting down again, creating chaos out of disorder, until Gert finally said, "Would you like me to take care of these things?" Kit welcomed the suggestion with relief, inviting Gert to stay in the house with Emma Jones and Simpson to look after her. She could see whoever she wanted and be leisurely about making plans for going back to California.

Gert got to work, religiously slicing open each envelope and marking its contents invitation, advertisement, bill, fan, personal, urgent, crank. On Friday Kit called from New Haven to say there had been applause at the opening and the play needed work and Guthrie was marvelous but she had several spots where she thought she could give him some good advice; why didn't Gert and Anne Tonetti drive up Saturday morning and see the matinee?

Gert had already said she hoped to get a job like Susie Hyde's. In New Haven she found a chance to tell Kit that among the letters she had opened was one from Susie in Santa Barbara saying she had been offered a job with Putnam and what she really wanted was to be with a publishing house. A few weeks later, on the first day of rehearsals for *The Age of Innocence,* Gert went to work for Katharine Cornell at a salary of twenty-five dollars a week.

———

Guthrie had agreed to play in *Jealousy* out of town before deciding whether or not to play in it in New York. He was satisfied with his work, saying he gave the performance that the part seemed to demand — "highly Continental in its rendition." No one agreed with him, but he would not change. Therefore he stepped out of the part and gave it to Richard Bird, Kit's erstwhile Marchbanks. When Bird had to withdraw, the part went to suave John Halliday, the most Continental of them all. Guthrie continued to direct, and the play was a success.

———

When Gert went to work for Kit she was completely unqualified for the job. She didn't know shorthand, she couldn't take any kind of dictation, she couldn't even type. But the job itself was rather undefined. She started out running errands and opening mail. Soon she was answering telephones, taking messages, relaying them, calling back and forth, making engagements and breaking them. Never too shy to say, "Would you like me to take care of this?" if she thought she could do it as well as or better than anyone else, she extended her duties even to picking out clothes for Kit as she used to do for her sisters, although it now meant trips to Hattie Carnegie. At 23 Beekman Place she found herself doing the marketing and checking the list with Emma Jones, paying the salaries and balancing the check books. Eventually she became what the theatre programs listed as "General Representative for Miss Cornell" which, in Kit's plainer language meant, "She runs the whole shooting match, as far as I am concerned." And cribbing from the Psalms: "May goodness and Macy follow me all the days of my life."

15

The Last of
the Tarnished Lady (1928-1930)

SET IN THE 1870s, *The Age of Innocence* tells of Ellen Mingott's return to New York's elite society as Countess Olenska after a disastrous European marriage. She has been removed too far from her old life ever to return to it submissively, but not far enough removed ever to be free of it. She falls in love with her cousin's conventional husband, Newland Archer, and he with her, but victims, both, of the tribal code, when she breaks their one assignation and returns to Europe, he does not follow.

While she was in Paris being fitted by Worth, Kit wanted to call on Edith Wharton, who spent her summers at Brice-sous-Foret, just twelve miles north of the city. But without Guthrie to push her she didn't have the courage, being afraid that she would not live up to the formidable author's image of the beautiful Ellen Olenska.

Mrs. Wharton was not altogether pleased with the dramatization of her novel. The difficulties were ironed out, however, and although she wasn't quite sure who Katharine Cornell was, her last visit to the United States having been in 1923, she was delighted with the play's success, her only other theatre venture having been a catastrophic production of *The House of Mirth* she herself had written with Clyde Fitch. Once the play was established at the Empire Theatre, Kit got up the courage to call on Edith Wharton's sister-in-law, Mrs. Cadwalader Jones, the closest she came to meeting Mrs. Wharton.

The Age of Innocence opened in Albany on November 8, 1928, and moved on to Pittsburgh for a week before opening at the Empire on

As Ellen Olenska in The Age of Innocence, *1928. (New York Public Library, Vandamm Collection)*

November 27, where it ran for twenty-six weeks, closing in June 1929. Guthrie was off in California doing "talking movies" and Kit went to a ranch in Yellowstone Park for a rest. In the fall *The Age of Innocence* toured for nine weeks, starting at Poli's in Washington, D.C., and ending at the Shubert Teck in Buffalo. In all that time its worst review came from Walter Winchell, who felt ennui setting in "ere the third episode unfolded," but that is really a compliment since it is hard to imagine Winchell sitting peaceably through even two scenes of a play in which the characters converse rather than assert. The other critics were so glad to see Kit not playing Leslie Crosbie that they couldn't contain their enthusiasm, and with the extravagance of the period clothes to delight them, the bustles and trains, the furs and velvets, the muffs and Parma violets, all so especially suited to her manner and bearing, and with her hair in bangs, they lost themselves in extolling her "dark, ivory-colored beauty that is almost Amerindian in its quality. Her dusky eyes have a stillness in them . . . the stillness of life so quick that the whole of a thought or a feeling can be expressed with the flicker of an eyelid." Such carrying-on by St. John Ervine, which continued for three more paragraphs in his *Daily World* review, made her uncomfortable, at moments actually unable to look in a mirror. It may have been at this time, covering embarrassment with a kind of bravado literalness, that she started saying that she did indeed have Indian blood, which came as a surprise to everyone, including her family.

On Gert's first day on the job she was introduced to Stanley Gilkey, a bright-looking fellow her own age who seemed so sure of himself and of what was going on that she decided to stick close to him and learn by observation. She soon realized that he was sticking close to her for the same reason, and it turned out to be his first day, too.

A Bostonian and a graduate of Harvard, Stanley Gilkey had spent his first year out of college in a Paris bank. When he returned to the United States, his old friend Mrs. Wolcott said what do you want to do with your life and he said he might be interested in the theatre. She sent him to Guthrie who interviewed him and then went off with Kit to talk about him. This was in the Lyceum Theatre where Stanley sat in a stage box waiting, while Kit and Guthrie were in a dressing room, unaware that he could hear every word of their utter lack of enthusiasm. They finally agreed they had to hire him because he had been sent by Mrs. Wolcott, and he came to work as assistant stage manager of *The Age of Innocence* with a small part and one line in the first act which never, during the entire run, was he able to make audible. (He perspired so much getting it out that he kept a blotter in his pocket to dry his upper lip before he went onstage.) Despite his inadequacy, he was so eager to succeed that he was kept on and eventually became to Guthrie what Gert was to Kit, his General Manager — and an important addition to the honor guard that was forming around Kit to escort her (and protect her) into the great years of her career.

With a friend from Pasadena Gert sublet an apartment (from Dorothy Parker) on East Fifty-fourth Street for a hundred dollars a month which she couldn't afford. Then the friend got fed up with New York and went home. Kit and a decorator friend Helen Irwin stormed R. H. Macy's (no relation) to fit up a place for Gert on the fifth floor at 23 Beekman Place, where she stayed for over a year, from late 1928 to 1930. The rent was generously within her means but it was a kind of dormitory existence.

With so few people living in the house it is astonishing that there could be so many different temperaments, schedules and modes of existence. Kit was all for coming straight home from the theatre, having something to eat, and going to bed, perhaps reading a while first. It was Guthrie's custom to leave a good bridge game to pick her up at the theatre, see her home, stay with her until she was asleep or settled down with her book, and then go back to his bridge game or step out on the town with his young men friends. Tallulah used to call him in the middle of the night and say, "For God's sake stop rubbing her back and get over here where the party is." When he was in rehearsal and kept more normal hours, he did not like sleeping in the dark and kept a light burning all night, or he prowled, and he insisted on a Spartan atmosphere for sleeping, with lots of cold air.

These divergent ways made it necessary for them to have separate bedrooms after the first five or six years of marriage. Kit kept the third floor and he moved up to the fourth where he had his sleeping cell and study.

Gert had to pass by and through all this ongoing life on her way from the front door to the fifth floor. She had her own key and tried to tiptoe past the stair landings, but there was always someone to hear her, someone to call out "Come in and talk!" Perhaps Kit wanted to be cued, or Guthrie would storm out of his quarters demanding to know what she meant by coming in so late, how did she expect to get any work done the next day?

And the top of the house finally reached, there was Simpson preening in his hall bedroom, straightening his hair, deciding which of his beautiful clothes to put on. For a time Emma Jones lived up there, too, wearing herself out to get up ahead of him so that she could say to Kit, see, your Black Prince is late again. Finally, for greater harmony, she moved to a place of her own in the neighborhood. Simpson was always a complete gentleman with his floormates, but he had such a complicated sex life, which today in his seventies he still delights to remember and to maintain, that he lived by the most erratic schedule of all.

One night Kit heard a noise on the stair outside her door and called out to Guthrie, or Gert, but it was Simpson, and she asked him to step inside and say hello. When he appeared in her door he was so resplendent that she couldn't help complimenting him and while she was at it, congratulating him on coming in so early for a change. He said he was not coming in, he was going out, and she asked where could he possibly be going at two o'clock in the morning and he said to a breakfast dance.

"What am I going to do with you, Simpson?" she said. "You're making money now and it doesn't cost you anything to live here, and yet you're not saving a cent." Banks only gave three- or three-and-a-half-percent interest on savings, and as an inducement she made an arrangement with him on the spot, refusing to let him go until he agreed, that whenever he put five dollars in the bank, she would add a dollar to it.

She always defended the servants to Guthrie, who came home once unexpectedly and found Simpson in his bathtub up to his neck in suds reading *The New Yorker*, and she always defended Guthrie to the servants. She was the considerate one, the peacemaker, the one who took everyone's side, smoothed the ruffled feathers and kept them all apart as much as possible, while Guthrie habitually brought home three or four extra people for dinner without warning and exploded at the dinner table, yelling at the servants in front of the guests and yelling at the guests in front of the servants.

And yet they found him an easier person to work for. Simpson loved Kit more than any woman, perhaps more than any person, and he was always polite and reverential with her, but he could gossip with Guthrie, and he did. Guthrie didn't mind being given the same meal two days running, in fact he didn't even notice, whereas Kit would send dishes back to the kitchen if they were not to her liking, even in the way they were arranged. Servants knew where they stood when Guthrie blew up at them, and he always forgot in the afternoon that he had blown up in the morning, and they found that easier to take than her austere, smiling, generously withheld criticism.

She always said she couldn't set one foot on stage without Eveline Drysdale, but for all her dependence on her servants and her concern for their welfare, she didn't really know them well or understand them. Had she been told how Simpson spent his money and time, she would not have believed it, waving aside tales of sexual derring-do with "Simpson likes to exaggerate!" It was that kind of benevolent innocence that endeared her to all who worked in her service and made them unwilling to let her down if it could be helped. Sometimes the stretch of keeping her buoyed up kept them on their toes too much for comfort. They felt more equal to Guthrie's kind of loftiness because they saw through it to his scruffier ways.

It was at the end of the pre-Broadway tour of *The Age of Innocence* that Gert moved up to the fifth floor. Expanding her duties to take a look at the household finances, she found that while Kit was wisely and grandly exhorting Simpson to thrift and planned saving, Emma Jones hadn't been paid her salary in weeks, not for want of money, especially, but because nobody had thought to do it. Not to face Kit with her delinquency until a system had been worked out, Gert herself paid Emma Jones who she then discovered had, in turn, been paying off various neighborhood merchants — not to face Kit with her delinquency.

One of the first letters Gert had to answer for Kit was from a fan deploring her Buffalo *r* and berating her for having come this far in her career without making an effort to lose it. Gert was critical of a fan who dared be critical of Kit, but as it turned out Kit was pleased to have her Buffalo *r* noticed since she was quite proud of it. At Mrs. Merrill's School she had studied speech (probably called "elocution" or "interpretation") with a man named Samuel Arthur King whose speciality was the importance of enunciating each consonant when two came together, such as the *n* and *d* in friend and the two *c*'s in eccentric, and who insisted that if you had a speech defect such as a Buffalo *r* you must perfect it rather than change it since you could only replace it with an affectation. Samuel Arthur King was well known in college circles and Gert had taken a course from him at Bryn Mawr. She began to feel more at ease in Kit's world.

Stanley Gilkey was undergoing similar indoctrination with Guthrie, with characteristic differences. Kit, for example, willingly gave Gert power of attorney whereas Guthrie lacked Kit's easy trust in people and never as long as he lived gave Stanley power of attorney, signing every check himself, no matter how small, up to his dying day.

———

Franchot Tone was the son of F. J. Tone of the Carborundum Company of America in Niagara Falls, and his maternal relations, the Franchots, were an old Buffalo family. He was attractive, soigné, and naturally talented as an actor, but it was as much out of consideration and respect for the Franchots that Kit gave him his first Broadway job in *The Age of Innocence*. In the last scene he played Newland Archer's son who visits the Countess Olenska in Paris twenty years after her affair with his father. It was a small part but one in which it was possible to make an impression, and he did.

During the run of the play he was asked to be best man at his Cornell roommate's wedding in Buffalo. For Franchot's benefit the ceremony was scheduled for a Monday afternoon so that he could catch the early morning train on Tuesday, bringing him back to New York late Tuesday afternoon, having missed only the Monday evening performance. The stage manager, Jimmy Vincent, could not give permission for him to miss a performance, that could only come from the star. Franchot was sure Miss Cornell would give the permission as she had given him his chance in the first place, out of esteem for an old Buffalo family. He was indeed surprised when instead the Buffalo girl give him a little lecture, saying how lucky he was to be on Broadway and how wonderful he was in the play, but if he intended to miss performances to keep social engagements, he had better choose another career.

He was sour-faced and disappointed when he left her dressing room, but he had no choice but to accept her refusal, especially since he was very serious about his career.

A month or so later Jimmy Vincent called Gert on a Monday morning to say Franchot had a touch of food poisoning. He had had the doctor but it didn't look as if he would be able to play that evening, and could Kit be at the theatre half an hour early to go through the third-act scene with the understudy. Kit was there with much solicitous inquiry about Franchot's condition, and the scene went well enough with the less-talented understudy.

The next morning Gert called Franchot's apartment to ask if he would be able to play that evening, and whoever answered the telephone said he thought Franchot was in Buffalo but would be back late that afternoon. When the too-recent best man arrived at the theatre that evening with powder on his face to make him look pale and ptomaine-stricken, the truth was apparent. Since the escapade was over and it would serve no purpose to tell Kit, Jimmy Vincent begged Gert not to tell her and she didn't, not until several years later when Franchot again became a subject of contention by abruptly leaving a play he was appearing in for Guthrie. Kit did not react in any way to the old story when she heard it. Perhaps she was relieved she had not known the truth at the time since it would have meant disciplining, perhaps firing, a young actor, which she always hated doing. Or maybe she did know at the time, maybe she had known all along and not let on — for the same reason. Responsibility brought contradictory emotions, and it did no good to let on what they were.

It was her third play as a full-fledged, above-the-title star, and her pre-performance stage fright had not let up, in fact had grown worse since it now included such a fear of getting sick that she was becoming a hypochondriac and such a fear of accidents that she was becoming, if fear can produce such a condition, accident prone. On the morning of the out-of-town opening of *The Age of Innocence* in Albany, she fell against a chair in her hotel room and fractured a rib (which she always preferred to say was broken), and by the time she reached her dressing room that night she was feeling so weak that for support she leaned against an object that turned out to be a hot pipe and seriously burned her arm. In her Worth clothes she stepped onto the stage that night taped together and smeared with Unguentine.

Guthrie was probably no help, since he would only remind her that things always happened in threes, and in this case he would have been right. The worst was yet to come.

In every city she ever played there were always local dignitaries and old family friends and zealous supporters of the arts all vying with one another to be her host, each assuring her complete privacy, etc., and independence to come and go. It was much more realistic and certainly preferable to stay at a hotel, and in years to come she reached the point where she wouldn't even stay with her father when she played Buffalo, but in 1929 she had not yet learned how to say no. When the post-Broadway tour of *The Age of Innocence* reached Cleveland, Ohio, she was the guest of Henry F. McIntosh, president of the Cleveland Trust Company and, as the *Plain-Dealer* reported it rather oddly, "this week accepts only informal invitations for luncheon."

It increased her uneasiness being so far from the theatre, and the McIntoshes and their four beautiful children put their Lincoln and their liveried chauffeur at her disposal for the long drive into the city each evening. She used to leave as early as six o'clock to give herself an hour in her dressing room, free from the rigors of gracious hospitality, and one evening she was riding along in the backseat and leaned forward to tell the chauffeur her door wasn't quite closed, it was rattling on its first hinge. The chauffeur stopped, got out and banged the door shut with her middle finger in the hinge. When he immediately jerked it open, her finger came out with the entire joint as flat as a nickel. There was no blood yet but her face went white and yellow and she said she was going to faint or be sick.

They were still twenty minutes from the theatre, but Gert had the chauffeur go to the nearest drugstore, where the druggist gave Kit aromatic spirits of ammonia and Gert telephoned back to Mrs. McIntosh to have her doctor or any good downtown doctor at the theatre in fifteen minutes. They converged on the theatre simultaneously, and the doctor took a look at the finger. A huge bubble was forming slowly but it had not burst yet, and he said for sure the middle joint had been crushed and she would not be able to play that night. Kit said she had to, it was their closing night and there would be no way to make up a missed performance to the Cleveland audiences. The pain was going up her arm into her elbow, and the doctor gave her an injection of novocaine in the middle of the arm. The finger was now like a black rubber bulb, but he couldn't lance it, saying there was going to be pressure but he wanted to see how far it would go or something of that kind — he did what he could and bound the finger and made an appointment to meet her at the hospital at eleven-thirty after the performance for X rays and further treatment. They would probably put a cast on it, which she thought would be all right since tomorrow was Sunday and a traveling day and she could probably have the cast off by the time they opened in Newark, New Jersey, on Monday. She refused to take a sedative for fear she wouldn't remember her lines, and she didn't want the audience to see her heavily bandaged finger, so she had Eveline tie a very thin yellow chiffon handkerchief the size of a scarf around the finger which she incorporated into Ellen Olenska's character.

There was only one difficult spot in the play involving her hands, a tête-à-tête with Arnold Korff in the second act, during which she served him tea. The tea could be eliminated with only a simple line change or two, but she would not hear of it, saying she couldn't possibly play the scene without serving the tea, so the stage butler brought it to her on cue while Korff, who was something of an elegant ham, thought to be helpful and hawked and sniffed and cleared his throat to take attention away from her, and she said a line of dialogue never imagined by Mrs. Wharton or Mrs. Barnes, "Do you mind if I serve your tea with my left hand?" and inflexibly right-handed as she was hefted the heavy, ornate silver teapot and poured with her left hand, keeping up the tea-talk intrigue of the plot, flicking the chiffon handkerchief aside to pick up the cup and saucer with her injured hand and pass them to her hawking, hemming, and spitting guest. The finger had been smashed at about six forty-five and this was nine-thirty, just time for shock and sickness to wear off and excruciating pain to set in, and backstage everyone was hanging on the prompt book in case she fainted or forgot where she was, but she did neither.

At the hospital they took X rays and found that three bones had been smashed. They put her finger in a plaster cast and gave her something to make her sleep.

The next day, bedded down and pampered in her train compartment, she sighed and winced and carried on, whispering for the second balcony to hear that she was in pain. In Gert's book no one kept insisting they were in pain; even if they were, that was for other people to figure out. Besides, she had seen Kit smilingly lift that teapot onstage and had little sympathy to offer, saying she could be wonderful enough when she had to be, and Kit sighed that she didn't have to be wonderful now, that there was nothing to be brave about in this train compartment and she was in terrible pain and went on proclaiming her pain all through Newark and up to Boston — except when she stepped onto the stage each evening to embody the serenity of Ellen Olenska. Mme. Olenska had taken on a lighter air with the attractive, ever-present chiffon scarf she now carried, waved, and couldn't do without. Countess Olenska simply had no time for anything as unimportant as a broken finger.

———

Ned Sheldon, debonair Edward Sheldon, was one of the brightest young playwrights to come out of Baker's class at Harvard. His Signora Vanucci in *Romance* had been Kit's first success with the Jessie Bonstelle Stock Company.

In 1915, when he was twenty-nine, Sheldon began to feel a stiffness in his joints, and by 1921 he was permanently crippled with progressive arthritis. Since he could not go to the theatre, his friends brought the theatre to him in the form of visits, readings, and news. It became a kind of official acceptance in the profession for a talented young person to be taken to meet Ned Sheldon in his sun-flooded penthouse on East Eighty-fourth Street. And no one ever came away from an hour in his presence without feeling that life had been enriched.

Woollcott took Kit to meet him after her success in *A Bill Of Divorcement*. Sheldon was never to see her on a stage, but he sensed at once in her the unusual combination of intense emotionalism and perceptive intelligence. That, along with her striking appearance, convinced him of her potentiality as an extraordinary actress.

He was still in a wheelchair at that time. It wasn't long before he was completely paralyzed from the neck down; eventually he could not even turn his head. His biographer, Eric Wollencott Barnes, writes that "by 1930 Sheldon's body was fixed in the rigidly supine position, with the head slightly raised on the pillow, in which he would remain for the rest of his life." Then the disease reached the optic field and his vision began to dim. Unbearable attacks of iritis wrung from him the only expression of suffering he was ever known to make to another human being: he begged the doctor to take his eyes out.

He made his adjustment by himself, no one ever knew how, not even his mother, and lived sixteen years stretched out in his famed Aquarium Room, a beautiful Paisley shawl usually draped over the lower part of his body, receiving friends, giving his life to them with wit and insight; counseling them in his soft whispering voice, advising them, collaborating with them, solacing them, entertaining them, scolding them, and above all listening to them. Barnes writes it was a privilege and a joy to be invited to dine with Ned Sheldon. He himself never ate in anyone's presence because his orderly had to spoon-feed him, but his luncheon guest would be elegantly served by the couch where he lay dressed in a stylish "white turtleneck sweater or a gaily patterned pullover." If one were lucky enough to be invited for dinner, he would be in dinner jacket, complete with boutonniere. He maintained such an air of normality that visitors often found it difficult to imagine the true nature of his condition. In the words of one actress friend, "He seemed like a young man just lying down for a moment."

He communicated with the world outside his apartment by means of telegrams and gifts, and in 1926 when he heard that his childhood friend, Margaret Ayer, now married to Chicago attorney Cecil Barnes, was in New York for a serious spinal operation, he proceeded to surround her with his own "imaginative goodness." Eric Wollencott Barnes, Mrs. Barnes's son, writes that Sheldon sent her books, special foods served on exquisite china, broths and fruit juices, jams and jellies, and one day to brighten the ceiling she must stare at all day, he send "an enormous cluster of colored balloons."

To fill her time, Sheldon asked her to write a sentence about each of the people they had known as children, telling him what had happened to them in the meantime. He was so impressed with the result that he urged her to try writing a play, suggesting, to give her some place to start, a dramatization of *The Age of Innocence*. When he read her first act he cabled his friend Mrs. Wharton for the dramatic rights and proceeded to guide Margaret Ayer Barnes, now out of the hospital, through the endless drafts that eventually make a play. It was her first writing effort. Three years later she would win the Pulitzer Prize for her novel *Years of Grace*.

He resolutely denied any credit for *The Age of Innocence*, refusing even co-authorship. Then he and his newly created author embarked in open collaboration on a successful comedy for Jane Cowl. After that, to satisfy some urge in Ned, who was an avid student of famous murders, they constructed a lurid murder-melodrama based on the notorious Madeleine Smith affair in Glasgow, a play entitled *Dishonored Lady*, which they intended for Ethel Barrymore. But Miss Barrymore dallied, and Guthrie, himself an ardent collector of the Notable British Trials series, snatched *Dishonored Lady*, which he persuaded Gilbert Miller to co-produce with him for Kit. It opened February 4, 1930, at the Empire Theatre where it ran for sixteen weeks.

In Glasgow of 1857 Madeleine Smith, in order to marry a man of her own station, dispatched her French packing-clerk lover by feeding him prussic acid in cocoa, which she handed him through the iron grill-work protecting her street level bedroom window from the sidewalk.

Dishonored Lady is set in New York of 1930. Madeleine Cary, in order to marry a titled Englishman, puts strychnine in the coffee of her lover, an Argentinian cabaret singer.

The similarity between fact and fiction is slim, and there was certainly no need for the authors to "gratefully acknowledge their indebtedness to Madeleine Smith" in the publicity, unless that is all it was — publicity. The most distinctive aspect of the Madeleine Smith affair was the famous verdict "Not Proven," sending her back into the world guilty but free. Even that could not be carried over because it was a quirk of Scottish law, and in New York Madeleine Cary was declared innocent, which turned the whole story into a simple and uninteresting miscarriage of justice.

Considering the almost patrician background of the authors, the refinement of their taste, and the impeccable example of their own lives, it is surprising (or perhaps not) that they chose to exaggerate the sordidness of an already sufficiently sordid story. Madeleine Cary goes to her lover's apartment late at night, intending to put the poison in the midnight coffee she will make him. But even with murder on her mind, she is so physically aroused by his nearness that she decides to spend one more night with him, proclaiming herself "Madeleine Cary! Your mistress and your nigger!", and with the knowledge that "I am going to hell and I can't stop myself!" turns out the fire under the coffee to be reheated in the morning. Looming over her lover as he stretches out on a divan, she encourages him to toy with her lips as the lights fade on a scene that would seem innocuous (and perhaps funny) today but which was shockingly explicit for a theatrical season in which the police closed Mae West's *Pleasure Man* simply because some men appeared on stage in women's clothing. After Madeleine and her José have had their morning coffee (José thinks it tastes a little bitter, which she explains is because she had to heat it up), he suddenly sees the empty strychnine bottle and cries out — how could she do it after last night? She rips out the telephone cord and goes on her way, a job well done, neither she nor Guthrie forgetting the old trick of almost forgetting her identifiable evening cloak.

In another scene her lover banged her one on the jaw, rousing Walter

As Madeleine Cary in Dishonored Lady, *1930. (New York Public Library, Vandamm Collection)*

Winchell out of the lethargy he had fallen into during Scene Three of *The Age of Innocence*. "Never in the history of the theatre," he reported, all agog, "has an actress of such distinction permitted such an exciting scene. She actually allows a man to crack her a powerful wallop in the face!"

Not all the critics were as thrilled as Winchell. The play was called "fifth rate claptrap" and Madeleine Cary "undoubtedly the most unsympathetic part ever played by a star." But this time they didn't stop at taking swipes at the play, as they had with *The Letter*. Stark Young began his review "It is time to stop saying she gives a fine performance in a poor play," and then caught himself, as if afraid he might be too cutting about an actress and woman he admired, ending up lamely, "The least said the better." That was in the *New Republic*, but at the other end of the spectrum, *Vogue* was not so considerate, saying Miss Cornell "has tarnished the Empire's great prestige and her own."

Blame (or credit) for the sensational aspects of the play must go to Ned Sheldon, for Mrs. Barnes was, after all, his pupil, merely tagging along. Even Sheldon's mother didn't understand it. A dignified, wealthy woman of great charity and compassion who loved her son so much that she was able to stay out of his life, even in his invalid condition, she finished reading the play at three o'clock in the morning and felt compelled to break her own rule of noninterference to ask in an anguished letter why it had to be "the kind of play which makes it questionable it could escape the censor, that draws that awful kind of audience that associates your name with just daring themes and situations, that makes people of the better sort leave the theatre dreading to think of the mire of a mind shut away from so many things in life."

Eric Wollencroft Barnes points out that "what Mrs. Sheldon could not realize was that *Dishonored Lady* was as much a part of the *real* Ned Sheldon as *Salvation Nell* or *Romance*." And what the critics could not realize, then or later, was that Madeleine Cary and Iris March were as much a part of the real Katharine Cornell as Candida, Sydney Fairfield, and Joan of Arc. She couldn't have played them had they not been. *Vogue* ended its diatribe with the conclusion that she must have done the plays from *The Green Hat* through *Dishonored Lady* because "she prefers . . . to be blunt, trash of a violent kind." It was meant as a severe reproof, but stripped of its condescension, it is a simple statement of the truth. There was a part of her that indeed preferred trash of a violent kind. Her integrity as an artist was the only defense such a preference needed. Every performance had to be as much a revelation of herself as it was an interpretation of a role, and therefore her choice of roles and the way she played them offer great insights into her nature, greater perhaps than can be inferred from her gracious, smiling, always agreeable, and increasingly guarded behavior offstage. One must look at her performances as one looks at the output of a writer or a painter.

During the run of *The Age of Innocence* Stanley Gilkey had an appendicitis operation, which in those days meant three weeks in the hospital and a month recuperating at home. While he was out, Gert persuaded Guthrie and Kit to let her take over his job. It was good experience and at the time unusual work for a woman, and her gratitude almost undid her. It was a whim of Kit's not to memorize any message, letter, or telegram brought to her on stage as part of a scene but to read it aloud from the prop paper put into her hand. Gert did not know this, and when a telegram was delivered to Ellen Olenska at a crucial moment Kit almost read aloud to the breathless audience, "Dear Kit, I love my new job. I haven't made any mistakes yet. Love. Gert." It was the kind of thing that did not happen twice in a Cornell company, but when *Dishonored Lady* was put together, Gert was given the job of assistant stage manager.

Dishonored Lady was the dressiest modern play Kit had ever done, even dressier than *The Green Hat* since Iris March was an outcast of society and Madeleine Cary was still in. Gert enlisted the help of her sister Louie, who had graduated from Smith and gone to work for Hattie Carnegie, to see that Kit was properly turned out. Between them, they picked out eight Carnegie creations (only four were needed) and then brought in Hattie Carnegie herself, who also had some pertinent suggestions. They ended up with a wardrobe that surely made Madeleine Cary the most striking woman on the American stage that winter, appearing in such numbers as a brown lace evening dress with a brown velvet bow set square on the fanny, a *big* brown velvet bow. It was the kind of gear that nobody but a clothes horse would have worn off the stage, which was all right for Madeleine, and it was so chic that they knew Kit could get away with it with her angular figure, long legs, and a sensational play like *Dishonored Lady*. To spare her the physical tedium of endless standing, Gert took her place at all the fittings

("Would you like me to take care of this?") until the last one. Their shoulders were the same breadth, and Gert knew she was half an inch larger around the waist and Kit's hips were a bit thinner. In time she could even buy shoes for her, knowing exactly where they had to pinch to fit Kit's narrower foot.

Guthrie was not sure he trusted the Macy girls from Pasadena to dress his wife on the New York stage, especially since he always preferred her in drapes, velvets, braids, and long classic folds, and they put her, if they got the chance, in crisper modern lines. Kit, who was agreeable to what anyone said, reassured Guthrie, saying she would like to see herself wearing the things Gert and Louie had picked out. Nevertheless, when a movie agent told Guthrie that a designer named Omar Khayyam at Saks Fifth Avenue made the most beautiful clothes in New York, he marched Kit off to Saks, where Omar made her a cream-colored satin coat with wide fur bands around it and a slinky satin evening gown underneath for the scene in which Madeleine first seduces José from Argentina. It was the most glamorous get-up of all and the one everyone wanted to photograph, but Gert had the satisfaction of knowing that when the play closed, Kit kept the Carnegie dresses for her own wardrobe and wore them all the time, big brown velvet bow notwithstanding.

It was always a joke in certain quarters along Broadway that Guthrie was able to direct Kit so masterfully because secretly he wanted to play all her roles. Stripped of envy and sniggers, the joke becomes a respectable and quite understandable explanation for the almost mystical, certainly spiritual fusing of their talents. The bulk of their work was done alone, usually at home, not to hold up the other actors in rehearsal, it was said, but also — obviously — to permit less inhibited communication between them. It is impossible to know what each contributed because they both had the same purpose in mind, to make the role hers.

She took enthusiastically to the wide-ranging movement of Madeleine Cary's predatory sexuality, bringing her own dash of sultry athleticism to the way she stalked danger and degradation. The physical side of a role was always easiest for her, especially if it was hard. The property man on *Dishonored Lady* was a European who had made his way to New York with Bernhardt. He believed that no artist should ever be struck and begged Kit to let him synchronize the wallop José had to give her with a handclap offstage. But she would have none of it, wearing a special protective hat, learning to stand precisely the right way in exactly the right position, instructing Fortunio Bonanova, who played José, to let her have it full in the face. On opening night her emotional involvement was so high that she came off the stage in almost a blackout, wet to the skin, to be ministered to by Eveline Drysdale.

There are times when it seems that having something to overcome, especially a physical obstacle like a broken finger or a crashing left to the jaw, brought her to a new and higher level of consciousness on the stage, by which is meant removal from herself. Maybe that was where her pre-performance nerves came from; maybe they were a necessary hurdle for the transition. If the simple physical act of walking onto the stage could be made difficult enough, she was certain to arrive with a magnetic command that the audience would find irresistible. Which is what always happened. Once out of the shadows of the wings, she lost her shyness, her reserve left her, and nurtured by the stage lights as if they were a thousand suns she grew in stature to the six feet that would-be actresses in the audience always thought she was.

Once out there, nothing could faze her. There was the matinee of *Dishonored Lady* when a fire broke out somewhere in the theatre. It was in the second act, just as Madeleine's father, brother and English fiancé were cross-examining her about her relations with José from Argentina. Suddenly the smell of smoke invaded the auditorium. They tried to continue but the audience began to stir. It was the only time in her entire career that Kit stepped out of character during a performance. She went to the footlights and told the audience the ushers were searching for the cause of the smoke and if in the meantime anyone wished to leave the theatre, please do so but do so in an orderly fashion. She would stand exactly where she was until they were all safe outside on the sidewalk, and if on the way out anyone felt the slightest panic, please take the time to turn and look back, and "you will see me standing here waiting until *you* are safely out of the theatre." There she stood unmoving, and needless to say, nobody else moved. Who would have dared desert such a protector? When the small blaze was found in the ladies' room on the mezzanine, it was extinguished and Kit invited a fireman onto the stage to assure the audience everything was all right. Then the curtain went down for a moment and went up again on the rather anticlimactic murder.

The critics had a highly personal image of Katharine Cornell that *Dishonored Lady* did not measure up to. What shocked and angered them was not that it was fifth-rate claptrap or that it was beneath her or that it was badly written or that it was a waste of time, what shocked them was that she did it so well and with such relish. Had she been terrible and had a miserable time, they could have been tolerant, forgiving a mistake they would all then forget. But she dazzled them, she thrilled them, and they resented it because here was no mistake; to use *Vogue's* word, she had really tarnished the image. To rescue her and keep peace with their own values they expended hundreds of words in overlong reviews turning her into a kind of enigma, forsaking her Duse likeness for one more up to the minute. Richard Watts, Jr., spoke for them all when he said she "was by way of becoming the Greta Garbo of the stage. She possesses the same inscrutable sort of fascination, and there clings to her that same aura of glamour and romantic illusiveness, that identical and fascinating combination of the strange, the sinister and the beautiful. About her there is that indefinable touch of the decadent which, allied to a certain vague eeriness and a certain very poetic loveliness, results in the irresistible, half fabulous quality that her colleague of the screen offers to such a valiant degree."

There would be a big, almost audible sigh of relief the following season when she appeared in *The Barretts of Wimpole Street*, for there were no enigmas here, they didn't have to excuse her by saying she was like someone else. She was herself, Katharine Cornell, the Katharine Cornell they always knew she would one day be. And having launched herself on her great roles, she never again permitted herself, or was permitted, to indulge the tarnished side of the nature and talent. And had she ever tried, after Elizabeth Barrett, Juliet, and Saint Joan, the critics, and probably the public, would not have tolerated it. Twenty years later with one distinguished role after another to her credit, perhaps deserving a little fling, she dared to play Somerset Maugham's well-mannered, witty play *The Constant Wife*. Well-mannered or not, even Brooks Atkinson took severe exception to it, claiming "it was impossible to believe" that she "would leave her husband and fly to the passionate arms of a lover." This of erstwhile Iris March, Leslie Crosbie, and Madeleine Cary.

16

Love and Money (1930)

WHEN SHAW DESCRIBED HER as "a gorgeous dark lady from the cradle of the human race," Buffaloans were pleased to think he meant Buffalo. When she came home for the first time as a star, in *The Green Hat*, it was a great social occasion and they clamored for a speech on opening night.

"For years I have planned what I would say were I ever called upon to make a speech," she began. But here was an obstacle that only ego could hurdle, and she panicked, bowed, and hurried off the stage. To show her affection for her hometown she always walked slowly when she left her hotel, turning her head to smile at everyone on the street, missing no one, so they could feel close to her and be able to say when they got home that night, "Katharine Cornell smiled directly at me." She was claimed, acclaimed, greeted, bragged about, and sometimes she received letters that began:

Dear Katharine, the stage is supposed to be uplifting. It is about time that someone told you that the good you contribute toward uplifting the thoughts and minds of the American people is so damn infinitessimal that you couldn't find it with a big microscope. Are you so rotten yourself or so immoral that you have to play these detestable plays? Have you ever played a decent play? Don't you think enough of your good father either not to engage at all or to play in productions that will enable the poor man to look people squarely in the face? You positively are rotten to the core if we can interpret through your plays the actual emotions that prompt you to devote your time to their production. I know you well, as well as the majority of your Buffalo friends. That is why I am writing these lines to you. I am a friend. . . .

Friendly letters like that, unsigned, went unanswered, and Kit probably never even knew she had received them. In answering the others, the grateful admiring letters, Gert tried to recreate Kit's voice on paper, even establishing certain guidelines for her thinking and expression. As time went on, the letters sounded more and more like Kit, or it is possible that Kit sounded more and more like the letters. Sometimes at the end of a letter to an old friend or an admirer who had sent a gift, Kit would want to add something personal and below her signature would scribble, "Thanks for the book" without having bothered to read the body of the letter which was detailed gratitude for the same book, pointing out the parts she had especially enjoyed and explaining why. These letters would have to be done over, and Gert would ask her please to read what she was signing, but Kit rarely did.

Gert also took on Kit's personal correspondence with her "good father." Because he was so short, reaching up to the average solar plexus, "the poor man" may not have been able "to look people squarely in the face," but nevertheless he survived his daughter's success magnificently, head as high as he could get it, full of advice, and his only complaint, ever, was that her choice of plays was too deep or intellectual for his taste. When he went to see her plays, often preferring to slip in quietly unannounced, he usually fell asleep, which was preferable to his staying awake because then he would cough through all her quiet scenes. Drained, she would come off the stage and say, "Father is out there tonight."

Periodically, dutifully, Kit would think it was time she wrote to tell him thus-and-so, and Gert would write the letter for her to sign. But more often than not Gert would have the letter written before Kit thought of it, a long chatty letter beginning "Dear Father" and regaling him with all the latest news, written as Gert thought Kit would talk to her father, which Kit would sign without reading, saying she was sure it was all right.

By the late 1920s, when he was in his sixties, Dr. Cornell had given up theatre-managing under the pressure of his other business enterprises, which were extensive. He never lost the golden touch of his younger days, in fact with the years it became surer, lighter, apparently infallible. Once during the Depression he arrived in New York and found a taxi shortage at the railroad station. Always affable, he gladly shared a cab with another man and being a gentleman under all circumstances, he offered his card and was informed in return that his traveling companion's name was Bulova. When he turned out to be *the* Bulova, Dr. Cornell asked, to be cordial, "How's business?" Mr. Bulova said it was very depressed but that six months would see a twenty-point increase on the board. Dr. Cornell got out at the Yale Club or 23 Beekman Place or whatever his destination, paid his share of the meter charge, the next day bought a thousand shares of Bulova stock, and in six months reaped twenty thousand dollars from a ten-minute taxi ride.

He was a pioneer investor in outdoor advertising when it was a brand-new idea, but the greatest coup of his life came early in the 1920s.

An enterprising young man named John O'Shei went to work as an usher in one of Dr. Cornell's theatres. In Horatio Alger–like style he was so quick and bright that he soon rose to become treasurer of the Majestic. One day he told Dr. Cornell about an acquaintance who had an invention O'Shei thought worth developing, but he lacked the capital. Dr. Cornell was willing to take a chance for a few thousand dollars (no more) on the invention, which was an automatic windshield wiper to replace the hand-operated wipers then used in all automobiles. With Dr. Cornell's money O'Shei secured the rights to the contrivance and set out to exploit it, forming the Trico Products Corporation in a tiny machine shop in the back of a Buffalo warehouse. In no time the business was expanding to meet the demand of every automobile maker in the country except Ford, who in the meantime had developed another windshield wiper, but eventually O'Shei convinced even Ford that it would be cheaper to buy wipers from Trico. With the Ford contract he made a clean sweep of the automobile industry. In the 1930s the descendents of the inventor tried to claim he had been duped into surrendering his rights, but they had no case. From the start John O'Shei proved to be an honest, scrupulously fair business genius.

Like his daughter, Dr. Cornell had a talent for attracting the right people. Despite his expansive talk, he did not have much business sense, he had only sense enough to put his faith in people like John O'Shei. He didn't even have a mechanical sense, and it is not likely that he ever understood what he had invested in. In the 1930s Trico expanded into automatic door-lock mechanisms and other features, and at one point they were the first on the market with a windshield washer which Dr. Cornell called "Two Little Squirts." He was very proud to have this new convenience installed in his own car, and driving down Delaware Avenue in Buffalo one winter night he wanted to show it off to Guthrie. Snow was collecting on the windshield, so he pressed the magic button. It never occurred to him that ethyl alcohol had not been mixed with the water, and the Two Little Squirts immediately created a sheet of ice on the windshield which he couldn't possibly see through. The two men were on their way to an opening of Kit's at the Erlanger Theatre and couldn't dawdle. At the best of times Dr. Cornell was one of the worst, inching drivers on the road, and that night he drove the entire distance with his head out the window.

Needless to say, he thoroughly enjoyed being a rich man, establishing the Peter C. Cornell Foundation, eating the best foods, drinking the best wines, ordering his suits from the best tailors (and always, as if it were a religion, selecting the most undistinguished patterns and fabrics). He enjoyed dispensing gifts of Trico stock up to the precise limit allowable by law (without being taxed) to other members of the family, exacting from them solemn promises to hang on to it, which they were glad to do since it paid excellent dividends. Douglas Cornell was fast becoming too old for his age in service to the city, and Dr. Cornell expressed fears that he would be forced out of his job. With the increasing financial worry of two healthy growing boys, now of college age, and the burden of Peter, the mongoloid son, Douglas had nothing put aside, nothing but his small salary to get along on, and Dr. Cornell was always helping out (which gave him the right to criticize extravagances) and seeing to the boys' allowances. Lydia suffered from, among other things, hives and needed constant medical attention. Besides which, she had entrusted her business affairs to a dear friend, Mrs. Reese in New York, who had managed, in Dr. Cornell's words, "to make cats and dogs of them," seriously curtailing her income and making it hard for her to get along decently, which, in Lydia's world at Cobourg, meant keeping a cook and two maids. Dr. Cornell would expand on all these family difficulties in his letters to Kit and then end up, "Do not want to bother you with these financial matters as I am able to take care of them myself, thank God." Apparently he meant it, for when he discovered that unbeknownst to him Kit had made some gesture to her young cousins, he would get downright uppity: "You know I will have to have a talk with you about these things for it is not necessary for you to do lots of the things you do or figure to do. I am perfectly able to do these things and want to. You must not butt into my territory. In other words, play your own side of the fence and let me worry along with the family."

Thus, in late middle life the father of Katharine Cornell found yet another identity. Arriving in Cleveland to see his daughter in *Dishonored Lady*, he was referred to in the press as "the windshield-wiper magnate."

On her side of the fence there was always someone in need of help, from an old character actor in *The Age of Innocence* trying to buy a farm in the wilds of Canada to retire to with his wife, to Ethel Barrymore whose audiences were no longer attentive enough for her to afford a limousine and chauffeur waiting outside the Drake Hotel in Chicago to take her to the theatre. Because she had never experienced material need herself, Kit was not quick to sense it in others, not until it was pointed out to her by Guthrie who, because of his poor beginnings, was even quicker to spot it than Gert, who had an eagle eye for situations involving money — or the lack of it. Ministrations to the old character actor continued for years, costing hundreds of dollars more than had originally been intended, and when Gert told Kit this, blaming herself for not being a better adviser, Kit's only comment was, "Isn't it wonderful what we are doing for Mr. Tavernier." Mr. Tavernier and his wife never made it to their farm in Canada, and true to his promise he left it to Kit in his will, but by then it had to be sold for unpaid debts and there was almost nothing left. After quickly dispatching a thousand dollars to Ethel Barrymore for unbroken limousine services, Kit wanted to hear nothing more about it, saying how dreadful it was to grow old in the theatre. (Miss Barrymore was fifty and presently returned the money.)

In *The Age of Innocence* old Mrs. Mingott was played by an actress named Katherine Stewart who fitted to the letter Edith Wharton's description of the character: "The immense secretion of flesh had descended on her like a flood of lava on a doomed city, changing her into something as vast and august as a natural phenomenon." When the play's run ended — and the tour — the stock market crash was cutting back theatrical activity. At best there were not many roles for an actress of Katherine Stewart's peculiar dimensions. She was growing old. She was diabetic and needed insulin shots. It was important that she keep money coming in.

She maintained an alcove bedroom (a sitting room with a bed in an alcove) at the St. James Hotel for thirty-four years, and there the enormous old lady waited among her things, a taffeta doll over the telephone and an old gold basket filled with imitation flowers on the table. She was well read, boringly so, even for Guthrie, with whom she delighted in having long literary discussions that gave him very little chance to say anything. She was very proud and very honorable and would get dressed up in gloves and a feather boa to go to the bank and meet the vice-president with the three dollars and thirty cents interest she owed on a loan, or to explain why she didn't have the three dollars and thirty cents. Kit was her co-signer many times on Morris Plan notes, a plan whereby one could be lent, on the spot, a thousand dollars to be paid back one hundred dollars a month for twelve months. When the money was needed right away, the interest rate did not seem so exorbitant and that nine hundred dollars (the first month's payment having been taken out) looked awfully good. The worst credentials were accepted because there had to be two co-signers who were in jobs and good for the money. Kit invariably ended up paying off Katherine Stewart's notes.

Kit had reached the point in her career where it was no longer possible for her personally to read all the play scripts being submitted to her, and while she was playing in *Dishonored Lady* it occurred to her that it would give a little income to Katherine Stewart to engage her as a reader at five dollars a script. Miss Stewart, who in the 1890s, it was rumored, had had an affair with a mittel-European Grand Duke, was delighted once she was convinced it was a literary task and not a menial one. She began waddling through the stacks of manuscripts, ably sorting, separating, discarding, setting aside, and summarizing them for Gert, who screened the results and according to the new system passed on only the best to Kit.

For months there was nothing at all to pass on. *Dishonored Lady* closed at the Empire, and Kit and Gert planned a boat trip through the Panama Canal to join Guthrie in California, where he was directing Ruth Chatterton in a movie. Kit was counting on the boat trip to rest up for her first appearance on the west coast (in *Dishonored Lady*). Just before sailing a messenger arrived with a parcel from Katherine Stewart, a manuscript, and a message saying please read at once. The script had the stamp of the author's agent rather than a producer, which meant that all the producers in New York had probably read it and turned it down, and a glance at the title and cast of characters explained all too well, all too boringly well, why Katherine Stewart would consider it wonderful enough to intrude it into their long-anticipated vacation — it was of all things a *literary* play. Someone had had the patience to write a play, and a long one, too, about Elizabeth Barrett and Robert Browning.

Kit read it and then couldn't wait for Gert to read it, and then could hardly wait for the boat to dock at Panama City to have Gert send a wire to the author's agent in New York securing the rights to *The Barretts of Wimpole Street*, by Rudolf Besier. It was too bad Katherine Stewart couldn't have found a play with a nice fat part for a nice fat old lady, but the five hundred dollars Kit later gave her as a finder's fee gave her independence from the Morris Plan for a while at least.

In June of 1930, four months after *Dishonored Lady* opened in New York, Mrs. Belloc-Lowndes, sister of Hilaire Belloc and author of superior horror stories, published a novel also based on the Madeleine Smith affair. For over a year Ned Sheldon and Margaret Ayer Barnes tried to turn *Dishonored Lady* into a screenplay for Metro-Goldwyn-Mayer, and when they repeatedly failed to satisfy Will Hays, the "Czar" of motion picture morality, MGM bought Mrs. Belloc-Lowndes's novel and made a movie of it with Joan Crawford, called *Letty Lynton*. Six weeks after it was released, the authors of *Dishonored Lady* filed suit against MGM (not against Mrs. Belloc-Lowndes, who was a friend-in-crime of Sheldon's and innocent of all wrongdoing) claiming copyrighted material from their play had been incorporated into the screenplay of *Letty Lynton*. The first decision, handed down in 1934, was against them, but on appeal that decision was reversed, and in 1940, after seven years of litigation, damages were awarded to Sheldon and Barnes of more than half a million dollars. At that time the settlement was one of the largest ever made in a plagiarism suit.

The triumph was considerably lessened when Guthrie, as producer of the stage play *Dishonored Lady*, promptly engaged the attorney Louis B. Nizer and filed suit against Sheldon and Barnes for the producer's share of their settlement.

It was Kit's everyday dread that Guthrie would offend someone with his perverse crotchets, that he would scream at an actor, fire a stage-hand, insult a friend, accuse Ned Sheldon, of all people, of trying to get away with something and drag him into court. She never expressed surprise when these things happened, barely pausing to acknowledge them, unless apologies were needed and would help. She did not go on about them — except once in the sitting room at Beekman Place when she shook Guthrie by the shoulders until his head banged against the wall. As a rule she moved around the incident, whatever it was, the way she briskly circled the lake in Central Park, not untroubled but sustaining her own relationships and many of his through the sheer force of her goodwill.

Gert was less goodwilled and more vocal. She did not subscribe to Kit's "live and let live" attitude, believing that when one behaved as Guthrie did, something should be done about it. The suit against Sheldon and Barnes was a devious trick, as if he had been lying in wait, biding his time, then stepping in at the kill to claim his share. Friendship was no deterrent to his actions, Gert felt, nor personal respect, admiration, or the wishes of his wife who would never sue anyone for anything, no matter what they had done. It did not help matters that the court vindicated Guthrie, that he won his suit. That only aggravated the situation, at least for Gert on Kit's behalf. A producer's share today would be as much as forty percent, and it was certainly no less then. It was bad enough to have taken a stand against Kit's friend Ned Sheldon, but to take half his money was beneath contempt.

Before the First World War the "director" was almost unknown, or at least unrecognized, in the theatre. Plays were "staged" by stars, producers, and sometimes, since it was considered a mere mechanical operation, by a stage manager. Probably because of the influence and example of Max Reinhardt, the director began taking his place in the theatre as an artist in his own right, and Guthrie McClintic was in the van, one of the most energetic and talented. From Winthrop Ames he had learned the importance of color and composition on the stage, qualities that "stagers" rarely gave consideration. He was one of the first directors whose personal taste put a stamp on each production. When the curtain went up on a Guthrie McClintic play, the audience knew they were in for an experience simply by what they saw.

Under the old system actors were expected to know their craft well enough to get up and give their performances with the stager simply directing traffic and seeing to it that they didn't bump into one another. Guthrie was one of the new breed who tried to help the actor give the best performance he possibly could, using his own talent in the best possible way. Actors and actresses responded to Guthrie's patience and care with them, from the oldest to the youngest, from Blanche Bates to Ruth Gordon. In 1927 when Guthrie cast Ruth Gordon in *Saturday's Children* (for the Actors' Theatre) against the wishes of author Maxwell Anderson, she responded to him so completely that she felt she learned from him to do her first real acting, as she points out in her book *My Side*, "acting in the deep sense." And even as he induced her performance, he made her believe she was doing it on her own.

Kit felt that talent such as Guthrie's was privileged. He was entitled to misbehave and be tolerated. You had to be very sure who you were before you faced a talent like his and criticized the man behind it. Whereas Gert, from the first rehearsals of *The Age of Innocence*, while admitting Guthrie's talent felt he would have been nothing without Kit. Later on she conceded what Kit maintained all along, that the reverse was also true, that Kit would not have been where she was without Guthrie. But that took a long time. In the early days, even before the Ned Sheldon lawsuit, Gert felt that Guthrie wasn't good enough for Kit and, in the word used by witnesses, brutally castigated Kit for putting up with him.

Other women adored Guth. Ruth Gordon's devotion was almost slavish. Margalo Gillmore's was wise, as she sensed when to take him seriously and when not to. If he Goddamned an actor, for instance, swearing an oath never to hire him again, he was sure to want that actor for his next play. Tallulah Bankhead found in him a fellow night owl, someone to sit up and "dish" with. Everyone, man and woman, loved his stories and the way he loved telling his stories, laughing so hard he had to press his hand against his hernia operation as if to keep himself from exploding. Even Gert's own sisters, Louie and Min, loved Guth and were entertained by him. But Gert wouldn't even call him Guth, for that was a term of affection.

In close quarters at 23 Beekman Place, Kit not only had to suffer Guthrie's perversity, she had to suffer Gert's intolerance of it. At the dinner table, especially after a few drinks, Guthrie would insult Gert, or so she would think, or he would insult an absent friend and Gert would take issue. The remarks would fly, and suddenly Kit would drop a curtain behind her eyes, in front of her mind. Who can say where she went? Perhaps she was looking out the dining-room windows on Beekman Place into the dining-room windows back on Mariner Street in Buffalo, watching her mother and father gesticulate angrily on Christmas night. More likely, that was the scene she was trying to escape. But for all her smiling presence and seemingly close attention to the heated discussion, she might just as well have been off striding around the lake in Central Park, so far was she able to remove herself. Once Gert was so incensed with Guthrie that she left the table and went up to her room to cry. Many years later, in another monumental dinner-table fight during which Guthrie threatened to leave Martha's Vineyard for good and Gert said it would be a far better island if he did, the situation was reversed and she reduced him to tears, to sobbing gasps of strangled emotion. On that occasion, Kit at once lifted the curtain from behind her eyes, rose and moved the length of the table to put her arms around Guth and lead him from the room, reappearing only to ask the servant to bring the remainder of her dinner and Mr. McClintic's to his bedroom. But on the night Gert cried, which must have been during the run of *Dishonored Lady* when she was still young and inexperienced, Kit did not emerge from behind the curtain to take her part. At that time Gert thought Kit counted on her for just about everything, but when she climbed the four flights of stairs to shed tears in her fifth-floor room, Kit did not follow with her dinner or even have it sent up to her.

It was true that Kit counted on Gert for just about everything. It was even true that Kit would rather play golf with Gert than go to a party with Guthrie, always providing that wherever he was she knew he was enjoying himself and seeing his crowd. Let him be thrown on his own, or let him be in trouble, let him be given the short end of a deal and need comfort, let him simply find himself alone for an evening at loose ends, and she forgot her own needs to see to his. Sometimes during the long run of a play, she would ask Gert to stay at home and play bridge with Guthrie when he needed a fourth, and to Gert it was simply part of her job. On one occasion, even as he was trying to impress a new player he had heard was very good, he behaved abominably the entire evening, Gert felt, got mad every time he lost, and at one point threw the cards at Margalo for making a wrong lead. When Kit came home, Gert told her she had had enough; she was not going through another evening like that ever again in her life.

She laid it on the line. "I've made my decision. I'm going to California to have a rest and then find another career or another job."

The part of Kit that was Candida might here have spoken the line Shaw wrote for her confrontation of Marchbanks and Morell: "Oh! I am to choose, am I?"

"That is sad for me," Kit said. "But if anybody thinks they are going to unseat Guthrie in my life, they have another thought coming."

Her choice was, perhaps, as Shaw divined it to be in Candida's case, "the weaker of the two."

Gert did not flee to California, of course. She sensibly moved around the corner to 414 East Fiftieth Street.

She and Guthrie continued to have flare-ups which he immediately forgot and she steadfastly refused to apologize for to anyone, to him or to Kit, and every once in a while when he showed up drunk and unshaven at an opening, as was his wont, she would threaten to drive him off the Palisades, saying the sacrifice of her own life would be worth it to exterminate him. Everyone laughed and said isn't Gert funny, but she would deny that it was mere rhetoric, even when Stanley Gilkey told her the admiring, affectionate things Guthrie said about her behind her back, even when Guthrie gave her an unexpected gift, not the usually frilly, useless, perfume-soap-man-to-woman gift but something she really wanted, something he had to think up especially for her, like four brand-new tires for her car. One time he found out she had no collision insurance and ordered for her every kind there was, an extravagant amount of insurance covering every kind of automobile accident, even, presumably, driving off the Palisades. Gert was grateful for the attention and the gifts and said so, but they did not sway her in her feelings. She got along with Guthrie, she joked with him, conspired with him, catered to him, ran errands for him, bolstered him up and never let him down because Kit loved him and for no other reason, but that was reason enough.

Thus they battled the next thirty years, and on the day before he died in 1961 when Kit asked if there was anyone special he really wanted to see, he said Gert. And when Gert, who was expecting dinner guests that night, received the rather surprised summons from Kit, she flew out of the house, posting a note on the door saying the dinner was off, and went to sit for a few hours with her old antagonist. It was

Guthrie's most endearing side that he never knew he was her old antagonist, or if the thought crossed his mind, he refused to accept it. Aside from Kit, Gert was the last person he spoke to on earth.

When strength cannot dominate where it loves, as it will first try to do, it is wise to serve, and Gert Macy has always looked on her years with Katharine Cornell as years of service, although sometimes at the beginning, because of her inexperience, it came out *dis*service. During the run of *Dishonored Lady* a woman called 23 Beekman Place and asked to speak to Miss Cornell. The number was still listed in the telephone directory and anybody could get it, so Gert asked the woman's name and she said, "Miss Braslau." There was a slight accent Gert did not care for and she asked for a first name. "Sophie." Gert had had just enough experience answering Kit's telephone to be sure by now that it was a saleswoman of some kind, probably underwear.

"I need to know one more thing," she said efficiently. "What is the exact nature of your business?"

"It is disgraceful," came the answer, "the way the younger generation has no knowledge of the great people of the previous generation."

Gert had sense enough not to wait for more and went to tell Kit there was a Sophie Braslau on the telephone who seemed who seemed to think everybody should have heard of her. Guthrie exploded with laughter. He told about it for weeks, how Gert had thought the Metropolitan Opera Company's greatest contralto was an underwear saleswoman.

Another doubtful service was the time she let herself be talked into playing Ella the maid in *Dishonored Lady* for seventeen weeks on the road. At each performance she would manage to get herself onto the stage, her feet planted, rather far apart but at least in the right position, and then with no amount of twisting or turning could she uproot herself and get off. She and the leading man were the only replacements in the original New York company, and a Philadelphia reviewer, mentioning them both by name, said "It is a pity that Miss Cornell had to cheapen the cast with these additions." It would have been funny were it not for the word "cheapen," which in Gert's language is not a funny word. She never acted again.

When *The Barretts of Wimpole Street* came along, she asked if she could put money in it.

The only other play Kit had ever bought, *The Age of Innocence*, she gave to Gilbert Miller to produce. Stanton Griffis was determined that she should produce *The Barretts of Wimpole Street* herself, and this time he was backed up by another old beau of Kit's, A. Conger Goodyear, the Buffaloan who had commissioned the Speicher portrait.

Griffis and Goodyear proposed to put up the thirty thousand dollars it would cost to produce *The Barretts of Wimpole Street*. If it failed, they asked for nothing in return. If it succeeded, they asked only that their investment be paid back, stipulating that all remaining profits be used exclusively for future productions by Katharine Cornell. It was further stipulated that Guthrie McClintic was to direct *The Barretts of Wimpole Street* and all future productions. At Gert's request to be included, she was considered valuable enough to serve as General Manager and was permitted to buy ten percent interest in the company. Thus together, Griffis and Goodyear put up twenty-seven thousand dollars, and Gert put up three. In December 1930 C. & M.C. (a simplified version of C. & McC. for Cornell and McClintic) Productions, Inc., was formed.

Unlike Gert, and despite his boasting, adventurous ways with money, the Windshield-Wiper Magnate did not ask to be cut in. It was one thing to help indigent members of the family, but a limit had to be put on sentimental philanthropy. "My Dear Miss Macy," he wrote in the mid-1930s,

> I sincerely hope you do not think that because I mentioned the fact that so many extra dividends were coming that it embarrassed me to know how to invest the money, it had affected my brain to such an extent that I would be crazy enough to think for one moment of building a theatre in New York, or any other place.... A memorial to Katharine would be a wonderful idea and I must confess that I have frequently thought of it, but have never considered anything of the kind as being a business proposition. I did, at one time, think rather strongly of building a theatre on the University of Buffalo property and presenting it to the University and calling it the "Katharine Cornell Theatre" in memory of her mother and a tribute to Katharine. But upon investigating the matter thoroughly, I came to the conclusion that the Socialistic tendencies are so rapidly creeping into all of our Universities, and particularly the University of Buffalo, which is decidedly Red, that I would not do it.

He can certainly be forgiven for not wanting to build a theatre, but neither did he ever consider her plays to be good business propositions, enjoying their success, basking in reflected glory, but never at any time granting her the same faith he could muster up at a moment's notice for, say, a perfect stranger he happened to share a taxi with. Which is interesting only because it proves his golden touch to be fallible after all. Starting with the formation of C. & M.C., his daughter successfully produced plays for twenty-nine years, her duration as a producer only exceeded in the history of the American theatre by the Shubert Brothers and the Theatre Guild, presenting in New York alone twenty-four productions to say nothing of revitalizing the road from one end of the country to the other. Starting at the depths of the Depression with only the thirty thousand dollars invested in her talent by Stanton Griffis, A. Conger Goodyear, and Gertrude Macy, she grossed in her time twelve million dollars.

V

Cornelia (1930-1934)

17

"The Barretts" (1930-1931)

WHEN KIT WIRED from Panama City for the rights to *The Barretts of Wimpole Street*, she was thinking of it as a present for Guthrie, for him to direct, not for her to act in. For her own immediate future, she was more interested in Philip Barry's new play, *Tomorrow and Tomorrow*, a modernized version — dramatically, biologically, and psychologically — of the fourth chapter of Kings II, in which the prophet Elisha brings about the miracle of the birth of a son to the Sunamite woman who thinks herself barren. With its elevated, all but immaculate miracle-morality conception of childbirth in the modern world, it was probably one of the few plays on the subject that could have attracted Kit. It also had its Candida theme, in that the woman in the play chose in the end to stay with her emotionally needy, cuckolded husband rather than go off with her wise, strong prophet-lover.

Kit and Gert arrived at San Pedro on a Sunday morning, and Guthrie drove them to the house in Beverly Hills where he and Stanley Gilkey were ensconced with Simpson in attendance. After breakfast, he announced that he would read the new play aloud. If Gert felt like bolting to Pasadena, she didn't.

Guthrie "cried like a fool" all through the first act, which isn't even the moving part of the play. It establishes the Barrett family: the invalided eldest child, Elizabeth, aged forty, confined to the couch in her sitting room overlooking Wimpole Street; her two sisters, Arabel the accepting and Henrietta the rebel; her six handsome, affectionate, ineffectual brothers, only one of whom, the stammering Octavius, or

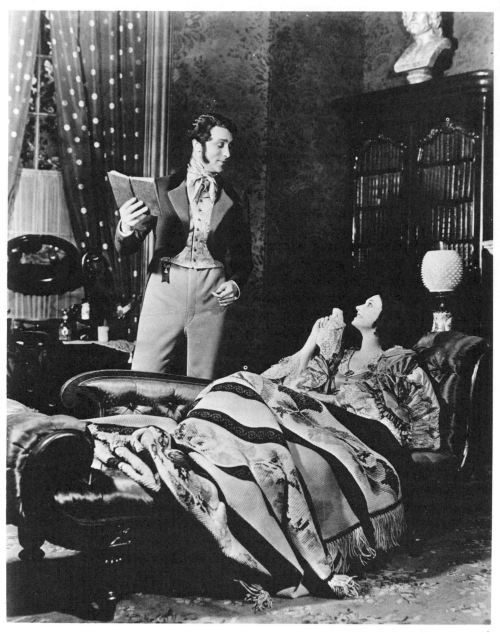

With Brian Aherne in The Barretts of Wimpole Street, *1931.*
(New York Public Library, Vandamm Collection)

"Occy," has a spark of spirit — all of them tyrannized by their widower father, Edward Moulton-Barrett, and only one of them loved by him, the first, the child born in love before his wife withdrew into terror, his daughter Elizabeth. There is what became the famous "porter scene" in which Father Barrett forces Elizabeth to drink the tankard of porter she hates so much, despite the doctor's permission to substitute milk. When Guthrie read a play aloud, which was every chance he got, he read the leading woman's part as Kit would read it had she rehearsed, taking on her intonations, inflections, and voice quality. When he brought the curtain down on Elizabeth Barrett alone in her prison, sobbing quietly in the moonlight, himself sobbing loudly in Beverly Hills, he stated emphatically that Kit had to play the part. Her only comment was that she found Elizabeth dull.

Act Two brings Robert Browning into the airless sickroom like a spring wind, and in his own words, "in a bare half hour we've talked intimately of art, and life, and death and love. And we've ordered each other about, and we've almost quarreled. Could anything be happier and more promising?" When he leaves, an hour into the play, Elizabeth struggles to her feet and leaning from chairback to table to window drape watches him disappear down Wimpole Street.

In the remaining three acts Elizabeth's health improves and her relations with her father deteriorate as his obsession with her sickness takes on a sinister quality. There is Henrietta's furtive love for dashing Captain Surtees Cook which her father aborts in his determination that none of his children shall every marry and become slaves to the "brutal tyranny of passion," "the lowest urge of the body." Woven into the scenes are the loyalty of Elizabeth's maid Wilson and the devotion of her spaniel, Flush. When accompanied by Wilson, Elizabeth finally escapes with Browning to Italy, Father Barrett decrees that her dog shall be destroyed immediately only to be told triumphantly by Henrietta that "Ba" has taken Flush with her.

Kit did not want to play an invalid, and there was even the chance that the healthy energy she conveyed to an audience would make her unbelievable confined to a sofa; nor had any of her other characters been as *submissive* as Elizabeth, a worrisome trait in a woman who only manages to escape her father's domination by becoming, albeit in a different way, submissive to another.

Guthrie was momentarily daunted when he learned that exactly twenty-seven New York producers had turned down *The Barretts*. But his faith in the play was so great — or maybe he had seen a sign in the way Kit found it and brought it to him — that he persisted. Eventually Kit turned down Philip Barry and agreed not only to play Elizabeth Barrett but to produce the play, backed by Conger Goodyear and Stanton Griffis. Gladys Cooper had been for many years her own manager at the Playhouse in London, and there was Eva Le Gallienne's brilliant example at the Civic Repertory on Fourteenth Street, to say nothing of Mrs. Fiske and her Manhattan Company thirty years before. Still it was an adventurous step for a woman to take at a time when most actor-managers were disappearing from the scene. The increase in responsibility was awesome.

While Guthrie worked at Fox during the day and at night hob-nobbed with Ruth Chatterton and other Hollywood greats, Kit played golf and lunched at Pasadena and they both began casting *The Barretts*. Rudolf Besier was surprised that an actress of Kit's caliber with at the time the largest personal draw of any actress on the stage would want to play Elizabeth when to him Father Barrett was clearly the starring role. So that was where the casting began. Lionel Barrymore was the first to be wooed, and he amiably closeted himself with the play, emerging grimly two hours later with the pronouncement that there may have been a time when *The Barretts* would have been a success, but it most decidedly was not 1930. As word of the new venture got around, others agreed with him. Al Woods pleaded with tears in his eyes that the public would "never buy Kitty as a virtuous invalid" and begged her to accept a new melodrama he had about a fallen woman who fell to save her brother from an unjust prison sentence — just the kind of vehicle the public was dying to see her in — again and still and forever.

In August 1930 Kit opened *Dishonored Lady* in San Francisco, where Ruth Chatterton's onetime sister-in-law, Brenda Forbes, was playing in *Fata Morgana* with Elsie Ferguson, who gave a party and said the McClintics were coming. Brenda was one of the privileged few who had seen Guthrie act in *Jealousy* when he played Los Angeles, where she also met him, but she had never met Miss Cornell. She was very young and excited and had a glass of wine for her nerves which worked so well that she had several and all her nerves were gone and she told the McClintics her glorious news that she was about to be in her first play in New York with Maude Adams. When Guthrie said it would never happen, that Maude Adams kept promising to come to New York and never did and never would, Brenda was crushed. It was typical of Guthrie. Before the party he had told Kit that Ruth Chatterton's young sister-in-law was talented and he thought she might make a good Wilson. Now, confronted with her, he created one of those abrupt clumsy moments Kit was always on the watch for. With years of practice she slipped into the conversation, "I can offer you something for sure." Brenda couldn't believe her good fortune. "Reeeeally?" she said. And Kit imitated her, "Reeeeally!' Later, Gert made a point of saying "Don't count on that," but Maude Adams didn't come to New York that year and Brenda Forbes ended up playing Wilson in *The Barretts*.

While Guthrie remained in Los Angeles to finish shooting his picture at Fox (called *Once a Sinner*), Kit worked her way back across the country, planning to close *Dishonored Lady* in mid-December, then to begin rehearsals for *The Barretts*. From Detroit she called Guthrie with Jessie Bonstelle's suggestion for Father Barrett, Charles Waldron, who had acted with Kit in *A Bill of Divorcement* and been directed by Guthrie in *Mrs. Partridge Presents*. They both knew him to be a good solid performer, and since no name character actor would touch the role, Stanley Gilkey, then back in New York, was directed to make Waldron an offer, which was accepted.

The Lionel Barrymores of the acting profession were afraid of Edward Moulton-Barrett's austere Victorian villainy, but young leading men were afraid of Robert Browning because he didn't have enough lines. He was the gusty emotional drive of the play, storming, captivating and carrying off the audience as he did his adored Elizabeth, but of the play's five acts he only appeared in three, with one long scene and two shorter ones, and to a certain kind of impulsive, short-sighted Robert Browning–type actor, that was simply not enough.

Time was growing short. Then as he was winding up *Once a Sinner* early in November, Guthrie was shocked to hear of Clare Eames's death (after an operation) in England at the age of thirty-four. Some time after leaving *Candida* to have her baby, she had gone to England with her husband, Sidney Howard, to be in his very successful play *The Silver Cord*, playing opposite Brian Aherne, whom she described on sight as "Hermes of Praxiteles." They soon found themselves involved in a deep and lasting love affair, and when Guthrie directed *The Trial of Mary Dugan* in London in 1928 (the spring between *The Letter* and *The Age of Innocence*) Clare Eames was devoutly sorry that when he saw *The Silver Cord* he missed Aherne, who had just left the cast. Now overwhelmed by the sudden, utter obliteration from the face of the earth of one as vital as Clare Eames, Guthrie had two thoughts: that it must be quite a man indeed to have been so completely beloved by Clare Eames, and that any man with stuff enough to inspire such love and to return it openly and forcefully, forsaking all others, could be just the man to play Robert Browning. He had never even seen a picture of Brian Aherne, but he resolved on the spot that as soon as he finished *Once a Sinner*, he would head straight for London for the sole purpose of seeking him out and signing him up. Kit was in agreement, feeling that even if Aherne didn't work out, there was a better chance of finding the right actor in London than in either New York or Los Angeles.

In London, through Joyce Carey's mother, Lillian Braithwaite, Guthrie was dismayed to learn that Brian Aherne was in rehearsal for a new play and wouldn't even be available for a meeting until it had opened. To fill in the time, Guthrie visited 50 Wimpole Street where he measured Elizabeth Barrett's bed-sitting room and drew a floor plan which the set designer he had engaged in New York, Jo Mielziner, later reproduced exactly on the stage of the Empire Theatre. Guthrie also had a rather formal meeting with Rudolf Besier who wondered that an American star like Katharine Cornell would want to perform in a play in which she was absent from the stage during the last scene. Taking this as a challenge, Guthrie assured him that for Miss Cornell the play's last scene was one of its great strengths. "Miss Cornell is not only a star," he added, rather indignantly, "she is also a great actress!"

Guthrie attended a performance of *The Barretts* which had just opened in London with Gwen Ffrangcon-Davies as Elizabeth and Cedric Hardwicke as Edward Moulton-Barrett. They were, to him, "appropriately Victorian," but he found the actor who played Browning so impossible that he sneaked out to avoid watching him when he was onstage.

Attending a performance of Brian Aherne's play, he was delighted to find it "drearier than words can express," but he was not at all pleased to be "singularly unimpressed" by Brian Aherne himself. It didn't help that the Atlantic crossing had been miserable and choppy and upon arrival he had been stricken with an internal ailment that forced him, with all he had to do, to spend most of his time in bed at the Ritz.

Which is where Brian Aherne found him. Lillian Braithwaite had informed him in advance of Guthrie's purpose in seeking him out, and he had been to *The Barretts* and found the part of Browning "short, difficult, and unrewarding." He was much more interested in a picture offer Fox was going to make that afternoon to star in the screen version of Noël Coward's *Cavalcade.*

Each trying to let the other down easy, they made small talk, and when Guthrie asked about the last days of his friend Clare Eames, Aherne spoke with such warmth and feeling that Guthrie reversed his opinion of him, responding with such warmth and feeling that Aherne suddenly saw in Guthrie a quiet, exceptional man, a genuine artist and a far cry from the high-powered American executives he knew at Fox. Guthrie drew up a quick contract on hotel stationery which Aherne signed before he left the hotel. Guthrie was so ecstatic that he decided to squander a small fortune (thirty dollars for three minutes) on a telephone call to Kit in Philadelphia, finally getting through to be told by the hotel operator that Miss Cornell was resting and couldn't be disturbed not even for a husband calling from London, England.

In frustration he went out to a shop in Dover Street and with a daring disregard for past experience bought the new actress-manager a gift of jewelry — a necklace, two bracelets, and ring of cabochon-cut garnets well over a hundred years old. In his mind's eye he pictured them on Elizabeth Barrett, and in all the seven hundred and nine times Kit played the part, she always wore them in the last act when Elizabeth leaves Wimpole Street for the last time. On opening night the backstage crush after the performance was so great that one of the bracelets got broken, half to be found later caught in the lace of her dress, the other half to be lost forever, and for once one could be grateful for Guthrie's little-boy greediness in having bought two. His immediate problem on leaving London was how to smuggle the jewels into the United States, for he was determined not to pay duty (probably feeling he had been robbed of thirty dollars in that transatlantic telephone call). He solved the problem by stuffing the necklace, two bracelets, and ring into an athletic supporter he purposely wore for the docking at Hoboken, New Jersey. Gert met him at the boat, and by the time he emerged from the endless standing, shuffling, and waiting in customs, he was in crotch-stricken agony, muttering about "a present for Kit." Nothing much about him ever surprised Gert, and she matter-of-factly led the bandy-legged arrival inch by inch to her car where he begged to be taken some place where he could remove his pants.

———

At the ordeal of Gert's Philadelphia debut as Ella the maid in *Dishonored Lady*, all her old friends from Bryn Mawr had shown up to applaud her first entrance, adding mortification to shame. Still she remained loyal to her alma mater and suggested to Kit and Guthrie for the rebellious Henrietta in *The Barretts* Katharine Hepburn, a recent Bryn Mawr graduate who had just made a success that November with Jane Cowl in a short-lived play, *Art and Mrs. Bottle*. She came to 23 Beekman Place to read, and Guthrie wanted to sign her to a run-of-the-play contract, but the young actress said she already had a job lined up for the summer as second girl in Jed Harris's stock company at Ivoryton, Connecticut, and could only play through the spring. Guthrie felt that if Miss Cornell ran through the summer — she rarely did, but if she did — he didn't want to have to break in a new Henrietta. Miss Hepburn persisted; Jed Harris was a brilliant producer-director and she couldn't pass up the chance to work with him and besides she was committed, all of which annoyed Guthrie. Gert, sensing that Hepburn had something of a crush on Jed Harris (he would later direct her most famous failure, *The Lake*) urged Guthrie not to take her attitude personally. But he was goddamned if he was going to let an unknown actress tell him the terms under which she would work for him, and thus the two great Katharines (the only two with two "a's") never appeared together. It is historically regrettable because as different as they were in talent, appearance, and temperament, they made their names in the same two roles, one on the stage, the other on the screen — Jo in *Little Women* and Sydney in *A Bill of Divorcement*.

Henrietta went to another Bryn Mawr graduate, Margaret "Beany" Barker, who had played well with Kit in *The Age of Innocence*. The irony is that when spring came and *The Barretts* seemed likely to run forever, Miss Barker wanted desperately to leave the cast to join the newly formed Group Theatre, and at Kit's insistence Guthrie had to led her go and "break in a new Henrietta" — no great hardship as it turned out to be Margalo Gillmore.

Also in the cast of *Art and Mrs. Bottle* was Joyce Carey, Kit's Meg in *Little Women* back in 1919. She had come to New York in 1925 to be in Noël Coward's *Easy Virtue* with Jane Cowl and stayed on (or gone home and come back) to be in six more plays with her. Jane Cowl and Kit were considered by some to be rivals: they were both dark and beautiful with velvet voices; they were about the same age (although for the public record Kit was seven years younger); Jane Cowl had given her Juliet to the world, and everyone was waiting for Kit's. There the likenesses and rivalry ended, but still to Kit there were professional rules about such things. In spite of what might be considered a previous claim dating back to 1919, Joyce Carey was a Jane Cowl actress, and had *Art and Mrs. Bottle* not closed after fifty performances, Kit would not have dared ask Joyce to play Arabel in *The Barretts*, which she was delighted to accept. Each star was always gracious and tactful to Joyce about the other, and Joyce managed to remain loyal to both, always sensitive to the differences between them, differences perhaps most explicitly evident in the different kinds of presents she gave them. For Miss Cowl it was always a fine linen handkerchief with a delicate lace border, something that looked pretty in a scented gift box, to be carried for effect or display and perhaps not quite ever used. To Kit she once gave a ham; on another occasion a rug.

In this their first venture into management, the McClintics established the standard of courtesy, care, and respect that in all future productions would be accorded to all members of each company. A cablegram of encouragement and bon voyage to Brian Aherne as he sailed on the *Mauretania* for what was only his second visit to the United States; another cablegram of welcome as he approached American shores; the company manager, Alan Attwater, dispatched to meet the boat, to steer him through customs, explain American money, protect him from the press, escort him to the New Weston Hotel, and see him settled there. And then the reassuring common touch of arriving for his first visit to Beekman Place at the moment of Guthrie's discovery that the chauffeur had taken the dog for a walk and lost it. The resulting outburst of pyrotechnical obscenities was unequaled in the young Englishman's experience to that date.

So much had happened since *Dishonored Lady* opened in California that Kit and Guthrie both forgot Brenda Forbes patiently waiting for some word in Los Angeles. Finally she heard from other sources that *The Barretts* was about to go into rehearsal and on her own packed up and traveled east, had her hair done, called 23 Beekman Place and was told to get herself over there at once. Simpson let her in as Kit was coming down the stairs. "Guthrie wants to talk to you," she said, "and I just want to say hello — and welcome." It was the beginning of another tradition — the ritual greeting of newcomers. Guthrie talked for an hour about everything but *The Barretts* and finally out of the blue offered her eighty-five dollars a week. Brenda was still so new to the profession that she didn't know that a show of disappointment usually led to embarrassed dismissal, and so it worked the other way for her and Guthrie was rather shaken by her disappointment. She said she had been expecting at least a hundred and she had already paid her own way east. Guthrie said the play was not going to be a hit. If it were a hit, she could expect a salary like that. She asked how long before one knew if a play was a hit? Six weeks, he said. Again with the fearlessness of the uninitiated, she bargained with him: she would play six weeks at eighty-five dollars, and if the play was a hit, from then on she was to receive a hundred. Agreed. The day after the opening in Cleveland, Guthrie said, "You'll not get one week at eighty-five! It's a hundred *now!*" Gert frowned at such profligacy.

The only real casting problem was Flush, Elizabeth Barrett's dog. Historically, Flush was a King Charles spaniel, a black and tan toy weighing between nine and twelve pounds. Aside from the rarity of the breed in modern times, it is not an impressive-looking dog for stage purposes, and a decision was made to go along with the traditional concept of Elizabeth's dog as the popular and recognizable cocker spaniel (twice the size of a King Charles). The first dog cast was a nervous, suspicious misanthrope whose good looks in no way compensated for his meager love of mankind, and he didn't even last the five-day trial period allowed an actor by Equity. Word was sent out for a dog with a beautiful disposition, handsome or not, and a few days later a Mr. Stoddard from Mount Kisco brought in an eight-month-old puppy who bounded into the middle of rehearsal to be greeted joyously, "It's Flush!" At first it was considered necessary to hire a professional dog trainer, but one could not be found who would sit patiently through eight- and ten-hour rehearsals. Without wasting time, Gert, who was also stage manager, took on the job. It took her exactly three days to housebreak the dog, and then he had to be taken to rehearsal every day until he became acquainted with the cast, especially Kit and Brenda, the ones who would have direct contact with him onstage. He was anxious to please and quick to learn, learning especially quickly that Gert carried little lumps of raw beef to give him when he behaved well. For the most part when he was onstage he sim-

*In the garden at Beekman Place. Simpson serving tea to the
McClintics and "Flush."*

ply had to lie still and snooze in his basket by the couch or on the couch itself, but he did have one exit to make on his own, on cue. Wilson (Brenda) would head for the door, calling, "Come, Flush!" He would look up at the sound of his name, and as she went out the door he would see Gert kneeling in the wings, out of sight of the audience, beckoning to him. He would hesitate a moment, squinting in the stage lights to make sure she had the bit of beef in her fingers, then perhaps scratch an ear in lazy anticipation, get out of his basket and trot off, always to thunderous applause.

A few days after Christmas, rehearsals began where they would begin for all Cornell-McClintic productions, in the dining room at 23 Beekman Place. For a week Guthrie kept the actors sitting around the dining table sipping coffee, reading the play, discussing it, exchanging ideas, getting acquainted. It was a rehearsal technique that an entire generation of directors in the 1950s would adopt, often claiming to have originated it. When it was time for the actors to get on their feet, Guthrie did not remove them to a rehearsal hall but directly to the stage of a theatre, if possible the theatre where they would eventually perform the play — in the case of *The Barretts*, the Empire. Set and properties were tangibly improvised from the start and costumes were simulated — hoops, shawls, and even the sword Father Barrett catches Henrietta lovingly buckling to the uniform of Captain Surtees Cook. The play was booked to play in Cleveland for half a week and for a full week in Buffalo before the New York opening on February 9.

With her elevation to manager, Kit's rehearsal nerves became a torment, in no way eased by her continuing doubts about the role of Elizabeth. It was a taxing role. Except for the last five minutes of the play, she was never off the stage from the rise of the first curtain. And yet it was not a role with meaty scenes for an actress; from start to finish she fed everybody else, Browning, her father, her brothers, her sisters. She builds them up and then they take over the scenes and she supports them. And long; as Kit put it, "She goes on like the brook — pages and pages." With never a scene of her own, except a quiet little moment with Wilson just before she goes away. Physically the role was all but unendurable, for she had to lie on the sofa for great lengths of time with her feet up, facing a side wall, and still project character, mood, and subtle emotion; project her voice to the last row of the top balcony and still remain a sick woman, a dying woman, the invalid Edward Moulton-Barrett has created for his own twisted satisfaction. Guthrie did everything he could to dispel any feeling Kit might have that she was being rushed. Even when the out-of-town opening was set, he assured her it could be changed, it could be postponed until she was ready. But with her new, oppressive responsibilities, the self-indulgence of a postponement was unthinkable. It did not help her to justify herself in what she was doing to have *Tomorrow and Tomorrow* open in the middle of January and become a quiet, substantial success.

In London, because the play was about Victorians, it was apparently treated as a Victorian play and given a Victorian production. The following summer Laura Elliot wrote to Kit after seeing it that the actors "slow up for the 'thesis' lines, point them more and *say them front*...." She had always felt that were she a stage director she would "ring a bell to warn the audience of pregnant lines." Even so, having seen both productions, she found Guthrie's fluid realism far more exciting, observing, "What you do in your production is to strip the play and characters from their special era and circumstances and reveal the essential, elemental and universal fundamentals in them — common to all."

It was partly through meticulous attention to period detail that Guthrie gave the play modern theatricality, and as always, he inspired his actors and production staff to follow where he led. Brenda Forbes, for example, patterned much of Wilson on her own Nanny, and Jo Mielziner dressed her in a Scotch plaid, an apron of black alpaca (her Nanny on her best days wore a black alpaca apron), a cap of ecru lace perched on top of curls with a cherry satin bow bobbing up and down. The first time she appeared fully costumed, she went to show Kit, who was on her couch onstage, suffering through lighting adjustments. "Too amber!" Guthrie was cursing. "Amber is *not* the right color for Miss *Cornell!*" Brenda peered through the huge entrance door of the set, the entrance door that would be so imposing and effective from the audience when Edward Moulton-Barrett walked through it but which would cause so much trouble at dress rehearsal, catching every hoopskirt going in or out, necessitating hours of precious rehearsal time for the women of the cast. Kit extended her arms to Brenda and said, "There's my little toy!" And Brenda walked to her like a toy, moving her feet in tiny hidden steps under the wide hoop skirt, therefore seeming to float across the stage telekinetically. She noticed that there was laughter from those who happened to be watching, and when she repeated the walk on opening night it delighted the audience and did much to keep the period of the play in its proper place as graceful, amusing, rather quaint background. The trouble was the audience wanted to laugh every time she moved, and she couldn't let them. The walk had to be controlled — as Guthrie controlled the rest of the Victorian background — and not allowed to intrude on the "elemental and universal fundamentals" of the play. Working with Guthrie was to learn how to act.

The Barretts of Wimpole Street was given for the first time in this country at the Hanna Theatre, Cleveland, on January 29, 1931, after a disastrous dress rehearsal lasting until four o'clock in the morning after which Kit, who had forgotten or garbled every third line, insisted the opening be delayed. She may have felt secure in this lapse of discipline, knowing that this time Guthrie would be the one to say no, they were sold out for their four performances and could not afford the black eye a delay would give them. Besides, a delay would only give them more time to worry, so the curtain went up as scheduled on the miraculously smooth performance that usually follows a disastrous dress rehearsal. There were three reviews: the first said it was a fiasco and suggested that Miss Cornell had chosen the play because she was onstage the entire evening; William McDermott, Kit's fan, wished she could have a stronger vehicle to sustain her through her debut as actress-manager; and Archie Bell in the evening paper gave the play and production a rave.

Fifteen minutes had to be cut from the performance to bring it within the three-hour limit allowed by the stagehands' unions, which was accomplished in time for the opening in Buffalo the following Monday night. It was another of Kit's traditions to take her plays to Buffalo before New York, often opening them there. There must have been a touch of masochism in the gesture, for everybody in her home town felt they had a stake in her career which raised them above the average audience and entitled them to tell her what she ought to do, and if she didn't do it, then she had gone grand on them. When he could, Guthrie acted as shock-absorber, and they let him have it on *The Barretts*. "You can't do this to Kit!" they said indignantly. "The audience will laugh at it.... The father is ludicrous.... Believe me, Guthrie, this is melodrama in Hoboken without the beer!"

It rained for the New York opening of *A Bill of Divorcement*, it rained for *The Dover Road*, and it rained for *The Barretts of Wimpole*

Street, this time a hard, driving rain dissipating any good luck it might bring by slowing traffic to a virtual standstill at midafternoon. To congest the situation even further, the Metropolitan Opera House, directly across the street from the Empire Theatre on Broadway at Thirty-ninth Street, was having an important premiere. Above the Empire, through the black torrential downpour, shone the white words "KATHARINE CORNELL PRESENTS" — instead of the usual "KATHARINE CORNELL IN." C. & M.C. Productions, Inc., the actual producing company, was never used on theatre programs and marquees, nor was it ever mentioned in newspaper articles and publicity. As far as the public was concerned, Katharine Cornell — the person — was the sole producer of her plays. Turning her natural modesty into a business and professional advantage, it was felt from the start that her designation as producer would permit her to list herself last as an actress, at the bottom of the house boards in front of the theatre, after everyone else, "and Katharine Cornell" almost as an afterthought, making her costars' higher billing an attraction to the best available talent.

Backstage, Kit arrived and gave out gifts. George "Empire" Pierce, an old-time, small-time vaudevillian, now the stage doorman at the Empire, handed Guthrie a telegram with a star on it for Frederick Voight, who played one of the Barrett brothers. The star on the envelope meant the message inside reported a death. Rather than upset even the least important member of the company, Guthrie opened the telegram and read that Voight's father had died ten days ago. Figuring three hours more wouldn't make that much difference, he pocketed the telegram. After the performance, when summoned to Guthrie's presence on the empty stage set, the young actor was afraid he was going to be fired and was relieved to hear, instead, of the death of his estranged father whom he had never known.

Because of the play's extreme length, the opening-night curtain was advertised for eight twenty-five. At eight-thirty only the two balconies had been filled. To enable the members of the press to meet their deadlines, the curtain could not be held any longer, and at eight thirty-two Gert, as stage manager, signaled the curtain to rise and Kit spoke her first line to Dr. Chambers with exactly fifty-two people seated on the lower floor. The play's five acts had been divided into three, with two scenes each in the first and third acts, and the actors played the long and terribly important first scene to the individual, consecutive, and simultaneous banging of eight hundred and fifty seats.

By the time Brian Aherne made his entrance in the second scene, forty-five minutes into the play, with his vigorous and historical greeting, "Dear Miss Barrett — at last! At last!", the audience was settled and at least ready to listen.

The play proceeded through to the end with only one hitch. In the out-of-town theatres the boxes had been separated from the stage by an orchestra pit, but at the Empire the boxes were so close that one could easily step into them from the stage. The second act curtain rose on Flush seated well downstage on the sofa while Elizabeth walked back and forth to show Dr. Chambers the improvement in her health. Suddenly spying the people in the boxes, Flush jumped down to investigate, and Kit had to change her direction and speed up slightly to pick him up in time to prevent him from joking with the paying customers. It was an error so "human" that it drew a round of applause and helped immeasurably to warm up the late, bedraggled, cranky, rain-soaked audience. Robert Litell said in the *World* the next morning, "Flush came perilously close to walking away with the play."

At the final curtain the hearty applause could be interpreted either as enthusiasm or congratulations on having gotten through this hellish evening. The usual hordes rushed backstage. Ina Claire stated with impersonal flatness, "It's in," but Stanton Griffis, with no regrets, only a backer's shrewd theatrical eye, said, "You kids are going to be crucified tomorrow." As soon as they could, the McClintics, Gert, Stanley, and Conger Goodyear escaped to 23 Beekman Place where they had drinks and snacks and waited. There were no television reviews in those days, no radio reviews, and because of the play's length even the newspaper reviews would not be out until the 5 A.M. editions. In his autobiography, Brian Aherne recalls going to Childs for something to eat after the performance, then walking to his hotel and going to bed. But both the McClintics (separately) always remembered him dropping in at 23 Beekman Place having just come from "21" where opinions were divided and everyone was reserving judgment.

At one-thirty Guthrie went downstairs to answer the doorbell, expecting another telegram, and there was Woollcott, looking more owlish than ever. It was not his wont to ring doorbells in the middle of the night, and Guthrie knew it meant one of two things: good news or bad news.

"Where is everybody?" he demanded with some asperity. Guthrie pointed upstairs.

Edging his portly frame through the door, Woollcott puffed up the short flight to address himself to Kit.

"How do you feel?" he asked. She made some incoherent reply. He looked around disdainfully at the half-filled glasses, thoroughly enjoying the dramatic suspense he was creating, building it as high as he could.

"You should be drinking champagne," he finally said, smoothly, as if he were on radio. "Corks should be popping. You have a smash hit. The reviews will be splendid." He let it sink in, then continued in his best avuncular, scolding manner, "And as for you, Miss Kitty, you should have your head examined for thinking Elizabeth Barrett wasn't the part for you. It's probably your finest performance."

18

Disciplined Fury (1931-1932)

THE NEXT MORNING Brooks Atkinson wrote of *The Barretts* in the *New York Times*:

> After a long succession of meretricious plays it introduces us to Kath-
> arine Cornell as an actress of the first order. Here the disciplined fury
> that she has been squandering on catch-penny plays becomes the vibrant
> beauty of finely wrought character.... By the crescendo of her playing,
> by the wild sensitivity that lurks behind her ardent gestures and her
> piercing stares across the footlights she charges the drama with a mean-
> ing beyond the facts it records. Her acting is quite as remarkable for
> the carefulness of its design as for the fire of her presence.... *The
> Barretts of Wimpole Street* is a triumph for Miss Cornell and the splen-
> did company with which she has surrounded herself.

Perhaps he had been considering for quite some time the two elements of her acting and weighing them against each other: the personal
quality she brought to any role and/or/versus her acting talent, the
craft she had to learn along the way. Perhaps he had been reserving
comment until the two elements caught up with each other and he
could say, at last, with pride in her accomplishment: "Her acting is
quite as remarkable for the carefulness of its design as for the fire of
her presence."

The other critics fell into line — "superb," "eloquent," "exalted,"
"dark," "rhythmic," "luminous," "haunting," "lyric," "ravishing" were
words they would use of her then and thereafter through the years.

Once she got over her wantonness of the twenties and emerged as the classic figure of the romantic cast they had in mind for her from the start, she could do no wrong, and the extravagance and regularity of their praise took on a kind of monotony.*

A witty and reliably caustic reviewer like Dorothy Parker, substituting for Robert Benchley in *The New Yorker*, might begin her review: "If you want to, you can pick me out of any crowd, these days. I am the little one in the corner who did not think *The Barretts of Wimpole Street* was a great play, or even a good play. It is true that I paid it the tribute of tears, but that says nothing, for I am one who weeps at Victorian costumes." But even she, having taken her stand, must veer off to assure readers that "Miss Katharine Cornell is a completely lovely Elizabeth Barrett — far lovelier than the original, I fear. It is little wonder that Miss Cornell is so worshipped; she has that thing we need, and we so seldom have, in our actresses; she has romance, or, if you like better the word of the daily-paper critics, she has glamour."

The play itself was criticized in as many ways by as many critics as any other play Kit had appeared in, mostly on the grounds that since it was a melodrama (although Besier designated it a comedy) the author had no right to keep the hero offstage during all the climactic scenes. The title of the play was the definitive answer to that criticism: the play was not about Robert Browning and Elizabeth Barrett, it was about the Barretts of Wimpole Street.

Mrs. Parker's other specific objection, surprisingly dainty, was to the suggestion of incest, in impulse if not in fact, in Edward Moulton-Barrett's last-act pleading with Elizabeth, in his passionate embrace, claiming "all your heart and all your soul!", sending her in fear even

---

* In preparing her exhaustive and illuminating 1974 doctoral dissertation, "A Historical Study of Katharine Cornell As an Actress-Manager, 1931–1960," Lynda Towle Moss, then of the University of Southern California, spent an entire summer in New York at the Lincoln Center Library for the Performing Arts sifting the Katharine Cornell material, the four hundred pounds of scrapbooks, programs, photographs, letters, and manuscripts. Members of the attentive library staff, most of them too young to have seen Katharine Cornell at her height, still recall, not with unmixed pleasure, Mrs. Moss reading into her tape recorder the play reviews, day after day through the long hot summer, the endless stream of adjectives so superlative that they lost meaning. One young assistant covers his ears at the mention of Katharine Cornell or wrings his hands begging for some unkind word of her, some slur, no matter how small. In an age when paragons are mistrusted, it is hard to understand the adoration and respect she inspired, let alone the universality of her appeal.

sooner than she had planned out of the house on Wimpole Street. In London, the Moulton-Barrett descendants considered the scene libelous and tried to have the play closed, succeeding only in having a few of the most offending bits deleted from the performance. There followed a clamorous brouhaha with much side-taking, and Shaw wrote angry letters which the *London Times* refused to print. The deleted bits were restored in the New York production, and Mrs. Parker, claiming they were surely apocryphal, lined herself up with the family against the writer.

In restoring the offending bits Kit struck a blow for creative integrity over domestic censorship, artist versus family, so to speak, a brave position for a Buffalo girl (think of the unsigned letters from angry Buffalo fathers!). But then she characteristically dismissed the unpleasant subject of incest by saying that the very little of it there was in the play was certainly not emphasized, not even nodded to, in her production. In short, having held out for incest, she denied it was there. "I always felt terribly sorry for Edward Moulton-Barrett," she said in *I Wanted to Be an Actress*, smoothing it all away. "As he saw it, Elizabeth had betrayed him. He thought that he was the only person who could understand her; take care of her. He had given up his whole life to her. For years she had allowed him to believe that; to keep her lying there. I never saw actual incest in it; only an overstatement of practically all father-daughter relationships."

Even, presumably, her own father-daughter relationship, for that is certainly what she found in *The Barretts* to make her own and enable her to play it. Peter Cornell never tried to turn his daughter into an invalid, but he did do his best to keep her his own "dearest little girl," bursted buttons and all. There were the times he sent her to her room after supper as a young suitor was about to arrive, then allowing the young suitor to think she didn't want to see him, even as Father Barrett came between Henrietta and Captain Surtees Cook. Dr. Cornell never exacted from Kit an oath not to marry, as Edward Moulton-Barrett tacitly exacted from all his children, but he did lock the door against her and her escort after the *bal masque*, and he did refuse to attend her wedding in an attempt to have her call it off. Of course Kit did not see the hint of incest in *The Barretts* because to do so would have been to see it in her own growing up. And of course she thought "Elizabeth had betrayed him ... for years she had allowed him to believe he was the only person who could take care of her," because that put a lot of the blame for the uneasy father-daughter relationship and the even worse interpretation of it onto Elizabeth's shoulders, that is, onto her own. And once again, by playing against the play, as she did in *The Green Hat*, she gave it a romance and dignity that brought the tribute of tears from Mrs. Parker and might even have elicited a nod from the stuffy descendants of Edward Moulton-Barrett.

Of all the plays Kit appeared in, *The Barretts of Wimpole Street* is the most easily related to her life and experience, that is, it required the least "twisting" on her part to make it her own, even to the circumstances of the artist suffering inertia from inner renunciation, suddenly awakened and given impetus to escape and bloom by the ministrations of an ardent lover. Perhaps that is why she didn't want to play Elizabeth at first, because it would require a stern look at her own life, something she was not inclined to do unless forced. And perhaps she was drawn into it at last by what had repelled her at first, Elizabeth's illness — surely an equivalent of Lalage Sturdee's crippled walk, Laura Pennington's grotesque plainness, and Sydney Fairfield's mental instability.

The cocker spaniel became the popular dog that year, and Flush was a pampered star of such magnitude that when a small pier collapsed under the celebration of a summer wedding at Sneden's Landing, the only cry to be heard as the guests were plunged into the Hudson in their white ducks and garden hats was to keep Flush aloft as he had to give a performance that night. He even invaded the literary world when simultaneous with Virginia Woolf's biography of Elizabeth Barrett's Flush there appeared Flora Merrill's biography of Katharine Cornell's. After the opening, he misbehaved only one other time, lifting his leg against a stack of leatherbound books on the floor beside Elizabeth Barrett's sofa, presumably the works of Robert Browning, leaving a visible cascade of wetness down their faun-colored spines.

But undamped, the works of Robert Browning experienced a resurgence of popularity, and healthy new chapters of the Browning Society sprang into existence around the country. Publishers rushed into print with new editions of *Sonnets from the Portuguese*. All the world beat a path to the Empire Theatre, and when Mrs. Herbert Hoover attended a performance, George "Empire" Pierce remarked with an odd ring of Victorian imperialism, "Mrs. Hoover may be First Lady of the land, but Miss Cornell is First Lady of the Empire."

Kit loved going to the movies and was more easily pleased than most people, but she had no wish to be in them. She had served a long apprenticeship in the theatre; it had taken years for her to begin to feel at ease with her talent. Useless to say that acting was acting, whether on the stage or on the screen; she knew that in her case it would be a hard transition. She admired actresses who could slip with ease from one medium to another — Tallulah Bankhead, Ina Claire, and Helen Hayes. But for Kit the movies would be like beginning all over again, learning a new set of rules, painstakingly evolving a new and perhaps more difficult technique. Would movie producers, let alone the public, be patient through still more years of apprenticeship?

Irving Thalberg, it seems, would. In order to get her to play Elizabeth Barrett for MGM on the screen, he offered to destroy the finished film completely, burn it and send it up in smoke, if she wasn't completely satisfied. Until he came along, Kit had had no trouble refusing the many persistent and generous movie offers made to her, but with courteous, gentlemanly behavior and the kind of dedication she always responded to, Thalberg met her every objection head on, offering so much money that even Dr. Cornell's eyes bulged in disbelief, smoothing away her fears, guaranteeing her relaxed, lengthy rehearsals, closed sets, the full Garbo treatment. Kit found it so hard to say no to him that one day when they were alone — Gert and Guthrie having momentarily left her unguarded — she said yes. Then she panicked, and Gert had to invade the studio and get her out of the verbal commitment.

Thalberg's main argument, the one he pressed most assiduously, did not impress her: he said she owed it to posterity to make movies. He claimed it was imperative that her performances be recorded for future generations of audiences to enjoy and for future generations of actors and actresses to study. With Kit's unwillingness to perpetuate herself by the natural means of having children, she was not likely to embrace it as a reason for making a movie. Besides, she didn't believe it. Once during a rehearsal Guthrie brought in a recording of Julia Marlowe's Juliet, and when it was played the young people present laughed at the extravagant readings. Bernhardt was not dead ten years, and yet audiences laughed at her death scene as Camille whenever the movie was shown. Kit saw no reason to let that happen to her; why should she inflict upon herself new anxieties making a movie for future generations to laugh at? — in her modesty, of course, always assuming that they would. She did not feel she was acting for historians or nostalgia fans of the future but for audiences of the here and now, people who came into the theatre tonight, sat in their seats and waited for the curtain to go up. Not only were they the ones she wanted to reach, but she wanted to be there when they responded, she did not want to be off in another part of the world while they gazed at a second-hand image on a screen. In fact, she was not sure she could give them anything to respond to without the inducement of their presence.

In this she may have been guided by instinct rather than intellectual judgment, for it is possible — there will never be any way of knowing — that her particular quality was theatrical rather than cinematic. Not that she was not photogenic; her face had the startling bone structure of a Garbo or a Dietrich, the planes and shadows a camera loves to explore, far more, in fact, than Helen Hayes's or Ina Claire's. But the largeness of her features, so explicit they could be seen in clear detail from the last row of the balcony, might have been less than an asset on the screen where the camera enlarges and exaggerates. Her voice and gestures were eloquent theatre props that might have been too much for the screen, necessitating adjustments so basic that she could not make them. And beyond physical equipment — and most important — it is possible that the quality she had as an individual, the unique something about her that transcended technique and craft and fifth-rate writing might not have transcended cameras; it would not have come through to an audience without her physical presence. (In the 1950s she made two successful appearances in live television, but that was another era, another time in her life, and only in the most superficial ways was live television ever comparable to movies.

Thus her decision not to make the movie of *The Barretts* — or, as it turned out, any other movie — may have been a matter of artistic selection, but not consciously so; and even with all the other possible explanations for her refusal — her fear, her modesty, her lassitude, what Laura Elliot called her "inner renunciation that often is inertia" — her real motivation was simpler: it was her love for the theatre. It can be described as "romantic" love (which Guthrie and Gert made practical), an idealization that no amount of unromantic experience ever seemed to diminish. She had no rivals in the theatre simply because she refused to compete, but sometimes other actresses of a more competitive nature, specifically Tallulah Bankhead, called her an amateur. In the popular sense of the word as "unskilled dabbler" the judgment is not so much preposterous as it is lacking in perspicacity, for Katharine Cornell's high degree of professionalism was the quality that any detractor had to admire, and in matters of consistency and reliability far outshone Miss Bankhead's. What Tallulah was criticizing — possibly because she envied it — was that with Kit's professionalism she never lost the romantic illusion that young girls find when they first start emoting for the bedroom mirror and lose the minute they come out from behind closed doors. Kit even managed to retain a suggestion of that youthful mirror-acting in the stage techniques of her maturity, which a sophisticate of Tallulah's advanced attitudes would find ludicrous. Ironically, that unsullied romanticism may have been a great part of what audiences responded to in Kit. Intending a brittle insult, Tallulah may have inadvertently hit on a truth and tossed a bouquet, for in its strictest sense the word amateur means lover, and of her time and her generation, Kit was the theatre's most ardent lover.

Which she demonstrated by continuing to turn down movie roles, many of which eventually won Academy Awards for other actresses, from Olan in *The Good Earth* (Luise Rainer), to Pilar in *For Whom the Bell Tolls* (Katina Paxinou), two roles which certainly attest to the range and versatility of her talent in movie producers' eyes. She knew that in years to come she risked being dismissed as "just a stage actress," but the soubriquet, because of its condescension, became part of the reason for her determination. With the onrushing popularity of movies, the theatre was being dismissed entirely too easily and it got her back up. More and more the audiences were deserting the theatre for the easier, faster, and more available escape of the movies, and critics began to say that the theatre was dying. At the end of each season they would add up the number of shows produced and point out significantly how many fewer there were than the year before, how many fewer hits, how many fewer new playwrights, how many fewer new stars, how much shorter the runs were, and how much less money was changing hands. (They still do it today.) The theatre was not by any means dying, but it had been seriously wounded. The movies certainly did not need her help to get along, whereas the theatre needed the strength of her commitment more than ever, and the more they willed it to die, the more determined she was that it shouldn't.

———

Helen Hayes was mentioned for the movie Elizabeth, and it seems to be the only role that either she or Kit ever played that anyone at any time ever considered them both for, so disparate were their talents. Then there was a bad moment or two when it seemed that through studio politics Marion Davies might be given the part, but Miss Davies was only one man's idea of a Victorian poet, and Elizabeth eventually went to Irving Thalberg's wife, Norma Shearer, a prototypical and oddly unphotogenic movie actress who with executive drive and a powerful husband was building a highly respected career on roles from the stage — *Strange Interlude, The Last of Mrs. Cheyney,* and others. Co-starring actors with solid stage training, Frederic March as Browning and Charles Laughton (not yet thirty-five and two years younger than March) as a chillingly sensual Edward Moulton-Barrett, the movie, released in 1934, was a success.

At that time Rudolf Besier, with whom Kit had become good friends mostly through correspondence, and who consistently misspelled her name in his salutations, wrote to her: "I feel a little like Judas Iscariot. For a bagful of dollars I betrayed a beautiful soul to her worst enemies — MGM and Norma Shearer — and they have done her to death. Happily for my conscience I have dear you to share my sin with. For you did dip your little hand into the bag and pocket a few of those accursed dollars. I don't want to be blasphemous, but the thought comforts me...."

The amount of money Irving Thalberg offered Kit to play Elizabeth on the screen hardly seems to have registered with her, and she was famous for never going into any production with the thought of making money, let alone for that specific purpose. Gert worried about money for her and kept a shrewd eye on it, finding personal satisfaction, for example, when Kit made enough from *The Barretts* to pay off the mortgage on 23 Beekman Place. Conger Goodyear also kept an eye on Kit's financial affairs and scolded Gert for paying off the mortgage; Stanton Griffis was always there with advice and guidance, and even Guthrie, but Kit herself admitted to being hopeless about money, even in her personal everyday life. There was the time Gert and Guthrie apparently got their wires crossed and Kit had to travel alone, unchaperoned and unattended, through Germany on a train. After a delicious meal in the dining car she discovered that she had boarded the train with an empty purse, containing neither money nor identification. Of course she had no trouble persuading the American couple at the table with her to lend her the price of her meal, and Gert was not at all surprised to receive a cable directing her to send this unexplained amount of money to these perfectly strange people in Kansas. It could all have been predicted.

Periodically, in an effort to reform and be wise about money, Kit would keep a scrawled record on the torn half of an envelope that had come in the morning's mail, dollar signs and illegible arrows and figures scratched across the address and cancellation, but she never improved. Once after World War II, out Christmas shopping alone, she went into the American Women's Voluntary Service, a fashionable boutique on Madison Avenue selling lovely antique furniture donated by wealthy women for charity. She found something she wanted for Guthrie or Gert but of course had no money. One of the women in the shop recognized her and offered her a blank check, showing her how to fill it out, first writing the name of her bank at the top. Kit was grateful and agreeable but couldn't remember the name of her bank, although she was sure it had the word "national" in it. National City, suggested the saleswoman. That was it, Kit agreed, and filled out the check, adding "Park Avenue Branch" in a proud burst of knowledge. Several days later the manager of the Park Avenue Branch of the National City Bank called Gert, rather bewildered by this check that had come through since Miss Cornell had no account with them. Gert, never having heard of the American Women's Voluntary Service and not having been informed that Kit had been out shopping alone, judged the whole thing to be a forgery and told the bank so, rather indignant that someone was going around posing as Katharine Cornell, all the same assuring the bank — half through a suspicious uncertainty about Kit when it came to money, and half through an instinctive effort to maintain good public relations at any cost — that Miss Cornell would make good the check. Kit was rather annoyed that she couldn't even do a little secret Christmas shopping without everybody getting on the telephone about it, but was rather taken aback to find that her checking account was with the Chase National Bank, not the National City Bank, and had been for twenty years. When Gert called the manager of the National City Bank on Park Avenue and apologized for all the inconvenience, he was not angry but rather charmed and suggested that since Miss Cornell liked the name of his bank and seemed to remember it, wouldn't it be wise to let him open an account for her and then this kind of thing couldn't happen again.

Her innocence about money being common knowledge among her friends and professional associates, Besier's letter has a slightly malicious ring when he says of the money paid by MGM for the movie rights: "For you did dip your little hand into the bag and pocket a few of those accursed dollars." He was a scholarly gentleman who loved her and usually filled his letters with domestic references to his wife's health and his own gout, so it is not likely that the observation was meant to be churlish, he was merely jesting about an opinion he shared with more than a few others who knew her professionally — that underneath her financially bland facade she was a knowledgeable businesswoman who understood in fine detail the ins and outs of every financial arrangement connected with her productions. An actor who toured with her in the early 1950s tells of coming upon her in her dressing room one night poring over a small black notebook which she said was a record of the house receipts for every engagement she had ever played in that theatre, and she was checking back and comparing to see how well she was doing this time.

The claim made on her behalf — certainly never made by herself — is that she was truly her own manager, making all managerial decisions but preferring to let those around her, her close inner circle, think they had made them because it kept everyone busy and happy. Despite Besier's touch of malice, the theory is still meant as a compliment, but it is hard to credit if only because the pose itself would have been next to impossible to sustain for so many years.

And yet besides Besier's intimating tone of voice, there is other tangible evidence, in her own hand, dating back to younger years, that she was not as oblivious to money matters as she always seemed. Mrs. Brock Pemberton was responsible for Kit's clothes in *The Green Hat*, and after the play opened in Detroit, Kit wrote her a routine thank-you note, almost formally social in flavor. It would be perfectly natural for her to tell Mrs. Pemberton how well the play was doing but, after her brief thanks, this is the way she phrased it: "We opened to $2200, the next night played to $2000, and Tuesday to $2100 and have kept it up ever since. We are breaking Detroit records — rather good."

That is a rather specific logging of figures — almost to the point of showing active research — to include in a casual note to your costume designer, written by one who in later years they would say was so vague about money that she couldn't make it up Madison Avenue without getting into financial trouble. With her documented sense of responsibility, if she had that much business awareness when it came to somebody else's production, it is not likely that she would have less when it came to her own.

Kit's house at Sneden's Landing was called the Log Cabin because Mrs. Tonetti, when she almost literally threw it together, ordered from John Wanamaker's catalogue a log cabin studio to be tacked onto a small old Colonial house she had bought and wheeled down from Tappan. Since then she had cut a skylight into the north roof to give any resident artist enough light, plastered the inside of the cabin, put something like plywood over the outside log curves to make the facade flat and solid, and built an enormous masonry fireplace into the wall connecting the cabin to the house. Aside from four bedrooms and two baths, all rather tiny and dark but comfortable, there was now a servant's room and bath, but the conglomerate was still called the Log Cabin. Mrs. Tonetti had long since given it to Anne, who rented it to Kit on a yearly basis. Then when Kit's erratic schedule precluded her using the house for extended periods of time, Anne rented it on a seasonal basis — other leaders in the arts were always willing to pay a good price to spend a few months in "Katharine Cornell's house" — and made enough for improvements and profit. This elastic arrangement lasted for twenty-five years, until 1952. Anne had the house painted every year and was constantly after Gert to find out if Kit was happy with the furniture and the fittings, was there anything she would like changed, what improvements should be made and even what repairs needed to be done. She knew that Kit would never complain on her own but that Gert would complain loudly on her behalf.

In midsummer 1931 *The Barretts* had run for six months and it was clear that if it couldn't run forever, it certainly could run a year, two years, three years, all stretching endlessly ahead night after night, performance after performance, season after season. The summer heat was excessive, and there was not the most primitive air conditioning in the Empire Theatre, not even the new process of directing electric fans into the auditorium over cakes of ice. Kit's costumes were heavy, silks and brocades over two or three petticoats, and even her head was bowed under the masses of false curls, like dark fibrous wood shavings, she wore. The first act, before Elizabeth tried to walk, ran fifty-five minutes and she spent it entirely on the sofa, with shawls draped around her shoulders and the lower half of her body under a heavily embroidered woolen afghan.

Even 23 Beekman Place was sunk in summer heat, and Kit's escape was the Log Cabin at Sneden's Landing where the Hudson generated cooler breezes than the East River. Mrs. Tonetti had a small inboard motorboat that occasionally served as a private ferry from Sneden's Landing to Dobbs Ferry where the New York Central could be taken into the city, so there was no justifiable fear of being trapped on the wrong side of the Hudson by a malfunction of the ferries at One Hundred and Twenty-fifth Street and Forty-second Street, but to minimize the risk of missing or even being five minutes late for a performance, it was Kit's usual practice to go to Sneden's only on weekends, even so leaving early enough on Monday afternoons to arrive at 23 Beekman Place by five o'clock at the latest for a lamb chop before the evening performance. In case of tire punctures and other breakdowns, there were two sister taxi drivers at Sneden's, Emma and Kathleen Stuart, who could take her to One Hundred and Twenty-fifth Street where she could board the ferry on foot and pick up a taxi on the New York side for the journey downtown.

As the summer progressed Kit began to feel a pressure at the back of her neck and a constant vibration developed inside her head at the base of the skull. Seeking relief, she started going to Sneden's Landing every night after the performance, her hair still wringing wet from the stage heat, drying in the car as Gert sped her across Forty-first Street from the Empire to catch the last Forty-second Street ferry at eleven-twenty. The next day Kit could do nothing but lie on her back listlessly reading, unaware that in addition to the other pressures, her eyes were bad and she needed glasses. Plagued by the fear of something happening to jeopardize the jobs of the sixty people dependent on her, she lost weight and the fear began to show in her eyes. An extra matinee was added on Thursday and both Saturday performances were omitted, cutting down the weekly performances from eight to seven (without cutting the actors' salaries, however, the management absorbing the loss) and providing almost a three-day weekend.

A lump developed at the base of her skull which was not her imagination as others could feel it, too, and she was close to panic at the thought of falling ill and failing in her responsibilities. Doctors were consulted who could find nothing physically wrong with her. What Brooks Atkinson called the "piercing stares" of her "disciplined fury" onstage now became part of her bearing offstage.

Margaret Barker's father was one of the first psychiatrists of distinction at John Hopkins, and on her own Gert called him and worked out a plan. He came to New York to see *The Barretts* and went through the formality of asking if he could come backstage to thank Kit for the many kindnesses she had shown his daughter. After a few minutes of the amenities, Kit became aware that he was studying her and asking too many unusual questions for this to be a casual visit. When he was gone, she accused Gert of subjecting her to a psychiatric examination without permission, and Gert had to admit the truth. Psychiatry was still in its infancy, and to the layman it was as frightening as the illnesses it treated.

Dr. Barker consulted with Guthrie the next day and said that Kit was not in a breakdown, but that she was too mentally and emotionally exhausted to keep up the pace and endure the strain of a long run. Were she his daughter, he would close the play for six weeks. In the middle of the Depression with greatly reduced theatrical activity, the actors, having thought themselves secure in a hit, would be put on the streets for six weeks at the beginning of the new season, too late to look for other jobs. Kit refused to think of it, saying it was inexcusable for the actors to be penalized for her defection. Finally it was agreed that the cast would be paid during the six weeks' lay-off, those receiving under a hundred dollars a week continuing at full salary, those being paid over a hundred dollars a week receiving half.

Quite a party traipsed off to Bermuda in October, including Margalo Gillmore, Brenda Forbes, and Joyce Carey. Kit and Gert took a house with Simpson to watch over them and pamper Kit and fix picnic baskets for the beach. Everything was supposed to be relaxed and fun, but instead of getting better, Kit got worse. Sometimes when the others went out sightseeing or partying, she and Gert would stay at home for a quiet dinner and an evening of reading or playing records, but suddenly in the middle of the meal Kit would get up from the table without a word, walk out the front door and not come back all evening, walking endlessly on the beach alone, moody, silent, severe in her silence. She got it into her head that she couldn't sleep and had to have a masseuse from New York. Miss Bjornsen was an enormous, powerful Norwegian who in her time had tended John D. Rockefeller, Sr., and massaged Paderewski's hands before he gave concerts, and according to Kit she had a special touch, a unique power in her manipulation. Miss Bjornsen arrived on the next boat, stepped ashore and announced that this climate would depress anyone and they must go to Lake Placid at once. They had been in Bermuda only two and a half weeks, but Gert packed Kit up and together with Miss Bjornsen they returned to New York where Gert got Kit's car out of storage and drove the party to Lake Placid with Miss Bjornsen constantly challenging her qualifications as a chauffeur and asserting that the cold air and massage would invigorate Kit and make her well.

They lived in a three-bedroom cottage off by itself on the grounds of the exclusive Lake Placid Club, where a boy on a bicycle brought their breakfasts each morning. Kit had her other meals sent in, too, leaving Gert and Miss Bjornsen to hike up the hill to the main dining room (with Miss Bjornsen telling Gert she was too young to be so easily winded) where everything on the menu was spelled in Basic English — "letus" was "lettuce" and "kantalope" for "cantaloupe." Miss Bjornsen was not the most scintillating dinner partner, being mainly absorbed in watching all the other diners for symptoms of physical degeneration and loudly announcing her diagnoses. Once she gave Gert a massage and told her she had tuberculosis of the kidney. Gert had a feeling she would spell it "kidnee."

But Kit adored Miss Bjornsen, as she seemed to adore so many physically imposing women, and responded to her treatment well enough to return to *The Barretts* on schedule. Broadway wisemen had predicted that no play could survive such a lay-off, no matter how big a hit it was, but the day after the reopening the box office was swamped with mail orders and there was an unbroken line out the lobby and down Broadway, waiting to buy tickets.

It is the logic of the theatre that when a play is dying and might be saved, at least for a time, by a little publicity, there is no money to hire a press agent, and when a play is a success that nothing in the world could kill, the first thought is to hire a press agent — only then he is called a press representative. *The Barretts of Wimpole Street* paid back its investment in the third or fourth week of the original

New York run, less than two months after its first performance, and Guthrie said, "What we need is a Ray Henderson." Somebody else said why not get Ray Henderson himself, an idea which had not occurred to Guthrie who, at times, still thought like a poor relation from out West.

Since he was Guthrie's ideal, it goes without saying that Ray Henderson had been Winthrop Ames's press representative during his last years in the theatre. Before that he had been with Forbes-Robertson, Maxine Elliott, Julia Marlowe and E. H. Sothern, William Faversham, and George Arliss and had become as distinguished in his field as his clients were in theirs, selecting them discriminately as much as they selected him, serving only one at a time with undivided loyalty unique among press representatives of the day who, promoting themselves as much as their clients, liked to have as many clients as possible. For that reason, Henderson was both honored in the theatre and respected by the press.

For the same reason, he was very expensive, but that was not a consideration. The main problem was his current professional arrangement with Ethel Barrymore which, upon investigation, turned out to be an unhappy association on the verge of dissolution. Miss Barrymore was touring in *Scarlet Sister Mary* and when, as her advance man, Henderson settled for an upright piano in her Boston hotel suite instead of the preferred grand, the ensuing altercation convinced him that it was time to move on to another client.

His active interest in Kit dated back to 1917 when Mrs. Wolcott may have thought she was the one to bring Kit to William Faversham's attention but Ray Henderson was the one who saw her in *Plots and Playwrights* and vouched for her talent. And part of Dr. Cornell's eventual acquiescence to Kit's joining the Jessie Bonstelle stock company was due to his faith in Ray Henderson, who had taken the time to write to him and tell him that his daughter was conducting herself like a professional with the Washington Square Players.

Henderson may have been honored in the theatre and respected by the press, but he was unknown to the public, for he did not think the public should think his talented clients needed a press representative. Therefore, having joined Cornell and McClintic, his name never appeared in any program for their productions. He didn't even look like the public's idea of a press representative as depicted in the popular movies and plays about show business. In his early forties, with straight brown hair parted on the side, a quiet, cultivated voice, dignified in English suits and rimless glasses but rather jaunty in bow ties and a mustache (before mustaches were taken seriously enough to be fashionable), he smoked a pipe and might have been in the diplomatic service. As a matter of fact, it was Guthrie's favorite way of describing Ray Henderson to say, "He is more than a press agent — he is an ambassador."

Laura Elliot had a theory that perhaps Kit's greatest talent was her sense of how to select the people around her. Kit wasn't aware of it herself, but by a miracle she attracted people who would serve her best and in so doing would allow her to bring out the best in themselves. To a great extent no one can go out and find such people, they must be drawn almost mystically.

"When she came into my studio on Fifty-seventh Street," Laura said, "I was supposed to be her singing teacher, but she didn't really want to sing — she drew something out of me that I saw helped her — and in so doing enriched my life beyond belief."

It was a theory Mrs. Elliot started advancing as one by one the members of the circle formed around Kit, from Eveline Drysdale and Wayne Simpson to Stanton Griffis and Conger Goodyear, with Guthrie and Gert in between. The acquisition of Ray Henderson was the final, triumphant, proof of her theory. Kit found press agents on the whole an unattractive lot, people she would like to avoid with their cheap sense of gritty newspaper columns and Broadway gossip, and the luck and instinct and wisdom and *talent* that inevitably compelled her to attract Ray Henderson — at just the right time — Laura said was god-given.

Kit presented problems that would have stymied the average press agent. There were no anecdotes, no funny stories, no crazy peccadillos, no Bohemian whims, none of the things to gladden a flackman's heart. She seldom gave parties and almost never went to them, and even when appearing every evening in a play and compelled to stay up late, she was asleep before New York night life began. If she guessed that she was the subject of gossipy speculation, she never let on. She valued her privacy. But she was not obsessively private, in the Garbo way, having a great reputation for smiling warmth and openness. She had no outrageous political beliefs, inclining to the conservative, or religious views, believing in God and life after death ("Or what is the point of all this?" she would ask), and the principles of her art — that it involved discipline and hard work — were not what the public wanted to hear about, being themselves slaves to discipline and hard work. She had no feuds with anyone. She was not jealous of her contemporaries, her predecessors, or of youth, and those who bore grudges against her could not be found, while those who harbored uncharitable thoughts about her kept them to themselves for fear of appearing churlish. She was a modest, thoroughly nice woman from Buffalo, daughter of a good respectable upstate family.

Above all she was one of a fast-disappearing breed: she was a lady. And it was Henderson's instinct to know that even in the midst of a great depression, perhaps especially then — with old values being questioned and slipping away — that was exactly what the public wanted her to be; it was the very quality the critics had been fussing and stewing about all through the twenties, causing them to stamp and cheer the transition — progression — from Madeleine Carey to Elizabeth Barrett.

Henderson was the first press agent in the business to evolve a system of reliable, interesting releases to every newspaper in the country every week concerning Miss Cornell's plans, Miss Cornell's activities, Miss Cornell's audiences, Miss Cornell's honors, Miss Cornell's holidays, and very often, Miss Cornell's thoughts. When he referred to her in his releases as Katharine Cornell, the second "a" in Katharine was always underscored to preclude the possibility of misspelling, but mainly she was referred to as Miss Cornell to such a degree that the press picked it up from him and often in straight news articles of their own about current theatrical events they would refer to Helen Hayes, Lynn Fontanne, Tallulah Bankhead, and Miss Cornell.

The theatre was Ray Henderson's passion, but music was his love, and he usually spent his summers abroad reporting the festivals at Salzburg and Bayreuth as special correspondent to the *New York Times*. He was certainly one of the last great letter-writers, not only writing brilliant, questioning letters to men like Bernard Shaw, but inspiring in them brilliant questioning answers, in Shaw's case precipitating such an onrush of thought (albeit irate) that the playwright turned Henderson's letter over and wrote his answer on the back as if not to waste time taking out a fresh sheet of paper. Of all those connected with *The Barretts*, Henderson sustained the longest and most personal correspondence with Rudolf Besier, and in his press releases he did not condescend to the public by sacrificing the language and mode of expression he used in reporting music festivals or corresponding with the world's leading playwrights. His releases for *The Barretts* — always marked "Special — Not Duplicated" — were given such titles as "What Happened to the Barretts After the Last Curtain Dropped," "The Author of Katharine Cornell's Play Is Not Like the Traditional Playwright," and "When History Invades the Theatre." When she returned to Broadway after her six-week lay-off, she had no trouble finding her audience again because Ray Henderson had never let them go. All the time she was gone they had been reading stories about her progress in Bermuda and Lake Placid. His articles always dispensed unusual information or made fascinating observations, sometimes including comments and contributions from audiences as well as provocative, well-parsed thoughts attributed to Miss Cornell, presented inside quotation marks.

Ray Henderson gave Kit a public voice in much the same way that Gert, in maintaining her correspondence, gave her a private voice. In the days of *The Green Hat*, Kit had learned to give buoyant, spontaneous interviews, always impressing the interviewers with her "black satin frock with a few ermines at the cuffs and the invariable scarf, red-violet, wound about her throat with two fluttering ends," as she gestured broadly with the hand on which she wore a square-cut emerald and chattered on in a surprisingly personal way, "I was born old, old — as sand! Guthrie is younger!" But with the dignity and weight of managership, the interviews came harder, perhaps, and she needed to be given words to say off the stage as well as on. Had she gone on about being born old as sand it might not have come out bright and amusing anymore but rather too truthful and just a bit complaining. In case she had other reactions too quick and opinions more arbitrary than her mentors would want attributed to her, they tried to establish guidelines, to indicate a philosophy or a sense of fairness they thought worthy of her — with which she seemed willing to have them endow her.

Kit always had at hand exactly the right people to help. In a way, the benevolent circle around her was made up of those she had instinctively chosen as extensions of herself, or she of them. Together, with love and a common point of view, they formed the entity, the theatrical phenomenon known as Katharine Cornell — or, more familiarly and affectionately, Miss Cornell.

"Gert darling," Conger Goodyear wrote when Miss Bjornsen's kneading and pummeling at Lake Placid seemed to be having results, "I am on my knees with thanksgiving that you are with Kit and will be with her, I hope, ad infinitum. Really, if you insist, I will marry you and then after a while you can cyanide me and there will be what little money I have left. . . . I agree with you that Kit will not know how really well she is until she begins work again. I have always felt that would be the way it would work out. And now that the nerves are conquered, I am confident of the rest, and I agree with you, too, about her needing more play when she gets back, only it must be play, and if I bother her or anyone bothers her, you must tell us. She never would. Anyway, we can talk about it when you arrive. I am not unselfish a bit, darling, I care for Kit, I love her more than anyone else — that's all there is to it."

"Gert dear," he wrote some time later, "I am beginning to really *hate* 'The Barretts' — it's growing into a Frankenstein [monster] that swallows and consumes so much of the joy of living. It has been a long while since there has been any ease and warmth among us — instead, a driving strain and weariness. . . . Don't pass this on to Kit. I need a shoulder on which to rest my ancient head and sob, and you are young and strong and understanding."

The monster in the new Hollywood movie *Frankenstein* provided a good analogy for the way everyone had come to feel about *The Barretts* — exactly a year ago they had wondered if it would be able to run a week, and now they wondered if they would ever be free of it — but it was not a question of passing the despair on to Kit, for she had passed it on to them. After only two months back on Wimpole Street, now without the deadly summer heat, now in the crisp, invigorating January cold, all the old symptoms and complaints returned, intensified: the constant vibration inside her head, now a drumming, the pressure at the base of the skull, the terror, the anxieties. What made it worse this time was that she could not or would not talk about it to anyone, and both her private voice and her public voice were struck dumb. In her disciplined fury the only things she could articulate was that the necessity of having to go to the theatre every night — ad infinitum — was intolerable.

A meeting was held. Guthrie, Stanton, Conger, Gert, Ray and Miss Cornell decided to close the play in New York City the second week of February and tour it until the end of June on a week-to-week basis,

with the cast, the crew and the out-of-town theatre managers understanding and accepting the condition that the play could be shut down
on two weeks' notice. The minute the old responsibility of having to
continue, no matter what, was removed, Kit felt better and embraced
with enthusiasm the new responsibility of taking the play to as many
cities as possible across the country. Her fascination with the road,
which had begun in *The Green Hat*, was intensified now that she was
her own manager, and she did not believe in slighting audiences simply because they did not live in New York.

A forfeit had to be paid the Empire Theatre for taking out a success playing to capacity, but even so *The Barretts* played 370 performances, a record for the Empire unbroken until *Life with Father* ten
years later. When the newspapers carried the story of the closing,
every seat for the remainder of the run was sold within three days.
During the final week, standees arrived at the box office in the morning
for the evening performance, and hundreds were turned away.

It rained for the closing, February 13, 1932, as it had rained for
the opening, February 9, 1931, but this time nothing could keep the
audience from arriving on time, and everyone was in his seat, with
the standees three rows deep, when the curtain rose promptly at eight-
thirty on Elizabeth's first scene with Dr. Chambers. There was no
time for the actors to linger sentimentally over this last performance
as their costumes were whisked away from them at the end of each
act by Joanna Klinge, the wardrobe woman, to be packed for travel
as she had once packed for Maude Adams in the same theatre. Jerry,
the property man, had made padded boxes for the properties and furniture, and Al Shea, the electrician, had extra men standing backstage
to "take the show down" when the performance was over. The play
was scheduled to open two nights later in Boston, and by the end of
the third act it was almost ready to go.

Many of the audience had seen the play before, some of them several times, and knew the scenes almost as well as the cast. As last-act
curtains came down on other shorter plays around town, actors rushed
from their theaters in full makeup to stand backstage for the last moments of *The Barretts*. Ruth Gordon (in *The Church Mouse* at William Brady's Playhouse), Pauline Lord (in Guthrie's *Distant Drums*
at the Belasco), and Alexander Woollcott (making his acting debut in
S. N. Behrman's *Brief Moment*) crowded in the wings with Mrs.
Patrick Campbell (recently closed in a new production of *The Electra*)

and when the final curtain fell joined with the audience in applause, cheers, and tears (even the ushers were crying). There were countless curtain calls, and even Flush, a new father, took a call with one of his pups. No one wanted to leave. As many friends and fans as were able crowded into Kit's dressing room for drinks and reminiscences, and it was a long time before anyone was aware of chanting somewhere, loud voices repeatedly calling "Cornell!" George "Empire" Pierce pushed through to say that the crowd outside the stage door had been waiting a long time and wouldn't leave until Miss Cornell said good-bye. She was still in her dark red silk dress from the last act — set off by Guthrie's cabochon garnets — and even with Elizabeth Barrett's shawl over her head she was prevented by the rain from going any farther than the stage door, which old George held open for her. The best she could do was stand in the light where at least they could see her from under their umbrellas, and speaking above the street noises, she thanked them for waiting and promised to come back another year. There were cheers of gratitude and cries of encouragement, and then she begged them all to go home, now, out of the rain, which they did.

19

Haus Hirth (1932-1933)

THE 1932 TOUR of *The Barretts of Wimpole Street* — known later as "the short tour" — covered eleven cities in twenty weeks, starting in Boston and ending in San Francisco. It was Ray Henderson's feeling that in order to give audiences across the country a chance to see Miss Cornell in her greatest role and to become familiar with the words "KATHARINE CORNELL PRESENTS," no less than a full week should be spent in any city. It was the customary practice of the day, if a play toured at all, to send out the star but scuttle most of the New York cast and substitute lesser actors (in talent and salary), and then, with as big a hit as *The Barretts*, to send out second and third companies, the words "second" and "third" referring not alone to sequence but to quality, and in all road companies to cut down the New York production, economizing on the size and number of sets, eliminating fripperies, substituting lighter, flimsier scenery to make travel easier (cheaper). There never was a second company of *The Barretts*, and the production Kit took on the road was the same one that had played at the Empire with one cast change, John Emery (Tallulah Bankhead's future husband) replacing John Buckler as Captain Surtees Cook. William Lyon Phelps wrote in *Scribner's* Magazine: "As 'Scribner's Magazine' is read in every town in America, let me urge the inhabitants of every city where this play comes, not to miss it. Go without three meals if necessary, but don't let this drama pass unseen." Apparently his readers took his advice and told their friends. It was the third year of the Depression, and because of the heavy production there had to be a $3.30 top for tickets, slightly higher than most touring companies, but even so every performance sold out and played to standees.

To ease the strain of traveling on top of performing, Gert saw to it that after the mortgage was paid off on 23 Beekman Place, Kit ordered a maroon Lincoln car for touring, an elegant affair with an open front seat for the chauffeur and a special leather covering to protect him from inclement weather. Lawrence Paddelford joined them as chauffeur and was accepted so completely that he was given one of Flush's puppies. It was undoubtedly a big moment in Guthrie's life to tuck Kit under the fur lap robe in the back seat of the maroon Lincoln, and she herself always enjoyed a bit of grandeur, but she also claimed to be a born hobo, for hoboes in the 1930s were riding the rails and that was what she longed to do. And so, while Lawrence Paddelford drove the maroon Lincoln in solitary splendor from city to city, she rode along in the Pullman with the other actors, poring over train schedules and arranging to have their sleeper shunted off the main line here and there to avoid arriving at their various destinations in the middle of the night.

To ease the strain of performing on top of traveling, Gert periodically suggested that Kit "walk through" a performance, giving it by rote, just once a week, or twice, sparing herself, not plunging in and reexperiencing the play to her usual physical and mental exhaustion. Kit's answer was her fear of not giving full measure to the one member of the audience who might need it at that one particular performance, but of course the fact was that she couldn't do it any other way. It didn't cheer her or depress her to be told that an audience — even that one person in particular, whoever it might be — might not know the difference. She knew the difference, and it would make her feel even worse than she did to give less than she could.

They played Boston, Philadelphia, and Washington, and by the time they reached Baltimore Kit's symptoms had returned and she was convinced she had a brain tumor or was going insane, or both. Dr. Barker suggested a thorough going-over mentally and physically at Johns Hopkins, recommending Dr. Sidney Miller, who was also suggested by a family connection of Gert's who was head of gynecology at Johns Hopkins. In addition to submitting her to every known test for every conceivable ailment, Dr. Miller had an early version of the concealed tape recorder in his office and took down every word she said, every thought she expressed, every fear she revealed, for study. He also sent a physical therapist to study performances of *The Barretts*.

Today it might be considered a reasonable psychological explanation of her illness to say she empathized so deeply with Elizabeth Barrett at every performance that she had assumed for herself Elizabeth's invalidism. This Dr. Miller rejected completely, offering a far less complicated explanation: that from lying on the stage sofa for a year and a half in exactly the same position, supine, facing a wall, projecting her voice to her left and not just straight out but up to the top balcony, she had brought continuous pressure on certain vertebrae of the spine, causing the congestion at the base of her skull and the vibration inside her head. The lump could have been produced by her own manipulation. Dr. Miller's report concluded that she was the victim of what was called an "occupational neurosis," like tennis elbow, housemaid's knee, or writer's cramp, and her particular variation, which Toscanini once had in his right arm, Dr. Miller likened to weaver's bottom.

He suggested changing the position of the sofa on stage, if possible turning it around completely to let her face in the opposite direction. But it was like telling Toscanini to conduct with his other hand. She would agree to it in the doctor's office, but the minute she was outside she began fearing all that would have to be done — changing the position of the sofa would mean changing the position of the entrance which would mean reversing all the action — and by the time she got back to the hotel she knew she couldn't go through with it. Guthrie said he would rather close the play.

They didn't close the play. They simply went on as they were, and suddenly, miraculously, all symptoms of illness disappeared, and before anyone could stop her Kit was out taking vigorous golf lessons from Ernest Jones. Since her only therapy in the play was to sit up straighter on the sofa, it can hardly be said that Dr. Miller effected a cure, but it can be said that his diagnosis induced a crisis. To tell a woman who tends to dramatize physical affliction that her incipient insanity is no more than a neurosis could conceivably make matters worse by seeming to belittle and minimize. But if she has good sense and an active conscience, she can find instead that she has been indulging herself and always, when put to the test, preferring good health to bad, become well. If she has a shred of humor, it is hard to sustain a brain tumor that turns out to be weaver's bottom.

One of Ray Henderson's press releases during the short tour was entitled: "Flush Finds a Dog's Life Is Pretty Swell Except for Kind 'Old' Ladies And Investigators." The old ladies were dog-lovers who could hardly follow the progress of Elizabeth Barrett's love for Robert Browning for keeping an eye on the stage behavior of Flush and coming to the conclusion at the end of the play that he was drugged for the performance. An indignant report would then be filed with the Society for the Prevention of Cruelty to Animals, and the management would be informed that Flush must be examined by their veterinarian and if the suspicion was correct that he was a drug addict, he would be arrested and taken from Miss Cornell, and she would be heavily fined. Gert would persuade them to carry out the examination in the theatre, and when the examiners arrived they would be greeted by Flush, wagging all his extremities and delighted to meet the kindly strangers. A ball would be thrown for him and he would scamper off to return it to whoever would throw it for him next, until all were exhausted with the game. Then came the dramatic part of the examination. The electrician would turn on all the stage lights and Flush would be placed in his basket onstage or on Elizabeth Barrett's sofa. With all the spotlights on him, in less than a minute he was snoozing away as he snoozed happily through hundreds of performances of Mr. Besier's stimulating play. In chagrin, the investigators would apologize and once presented Flush with a handsome pewter drinking mug, suitably inscribed. In Detroit the Michigan Humane Society was so delighted with him that he was made an honorary member and given a button to wear on his collar as proof of his good standing. To forestall his arrest, in each new city he was taken for walks during intermissions so that members of the audience who might be suspicious could see him frolicking hilariously on the sidewalk outside the theatre.

On opening night in Los Angeles, Douglas Fairbanks, Sr., decided at the last minute to bring a party, and since there were no seats left, a row of gilt chairs was stretched across the front of the orchestra. In his autobiography (*A Proper Job*) Brian Aherne recalls the intimidating effect of looking down to see, their chins practically resting on the edge of the stage, Douglas Fairbanks, Sr., and Mary Pickford, Douglas, Jr., and Joan Crawford, Irving Thalberg and Norma Shearer,

Norma Talmadge and Joe Schenk, Constance Bennett and Gilbert Roland, Ruth Chatterton and Ralph Forbes, and Charlie Chaplin.

But for Kit the most memorable moment of the tour came in Chicago. During the four-week run there had been more demand than usual for the dollar seats and literally thousands were turned away. Ray Henderson, who always worked to have Miss Cornell's productions complement whatever was happening in the cities where they were playing, pointed out to her that the Chicago schoolteachers were being paid in scrip and were practically destitute. He suggested, and she agreed, that at the end of the run they give one final Sunday matinee performance at the biggest auditorium in town, the Civic Opera House (capacity four thousand), for a dollar a ticket, general admission, no reserved seats, donating the proceeds to the Teachers' Sick Fund. Samuel Insull, the public utility magnate, charged them five hundred dollars for the rental of the house, and the stagehands insisted on full pay, but the actors and staff donated their services, Besier waived royalty, and there were no paid advertisements. The announcement was made on Thursday afternoon in the newspapers, on the radio, and at the schools that tickets would go on sale at the box office at ten o'clock on Sunday morning on a first-come first-served basis, with not a ticket to be sold in advance or through an agency.

Miss Cornell herself was to sell the first hundred tickets, and at nine-thirty on Sunday morning when she and Gert left the town house she had rented for the run of the play, she was apprehensive that no one would show up, but as they crossed the bridge they overtook a line of people ten feet wide, three blocks long, going around the Opera House and out over the bridge. It had begun forming at midnight the night before. Kit's first thought was that she should get out and walk, that with the teachers destitute and all these people standing in line all night there was something wrong about driving up to the box office in the maroon Lincoln with Lawrence Paddelford at the wheel. Gert convinced her that was the way the crowd *wanted* to see her arrive — which was true, judging from the cheers that greeted her.

In the box office she found a pile of dollar bills with slips of paper pinned to them "for the directors," which she put aside with the remark that if the directors wanted tickets they would have to stand in line. The fire chief said he would stop the performance if he didn't get seats, but he didn't get seats. Before the performance Kit went to every member of the company and asked him not to smoke backstage that afternoon, no matter how much he wanted to, not even to light a match, not to do anything that would give the fire chief a chance to make trouble. The cast complied, and the performance was not stopped.

The entire house was sold out within an hour and the hundreds still waiting in line had to be turned away. As many standees as possible were admitted without breaking the fire laws, and the cheering at the end of the performance was gratifying, although the auditorium was so large that it was doubtful that everyone heard the play, let alone appreciated the nuances. But the thrill of the afternoon was that it happened. After Mr. Insull got his five hundred dollars and the stage-hands got their cut and ten per cent of the gross was donated to the Actors' Fund Of America, the stricken schoolteachers received an unexpected windfall of $2,761.20.

When the tour ended in San Francisco on July 2, 1932, no one would have guessed that it wasn't the end of the production for good. Only six months before it had become a Frankenstein's monster, but now there was a reluctance to let go of it, and the final performance was a sentimental one. Kit, with the threat of illness and breakdown still darkening the back of her mind, but at last freed from her painful confinement to Elizabeth Barrett's sickroom, found herself moved by her line to Wilson in the last act: "It's impossible to believe that in a little more than an hour I shall have left this room, never, in all likelihood, to see it again."

———

July 1932, Bavaria, in the shadow of the Zugspitze. As a mountain thunderstorm broke over Garmisch-Partenkirchen, a car drove up to Haus Hirth near the village of Grainau, and a skittish man clutching books and manuscripts to his bosom scampered through the downpour into the pension. When the genial, white-haired host and proprietor, Herr Hirth, offered the protection of an umbrella and suggested putting the car in the garage for easier unloading, the new arrival was too concerned about his books — whether or not they had gotten wet — to more than grunt that he didn't drive. Herr Hirth, concluding that there must be someone still in the car who did drive, went out with his umbrella and offered assistance to the smiling, dark-eyed woman he found waiting patiently behind the wheel of the car for the rain to stop. He knew at once that she was the American actress his friends the Kleibers had asked him to make welcome.

Months before in New York, when all of Kit's friends were concerned for her well-being, Woollcott, dismissing the meager curative powers of a Bermuda or a Lake Placid, sounded the call to the colors at a small gathering, asserting that a Happy Valley must be found for Kit to get away to. Ruth Kleiber, wife of the Austrian conductor Erich Kleiber, turned to Kit and said, "Go to Grainau, to Johanna Hirth. That is the only place where you will get well."

Johanna Hirth originally came from Darmstadt where her father was attorney for the Grand Duke of Hesse, the grandson of Queen Victoria. Born in 1889, Johanna grew up on familiar terms with European aristocracy and was even allowed glimpses of Victoria, on her visits to the castle at Darmstadt, patrolling the grounds in a Bath chair drawn by two ponies. After an early marriage and the subsequent loss of her young husband in the Great War, Johanna married Walther Hirth at about the time Kit married Guthrie.

Walther had grown up in Munich where after the war he sold his family's profitable newspaper interests for a fortune he then lost in the first big inflation. With the loss of the family house in Munich, he removed to Grainau where some years before he had designed and built a Bavarian country house for his mother. Walther's endeavors, like his girth, were likely to expand, and even his mother, accustomed to a life of city luxury and elegance, found Haus Hirth at Grainau too overextended for comfortable living. Walther and Johanna now took refuge there with family treasures salvaged from Munich, magnificent Biedermeier furniture, carpets, books, paintings, linens, and fine china. With very little money and too many rooms, they decided to encourage visits from paying guests among their urban acquaintances seeking peace and leisure in the country. Johanna's brother, Emil Preetorius, was a brilliant scenic artist celebrated throughout Europe, designer at the Bayreuth festivals; another brother was a Bavarian senator and teacher at the Academy. Both recommended Haus Hirth to their friends. Soon an elite sampling of musical and theatrical personages began mingling with Munich affluence and Hesse-Darmstadt aristocracy at Haus Hirth. But guests were not limited to the German nationality. Conger Goodyear, who followed Kit there and became a regular guest, recalled years later: "The company was various; a snooty British fishing curate and his handsome curatess; keen clicking Ellen Tennant; the handsome captain of the Oxford Rugby team." Nor were the guests limited to adults. Among the teenagers who smile out from the scrapbooks of the 1930s were Philip Mountbatten of Greece (later Duke of Edinburgh, Prince of Great Britain), and Eugene List of the United States (a frequent visitor with his piano teacher Olga Samaroff, Leopold Stokowski's first wife). There was only one restriction on guests: they must be friends or friends of friends.

Ruth Kleiber wrote Walther and Johanna Hirth to make room for Katharine Cornell, should she seek it. After *The Barretts* closed in San Francisco, Kit and Guthrie headed east, then on to Europe. Kit had once driven through Garmisch and, intrigued with the idea of staying there, wired Haus Hirth from Venice specifying the time she and Guthrie would arrive. Rain was such a part of important days in her life that it is too easy to see bright foreshadowing in the thunderstorm that broke as they drove up to Haus Hirth. Besides, even Guthrie was too busy protecting his precious books and manuscripts from the downpour to look for signs.

The logotype for Haus Hirth, used as a letterhead — a kind of coat of arms also appearing on the facade of the establishment, under the eaves over a second-story window — was a dachshund, assis, bearing like a banner or a picket sign a large "H" on a long staff. Frau Hirth bred and trained dachshunds, and on the night Kit and Guthrie arrived one of her bitches was whelping. She and Walther were sitting up with the dog, and Kit, unable to sleep, heard their voices and joined the vigil, helping, when the time came, to give birth to the litter. It was a significant action with consequences — Johanna Hirth has always maintained because it gave her a feeling of usefulness — instilling in Kit overnight two new and driving loves: one for dachshunds, the other for Haus Hirth, or, more specifically, for Johanna Hirth herself. That first year, Kit arrived intending to stay two weeks. She stayed three months and came back five years straight running.

In an atmosphere of decorous informality there were never more than twenty guests at Haus Hirth and they all dressed for dinner, sitting at one candlelit table presided over by Walther at one end in lederhosen and Johanna at the other in exquisitely embroidered Bavarian dirndls with a delicate lace headgear replacing the kerchief she wore during the day. After dinner she sat by her workbasket in the main salon, mending the house linen while her talented guests performed for one another — sang, played, recited, read aloud. On occasion Walther, for all his heft, would dance, to everyone's amusement. Everyone was indeed a houseguest. No account was kept of food or drink or other services, although there was some kind of daily rate, which was never referred to, and payment was made at the end of a visit discreetly, not to offend anyone's sensibilities. Walther was in charge of the business affairs, and perhaps it was never a profitable operation or perhaps that was only Kit's impression, because to help out, discreetly, at least once she left behind the car in which she had arrived, a Model A Ford convertible coupé, donating it for general use at the pension.

Kit was up early each day, before anyone else, reading downstairs in a comfortable windowed corner. To please Johanna, she always breakfasted on a soft-boiled egg. Johanna was proud of her eggs, which were better than anyone else's because she knew the best way to feed chickens. After breakfast there were the dogs to be seen to, and then perhaps sunning on the loggia, where grapevines grew over trellises. Walther was the official greeter and genial host, the fixer of things, the planner, builder, and expander, the decorator and arbiter of taste, while Johanna saw to it that the house and grounds ran silently and well. The gardens beyond the loggia were hers, and there were always fresh vegetables on the dinner table. Kit followed Johanna into the kitchen, where Johanna did not actually do all the cooking but strongly supervised Vevi, the plump Bavarian cook who became a favorite of Kit's, and one of Kit's greatest pleasures was being allowed to put the freshly laundered linen away. If the morning chores were finished in time, there was a ritual walk with the dogs to a cliff high up on the mountainside. Other guests vied for the privilege of taking this walk with Johanna, and if it was not Kit's turn, she had time for letter-writing, telling everyone in New York in her indecipherable scrawl how happy she was, until lunch at one or one-thirty.

Afternoons were for reading and line-study. Or Kit and Johanna read Shakespeare's plays aloud to each other — and others — with Kit reading a scene in English and Johanna reading the same scene in German, following it up with a discussion of the translation, a comparison, pinpointing where subtleties had been missed and where the original text had been, perhaps, improved upon. Or Kit would read aloud in French, at which she had been proficient since writing her play "Patty en tension" when she was fourteen. She understood German and learned to get along with the servants and other guests whose language it was, but she never became fluent. What was important, however, was the sense of the language she developed, the feeling for its nuances which would give validity to her portrayal of Elsa Brandt in *Alien Corn* the following year.

Late in the afternoon there were other walks to be enjoyed, carefully tended gravel paths from one village to another along mountain streams, away from the road. There might be a twenty-five-minute walk to Grainau for shopping, or a longer one to Unter Grainau (Lower Grainau) where the railway station was. On some days there were motor trips, to Darmstadt where Kit became friends with Johanna's friends, especially the Princess Hesse, or a whole group might pack off to distant concerts in a baroque country church.

On morning walks that summer Kit described for Johanna the torment of the past year and confessed that she didn't think she could go on the stage anymore. At that point she may have been dramatizing a bit for a new audience, but if so, even so, she received the answer she needed, one that confirmed her own resolution of the problem. Johanna reminded her that she had a God-given gift and must use it, appealing to the artist's sense of responsibility to his art, rather than to himself. Frau Hirth maintains today, with no immodesty, "I gave her strength," which is undoubtedly true. Kit might have survived the torment of the past year; the drumming inside her head might have subsided, the pressure at the base of the skull might have let up, and she might have gone on working, if only because she had to, but the underlying upheaval was not eased. It may have been a sense of having reached a point of no return in both her career and her personal relationships, a realization that they were irrevocable. But her repressed dissatisfactions were not assuaged, and she did not reestablish a hold on her existence, until she met Johanna Hirth and established an emotional new friendship.

It was not easy for those around her to understand what she found there. At Kit's insistence, Gert went alone one year to "experience" Haus Hirth. After dinner on the first evening she was subjected to a flute player as the guests sat around being impressed with one another, it seemed to her, and Walther, "a flower just tied to his wife," had to be told who everyone was and even then couldn't remember and got their titles mixed up. Gert found Frau Hirth disingenuous in her expensive peasant costume, a noble and boring headmistress who dispensed spiritual manna as she darned the bed sheets. The next morning, when all the neophytes clustered around, bidding for the ritual walk by the side of the mighty one, Gert, who would have hidden under a tree to get away until lunch, said she wanted to see the village. Shunning those picturesque gravel paths along mountain streams, she gratefully hugged the road they avoided and drove her little car to the nearest outside telephone where she called her sister Min in Paris and gave her instructions: "Call me and say you have pneumonia and I have to leave." She arrived intending to stay four days and left at the end of two. She did not tell Kit precisely why she had left, but was too honest not to say there was a cult there she just couldn't join. Kit was very gentle with her, as if she were a handicapped person.

Kit never gave up wanting those she loved to love one another, and perhaps she didn't realize how fortunate it was, at times, that they didn't. It seems fairly clear that apart from the emotional stimulation of Johanna Hirth's presence, the therapeutic value of Garmisch was that it was not Broadway, that Haus Hirth was as far removed as possible from 23 Beekman Place, and that the Zugspitze bore no resemblance to Sneden's Landing. Surely Garmisch would have been less a haven had it been taken up by the very ones she needed — consciously or not — to escape from.

Guthrie was always welcome at Haus Hirth, and sometimes in the evening after he read aloud a play from his traveling stock, Frau Hirth would be so impressed that she would ask to read it for herself, later, and finding it deplorable, would marvel at the brilliance of a man who could give life to such ineptitude. Guthrie enjoyed being thus appreciated, and there were other attractions at Haus Hirth to bring a bloom to the tender plant. Unlike Gert, he enjoyed being associated with — and accepted by — titles, affluence, and inbred gentility, but like her he was too restless to calm down among them for long. On the first visit in 1932 he stayed only the scheduled two weeks, returning to New York to direct Emlyn Williams in the successful London thriller *Criminal at Large*. Another routine was thus established: Guthrie would escort Kit to Garmisch, linger a few days — mainly for sessions with a woman dentist he discovered there who was cheaper than his dentist back home — and then go off to seek his own brand of pleasure. At the end of Kit's stay, he might return to take her home, or she might be trusted to travel alone on the train from Munich to Bremerhaven, sometimes, as has been noted, forgetting to take money and being delivered on board her homebound steamer by smitten strangers. At the end of that first visit she carried on board four dachshund puppies, only one of which actually belonged to her — Sonia, the first of a long line that ended almost forty-five years later with Casper, who outlived his mistress.

It must have appealed to Kit's sense of drama to find such completeness in Germany where her mother had grown up, learned to smoke cigarettes and play the mandolin, the country where Alice Cornell spent the only happy years of her life. It must have appealed to Kit's sense of dramatic form to return thus to the land of her own birth for a kind of rebirth, to complete the circle. It was that kind of all-inclusiveness in Kit's nature that moved Johanna to say that "Kit" was too small a name for her, a trifling diminutive, and she would never use it. Instead she called her "Cornelia," not only to create a more powerful and fitting name from the root "Cornell," but also to honor Goethe's sister with a worthy namesake.

Once Kit was established as her own manager, with Gilbert Miller, Al Woods, and other producers no longer reaping the benefits of her work, Conger Goodyear said it was equally pointless to go on paying huge percentages (usually forty percent of the gross) to theatre owners. When David Belasco died in May 1931, his theatre on Forty-fourth Street became available, and at the end of August the McClintics took it on a two-year lease with an option to buy.

Gert and Stanley Gilkey refurbished the dressing rooms a bit, and Guthrie inaugurated their tenancy in November with his production of S. N. Behrman's third play, *Brief Moment*, featuring Francine Larrimore. One of the play's leading characters, as described by the author, "is very fat, about thirty years old and lies down whenever possible. He somewhat resembles Alexander Woollcott, who conceivably might play him." Even with that in the script, Behrman claimed to be surprised — and not altogether pleased — when Guthrie took him literally and cast Woollcott in the part. It was a shrewd move, however, for the play drew less than enthusiastic reviews but Woollcott's presence in the cast kept it running so long that it had to move to another theatre to make way for Guthrie's next production, *Distant Drums*, a failure that closed after forty performances. Then the house was dark almost two months until Guthrie revived A. A. Milne's 1922 comedy, *The Truth about Blayds*, which also failed, leaving the house empty five months more until *Criminal at Large* opened in October 1932, and was such a hit that it had to move to another theatre to make room for Kit's first production in her own theatre just before Christmas.

Perhaps the phenomenal success of *The Barretts* gave the group around Katharine Cornell too lofty a sense of mission in the theatre; it certainly gave them a feeling they could do no wrong, which they promptly did. In 1931, *Lucrece*, French playwright André Obey's re-telling of Shakespeare's *The Rape of Lucrece*, had been successfully produced in Paris and London by La Compagnie des Quinze. Conger Goodyear went to the London production twice, once with Clemence Dane and once with Mrs. Patrick Campbell, both of whom agreed with him that it would make an excellent piece for Katharine Cornell. He sent her a copy of the play which Joyce Carey read aloud one afternoon, in French, and Kit was enchanted. Goodyear went to Paris to negotiate the terms of production with the author, and even before *The Barretts* closed, *Lucrece* was settled on as Miss Cornell's next production. If it can be said that with her elevation to managership Katharine Cornell became an institution, then *Lucrece* was surely an institutional choice — with a nod to the classics, a bow to the contemporary, and a highminded introduction of the best European art to the commerce-ridden streets of Broadway.

La Compagnie des Quinze opposed realism and with the simplest staging sought to bring poetry back to the theatre. Their production of *Lucrece* had been unaffected to the point of austerity, with young dancers, against drapes, playing out the scenes, most of them wordless, as their movements were described, defined, and interpreted by two narrators, a man representing history and a woman presenting the more compassionate view of poetry. Guthrie maintained that a Cornell production demanded magnificence, and everyone agreed.

Thornton Wilder, who had won his first Pulitzer Prize in 1928 for his novel *The Bridge of San Luis Rey*, was persuaded by Guthrie to come into the theatre and do the translation. Heretofore, Wilder had dabbled only in one-act plays, even those being of a literary nature not suitable for professional production, but Guthrie thought that

Lucrece needed his literate use of English as well as his knowledge of French — and thereby performed a profound service to the American theatre of the next three decades.

For the stage set Robert Edmond Jones created, against gray velvet, a spacious Roman colonnade within which the actors, dressed in rich, warm Renaissance colors, moved through imaginary doors, wielding imaginary props. The first-act picture of Lucrece and her handmaidens spinning was the loveliest tableau New York had seen in years, and the entire stage seemed a magnificent renaissance tapestry come to life. It will be remembered that Jones was one of the original backers of the Washington Square Players where Kit said her first four words on the professional stage in *Bushido*. Since then he had become especially esteemed for the stark eloquence of his settings for O'Neill's plays, and he was now so taken with *Lucrece* and so eager to work with Miss Cornell that in his enthusiasm he almost violated an exclusive contract he had signed with the new Radio City Music Hall.

The theatre was moving into the 1930s along with the rest of the country, and unions were a growing consideration, sometimes a concern. Actors' Equity at first maintained it was too soon after the closing of *The Barretts* for Brian Aherne, an English actor, to be given another leading role in a New York production. But, as in the dispute between Robert Edmond Jones and the Radio City Music Hall, a concession was made, and Aherne, costumed by Jones, was magnificent to look at and listen to as Tarquin, the young prince who determines to test the virtue of Collatine's wife, Lucrece, thus generating the action of the play. As usual, Kit surrounded herself with as many actors as possible from past productions. From *The Barretts,* in addition to Aherne, the new cast included Joyce Carey, Brenda Forbes, and Charles Waldron. Pedro De Cordoba, Morell in her 1925 *Candida,* played Collatine, and even Robert Loraine, the only actor she ever admittedly didn't get along with, apparently had established a bond simply by being with her in *Tiger Cats* and joined *Lucrece* (at the same theatre) as one of the narrators. Blanche Yurka was the other, and in half-masks of dull gold and bronze-green draped robes, they set the classic, sculptured tone of the play.

Deems Taylor, who had done incidental music for *Will Shakespeare* and *Casanova* and had since made a great success in modern opera with *The King's Henchman* and *Peter Ibbetson,* composed preludes for each act which in performance were played by the New York Little

As Lucrece, costumed by Robert Edmond Jones, 1932. (New York Public Library, Vandamm Collection)

Symphony Orchestra. A stage box had to be enlarged to accommodate the musicians, who were conducted by Taylor himself. It must be clear by now that in the production of *Lucrece* nothing was spared in the way of love or money, with some of the finest talents in the American theatre contributing their best — and then trying to better it.

Arturo Toscanini rarely went to the theatre but attended the opening-night performance of *Lucrece* under pressure from a close friend who also happened to be the mother of Kit's oculist. He sat in the second row and at the end of the play stood and cheered, turning his white head to exhort the entire audience to do the same, waving his arms expressively, leading the acclaim as if conducting the philharmonic. He came back on closing night, too, joining the audience as they moved down the aisles to lean across the footlights and touch the actors.

The time between the two occasions, however, between the opening and the closing, was startlingly brief, just four weeks, or thirty-one performances, and the play only ran beyond the first Saturday night because Guthrie said it would be a humiliation for a Katharine Cornell production to close in one week. Of the twenty-four plays that appeared in New York under her name, *Lucrece* was one of the few out-and-out failures and one of only two pre–World War II productions that did not show a profit.

It played three weeks out of town, in Cleveland, Detroit, and of course Buffalo, before opening in New York on December 20, 1932, and everywhere it went, Toscanini notwithstanding, critics and audiences found it "stilted, too conscious of its own art, and quietly, but firmly tiresome." Kit said years later, "It seems to me now that the thing was killed by too much love. Too many people were enthused about it and wanted to do things for it. . . ."

All of it is probably true, from the critics' carping to Kit's hindsight wisdom, but there may have been another, far subtler reason for the failure of *Lucrece*. One critic, John Anderson in the *New York Journal*, suggested that since the critics had scolded Miss Cornell for playing such gaudy ladies as Iris March, she was now seeking revenge by forcing upon them "this solemn saga of deathless chastity." It was an amusing observation, but there was an edge to it, and just possibly a grain of truth, that a strain was showing in the promotion of the new institutional Katharine Cornell, uplifted manager and great lady. Another critic smirked a little, observing that for all Miss Cornell's voluptuousness and Brian Aherne's heroic manliness, the rape scene suggested "no more than a couple of Vassar girls having a pillow fight." This of the Katharine Cornell who a bare three years before had shocked (and delighted) Broadway with her predatory sensuality as Madeleine Carey. There was something aggressively removed about the star who starred in *Lucrece*.

One of her greatest physical assets on the stage was her voice, with what Atkinson called "its high white tones." But in *Lucrece* she played most of her scenes in pantomime while a narrator spoke on her behalf, vocalizing her thoughts, commenting on her actions, and, in short, playing half of her part. It was a literal symbol of what was happening in the transition from Katharine Cornell the actress to Miss Cornell the actress-manager. Her private voice had been given over to Gert in her letters, her public voice given over to Ray Henderson in the press, and now her professional onstage voice was given over to André Obey, Guthrie McClintic, and Blanche Yurka. Not that any of those involved in any way conspired to diminish her presence. Their only idea, ever, was to protect her, to nourish her, to build her up, to ease the path of her art, to serve her. It was as if, in spite of their efforts, her very success itself, her eminence, the pinnacle she had reached, sought to remove her, as if the entity known as Katharine Cornell was out to sabotage the woman and the actress, and she, in her conscience and eagerness to please, with that "inner renunciation that is often inertia," was the most willing conspirator of all.

Had Katharine Cornell been felt at the heart of *Lucrece*, the flaws of the play would have been forgiven as they were in *The Green Hat* and even *Dishonored Lady*. But she was not there, and it was not so much that she had been removed and her voice given to Blanche Yurka, she had never been there in the first place. *Lucrece* was an institutional choice, and there was nothing in it that she could "twist and turn around in her mind until she made it into something of her own."

Fortunately, the opposite was true of her next production.

In Sidney Howard's *Alien Corn* she played Elsa Brandt, a brilliant young pianist whose German parents, a violinist and an opera singer, were interned during the Great War, when Elsa was five or six, in a Georgia camp where the mother died in the flu epidemic and the father, impoverished by the U.S. government, tried to take his own life but only succeeded in smashing his left arm so that he could never again play the violin.

Fifteen years later Elsa finds herself teaching music at a small women's college "a few miles west of Chicago," correcting endless examination papers and trying to endure the smugness and provincialism of the great American Middle West that in the previous decade Sinclair Lewis had laid bare in *Main Street* and *Babbitt*. Elsa yearns to go back to Vienna, her birthplace, there to resume her studies and pursue a career as a concert artist, but she must cling to her hated job to support herself and her half-paralyzed father. A fervent, idealistic, radical young suitor shoots himself for love of her, which means she will be dismissed from the college for attracting "untoward attention" to herself. Only then is she able to bid farewell to the married man she thought she loved and whose proffered security she was about to accept, and to wrench herself free, regardless of consequences. When a policeman comes to the house to investigate the suicide, he asks if this is her home and Elsa responds, "No. Vienna." The curtain falls.

In a dramatic imagination it is no more than a step from Vienna to Garmisch-Partenkirchen, and with the recent spiritual and artistic regeneration Kit had experienced in that part of the world, Elsa's longing could have been her own. No other play she had done seems to have been so closely related to her own emotional state at the actual moment of production. It must have taken very little twisting. Percy Hammond shrewdly observed in the *Tribune* that without her the play would have been "just another exhibition of actors in deliberate attitudes, reciting lines from a Times Square rostrum." The play had many faults, easy melodramatics (the minute the gun is brought out in Act One, one knows that someone will get shot in Act Three), and pasteboard characters (a woman's husband cannot "carry a tune across a tennis court," and yet she hears him whistling a theme from a César Franck Chorale, of all simple things, later hears Elsa banging it out on the piano, and immediately guesses that they are having an affair or are about to). But because of the star's "dark and rhythmic" presence as the "beautiful but frustrate pianiste," critics and audiences tolerated the flaws as they would not tolerate them in *Lucrece*.

After a tryout in Baltimore, *Alien Corn* opened at the Belasco on February 12, 1933, and played twelve weeks. Then, because Ray Henderson always advocated closing a play while the houses were still crowded, it closed May 15, toured Boston and Philadelphia, then headed for the alien corn of the great Middle West.

Arriving in Chicago with the World's Fair, called that year "A Century of Progress," *Alien Corn* settled in for a hot summer month. Guthrie had devised a clever trick with the set of the play. The concert grand piano, which Elsa played off and on during the course of the action, ran along one wall of the Brandt living room. To get away from the phony offstage effect that most onstage playing has in the theatre, the onstage piano was hollowed out and so placed that the movement of an offstage baby grand could be fitted into it, and the two pianos became one.

Doris Madden was the offstage pianist, and during rehearsals Kit spent at least two hours a day watching her fingering and then practicing at a dummy piano, learning what to do with her hands and feet. She even crossed hands, which was most impressive.

In performance, the pianos were so arranged that when Kit sat at her onstage piano, she could see her offstage counterpart, a fortunate arrangement because there came the performance during a stifling hot spell when Doris Madden fainted at her job. Kit saw it coming and was able to stop on exactly the right note.

"Oh, I'm tired," said the indefatigable Elsa Brandt that day.

The Depression was shaking the theatre up, and the movies were breaking it down. Guthrie cast *Alien Corn* with actors from such different theatrical backgrounds and with such divergent acting styles that five years earlier, in the days of lingering tradition, graceful gesture, and standard speech, he would not have dared put them all on the same stage, let alone in the same play. James Rennie, who played Elsa's moneyed suitor, was a typical leading man held over from the 1920s, the kind of very nice, well-spoken, straight-featured fellow that critics and audiences were finding it harder and harder to imagine Katharine Cornell attracted to. His wife was played by Lily Cahill, a gracious drawing-room actress, the kind for whom the word "comedienne" might have been coined. Miss Cahill's greatest charm was that in the second act when she sang "Vissi d'arte," she, with the character

With James Rennie in Alien Corn, 1933. (New York Public Library, Vandamm Collection)

she played, thought she sang it well. The only other woman in the cast was one of Guthrie's dear, resurrected older actresses, Jessie Busley, who came to Elsa of the Middle West by way of *Beverly of Graustark*. The robust German actor Siegfried Rumann was Elsa's father, his withered arm and Sturm und Drang brusquely shattering the accepted Broadway picture of a gentle German "Music Master" perpetuated for so many years by David Warfield in the play of that name. And Kit's third leading man, impressive and sullen as the intense, muttering, explosive young radical who shoots himself with the agonized cry, "I love you, Elsa!", was an intense, muttering, explosive young actor raised in the glorious tradition of the Yiddish theatre, Luther Adler, now on a flier from the Group Theatre, where the Actors' Studio would one day be born. Too short for such elevated drama, he wore lifts that were veritable cothurni, giving him what seemed to be an extra joint halfway up the calf.

Alien Corn opened at what may have been the lowest point of the Depression, less than two weeks before the first inauguration of Franklin D. Roosevelt. There were breadlines of unemployed, mounting mortgage foreclosures, failing banks, and widespread fear that the country's affairs had become so complicated that they might never be completely understood, let alone resolved. It was deemed wise to keep more ready cash on hand than usual, and there was a rumor that gold, still much used as common currency, might become scarce. On the advice of Conger Goodyear and Stanton Griffis, Gert instructed the box office at the Belasco to put aside all gold pieces, and when several hundred dollars' worth accumulated, she cached it away in a bottom drawer on the top floor at 23 Beekman Place. It disappeared. Aside from Kit and Guthrie, only Emma Jones was living in the house at the time. Simpson had been let go, finally and reluctantly, to be taken on immediately by Conger Goodyear who said he liked the way Simpson remembered what guests drank (he most likely wanted to ease Kit's discomfort at having to fire someone). There had been a few workmen in and out of the house on the lower floors, but the mystery of the missing gold was never solved, although it was Gert's firm, if secret, conviction, still cherished after forty-five years, that Guthrie pinched it.

Alien Corn miraculously prospered from the start, despite the times, and in the second week of the run Gert took off for Florida with Margalo Gillmore to spend a few days on board Stanton Griffis's yacht. She arrived to plague both Griffis and Conger Goodyear, also aboard, with a story that on the train, just out of New York, she and Margalo had met up with Morris Ernst, the civil rights lawyer, who said he was on his way to Washington to advise the President-elect to close the banks throughout the country for federal inspection, thus averting a disastrous run on them and saving what banks might still be solvent. Griffis said Gert would fall for anything and was furious with her for spreading such a preposterous fabrication, saying that was the way panics were started. She, in turn, suggested that he was the kind of man responsible for the country's crisis in the first place and wondered if the bottom of his yacht wasn't filled with hoarded gold. He was so enraged that he threw their bridge money into the ocean. Roosevelt had been inaugurated that day, and the next morning they heard from a woman on the beach that his first official act as President had been to declare a "Bank Holiday." Griffis went very calm and took charge of the party's activities. When they went to the races that afternoon, he insisted they place their bets with him, not at the windows, to keep all cash within their own circle.

He also telephoned Kit in New York and told her to close *Alien Corn*, at least until the bank crisis was over.

On the morning of the day the Bank Holiday was declared, Guthrie sailed for two months in England, Scandinavia, Germany (where he stayed overnight at Haus Hirth), and Russia. Ray Henderson was also out of town, and it was one of the few occasions when Kit was completely alone, with none of her advisers physically present, to make major managerial decisions. Other plays were indeed closing, but when she found that Gert, with foresight, had not banked the previous week's box office receipts and that there was enough money in the safe to pay the actors' salaries, she decided to keep the play open and instructed the treasurer to accept any form of payment for tickets, whether it be check, IOU, or barter, reasoning that at such a time the public needed theatre more than ever, and anyone who wanted to see a play should be allowed to, if he had the dollars in his pocket or not. From Florida Griffis yelled that she was insane, the checks would bounce, one could not legally enforce payment of an IOU, and she would be unmercifully, if not criminally, taken advantage of by the public. She, on her end of the line, got grand about human nature and how it responds to stress, firm in her conviction that "People don't cheat in crises."

She was right, but one wonders if credit should go to human nature or to her powerful influence on human nature. Every IOU at the box office was paid off, and if a check bounced because a bank did not reopen, it was eventually made good. Along Broadway, her actors were not the only ones who kept working, but they were among the few who got paid for it.

Of all the characters she had played up to that time, Elsa Brandt was only the third with a talent (after Mary Fitton and Elizabeth Barrett), and it is likely that Kit saw in her some of her own contradictions and even found some welcome corroboration of more obscure feelings and attitudes. Certainly Elsa's contention that "When you've got a talent it's a demon that drives you and drives you and leaves you no peace!" coincided with Kit's own sense of being obsessed, oppressively bound and relentlessly swept along, although she put it more gently: "Art isn't a profession, it's a necessity that's wished upon you." Perhaps Elsa expressed the extreme she reached for.

It is not certain at the last curtain of *Alien Corn* whether or not Elsa will succeed in making her way back to Vienna, but when the final last curtain fell in Chicago on July 2, 1933, there was no doubt that Kit would make it back to Garmisch (on the *Europa*) for another perfect summer. There was music that year, Wagner at Bayreuth — *Lohengrin* and *Die Meistersinger* — village festivals, and more music at Salzburg.

Elsa Brandt longed for Vienna to resume her career, to get into the thick of it; Kit longed for Garmisch as a respite, refuge, healing place, escape. But in the summer of 1933 she was well again and there was no escape. She brought the pressure with her in manuscript form. In the late mornings, after the ritual walk with Johanna, and often in the quiet afternoons with Johanna to cue her, she was learning lines. Elsa said, "My talent is a demon child that has to be born!" To extend that very 1930s metaphor at the risk of ridiculing it, Kit, with Guthrie as faithful midwife, was about to give birth to a demon child that both her admirers and detractors claimed was long, long overdue: Juliet.

20

The Long Tour (1933-1934)

KIT TOOK A HOUSE on Mt. Vernon Street when *Alien Corn* played in Boston, and one afternoon, when she was confined to the living room couch with a bad cold, H. T. Parker, the revered drama critic of the *Boston Transcript* (since 1905) came to call for the purpose of urging her to play Juliet, with a special plea that she include the "Gallop apace ye fiery-footed steeds" speech, which almost every Juliet since Adelaide Neilson had left out. For some time Ray Henderson had been saying to her that no actress is really tested until she does Shakespeare. When Kit maintained she was not a Shakespearean actress, he said she had to do it to round out her career, even if she only did it once, and Juliet, while she was still young enough, was the *platter* piece, waiting to be served. He tried to assure her from his experience with Sothern and Marlowe that Shakespeare never let you down. Guthrie said it was the next logical step in her career and could not be avoided. The sooner she did it and either took her beating or pulled it off, the sooner she would be free to think of other roles, other plays.

Dorothy Parker, herself a very sharp poet, said of Kit in *The Barretts* that "she presents, for the first time, to my knowledge, on any stage, the portrait of a poet who could really have written poetry." The irony is that Kit disliked poetry. From Shakespeare to Robinson Jeffers she found poetry difficult to follow, hard to understand, impossible to speak, and she never read any unless she had to. When she leaned to a classic, it was a prose classic and never, surprisingly, in the romantic tradition. She never saw herself as Marguerite Gauthier, for example. She inclined toward Ibsen, and the one great role she was drawn to was Rebecca West in *Rosmersholm*. She only hesitated, she claimed, because it was impossible to equal the memory of Mrs. Fiske in the part. Since Mrs. Fiske had only played Rebecca West on Broadway for a scant three weeks in 1907, Kit's reluctance is suspect.

She also felt she could not embark on the project without a satisfactory translation. At that time Thornton Wilder, who loved travel and people and sociability, wrote to her, "The very sight of your single-mindedness and dedication has helped me to make some decisions. I hereby resolve to be a better boy and a more serious one." He was ready to do anything in her service and was well qualified to adapt Ibsen as he would prove in a very few years with his excellent version of *A Doll's House* for Ruth Gordon. Kit was right to reject the existing translations of *Rosmersholm*, but instead of commissioning a new one from Wilder, she gave the assignment to an inexperienced writer named Eugene Gay Tifft, a distant cousin on the Plimpton side of her family. The result was unsatisfactory.

It seems clear that unconsciously she was undermining her own efforts to play a part she very much wanted to play. Since there is no reason to question the sincerity and depth of her feeling for Rebecca West, the trouble seems to have been that nobody close to her backed her up, and she could not take a stand as she had eight years earlier for Iris March. That was before she was a star, before she was her own manager, before she was Miss Cornell. Now, with all that added responsibility, she hesitated to take an artistic stand without the unanimous support of the others who made up the Katharine Cornell Establishment. Everyone was polite and respectful of her interest in Rebecca West, but they urged Juliet, and she went along with them.

It is not surprising that flamboyant Guthrie was unenthusiastic about *Rosmersholm* with its chill Nordic air, its murky daylight in which candles are used for illumination, not decor, its boxed-in action that narrows as it broadens, its gracelessness, and its layer upon layer of meaning so concealed that even Sigmund Freud needed a learned essay to unravel it all. What is surprising is that Kit was drawn to it. Whether or not she actually saw Mrs. Fiske play Rebecca, she certainly knew historically that the basis of Mrs. Fiske's interpretation was her courageous (for 1907) emphasis of the incest motif in Rebecca's past, never put into words in the course of the play or guessed at by the other characters, but definitely perceived by audiences and critics who could "hear Mrs. Fiske think." It was an historic performance because never again could the part be played without this emphasis. That Kit, especially after the way she smoothed away the darker side of *The Barretts,* wanted to undertake such a complexity of extremely modern motivations suggests that she was ready to go off in a completely new theatrical direction. Had she played Rebecca West and been successful, it is unlikely that she would then have gone on to Juliet. Freud couples Rebecca West with Lady Macbeth, and perhaps the one role would have led to the other and a completely different kind of theatrical career would have followed. When she returned to Shaw in later years, for example, it surely would have been to *Heartbreak House* rather than *The Doctor's Dilemma.*

Her attraction to *Rosmersholm* is significant for two reasons. First, the play was written when the world was just awakening to the quality in certain individuals that was sometimes called "magnetic influence," the ability to influence the mind and thinking of other individuals or groups of individuals. It was a subject that deeply interested Ibsen, who endowed Rebecca West with a strong magnetic influence over John Rosmer and his invalid wife, Beatë, a quality that Dr. Kroll recognized and half admired when he said to her, "Whom could you not bewitch when you set your mind to it?" It was also a quality that Kit had recognized in herself as a young girl on the night of the *bal masque* when she stood outside the locked house on Mariner Street and knew that if she chose, she could induce in Karl Sprague a wish to marry her. It was a frightening power because it could be mis-used, and she had fled then to spend the night with friends rather than go back to the Sprague mansion. It is certainly doubtful that she ever gave conscious thought to this power of hers, except to wonder sometimes, quite seriously, what people saw in her to attract them, but the power is quite clear in all her personal relationships, and it is a great part of her influence over audiences. It must have been at the bottom of her instinctive compassion for Rebecca West, the flawed one, who mis-used her magnetic influence to create her own destruction.

But her attraction to *Rosmersholm* is most significant in that Rebecca West, unlike Elizabeth Barrett, had all the physical passion of an Iris March or Madeleine Carey, with the difference that it is suppressed — in disciplined fury — *re*pressed, so controlled that even though Rebecca herself says it is "uncontrollable," she is never once permitted to touch Rosmer, the object of her passion, until they clasp each other in their death-plunge into the millrace. One cannot help wondering if Kit's instincts had not sharpened to a superb peak in sensing in Rebecca West's removal, first emotional, then physical, a correlative to her own development as an actress and as a woman.

But her friends and admirers — and advisers — wanted her to do Juliet.

She might have held out even longer had it not been for a speech toward the end of *Lucrece* which began, "Oh, Rome! Roman legend, history! Latin tongue and Latin dignity! Roman soul! What preparation and what example you have given us for misfortune . . . !" It was the first blank verse she had spoken on a stage since playing Mary Fitton playing Juliet. The bravura spurt of poetics came too late in *Lucrece* to win over the critics, but they were pleased with her reading and she was aware that she held the audience by presenting the speech simply, *without* bravura, the aspect that scared her most about poetry in the theatre. She was encouraged to think maybe she was, at last, ready to try Shakespeare.

Her sometimes flat-footed practicality also played a part in her decision. Four days after *Alien Corn* opened, as twenty-year-old Elsa Brandt she reached her fortieth birthday, and she felt that if ever in her life she was going to play Juliet, it had to be then — that year. Immediately, her age became one of the challenges of Juliet, the kind of challenge she relished. Undefined but perceptible gray streaks were beginning to appear in her hair, and when someone at Garmisch untactfully asked if she would wear a wig as Juliet, she, who in any other play where it didn't matter was always eager to change the shape of her head with a rat, fall, braid, or bonnet, responded rather grandly that an actress who had to wear a wig as Juliet shouldn't play the part.

The one thing she insisted on was time to study the part, time to rehearse it and then build it, polish it, and perfect it in front of audiences, not just two weeks out of town, but many weeks — months, if possible — before facing the New York critics. This stipulation on her part fitted in perfectly with a plan Ray Henderson had been evolving for a transcontinental repertory tour which, when it was concluded, *Variety* would refer to as "the most outstanding dramatic accomplishment in recent years." While she was absorbing the role of Juliet, she would alternate it with *The Barretts*, which, Henderson figured, a hundred cities and towns across the country had not yet had a chance to see. A third offering would be *Candida*, a legend to the theatre-going generation that had grown up since her 1925 production. The tour, as Henderson envisioned it, would sustain her entire 1933–1934 season, and not only would it answer Kit's need for time with Juliet, it would demonstrate her faith in the road, where she was often more comfortable than in New York. With the growing popularity of the movies, the annual number of theatrical road shows had decreased from over three hundred in 1900 to less than twenty in 1933. Two distinguished theatre practitioners were still touring — Eva Le Gallienne with Ibsen and Shakespeare, and Walter Hampden with a repertory of four classical plays — but everyone else said the road was dead. Katharine Cornell's seventeen-thousand-mile tour in 1933–1934 would prove them wrong.

In the two years the McClintics leased the Belasco Theatre, they had to pay out more in rent and carrying charges than they received in income. The Katharine Cornell productions more than covered the overhead, but the money received from the others (Guthrie's) was unequal to the cost of maintaining the theatre, and the weeks it went dark were a complete loss. They had also come to realize that any time Miss Cornell wanted a theatre in New York, she had only to ask to be given her choice, and on terms more advantageous than those extended to other producers. Besides, Kit never felt at home in the Belasco, preferring the Empire and, in the years to come, the Martin Beck and the Ethel Barrymore. When the lease on the Belasco terminated in the summer of 1933, it was not renewed and no move was made to pick up the option to buy.

Offices were then taken in the new RKO building in Rockefeller Center and filled with as many employees as possible who had worked for Winthrop Ames, still the ultimate to Guthrie. Ray Henderson was at his desk at eight o'clock every morning answering mail, sending out releases, keeping meticulous records of every financial transaction involving as much as a two-cent stamp. Ames's ex–switchboard operator, Margaret "Sully" Sullivan, was there to answer the telephones and could identify every actor in New York after he called once. William Worthington, Ames's ex-playreader and a Baltimore gentleman, also joined the staff, writing comprehensive critiques of all scripts submitted to the office, grading them A, B, or C, passing on only the A's, which were few and very far between, to Guthrie.

Guthrie would also like to have hired Ames's stage manager, Maude Howell, probably the first woman stage manager on Broadway, but she was set on going to Hollywood to become a director, and as Gert puts it, looking back, "Guthrie had to settle for me." But before she left, Maude Howell — for no other reason than love for Guthrie — passed on to Gert many of her tricks for expeditious touring. For example, Ames had permitted her to buy a ground cloth on which she marked with a circle where every spotlight had to hit so that she could light a stage with no furniture on it, before the walls of the set were in place, even before the set was brought from the train to the theatre. This kind of short-cut information was invaluable to Gert as company manager for the short tour of *The Barretts*, and now, elevated to general manager, she was learning the business side of touring sitting with Ray Henderson plotting the long tour, determining which cities would be included and how many performances would be given in each, booking theatres, negotiating the terms of booking, working out rest dates for the actors, and mapping travel routes with the railroads.

Guthrie did not find it easy to come up with one set of actors for three plays. Of the basic *Barretts* cast, Brian Aherne was in Hollywood, Joyce Carey had returned to England, Margalo Gillmore was preparing to be in Woollcott's first playwriting effort (with George S. Kaufman), *The Dark Tower*, and two other cast members had died. But Brenda Forbes was ready to go, and Guthrie made his first brilliant, triple-threat piece of casting by assigning her to Wilson in *The Barretts*, Prossy in *Candida*, and Lady Montague. Charles Waldron came back as Father Barrett, doubling as Friar Lawrence, and new actors were soon recruited, among them George Macready, John Hoyt (then Hoysradt), and Alice Johns as Juliet's Nurse. Merle Maddern as Lady Capulet was a special comfort to Guthrie because she was the niece of dear Mrs. Fiske, who had died the year before, and because she read fortunes in the cards better than most professionals.

Romeo, Robert Browning, and the Reverend Morell were all played brilliantly by Basil Rathbone, who went to Garmisch in the summer of 1933 to get a head start rehearsing with Kit.

Because of the doubling, not all the casting was so inspired. A. P. Kaye, for example, was fine as Candida's father and totally inept as

Romeo's. The most interesting bit of casting was an eighteen-year-old Wisconsin boy, Orson Welles, who had made his theatre debut the year before with Michael MacLiammoir's Gate Theatre in Dublin. Thornton Wilder had given him a letter to Alexander Woollcott, who had passed him on to Guthrie who cast him as Mercutio, Eugene Marchbanks, and Octavius Moulton-Barrett.

It was Guthrie's first experience with Shakespeare as well as Kit's, and conscious of his lack of education, he was both flattered and insecure to have such a great literary trust placed in his talent and judgment, especially by scholarly Ray Henderson who urged the project in the first place. When Henderson put at his disposal one of his most treasured possessions, Sothern and Marlowe's original prompt-book for their production of *Romeo and Juliet* in 1904, Guthrie accepted it as law. He also plowed through Furness's *New Variorum*, that synthesis of all previous Shakespearean criticism, including variant readings.

Having absorbed all this material, it is not surprising that he approached *Romeo and Juliet* traditionally and conservatively. It is said in the text that Juliet will be fourteen in a fortnight, but as Miss Marlowe, Jane Cowl, and all other Juliets going back to before Ellen Terry had raised it to eighteen, so Guthrie raised it to eighteen. He found it was true that the "Gallop apace, you fiery-footed steeds" speech had not been acted since Adelaide Neilson decided not to in 1872, and H. T. Parker of the *Boston Transcript* notwithstanding, he saw no reason to reinstate it. All the vignettes of preparation for Juliets' wedding to Paris, the Nurse's discovery of Juliet's body, Friar Lawrence's discovery that his letter to Romeo has not been delivered, whatever greater minds than his had cut, Guthrie cut. In his reverent mood, he naturally thought of Winthrop Ames and commissioned Woodman Thompson, whose main qualification seems to have been his designs for Ames's tasteful revival of Gilbert and Sullivan, to provide practical and beautiful scenery in restrained, muted colors, a fitting and somber background for two hours' traffic in iambic pentameter. His most original idea was to have Martha Graham arrange the dance, to Paul Nordoff's music, which gave Romeo his first sight of Juliet.

Equity allowed five weeks' rehearsal, time to prepare *The Barretts* and *Romeo*. *Candida* would be rehearsed on the road and enter the repertory in the fifth week. Kit wanted Buffalo to be the first to see her Juliet, so it was chosen over *The Barretts*, for the opening on November 29, 1933. The three days leading up to it were nightmarish. When it was too late to do anything about it, it was discovered that Juliet's nightdress was not suited to the play, the period, or the actress wearing it. While others fussed and blamed each other, Martha Graham went out and bought some soft white nun's veiling from which she fashioned a flowing robe of beautiful and authentic design. Miss Graham dismisses with vague asperity any suggestion that she actually pedaled the sewing machine, but the robe was ready for the opening-night curtain, and in *I Wanted to Be an Actress* Kit said, "When I got to the theatre at half past seven I found her still there in my dressing room, sweeping up the threads."

Despite the fact that the Erlanger Theatre billed Kit as "Buffalo's Own," playgoers stayed away from *Romeo and Juliet*. When *The Barretts* was substituted, they filled the Erlanger to capacity, even though they had seen it the year before. Ray Henderson had warned the McClintics that this would be the case throughout the tour. Audiences had not gone to Shakespeare since John Barrymore's Hamlet and Jane Cowl's Juliet twelve years before: he was not fashionable. But no one had ever done well in Shakespeare at first, not Barrymore, not Cowl, not even Sothern and Marlowe, until word got around that their productions were good and their names became synonymous with quality. It was for this reason precisely that Henderson had insisted they tour with three plays, so that while Kit was floundering as Juliet, *The Barretts* and *Candida* would pay the bills.

After four days in Buffalo the troupe headed west, traveling in two private Pullman cars, one with a drawing room, three compartments, and eight sections and the other with nothing but sections, to accommodate forty actors, two stage managers, six stagehands, two electricians, two carpenters, a property man, Joanna Klinge and an assistant, Eveline Drysdale, Mrs. Basil Rathbone (Ouida Bergere), four other wives, three dogs (Flush, Sonia, and the Rathbones' German shepherd police dog, Moritz), Gert Macy, and at times, Guthrie. They were watched over by Si, who claimed to be the "onliest" porter with a beard in the United States.

The wardrobe of one hundred and twelve costumes, all of them period, for the three plays, was packed in elegant old wicker costume baskets, and two baggage cars were needed for the baggage, scenery, furniture, properties, and electrical equipment.

From Buffalo they shot straight across the top of the country to the West Coast, south as far as Los Angeles, back up to Oakland and Sacramento, east to Salt Lake City, Cheyenne, south to San Antonio and Houston. Then they zigzagged north to Sioux Falls, east to Columbus, south to New Orleans, east again to Savannah and worked up the coast to New England and New York State, avoiding all the cities where *The Barretts* had played on the short tour, ending up at the Brooklyn Academy of Music on June 20, 1934, after seven months on the road.

The railroads cooperated marvelously, putting on special engines late at night and holding up other trains when necessary to get the troupe into and out of seventy-four stops for seventy-five stands (Buffalo twice), thirty-eight of them one-nighters. At each stand ten trucks had to be waiting to cart everything from the railroad cars to the theatre, and back. Simply to watch an arrival or departure was thrilling, and in years to come various theatre luminaries would credit the sight with first turning their heads in the direction of their calling.

After the opening in Buffalo, Chicago was bypassed because *The Barretts* had played there and because Kit was by no means ready to have her Juliet seen by the Chicago press, a ploy the critics got around by traveling to Milwaukee for a performance and returning to their desks to write the expected grumbling, carping — if respectful — reviews. The Milwaukee press, on the other hand, declared that her "superlative accomplishment," "the loveliest and most heartbreaking of all Juliets," "served to demonstrate, if further proof was needed, that Miss Cornell is one of the great." Still audiences stayed away from *Romeo* and flocked to *The Barretts*, and when thrifty Gert suggested parceling out tickets at reduced prices to schools and civic groups, Ray Henderson reprimanded her sharply, reminding her that Miss Cornell was not a bargain basement item to be offered at cut rates.

After Milwaukee came Madison, Wisconsin, for two days, and a week split between Minneapolis and St. Paul (she always played both cities to avoid offending either), and then on to Duluth. Guthrie, who had gone back to New York after the Buffalo opening to rehearse Owen Davis's drama of the old South, *Jezebel*, caught up with them there in time to rehearse *Candida*, which would go into the repertory at the next stand, his hometown, Seattle.

Guthrie's parents were both dead, but there were still families in

Seattle he had known, people he had gone to school with, and probably many who had snubbed him and his mother and father in the old days. He had been back to his hometown a number of times in the twelve years since his marriage to Kit, but this would be his first return as a celebrity.

It seems contradictory that from Duluth to Seattle, over half the length of the country, a tour whose principal aim was to bring the living theatre to out-of-the-way places made not one stop, gave not one performance. But all possible stops along the way, every city in Montana — Billings, Butte, Helena, Great Falls, Missoula — had by agreement and prearrangement closed their doors to the living theatre. Movie theatres, and their owners, had become so powerful — and were so afraid of the competition — that they were able to effect such a boycott. Not only were movie theatres in these cities made unavailable to Katharine Cornell, but all public halls and auditoriums where a play might have been performed were paid to remain empty.

Scheduled to open on Christmas night in Seattle with *The Barretts*, the troupe departed Duluth on Saturday morning, December 23, attached to the "Orient Express" on the Great Northern Railway, which would get them into Seattle early Christmas morning. Six hours were needed to set up the stage and distribute the costumes for the performance that evening. It was an easy schedule.

But even as they sped through Minnesota and North Dakota there were rumors of trouble ahead, of washouts in the state of Washington where it had been raining for twenty-three days straight. On Sunday, as they puddled through an endless downpour across Montana, already behind schedule, Kit decided the company needed a Christmas Eve party to cheer them up. The dining steward agreed to close the diner to other passengers at eight-thirty and sent ahead to the next stop for turkeys, but none were to be had so they settled for twenty chickens. Prohibition had been repealed earlier that month, just after the tour left Buffalo, and so a Christmas punch of sorts was available. For some it was the first time they had ever been served an alcoholic beverage by legal waiters in a respectable public place.

Kit and Basil sat with the crew, Guthrie sat with Eveline Drysdale and Joanna Klinge, and Gert with the stage managers. Some of the younger members of the company, led by Margot Stevenson (who played Bella Hedley in *The Barretts* and ran across the stage shouting "Down with the Capulets!" on alternate nights), had the foresight in

Duluth to buy ten-cent presents for everybody, and after food, toasts, gift-giving and caroling, with Si and all the waiters and even the conductor joining in, that feeling of warmth grew that Kit called "gemutlichkeit," at that time so much a part of the romance of the theatre, especially the theatre on wheels. A band of players, fifty-odd, speeding through the night, hundreds of miles from home — "Silent Night, Holy Night" — Christmas Eve in the middle of a flood.

They were due in Seattle at eight o'clock on Christmas morning, and they pulled into Spokane, on the eastern side of the state, at eight-thirty. A telegram from the anxious theater management in Seattle: with every ticket sold for that night, would it be too optimistic to announce on the radio that whatever the delay, the troupe would at least arrive in time to give the performance at the scheduled hour? Telegrams back and forth, progress reports. In the best of conditions Spokane was nine hours from Seattle, and beyond Spokane the going was slow, increasingly dangerous and unpredictable. The news of what lay ahead was alarming: the tracks of both the Great Western and the North Pacific Railroads were washed out. Permission was granted for the "Orient Express" to use the tracks of the Chicago-Milwaukee, and the hours inched by as slowly as the towns — Wenatchee, Yakima, Walla Walla — for Guthrie, the scenes of his childhood were passing before his eyes. The day went, night came, the train crept through the Cascades, then stopped altogether. Hope was abandoned of reaching Seattle at all that night, but the wires were long since down, telegraph poles uprooted, and there was no way to send word ahead or receive any.

A trestle had been washed away up ahead, and railroad workers were flinging up a new trestle over which the train must creep past the wreckage of the one that had fallen. As the cars moved slowly out into space, the actors peered through the windows, looking down unexpectedly into the faces of the emergency workers, lit by acetylene torches, staring upward to see if the tracks would hold, watching to see that the wheels didn't slide. There was an infinite quiet. The tracks held. The train moved on.

Eight o'clock. Nine o'clock. Ten. The actors, with the crisis past, had time to get bored and scratchy, knowing that on the following Saturday one-eighth of their salaries would be missing from their pay envelopes. It was a ruling of the theatre that such a deduction could be made when a performance was canceled by an act of God, and if any member of the company had previously wondered what constituted an act of God, he knew he was in the middle of one that Christmas night between Spokane and Seattle. Kit sent out word from her drawing room that they would give an extra matinee so that no one would suffer a loss, neither the actors nor the theatre management, but it did little good. It was a glum, exhausted, disgruntled troupe that pulled into the King Street Station, Seattle, at eleven-fifteen.

Hordes of people in raincoats searched the train windows for long-awaited arrivals, and as Kit stepped onto the platform cameras clicked, light bulbs flashed, and a man pushed his way out of the darkness calling her name. He introduced himself as Hugh Pickett, manager of the Metropolitan Theatre, and informed her that the audience was still waiting.

There was a blank silence broken only when Guthrie, picturing a handful of derelicts seeking refuge from the storm, asked, "How many?"

"The entire house," was the reply. "Twelve hundred people."

"Do you mean they want a performance at this hour?" asked Kit.

"They're expecting it."

The cast and crew, all fifty-odd of them, were galvanized into action. Every truck that could be inveigled out into a downpour on Christmas night was waiting, and suddenly unknown hands were holding a hundred umbrellas over canvas flats as they were hauled from the railroad cars, and tarpaulins out of nowhere were thrown over Elizabeth Barrett's couch and writing table to keep them dry in transit. The actors, instructed not to go to their hotels but to head straight for the theatre, piled into waiting limousines, and police sirens escorted them (rather needlessly) through otherwise silent, empty streets. For Guthrie it was a homecoming beyond his wildest dreams, and to top it all, as they screamed up to the Metropolitan Theatre he saw that Ray Henderson, as a gesture, had put his name on the marquee along with Kit's.

At the theatre, seated in the auditorium, milling through the lounges and lobbies, spilling over into the public rooms of the Olympic Hotel across the way, over a thousand people, mostly in evening dress, conversed, read, played cards, drank, dozed, ate, or just waited. They now began streaming back to their seats, and Kit worried that unused to the ways of the theatre, they might reasonably think that now the actors had arrived the play could begin, when, as they knew on their side of the curtain, there was almost insurmountable work to be done first.

She said they could not be kept waiting any longer, and Guthrie, always able to sense a theatrical moment, suggested the audience be allowed to watch the play being unpacked and set up. Ringing up the curtain as the first trucks began to arrive from the train, he pushed his old hat back on his head, jammed his hands in his pockets and strolled out to explain everything that was going on, filling in with theatre lore, anecdotes, reminiscences, giving a tour de force performance that held the audience enthralled while the stage hands and electricians worked to accomplish in an hour what their union officials said could not possibly be accomplished in less than six.

Flush was sent out many times, whenever Guthrie's inventiveness flagged and the proceedings began to get dull, to keep the audience's spirits up. The massive entrance, the fireplace, the furniture slid into place, and then began the process that theatre people find tedious but which the audience that night found most exciting of all, the lighting of the set, bringing out the texture of the painted woods and fabrics, giving depth and darkness to the corners, bringing the sunlight into the room from Wimpole Street. Through it all, Jimmy Vincent, the chubby, rather Asian-looking stage manager, had to lie on the sofa and assume for the lighting experts, to the great amusement of the audience, every pose, every gesture, every uplifted chin, downcast eye, and every outflung hand that Elizabeth Barrett would assume in the course of the drama, informing the audience sheepishly as he finally rolled off the sofa, "Miss Cornell looks prettier."

It was almost midnight when the first scenery truck pulled up to the Metropolitan Theatre, and at one o'clock, miraculously, the job was done. A calm fell over the house, a hush. The warning bell was rung for the actors in their dressing rooms, the lights in the auditorium were dimmed, and the curtain was lowered. The auditorium lights faded out completely, there was blackness for a few moments, and at five minutes past one in the morning the curtain rose briskly and Kit spoke her first line to Dr. Chambers.

It was an intoxicating first act. The audience had paid the actors the supreme compliment of having the faith to wait for them, and the actors responded with the kind of performance actors wish they could give every day of their lives. At the end of the brutally long first act, delayed fatigue set in, with the bulk of the play yet to come. As Kit hurried past a watchful Guthrie on the way to her dressing room, she said, "Get me an agg."

There was an all-night lunch wagon nearby, but in their long wait the audience had eaten everything it had to offer. They had also stripped clean a twenty-four-hour drugstore, and the facilities at the Olympic Hotel were shut tight, perhaps in self-defense. In desperation, Guthrie started looking up old high-school friends in the telephone directory, and at two-thirty — he roused a man named Zell Nelson, living nearby on Denny Hill, who agreed to give him an egg if he would come and get it.

Kit downed the egg raw, and the play continued until almost four o'clock when the final curtain came down, and, as Woollcott later wrote of the occasion, "that blessed audience, feeling, perhaps, that it was by this time too late to go to bed at all, stayed to give more curtain calls than the exhausted troupe had ever heard."

Ray Henderson was in San Francisco but still managed to get the story of the Seattle opening into every newspaper across the country the next day. Woollcott's article, "Miss Kitty Takes to the Road," appeared in the *Saturday Evening Post* in August 1934, perpetuating the story with far-flung results in unexpected places. At a heated public meeting in Saint Louis, protesting that Daylight Saving Time would necessitate a later curtain for the open air St. Louis Municipal Opera, a rebuttal began, "Is St. Louis less civic minded than Seattle where they waited until one o'clock in the morning . . . ?" And so on.

The story reached the largest audience of all and entered theatrical legend when Woollcott took to the airways as "The Town Crier," and with his mellow, bedtime-story manner became a national darling. Establishing a radio tradition at Christmas that for many listeners rivaled Lionel Barrymore's performance as Scrooge, each year Woollcott retold, yet again, the thrilling events of the Christmas night in Seattle when the audience sat in their seats until one o'clock in the morning waiting for Miss Kitty to emerge from the flood.

Ray Henderson was always ahead of the troupe, preparing for their arrival with the hotels, smoothing the way with local dignitaries, establishing rapport with the press. At each new theatre he saw to it that the dressing rooms were scrubbed and cleaned throughout, and that Miss Cornell's had (1) a carpet on the floor, (2) a comfortable couch, (3) a comfortable chair, and (4) a large mirror. In his concern for the company's comfort he never let them know that the black Packard limousines that met them so stylishly when they arrived usually came from the local funeral parlor. Every theatre manager was given in advance a stern warning: "It is necessary and exceedingly important that the stage of your theatre be heated to a high temperature. It must be *hot*. If there are draughty doors or windows, they must be repaired so that there are no draughts and the stage can be KEPT HOT. This is IMPERATIVE. Miss Cornell is very susceptible to taking cold. If she is ill, the theatre has to be closed. So please take every precaution to safeguard her health. Thank you."

This kind of precaution could be expected, and was taken, in modern, well-equipped legitimate theatres, but with the exception of four or five in the large cities, such theatres no longer existed. For the most part the company performed in movie theatres, community halls, high-school auditoriums, and endless variations. In Oakland (a "three-in-two-days" city with *Romeo* Monday night, *Candida* Tuesday matinee, *The Barretts* Tuesday night) they were separated from a basketball court by a thin partition, with the referee's whistle punctuating Mercutio's death and the balcony scene. In Denver they performed in a structure where cattle shows and rodeos were usually given, and a small dressing room, like a packing crate, had to be built for Kit near the stage, since the actual dressing rooms were a good five minutes' walk away. In Colorado Springs there were only two dressing rooms, one for men, one for women.

A Shriners' Hall in Des Moines. In Nashville, the famous Ryman's Auditorium, built as a church by a retired riverboat captain who got religion, with the stage where the altar used to be, surrounded on four sides by pews. The actors, separated from the audience by loosely hung curtains, made up in mirrors propped up on prayer-book stands, in full view of the balcony trade above. For contrast, everybody in Amarillo dressed under the stage but Kit, who was isolated in a dressing room the size of a concert hall — which, apparently, it was, containing as it did a grand piano, two bass kettle drums, thirty ballroom chairs, a couch, a roll-top desk, a dressing table, and three potted palms. In a touching effort to make her comfortable, the management also wheeled in a wooden bathtub and donated several pitchers which had to be filled with water at the one tap (cold) under the stage. To ease her exile, John Hoysradt came in and played the piano while she made up. In Utica, an old-time burlesque house — a note attached to her dressing table mirror asked her please not to swipe it like the last New York star did.

Movie theatres were often the worst of all, either small art houses with no backstage space or giant palaces with Wurlitzer organs. Often the current movie attraction ran until six o'clock on the day of performance, which meant setting up silently in the dark behind the silver screen and constantly losing the stagehands who would sneak out front to enjoy the movie. Some of the palaces were so immense that a choice had to be made: to shout for the back half of the audience, ruining the play for the front half, or to play normally for the front half, inaudible to the back. Usually, the system of reserved seating was a mystery to the management and to the ushers.

Movie theatre managers were opposed to the living theatre for economic reasons, claiming that after a play came to town and everybody laid out his three dollars for a ticket, it would be weeks before anybody had twenty-five cents for a movie. It was the Depression, and there was justification for their grudge, but in all other ways the arrival of a legitimate play stimulated an economic boom. Whole families would make the trek in from the country to see the play, while they were at it staying two or three days to shop, filling the hotels, stores, and restaurants. Sometimes they came by the busload from hundreds of miles away, and throughout the tour the Katharine Cornell management kept receiving letters of thanks from merchants, grateful for the touch of prosperity.

At some stops a legitimate play had not been seen since the First World War, at others, never. Some of the audience still didn't know what to expect when they sat down in their seats and, if they were too far down front, worried about the "flicker." It was not uncommon for a box office to receive a call asking, "Is Miss Cornell a soprano or a contralto?" and when told she was neither, asking, "Then how does she entertain the audience?" But whatever the doubts, they came to find out. At the Tulane Theatre in New Orleans, where the last stage production had played to empty houses, women rioted when there were no tickets left for the matinee, and the police were called, one of whom had to be given first aid when a disappointed patron stabbed him with a pin. At Lincoln, Nebraska, Kit was whisked into the governor's office because he wanted to meet her, but the movie theatre manager in Memphis asked Gert, rather accusingly, "Who is this Miss Cornell? I've never heard of her, but a lot of people around here have. The day we announced this we got three hundred letters asking for tickets." With that kind of response, movie theatre managers sometimes slyly oversold the performances, playing on Miss Cornell's sympathy to give extra performances and bail them out, which she always did.

On the one-night stand in Amarillo, a sandstorm came up during the performance, so strong that when it was time to leave the theatre, taxis had to climb the sidewalk and back up to the stage door so that the actors could be pushed forcibly into them and driven blindly, hell-bent, to the hotel. In the middle of the square there was a heavy chain attached to a flagpole, and the townspeople said the wind was nothing if that chain didn't stand out straight from the pole. There was sand in everything — food, hair, eyes, mouth, clothes. During most of the play the wind was so strong that the actors couldn't hear their cues. But at the end of the play the wind, like every hazard of the tour and every hurdle of the road, was drowned out by the applause.

In Waco, Ray Henderson put Kit in touch with Dr. A. Joseph Armstrong at Baylor University. A Robert Browning scholar, Dr. Armstrong was devoting his time, which turned out to be his life, to the formation of a Browning Center on the campus of Baylor which would eventually house the greatest Browning collection in the world, of letters, books, manuscripts, furniture, and memorabilia. Dr. Armstrong gave Basil Rathbone a ring of Browning's to wear during the performance, and Kit a brooch of Elizabeth Barrett's. He also wanted her to use one of Elizabeth Barrett's own books as a prop, but her old habit of never learning things she had to read aloud on stage prevailed over historical and theatrical sentiment, and she had to stay with the volume in which Gert had pasted her lines.

On the longer stands the company stayed in hotels; on the shorter, they slept in the Pullman cars. Some were better troupers than others. Often on the one-night stands the cars wouldn't be shifted to outgoing tracks or hooked onto a departing train until two or three o'clock in the morning, and then, above the slamming and banging, Mrs. Basil Rathbone could be heard exhorting her husband to tell the engineer not to bounce her around so much. Whereupon the dauntless Romeo and intrepid Browning, not to mention the fastidious Morell, would emerge obediently from his compartment, climb down to the tracks in the cold, and run ahead to the locomotive for a word with the engineer. He was such an affable man that it usually worked, and his wife felt justified in her self-indulgence.

The Rathbones also never seemed able to cope with the economics of touring and found themselves in constant need of money, asking for all or part of the Saturday pay check to be in cash. On one of the longer stands, they took Gert to Saturday night supper and over the meal told her they couldn't afford the sumptuous spread they were treating her to, that they had no money to pay their way out of the hotel the next day because Basil's pay envelope had been stolen. Kit insisted on reimbursing him, prevailing over Gert's conviction that Ouida Rathbone had simply spent the money and invented the theft.

There were other actors more suited to play each of Rathbone's roles, but there was no other leading actor of the day who could have played all three so well. With his handsome Velásquez head, he brought distinction and high theatricality to each interpretation and every performance. But in his surviving correspondence with Katharine Cornell there is no letter not devoted to explaining why he was broke and seeking financial help once again or apologizing for not discharging his current indebtedness. This may explain why he was forced to make the Sherlock Holmes movies for which, despite other excellent screen performances and impressive stage appearances later in his career, this fine actor is best remembered.

The management was required by the unions to supply the stagehands and wardrobe women with lower berths, while the actors paid for their own accommodations out of their salaries. Orson Welles and John Hoysradt always insisted on a compartment when everybody knew that even between them they did not make enough to afford it, while at the other extreme, Charlie Waldron hardly ever bought a berth at all. He was sixty, the oldest member of the company, the most seasoned trouper, and knew every trick of economy, even to manufacturing his own gin in hotel bathtubs. On a long stand, if he didn't need a bathtub for brewing purposes, a cheaper room could be had at the YMCA, which was also cheaper than a Pullman berth on a short stand, providing they were not due to pull out in the middle of the night.

Nights spent traveling between stands presented a problem, but Waldron had learned that there was always a coal stove in the freight car, and when Si made up the berths for the night, that was where Charlie Waldron could be found, in the freight car, toasting the crackers or rolls he had bought at the grocery store at the last stand, then mixing an orange powder (from the same store) with his homemade gin for what he called orange blossoms, enjoying a snug little late night supper.

On one occasion he decided to splurge, not only to buy a lower berth for a night, but to reserve a whole section and settle in after the performance with a good supply of orange blossoms and the new issue of his favorite magazine, *Popular Mechanics*. When Kit and Gert drove up in a taxi at one-thirty, the entire Pullman car was in darkness with only a small flickering light in one of the windows. Charlie Waldron had picked one of the two nights during the long tour when they were too far out from the station to be hooked up to the generator, and there were no lights. He had been making do with a candle stub he packed in his suitcase for emergencies, but it was almost gone, and since Gert was dressed, he asked if there wasn't some place she could get him another candle. She tried, but it was the middle of the night and Charlie Waldron's celebration soon ended in darkness.

There were all the intrigues, romances, alliances, and disputes that could be expected among any fifty people thrown into such close proximity for seven months, and Kit participated or withdrew — or was included or excluded — according to a tacit, barely perceptible, protective code. She could call Margot Stevenson into her dressing room and have a talk with her when she felt the younger actress was spending too much time with the wrong boy. But when Gert had to arrange an abortion for another actress, it was kept secret from Miss Cornell, as if it would be a shock or an affront. Kit said, "We are not strong with a few weaknesses, we are weak with a few strengths," and discipline was a strength that could — and should — be developed. Lapses disheartened her more than they angered her, and perhaps it was only considerate to keep them from her.

When they were too flagrant to be concealed, however, Kit dealt with them efficaciously and charitably. Orson Welles, who at the time described himself as emerging "noisy and faltering out of the age of insolence," was prone to be late for half-hour calls and at least once missed a train connection and had to hire a private plane to reach the next stand on time. (Several years later, when Welles was late for a broadcast rehearsal with Alexander Woollcott, Woollcott confronted him angrily, "Who the hell do you think I am? Katharine Cornell?") In San Francisco, Kit and Gert were having late supper one night at the Mark Hopkins Hotel when two men in capes and mustaches came in and created a stir with their outrageous accents and flamboyant manners. Kit recognized Welles and a fellow actor named Bill, but rather than embarrass them on the spot, she and Gert departed. Shortly, a note was delivered to the two bizarre strangers suggesting it was time to return the comic clothes to wardrobe and go to bed. The next night they were called into Miss Cornell's dressing room and told to remember they were not the Katzenjammer Kids, they were members of the Katharine Cornell company and personal representatives of Miss Cornell; in future they would conduct themselves as gentlemen with decorum and dignity at all times.

"About twice a year I wake up and find myself a sinner," Welles wrote to Kit from the Claypool Hotel in Indianapolis after another reprimand. "Somebody slaps me in the face, and after the stars have cleared away and I've stopped blubbering, I am made aware of the discomforting realities. I see that my boots are rough-shod and that I've been galloping in them over people's sensibilities. I see that I have been assertive and brutal and irreverent, and that the sins of deliberate commission are as nothing to these. This of course is good for me . . . just as the discipline of this tour is good for me. . . ."

Two weeks after the incident at the Mark Hopkins, Welles's friend Bill was in trouble again, this time seriously. Driving down Sunset Boulevard in Los Angeles late at night, on the way home from a party in a rented car with three other members of the company as passengers, he was struck by another car turning suddenly out of LeBrea. The two girls in his car landed in the hospital, Margot Stevenson with a broken nose. There were four understudies playing in the next day's matinee performance. Bill was arrested for drunken driving, as dire an offence in California then as it is now, and bound over for trial. Kit went bail for him, against the advice of her attorney who had no sympathy for Bill's situation and thought he would become fearful of the final outcome and attempt to get away. The troupe moved on to Oakland, and Kit continued to make herself available for assistance, only surrendering the responsibility, financially and morally, to Bill's father. In letters and telegrams, Bill hoped and pressed to be allowed to rejoin the company when his trial was over, to "redeem myself not only in your eyes but in my own." Against Gert's advice, Kit was inclined to take him back.

Bill was found guilty and given two weeks before sentencing to apply for probation. From Columbus, Ohio, Kit wrote on his behalf to the probation officer of the Los Angeles Superior Court, and finally, two months after the accident happened, he was sentenced to one year in the county jail but granted probation for two years on condition that he pay a fine and make restitution for property damage. He did not rejoin the company.

In Los Angeles an encounter took place in Kit's dressing room that became another of Woollcott's favorite stories. It happened that Mrs. Patrick Campbell and Mrs. Leslie Carter, who had never met, arrived at the same moment after a performance. As Kit told it in *I Wanted to Be an Actress*, she introduced them, and "Belasco's Du Barry bowed to Shaw's Eliza and turned away. And Shaw's Eliza bowed to Belasco's Du Barry and turned to *me*. 'But,' she whispered in that famous whisper which *can* — and at that moment *did* — shatter the rafters, 'I thought she was *dead!*'"

Guthrie was in and out of the tour, busy with his own production of Sidney Howard's *Yellow Jack*. Written with Paul de Kruif, it was a dramatic transcript of Walter Reed's search for the fever-breeding mosquito in Cuba. (One of the volunteers to be bitten, a small part, was played by James Stewart.) To date, it was Guthrie's most prestigious and successful production on his own. Determined to see it, Kit took the train from Roanoke after the performance on Friday night, attended the *Yellow Jack* matinee on Saturday in New York, and took the train for Princeton for a performance of *The Barretts* Saturday night. As if the day weren't full enough, she had supper afterwards with Albert Einstein and his wife.

"I couldn't talk to Professor Einstein about his work," she said, "but he was lovely about mine."

It was estimated by *Variety* that in two hundred and twenty-five performances, Katharine Cornell's 1933–1934 repertory tour played to five hundred thousand people. She set box office records wherever she went. She proved that lost, neglected, uncultivated audiences in thirty-four states would patronize the living theatre if given the chance. She established precedents for other productions and standards for her own. In the course of her career as actress-manager, she would eventually tour an overall hundred thousand miles for three hundred and thirty-six weeks, or altogether almost six and one-half years on the road. By never giving audiences less than her very best, she instilled in them a faith and affection as indisputable as the high quality of her productions.

She not only played fair with audiences, she played fair with theatre managers, often in spite of their open hostility and against the arrangements of her own business advisers.

The 1939–1940 tour of *No Time for Comedy* arrived for a one-night stand in Birmingham and found the theatre filthy. The toilets had not been cleaned and the dressing rooms hadn't even been opened for years. As the company stood forlornly amid the squalor, the manager arrived, gum-chewing, insolent, arrogant, his hat rudely pushed back over dirty hair. Kit asked why he couldn't at least have had the backstage aired out and the toilets cleaned for the actors.

"Why should I?" he asked. "I don't make any money out of you. Why should I spend one cent getting this place cleaned?"

Margalo Gillmore and the other actors were ready to kill him, but remembering they were civilized members of a Katharine Cornell company, were more ready to walk out of the theatre and refuse to play under such conditions. But Kit's focus had suddenly shifted.

"What do you mean you don't make any money?" she asked.

He explained that with the deal her representatives had wangled, he barely broke even, that he could at least make a buck if he put a movie in the house. She asked what the deal was, and he told her. His contempt did not diminish one bit, in fact it increased as he warmed to his subject. But to everyone's surprise, Kit no longer seemed affronted. If they hoped she would go on standing up for their offended sensibilities, they were disappointed, for here she was, her own sensibilities equally offended, suddenly contemplating this rowdy almost with favor. What they didn't grasp right away was that she had gone beyond the man's manner to his meaning.

"That's terrible," she said. "If theatre managers don't make any money, then theatre across the country will die. There is no point in touring if everybody doesn't make money out of it. We'll change your percentage. Gert . . . ?"

It may be true, as some say, that she did not always know much about the business arrangements of her productions, but when she was aroused by what she did know, her actions were, in Margalo Gillmore's words, "quick, instant, and right."

The immediate effect of the 1933–1934 repertory tour was to inspire other major productions to take to the road — Helen Hayes in *Mary of Scotland*, George M. Cohan in *Ah, Wilderness!*, Alfred Lunt and Lynn Fontanne in *Reunion in Vienna* and later in *Idiot's Delight*, Ina Claire in *End of Summer*, Jane Cowl in *First Lady*, Katharine Hepburn in *Jane Eyre*. But as fine and long and profitable as these tours were, they were all single shows and not repertory, and loyal survivors of the 1933–1934 tour maintain that nobody in the theatre ever, either before or after (except in subsequent Katharine Cornell tours), traveled with such distinction, security, camaraderie, and comfort. In the set of every play there is a peephole, invisible to the audience, through which the actors backstage can see what is happening onstage or in the audience. In Katharine Cornell productions, the peephole was always encircled by a brass ring.

A brass peephole. That was class.

⸻

The first question at every stand was, "Where is the park?", where Flush would sometimes be more welcome than he was at the hotel. In Seattle he may have been an actor-hero like the other members of the company, but the Olympic Hotel would have none of him and Kit had to take an apartment on First Hill for herself, Flush, Sonia, Guthrie, Gert, and Eveline Drysdale. The biggest hotel in Oklahoma City denied admittance to dogs, so everybody had to stay at the second biggest, and in Houston they wouldn't let him use the front elevator, insisting he be sent up with a bellboy like a piece of luggage. "Where he goes, I go," said Kit. Clemence Dane was there, too (on a lecture tour), and imperious in evening dress she followed Kit and Flush into the service elevator with the maids, the mops, and the extra rolls of toilet paper.

Clemence Dane saw Kit in all three plays, and a week later wrote to her from Chicago:

I've always had this instinct about your work, that you are one of those artists who *can* tackle the big stuff — in fact, who are at their best *only* when tackling stuff bigger than they are themselves. It is a very rare form of acting ability — I can think of only four among our moderns at home of whom one can say it — and only two in whom it approaches great acting. I *like* you in all your work — you have grace, beauty and a mastered technique, but not until I saw your potion scene was I satisfied, did I feel here is something splendid and apart. Don't misunderstand me — no, you won't, of course: but I do mean that other people could have played your other parts — they are in the range of any first class actress. You gave your special quality to them, but other actresses could do the same — but Juliet is the test of the great actress — and to me in the potion scene you gave something, in your own way, unique. *I* know what you mean when you say you want to work on and on in the part — of course you do and will: but you *are* in your big scenes already a Juliet, not merely an accomplished actress playing Juliet. . . . I see such a range of great parts opening out before you. Of course they won't make money, and of course people will attack your interpretation of every part in turn, gracelessly and ungratefully, as they've done with all the big interpreters. . . . But if you go *on* — they'll remember you for a little when you are dead — and maybe say "I saw Katharine Cornell" in the same way an old lady said to me wistfully "I saw Irving". . . . Go *on*, Kit, go ON!

Kit sent this letter to Haus Hirth with a notation scrawled in the top corner: "Please Johanna keep this for me. I am proud of it. C."

VI

Miss Cornell (1934-1936)

21

Wanton Juliet (1934-1935)

AS RAY HENDERSON HAD PREDICTED, *Romeo and Juliet* drew less than the other two plays, as a rule attracting only one-fourth the audience of *The Barretts*, although in places where it was performed a second time, that performance usually approached capacity. As the tour progressed and the company's reputation preceded it, audiences became less frightened of Shakespeare, and in San Francisco, the tenth stand, the plays were drawing almost equally. But the bootleg reviews of the Chicago critics, while not unexpected, were eye-openers to the Mc-Clintics, and despite the growing audience acceptance, they knew their *Romeo and Juliet* needed a lot done to it before it could be taken to New York. The problem was where to begin.

At a matinee in San Francisco, Guthrie sat in front of two noisy, talkative women. As the lights came up on the final scene in the tomb of the Capulets, he was about to turn and hiss at them, crooking his finger in their faces, when one of the women said, "I knew it! When the curtain went up I knew this show would have a bad end!" The ingenuousness of such a remark is hard to credit, but whatever the woman's tone of voice, ironic, bored, or joking, taken literally it was a criticism that Guthrie found valid. Drama should be inevitable. When the curtain comes down on a tragic ending, the audience should realize that no other ending is possible, but they should not realize that when the curtain goes up. Guthrie had the uneasy feeling that in his solemn staging, in his reverence for iambic pentameter, in his toadying respect for great artists of the past, and in the somber Woodman Thompson sets, he had committed an unpardonable sin in the theatre: he had given away the plot too soon.

He rushed out and bought an unmarked copy of the play and read it through as if it had just been submitted by a new playwright and passed on by Bill Worthington with an A rating. As he recalled in *Me and Kit*, without the Sothern and Marlowe promptbook to prompt him he found "a drama of hot blood, high passion, exhilaration! Tragedy, springing from recklessness — from youth's fervor — its refusal to turn back — to pause and reflect; had either one of the lovers ever stopped to think, there would have been no tragedy."

In his zeal for scholarship and tradition, Guthrie had put the play on display in a museum instead of up on the stage in a theatre. He had allowed Sothern and Marlowe, the New Variorum, Adelaide Neilson, and Jane Cowl to stand between him and the play, as had the dread iambic pentameter. From now on the verse should be read for meaning, sense, and emotion, and let the poetry take care of itself.

He decided that everything in the touring production had to go except, with Kit, a small cadre of actors — Basil Rathbone, Brenda Forbes, Charles Waldron, and Orson Welles. Starting with the sets, he called Jo Mielziner out from New York. They met in the Middle West and Guthrie outlined what he wanted — "light, gay; hot sun, spacious, ending in a marvelous dark Capulet tomb where 'no healthsome air breathes in.' " Not until then must the gloom be allowed to settle over the action. The Woodman Thompson sets were given to a grateful little-theatre group in Cincinnati, and *Romeo and Juliet* was taken out of the repertory. It had played thirty-nine performances. That was in April, and so confident was Guthrie of his new approach that the minute the long tour ended in June, Ray Henderson announced on the marquee of the Martin Beck Theatre:

OPENING, DECEMBER 20TH, AT 8:15 SHARP
MISS CORNELL'S SEASON

Noting this, during the summer, *The New Yorker* commented: "In this uncertain world, where values change and friends depart, it is reassuring to discover someone who knows precisely where he is going. . . ."

With Basil Rathbone in Romeo and Juliet, *1934. (New York Public Library, Vandamm Collection)*

At the end of the long tour, the cast gave Miss Cornell a silver box with their names engraved on it, and then Cornelia set off, the long way round, for Garmisch. With Guthrie, Gert, and Katherine (Kay) Wilson, an actress friend who had played parts for Guthrie in *Criminal at Large* and *Yellow Jack*, she sailed on the *Exeter*, an American export boat, for Majorca. There they all lived for a month in a dream villa of white stucco, high on a rock overlooking the bay. At midsummer, Guthrie had to return home for rehearsals of *Divided by Three*, a play by Beatrice Kaufman (George S.'s wife) and Margaret Leech, starring Judith Anderson with James Stewart, James Rennie, and Hedda Hopper in the cast. Gert and Kit drove up through Barcelona and Andorra to Carcassonne then Gert went to visit relatives in St. Jean de Luz, and Kit spent two weeks in St. Paul, a village behind Cannes, with a Garmisch friend, Nancy Gates. She met up with Gert again in Geneva, where Ray Henderson was waiting to introduce her, at last, to Rudolf Besier, on holiday from his home in Guernsey. Besier was the tallest playwright anyone had ever seen, six foot four, at least, and Mrs. Besier had a stammer which she insisted, delightfully, had been brought on by an appendicitis operation. They talked about everything but *The Barretts of Wimpole Street*. The Besiers also met Johanna Hirth that summer and caught from her the habit of calling Kit "Cornelia."

While in Geneva, with Ray Henderson to lead and suggest, Kit worked out the details of Miss Cornell's forthcoming season. The original plan had been to play *Romeo and Juliet* for a limited run (even Jane Cowl managed only one hundred and fifty-seven performances; Ethel Barrymore, twenty-nine), and then, to foster the idea in the public mind that Miss Cornell was working toward the establishment of a repertory theatre, to alternate *The Barretts* and *Candida* while rehearsing *Rosmersholm*, which would be introduced into the repertory to climax the season. In Majorca, however, Kit and Gert had read John van Druten's antiwar play, *Flowers of the Forest*, and felt it was a moving, important play that Miss Cornell should do. At first she and Ray and Gert toyed with the idea of cutting her New York season short to make her first London appearance in fifteen years in the van Druten play, but complications with van Druten's schedule finally determined that after *Romeo* they would revive *The Barretts*, as scheduled, while rehearsing *Flowers of the Forest*, which would then climax the season in place of *Rosmersholm.* Rebecca West was put off for one more year; as it turned out, forever.

———

At Garmisch, a new large room had been added onto the third floor at Haus Hirth, especially for Kit. Designed and engineered by Walther, it was almost a suite, with a magnificent porcelain stove, a couch with a formal eighteenth-century portrait above it, and, partitioned off from the rest of the room by a curtain, a bed that had been hand-carved locally. It was a quiet room on the back of the house, away from the road, with a balcony overlooking the driveway court, a room suitably removed for the study of Juliet in the afternoons, cued by Johanna. It was officially called, in the house books, the Cornelia *Zimmer.*

Everything was geared to the upcoming *Romeo and Juliet.* The Rathbones came again, as they had the summer before, for leisurely rehearsal talks, first wiring from London that they were short of money and being funded by Kit. Paul Nordoff was a regular at Haus Hirth and that year composed a song in honor of Johanna's birthday which Kit agreed to sing at the evening entertainment. In the afternoon she appeared before Johanna, pale and shaking with stage fright, and said, "You see, Johanna, what I go through for you?"

But she was relaxed enough to act up a bit, too, playing Juliet's balcony scene (presumably either before the Rathbones arrived or after they left) with one of the other guests from the balcony outside the Cornelia *Zimmer.* Her Romeo, Dr. George Vincent of the Rockefeller Foundation, used a ladder to ascend from the driveway court, and Johanna, observing the demonstration, pronounced him too old for the part. (Dr. Vincent's wife, then sixty-nine, was out climbing mountains.)

Kit and Johanna motored down to Verona in the old Ford, in Vicenza visiting the ancient castello where, legend has it, Juliet lived. With her combined sense of high romance and earthy practicality, Kit was moved to be standing under the sun that had shone on Juliet but observed that the balcony inside the walled garden was much too high for immortal whisperings. She said later that her biggest thrill came in climbing around the Roman amphitheatre where Duse had played, "and thinking of how, after her Juliet there, her emotional excitement was so intense that she ran through the streets all night with her hair blowing in the wind."

In October it was time to go home for rehearsals, and as if trying to take the peace and security of Garmisch with her, Kit persuaded Johanna to make her first trip to New York, saying she couldn't possibly go into rehearsal without her since Johanna was the only one who knew how to cue her properly. It was a bad idea from the start. They sailed on the *Europa* and Kit was immediately unwell, probably in nervous anticipation of at last facing New York as Juliet, and Johanna was seasick the entire voyage, able to take nothing but mineral water.

It was one of the rare times when Guthrie was unable to meet the boat. He was always solicitous when Kit traveled, almost a show-off about it. On a cross-country train trip he would arrange to have telegrams delivered to her at almost every stop, even Douglas, Arizona, and Liberal, Kansas, with messages varying from "Darling, I miss you, I love you, how are you?" to "How are you darling? All my love!" and sometimes, urgently, "Wire exactly how you are! I miss you I love you!" Gert always felt it was an act he put on to impress the Pullman porters on the train with the importance of the personage in Drawing Room A, Car 24, Eastbound, "Golden State Limited." But whatever his motives, the fact is that Guthrie loved being consistently thoughtful and Kit came to rely on it. Whatever his other, counterdomestic involvement, whatever devilry he found himself up to, it was dropped in a hurry as he scurried off to meet her train or boat, neatly dressed, shaved, sober, and smiling. And if he did not meet the *Europa* in October 1934, the chances are that he was at 23 Beekman Place waiting to rush out and open the door of her taxi as it drew up.

But since he was not on the dock, Kit had no one to wave to, and as if to rub it in, Johanna, the stranger to these shores, immediately spotted someone she knew in the crowd waving a Bavarian flag.

Still pale and gaunt, with her hair pulled back under a scarf, Kit was not recognized as she landed, and the customs inspector gave both women a difficult time, wanting to know what was in the boxes they carried. When Kit said, "Heads," he suspected levity, which he did not appreciate, and insisted on opening the boxes. Inside he indeed found two recognizable heads of Katharine Cornell (sculpted by a fellow guest at Garmisch) and he became gracious and gallant. His name was Barrett and he felt such a great kinship that he kept in touch for years, and Gert would send him tickets for his wife and children.

As soon as they landed, Johanna decided to go home again on the

Europa's return voyage, which she did, spending a total of forty-eight hours in New York. Perhaps she never intended to stay in the first place, perhaps the difficult crossing had strained the friends' relationship, or perhaps New York was overwhelming. At Garmisch Johanna reigned, creating a sophisticated simplicity for the elegant and the honored, which is what they went there for and, in Kit's case, wanted to take home. But perhaps she couldn't thrive outside her domain and felt confused and out of place. In Garmisch, Kit could play Ruth to her Naomi, but in New York she couldn't return the gesture. Everybody made light of her quick turnaround and suggested she write a travel book about New York. Kit asked what gift she would like sent to the ship for her sailing. Johanna was unfamiliar with that custom and did not know what to suggest, but since she had a passion for neatly wrapped parcels, she said she would like some string. Kit sent a package eighteen inches square filled with balls of string. In 1975 Johanna had not yet used it all up. She never saw Kit play Juliet or any other role.

Orson Welles had joined the long tour on the assurance that it would culminate in a New York stand, thus enabling him to make his Broadway debut in contrasting juicy roles. He was hurt, almost personally, when Miss Cornell's New York run, which he felt had been held out to him, was postponed, but he recovered sufficiently to be on hand in the fall, expecting to resume his roles. Guthrie, however, had never been completely happy with Welles's youthful Mercutio, and when Brian Aherne was unexpectedly available and anxious to play it, Guthrie jumped (providing, Aherne adds in his autobiography, he accepted Welles's small salary). Twice thwarted, Welles was furious, but it is a mark of the impatient young giant's wisdom, if not his humility, that he was willing to stay on in the lesser role of Tybalt.

Edith Evans came over from England to play the Nurse. When she saw what Guthrie was trying to do with the play she was so pleased that she wanted to accept the salary she had been offered instead of the one she had demanded, but nobody held her to it. Other newcomers to the cast included Moroni Olson as Capulet, George Macready as Paris, and John Emery as Benvolio.

Encouraged by Guthrie, Jo Mielziner abandoned traditional Elizabethan or Renaissance design in favor of an earlier Italian primitive style, copying the manner of Giotto di Bondone, the thirteenth-century artist noted for his lightness, gaiety, and purity of color. With brightly colored walls and turrets standing out against deep-shadowed recesses and passageways, all free from the restriction of true perspective, a modern "revue" ground plan was used, the kind that in musical revues permitted transition from songs to sketches to dances without a break, often with overlaps. Guthrie restored to the script everything that had been left out for the past seventy-five years, cutting only the obsolete comedy of the musicians and servants, and feeling that all twenty-three of Shakespeare's scenes were needed to make the story hang together, played them (with one twelve-minute intermission) at a spirited clip that left the audience no time to think or applaud disruptively between scenes (and got the curtain down under the three hours allowed by the unions). Juliet, the sun, was fourteen again, graying hair and all, and in the exhilaration and youthfulness of the production it mattered not to give away the plot, so Guthrie even reinstated the Prologue with its foreshadowing that the star-crossed lovers "do with their death bury their parents' strife," and fittingly (and perhaps in amends) let it be spoken by the youngest member of the company, Orson Welles.

Guthrie yelled his head off twice over the production. The first time came during dress rehearsal for the Detroit opening when Jo Mielziner's balcony, a slim tower rising into a blue sky toward the stars, turned out to be, fully lighted and occupied, so narrow and dumpy that it made fourteen-year-old Juliet look like a Valkyrie hovering over the field of battle, choosing those to be slain and those to be carried off to Valhalla. Guthrie had had misgivings all along which with great strain he had kept to himself, and even now he let the scene finish and magically dissolve to Friar Lawrence's cell before letting out an agonized "Jo!" At the sound of it, Charlie Waldron, who had dress rehearsed with Guthrie before, calmly sat on Friar Lawrence's cot to wait out the storm, and Kit beat a retreat to her dressing room and closed the door, presumably standing in a corner with her hands over her ears.

Jo Mielziner, with the patience and good manners that never deserted him, painted down the offending shaft to drab and lighted only the lovers' faces for the opening in Detroit, the four performances in Cleveland, the week in Pittsburgh, and the two days in Toronto. For the New York opening he came up with a balcony ten feet wide made of blue velvet to absorb the light and still let the actors' faces shine through "the mask of night." It was all that Guthrie had dreamed it would be, but there was only time to light it before the first performance. To let Kit rest at home, he had one of the citizens of Verona, Ruth March, stand in for her. In the middle of the session, however, Kit appeared, unable to stay away, and asked to stand in for Ruth March. To play the delicate balcony scene on a set she had scarcely seen before except as a sketch, an elevated platform she had stood on for only an hour while a spotlight experimented around her, a perilous ledge from which she might literally fall flat on her face before a New York audience come to pass judgment on her, was the kind of challenge to her physical dexterity, the kind of obstacle to be overcome that could make an opening night bearable and help her forget her stage fright. The last-minute decision of the carpenter, made after the curtain was up and relayed to her by a shaking Guthrie during the performance, that it would be easier if she clung to the balcony at the end of the scene, to be wheeled off with it, was like adding another welcome heat to the race.

She was not nervous. After a year and a half of performing, travel, and study, she felt she was prepared. She visited all the dressing rooms and chatted with each actor. Guthrie, as usual, superstitiously dressed down to the occasion in a shiny, grubby old suit, hiding behind a miserly two days' growth of beard. The actor playing Montague might well have done the same, for he was too nervous to make his crepe beard stick, and at 8:14 Jimmy Vincent, the stage manager, informed Miss Cornell that they would have to hold the curtain five minutes. Her reply was that on this occasion Romeo would have to have a beardless father because they couldn't wait, and at 8:15 sharp, as advertised, a resplendent Orson Welles, shielding his face with a gold Benda mask, stepped through the sage green curtains with the crest of the Capulets embroidered on one side and the Montagues on the other, and Miss Cornell's season began.

It may have been just an exaggeration of Guthrie's to embellish his account of the opening in *Me and Kit*, but if it didn't happen it should have, that at the end of the performance the audience was silent, and Kit, in the great purple cape she wore for curtain calls, whispered to him, "We can't take curtain calls if no one applauds." When the applause broke it was prolonged by cheers and bravos until Kit, unable to run through the streets like Duse with her hair blowing in the

wind, wept openly and decreed there would be no more curtain calls
— "If the audience sees me like this, it will look as if I am asking
for something."

It was Guthrie's reward for breaking with the past that Miss Cornell's arrangement of the text, as it was billed in the program, was
given credit for breaking new ground. John Mason Brown wrote in
the *New York Post* the next day:

> It is not often in our lifetime that we are privileged to enjoy the pleas-
> ant sensation of feeling that the present and the future have met for a
> few triumphant hours. . . . Yet it was this very sensation — this uncom-
> mon sensation of having the present and the future meet by witnessing
> the kind of event to which we will be looking back with pride in the
> years to come — that forced its warming way, I suspect, into the con-
> sciousness of many of us last night as we sat spellbound at the Martin
> Beck.
>
> Miss Cornell's Juliet is luscious and charming. It finds her at her
> mellowest and most glamorous. It burns with the intensity Miss Cor-
> nell brings to all her acting. It moves gracefully and lightly; it is end-
> lessly haunting in its pictorial qualities; and reveals a Miss Cornell who
> equals the beauty of the lyric lines she speaks with a new-found lyric
> beauty of her own voice. . . . To add that it is by all odds the most
> lovely and enchanting Juliet our present-day theatre has seen is only
> to toss it the kind of superlative it honestly deserves.

Burns Mantle called her "the greatest Juliet of her time," and all the
critics went on at length about every element of the production, the
direction, the sets, and the acting of the entire cast, although it was
generally agreed that Brian Aherne, with "the brilliance of a diamond,"
overshadowed Basil Rathbone's "good, workmanlike, conventional job"
and "would have made a Romeo to match her Juliet."

But John Mason Brown was more astute than most critics, able to
see beyond the "acting wonders and scenic splendors" on display at
the Martin Beck to the larger meaning of the event in the overall life
of an artist. With an almost clairvoyant awareness of Guthrie's, Gert's,
and Ray Henderson's aspirations on behalf of Katharine Cornell, he
wrote:

> The evening was an important one in Miss Cornell's career. It came to
> New York audiences as a testing-point in her development as an actress.

It was the ordeal by means of which she was to demonstrate to a public that has long had cause to admire her in several good plays and many more trifling scripts whether or not she could meet the challenging demands of one of the greater classic roles. It was a nerve-wracking night which was fated either to bring her disillusioning failure as a player or to crown her with a new significance in our theatre. To say that she emerged triumphantly from the evening both as an actress and a manageress is but to state an agreeable truth.

Lynn Fontanne wrote to her, "I would crawl on my hands and knees to see the Juliet that Atkinson describes. They all make one crazy to see it — even Burns Mantle seems interesting and intelligent. Well, darlings, how happy you must be — Alfred and I send our love and our delight that the dread night is over."

Once freed from strict adherence to the meter of verse, the next step in routing the ghosts of Modjeska and Marlowe and Jane Cowl undoubtedly came in the reinstatement of all that had been cut, especially the lines H. T. Parker had begged her to include, which were not included in the Buffalo opening, the "Gallop apace, you fiery-footed steeds" speech in which Juliet begs night to hurry on so that Romeo may

> *Leap to these arms, untalk'd of and unseen.*
> *Lovers can see to do their amorous rites*
> *By their own beauties; or, if love be blind,*
> *It best agrees with night. Come, civil night,*
> *Thou sober-suited matron, all in black,*
> *And learn me how to lose a winning match,*
> *Play'd for a pair of stainless maidenhoods:*
> *Hood my unmann'd blood, bating in my cheeks,*
> *With thy black mantle; till strange love, grown bold,*
> *Think true love acted simple modesty.*

It is not surprising that Adelaide Neilson, burning to succeed in the middle of the Victorian era, cut such shocking lines of youthful, untried passion. No literary, mid-Victorian angel in the house would even think such thoughts, let alone speak them on a stage. Nor is it surprising that the Juliets who followed, the imperious, ladylike Juliets, all too aware that they were playing in a classic, would not want that classic besmirched by such evidence of carnal desire. But for Kit, here, at last, of all things in all places — where it could not possibly sully Miss Cornell's institutional image — was some of the lusty, romantic earthiness that she had not been permitted to play since the days of the tarnished ladies.

If passion was the key to her interpretation of Juliet, youthfulness was the key to passion. One of the few apologetic criticisms of the staging questioned if it was necessary for the director to send Juliet *running* off the stage in the blackout at the end of each scene, and the answer seems to have been that it was necessary, absolutely necessary, because it was through physical movement and bodily action that Guthrie gave Kit the key to youthfulness, which in turn was the key to passion. It was the first role since Mary Fitton in *Will Shakespeare* in which her gift for athletic balance and her skill at swift, poised movement were indispensable elements of the performance. What a relief and release it must have been after the cramped years on Elizabeth Barrett's couch to go darting in and out of the dancers at the ball, through the Capulets' orchard, up to the tower of her balcony, then wheeling off into the darkness of the wings where the youthfulness did not always stop and sometimes took the form of an uncharacteristic prankishness. At least once she was seen to kneel in a sprinter's starting position in a hoydenish, show-offy way before making her first winged entrance into the orchard in her vivid red dress (always to audible gasps from the audience). Usually before her first entrance she could be found in the wings with her arms raised high above her head, clenching and unclenching her fists to send the blood down her arms and out of her hands, giving them the smooth, veinless look of a young girl's.

It may be true to say that the physicality of the emotions and the athleticism of the action formed the basis of the youthfulness and passion of her interpretation, but it is an oversimplification that unjustly and incorrectly discounts the acting miracle of a performance in which all the facets of a great artist came together and reached their peak at the same time. The craft she had learned from Jessie Bonstelle and the intense emotionalism of her own character here merged with her romantic aspiration for the beauty and elevation of the theatre. How such things happen it is impossible to know, just as it is impossible to know exactly what it is that happens. There is no explanation for the "ecstasy of her eyes" which one critic noted. In the *New York Sun* Richard Lockridge called her Juliet "an eager child, rushing toward love with arms stretched out." Kit herself said after playing Juliet that the biggest secret of acting is to do away wtih all excesses and embellishments, to bring an interpretation to its utmost simplicity. That could explain how she managed to convey "an eager child rushing with arms stretched out," but it in no way explains how a critic knew the rush was "toward love." And that was the part of the performance that captured and held the audience. To everyone she was not "an eager child." Margot Stevenson from the original company to this day becomes almost inarticulate in trying to convey the quality of the performance, and finally comes out with, "She was just this big Italian girl in love!" Surely no other Juliet has been so described, and yet with eager child or big Italian girl, the constant is love.

Stark Young in *The New Republic* was one of three out of eighteen critics to give the production a mixed review, and as is often true in such cases, he was the one to hit upon this intangible element of her performance, the part that gave it greatness: "She makes you believe in love, that Juliet loves, and that the diapason and poetry of love are the reward for its torment. Of various Juliets this must have been one of the last things to be said." And it came from a place beyond the reach of critics, lesser actresses, and determinedly explorative biographers.

In the middle of the run Edith Evans's husband died unexpectedly in England, and without warning on a Saturday morning the actress embarked for home. Brenda Forbes went on as Juliet's Nurse at the matinee and continued until Blanche Yurka was ready to take over the role, and in the wings before those performances Brenda could be seen bending herself double, gnarling herself, hobbling herself, getting old, while a few feet away with her hands raised over her head, jiggling her fingers, Kit was getting young.

The second time Guthrie yelled his head off came a few weeks after the opening.

The cost of the set that was given away in Cincinnati was over eleven thousand dollars, and the abandoned costumes represented a further loss of almost sixty-five hundred. Starting from scratch, the new production of *Romeo and Juliet* opened in December 1934, at a cost of forty-three thousand dollars. On top of these heavy losses and expenditures, *Variety* commented, "There has probably never before been a 'Romeo and Juliet' so handicapped from a gross standpoint. Because, no matter how fine, how beautiful, how well done, Shakespeare is still Shakespeare, and $3.85 top is a lot of money. . . ."

Confounding such dire head-shaking, *Romeo* sold out at every performance, even at matinees playing to over a hundred standees, and a cry was raised when it was announced that the play would close at the end of its scheduled six weeks. The loudest cry came from Guthrie. In theory, he believed in Ray Henderson's exalted idea of repertory for Miss Cornell, both as a theatre ideal and as a way to survive the crass commercialism of Broadway, but in practice to close an already debt-ridden production at the lucrative height of a phenomenally successful run was too much for him. Ray Henderson was of the conviction that once a plan was announced, it was like a promise that must not be broken.

Kit had a less elevated and more distressing reason for dreading an extension of the run, although she would never have used it as a plea for cutting the run short. The cough Dr. Cornell habitually brought to the theatre that disrupted his daughter's quiet scenes was a chronic condition that ran in the family. His sister Lydia had it, and it had also been passed on to Kit. Called a trigger cough, it was brought on by a sudden lack of air in the lungs, almost like a choke. It first began to bother her on the stage in *The Barretts*, and not to make it worse, she gave up cigarettes after smoking heavily all her adult life.

Although the cough was probably eased by not smoking, it never went away. But at least audiences found it reasonable for Elizabeth Barrett to cough once in a while, and she was able to use it to good advantage in her performance. As Lucrece, Elsa Brandt, Candida, Juliet, and every part she played thereafter, she had to control it, to hide it, to cover it; she learned a dozen tricks to keep the audience from knowing of her affliction. The most dreaded moments in *Romeo and Juliet*, moments she had to look forward to with growing anxiety all through the performance, thereby increasing the likelihood of a spasm, came in the last scene of the play in the tomb of the Capulets. First she had to lie completely still in mock death while Romeo discovered her, killed Paris, and then took his own life, and then she had to stab herself, fall over his body and remain perfectly still in actual death while the Montagues and Capulets trooped in, discovered the bodies, grieved, and resolved to end their conflicts. Since Guthrie had put back all cuts, the scene was endless and every merciless word an agony. Actors who played near her reported that perspiration poured from her face in her determination not to give way to a cough.

There were times when she vowed to quit the theatre for good rather than suffer through the last scene of *Romeo and Juliet*, but to satisfy Guthrie, the run was extended three weeks, a week at a time, and then to satisfy Ray Henderson, the play closed on February 23, 1935, after nine weeks and seventy-seven performances, still playing to capacity. Two nights later Miss Cornell's season continued with the revival of *The Barretts*, which could be resurrected so expeditiously because it was all stored in a warehouse just a few blocks away.

Lighting was the most expensive part of a production, so expensive that at the end of the original New York run of *The Barretts* Gert and Stanley Gilkey decided it would be a great saving to own their electrical equipment, instead of renting it for each play, and store it when not in use. The Reilly sisters, who did their trucking and hauling, recommended a warehouse next to their own headquarters in the West Forties, where C. & M.C. rented two floors and began storing not only electrical equipment but scenery from every play, as well as costumes, props, drapes, large ceilings, small ceilings, and since Kit would not act without a carpet on the floor and Guthrie couldn't stand the sound of feet on a stage, there was even a wide selection of rugs and ground cloths. Nothing ever went to Cain's from a Katharine Cornell production, and as the collection grew it became a kind of lending place for other producers. In her own plays audiences never caught on that the back wall of Candida's living room had once been, perhaps, the back wall of Elsa Brandt's. It was through such sound economy measures that Katharine Cornell was able to avoid the cheapening necessity of being commercial in outlook. And the warehouse arrangement gave a practical basis to Ray Henderson's hopes for establishing a repertory of alternating plays.

The press reception of *The Barretts*, although lacking the excitement of discovery, was better than for the original production, with the conclusion that it had "grown richer and more satisfactory." But it was

Curtain call, Romeo and Juliet, *1935. Left to right: Ralph Richardson, Katharine Cornell, Maurice Evans, Edith Evans, Charles Waldron. (Richard Tucker)*

Katharine Cornell with "Sonia," Johanna Hirth with "Illo," Walter Hirth standing, at Garmisch, 1936.

fortunate that *Flowers of the Forest* was put into rehearsal immediately after the opening, for with the unpredictability of Broadway, audiences stayed away from *The Barretts,* and it closed in three weeks after a disappointing twenty-four performances.

The cast of *The Barretts* was a mixture of the original company and the touring company, with Brian Aherne taking over again as Robert Browning (when *Romeo and Juliet* shut down, Basil Rathbone hurried off to Hollywood where he gave one of his best performances in *David Copperfield*). There was one important newcomer playing Occy, Burgess Meredith, who had apprenticed with Eva Le Gallienne's Civic Repertory. In an article for the *New York Times* after Katharine Cornell's death in 1974, he recalled the day he was cast. He had been asked to come to the Cornell-McClintic offices in Rockefeller Center for an interview, which to a young actor in 1934 was the equivalent of a royal command:

> Kit was sitting there looking quite beautiful; a gentle-mannered lady, very quiet. Incidentally, this sense of repose, this lack of temperament is a quality I've never seen, to such an extent, in any other star. Guthrie, on the other hand, was talkative, nervous, and very witty. I recall at that first meeting he launched into an abrasive discussion of the Group Theatre and the method actors who were looming on the horizon and whom he did not like. Since I was then studying with Strasberg and Benno Schneider I wondered what was coming next. I felt Kit watching me and smiling and finally she touched her husband's hand and interrupted him. "Guthrie, I must go. Persuade this boy to come into *Barretts* next week so we can get acquainted before we rehearse the van Druten play." Guthrie looked a little miffed at not finishing his tirade but he said "Fine." When Kit left he said, surprisingly, "She's a marvelous woman. You've no idea." Afterward I was to hear him say that many times. I finally figured out he was simply a fan of hers; that is, aside from being her husband....

Thus in a few minutes, with no bargaining, no stalling, no patronizing reluctance or pandering flattery, with Guthrie fronting and Kit backing him up with smiles and then suddenly coming crisply to the point, the young actor was cast in two important roles and a splendid career was given a leap forward. What's more, it was made to appear that he made the decision to join them, not the other way around, that he had to be "persuaded." Both Kit and Guthrie always showed this consideration for an actor's vulnerable self-esteem. When an actress like Marian Seldes came to see Guthrie about being in *That Lady*, so full of worship for Miss Cornell and so miserably, painfully aware of what she considered her ungainly height, Guthrie squinted at her appraisingly, "Why you're just about the same height as Miss Cornell, aren't you?" (Actors all had a rude awakening when they went to talk to Gert about salary, but by then they'd have worked for nothing.)

In *Flowers of the Forest* Burgess Meredith played Leonard Dobie, a dying young poet with second sight. In a trancelike spell he repeats the last words, spoken seventeen years earlier, of another dying young poet, a soldier killed at the front for the glory of doing his duty, words of solace and affirmation for Naomi (Katharine Cornell), the woman who loved him and has always believed he died embittered with living:

> *Their deaths we called their glory. We were lying.*
> *The glory was in living, not in dying.*

The rest of the cast was, as usual, top quality. Brenda Forbes played Leonard Dobie's sweetheart, Margalo Gillmore was Naomi's frustrated sister, Moffat Johnson played Naomi's understanding husband, and Hugh Williams came from England to play the dark, brooding, romantic soldier-poet-lover in the second-act flashbacks.

If Kit needed something in *Flowers of the Forest* to twist around to make the part of Naomi her own, there was the operation Naomi underwent not to bring the dead poet's unborn child into a world that countenanced war, an action straight out of Kit's own experience. But it is doubtful, oddly, that this most obvious parallel occurred to her, at least consciously. It was the kind of moral unseemliness, in this case happening between acts and referred to only once, that she was beginning to glide over in plays and perhaps in life, almost as if it wasn't there. Many years later a friend, having watched a television rerun of Garbo's movie version of *The Green Hat* (*A Woman of Affairs*), referred to the scene in the hospital where Iris March has just lost her baby. Kit remembered the scene but did not remember and would not be told that Iris March ever lost a baby, although it was the single most important dramatic event of the play.

When Brooks Atkinson pointed out that in *The Barretts* the "carefulness of the design" of her acting had merged with "the fire of her presence," he indicated, as noted earlier, that her craft had caught up with her personal magnetism and was contributing equally to her performance. And so it is possible that she did not feel the need to twist Naomi into something of her own, that she was able to play it on technique.

She said she wanted to do *Flowers of the Forest* because it was a moving antiwar play, a laudable, institutional reason, and maybe that was all she needed to create a characterization. If so, it was a sign of her maturity as an actress. But unfortunately her craft had not developed to the point where it could carry a straight thesis play for a whole evening without adequate support from the playwright, and van Druten, for all his deft, silky-smooth theatrical know-how, did not give the actors or audience much else to hang on to. Even his thesis was not very clear or exciting, and one wonders what it was, exactly, that struck Kit with such force. If asked at the end of the play for van Druten's views on war, about the most one could say was that he was against it.

Her misguided attraction to the play was strong enough to sustain her against great odds (and, as has been noted, to the exclusion of *Rosmersholm*). Guthrie did not like the play, but Gert did, and maybe it was her encouragement that kept Kit at it. Guthrie's distaste for the play was undoubtedly colored by the fact that van Druten insisted on having his old friend Auriol Lee direct it, as she had directed all of his plays both in England and the United States. This was also a serious drawback to Kit, who had been directed by Guthrie for ten years and claimed she couldn't work without him. Van Druten insisted. Auriol Lee was suffering through the early stages of a form of encephalitis, a kind of sleeping sickness, and perhaps out of loyalty and compassion van Druten was determined not to exclude her from his plans. An agreement was finally reached that Auriol Lee would direct the play, but Guthrie would always be in evidence as production supervisor. One has a picture of him pacing the foyer outside the auditorium where rehearsals were being held, now and then peering inside, waiting for Auriol Lee to drop off so he could hurry in and redirect the scenes before she came to.

Flowers of the Forest was cheered in Baltimore, and everything pointed to a similar reception in New York. It rained for opening night, by now a sign of good luck, and another sign came when one of those catastrophes happened that by simply having to be dealt with always seemed to steady Kit's nerves. Burgess Meredith, who was having his first experience with her pre-performance stage fright, tells what happened: "A few moments after the curtain went up and just as I started my first speech, a woman in the second row of the audience had an epileptic fit of some sort. She started to scream and snort as though possessed. The ushers raced down the aisles and the audience and myself were traumatized. Only Kit Cornell, so fearful an hour before, became calm. As calm as Mother Earth. She took me gently by the shoulders and began to ad lib 'You're not well . . . lie down and let me rub your forehead.' I lay down on a sofa as if I were hypnotized. Kit, still talking, put a pillow underneath my head and cajoled me and somewhat miraculously rubbed my head with some cologne she had conjured up from somewhere on stage. By and by the ushers carried the now catatonic lady up the aisle and out of the theatre and the audience resettled itself, probably wondering if it were all part of the plot. Kit, still in character, said to me, 'Now Gerald (or whatever my stage name was), you're fine now, your color's back, now tell us that lovely poem again.' " The cologne was on the stage for a similar scene of forehead-rubbing in the third act, the effect of which may have been somewhat weakened that night by the improvisation in the first act, but how lightning quick was Kit's mind to think of it.

Perhaps the torrential downpour on the Seattle Christmas of 1933 had exhausted the elements of all further good fortune, for the reception of the play was as dismal as the weather, and it only managed to last forty dreary performances. In one season Miss Cornell had experienced her peak and a great depth. Of her New York productions in the decade of the 1930s, only *Lucrece* was a greater failure, critically and financially, than *Flowers of the Forest*.

22

Smiling Joan (1935-1936)

THE POPULAR GERMAN ACTRESS Elisabeth Bergner came to New York to make her American debut in her London success, *Escape Me Never*. She saw Kit's Juliet and at once told her she ought to play *Saint Joan*, a role Bergner herself had first played in Berlin in 1924, which had given her an immediate international reputation. It was rare in the theatre of that or any other day for one star to press her favorite role on another. The suggestion was sincere homage, and Bergner backed it up with charming notes and telegrams and even offered to delay the release of her projected film version of the play until after Kit's production, should she decide to do it.

At the same time, Brian Aherne suggested to Kit that one day she do *Saint Joan* as he would dearly like to play Warwick. The play had been at the back of everyone's mind since 1923 when Kit had been the logical choice to play it in New York but couldn't even "try out" for it because of her commitment to *Casanova*. Always susceptible to the influence of those around her, she now began to think seriously about Joan, and that was all Ray Henderson needed. When *Flowers of the Forest* closed in May 1935, and they all went their individual ways for the summer, he headed for Rouen, as Kit later put it, "to steep himself in the wonder and the terror of the Domremy legend."

Gert had become an ardent Francophile and went to France that summer, while Guthrie escorted Kit straight to Garmisch. It was her fourth consecutive season at Haus Hirth, and in the course of the long spring and summer she found, in a Munich pet shop, Illo, her second and most adored dachshund. Guthrie squinted distastefully at the Zugspitze for a few days, then moved on to the night lights of London.

The plan was to open Miss Cornell's fall season with a ten-and-a-half-week tour of *Romeo and Juliet* before going into rehearsal for *Saint Joan*. With Brian Aherne temporarily in Hollywood and Basil Rathbone permanently there, Guthrie had to find actors to play Romeo and Mercutio, as well as give serious thought to casting the Shaw play. It was always the McClintics' policy to replace an actor with another of equal, or sometimes greater, caliber, and Guthrie started off by persuading Ralph Richardson to make his New York debut as Mercutio and the Chorus.

In the spring of 1931, just after *The Barretts* opened in New York, Guthrie had seen Sybil Thorndike's *Saint Joan* revived in London and had admired Ernest Thesiger's Dauphin, the most difficult supporting role to cast and to play. He now heard that Maurice Evans, a much younger actor, had repeated Thesiger's brilliance as the Dauphin in the Old Vic–Sadler's Wells production of *Saint Joan* the previous fall. He meant to have him play the same part with Miss Cornell, and Conger Goodyear was anxious to have Evans play Romeo. He was engaged for both roles, and so was launched one of the most distinguished Shakespearean careers in the American theatre of the twentieth century.

While in London, Guthrie had an audience with George Bernard Shaw which Ray Henderson wrote up for the *New York Tribune*:

As Katharine Cornell was planning her production of *Saint Joan* in America this season, her husband, Mr. McClintic, expected some advice, not to say admonition and instruction, but the playwright was for leaving everything in the hands of Miss Cornell and her husband. He was vocal on other topics — the belief that a butcher had helped Shakespeare write *Romeo and Juliet*, for instance. Why, didn't the bard speak of "joints"? And who else but a carver of meats could have been responsible for that line? He wondered when producers would realize that there was nothing alluring in bare flesh on the stage, clothing being much more provocative. Who is this "Kit" to whom Mr. McClintic continually referred? In his land that was the familiar name for Christopher. When it was explained that "Kit" was Mr. McClintic's wife, he exclaimed:

"What a disrespectful manner in which to speak of a great lady."

As Guthrie said good-bye to Shaw, the old Irish playwright asked, "And now that I have met her husband, when am I going to see Katharine?"

"Come to America," said Guthrie.

No one seems to know why she never acted in London after *Little Women*, so it is an interesting matter for conjecture. There are indications that her Buffalo *r* kept her on the home side of the Atlantic. Even her most devoted critics sometimes took exception to her native speech patterns and inflections. Dorothy Parker, after complimenting her Elizabeth Barrett extravagantly, went on to say, "Her voice is more thrilling than ever, so it is perhaps cavilling to say that, thrilling though the music may be, it would be nice, now and then, to distinguish some of the words. Perhaps cavilling it is, but here I am saying it." John Mason Brown noticed in her Juliet that occasionally "when she is called upon to utter such words as 'prayer' or 'fear' her diction is blurred with a flattened 'r'." Most playgoers and critics did not cavil, feeling, with Arthur Pollock of the *Brooklyn Eagle* that "even when you can't understand what Miss Cornell says — and she could often be more intelligible — you get what you need to know from the ecstasy of her eyes and the eloquent curling of her wide red lips." Perhaps in deference to Guthrie's awe of the great British actresses with their classical background and idealized speech, she did not wish to invite comparison with Sybil Thorndike and Gwen Ffrangcon-Davies. When she risked it in *Little Women* she had been an unknown, intrepid young actress from nowhere. Now she was Miss Cornell and must be more cautious.

Maybe the truth, as it is in many artistic decisions, was more down-to-earth. Maybe she never acted in England because they would not let her bring in her dogs.

———

Florence Reed played Juliet's Nurse with an Irish brogue, and Charles Waldron was back to play Friar Lawrence.

The small but noticeable part of Benvolio was played by a young actor out of the Chicago Civic Shakespeare Company, Tyrone Power, Jr. (His famous father had died in 1931, but apparently it was not until the movies took over his career that the "Jr." was dropped.) He was first taken on as Burgess Meredith's understudy in *Flowers of the*

Forest, and after the *Romeo* tour he was kept on to play Bertrand de Poulengy in *Saint Joan.* During that run, Power received an offer of a seven-year contract in Hollywood and sensibly went to the other, more established, actors for advice. Brian Aherne advised him to stay in the legitimate theatre and build a solid reputation as a stage actor, while from the next dressing room Maurice Evans advised him to grab whatever chances came his way while he could.

In productions the size of *Romeo and Juliet* and *Saint Joan* there were chances to give chances to new young actors. Guthrie and Gert and Stanley were constantly canvassing nonprofessional productions and drama schools, most notably the Neighborhood Playhouse, to see who was new and coming along. Most of their choices for smaller parts, walk-ons, and extras would later go on to better things.

In addition to being exposed to the finest acting and directing in the theatre of the day, by example the young people were "brought up" to assume the responsibilities of their art and their profession. "Promptness is a courtesy even Kings extend," and Kit, uncertain of unkinglike Guthrie, used to leave home long before he did to be sure of getting to rehearsal on time. Respect for fellow actors was essential; and so was self-respect. Sometimes an inexperienced actor, playing his big moment with Miss Cornell, would nervously play it safe and reverentially turn three-quarters away from the audience so that she could remain full front, only to hear a gasping, spluttering explosion from Guthrie in the auditorium, "Get *above* her! Upstage her! It's your moment! *Take* it!"

While the novices learned, they were protected and cared for. *Romeo and Juliet* opened in Chicago in late November 1935, and Kit arranged for the entire company to have Thanksgiving dinner as her guests at a local private club. After Chicago, the last two weeks of the tour were devoted entirely to a staggering schedule of one-night stands, twelve of them, and when Gert, as advance man, came back and reported to Kit that everything on the road ahead was very expensive, especially meals and hotel rooms when taken for only one night, and that the kids in the company would not be able to live decently on their pay, the management, without any suggestion from either the cast or their union, gave a ten-dollar raise to all the Citizens of Verona, Kinsfolk of Both Houses, Maskers, Watchmen, Attendants, and Guards.

Maurice Evans was physically too small to play opposite Kit, but his heels were built up and John Mason Brown spoke for all the critics when he said that his Romeo was "a great improvement over Mr. Rathbone's. He is indeed the best, the most persuasive, the most likeable and the most understandable Romeo that I, at least, have ever seen. Where Mr. Rathbone was sad, sinister and extremely arctic, Mr. Evans is gay, open-hearted and almost tropical." Part of his open-hearted tropicality was the lilting way he had of singing many of his lines, almost putting the longer speeches into an aria form, which amused many of the younger actors in the cast who would group backstage like a medieval chamber group, especially during the tomb scene, and croon softly along with the aria ending "Thus with a kiss I die." Evans heard about it and one night delivered the speech in a different rhythm to a new melody, just to throw everybody off. But then he couldn't remember the new tune and eventually went back to the old one, to everybody's satisfaction. Juliet was undoubtedly too agonized controlling her cough to be aware of what was going on.

Steps, levels, and ramps were identifying features of Jo Mielziner's sets, adding interest and vitality to the stage picture and providing an opportunity for stunning effects of lighting. They also gave a lift to the action, an agitation or a majesty, depending on which was wanted and providing the actors knew exactly what they were doing. Kent Smith, who played Dunois in *Saint Joan*, spent some time with Kit on the set for "the bank of the River Loire" waiting for the curtain to go up on the second act, and no matter how many performances they had given, she still spent the time counting the steps from here to there and gauging once again the leap from this level to that.

But the platforms for *Romeo and Juliet* were too heavy and cumbersome to be transported for the one-night stands, and for the last two weeks of the tour Guthrie went to Chicago to restage the action on a level, especially the fencing scenes (originally directed by Georges Santelli). In one scene Tyrone Power had to separate a fighting Montague from a fighting Capulet with a single upsweep of his sword between theirs. At rehearsal, in his desire to show Guthrie how hard he had been working and how deft he had become, the young and future Zorro raised his foil as directed and then for a fillip brought it down in the X that formed when the other two swords came together again, forcing one of them across the eye of the young actor playing Romeo's man Balthasar, Shelton Earp (who was, in this distinguished company, nothing less than a descendant of Wyatt's). The point just brushed his forehead and cheek, and when he was carted off to the hospital and dabbed and stitched, his eye was found to have escaped all injury, but he was never able to face the hazard of the duel again and happily retired to civilian life in Baltimore, where he came from, sending Miss Cornell a good-luck telegram on opening night in New York.

When Guthrie traveled with the production, he eschewed compartments and drawing rooms for a berth out among the small-part actors whom he loved because they would sit up with him all night while he drank, listening to his long old stories and laughing at his imitations of Mrs. Fiske, Mrs. Carter, Mrs. Campbell, Blanche Bates, and Ethel Barrymore. Kit was not necessarily more exclusive, she was just less aggressive. Nor did she drink much. Sometimes when she did have a drink or two with young cast members she invited into her compartment, she would favor them with a rendition of "Burlington Bertie from Bow," her favorite English music hall number, but mostly while Guthrie's contacts with the company gave him a chance to go on teaching, hers gave her a chance to go on learning. Through her friendship with Ruth March, begun on the *Romeo* tour when they would take long walks together, she developed an interest in modern art and bought her first painting, a Charles Burchfield that Ruth March had admired at a gallery. Kit's interests were almost always formed that way, by the enthusiasm of someone she wanted to please, just as she had become serious about acting to please Guthrie. Consequently, interests she might be expected to have cultivated early often came late. After Kirsten Flagstad made her historic New York debut at the Metropolitan in 1935, Bill Roehrick, a young actor in *Romeo*, managed to obtain two hard-to-get tickets for a performance of *Tristan and Isolde*, and Kit was delighted to go with him. But toward the middle of the last act she pulled her coat around her and suggested they move to the aisle because her car was picking her up to take her and Ruth March to Sneden's Landing. When asked if she did not want to hear the Liebestod, she seemed surprised to find that she had not already heard it and said of course she wanted to hear it, but from the back of the auditorium, and hurried up the aisle. Even with her love of music, apparently her time had not yet come for Wagner. Years later, after the Second World War, in order to share the enthusiasm of her friend Nancy Hamilton, she became not only an ardent devotee of Wagner's music but a close personal friend of Kirsten Flagstad's.

Ruth March was Armenian by birth and carried on her breast the scar of a bullet wound inflicted by her father when she was a child. Seeing in this a wild exaggeration of her own unhappy childhood, Kit was moved by the emotional scar as well as the physical one and sought to include Ruth March in all her plans for plays, relaxation, and travel. Just out of the Neighborhood Playhouse and perhaps too young to deal with the celebrity of Katharine Cornell and the all-inclusiveness of her attentions, the younger actress fell into moods so intense that Kit said they permeated entire rooms. With all love and gratitude, all Ruth March really wanted was to be completely American and accepted by Americans of her own age. She eventually married an architect (as both Anne Park and Anne Tonetti had) and left the theatre, but she never lost touch with Kit.

Having come into *Romeo and Juliet* in the middle, so to speak, Maurice Evans had never seen Kit rehearse from the beginning and was taken aback at the first reading of *Saint Joan*. He knew she had been studying the part all the previous summer, going so far as to trace the Maid's life on a motor trip from the Maison Rouge in Strasbourg to the marketplace in Rouen where the burning took place, and still she stumbled over the words, lost her place, worried about her glasses, and seemed unable to convey either the emotional or intellectual content of what she was reading. A volatile born actor like Evans, used to making sense out of any script he picked up, on sight, was appalled at what he heard and confided to Gert that the great Miss Cornell may have been a lovely Juliet, but surely this time she had taken on more than her talent could bear.

Saint Joan offered one of Guthrie's most luxuriant casts. In addition to Evans as the Dauphin, there were Brian Aherne as Warwick, and Tyrone Power, Jr., as Bertrand de Poulengy, Arthur Byron as the Inquisitor, Eduardo Ciannelli as Cauchon, Charles Waldron as the Archbishop of Rheims, and George Coulouris as Master John de Stogumber. Cornell "alumni," as they were called, included William Roehrick, David Orrick, Arthur Chatterton, and David Vivian, with Ruth March and Lois Jameson alternating in the only other woman's role, the Duchess de la Tremouille. Kent Smith, who was in Hollywood being tested by Irving Thalberg to play Romeo on the screen, preferred to go back to New York and be in his first Cornell production as Dunois, the Bastard of Orléans.

After several weeks of rehearsal, Maurice Evans was incredulous at Miss Cornell's growth in her part, but even her industry could not save the bad dress rehearsal at the Cass Theatre in Detroit. Usually on such occasions, the minute the curtain hit the floor Guthrie would roar from out front, "Take it up!" and leaping onto the stage would start laying out the actors, "First of all, *you* . . . !", crooking his finger accusingly, then "You!" and once again, "*You!*", entwining his legs into knots. But this dress rehearsal was so excruciating that when the final curtain came down, silence descended with it. No one dared move. Even Miss Cornell stood downstage center, her face practically in the curtain, transfixed to her final position. A quiet Guthrie came through from the auditorium, walking like a reasonable man, and without looking to the right or left directed himself center stage where he put his arms around Kit for a moment. Then he began softly, genuinely polite, "Ladies and gentlemen, we have a great deal of work to do, so let us begin . . ."

Bad luck plagued the out-of-town tryout. In Buffalo Kit's worst dream came true and she caught the flu. In Pittsburgh it worsened into laryngitis, and by Friday of that week she could not speak at all, not even in a whisper. She was staying with old Cobourg friends of Dr. Cornell's and Aunt Lydia's in a gracious house in the residential part of the city, and they put her to bed and called in their own doctor. The Friday and Saturday performances, both nights a sellout, had to be canceled. Her hope of still opening in New York the following Monday, March 2, was dashed when the doctor ordered her to stay in bed for a week. It was the first and only time in her career that she ever missed even one performance because of illness, and it was the first and only time she had to postpone a New York opening, once it had been promised, for any reason whatsoever. The shock to her sense of responsibility was much harder to accept than the laryngitis.

Saint Joan finally opened at the Martin Beck on March 9, 1936,

As Saint Joan, 1936–1937. (New York
Public Library, Vandamm Collection)

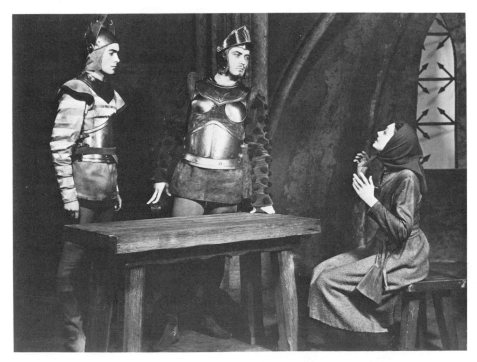

With Tyrone Power and Joseph Holland in Saint Joan.
(New York Public Library, Vandamm Collection)

and the next day Burns Mantle said the triumph belonged to two maids, "the Maid of Domremy, France, and the Maid of Buffalo, N.Y." John Anderson wrote in the *New York Journal*, "Before there is any haggling, let it be said that it is Shaw's greatest play and that Miss Cornell is superb in it. She is beautiful to look at and her performance is enkindled by the spiritual exaltation of a transcendent heroine."

His only qualification was to wonder, "occasionally, if Joan smiled so often." The answer is she must have, because the smile he was talking about Kit brought to the part from her own childhood when, to the cry of "Follow the leader!", she led the neighborhood buckoes up the church walls and across the crest of the roof in her own individual siege of Orléans. Her performance defied analysis and didn't need it any more than it needed defending, for Joan seems to have been the one great stage role she was fated to play from the beginning. Not that she *was* Joan, for she wasn't, with her aristocratic mien and well-bred physicality — even dressed as a soldier it would be hard for Dunois to forget she was a woman and a lady. But paradoxically, she did not have to "twist the part to make it her own." It was simply hers by some inborn sovereign right, a claim that can hardly be made for any actress since. If her wanton Juliet was the peak of her career, her smiling Joan was a leap into the vault of the sky. It was her zenith.

Ray Henderson was not a man to drop old threads of public interest, but to keep weaving them into the present patterns, giving the satisfying sense of continuity he wanted Miss Cornell's career to have. The program of a special benefit performance of *Saint Joan* for the Actors' Fund of America on May 1, 1936, contained the following note:

> Flush, the cocker spaniel actor who won national fame by his urbane and distinguished performance with Miss Cornell in *The Barretts of Wimpole Street*, is six years old today. By your gracious consent he will emerge from his retirement this afternoon to take a bow at the end of *Saint Joan* on the stage where he said farewell to his art some time ago.
>
> It is perhaps a sentimental occasion upon which the most severe members of our audience may frown, but, aside from his undeniable personal charm, Flush was a loyal and faithful servant of the drama. He never missed one performance in the 709 times we acted *The Barretts of Wimpole Street*. Only twice did he err behind the footlights. He traveled over 25,000 miles to carry the speaking theatre to the one-night

stands and to the metropoli of the nation. He was jealous of his understudies, his most grievous fault in our eyes, but what he felt about them he expressed. He never gossiped and he never carried any tale but his own.

So we beg of you who may not share our love for our fellow actor that at least you will not boo him when he trots before the curtain, perhaps for the last time, but will remain silent, while those of you who love him, as we do, will applaud him as once you did when he delighted you by his talent and by his modesty as he embodied the adored Flush of Elizabeth Barrett.

The whole house cheered him and applauded, and when he died in July 1937, the Associated Press sent the story out over its entire network. Rudolf Besier wrote from Vevey, Switzerland: "It was only today that we had the news of Flush's death. Dear, good, faithful, industrious Flush, there in a London paper was his obituary notice together with a little biography and a beautiful portrait of 'Himself.' All of our sympathy dearest Cornelia. Though we never met him we mourn his departure only less deeply than you must."

Flush was buried at Sneden's Landing, wrapped in an actor's coat.

Not expecting *Saint Joan* to be a commercial success, the McClintics had bought Maxwell Anderson's play *The Wingless Victory* for the fall. If Kit were to have the summer off, which was imperative for her health and well-being, and before that if she were to take *Saint Joan* to the road, she could not play it in New York more than three months. This meant closing one of the three biggest commercial hits in town (the other two being Helen Hayes in *Victoria Regina* and Lynn Fontanne and Alfred Lunt in *Idiot's Delight*) and paying a penalty to the Martin Beck Theatre for ending the run before the box office receipts warranted it. But commitment to an ideal will always dig into profits. Determined not to cheat audiences outside New York, in the spring of 1936 Kit closed *Saint Joan* and maneuvered the massive production through a seven-week tour of five major cities: Boston, Philadelphia, Chicago, Los Angeles, and San Francisco.

Kit had wanted to take Ruth March to Majorca that summer, but prevented by the outbreak of the Spanish Civil War, she started looking for a summer place closer to home. Anne Tonetti (now married to Eric Gugler) had long been a "finder" for Guthrie, tracking down furniture and decor to dress the sets of his plays, and having also found a house for Kit at Sneden's Landing, she set out to find another for her on Martha's Vineyard, the large island off the coast of Massachusetts. Kit had pleasant memories of having visited there as a child; now she was offered the rental of a small property owned by Anne's sister Lydia. Called The Camp, it was on the water near Vineyard Haven, isolated, tiny, with no electricity or plumbing.

Perhaps at Martha's Vineyard Kit found an echo of the camping days of her youth, for she enthusiastically embraced the remoteness, the primitiveness, the inconvenience, the inaccessibility, and the artlessness of days at The Camp. Toward the end of her stay with Ruth March, she walked down the beach and selected the site where the next year she would build her own island home.

Then she went off to Garmisch for a month, but as a kind of afterthought, as a gesture to assure Johanna Hirth that she was still loyal, which indeed she was and always would be. But in five years her passionate attachment to Garmisch had lived itself out. In Martha's Vineyard she had found more than a holiday retreat, more than a safe resting place, more than a haven, more than a home. She had found the place that forty years later she would ask to be taken to when she knew it was time to die.

23

Magnetic Influence (1936)

It would gladden Clemence Dane's heart to see me write the words "I saw Katharine Cornell." My brother and I were taken to see *Saint Joan* at the Saturday matinee, April 25, 1936. I was one week short of my fourteenth birthday. Before that I had been taken to the theatre four times, to two musicals and two plays. The musicals were *The Band Wagon* and *Jubilee*. The straight plays were thrillers, *Double Door* and *Post Road*.

I have always been grateful to the random taste that led my parents to take me next to *Saint Joan*, although my theatregoing had in no way led up to or prepared me for the intricacies of George Bernard Shaw. The play was very long, practically uncut. Twenty years before, Ray Henderson had written to Shaw protesting his insistence that William Faversham not cut *Misalliance*, and Shaw had replied, a full page on the back of Henderson's letter, ending, "I believe I know my own business. Excuse me for saying that you do not." Guthrie was convinced that Shaw had spies attending all performances to make sure the actors spoke every word, but still he courageously pruned the scenes as he saw fit, although it was not so much an artistic defiance as it was a reluctance to pay the stagehands overtime if the performance went beyond three hours. When it came to cases, Guthrie's parsimony would always be stronger than his fear of authority.

Children were taught more patience in those days, and from the beginning of the afternoon there were wonderful things to watch. Outside the movies I had never seen anything as magnificent as Jo

Mielziner's three-arched unit set that could first be a castle at Vaucouleurs, then the throne room at Chinon, and just as easily become the bank of the River Loire near Orléans or the Earl of Warwick's tent. Joan the Maid made her first entrance up through a trapdoor in the stage floor, and on the bank of the Loire there was a fascinating trick flag waving in the breeze which suddenly jerked around a hundred and eighty degrees when the wind changed in answer to Joan's prayers. I liked the scene in which Joan ferreted out the Dauphin from the crowd where he was hiding to deceive and trick her. The political-religious dialogue between Warwick and Cauchon was way beyond my comprehension; and although the trappings of the Inquisition were striking, the high benches and fire-reflections offstage, the scene came toward the end of the long afternoon and seemed repetitious and hard to follow.

Then came the epilogue, the disputed epilogue that critics and scholars frequently urge should be omitted. Shaw would not have it omitted, of course, and with a child's perverse ability to have two opposing reactions, I loved it both because it prolonged the play and because it was the last scene and the play would soon be over. The Shavian levity was delightful after what had gone before. Set in the Dauphin's dreams twenty years after Joan's death, many of the major characters reappear as at a school reunion to tell what they have been doing since. A gent walks in from the twentieth century to say Joan has at last been canonized, but it is generally agreed that if she returned to earth, she would be burned again. Having seen Joan led off to be roasted in the previous scene, I was enchanted with her reappearance in a lancet window, illuminated by a streak of summer lightning, reassuring the frightened Dauphin, "Easy, Charlie, easy!" I was pleased to see a character I had only heard about so far, the soldier who tied two sticks together to make a cross for Joan to hold and look upon as she died, the man now doomed to eternity in hell but allowed out one day a year as a reward for his good action. As for the appearance of the man in 1920 clothes amid all the medieval panoply, that was the kind of theatre I liked and understood.

Then at the end of the epilogue came the moment that some fate or force had sent me to the theatre that afternoon to see and hear. The other characters faded back into the shadows, leaving Joan alone. In her golden armor she moved downstage center, and with just a pin spot lighting her face looked up to the balcony where I was sitting and spoke the last line of the play: "O God that madest this beautiful earth, when will it be ready to receive Thy saints? How long, O Lord, how long?" The curtain came down, and something had happened. I had been changed.

Perhaps led is a better word, or drawn. Directed. In the given circumstances, an impressionable boy could go in any one of many directions. A backsliding Presbyterian even at fourteen, he could become converted to religion, assimilating the lives of the saints and perhaps trying to become one; with Joan as a starting place he could become an historian; he could set his sights on soldiering; he could become obsessed with and perhaps practice the art of witchcraft. Or, as in my case, instead of falling for Joan he could fall for Katharine Cornell and pursue the art of the theatre, a pursuit which would lead, forty years later, to the writing of this book. The point is that the effect of the performance did not end with the final curtain.

S. N. Behrman said "it was something essential in herself, as a person, that the audiences sensed and reached out to." As true as that sounds, I feel it would be truer the other way around, that it was something essential in herself, as a person, that *reached out to me* directly across the footlights, as if we were the only two in the theatre. A Boston interviewer once likened the phenomenon to "radium, flashing its healing rays," but the most apt term for it is the old-fashioned "magnetic influence" of Ibsen's time. Not everyone in every audience was so influenced, of course.

But the member of the audience Kit sometimes talked about, the one for whose sake she never gave less than her best, the one for whose benefit she withstood the terror of stage fright, the one without whom there would have been no purpose to acting at all, that one was magnetically influenced, led, changed, even awakened, and it was her chronic modesty that limited his number to one per audience, for he still survives today in large numbers, sprinkled through every gathering of knowledgeable theatre people past the age of fifty.

The influence is best defined by its effect, but not every case is as clear-cut as my own. Usually the subject's eyes light up at the mention of her name and he feels a sudden, urgent need to tell anyone who will listen about the time he saw her. Almost always that is exactly what the experience turns out to have been: he saw her in a play, no more than that. Even the name of the play is forgotten, and the year. But since then he has carried with him an image of something inexpressibly beautiful, sometimes synthesized by memory into an ordinary piece of clothing or jewelry, a ring constantly twirled on Elizabeth Barrett's finger, Masha's tiny, gold bell earrings, Iris March's hat, Jennifer Dubedat's blue velvet dress; even the lint Linda Esterbrook kept flicking from her jacket, the blouse Constance Middleton kept tucking in at the waist; a stance, a gesture, the sudden clasping of her hands beneath her chin, the clutching of a drapery, the leaning in a door; a line of dialogue — "Boy died for purity!"; "If you bark now, Flush, we're lost!"; "Easy, Charlie, easy!" The magnetically influenced will catch himself, puzzled and rather impatient that the ordinariness of the memory is inadequate to the feeling. Martha Graham says that when Kit left a stage she took the grand piano with her.

A young man signing himself "Richard Ritter" in a bold artistic hand first writes to her in the 1930s, confiding his ambition to become a director and thanking her for setting such high theatrical standards. As the years pass he settles for something less than his original goal, but still he sends her birthday wishes, Christmas greetings, and get-well cards, as if contact with the ideal can make up for whatever disappointment his own life has brought. If he ever realized that Miss Cornell's prompt, but brief, replies were written by Gertrude Macy and others, it might have annoyed him, but it would not really have mattered. As another audience member once wrote, "Dear Miss Cornell, how glad I am to be alive in the same world with you." For the magnetically influenced, her existence seems to have been enough.

The influence did not necessarily have its beginning in a darkened theatre. Although Kit never traveled alone, if her traveling companion went off to see about tickets or to ask directions and left her sitting alone — on a ferry between Woods Hole and Martha's Vineyard, for example — she invariably struck up a conversation with whoever was handy, and they in turn rarely forgot the encounter, quoting the not unusual conversation word for word and handing it on to friends and children like an heirloom. As it was with the letter-writers, the need to perpetuate the contact and perhaps bring her existence closer was irresistible.

Early in World War II a young Amherst man was injured and stranded on the rocks below Kit's house on Martha's Vineyard. She heard his calls, rescued him, drove him to a doctor, and afterwards invited him and his friends to lunch. The incident was reported in the local press and picked up by a national news service; news magazines made note of it. Thirty-five years later the young man, now middle-aged and successful in business, will tell you impressively that Katharine Cornell once saved his life, and from his complex, well-ordered business files will extract a manila folder marked "Katharine Cornell," containing a handful of old clippings, to prove it.

It is acknowledged by all that Kit was apolitical, but an English-woman recalls spending some time at Haus Hirth as a young girl in the mid-1930s and being aware of Kit's deep concern with the threatening political situation and the menace of Hitler. She recalls an afternoon when Kit withdrew to a secluded room with another guest for an earnest conversation in low voices; she remembers, vividly, being convinced at that moment that this dark, intense American who posed as an actress was in reality a spy for the United States government. Today the girl, now a woman in her late fifties, tells of the old encounter, adding that she has never found reason to change her mind. She does not find it at all inconsistent that Katharine Cornell had a long, distinguished, to say nothing of time-consuming, career in the theatre: what a perfect blind for her more important activities fighting the forces of evil.

Katharine Cornell's effect on people often revealed more about them than it did about her.

———

Unlike Rebecca West in *Rosmersholm*, Kit never misused her magnetic influence for self-serving ends, not even to persuade her advisers and protectors to let her play Rebecca West in *Rosmersholm*. Unconsciously she used it to secure the love of all those around her, from the lowest stagehand to the most exalted co-star, but since both sides benefited by that, it can hardly be called manipulative. A few actors, Basil Rathbone among them, eventually felt themselves diminished, professionally, by her magnetic influence. As a courtesy Rathbone was invited back to play Romeo for the twelve-week tour (and the second New York run) in the fall of 1935, with the possibility of going on to play Rosmer in the still-projected *Rosmersholm*. Still smarting from his rather cold reviews the year before and searching to justify them, he wrote: "Much as I sincerely love playing with Kit, her success and position are so terrific that it is almost impossible for anyone like myself to progress, to make any advancement. It is almost as if the press and a large portion of the public resented anything but just good workmanship from her company, an attitude Kit would resent I know were she aware of it, *because no one in the theatre is more fair and well-wishing to her fellow players than Kit*. But Kit is so mesmeric that beyond a certain point one cannot progress with her." He called it mesmerism and felt so guilty about resenting it (all that underlining!) that he only confided his feelings to Gert, who did not pass them on to Kit.

If her magnetic influence ever worked negatively for someone, it was, paradoxically, because it was too positive: because the need to live up to the ideal she represented exceeded the ultimate ability to do so.

That is the story of Jimmy Vincent. It warrants telling because its melodrama clearly outlines the nature and power of the magnetic influence, for good and for bad, pointing up her detachment from it, as if it were an independent phenomenon. The story also makes an oblique comment on the tie between Kit and Guthrie, which may be the only way to approach that complex, impenetrable, and beyond a certain point inexplicable, relationship.

Jimmy Vincent was born in Durban, Natal, South Africa. Nothing is known about his parents, but he grew up a devout Roman Catholic and as a boy of eight or nine was running errands for a butcher and sleeping on a blanket in his back room. His youth paralleled Guthrie's in that he was apprenticed as an office boy to a law firm, a mark of his ambition since he had no formal education, and spent all his money on balcony tickets for the local stage shows on Saturday afternoons. When he was old enough, he struck out on his own to become a chorus boy, later graduating to small parts in touring companies.

With a willingness (which amounted to eagerness) to better himself by the performance of menial tasks, he became servant to a man sailing for England, an arrangement which apparently lasted only for the duration of the voyage. Arriving in London in the spring of 1926, he got a job stage-managing for Jane Cowl in *Easy Virtue*, using every moment to learn the theatre and improve his speech. That job was followed by another, with Tallulah Bankhead in *They Knew What They Wanted*, which suggests how and where he met Guthrie, who brought him to the United States.

He was too intelligent to have an inflated idea of where he was headed in life, but even his modest attempts to keep up with his improved lot seemed, rather, to betray it. His new good suits invariably looked like hand-me-downs, his patent leather shoes like shiny cardboard. He was not an attractive young man, not good-looking. He was fat and rather damp and, although only in his twenties, practically bald. Perhaps he had an oriental cast to his eyes, or else Guthrie was molding him into something, for he cast him in *The Letter* as Ong Chi Seng, the bright and cunning Chinese law assistant. He was so successful in the role that it became the central character in a radio series, which he played for fifteen months. In his hardworking gratitude, he became Guthrie's factotum, performing every service from shining shoes to typing letters (self-taught).

From this distance it is safe to guess that the original relationship between Guthrie and Jimmy Vincent was sexual. Where Guthrie was indiscreet, he was also secretive, and one could not always be sure which of his young male friends were or had been lovers. His affairs seem to have been of fairly short duration, ending without rancor or unpleasantness, the young men often staying on to perform peripheral production jobs.

If the subject of homosexuality came up in Kit's presence, she waved it away as no more than a gossipy word. In her view, love was love, whether between man and woman, man and man, or woman and woman. She discussed Guthrie's clandestine sexual activities with no one; whatever she knew of them she kept to herself. Only one thing was apparent to an outsider — that she took special pains to be pleasant and agreeable to all his young male friends, going out of her way to see that they were never excluded or slighted, inviting them to dinner at 23 Beekman Place or to weekends at Sneden's Landing, often in preference to her own friends. Perhaps her consideration grew out of compassion for what she knew could be Guthrie's lack of consideration where the emotions were involved. It is not surprising that Jimmy Vincent, fat, balding butcher's boy from the ends of the earth, when smiled upon, should shift his total loyalty and devotion from Guthrie to Kit.

He did not fit in at the dinner table at 23 Beekman Place or on weekends at Sneden's Landing, but it didn't matter because his dedication to service was far greater than any social aspiration. He much preferred running to the corner for a newspaper somebody wanted, staying up all night typing revised script pages for next day's rehearsal, keeping records in his painstakingly acquired, perfectly formed high-school hand, or walking on for twenty weeks as a messenger boy in *Criminal at Large.* He might have continued that way indefinitely if Gert had not realized his capabilities. When she became Kit's general manager in *The Barretts* she insisted that Jimmy Vincent be made stage manager.

On the short tour of *The Barretts* he was given the chance to demonstrate his devotion. When Kit was driven frantic by the pressure at the base of her skull and the obsession that she was suffering from a brain tumor, her greatest fear was that she would suddenly not be able to remember her lines in the middle of a performance. In the arrangement of the set, Elizabeth Barrett's couch was left of center (facing the audience), and she asked Jimmy Vincent to stand on that side of the stage with the promptbook in his hands every minute of the play. He did better than that. The fireplace was in the left wall of the set with its papier-mâché coal basket. A small fan blade rotated slowly in front of a tiny spot with a reddish-colored gelatin, giving the illusion of flickering fire. Next to the coal basket, just out of the audience's vision, there was a space so narrow and low that seemingly only a double-jointed mischievous child or an amiable trained animal could have crouched there. But the great advantage of this hiding place was that it was within a few feet of Elizabeth Barrett's couch, as close as one could come to her without actually being on the stage, with no wall or other obstruction to mute the voice should a whispered prompt have to be given. Into this space Jimmy Vincent climbed and there concealed himself at every performance, jack-knifing his flabby torso against his legs in what must have been torturous constraint, shining a pencil flashlight on the script with barely room to turn the pages. On her couch, Kit could almost touch his assuring presence.

Kit always claimed she could not have gotten through the short tour of *The Barretts* without Jimmy Vincent, and the claim may have been justified to the degree that probably no one else would have had the devotion to squat in that painful and humiliating chimney corner night after night for the length of that interminable play.

Jimmy Vincent's devotion to Kit increased in direct proportion to his contempt for Guthrie, who had been kind and even generous at the beginning but who now, with time, began to emerge in a rather shady light. Jimmy's basic complaint was professional and much the same as Gert's. Trying to keep a production rolling smoothly and efficiently, to get things done properly and on time, he felt he was constantly being plagued by this privileged madman's supercilious un-predictability. Whereas Kit's dedication to a production increased with every performance, no matter how long the run, Guthrie felt his responsibility ended with rehearsals, and after opening night could not be wheedled back to look at the show, tune it up, sharpen the action, gives notes to the actors, take up the slack in the performance, or do any of the things necessary to keep a long-running show up to its reputation. In Guthrie's own writings he refers often to "seeing a play for the thirtieth time" or "dropping in to see how the performance was holding up," but he relied on the stage manager to enforce the necessary discipline, which in a way made him all the more infuriating, for if it was not done he was likely to fly into one of his rages. Jimmy Vincent was proud to be entrusted with responsibility and carried it well, but he would gladly have surrendered it to see the man Katharine Cornell loved live up to her standards of professionalism. From where he stood, he felt that Guthrie was not quite good enough for his lady. And since she would never criticize Guthrie nor hear of it from anyone else, Jimmy Vincent's resentment was more on her behalf than his own. It was almost a point of honor.

As the short tour progressed, his professional contempt turned to black personal hatred. *The Barretts* was so written that the six young Barrett brothers appeared in the first scene and not again, as a group, until the last, leaving all of them but Occy offstage almost two hours in the middle of the play. When Guthrie joined the company on tour, he became briefly enamored of one of the young actors, who would change into street clothes after the first scene and go off with Guthrie, returning just in time to climb back into costume and go on for the last scene of the play. Jimmy Vincent was the kind of omniscient stage manager who misses nothing, and even confined to his chimney cor-ner bent double over the promptbook, he knew or sensed or was told and confided to Gert in wrath that Guthrie took the boy to a nearby Turkish bath.

No other stage manager or assistant stage manager, no actor or actress, no one of either sex connected with any other production ever suggested or implied that Guthrie imposed his amorous leanings on his professional behavior, and yet there is something that rings true in Jimmy Vincent's claim. To begin with, even considering his prejudices against Guthrie, he was not a liar or a troublemaker. In fact as time went on his sense of honesty would be, in a way, his downfall. And

Guthrie, for all his secretiveness, was not always discreet, nor was he inhibited by an overweening sense of propriety. He thought nothing of leaving an assignation just in time to call for Kit after a performance, allowing her to think he had been out front watching the play all evening. And recalling the party they attended in their younger years where he insisted on making love to her in the bathroom, there is something ribald, risky, and even cheapening about an affair carried on in a public steam room that might have appealed strongly to him. It might have been just his style. A cautious man's mistrust can lead to incautiousness; fearing loss where he cannot gain, he will seize what is available, the physical side of a relationship, the quick flagrant indulgence, the immediate gratification of feeling with very little, or no, emotion.

Kit could hardly have lived so many years with Guthrie, sympathetically tolerating his "other" life, if she had not had a separate emotional life herself. It differed from his in significant ways.

There was nothing secretive about her emotional attachments. It was always quite evident whom she loved at any given moment. Her letters to her "bewitching, beguiling," and sometimes "exasperating" young women friends were typical of the lack of restraint that even to outsiders represented an emotional concentration.

Also, unlike Guthrie, she found rapport and spiritual affinity more important than physical gratification. There may even have been some sexual repression (which she recognized in Ibsen's Rebecca West and Elizabeth Barrett). Not that the physical experience didn't matter, for it did; and it could be open and unrestrained. One recalls the random afternoon she decided to have an affair with a man simply because his love for her had been so lasting and loyal that she felt it deserved gratification. It was an easy, spontaneous offering — which he was unhappily unable to return.

But the incompleteness did not mar the relationship. Years later, in a letter that began "Dearest Kitten," he wrote: "I wonder if even your great understanding tells you how much you gave me in a gesture one summer afternoon — of what importance is it that dull candles gave no light in such a white blaze of spirituality — that day — you made me whole — "

Her closest relationships, more often with women as the years went by, might aptly be called "passionate friendships."

Like many others, Jimmy Vincent could not see that with their strengths and weaknesses Kit and Guthrie complemented each other like interlocking pieces of a picture puzzle. Had they been strong in the same places and weak in the same places, they would not have fitted together so exactly; certainly would not have been able to give each other so much. Without her, Guthrie would have had little dignity as a human being; without him, she would have had little security as an actress. All Jimmy Vincent could see was that he should reprimand the errant Barrett brother and insist that he remain in the theatre throughout the performance. But he couldn't do that without involving Guthrie, which he had too much respect for Kit to do.

To be thus frustrated was aggravating enough to a perfectionist, but what really offended Jimmy Vincent was that while Kit was out on the stage being beautiful and courageous in the face of panic and a throbbing head, her husband was off behind her back, not debasing himself, for in Jimmy Vincent's eyes he was already beneath contempt, but cheapening her. He criticized Guthrie to Gert, and to Stanley, in a way that was becoming dangerous.

"If I had a gun I would shoot him and not care what happened," he said. "I would feel purged to have killed him."

Such thoughts were, idly, not new to Gert, but Jimmy Vincent scared her a little (Stanley scoffed at the whole thing), and she calmed him as best she could. He trusted her, and perhaps her counsel helped, for he never let Guthrie know how he felt. But what actually pulled him through and sustained him was the evolving nature of his adoration of Kit. He told Gert that as a little boy he had been taught to pray to the Virgin Mary. When, as a young man he found (or decided) that the Virgin Mary did not exist, he still went on praying to her, to nothing, that is, and his life became empty. Now he had found the Virgin at last, not again but for the first time, in Kit, and his life was full. It was to her that he prayed, got down on his knees every day, and in her grace he felt safe from the evil within himself.

Apparently Norma Shearer and Irving Thalberg were set on becoming the McClintics of Hollywood. With the movie of *The Barretts of Wimpole Street* a success, they turned to *Romeo and Juliet*, and in one week during Kit's first New York run they saw at least three performances, always in the same third row center seats. Suspicious

Guthrie was sure they were out to swipe all his ideas, Martha Graham's dances, and Paul Nordoff's music, but as it turned out, all they wanted was Jimmy Vincent. He had a reputation now as a stage manager, and they had heard how much the McClintics relied on him. He was invited to meet the Thalbergs at their apartment in one of the fashionable Fifth Avenue hotels. He put on a tie, shined his shoes, combed his few remaining hairs, and impressed their Hollywood sensibilities mightily with his knowledge of Shakespeare and the genteel English accent he had been cultivating since his days in London. He was making one hundred and seventy-five dollars a week as the McClintics' stage manager, and the Thalbergs offered him five hundred, a contract with the prestigious MGM, and an assignment as dialogue director on *Romeo and Juliet*, working exclusively with Miss Shearer, all to begin at the end of his current season with Miss Cornell.

Jimmy Vincent was dazzled, seduced, and apprehensive, certain that Guthrie would do something terrible when he heard. He confessed to Gert, who would feel his departure more than anyone since it would be up to her to find his replacement for next season, and she urged him to accept the Thalbergs' offer. He had worked hard for eight years, she said, starting as a lackey, which is what he would be still had his fate been left to Guthrie. He could not give up a chance for advancement out of a misplaced sense of loyalty. He had served his apprenticeship. It was time to move on.

Jimmy Vincent couldn't face Guthrie with his decision, or Kit. He honored her for her integrity, and here he was, doing what she had too much integrity to do, grabbing the first chance he had to leave the stage for the movies. He felt like a deserter. When the season ended he said he had saved some money and was going to the West Coast for a summer vacation, which was as near as he could come to telling the truth to their faces. From Los Angeles he wrote a letter which must have taken days, awkward, stunted phrases in gracefully formed schoolboy script. Guthrie went into the expected tantrum, vowing never to speak to or of Jimmy Vincent again as long as he lived. Kit had always felt that Jimmy Vincent was worth more than he was paid and on several occasions had slipped him a hundred dollars when Guthrie and Gert weren't looking, but whatever she felt, she knew better than ever to defend him in front of Guthrie, for fear of bringing on a new torrent of invective.

And so with a mature step Jimmy Vincent went to Hollywood. It was right that he did. He was a hard worker, not untalented. He deserved good things, he deserved success and prosperity. He deserved esteem. But it didn't work out that way. Until then he had been on his way up, but it was as if he had suddenly turned his back on the mater dolorosa in the Pietà, the blessed saint to whom he prayed, the highest of all created beings, and from that moment on he was on his way down.

Miss Shearer was fair to him and pleased with his work. It was even said that she came to rely on him. But as seductive as the title dialogue director had been, the job involved little more than cuing the star, with not a fraction of the responsibility he had been used to in New York. He was so willing to work that no sensible employer wouldn't have hired him if he became available, and after *Romeo and Juliet* he stayed on at MGM working for George Cukor on Garbo's *Camille* and a string of other pictures.

After World War II a Cornell "alumnus" wrote to Gert that Jimmy Vincent was in the Los Angeles County jail accused of molesting a minor. Remembering that Gert had lived in California for many years, he wondered if she knew anyone who could help. Gert was unfamiliar enough with such drama to be shocked, so she called Conger Goodyear, who was square enough to be shocked but who, as president of the Museum of Modern Art, knew influential lawyers in Los Angeles who took over. No one remembers the disposition of the case, but Gert does remember a letter she received from Jimmy Vincent in jail, in which he admitted that he had asked three young boys to his single room in Santa Monica, and that the mother of one had gotten worried as evening came on, that she had called another mother and together they had called the police. He said he was guilty of nothing, but the circumstance itself was odd, and since California law was notoriously hard on that kind of offense, he had been arrested. Many of his words with their full open loops and symmetrically rounded curves were crossed out with a censor's crayon, and after a few further deletions on Gert's part, the tale was told to Kit, which Gert felt was due since she had involved Conger Goodyear. Kit said, "You know how people make things up; it isn't true. . . ." This time Gert was inclined to agree.

When the ordeal was over, George Cukor heard about it from Guthrie, and knowing how responsible Jimmy Vincent was, so solid that he didn't even drink or smoke, Cukor moved him into his gardener's cottage. A loner with no life of his own and no needs beyond a cot to sleep on and a place to hang his clothes, Jimmy Vincent plugged away at his menial studio jobs and when there was a party up at the main house served the drinks and got out the ice. He couldn't drive a car, but with a houseful of guests he knew whose coat was whose and once again made himself indispensable. Cukor wrote enthusiastically to Guthrie that Jimmy Vincent was a treasure, that he was even learning how to cook. Guthrie was not gratified to hear Jimmy Vincent's praises sung so loudly, but he was impressed to find himself enjoying a letter-writing intimacy with George Cukor.

It was but a step from serving drinks to sampling them, and once Jimmy Vincent developed a taste for gin and tonic, in no time at all he was a full-blown alcoholic. He eventually went to a clinic for help, committing himself for treatment. George Cukor wrote to Guthrie that he had straightened himself out but was very poor and needed work. Cukor wasn't doing a picture, so Jimmy Vincent was returning east. Cukor hoped Guthrie would hire him or find something for him.

It was a kind letter, but Jimmy Vincent had too much shame (or good sense) to present himself to Guthrie. Instead he appeared, scrubbed and uncertain, before Stanley Gilkey and Gert, who took him to lunch. He was living at the Hotel Diplomat on West Forty-third Street and said he had brought all his savings east, but he was down to five hundred dollars and needed a job right away. Once started, he talked so honestly about his problems that they were embarrassed not to have anything in production to offer him.

By then (the early 1950s) Gert was living at Sneden's Landing in a house she had built and, like Kit and Guthrie, filled with mementos of past productions, remnants of old stage sets, pieces from long broken-up, imaginary drawing rooms. She invited Jimmy Vincent out for dinner, and as they drove across the George Washington Bridge she told him she had seen a sign in her local Grand Union advertising for workers, full or part time. She knew that whatever he did he would do well, be it only unpacking groceries or punching a cash register, and she knew it would be a comedown for him, but she hoped he wouldn't let it stand in his way that he had been dialogue director for Norma Shearer and stage manager for Katharine Cornell. She hoped he was not too grand to do whatever work he could get if he really needed the money. She thought that for the time being he shouldn't even try for a job in the theatre, he should get hard work with long hours involving strenuous physical exertion. His spirits seemed to lift and he thanked her for having faith in him, and although privately she didn't think it took much faith to think he could be a grocery clerk, she refrained from saying so. It was October, beautiful driving up the Palisades Parkway, and she said everything she could to keep his spirits high, even wildly assuring him that Kit, of course, would want to see him. She brought up old jokes, and Jimmy Vincent went so far as to recall his past laughter, if not to echo it.

But when he stepped into Gert's house, the first thing he spotted was some ordinary object from the set of *The Barretts* (so ordinary that its identity has now been forgotten), a prop or piece of furniture, something he had meticulously squared on its marks every night before the curtain went up. Perhaps it was a chair he had been used to sit in to give the crew someone to focus their powerful lights on in a new town. He had done that on the famous Christmas night in Seattle to help light Elizabeth Barrett's couch, and Alexander Woollcott had actually written him up. "To the rapture of Seattle," Mr. Woollcott had written, "Jimmy Vincent, the stage manager, stretched himself out and assumed, one after another, all the postures he knew Miss Cornell would later assume. As Mr. Vincent is stocky and Oriental in appearance, and as the visible gap between his trousers and his waistcoat widened horrifically with every languorous pose into which he tried to fling his arms and head, the effect was stupefying." Imagine being written up, so humorously, by Alexander Woollcott! Why, how, in the years since then, had he dropped out of the light into darkness? — because he had stopped assuming Miss Cornell's "postures" and tried to assume his own? There it was before him, his loss, his infidelity, his betrayal, suddenly materialized in an old stage prop from an out-of-use set. While Miss Cornell had gone on all these years, as shining and erect as Joan of Arc in her golden armor, he had ducked off into the dark behind her back. He confessed to Gert, his confessor from the start, that no one would ever give him a job again because it was on his record that he had been in jail. She fed him a steak and tried to divert him, gabbling on about her other souvenirs, a chandelier from this play, an end table from that, almost apologizing for the pleasant comfort in which she lived, knowing what his room must be like at the Hotel Diplomat. She urged him to spend the night and drive in with her the next morning, which he didn't want to do, but rather than simply dump him on a bus, at about ten o'clock she drove him as far as the George Washington Bridge.

Two days later Stanley was called by Bellevue Hospital saying they had admitted a man named James Vincent who had been found by a maid dead drunk on the floor of his room at the Hotel Diplomat, lying in pools of blood with his wrists cut. In a pocket of his clothes they had found a slip of paper with Stanley's name and telephone number on it as well as Gertrude Macy's. Stanley and Gert went to Bellevue and were admitted by a prizefighter of a woman who locked them in the ward with the patients behind a heavy sheet-iron door. In a two-by-four waiting room Jimmy Vincent was produced, shaved, looking shy and awful in a flannelette wrapper and paper slippers. He had a small Band-Aid on each wrist. He said they shouldn't have come, that he wasn't worth it. Gert said that when he got out of this place, he must come out to her house again. He must forget everything that had happened and start looking for the kind of job they had talked about.

Soon after this, Stanley had a call from the Yonkers police saying they had pulled a body out of the Hudson River and would he come to the Yonkers morgue to identify it. Jimmy Vincent had taken a bus to the George Washington Bridge, the place where Gert had given him his last fleeting hope for himself, and there, unable to live a moment longer with nothing to pray to, had thrown himself into the river.

———

Guthrie's partisans claim that because of his indigent background he was quicker than Kit to respond to others' material needs, but Gert maintains he was cold and stony when it came to Jimmy Vincent, not even offering a nickel toward a decent funeral. George Cukor wired from Los Angeles that he would pay all burial expenses and any outstanding debts Jimmy Vincent might have left.

Kit, of course, knew only what she was told, which doesn't seem to have been much. She was sympathetic and commended Gert and Stanley for all they tried to do. If it seems odd that a woman of such renowned compassion would let it go at that without asking a hundred questions, without pursuing the subject for her own satisfaction, without demanding to be told what had happened to a man who had once been such a profound help, so she claimed, in her own time of need and despair, it is simply part of the gradual removal that began when she became an actress-manager, the moment when the theatre, on the word of many of her co-workers, stopped being fun.

By the time Jimmy Vincent died she was in her late fifties, but an actor in *Saint Joan*, when she was still in her early forties, asserts that even at that point in her career she was already "wrapped in cotton wool," to be picked up carefully and moved from place to place and just as carefully set down again to work or to eat or to rest or to read. The actor played a small part, and not being close to her was only an observer, but it may be true that one sees more from a distance, and it certainly was true that while Judith Anderson and Ruth Gordon had to step to the curb to hail a taxi, for Miss Cornell a taxi simply materialized. Another Cornell alumnus of the 1930s says her removal was facilitated by Guthrie's young male friends on special assignment to surround her, protect her, guard her, and tend her, in squads — when they were not busy escorting Guthrie himself to and fro and holding taxis for him while he philandered or waged business.

Allowing for gossipy coloring in those reports, the impression remains that with Ray Henderson acting as her public voice and Gert Macy serving as her private voice, with a capacity to endure only so much responsibility and travail, "Miss Cornell" seems to have become distant, and then remote from everyone but those to whom she was a passionate friend. Gert was not aware of it, but others were. It certainly does not seem to have been intentional, but it was there, a marked reflexive closing in around her as the pressures of stardom and managership increased, a loyal showing of the protective instinct she brought out in people.

Onstage it was another matter. All her emotional vitality had always gone into her acting, leaving her drained and exhausted, and it increased with the years, if possible, along with her energy for direct communication. Every actor who ever played with her will swear that her spontaneous participation and involvement with him and his role was as great at the three hundredth performance as it had been at the first, and the rapport was not only visual and verbal, it was physical. In the last act of *Saint Joan*, David Orrick was one of two soldiers who had to step forward and grab Joan, to be stopped by Cauchon calling out, "Not yet!", then to stand waiting while the scene was finished, and finally drag Joan off to the stake. It disturbed Kit that they did not take her arms forcibly, that they treated her with too much loving care, and she kept urging them to be harder on her. As a result they used to grab her so fiercely that they forced from her a small whimper, audible only to them and so demoralizing that the two staunch, vengeful soldiers had to steel themselves not to put their arms around her and assure her they were only playacting.

That was only within the limits of performance, however, and there seems to have been a sharp line of demarcation. In Dunois's important scene with Joan on the bank of the Loire, when he is won over to her side, he would put his hands on her shoulders, not as a man to a woman, but as a soldier to his comrade, accepting her. It was a moving moment. When the picture call came along, Ray Henderson had not selected the exact moment of that scene that he wanted photographed, so Kent Smith — and Kit — suggested the moment he put his hands on her shoulders because the photographer could get in close for a tight shot. But Henderson said no, he felt that Joan should be a person apart, that no one should touch her. Since the shoulder clasp was given to the paying customers at every performance, eight times a week, what Henderson must have meant, consciously or not, was that Miss Cornell should be a person apart, that no one should touch Miss Cornell.

It was just as well that she was not told all the details of Jimmy Vincent's story. Not that she would have been shocked or that she would have heard things she didn't want to know, but because she would have been disturbed, maybe deeply distressed, by any suggestion that she had played some part in it. She never understood her effect on people and said so, often, to friends.

What began as a fear of mis-using her power by manipulating others became an unwillingness to mix too deeply, indiscriminately, in people's lives and perhaps influence them without knowing it; eventually, with the new responsibility and further power imposed upon her by stardom, and with the loving cooperation of her protectors, she settled into a kind of smiling, gracious, and comfortable isolation.

VII

First Lady (1936-1945)

24

Degrees of Fame (1936-1937)

As FAR BACK as *Dishonored Lady* Richard Watts, critic of the *Tribune*, had pronounced Katharine Cornell "our First Actress." It was not a catchy phrase, so another was coined from the political scene, apparently about the time Mrs. Roosevelt moved into the White House, and by the mid-1930s partisans were claiming the title "First Lady of the American Theatre" for half a dozen leading actresses. But the contest — or rivalry — unofficial though it was and certainly never entered into by the participants themselves, actually centered around only two, Helen Hayes and Katharine Cornell. In the *New York Post* John Mason Brown berated himself and his colleagues for being "tempted to express their admiration for the one in terms of superlatives tossed off, by implication at least, at the expense of the other." He deplored the idea that there had to be a "first" or a "best," since "there is plenty of room in our stage for both Miss Hayes and Miss Cornell. And there is no reason why either one of them should be forced to wear Eleanor Blue to the other's discomfort or disadvantage."

The whole thing, he said, was "silly (because meaningless) and ungracious (because unnecessary)." The only possible reason for contrasting the two actresses was not to rate them but to enjoy their differences:

What I, for one, admire unstintingly in Miss Cornell is everything exceptional about her, everything uniquely hers, which sets her apart from all other women on or off the stage. I prize her Mrs. Siddons tension; her tragic majesty; her dark allure; her midnight pallor; and the sense she gives of being so fateful in her own person that when she comes through a door you are gladly persuaded she could never have entered to answer anything so mundane as a telephone but must have emerged because she has a date with destiny. In the presence of Miss Hayes it is just the opposite qualities I admire. She, too, is exceptional and in no way more than in her radiant averageness. I like ... the simple humanity which has no connection with the unearthly attributes of the muses; the technical virtuosity she unquestionably possesses; the feeling she so reassuringly creates that she is just like any number of earnest, attractive, intelligent, and hard-working young American women — with this glowing exception — she happens to be the one who made good, and who for countless reasons deserves to have done so.

The two actresses never could have played the same roles (as d'Annunzio made Duse play Bernhardt's, to force a comparison), but oddly enough in the course of their long careers they played variations of the same character. Cleopatra was the most obvious one, and with no character could their individual qualities have been more neatly contrasted: a young Miss Hayes was fine as Shaw's frisky kitten, and an aging Miss Cornell was eloquent as Shakespeare's serpent of old Nile. But less obviously — and more interestingly — a comparison reveals that Candida Morell and Maggie Wylie (Miss Hayes's great role in James M. Barrie's *What Every Woman Knows*) are basically the same character, stemming at least from the same prototype: the patient, loving, industrious woman behind the important, successful man. Here again the specifics point up the differences — and distances — between the temperaments, talents, and appeal of the two women and the actresses who played them. When the husband in each play is faced with the truth about himself and his marriage, he is indignant and hurt. Candida comforts her James and secures his love by her compassion for him ("I give myself to the weaker of the two"); wily Maggie begs her John to have compassion for *her* ("Oh, John, if only you could laugh at me!"). The one so wise, all-seeing, enveloping; the other so humble, so eager to be enveloped.

Although Miss Hayes was nine years younger than Miss Cornell, she had been on the professional stage longer and arrived at stardom earlier. (Recall that the critics did not attend Miss Cornell's opening in *A Bill of Divorcement* in 1921 because, led by Woollcott, they flocked to Miss Hayes's opening in *The Wren*.) Nevertheless, their careers peaked simultaneously, for Kit opened in *Saint Joan* just a few months after Miss Hayes opened in *Victoria Regina*, and the two plays ran triumphantly almost side by side. Since Miss Hayes arrived at Victoria by way of Maxwell Anderson's *Mary of Scotland*, it may seem odd that with her "radiant averageness" she had cornered the royalty market over Miss Cornell with her "tragic majesty." One might have thought it would be the other way around. But in this circumstance lies the most easily grasped delineation of the two actresses by contrast.

There is a scene in *Victoria Regina* in which Victoria, angry with Prince Albert, beats on the door of his room demanding admittance as "Her Majesty, the Queen!" When he replies that Her Majesty, the Queen, must wait, she is shocked, further angered, indignant, even wrathful. But after a moment she fights to keep back the tears, raps on the door softly, and when the voice within asks who is there, she replies in a small voice, "Your Wife, Albert! Your poor unhappy wife!" Laurence Housman's play consisted of thirty scenes, only ten of which could be included for an average evening in the theatre, and this scene was not performed by Miss Hayes, probably because she didn't need it; its single point was made quite clear in the way she played all the other scenes, in her person, in her presence, in her manner. It epitomized the tremendous appeal she had for audiences. Helen Hayes played queens as if they were women.

Katharine Cornell played women as if they were queens.

The only time the matter was ever put to the critics for an official vote, Ethel Barrymore was chosen First Lady of the American Theatre, hands down. Miss Barrymore's seniority — she was eleven years older than Kit and twenty years older than Helen Hayes — may have given the critics a chivalrous, gentlemanly way out of their dilemma. Howard Barnes, however, for one, split his vote three ways: Barrymore for voice, Hayes for technique, Cornell for personality.

———

The First Lady of the Land, when she attended one of Kit's plays, usually mentioned it in her newspaper column, "My Day." The two women met when Kit was trying out *The Wingless Victory* in Washington in the fall of 1936, and on an official occasion the following spring Mrs. Roosevelt's empathy for Kit's agonizing shyness in public was so genuine that it could only have risen from a similar shyness she herself had overcome.

The occasion was the presentation at the White House of the Chi Omega Sorority's National Achievement Award to Kit in March 1937. She was the first actress to be so honored.

Mrs. Roosevelt made the actual presentation. With an eye to the quivering recipient, she extemporized, "I hope that while Miss Cornell probably wishes now that she might have this evening only as a memory, that she will carry away the feeling that she has had a happy time, because we, all of us here tonight, many of us just playgoers, would like to give back to her some of the pleasure she has given us." Kit rose and inarticulate sounds emerged from her throat instead of Miss Cornell's famous "high white tones," and the First Lady of the Land pushed the medal at the First Lady of the Theatre with a laugh and some such remark as, "Well, anyway, here it is!" Then she put her arm around Kit's shoulder and suggested to the guests at large that they adjourn. Kit stepped down from the platform with relief, completely forgetting the medal. After it was firmly put into her hand, she and Guthrie were taken upstairs to the President's study.

The Chi Omega Award was not the first of the many honors bestowed upon her. In 1935 there was the New York Drama League Award for her performance as Juliet, and the Chancellors Medal from the University of Buffalo. Even before that, as soon as *The Barretts* opened, Conger Goodyear had suggested that Yale, his alma mater, should be the first to confer upon Miss Cornell an honorary degree, but the Chairman of the Committee on Honorary Degrees, a conservative clergyman, said he could not recommend a degree for a woman, "least of all an actress."

Other institutions were less narrow-minded, and the avalanche began while she was touring *Saint Joan* in 1936, when she accepted the degree of Doctor of Letters from the University of Wisconsin. Ten other honorary degrees followed in the next twenty years: Elmira College, Smith, the University of Pennsylvania, and Hobart (where her great-great-grandfather, David Bates Douglass, had taught mathematics and where her grandfather, Colonel S. Douglas Cornell, had spent his undergraduate years) in the 1930s; Clark University, Ithaca College, and Princeton in the 1940s; and Baylor University, Middlebury College, and Kenyon College (where David Bates Douglass had once been President) in the 1950s.

———

C. & M.C. Productions was chartered with a capital of six hundred shares. Kit received two hundred shares for her interest in *The Barretts*. Stanton Griffis and Conger Goodyear took one hundred and eighty shares each and Gert Macy the remaining forty, for which the three put up a total of $30,000. That money, which went to finance *The Barretts*, was all that was ever put into C. & M.C. It was agreed that when it was paid back, the investors would take out no profits, but that all profits would be held for future productions. If no profits materialized and more money was needed, they would furnish it.

It didn't work out that way. *The Barretts* was so successful that the government stepped in and would not allow a corporation as small as C. & M.C. to accumulate such large profits. Griffis called in a tax expert who explained to the government that C. & M.C. planned to produce more plays with the profits, planned to grow into a bigger business, which was the point of accumulating the money. But it was not allowed. They were forced to declare $110,000 in dividends, $11,-000 to Gert, the rest fifty-fifty between Griffis and Goodyear. Since the two men had no desire to make money out of the venture and had not entered into it for that reason, they asked only for their investments to be returned plus the usual six percent interest. The rest, as well as all future profits, they used to establish and maintain the Katharine Cornell Foundation. C. & M.C. was allowed to keep $75,000 or $80,000 as working capital, and with this money, supplemented by the profits from Kit's shares of stock, they produced *Lucrece* and all subsequent plays. It was stipulated from the beginning that if the corporation should ever be dissolved, its remaining "assets and property of every nature and description" were to be divided into three equal parts and transferred to the Museum of Modern Art, to honor Conger Goodyear, Cornell University's theatre department, to honor Stanton Griffis, and the Actors' Fund of America, to honor Katharine Cornell. The corporation was not dissolved until 1963.

When papers were filed establishing the Katharine Cornell Foundation in 1935, the press reported its chief purpose to be "to encourage and further the kind of theatre toward which Miss Cornell and Guthrie McClintic have worked during the past years."

———

If Kit reached her peak with *Romeo and Juliet*, so did Guthrie. Then, having proved himself with a classic, he turned once again to the succession of new plays he had begun with *Yellow Jack*. Early in 1935 he staged Edith Wharton's story *The Old Maid*, as dramatized by Zoe Akins, with Judith Anderson and Helen Menken in the cast.

Before *Saint Joan*, Guthrie directed another Edith Wharton story, *Ethan Frome*, this one dramatized by Owen Davis and his son Donald. Raymond Massey was Ethan, with Pauline Lord playing Zeena and Ruth Gordon as the poor-relation hired girl. Guthrie, for all his love of theatrical extravagance, was famous for driving stage managers wild in his pursuit of authenticity when it came to realistic plays. In *Ethan Frome* he insisted on, and got, snow that crunched underfoot when Ethan walked across the dooryard from the house to the barn.

After *Saint Joan*, Guthrie stayed with the classics for his next project. It took professional courage for him to bring John Gielgud over from England to play *Hamlet* because Gielgud was not yet well known in New York and Leslie Howard, with his captivating charm and tremendous movie following, had been contemplating a *Hamlet* of his own for a year and suddenly decided to bring it to town simultaneously with Gielgud's. Guthrie surrounded his sensitive, civilized Hamlet with the patrician authority of Judith Anderson as Gertrude, Lillian Gish as Ophelia, and Arthur Byron as Polonius. Howard played a subdued, modern, amiable, intellectual, and rather rambling Hamlet, while Gielgud's was brilliant, sharp, and traditional. Those who were there and have seen all Hamlets since still acclaim him as the finest Hamlet of his own generation and the generations that have followed. With the handwriting on the wall, Howard quickly closed his production, simplified it for travel, and took it on a long tour to recoup his financial losses and reestablish his popularity across the country, while Gielgud went on to play one hundred and thirty-two performances in New York, thirty-two more than John Barrymore and at that time a record for the role. The revival of interest in Shakespeare that began with Kit's *Romeo and Juliet* would really bloom the following year with Maurice Evans's version of *Richard II* and Orson Welles's *Julius*

Caesar, and it is quite clear that Guthrie McClintic was instrumental in bringing it about, both indirectly and directly.

But in the progression of Kit's career immediately after *Saint Joan*, the most important aspect of Guthrie's activities (away from her) was his professional relationship with Maxwell Anderson. It had begun in the twenties with *Saturday's Children*, and since then Anderson had won a Pulitzer Prize for *Both Your Houses* and changed his writing style completely to what Brooks Atkinson called "dark passionate poetry on a lofty artistic plane" in the plays *Elizabeth the Queen* and *Mary of Scotland*. Every successful playwright of the 1930s had a distinct, clear, recognizable voice of his own, from Clifford Odets to Philip Barry, but only Maxwell Anderson dared the heights of blank verse. And firmly believing that verse need not be limited to classical or historical themes but could and should be used to dramatize current life and attitudes, he fashioned a play about the aftermath of the Sacco-Vanzetti trial, called it *Winterset*, and let Guthrie produce and direct it with Burgess Meredith in the leading role. If even halfway feasible, Guthrie would offer every woman's part that Kit couldn't play to Judith Anderson or Ruth Gordon, and he wanted the latter for Miriamne, the girl Meredith finds living under the Brooklyn Bridge. When she refused it, he demonstrated his unpredictable dramatic flair at its best by giving the part to a young Mexican dancer from the movies, a one-time partner of George Raft's at the Paramount Theatre, named Margo. She was a tremendous success, along with Richard Bennett, whom Guthrie coaxed back to the stage for one farewell appearance. Another play the same season, Sidney Kingsley's *Dead End*, had almost the same setting as *Winterset*, the Lower East Side riverfront. In *Dead End* Norman Bel Geddes had the audience face into Manhattan, confronting the cluttered streets and tenements. In *Winterset*, Guthrie had Jo Mielziner face the audience out, or on a bias, with the gigantic span of the bridgehead soaring over their heads into the dim sky at the back of the stage.

Anderson had been in the front rank the year before with his *Valley Forge*, along with Lillian Hellman's *The Children's Hour*, Robert E. Sherwood's *The Petrified Forest*, and Clifford Odets's *Awake and Sing*, but the Pulitzer Prize had gone to *The Old Maid*, outright sentimentality made palatable and popular by Guthrie's staging. The critics were so incensed by the choice that they formed their own award-giving body, and the following year when the Pulitzer Prize went to

Robert E. Sherwood's *Idiot's Delight*, the New York Drama Critics Circle gave their first award to *Winterset*. It was ever Guthrie's place in the scheme of things, personal and professional (even when it came to Kit), to be part of the problem and part of the solution.

Guthrie, Anderson and Meredith were quick to repeat their success with two more collaborations, *High Tor* and *The Star-Wagon*. But first the prolific Anderson came up with *The Wingless Victory*, a retelling of the Medea legend set in Salem in 1800 (a favorite dramatic device after O'Neill reset the Electra story in New England of the Civil War period). Also reminiscent of Joseph Hergesheimer's popular novel *Java Head*, *The Wingless Victory* told of Oparre, a Malay princess brought home by sea captain Nathaniel McQuestion as his wife, to be snubbed and scorned by his relatives. With their racial and religious bigotry and their greed for McQuestion's fortune, they force him to send Oparre back to the East, virtually consigning her to life in a brothel. Before that can happen, however, she takes her own life and her children's lives in the cabin of her husband's ship, the *Wingless Victory*.

It is doubtful that Maxwell Anderson, when he wrote *The Wingless Victory*, had the elegant First Lady of the American Theatre in mind for Oparre. But in allegiance and trust he automatically gave the script to Guthrie, who unexpectedly saw it as Kit's next play.

———

Walter Abel had been in Guthrie's production of *The Square Peg* in 1923 and had almost had Tom Nesbit's part in *The Way Things Happen* in 1924, but until he played Nathaniel McQuestion in *The Wingless Victory* he had not actually appeared on the stage with Kit since the old Jessie Bonstelle days. He had never lost touch, of course, as no one ever did, and when he married Marietta Bitter in 1926 he even felt it necessary to obtain Kit's approval, which she was glad to give, enchanted that he was marrying a beautiful harpist.

Remembering the lusty days of *Lombardi, Ltd.*, Abel was a little impatient with Guthrie for keeping McQuestion separate from Oparre in all their scenes, at different ends of the room, on different levels, on opposite sides of a table, seated at the far ends of a sofa, as if Oparre were a person apart, not to be touched by anyone. It seemed to belie the script, which implied that Oparre's physical magnetism was the quality the tight-lipped New Englanders found most reprehensible and that the "lusting" McQuestion found most irresistible. Again recalling the days of *Lombardi, Ltd.* when Kit seemed not to have a serious thought on her mind and even enjoyed a bit of rowdiness onstage, providing the audience didn't notice, he kept threatening, with appropriate leers, to move in on her in their biggest, most intimate scene, and at the last performance before he left the company to go to Hollywood (to become a fine screen D'Artagnan), he told her that at last he was going to play that scene the way it was meant to be played, and to be prepared. But she did not enter into the spirit of it as once she might have, and actually seemed apprehensive during the scene, eyeing him sidelong, backing off whenever he made an uncharted move, carefully maintaining the distance between them that Guthrie had prescribed.

Jo Mielziner had collaborated on so many sets for Kit that by now he was as deft as Guthrie at providing a milieu in which her magnetic influence would be most keenly felt. The principal setting of *The Wingless Victory* was the living room of the McQuestion house in Salem, a broad formal room two steps down, through a wide, brightly lighted entrance, from a great hallway in which a curving staircase could be seen leading to the upper floors. Upstage right, almost out of sight, tucked away in the shadows, was a small door to the kitchen quarters, so disguised that it seemed to be part of the wall. As much as Kit hated the star system, it was the day when audiences came to see the star and eagerly awaited the star's first entrance to let loose a resounding hand of welcome. Plays were constructed for that entrance, especially by knowledgeable playwrights such as Maxwell Anderson; plays were designed for that entrance by theatre-wise designers such as Jo Mielziner; plays were staged for it by sophisticated directors such as Guthrie McClintic.

The first-act curtain of *The Wingless Victory* rose on a family gathering to welcome home Nathaniel McQuestion after twenty-seven years at sea, and his entrance was built up to as if it were the star's, until he was practically carried onto the stage through that grand archway. Then the stage gradually cleared and the audience waited, all lights and attention focused on that same grand archway, for the real star to make her entrance through it. Suddenly one became aware of a slight rustle, no more than a stirring, in the dark shadows upstage right, and as one peered into them one became aware of the stunning presence: someone of import had arrived, slipped in, and the subtly changing lights gradually revealed it to be Oparre, seemingly half naked, a contrast to the primly covered inhabitants of Salem who had recently peopled the stage, moving through the little trompe l'oeil door from the kitchen, feeling her way on bare feet across the deep oriental rugs to the center of the salon, perhaps carrying a child, leading another — the memory dims. The audience was so mesmerized that they almost — not quite — forgot to release their pent-up applause.

It was a directorial coup typical of Guthrie, theatrical, thrilling, and above all unexpected, without making Kit uncomfortable with an irrelevant trick or sacrificing the reality of the moment. Given her choice, she would always make her entrance through the smallest, most obscure door on the stage, so he simply let her. By confirming her attitude toward star entrances, he gave her the greatest star entrance of them all — the surprise. And to do it he didn't have to intrude on the play or violate its content; in fact he contributed immeasurably to it. In one striking moment he visualized for the audience the irreconcilable difference between Oparre and her adopted clan and established the position she would hold in that house.

In the *New York American*, Gilbert W. Gabriel wrote of her as Oparre: "As ever, she is most beautiful to see, most thrilling to hear, most memorable to meet in angry passion, in eloquent death. Confirm her is all we can as the foremost actress of our land." He found the play "a thrill of spacious, poetic writing, of marching metre, of images lifted high against the sky, that is superlatively pleasureable."

Not all critics were so generous. In *The New Republic*, "highty-tighty" and "semi-tosh" were Stark Young's words for the "tired, rhythmic patterns, superfluous images and lyric clichés" of Anderson's writing. He then went on to raise the old cry heard years before over *The Green Hat* and *Dishonored Lady*, when *Vogue* had said that Miss Cornell must have acted in such plays because "she prefers, to be blunt, trash of a violent kind." Implying that Miss Cornell must have acted in *The Wingless Victory* because she preferred semi-tosh highty-tighty, Young addressed her audience: "Miss Cornell has to deliver some of the worst speeches in recent playwriting, and seemingly does not shirk the onus of delivering them. This may be due to her loyalty to the text and sincerity as an actor or to her mediocrity or lack of distinguished instinct as an artist — the risk of your decision is hers."

It was with her "loyalty to the text and sincerity as an actor" that Kit sustained until after World War II the peak she had reached with *Romeo and Juliet* and *Saint Joan*. If she never went higher than those two performances, each role she took on after them represented a significant variation of her achievement, the highlighting of a new area of her talent, or the illumination of a further aspect of her aspiration for the theatre as an institution. Maxwell Anderson was a serious, passionate playwright whose artistic searching led him to believe he had found the simple secret to writing great tragedy, and he evolved a formula which he applied in like manner to the Sacco-Vanzetti case and Medea. If his talent proved, with time, to be facile, he had at least aimed for "images lifted high against the sky"; John Mason Brown wrote, "His contribution as a dramatic poet may be indifferent, but no one can deny that in theory the religion which is tragedy finds him among the faithful." And in a world of Depression moving inexorably toward war, he was one of the few major popular playwrights (along with S. N. Behrman in silken comedy) to sound the alarm against bigotry and injustice.

Kit's powers were at their zenith. Craft, technique, and knowledge had at last blended with her personal emotions, aptitudes, and limitations. By whatever secret means she and Guthrie had devised, she could induce a performance in whatever play she chose, twisting whatever part she played to make it her own. And as it had been true that there was something in her that liked the "trash of a violent kind" in *Dishonored Lady*, so now there was something in her that rose to the "semi-tosh highty-tighty" of *The Wingless Victory*, otherwise she would not have been able to act it with such "loyalty to the text and sincerity as an actor." Stark Young cannot have it either way, it has to be both. But he was right to say that the risk of the audience's decision (for or against her) was hers. She risked what had to be risked, and the audience, supporting her with patronage and attention, decided in her favor.

It is one thing to keep the loyalty of the audience; it is quite another accomplishment to command it among one's peers.

When *The Wingless Victory* opened at the Empire Theatre on

December 23, 1936, Noël Coward had opened around the corner at the National Theatre (today the Billy Rose) a month earlier in his collection of one-act plays *Tonight at 8:30*. Each wanted to see the other's performance, and to make it possible they tossed a coin to see who would switch one midweek matinee from Wednesday to Thursday. Kit lost, and on the free Wednesday asked Walter Abel to attend Coward's matinee with her. As soon as the curtain rose she began to fidget in her seat, to twist and sigh, putting her hand to her face as if reluctant to watch Coward and Gertrude Lawrence at their most dazzling. When he could, Abel whispered, "What's the matter?" She whispered back, almost with a groan, "Tomorrow *they* are coming to see *us!*"

Oparre was a tiring role. The scene at the end of Act Two when she turns on her Puritan in-laws was, according to Kit, "as wearing as singing Isolde eight times a week," and then it had to be topped by the double infanticide and suicide in Act Three.

The problem of makeup added to the strain. Kit's features were so prominent and distinct, even from the top of the balcony, that she usually did not give much thought to makeup, relying mostly on the emotion behind her unadorned face to create the necessary illusion. But as Oparre she had to use a body makeup, which took hours to apply, and after each performance Eveline had to go home with her and put her in a tub to scrub her back, shoulders, and arms. This meant appearing on the street outside the theatre in makeup, one of her particular professional aversions, and on matinee days she could not leave the theatre between performances at all, not even to eat, since the job took too long to be done twice. Also, her skin was becoming hypersensitive.

When the demand for tickets began to let up, it eased the situation to alternate *The Wingless Victory* with *Candida* on Monday and Saturday nights and Wednesday matinees. From the cast of *The Wingless Victory*, Kent Smith played Morell. A. P. Kaye was Mr. Burgess, and Marchbanks was played by Robert Harris. Mildred Natwick, a young character actress who had just finished playing Ina Claire's mother in *End of Summer*, was Prossy.

After one hundred and ten performances, *The Wingless Victory* went on a tour that was short but even more of a strain than the New York run.

It will be remembered that in Kit's first production of *Candida* Sidney Howard's wife Clare Eames had to give up her role of Prossy to have a child. Eleven years later that child, Claire Howard, played Oparre's daughter in the New York run of *The Wingless Victory*. It was the kind of casting to delight Guthrie, and the kind that only he would have thought of (although it was Gert who found Claire Howard in the King Coit School). She was a talented, well-behaved child, brought to rehearsals by a sensible aunt who always saw to it that her charge learned exactly as much as Mr. McClintic asked, never more, never less.

But when the play went on tour, the child labor laws in most states prohibited the "exhibitioning" of children under the age of twelve, and a midget had to be hired, or a "little person," as Gert, who did the hiring, quickly instructed everyone to say. The little person was thirty-five years old, traveling with a guardian or companion who also, by contract, had to be on the payroll, and when she spoke it was a high, harsh middle-aged voice talking baby talk, as opposed to the pure, childlike music of Claire Howard's voice. And even with all Kit's training on the slack wire in the backyard on Mariner Street, it was physically taxing, on top of the big emotional scenes, to carry the little person (who weighed twice as much as an average child) up the long curving staircase, keeping a straight back and maintaining Oparre's majestic balance. Kit was never for a moment at ease with the grotesque situation, feeling it seriously undermined the believability of the play, and at the opening in Washington, where the little person was to make her début, Walter Abel came out of his dressing room to find Kit lying on the floor of the stage with everybody dancing around her frantically. But just in time, of course, as he still remembers it, "like a racehorse she was on her feet, her nostrils distended, the blood rushing to her every nerve — and *on!* Such drive, such adrenalin, such energy — from the source of all emotion!"

Claire Howard was taken on tour because there were several cities where the state laws allowed her to perform, and in Detroit Dr. Cornell's old friend Ed Stair, from the *Detroit Free Press*, pulled strings and special permission was granted. It was a great relief, in those places, to send the little person and her keeper back to New York for a few days, but it didn't really lighten the atmosphere, which remained heavy and strained. It was typical of the whole tour that in Pittsburgh an intense young member of the company whose magnificent name, Theodora Pleadwell, had a Puritan ring that might have entitled her to be a character in the play, would countenance no levity among her fellow actors because it was in Pittsburgh that Eleonora Duse had died. Kit was once heard to murmur, perhaps after satisfactorily dispatching the little person at the end of Act Three, "Something should be done about Theodora Pleadwell."

Part of the heaviness was Kit's own. At about that time a Dr. Dunlop of Johns Hopkins devised a questionnaire which he asked her to complete. His purpose is lost as are his conclusions, but the questions and Kit's answers give a clear picture of her state of mind:

QUESTION: You make a quick survey of your whole life, reliving all your pains and all your pleasures, your humiliations and triumphs, your regrets and satisfactions, your miseries and the happiness, and suppose you were compelled to make the following decision, with no alternatives — live through your life once again, exactly as before, with no opportunity to better it by your present experience, or die instantly. Which would you choose?

K.C.: To die at once.

QUESTION: Do you think the more sensitive a person is, the more likely he or she is to choose instant death?

K.C.: Yes.

QUESTION: Do you think that the average human being would prefer to live again or to die at once?

K.C.: Fifty-fifty.

QUESTION: Do you think that the wiser, more philosophical a person is the more he would choose to live again? Or to die?

K.C.: To die.

QUESTION: Name the particular event or factor which most influenced your decision.

K.C.: Unhappy childhood.

QUESTION: Do you think that the great majority of people in past ages would have chosen to live again?

K.C.: Yes.

QUESTION: Do you remember any time in your life when your answer would have been different from the one you give now?

K.C.: No.

She had gone many years without stopping, years filled with work. Even the holidays at Garmisch, the weekends at Sneden's Landing, and lately the summers at Martha's Vineyard had been spent in preparation for work, resting up for more work, and making plans for still more work, with no time spent simply recovering from work. In the spring of 1938 when *Stage*, a dying magazine seeking to revitalize itself, asked to publish her life story as told to *Stage*'s editor Ruth Woodbury Sedgwick, Kit's immediate suggestion was that the series be called *Twenty Years of Hard Work*. With Juliet and Joan she had reached a plateau. By its characteristic elevation a plateau is remote; by definition it is monotonous and flat. In her own words as they eventually appeared in *Stage*, she was bored with herself at the end of *The Wingless Victory* tour and decided to take a year off.

25

Time for Comedy (1937-1939)

HER NEED FOR A SABBATICAL YEAR must have been great indeed for her to insist on it when she knew it would displease her beloved Ray Henderson. He felt that one had so few productive years that one could not afford to waste any of them on rest, that one had to push on without stopping. Unhappy to see him unhappy, to assure him that she had no intention of stopping for good, and — far more important, considering the nature of the man — to give him something to plan for, she suggested that the time had come to put into action his greatest dream for her outside a repertory theatre: a world tour. No other actor or actress from any country had ever attempted anything so comprehensive in its artistic ambition and so staggering in its logistics.

A full-page announcement appeared in the July issue of *Theatre Arts Monthly*, listing thirty-three countries to be visited, from Australia to Finland, from Java to Ireland, from Russia to Mexico. Henderson loved to travel and he set off around the world to talk about Kit, to sell her, to bring her name to places that had as yet not even heard of her; to plumb theatre practices, scout stages, test receptivity, estimate budgets, and make friends. Guthrie always said Ray Henderson had the manner of an ambassador; now he assumed the function. It is the way of many great stars to diminish those around them as they themselves move upward. Not so with Katharine Cornell, who pulled everyone up with her. At her peak, she instinctively saw to it that Ray Henderson reached his.

The site Kit chose for her house on Martha's Vineyard was between Vineyard Sound and Lake Tashmoo, a tiny peninsula trying to be an isthmus and falling short by several hundred feet, a spit of land with water on three sides and a primitive path down the middle. Anne (Tonetti) Gugler's sister Lydia, who owned The Camp where Kit stayed with Ruth March in the summer of 1936, warned her that the price of the land would treble if the natives knew a famous stage actress wanted to buy it. Therefore, since it was near The Camp and it would be logical for Lydia to want it, she pretended to buy it for herself, and since the natives knew she was poor, they let her have it for a fair price. Years later Kit would make up for her part in this initial, mistrustful collusion in an unintentionally amusing way. Gert was touring Europe with the Martha Graham troupe, and Kit cabled her in Stockholm that the four hundred feet of property beyond hers, with a shack on it, could be bought for seventy-five hundred dollars — and did Gert want it? Gert, ever the wily bargainer, wired back that she did, but to offer five. Kit showed the cable to the owner and without waiting for acceptance or refusal assured him, "I know Gert — she'll come up to six."

Eric Gugler designed the house (built and ready for the summer of 1937) to Kit's specifications. There was a living room and a bedroom with an enormous bed at one end, with a wooden frame around it wide enough to store magazines and books. The bed itself was on casters to slide out easily for changing, and Gugler instructed Anne to get "hundreds" of cushions for it. Sitting on the bed among the cushions, one's feet didn't even have to touch the floor. There was a bathroom with a shower but no tub (Kit insisted on no cheap fripperies) and a kitchenette with a stove, sink, ice box, and worktable. There was a fireplace for warmth, a cesspool, no telephone, no electricity, and a dug well with water so brackish it was hardly drinkable. Gugler gave the small house a square, competent whitewashed chimney rising above a steep gable of silver weathered shingles. Inside, the rooms were fourteen feet high at the center, and from the outside the roof swept low and dramatically into its setting almost without a break. Most houses were set back from the water for protection, but Kit was impatient with a long walk through pebbles and beach grass after swimming and put her house as close to the water's edge as she dared, with only gentle sloping sand between. It could be said that the site formed the third corner of a triangle with East Chop and West Chop, headlands each with its lighthouse, so she called her house Chip Chop.

Throughout the planning stages and into the construction the dramatic cry was raised that all she wanted was a place to be alone; all she needed was a hideaway big enough for just herself, where she (and the dogs, of course) could disappear to read, study lines, and tramp the woods and beaches. But it is not surprising that off the kitchenette she saw to it that there was a small extra bed, no more than a ship's bunk, with its own toilet and wash basin, for Guthrie, if he chose, or for Gert, or Ruth March, or whoever; room for the "someone in the next room" she could not live without for long. Nor is it surprising that when Guthrie could overcome his fear of storms but not his distaste for living without a telephone, she put in a telephone. Next came a generator to make electricity.

Guthrie found he was — or became — a sun worshipper. He loved to swim nude and delighted that he could walk down the beach for a mile or more, naked, and not worry about encounters. With a telephone within reach, he didn't mind the other asceticisms, least of all the little sleeping bunk off the kitchenette, and he was at Chip Chop more and more often.

Even before Gert acquired her shack, Kit too was extending her property, and when the house beyond Gert's became available, she bought it and rented it for several years to I. A. R. Wylie, the writer, who improved the property with a separate cottage for her maid whom she couldn't bear to leave behind in Princeton. Eventually the property, which for obscure reasons had always been called The Swindle, was sold to Brenda Forbes, who improved it with a cedar pine room and tile bath for her mother, and who still owns it today. The immediate benefit to Kit in acquiring The Swindle was that she could tap its delicious and abundant water supply for Chip Chop.

Guthrie became so proud of Kit's Chip Chop that he wanted Noël Coward and Clifton Webb and Laurence Olivier and all their other friends to see it, so they added what was known variously as the Great Big Room, the Picnic Room, and the Ping-Pong Room. Forty feet by seventy-five, it was so spacious that carpeting out of a Mellon ballroom had to be bought at the Parke-Bernet Galleries, carpeting so extensive that no other room had ever been found to accommodate it. There were high Gothic fireplaces at the far distant ends of the room, and an admirer of Kit's presented her with huge, matching fire screens bearing in heavy brass the monograms K.C. and G.McC. Big enough to enclose a four-room house, with long, evenly-spaced windows in opposite walls, therefore looking out onto both Lake Tashmoo and Vineyard Sound, the room was able to absorb all Guthrie's decorating whims. Even Kit caught the decorating fever, since there was so much to be decorated, and visiting Aunt Lydia in Cobourg she found a long, low table fifteen feet long where nuns used to sit doing their tatting and other needlework. There was a little drawer at each place for lace and string and needles and hooks, and in front of each little drawer a little white pine chair. Kit bought the table and all fourteen chairs. Olivier sent them a gigantic clock with no works, a huge empty Elizabethan clock case that wouldn't fit anywhere else. Johanna Hirth sent the Bavarian porcelain stove from the Cornelia Room.

The Great Big Picnic Ping-Pong Room was connected at one end with the original house — on the diagonal — by a screened-in dining porch, and at the other end a flagstone terrace connected two handsomely fitted guest houses, each with a full bathroom. On the other side of the original structure from the Great Big Room, a great big kitchen was added with skylight windows, and beyond that, along a corridor, a room for Dr. Cornell or Guthrie with a window bay onto the Sound and a fenced-in private terrace for nude sunbathing. Beyond that still, down several steps from the main floor, was a separate apartment for a live-in working couple.

Even when the house — or establishment, as it became — was operating full tilt, Kit always went to bed early to read, no matter who the guests were, while Guthrie stayed up late playing cards and telling stories. On one occasion Mildred Knopf was in one guest cottage; Neysa McMein, the artist and illustrator, in the other. Guthrie was escorting them to their respective doors in the small hours of a late night. On the flagstone terrace outside the Great Big Room were two enormous peacock blue urns, narrow-mouthed and squat, very old, very beautiful. Guthrie, in a silly mood, popped himself into one of them with his grinning head sticking up like one of Ali Baba's forty thieves. The sight was good for a big laugh until he realized he couldn't get out, which was good for an even bigger laugh until the situation suddenly became threatening and serious. Neysa McMein was all for getting an ax and heroically smashing Guthrie free, but he was horrified at the thought and begged her, "Oh my God, don't do that, Kit will kill me!" Finally the women managed to upset the urn onto its side on the flagstones and Guthrie wriggled out, first one skinny shoulder, then the other, his scrawny boneless frame for once standing him in good stead.

In the dawn's early light of all next mornings at Chip Chop, heavy-headed guests were only dimly aware of cottage doors being quietly opened by the First Lady of the American Theatre on all fours pushing a coffee tray as far as possible into the room without making noise, then silently slipping away.

On the grounds, away from the water, there were a garage and a tool shed that one day would become a workroom where Kit, with the patience of years' practice, would learn the meticulous, restorative pleasures of marquetry; when given a loom she would weave fabrics for Guthrie's sports jackets. But in the early days at Chip Chop, garbed in work shirts and pants ragged with wear, slicker and sou'wester, it was her delight to breast the rising forces of nature, no matter how they rose, and in the historic hurricane of 1938 the Great Big Room afforded what was probably her finest hour. On that memorable afternoon she entertained at lunch two women, if not elderly then at least of a retiring nature, who had founded or ran the Country Day School on Tenth Street in New York and had a summer house in Chilmark. They were in the Ping-Pong Room when the hurricane struck, and immediately sensing that its force was enough to knock down the walls, the first thing Kit did was to throw open all the windows on both sides of the room so that the ferocious waves could sweep through unimpeded. Before they knew it, the water was two feet high, showing no sign of letting up, and Kit got the old ladies onto the piano. She herself was on the piano stool; the cook was passing up the drenched and frightened dogs, and Kit was making plans for the next step, somehow to get everybody onto the roof, when the Coast Guard arrived with a rescue party.

———

All that was still in the future in the fall of 1937 at the beginning of her sabbatical year. Ray Henderson was submitting regular, enthusiastic reports of his trip by letter, telephone, and cable. His notes were beginning to show that the projected tour was logistically feasible and financially practicable. Perhaps because of the sense of mission with which he traveled, even politically problematical areas seemed ready and waiting for him, eager to be included in his plans.

On Friday, October 1, Kit was alone at Chip Chop. The James Cagneys and several other friends dropped by in the afternoon and she read them a cable she had received that morning from Ray in Cairo: "Egypt keen flying London tomorrow." The next morning, Saturday, October 2, Guthrie and Gert arrived unexpectedly from the mainland. They, too, had received a cable in New York the night before, theirs from the American Consulate in Athens, beginning: "Henderson trapped and drowned in submerged seaplane. . . ."

Only three passengers on the small plane — those seated in the front of the cabin — were killed. They were immediately buried in Athens with plain markers. On behalf of Ray's only living relative, a brother in Colorado Springs, Kit communicated with the Athens authorities and asked that the body be exhumed for return to the United States. She was informed that the body would have to be claimed personally and then accompanied home.

Guthrie heard the news of Ray Henderson's death standing in the lobby of the Empire Theatre, on the exact spot where they had met six and one half years earlier during the run of *The Barretts of Wimpole Street*. At the time of Ray's death, Guthrie's production of Maxwell Anderson's *The Star-Wagon* was playing successfully at the Empire, starring Burgess Meredith and Lillian Gish, and it was Miss Gish who found a way to bring Ray Henderson home. She had a lawyer friend in Athens, an American, who claimed the body and escorted it across the ocean on an Italian liner. Cremation followed, and, as Ray had directed in his will, his brother hired a small plane to strew the ashes over Pike's Peak.

The body of people that surrounded Kit and in actuality formed the entity known as Katharine Cornell had lost a vital limb. The body recovered and continued on, seemingly in exuberant health, but something intangible, a spirit, had been stilled. All plans for the world tour were immediately dropped. The threatening world situation was sufficient reason. But when the situation cleared again after World War II, the idea of a world tour was never revived, not even as a wishful thought. Ray Henderson would not have said it was too late for this great adventure. He would have said it was high time.

Kit apostrophized him in the *New York Times* on October 10, 1937: "Dear Ray, you have left us high responsibility. . . ."

But a tiny, imperceptible chink had appeared in Joan's gold-plated armor.

In that same October the young Prince of Hesse-Darmstadt was to be married in London to an English girl when his father, the Grand Duke, died and the wedding had to be postponed for a month. In November the family, all friends of Kit's through Johanna, set off by plane across the English Channel — the Grand Duchess, another son (the Prince's brother) and daughter-in-law, several children, their governess, and a Baron who was to be an official witness at the ceremony. One child, Johanna's namesake, was too young to travel and stayed behind at Haus Hirth. It is believed that after starting across the Channel, the party turned back to collect someone who had missed the plane; the story goes that the plane crashed into a chimney. Everyone on board was killed.

Johanna and Kit usually talked on the telephone every few weeks, and when Kit heard of the stunning accident she sailed immediately for Europe, to be there if needed. The young couple in England were married quietly and returned to the Continent for the mass burial. The young Prince was so numbed that it was difficult to get through to him, even for Kit, but she became good friends with his wife, the new Princess. Coming one month after Ray Henderson's similar death in a plane over a body of water, it was as if some ungenerous fate had deliberately postponed the Hesse-Darmstadt wedding so that Kit could experience the full, unalloyed impact of both tragedies. It is no wonder that she always suffered an excessive fear of flying, even through her airborne U.S.O.–American Theatre Wing tour in World War II.

It was the only time Kit ever visited Garmisch in the winter, and from then on her visits became less frequent because of the political situation. Munich and the surrounding territory, including Grainau, was the seat of the Nazi movement, and at about this time (1937–1938) Frau Hirth was ordered to post a notice that no Jews were allowed at Haus Hirth. She asked to be given a few days first, and wrote a letter to von Ribbentrop, enclosing a guest list, informing him that if she were to post a notice forbidding Jews, all these distinguished representatives of many nations would leave in protest. A few days later she received a directive from von Ribbentrop actually forbidding her to post such a notice. Apparently it was against protocol to grant a request; the incentive had to come from him in the form of a directive. When the war ended she destroyed that directive lest the occupation forces think she had an in with von Ribbentrop, which couldn't have been further from the truth. After her communication with him, she became an object of special scrutiny and had to tolerate a Nazi officer billeted at the hotel.

When the war began, Haus Hirth became a haven for refugees from the Munich bombings, and at the end of the war it was taken over by the American Army of Occupation for ten years. The genteel house party of the 1930s was ended.

Much was made of Kit's "fortieth" birthday in February 1938. Douglas Gilbert reported on her New York activities for the *Buffalo Times*: "Enjoying a much-needed sabbatical from the theatre, she romps around doing what she pleases — a flitter-budget. Sneaks out to the movies every day. Sobs unashamedly at the sad scenes and laughs like an apple-knocker at the comedy. Miss Cornell is, in fact, having the time of her life. . . ."

By dropping her curtain, Kit was able to elide certain emotional exigencies and philosophical truths of her existence, but one wonders if — flitter-budget though she was — she was laughing like an apple-knocker at the fact that she was really forty-five.

In extension of the birthday festivities, her life story as told to Ruth Woodbury Sedgwick began appearing in *Stage* in September 1938. The previous May Mrs. Sedgwick went to Martha's Vineyard armed with an antediluvian recording device into which Kit, sitting cross-legged in blue denim slacks on an old pine table in the Great Big Room, spoke her piece. Mrs. Sedgwick counted four dachshunds present: Hanie, Trudie, Sonia, and the ever-favorite Illo.

Called *I Wanted to Be an Actress* instead of *Twenty Years of Hard Work*, the memoir is brief, less than fifty thousand words, even with extra material judiciously added by Gert when the recording sessions were over, to clear certain points and stress other impressions. Mrs. Sedgwick sticks as much as possible to Kit's actual words, and the result is gracious, charming, uninformative, and not very illuminating, rather like a friendly report to an alumnae association. There were few theatrical autobiographies published in those days, and none of the braggadocian, tell-all-and-then-some kind we have today, so Kit's served its purpose well, although it did not, in the long run, save *Stage* from oblivion.

In the spring of 1939 the work appeared in book form, published by Random House simultaneously in a regular edition and a limited signed edition. Dr. Cornell wrote from Buffalo: "Ulbrich has a window display of your book. $3.00 without your signature and $6.00 with. I suppose the extra $3.00 they charge for the one with the autograph is to pay a handwriting expert to decipher it."

After two calamitous plane crashes resulting in almost ten desolating deaths and the loss of as many friends; and now on the downhill side of forty-five and sliding into fifty, Kit crowned her recuperative sabbatical year by returning to the theatre in October 1938, with a failure so complete that for the first time in her career she did not even bring it into New York. It was a German classic, *Herod and Mariamne* by Friedrich Hebbel, telling of the bloody tyrant's psychopathic jealousy of his innocent wife's imagined infidelities. Although Kit was not a Bible reader, she loved biblical stories and titles like *Alien Corn* taken from the Bible, but her real interest in *Herod and Mariamne* was that Clemence Dane had written the English adaptation. It is impossible to say if the loss of Ray Henderson's guidance had anything to do with it, but Kit seems to have reverted to her 1920s, pre-Henderson way of selecting a play. She was indebted to Clemence Dane for *A Bill of Divorcement* and *Will Shakespeare*, therefore she must do *The Way Things Happen* and *Herod and Mariamne*.

That may have been part of it, but certainly not all. Because Clemence Dane had adjured her to tackle the "big stuff" and this play was Clemence Dane's own "big stuff," perhaps she could not refuse for fear of being thought craven by her robust friend. Or perhaps that was it, that Clemence Dane was her friend, and she didn't want to offend her. Perhaps she didn't know how to say no.

Simpler still, perhaps she didn't want to say no. It is very possible that she liked *Herod and Mariamne*.

Dorothy Thompson is supposed to have suggested her very close friend Fritz Kortner for the role of Herod. Guthrie was prodigious in his knowledge of theatre outside the United States. There wasn't an important actor or actress in Europe that he didn't claim to have seen, citing in sharp detail their acting styles and doing devastating imitations. Whether Dorothy Thompson suggested Kortner or not, it was

Guthrie who convinced Kit that the fierce German star would be a tremendous asset to the production.

It was one case in which his unpredictable dramatic flair misfired. A Cleveland critic observed that there was "hardly a note in the scale of human feeling that is not touched in the play," which should have made for theatrical fireworks, at least, had the two stars not been so mismatched. Opposed to what one of her fellow actors calls "Kit's grand naturalistic style," Kortner played in the completely unnatural, declamatory style of Alexander Moissi of the Reinhardt theatre, the style known as the "tirade," which was exactly that, often ranging within a single speech from a harsh, prolonged, guttural whisper to an ear-splitting shriek. In movies he performed perfectly sanely, playing in concert with his fellow actors, but in *Herod and Mariamne* he was in his prime — fresh from his doings with Miss Thompson — and no matter what anyone else was doing, he was determined to play Herod as he had played it at the Berlin Stadttheater, even to the extent of having his own personal prompter (a cousin or a nephew) always in the wings on one side of the stage or the other, or at the back, depending on where Kortner was, murmuring in a low voice Kortner's every line, always exactly one sentence ahead. Apparently he was inaudible to the audience, but on the stage it was like hearing Herod's voice twice, a reverse echo. Agreeable Kit plowed on as if schizophrenia were the norm.

Kent Smith didn't have much to do but stand around looking handsome and Roman as a centurion; Ruth March was an attendant, Florence Reed Kit's mother.

Another extra, Mildred Dunnock, confided to Gert on the way to Eaves Costume Company that she was pregnant and didn't think it fair to be fitted for her beautiful Valentina costume when she knew that in time it would have to be let out or refitted to another actress. In tears, she thought it only honorable to quit. Gert said to keep her pregnancy a secret from Miss Cornell and go on with the fitting. She had several months before her condition would become a problem, and the play might not even last that long (perhaps Gert had been watching rehearsals). Having conspired this way with a young member of a company, as she often did, Gert always felt it her responsibility to keep an eye on the situation. At one performance out of town she was sitting with Guthrie in a stage box watching a very long scene between Kortner and Kit during which the supporting actors stood endlessly and listened. Something in Miss Dunnock's stance suddenly alerted Gert, who — as if a pistol shot had been fired — sprinted out of the stage box through the passdoor backstage, careened around the back of the set, extricating as she went the ammonia capsules she always carried in her purse as protection against her own backstage claustrophobia, and arrived at the opposite side of the stage just in time to help a stagehand reach in and catch the fainting expectant mother as she collapsed, haul her discreetly into the wings, and break an ammonia capsule under her nose. Such was the stupefying effect of Kortner's tirade that nobody on the stage or in the audience noticed.

Guthrie's attention to period and background, so essential to the success of *The Barretts* and other period productions, in this case came across as fussy. "The play is cluttered with distracting detail," the critics complained in Cleveland and Pittsburgh. "Interesting characters are introduced and then whisked off before you are sure of their names." Audiences were coming to the theatre prepared to worship Miss Cornell as always and going away dissatisfied, without the critics' articulate ability to say why.

In rehearsal the actors sensed that the play was not going to be a success, and the stagehands out of town referred to it as "Heroin and Marijuana." But once committed to a role and a production, Kit's faith became unshakable, and Guthrie encouraged her inflexibility in the belief that she could not perform without it. After a performance one night in Pittsburgh, Gert flat-footedly told them they had better face the fact that the play was a flop and close it, canceling Washington, the next and last stand before New York. Guthrie was incensed, saying that Kit's performance that very evening had made him "cry like a fool." As always in the face of Guthrie's assertions, Gert became more dogged in hers. She said the audiences were going away disappointed and unhappy, she had heard them in the lobby; they were coming only out of blind loyalty to Kit and then getting stung for it. It was cheating to take advantage of their loyalty, and the next time they went on tour they would be unable to play Pittsburgh because audiences would not be made fools of twice in a row. This was not the kind of integrity she and every actor and every member of every audience had a right to expect from Katharine Cornell. As might be expected, Guthrie flew into a rage that made Fritz Kortner's tirade seem like underplaying.

The unusual aspect of the scene and the reason for examining it here, is that Kit, for once in such circumstances, did not lower the curtain behind her eyes and remove herself from the squalid fight but stayed very much within it. At that time Gert was planning to make her theatrical debut as a producer with a musical revue on Broadway called *One for the Money* by Nancy Hamilton and Morgan Lewis. Kit may have felt that her own territory was being encroached upon or, quite the opposite, she may have felt that Gert needed a nudge. She pointed out that Gert might be expected to dislike *Herod* because her own interests were now obviously shifting to the musical theatre, but she and Guthrie would always be committed to the theatre of high drama. She felt that Gert had served her apprenticeship long and well, and perhaps it was time to free herself from service to others.

This was different from Guthrie's habitual crooked finger and cry of "Out!" Gert went to bed that night believing her days with Cornell-McClintic were over. The next morning she arranged for train accommodations back to New York and after years of scrimping on room service bills on the production budget, called downstairs and ordered the biggest breakfast on the menu, which she thoroughly enjoyed. It was interrupted, however, by a call from Kit feeling morose about the night before. Gert admitted to her own sad feelings, not because of Guthrie and the things he said, but because Kit herself had fired her. Kit dismissed the idea, saying they couldn't any of them begin to get along without Gert and Gert knew it; they couldn't even get to Washington without her. Gert said that was simply not true, that Alan Attwater, the company manager, could handle everything efficiently and could take over on a moment's notice. Gert furthermore admitted that her theatrical taste might be plebeian, but if Kit and Guthrie thought *Herod and Mariamne* was great theatre, then she didn't want to be connected with them. Kit willingly confessed that the night before Gert had put into words what she and Guthrie were trying not to admit to themselves and each other, and they had reacted accordingly. Alan Attwater could indeed manage the production, but she, Kit, could not possibly set foot on a stage without Gert, couldn't go to Washington, couldn't even get herself out of Pittsburgh. Would Gert please stop by her suite for a moment before making any further plans . . . ?

For all Guthrie's protection of her fragile sensibilities, Kit was the one who first accepted the failure. It was too late to cancel Washington, but it was announced at once that *Herod and Mariamne* would not open in New York.

Gert stopped by Kit's suite as requested and was not fired and did not quit.

One for the Money, the musical revue Gert produced with Stanley Gilkey, opened two months before *No Time for Comedy* with a cast of unknown young performers including Gene Kelly, Alfred Drake, and Keenan Wynn. Its success was enormously satisfying to everyone and brought Nancy Hamilton into the circle of Kit's friends.

Mildred Oppenheimer Knopf's son had been named Christopher in the hope that he would be called "Kit" after his godmother, and Mildred Dunnock Urmy's daughter was named Linda after Kit's role in her next play, S. N. Behrman's *No Time for Comedy*. While *Herod and Mariamne* was dying out of town, the Playwrights' Producing Company was being born on Broadway with Raymond Massey in Robert E. Sherwood's *Abe Lincoln in Illinois*. Behrman's first contribution to the new company's agenda was another of his smooth, polished, clever, articulate, literate social comedies, this one having to do with a smooth, polished, clever, articulate actress whose playwright husband has for years supplied her with smooth, polished, etc., comedies and suddenly decides he must write a plunging tragedy about war and death and the deplorable state of the world. The role of "Linda Esterbrook, known on the stage as Linda Paige," was written for and offered to Ina Claire, who in *Biography* and *End of Summer* had become identified with Behrman plays. Miss Claire couldn't settle down to say yes, so the play was offered to Lynn Fontanne with the hope that Alfred Lunt would play the playwright, Gaylord Esterbrook, but they were off on a long tour. Even Gertrude Lawrence was given her turn to say no before Robert Sherwood recklessly suggested Katharine Cornell. Her name would not ordinarily be found on the same list with these other actresses, at least not with the implication that their talents were synonymous. Her modern plays — *Alien Corn* and *Flowers of the Forest* — had not been her most outstanding successes, and the smiling period style of her one and only comedy, *Candida*, was no match for the smartly dressed and stylishly designed repartee of a Behrman play. As John Mason Brown put it after *No Time for Comedy* opened,

With Laurence Olivier in No Time for Comedy, *1939. (New York Public Library, Vandamm Collection)*

"Where comediennes shine in the brightness of the noonday sun, she [Miss Cornell] has been a daughter of the night; pallid, glowing and compelling. 'Il Penseroso' and 'L'Allegro' could not be less alike, for example, than Miss Cornell and Ina Claire." And yet here was Robert Sherwood personally putting into her hands the script of *No Time for Comedy* and asking her to play it. If Kit remembered that she had once brought down the house with her comic antics in *Lombardi, Ltd.*, it was also to remember that nothing had been at stake. When Sherwood asked her to join forces with the Playwrights' Company, her immediate reaction was to say no.

But Guthrie was like a CO in the Air Force — the minute you crashed, he sent you up again. After *Lucrece* he urged her immediately into production for *Alien Corn*, after *Flowers of the Forest* into plans for *Saint Joan*. Now, after *Herod and Mariamne*, *No Time for Comedy* was there to be done, and right or wrong, he urged her to do it.

Kit's fear of comedy was no secret. Lynn Fontanne advised her, "If the lines are funny, just give them a chance — say them loudly enough." Everyone wanted to help, but not everyone succeeded. Being driven down from Sneden's Landing one afternoon, Kit was sitting in the middle of the backseat with Guthrie on one side and Gert on the other. Speaking of *No Time for Comedy*, Gert had to lean forward and talk across Kit to say to Guthrie that the trouble was that Kit didn't have much humor. And Guthrie had to lean forward and talk across Kit to agree impatiently that of course Kit didn't have much humor, everybody knew that, but if she would just learn the lines and take it from him how to say them, he would bring out the comedy with his staging of the scenes and his direction of the other characters. It is historic proof of her comedic perceptions that Kit did not crack their heads together and tumble them out of the car, as the humorless person they described would surely have done.

Katharine Cornell's was the dignified, established producing organization, and at first she, or rather her advisers and spokesmen — in this case, specifically, Stanton Griffis — insisted on the lion's share of the production. But the upstart Playwrights' Company was a sturdy adversary, too big to be pushed around, despite Griffis's contention that they were just "a bunch of boys with some plays to sell." Behrman seems to have been the deciding factor in the negotiations. He became so enamored with the idea of Katharine Cornell that had the Playwrights' Company not come to terms with her, he might have taken his play away from them and they knew it. Since the whole point of establishing the Playwrights' Company was to side with the playwright, they gallantly acquiesced, as did Griffis. It was agreed that C. & M.C. would have fifty-one percent of the production, with the Cornell name listed first as producer above the title.

Kit and Guthrie also reserved the right of casting approval, but it was Harold Freedman, Behrman's agent, who solved the first and most important casting problem by suggesting Laurence Olivier for the role of Gaylord Esterbrook. At one point Guthrie had wanted Walter Abel, but Abel thought the character totally unresolved, a man incapable of coming to conclusions about himself. Guthrie said, "Isn't that the point?", and in Olivier found an actor able to raise irresolution and indecision to a supreme comedic art.

Guthrie further backed Kit up — and Olivier — with two other English actors, both masters of high comedy, John Williams and Robert Flemyng. Flemyng had just made his American debut with Gladys Cooper in *Spring Meeting*, and Equity would only waive its six-month rule for alien actors if he would agree not to appear on Broadway for one year after *No Time for Comedy*. The situation in Europe so threatened the future that such a stipulation would probably have little meaning, and Flemyng agreed.

The part of the "other woman," the ultra-feminine visionary inspirer of talented men who urges Gaylord to plumb the depths of his soul in search of dark tragedy, was played with impeccable wit by Margalo Gillmore, and the small cast was rounded out with Gee Gee James as the amusing maid.

Her three leading men all fell for Kit and worked with Guthrie to ease her through the precision comedy timing, the offhand delivery, the gaiety of spirit, and the kind of projection John Mason Brown calls "triple exposure — that sense of harking back to what has just been said and anticipating what is to come even while speaking" that go to make up an alert comedy performance. In the sequence of scenes in the play, John Williams was the first at bat with her, and he would stagger offstage where the other two were keeping score, shake his head, and murmur "Poor old Kit!" all the way to his dressing room. Olivier would come off at the end of the first act slapping his forehead, "Poor old Kit, oh, poor old *Kit!*" Flemyng's turn didn't come until the second act when he too would join the offstage chorus of "Poor old Kit!" until finally Olivier exploded. "Poor old Kit! What are we saying? *Poor old Kit* is the most successful woman in the American theatre! The richest, the most beautiful, the most sought after, the most distinguished, the most loved — ! Poor Old Kit, *indeed!*" Nevertheless, in all the years since then, when either Flemyng or Olivier refers — in conversation or letter — to "P.O.K.," the other knows without question who is meant.

Now and then Behrman would take Gert out for a discreet drink and a tête-à-tête to hint most kindly that Kit was perhaps not reaping all the comic rewards inherent in her lines. Gert did not pass his gentle reprimands on Kit; she didn't have to. In his memoir *People in a Diary* Behrman recalls that after the first out-of-town performance in Indianapolis he went backstage and found Kit in tears, saying she had let him down. He assured her as airily as he could that "the others think the play got over."

"Thanks to Larry," was her response.

It was that precarious moment when Behrman and the Playwrights' and all those who did not know her well feared she might quit. Olivier had finished the movie *Wuthering Heights*, and after its release his name and face would become famous across the country. But until then he was relatively unknown in the United States; even habitual theatregoers forgot they had seen him in support of Noël Coward and Gertrude Lawrence in *Private Lives* and as the charming, ingenuous victim in the sinister homosexual ménage of *The Green Bay Tree*. Kit was known and loved, but Olivier was brand new, and as Behrman wrote later, when he appeared on the stage of the English Theatre in Indianapolis, "there was a stir in the audience about him that lasted all evening."

As if the clear-cut deftness of his acting were not enough to unsettle Kit, Olivier was fourteen years younger than she, although the characters in the play were meant to be the same age — his. No one, no critic or gossip or columnist, no jealous actor or dissatisfied member of the audience ever openly took notice or made reference to the fact, because to see them together eliminated the discrepancy. But in her unhappiness Kit cannot help but have thought of Candida's parting injunction to Marchbanks. To help him forget that he loves her and to convince him of their incongruity as romantic figures, she asks him: "Will you make a little poem out of the two sentences I am going to say to you? 'When I am thirty, she will be forty-five. When I am sixty, she will be seventy-five.' " At the time of *No Time for Comedy*, Olivier was thirty-two, and Kit was forty-six.

In other difficult roles, her supporters had always been able to rely on her beauty to shine through when all else failed, and here was her first chance since *Dishonored Lady* to emerge in high fashion from rats and falls, shawls and petticoats. Although Gert preferred her to be crisp and tailored, Guthrie liked the sweeping classic lines Valentina had draped her in as Mariamne and asked her to come up with modern equivalents for Linda. But as if to pull all possible rugs out from under her, for all Kit's sudden newfound style, here was a leading man as beautiful among men as she was among women, and in a more immediately striking, popular way. Behrman, whatever he felt about her comedy playing, was her strongest partisan from the start, and even he had to admit after the Indianapolis opening, "Kit looked wonderful; she had her beauty, but beauty is a static thing. Larry had the most engaging and volatile good looks."

It is no wonder that the Playwrights' and others who did not know her well thought she might quit. Almost any other leading actress in similar circumstances would have, or would have had Olivier replaced with an older actor who would make her look better. Behrman continues: "The apprehensive ones did not know Kit. She did not quit. She stuck. She got better and better as she vanquished her nervousness. The company was her responsibility. She mothered it. They all blossomed under her ministrations." Far from resenting Olivier, she felt that his brilliance saved the play and kept it alive while she "vanquished her nervousness," that he dazzled the audience into not noticing that she was still pursuing the evanescent craft of comedy.

One form of her ministrations, more godmotherly than motherly, was her active interest in Olivier's transcontinental wooing of Vivien Leigh, much as she always took an interest in romances that bloomed between young people in her touring companies. The lovers were both still tied to other people, both trying to obtain divorces to marry each other, and while today such a situation would hardly even classify as a news item (except for their desire to marry, which would create a freakish kind of curiosity), this was 1939 and Miss Leigh was in the middle of filming *Gone with the Wind* in which David Selznick, the producer, had too much at stake to risk the open scandal everyone thought would result should the public find out that Scarlett O'Hara was having an affair with Heathcliff. Consequently, Selznick did everything he could to keep the lovers apart, while Kit, without offending the public sensibility or violating her own standards of decorum, did what she could to bring them together.

In his biography of Olivier, John Cottrell says that after *No Time for Comedy* opened at the Ethel Barrymore Theatre on Monday, April 17, 1939, and seemed assured of a long run, on one occasion Olivier tried "weekend commuting to California, making a sixteen-hour flight after his Saturday night performance and flying back late on Sunday." Gert Macy remembers this happening the weekend before the play opened when Kit, despite her own mistrust of air travel, let Olivier miss one dress rehearsal to fly west while Miss Leigh, forbidden by protocol to be seen with him in public places, flew east as far as Albuquerque — or one of the other southwestern cities — where the lovers met for a few moments together. Guthrie was horrified by Kit's leniency and stewed the entire weekend, certain the return flight would be grounded.

In June Miss Leigh finished filming and rushed to New York to be with Olivier. Since they could not stay at the same hotel or, even worse, be seen sneaking in and out of each other's, Kit gave them the Log Cabin and all its privacy at Sneden's Landing. Olivier couldn't even openly meet the plane at Newark, and Gert was chosen his surrogate. In an ecstasy of anticipation, Miss Leigh kept wiring revised, detailed descriptions of what she would be wearing so that Gert would be able to recognize her when she deplaned, quite charmingly unaware that on arrival she would be besieged by reporters with flashbulbs and not at all difficult to single out. On the appointed night Olivier couldn't wait and insisted on riding to Newark with Gert, but once started couldn't wait until they reached the airport to find a men's room, and Gert gladly dumped him at a service station just outside the airport, sternly instructing him to wait there until she picked him up on the way back. Later, when she departed the airport with her charge in the backseat, the impatient swain was in the middle of the highway all but flagging down cars for fear of missing hers. He had been heard days beforehand sighing like a furnace that he wished Kit had a double bed at the Log Cabin, and as a surprise she had her twin beds moved out and a double bed moved in to make his wish come true. So much for any resentment she might have been thought to bear against her too talented, too handsome, too young co-star.

———

No Time for Comedy was one of her great authentic hits, by which is meant that it not only succeeded to everyone's satisfaction theatrically and artistically, but it exceeded everyone's most extravagant hopes financially. It was the third largest money-maker of her entire career, topped only by the 1931 production of *The Barretts of Wimpole Street* and the 1951 production of *The Constant Wife*, and it was her second production, after the 1931 *Barretts*, to gross over a million dollars.

S. N. Behrman had written a lighthearted examination of his own deeply troubled conscience as a playwright, and shortly after the opening Woollcott wrote in a note of congratulations to Kit, "I ran into Behrman Sunday night at Voisin's. He looked shockingly happy. He can't see Hitler for the standees." By midsummer Robert Flemyng couldn't see the standees for Hitler and left the cast to have an operation on a varicose vein, which would make him acceptable for active military service. He returned to England to join up for the duration and was replaced by Tom Helmore.

The standees continued, and when Olivier left the cast to return to England (reporters were told it was pure coincidence that both he and Vivien Leigh were sailing on the *Île de France*), his role was taken on by Francis Lederer, the curly-headed young Czech actor known for his huge success in Dodie Smith's sentimental Tyrolean comedy, *Autumn Crocus*. He was undoubtedly a talented actor whose success was deserved, but his Gaylord Esterbrook was an unhappy piece of casting for which Gert had to assume responsibility. She was the one who went to Chicago to see him in a production of *Seventh Heaven* and sent back word that he was the man they were looking for.

No matter what her personal responses, it was Kit's way to be as considerate of all her leading men as she was of Olivier and Brian Aherne, whom she adored. In a tour of *The Barretts* after World War II, Father Barrett was played by the extraordinary English actor, Wilfred Lawson. In her experience Kit felt she had never been given more truth from an actor. He generated such belief in what he was doing that it was impossible to answer him mechanically with a mere reading of lines; his resourcefulness demanded other actors constantly to rethink and react anew. Out of respect for this great talent, Kit tolerated his excessive drinking, warning him, pleading with him, and finally threatening him. There came a matinee performance in San Francisco when he put his trousers on backwards and, finding it difficult to zip them up, called Gert into his dressing room for help, saying he couldn't go on stage with his trousers unzipped. Only then did Kit find it impossible to keep him in the company, and even then she had the patience to listen to his pleading, the fortitude to witness his tears, and the courtesy to acknowledge his written apologies.

Henry Daniell, her leading man on tour with *That Lady*, was at the time an austere religious zealot and not popular with either the cast or the public. When asked for his autograph at the stage door, he coldly refused. When told by fans "We've seen your pictures," he replied, "I can't help that," and moved on, chin high in arrogance. It was not entirely surprising that he did not get a hand on his first entrance, but it was surprising that he was disheartened and hurt by it. At one performance Kit asked David Orrick, who did not appear in the first act, to go around front and start the applause, and after that it became Orrick's nightly chore. Daniell was a star, and Kit felt he had that courtesy coming to him.

There were no such problems with Francis Lederer, but he was not an easy man, and *No Time for Comedy* lost some of its silken smoothness. His recent marriage to Margo did not seem to be going well (with Gert, as usual, acting as confessor to the bewildered young actress over tearful lunches), and it may have been that he was simply going through a difficult phase of his life. Whatever the cause, he seemed to have left his charm in Dodie Smith's Tyrol and, furthermore, had secured for himself a run-of-the-play contract (which as a rule Gert did not favor, but in this case had magnanimously granted). With half the New York run still to go and a long tour projected after that, Kit saw to it that everyone got along beautifully and that Lederer was made as comfortable as possible. By then she was able to carry the play on her own, filling in with her growing wit for her leading man's odd abrasive lack of it — just as Olivier had filled in for her at the beginning.

At the end of twenty-four weeks, *No Time for Comedy* set out on a tour of more than seven months (two weeks longer than the history-making repertory tour of 1933–1934), playing in fifty-seven cities (Chicago twice), with nine weeks of one-night stands (not consecutive; all told). Professionally her year was looking up, and even the loss of Ray Henderson was somewhat balanced by the addition to the staff of Francis Robinson. Several years before, when Robinson was working on a Nashville newspaper, Ray Henderson had seriously suggested him for his own job, should a successor ever be needed. Since then Robinson had come to New York to work with William Fields in publicity for the Playwrights' Company, his first assignment being to draft the original announcement of the company's formation.

Richard Maney, the most widely known public relations man of the day — perhaps because he always seems to have believed in publicizing himself at least as much as his clients — was the press representative for *Herod and Mariamne*, but he was Ray Henderson's direct opposite and it was not a happy arrangement. He was "chilled" by Miss Cornell, found her performing deficient in "warmth, humor and humanity," and in the line of duty deplored the fact that "you'll not catch Miss Cornell doing cartwheels on the mall." In his autobiography *Fanfare* he explains further that he found "the company of tipplers less trying" and concluded that "Tallulah makes better copy than Katharine Cornell." Guthrie probably hired him because he was supposed to be the best, but he was part of the aberration of that entire production. Publicity for *No Time for Comedy* was handled by the Playwrights' Company and William Fields.

When as a young man Ray Henderson worked in the box office of a theatre in Colorado Springs, it was Allan Attwater who brought him to the attention of Sothern and Marlowe and started him on his career. Now it was Allan Attwater who brought Francis Robinson to Kit's attention, recommending him for his own job as company manager while he fulfilled a prior commitment to the D'Oyly Carte Opera Company. When he returned to *No Time for Comedy*, it was arranged with Fields that Francis Robinson would stay on as press representative for the road tour.

On Easter Sunday in Chicago (the second visit), having met her at the train and checked her into the Drake Hotel, Robinson was helping Kit walk the dogs along the lakefront. It was the coldest day he could remember. She wore a big sheepskin coat. Suddenly she asked how he would like to come into her office. When he said he would like it very much, she said, "Talk to Mr. McClintic." So it was settled, in less than a minute.

Dog-walking was a favorite time for making decisions and exchanging confidences. She told Francis Robinson that day that Moss Hart was writing a play for her, a strange, unconventional play with music in which she would have a chance to do everything — sing, dance, even appear as a child. She was delighted with the prospect. (But when the play was finished, it had acquired a full-length score by Kurt Weill. It became Gertrude Lawrence's *Lady in the Dark*, which ran simultaneously with Katharine Cornell's *The Doctor's Dilemma* in the spring of 1941.)

Linda Esterbrook, known on the stage as Linda Paige, is another variation of Candida, the wise, all-seeing woman behind the strong, gifted, but rather bumbling man. Coming in another era in another society, Linda is not economically dependent on her man, as Candida was on hers, and is therefore all the more wise and all the more all-seeing because more dispassionate and less sentimental. It is these qualities of superiority that infuriate her husband and drive him, temporarily, into the arms of a clinging builder-upper, an artfully sweet and docile inspirer of superior men. As Kit "discovered" her role, Behrman says, "I made a discovery myself; that the woman she was playing *was* Kit, though I had hardly known her when I wrote the part."

Linda did indeed reflect the image of Miss Cornell the Establishment, Miss Cornell the Personage of Ray Henderson's press releases, Miss Cornell the Being in Gert Macy's letters, but if Linda really *was* Kit it was in a way that Behrman, perhaps, did not have in mind and that Kit, perhaps, was not aware of herself and simply projected intuitively: she gave Linda the serene flexibility an emotional woman acquires in order to survive.

It is the action of the play that Gaylord Esterbrook writes an appalling tragedy dealing with death, immortality, and the Spanish Civil War. With adroit lack of action, Linda maintains her opposition yet shifts with the sands of his creativity and his love affair until he is forced by his own talent back to what he writes best — comedy — and by his own need back to the woman he loves most — herself. In appraising Gaylord's play in the third act, Linda says to him:

Your hero says that in Spain he's learned how to die and that now he will practice what he has learned — that does not impress me — that he knows how to die. Millions of people know how to die — in any case it is an art that sooner or later Nature imposes on us all — no, Gay, the difficult thing is to *live* — that requires skill. That requires imagination — that's the index of civilization — the ability to live, not the ability to die. Don't spin for me fantasies of death — imagine for me variations of life.

Kit had been living variations of life since she first learned how to do a balancing act on a slack wire back on Mariner Street. With an early inclination to become all things (rather indiscriminately, as she herself admitted, looking back), she was led by people and circumstances to become a teacher, an athlete, an artist, an actress, a manager, a daughter, wife, godmother — *et aliae* — and passionate friend. With flexibility that came from experience she never gave up being one to become another, accumulating them all in her own skin. As Behrman said, through Linda, that took skill; and Linda knew, from Kit, that it took balance. It required imagination — it was the index of civilization — to become so many disparate individuals, without ever betraying one for the other.

If, as Behrman discovered, the woman she was playing really was Kit, it was due less to his own omniscient writing than it was to her (now) consummate ability to twist a part and make it her own. Perhaps she had perfected her art to the degree that she could now convince a writer that he had written what she created.

Despite the play's great success, not everyone was pleased with the way she twisted this particular part. Brooks Atkinson was. He wrote: "The cast is the most springlike event that a sullen April has borne this season." Of Kit he said, "After two years of silence in New York, which does not enjoy the quiet, Katharine Cornell has returned in all her magnificence playing comedy with effortless skill and personal sincerity — she has been wearing the black vestments so long that we hardly know how beautifully she can manage the smartly colored frocks of comedy. She can manage them superbly."

Other critics were full of praise, but with shadings. The first act of *No Time for Comedy* opened with an amusing telephone scene, and it was this scene that John Mason Brown had in mind when he wrote (in another place), "When she comes through a door you are gladly persuaded she could never have emerged to answer anything so mundane as a telephone but must have emerged because she has a date with destiny." In his review of the play, he wrote, "Although she smiles, her spirit is gay, and she is irresistible, she is not witty. She has found her satisfactory substitutes for comedy, chief among them is her all conquering sincerity."

He proves his own wit by continuing, "She throws away laughs as profligately as Madame Ranevsky threw away money," and many of Kit's closest friends and admirers in the audience on opening night winced at the propensity, murmuring "Poor old Kit" — thereby missing the essence of the performance. To this member of that audience — by then seventeen and rather unsophisticated, granted, in the subtleties of sophisticated comedy — it seems that by looking for the glory that was missing, they missed the glory that was there. Had a great comedienne spoken the speech quoted above, she would have infected the audience with a joy of being alive springing from her knowledge of living and life. Kit, by endowing Linda with her own emotionalism — which Brooks Atkinson and John Mason Brown both called her "sincerity" — communicated joy, too, but it was harder won, springing from an uncanny knowledge of the millions who would know only the art of dying imposed upon them by Nature. A great comedienne would have enchanted the audience. Kit thrilled them.

S. N. Behrman had learned Gaylord Esterbrook's lesson. He stayed with comedy; he dazzled with intellect. But he cannot have been displeased that Kit, in her Valentina gown and her Saint Joan smile, managed to suggest — with brightness — the trembling of his heart.

It was true, as Laura Elliot claimed, that Kit had the talent for attracting the right people at the right time, and sometimes the talent extended to her plays. After somber years with Lucrece, Elsa Brandt, Juliet, Joan, and Oparre, climaxing in the double doom of Mariamne — her own and the play's — it was time for Linda Esterbrook and *No Time for Comedy*. And after her morose sabbatical year, Ray Henderson's death and the virtual extinction of the Hesse family, it was time for laughter outside the theatre, too. Kit always gave back the essential quality that people brought to her. Guthrie brought the art of acting, and she gave him her talent; Ray Henderson brought dedication — "high purpose" — and she assumed her place in the theatre; Gert brought equilibrium, and Kit responded with stability.

But until Nancy Hamilton, co-author of *One for the Money*, the revue Gert had produced, no one had ever brought the simple gift of laughter. Kit always enjoyed the fun in other people, starting back as far as Lowell Sherman's silly antics over *Casanova*, but of those close to her, Guthrie was perhaps too tense and worrying, Gert too soberingly level-headed, Ray Henderson too solemn and reverential.

A generously talented Smith graduate from Sewickley, Pennsylvania, Nancy Hamilton began her writing career in New York with sketches and lyrics for Leonard Sillman's first great *New Faces* revue in 1934. Also a clever actress, she played a small part in *The Warrior's Husband* with Katharine Hepburn, whom she later parodied in a *New Faces* sketch, and acted Miss Bingley in Helen Jerome's dramatization of *Pride and Prejudice* (with Brenda Forbes playing Charlotte Lucas). Considering the smart pertinence of her lyrics, it is not surprising that she wrote a most impertinent critique of *Lucrece*, castigating its pretentiousness, and got it published. A prodigious maker of plans and planner of junkets, an indefatigable mixer, collector, and maker of friends, she has always been unable not to bring people together and loosen them up — to their own delighted surprise. Kit, the most reserved of party-goers, loved the originality of Nancy's gatherings, where no one was given a chance to be reserved. An unsuspecting arrival might be given a nine-inch square of canvas, brushes, tubes of paints, and an inspirational libation before being turned loose to mingle with the other guests; or be handed a long pole with a crosspiece nailed to it and directed, drink in hand, to a trunk of old clothes to make a scarecrow. At a birthday party for Guthrie, who adored having his birthday fussed over, a pink parachute dropped from the sky with his presents.

In the years to come Nancy Hamilton would bring many diverse elements into Kit's life — remarkable new friends, original ideas, challenging quests, not always for amusement. There would be the film on Helen Keller, written by Nancy Hamilton and narrated by Katharine Cornell, which would win an Academy Award; there would be the active support of Kirsten Flagstad's art which the rest of New York refused to hear in postwar political deafness; there would be the preservation of Mme. Flagstad's own translations of lieder, spoken by Katharine Cornell and painstakingly edited on tape by Nancy Hamilton. But however serious the adventure, always the dashing humor. Even in the last wakeful nights of Kit's life, it was Anthony Trollope that her friend read aloud.

As Guthrie brought his art, Gert her probity, and Ray Henderson his aspiration, Nancy Hamilton brought a talent for fun — and has always said she found in Kit one of the funniest women she has ever known.

26

"Kit Cornell
Is Shellin' Peas...!" (1939-1944)

AFTER THE HESSE FAMILY FUNERAL in the winter of 1937, Kit had joined Guthrie in London and at last screwed her courage to the point of meeting George Bernard Shaw. Forced to decline Mrs. Shaw's invitation to lunch because of a full schedule, she called one afternoon instead and later described the meeting: "I was frightfully nervous but Mr. Shaw put me at ease immediately. I expected all sorts of cleverness and snappy rejoinders. But he probably summed me up immediately; saw I wasn't up to it, so he didn't try. He was charming and easy. When I got back to the hotel, Guthrie asked, 'What did he say?' And I said, 'I can't remember a thing.'"

Three years later, Shaw was surprised to learn that Kit wanted to play Jennifer Dubedat in *The Doctor's Dilemma*. Not only was it a nonstarring role but, as he wrote to her and as he had written to Lillah McCarthy before her, Jennifer was "the sort of woman I hate." His favorite female in the play was Minnie Tinwell, the serving girl at the Star and Garter where the doctors congregate in Act Two, "daughter of joy and shyboots, who can steal the play in two minutes if she is put to it. In the original production she was played to perfection by the daughter of an American bishop." He suggested that if the play toured Kit should double in both parts, since there was plenty of time between Jennifer's exit and Minnie Tinwell's entrance to change costumes. As an actress, the two roles would give her a decent night's work, and as a manager she would save a salary. "I could find a dozen Jennifers more easily than I could find one Minnie Tinwell."

In The Doctor's Dilemma, *with Raymond Massey, 1941.*
(New York Public Library, Vandamm Collection)

With Alexander Woolcott and "Illo," 1941.

But Margaret Curtis played the small part of the serving girl at the Star and Garter, and Guthrie surrounded Kit with a stalwart honor guard of leading men: Clarence Derwent, Whitford Kane, Ralph Forbes, Cecil Humphreys, and Colin Keith-Johnston, with Bramwell Fletcher as Jennifer's dying husband and Raymond Massey as the newly knighted Sir Colenso Ridgeon who has the power to save Dubedat's life.

Raymond Massey was at last keeping the promise made to himself in a Cobourg, Ontario, stable in 1914: one day to act on the same stage with Katharine Cornell. What is more, he says, when the time came, she actually saved his career from foundering. He had become so closely associated with the title role of *Abe Lincoln in Illinois* that no one would cast him seriously in any other part, and Kit rescued him from oblivion and/or bad movies. As he likes to put it, he left the stage in a stovepipe hat and under her auspices reentered in a gray top hat.

He repaid her kindness by providing her with one of those in-performance scares she was so good at rising above. In Cincinnati, on the post-Broadway tour, Massey was given a sulfa drug to stave off the flu, which induced a not uncommon period of sulfa-amnesia. Admiring Dubedat's paintings at the end of the first act, he held one up to cover his face and muttered under his breath, "You'd better get the rag down because I don't know where I am or what I am doing or what comes next." Get the rag down, indeed! She sailed on, delivering his lines as well as her own, prefacing his with a waggled finger and "Sush! I know what you're going to say" and then saying it, or, with a laugh, "I can see what is going on in your mind!" and articulating his thoughts. She covered for him so well that in the intermission, a doctor who had been called up from the audience was surprised to be told the actor was having trouble remembering his lines.

Jennifer is a small role, but in one way it is an actress's dream. As the first act begins, she is offstage waiting in Sir Colenso's reception room. For one-half hour a stream of worldly, morning-coated men enter and, having passed her on the way in, talk about her effusively until the audience is in a fever of impatience to see her. And when Kit finally did appear, Guthrie had arranged that she was a sight that topped her buildup. Inspired by fashion plates of 1903, her first-act ensemble was rose-pink crepe de chine, the skirt falling in small accordion pleats from hip to floor, the sleeves from elbow to wrist, with just the suggestion of a bustle or a hoop to flare the skirt; a huge hat, black straw with a brim curving upward at the sides, was laden with cabbage roses of the same pink.

Kit set a record of fifteen weeks for the Shaw play in New York and in the fall took it on the road for fourteen weeks more, visiting twelve cities. Raymond Massey says of her at that time: "Whatever anyone else tells you, Kit ran her own show. They will say everything was managed by those people around her, but it is absolutely not true. She knew everything that was going on and she made all the decisions. At the end of the day you could find her poring over the box office receipts. She was a shrewd and intelligent businesswoman." Rudolf Besier had given her the same credit back as far as the motion-picture sale of *The Barretts of Wimpole Street*, but such protestations of her business acumen may actually have been tributes to an organization so smooth running that it did not seem to exist, like the engine of a Rolls-Royce.

In discussing terms for the production of *The Doctor's Dilemma*, Shaw wrote to her: "I notice that you take a percentage on profits. Have you noticed that I take a percentage on receipts? There may be no profits; and there are always receipts; and the profits can never exceed the receipts. And the receipts can always be ascertained, whereas it may take ten lawsuits to settle what the profits are." He seems to be treating her as a business equal (a rare equality in his eyes), but then he acknowledges the organization around her by adding, "Ask Guthrie whether he has considered this." His afterthought is interesting, not so much because of his fear that he had given a woman — even Katharine Cornell, from the cradle of the human race — credit for too much sense, but because of something Conger Goodyear once wrote about his first meeting with Shaw: "He warned me that, in the long run, no one could make money producing, and advised me to see that Kit put her profits in annuities or sound securities. He seemed to assume that I was her 'protector.' I didn't disabuse him." Of course Conger Goodyear didn't disabuse Shaw, because he, too, liked to think of himself as Kit's protector. And what is more, Kit probably encouraged him to. But then note that Shaw, having been led to believe that Goodyear was Kit's protector, has the wisdom to sense that she would like him to think of Guthrie as her protector, and advises her to consult him rather than Goodyear. And all the time it was Gert who was actually putting Kit's profits into annuities or sound securities.

From that round robin of tact and concealment, it seems clear that at the time of Raymond Massey's keen observation and conclusion, Kit had become more an accomplished executive than the "shrewd businesswoman" he suggests, not alone because of her evident ability to delegate authority, but because of her ability — through the persuasive charm of her magnetic influence — to delegate the illusion of authority. Where one began and the other ended, and exactly who was protecting whom, from this distance and through such protective veils it is impossible to say.

The Establishment — the entity known as Katharine Cornell — was functioning so smoothly that even failure could be absorbed without serious shock, even a failure as great as *Rose Burke*, by the French playwright Henry Bernstein. It was the second of only three plays in her career that she did not bring to New York.

After seeing her play Elizabeth Barrett, Bernstein had said he would write a play for her, and when Conger Goodyear was in Paris negotiating with André Obey for the rights to *Lucrece*, Bernstein described the play he had in mind. Goodyear reported, "I think it had spirits in it. I preferred *Lucrece*."

Bernstein was a boulevardier with wild ideas, most of which became boulevard plays sooner or later. He was prolific, dramatic, and theatrically persuasive. Through the years he sent pressing love letters to Kit, flowers, pronouncements, and promises, and at last, during the run of *The Doctor's Dilemma*, appeared in New York with the play he had promised, or at least half of it. His arrival followed upon his escape from France as a refugee from the Nazis, and of course he appeared wrapped in a combustive dramatic aura with tales of smuggling his private art collection out of the country by sending himself a tire — *un pneumatique* — with the canvases rolled up inside.

His play was no longer about spirits but about the complicated emotional life of a glamorous sculptress who in her big scene smashes a plaster figure of Britannia. In honor of the great American actress who would play his wild Gallic Rose, he was writing the play directly in English, instead of first writing it in French and then having it translated. Once arrived and settled at the Waldorf, he frequently summoned Kit to his suite to hear new scenes, additions, and revisions, always convincing her and Guthrie that he knew infallibly what held and what didn't hold on the stage. The plan was to put *Rose Burke* into rehearsal in New York after *The Doctor's Dilemma's* post-Broadway tour.

On Monday, December 8, 1941, the day after the bombing of Pearl Harbor, *The Doctor's Dilemma* began its second week at the Curran Theatre, San Francisco. It was almost the only entertainment in town not to be canceled, and Kit, Francis Robinson, Eveline Drysdale, and two dachshunds walked down from the Fairmont Hotel in a complete blackout, unable to see one step ahead. The theatre held eleven hundred people, and that night three hundred and forty-seven groped their way to their seats. The blackout was over before the performance ended, and from then on there were only dimouts, but a notice was posted in the theatre that in the event of a blackout prior to the eight-thirty curtain, the curtain would be held one-half hour past the all-clear signal. The management promised to refund money if patrons were unable to attend and returned the tickets within forty-eight hours after the missed performance. The box office receipts dropped by half in the second week, and *The Doctor's Dilemma* concluded its tour while a dazed public drew breath and groped for the rhythm of wartime existence.

Since they were there, the McClintics decided to stay on the West Coast and go into production immediately for *Rose Burke*, opening it in San Francisco and touring it back across the country to New York. Guthrie having had his way with Jennifer Dubedat's clothes, to say nothing of Linda Esterbrook's, Rose Burke was Gert's turn. They had met with Main Bocher in Chicago, and he now came to San Francisco with his best fitter. Donald Oenslager came out to supervise the construction of his sets and find the necessary furniture in the local antique shops. Gert herself was dispatched to New York to escort the excitable playwright across the country.

The play was not well received. Critics and audiences, distracted by war news, were impatient with boulevard drama. Jean Pierre Aumont, playing Kit's lover, received the most favorable reviews which, considering the natural ineptitude of his debut performance in English, was an implied criticism of the rest of the production. Even bucking cross-country opposition, the Cornell name was bringing in money at the box office, but it was Pittsburgh and *Herod and Mariamne* all over again; she could not impose on her New York audiences, or let them down, with an inferior play. Kit smashed her last Britannia in Toronto.

After Pearl Harbor the energies of the entire country were directed toward the war effort, and in the theatre Katharine Cornell was one of the first to volunteer her services. Taking no time to indulge in regrets over the failure of *Rose Burke*, she decided on a revival of *Candida* at the Shubert Theatre for the benefit of the Army Emergency Fund and the Navy Relief Society. The production was under the auspices of The American Theatre Wing War Services, Inc.

Candida had become so closely associated with her that when *Theatre Arts Monthly*, a literate and un-show-businesslike magazine, printed a full-page color photograph of her in Candida's red dress, sitting in a Victorian chair with her cheek resting on her hand, no caption was needed to identify either the actress or the play; the legend simply read: "In her most endearing role." Of the five versions of *Candida* that she eventually performed, this one (the fourth) was considered to be definitive — the most perfectly cast and acted, the most star-studded, and the most popular. Raymond Massey played Morell, Burgess Meredith was Marchbanks, Mildred Natwick was Prossy, and Dudley Digges, who had directed her first *Candida* in 1925, was Mr. Burgess.

It has never been unusual for actors to donate their services, as they all did for this production, but for the Shuberts to give the theatre rent free and for the stagehands' union to waive compensation for its members suggests how completely the country was rising to the war effort. Even Shaw waived his royalties, an absolutely unheard-of concession. And the musicians' union did not make them hire an orchestra.

The original idea was to give a series of four matinees and one Sunday evening performance, but each of the performances played to standees up to the limit of the law, and so many crowds were turned away, so many mail orders rejected (a thousand a day) that a second week was added to the schedule, and then two more weeks. Still it was not enough, and twelve additional performances were given, with Ernest Cossart taking over the role of Mr. Burgess and Brenda Forbes stepping into her old familiar role of Prossy. Finally, the production was taken to Washington for one week's engagement at the National

Two views of *Candida*, the 1942 all-star production.
Burgess Meredith as Marchbanks (Bob Golby)
Raymond Massey as Morell (Bob Golby)

Theatre. At popular prices of $1.10 to $4.40, the Army Emergency Fund and the Navy Relief Society each received $36,817, while the American Theatre Wing received almost $10,000.

Burgess Meredith was already a private in the Army, on special orders to be in the play. After a performance in Washington there was a knock on his dressing-room door and he yelled out, "Who the hell is that?" From the other side of the door came a clipped answer, "General Marshall to see Private Meredith!" Private Meredith, the story goes, snapped to attention in his undershorts to receive the congratulations of the Army Chief of Staff.

Ruth Gordon wanted Guthrie to do *The Three Sisters* so that she could play Masha. It was typical of him that he took her suggestion but gave Masha to Kit; it was typical of Ruth Gordon that she didn't take offense and was delighted to play Natasha, the sisters' intrusive sister-in-law. To round out what surely would have been the most theatrically aristocratic cast of the decade, Guthrie invited Alfred Lunt to play Virshinin, Masha's lover, and Lynn Fontanne to play the smaller, more neglected role of Olga, the eldest sister. Lunt jumped at the idea, contributing with enthusiasm the thought that Lynn would be better as Masha, while Kit, with her emotionalism, would bring a new and surprising dimension to Olga, the spinster schoolmistress. Guthrie's explosion rocked 23 Beekman Place.

Kit herself was pleased with the idea of playing Olga, who had fewer lines, but Guthrie was damned if he would direct the play unless she played Masha. Lunt acquiesced, but the plan broke down at Miss Fontanne who, while perfectly willing to play Olga, felt that every time Lunt embraced Kit — with herself peering at them from behind a pillar — the audience would laugh.

The two actors finally settled on instead of the Lunts were in no way a compromise: Judith Anderson as Olga and Dennis King as Vershinin. Gertrude Musgrove, a young English actress who had made a success the year before in a play about a blitzed London music hall, was chosen for Irina; Edmund Gwenn played Chebutykin, the old army doctor, and Alexander Knox played the Baron. Other roles were taken by Tom Powers, McKay Morris, and Eric Dressler, and there were always the newcomers at the bottom of every Katharine Cornell cast list — Gregory Peck had toured as "a secretary" in *The Doctor's Dilemma*, and in *The Three Sisters* "an orderly" was played by Kirk Douglas.

Clifford Odets had been preparing a translation which seems to have gotten lost in the shuffle, and Valentina suggested that Guthrie acquire the services of Alexander Koiransky, a scholar and critic in Moscow before the revolution, a fine artist who had known the Moscow Art players.

The work took six months. Koiransky would translate aloud from the Russian text while a secretary took it down in English. Guthrie questioned all nuances, to the translator's annoyance, but since his experience with *Romeo and Juliet* Guthrie was not hampered by tradition and insisted that Koiransky clarify the exact meaning and intention of every word. Thus they evolved an extremely workable — and if not colloquial, at least speakable — play. Woollcott, a fussbudget when it came to words, said he wasn't even conscious of its being a translation.

Koiransky was helpful in other ways, even in casting. Andrey, the three sisters' brother and Natasha's husband, is spoken of in the text as being stout, but Guthrie could find no stout actor who was also suitable emotionally. Koiransky explained that Chekhov had so described the character because the actor he wanted to play it in the Moscow Art Theatre was fattish. Eventually, when that actor left the troupe and another actor took over his role, all "fat" references were taken out of the dialogue. Guthrie took them out, too, and cast slim Eric Dressler whom he had wanted all along. Koiransky unearthed the march used in the last act in the original Moscow production, and did much to infuse the production with authentic atmosphere. Apparently without contract, he was paid what amounted to an honorarium, which would seem shockingly inadequate to a writer today. But when the production became a success — unexpectedly, for no one really expected Chekhov to be financially profitable, especially in wartime — the scholar was found teaching Russian literature out west and on several occasions bonuses were sent to him.

Washington, D.C., was crowded, unpredictable, and an exciting place to be when *The Three Sisters* tried out there in December 1942.

Gert's sister Louise had worked in Paris as fashion editor for *Harper's Bazaar* until the office was closed by the war in 1939. Returning to the United States (and refusing to work any longer for a Hearst

The Three Sisters: *Katharine Cornell with Gertrude Musgrove, Ruth Gordon (standing), and Judith Anderson, 1942. (New York Public Library, Vandamm Collection)*

publication), she went into war work where she met and married Harry Hopkins, special assistant to President Roosevelt. In wartime, such figures had more romantic glamour than theatre people, and in a party with Mrs. Roosevelt and Maxim Litvinov, the Soviet ambassador, Mr. and Mrs. Hopkins vied with the actors for radiance at the opening of *The Three Sisters.*

Later in the play's stand, invited by the Hopkinses to supper, Kit, Guthrie, Gert, and David Orrick found themselves standing in a blizzard outside the National Theatre with no way to get there. Even Orrick's second lieutenant's uniform was ineffectual. In wartime, taxis simply did not materialize, not even for Katharine Cornell, an intolerable situation to Gert Macy who stepped in front of the next passing vehicle and informed the young officer behind the wheel, "I have Katharine Cornell here!" "Sure, lady," he replied, "and I'm Dwight David Eisenhower." It was futile of him to resist, for Gert piled her charges into his car and when he meekly asked "Where to?" and was told "The White House!", he was convinced he was being abducted by a band of maniacs.

———

The cast of *The Three Sisters* was so heavy that they were billed alphabetically in publicity, always with "and Miss Cornell" at the bottom, while in the program for the New York opening on December 21, 1942, it was easier — and more fitting — not to bill anyone at all, to feature the play instead of the players. Backstage, a management that prided themselves on upholding theatrical tradition and respecting each actor's rightful place in the hierarchy found the hierarchy not easy to determine.

Because of Edmund Gwenn's age (sixty-seven) and years in the theatre (forty-seven), he deserved (certainly did not demand) greater veneration than Dennis King (forty-five years of age, with twenty-five of them in the theatre), but Dennis King rated (certainly did not demand) first consideration because he was a bigger star. And whereas King's rank could have been pulled over Ruth Gordon, it could not be forgotten that she had been billed over him in *A Doll's House* — if only because Nora *has* to be the star of that play — and where did he stand in context with Judith Anderson: before or after? higher or lower? equal? Equality only made the problem more difficult. Edmund Gwenn and Ruth Gordon were, perhaps, the same size stars, but which should be given preference — his years or her sex? The assignment of dressing rooms took as much diplomacy as the Atlantic Charter.

The Ethel Barrymore Theatre had two dressing rooms on the ground floor — at stage level — forming a kind of suite consisting of one grand dressing room and a smaller receiving room or antechamber, the whole meant for one grand personage such as the theatre's namesake, or a couple such as the Lunts. Traditionally it was a sign of stardom to dress on the ground floor, at stage level. There were five accredited stars in *The Three Sisters*, three of whom would have to dress on the second floor. Which three?

It was the kind of problem Gert tackled with relish and authority. Since the key to a congenial arrangement of actors obviously rested in the placement of Miss Cornell, Kit was banished forthwith to dressing room #3 on the second floor. Judith Anderson and Ruth Gordon, who were fortunately compatible, were given #1 and #2 on the ground floor, Dennis King was billeted on the second floor in #4, and Edmund Gwenn in #5. On the afternoon of the opening, King's dresser, arriving at the theatre to arrange the master's amenities, greeted the arrangement with a chilly, "Mr. King does not go upstairs," until he saw Eveline Drysdale laying out Kit's amenities — upstairs.

After the opening of *The Three Sisters* it would have been impossible for Kit to receive her visitors on the second floor in dressing room #3, not only because the traffic jam on the staircase would have been unmanageable (hers mixing with Dennis King's and "Teddy" Gwenn's), but because so many of her first-night friends were from Buffalo, elderly friends of the family who simply could not negotiate stairs. Kit solved the puzzle by standing in the middle of the stage to receive. Among the well-wishers was Ruth Gordon's thirteen-year-old son, Jones, who had not been to a play before.

"You're Ruth Gordon's son, aren't you?" Kit asked, leaning forward to shake hands. He admitted that he was. "Wasn't your mother wonderful?" she prompted.

"I thought you were all good."

Those who were there agreed it was one time in her life when Kit met her match in charm, and the critics could have used him as their reference, for he summarized all their glorious celebrations the next day. For all their fine words, Jones put it best: the actors were all good.

After one hundred and twenty-two performances in New York, *The Three Sisters* went on the road, running from beginning to end a total of thirty-nine weeks, the longest run any Chekhov play had achieved in the United States, and the longest run for *The Three Sisters* anywhere.

Kit had always been surrounded by fine contemporary actresses in supporting roles — Edith Evans, Margalo Gillmore, Brenda Forbes, Mildred Natwick, Joyce Carey, Margaret Barker. But until *The Three Sisters* the big guns playing opposite her had been men — Brian Aherne, Laurence Olivier, Raymond Massey, Burgess Meredith, Charles Waldron, all the way back to Leslie Howard. In *The Three Sisters*, for the first time, she was face to face, on equal terms, with the formidable talents of Judith Anderson and Ruth Gordon. It was undoubtedly a delight for Guthrie to have his three favorite actresses on the same stage, but it may also have made him more protective of Kit than usual. White, at that time, was almost never used on the stage because the audience's eye is drawn to it in hypnotic fascination. In the third act (the second in the McClintics' production), while Kirsanov Street blazes outside the windows, Masha, according to the text, rests her head on a cushion which she carries with her when she moves restlessly around the room. In most productions it is a sofa cushion, covered in dark green or brown, and unobtrusive. Guthrie put into Kit's hands — against Masha's black dress — a white bed pillow. It could be defended by pointing out that the scene takes place in the sisters' bedroom.

Actually, Kit did not need such theatrics, for she brought to Masha a quality that every actress since then seems to go out of her way to deny: nobility. Nobility of spirit without ostentation. Without it, Masha is a bored suburban housewife having a fling with an army officer. Kit denied that Masha and Virshinin went so far as to have a physical love affair, a concept other actresses would scoff at, but when she came into the final scene with a haunted face, searching for "my man" — a phrase later actresses seem to abhor as much as the emotion of the moment — perhaps because of her frustration she was a bereaved specter on the verge of madness. Kit's Masha was the sister the audience came away remembering, which is the way Chekhov put the play together; in later, more "realistic" productions, either Olga or Irina is often more memorable because she is less ordinary.

Kit's Masha was also extraordinary in that she found, played, and savored the wit. Masha is written as a woman with far more wit than anyone around her, certainly more than Virshinin, and even — especially — her sisters. It is one of her prides. There are two specific, very obvious instances. In the first act when she is so bored that she decides to go home before the tedium of lunch begins, she listens to Virshinin expound at length on the beautiful effect the sisters' lives will have on the village in two or three hundred years, she pauses, removes her hat pin, and announces, "I'll stay to lunch." Kit played the moment with a timing S. N. Behrman would have been proud of. The second instance occurs when the sisters watch Natasha come in one door, cross the stage and exit through another, whereupon Masha comments, after another Behrman pause, "She walks as if she started the fire."

In another less important but not negligible way, Kit made Masha her own. Of all the Mashas from Chekhov to the present, she was surely the best whistler.

In 1925, *The Green Hat* drew references in the current musicals; fifteen years later Katharine Cornell herself was supplying material for comedians and nightclub entertainers.

On tour Kit once stayed in a hotel where Sophie Tucker was opening a cabaret act and suggested to Stanley Gilkey that they attend the opening. Past her prime, Miss Tucker made a new career out of being "the last of the red-hot mamas!" Growing fat and old and losing her voice gave her a whole new repertoire of jokes, sentimental stories, and monologues from the point of view of "us old girls." "Speaking of old girls," she ad libbed that night, "I see we have in our midst one of the great old girls of show business — Kit Cornell!" Kit was made to stand and take a bow — a fellow red-hot mama — and after the show stood in the lobby signing Sophie Tucker's record album because Sophie Tucker told her to. She was ten years younger than Miss Tucker.

The choicest unofficial accolade in all show business came early in the 1940s when she was written into a Cole Porter lyric. Noting the trend out of the city and back to the country chronicled by Kaufman and Hart in *George Washington Slept Here*, and never one to let a fad or a fashion go unmocked, Porter wrote for Danny Kaye to sing in *Let's Face It*:

Farming, that's the fashion,
Farming, that's the passion
Of our great celebrities of today.
Kit Cornell is shellin' peas,
Lady Mendl's climbin' trees,
*Dear Mae West is at her best in the hay.**

Cole Porter probably meant the image of the First Lady of the American Theatre shelling peas to be wittily outlandish, when in truth it was quite accurate, in fact, understated. She had settled in at Martha's Vineyard not only because she loved it but because — for once — everyone she loved loved it. She couldn't make them all love one another, but it helped if they all loved being in the same place. She even brought Laura Elliot to the Vineyard to stay one summer, and when Mrs. Elliot died in 1940, her ashes were buried under a juniper tree by the front door of Chip Chop.

Not since Buffalo had Kit become involved in community activities, but at Martha's Vineyard she pitched on the local baseball team in a game to benefit the Martha's Vineyard Hospital, and sang a solo in a benefit for the local U.S.O. at the Vineyard Haven High School.

With the onset of wartime shortages, vegetable patches called "victory gardens" were springing up across the country. Kit bought an acre of land nearby on Lake Tashmoo with a tumbledown barn, and was soon farming so seriously that she borrowed a stable and farmer's cottage to house the chickens she acquired, the two pigs, and the elderly horse named Silver. She bought a separator and a sterilizer and soon had all the equipment needed to run a good-sized dairy, all for a cow named Winnie that she milked every morning, cajoling Guthrie into holding a pan or operating the sterilizer. With the acute gasoline shortage, Silver was hitched to a buggy and driven to town once a week for supplies, at least until he got sick and had to be shot. Not only was Kit Cornell shellin' peas, she and Nancy were plantin' 'em, along with beans and carrots, and priding themselves on the smallest, tenderest baby scallions, beets no larger than large peas, and corn so tiny and tender that hearty eaters didn't know if they were biting into the kernel or the cob.

Her farming was typical of all wartime existence, random, without

* Copyright 1941 by Chappell & Co., Inc. Copyright renewed.

much sense of sequence or consequence, which may explain why Kit embarked on what was probably the most inconsequential play of her career, *Lovers and Friends*, by Dodie Smith. It was a charming, genteel, marital mix-up kind of play, a triangle — or rectangle or pentangle — involving Raymond Massey, Henry Daniell, Carol Goodner, and Anne Burr.

Its literary quality is best defined by a line of Carol Goodner's — "Don't you ever take out your youth and play with it?" — which everyone wanted to cut except Guthrie, who took a strong liking to it. Raymond Massey recalls that at every tryout performance Carol Goodner would realize the line was coming about five lines earlier and begin to giggle, at the same time struggling to control herself. By the time she got to the line itself, tears were streaming down her face and she uttered it in a strangled voice, which the enthralled audience interpreted as some peculiar emotional emphasis. Kit kept saying, loyal to Guthrie and the author, "The line's a hazard, a risk we must take." Abruptly, on the eve of the New York opening, she had Carol Goodner cut it.

The day after the New York opening on November 29, 1943, George Jean Nathan wrote: "To praise Miss Cornell and her company for their performance in a play to which they were so embarrassingly superior would be to praise the Notre Dame backfield for a performance against Miss Spence's school." Nevertheless, it ran for twenty-nine weeks in New York and, even with wartime travel restrictions, toured for six weeks. After *No Time for Comedy* it was her fourth most profitable production, but it was the last play of her career that audiences in New York would flock to simply because she was in it. She had never used — or mis-used or abused — that loyalty, but had she chosen to bring *Herod and Mariamne* or *Rose Burke* to New York they might have had healthy, successful runs because of her name and, more importantly, her presence.

After the war, the world would be changed.

In the sum total of her plays, *Lovers and Friends* is one that even her most ardent admirers are inclined to forget that she ever did.

27

The Barracks
of Wimpole Street (1944-1945)

It was Margalo Gillmore who, through her friendship with the American Theatre Wing's Antoinette Perry (for whom the "Tony" Award was named), paved the way for Kit's eventual significant contribution to the war effort.

The American Theatre Wing (its name a double-edged play on the word "wing" as a tactical unit of the new Army Air Forces and as behind-the-scenes work space in a theatre) had successfully sponsored *Candida*. Kit then waived her prejudice against movie acting to appear with Tallulah Bankhead, Edgar Bergen, Benny Goodman, Merle Oberon, Yehudi Menuhin, Alfred Lunt, Lynn Fontanne, and Ina Ray Hutton's All-Girl Orchestra in *Stage Door Canteen*, a celebration of the Wing's center for enlisted servicemen on West Forty-fourth Street where the theatre great were serving the troops as waiters, countermen, dishwashers, and entertainers. In Kit's vignette, she spoke a few lines from *Romeo and Juliet* to Lon McAllister, while serving him an orange.

The Wing was anxious to use its share of the film's proceeds to send a stage production to the armed forces overseas that would represent the best the American theatre had to offer. When asked for an opinion by her friend Antoinette Perry, Margalo Gillmore suggested Kit, who was in Philadelphia touring in *Lovers and Friends*.

Kit's first — and only — thought was to take *The Barretts of Wimpole Street*, and she hesitated only long enough to determine that Brian Aherne was available to play Browning. Despite the wartime shortage of actors, and perhaps because of the prestigious aura that immediately surrounded the venture, the rest of the cast fell easily into place: Brenda Forbes as Wilson, Margalo Gillmore as Arabel, McKay Morris as Edward Moulton-Barrett, and Margalo's husband, Robert Ross, doubling as a Barrett brother and one of Elizabeth's doctors. By further doubling and the elimination of two Barrett brothers, the cast was reduced from eighteen to thirteen.

Guthrie had revived his acting career in *The Three Sisters* by playing the drunken army doctor for four weeks while Edmund Gwenn was out of the cast with pneumonia. In *Me and Kit* he admits modestly that he was "very good indeed" and documents his claim with a list of actors, actresses, and writers who came backstage to agree with him. His acting luck was holding. If he wanted to go overseas with Kit he had to pull his weight and fill his space — he had to have a job to perform. He did not need much urging to accept the part of the Barrett family physician, Dr. Chambers. Nancy Hamilton took on the job of wardrobe mistress. She also arranged, rehearsed, acted, and sang in the small musical revue to be performed by cast members in hospital wards wherever they went. Antoinette Perry's daughter Elaine was taken on as stage manager, and William Noon as technician. Everyone was given the assimilated rank of captain, and with Gert Macy as the ranking general manager, they numbered seventeen. Small as the group was, it still was twice the size of the average U.S.O. troupe. The set was simplified to a drape with insets for windows, fireplace and door. To save every possible inch of space and every conceivable ounce of weight, Flush was played by a Yorkshire terrier not half the size of a spaniel.

The American Theatre Wing was paying for the production, and the U.S. Army's only responsibility would be to transport, billet, and feed the company. Nevertheless, the Special Service Division — and the U.S.O. — aside from complaining about the size of the troupe, made it quite clear that they did not think G.I.'s overseas (or anywhere, for that matter) would want to see a three-hour costume drama about the literary love affair of two middle-aged Victorian poets and insisted that the play be screened at Mitchell Field on Long Island before an audience of twenty-five hundred G.I.'s. Not to increase the actors' nerves, they were told it was a routine tryout — like Philadelphia. After the performance, the local Special Service Captain volunteered the following report to his superior at the Special Service Division headquarters in New York:

1. It is believed that your office would be interested to know of the very many calls which we received after the presentation by Miss Katharine Cornell and Mr. Brian Aherne in *The Barretts of Wimpole Street*.

2. Such a situation has never come up before. All the many calls received were high in their praise, and the various individuals stated that they were anxiously looking forward to entertainment of this sort from time to time.

3. The ovation given the cast by those attending the performance together with the many compliments offered for several days thereafter to this office seems to indicate that this kind of entertainment is definitely practical.

What had been unwieldy a few days before was now deemed practical, with the stipulation that an alternate play be prepared — a ribald farce, if possible — in case of the dismal failure that was still predicted. *Blithe Spirit* was as far as Miss Cornell would go, with good parts for seven members of her company but nothing for herself since, in that exigency, she would not be considered hilarious or bawdy enough to participate. *The Barretts of Wimpole Street* unit — or "the B.O.W.S.," as it came to be known in the army's acronymic jargon — was dispatched to Camp Patrick Henry, Virginia, where the actors christened their quarters "the barracks of Wimpole Street." After indoctrination, they departed the Hampton Roads Port of Embarkation aboard the S.S. *General Meigs* on August 11, 1944, under orders to NATOUSA, the North African Theater of the United States Army, which, with the mysterious logic of the military, landed them in Naples.

After four performances in Santa Maria, a small town fifteen miles north of Naples, the army brass conceded that the venture seemed to be working. The G.I.'s lined up three hours ahead of time for each performance to be sure of getting seats, and they lined up again afterwards to say hello to the actors and thank them, with Kit insisting they be allowed backstage, contrary to Military Police regulations for all previous U.S.O. productions. The actors were told time and again "It was like a letter from home" and "It was like a family reunion." One tough paratrooper, who had apparently seen the show once, came back with a buddy and was heard to crow triumphantly on the way out, "Didn't I tell you it was better than a whorehouse?"

Only then was the venture pronounced an official success. Kit and Brian had originally committed themselves to two weeks overseas.

On wartime tour, Italy, 1944. Katharine Cornell at the wheel. Clockwise from her: Gertrude Macy, Margalo Gillmore, Brenda Forbes, Nancy Hamilton. (U. S. Army Air Force Photo)

Brian Aherne and Katharine Cornell with busts of the Brownings in Florence, 1944.

After performances in Caserta, the next stop after Santa Maria, they were asked to stay six months and agreed so quickly that they might only have been waiting to be asked.

During that six-month period, from August 1944 through January 1945, Margalo Gillmore wrote long, detailed letters home to Patricia Collinge, the actress and writer, and later the letters formed the basis for a book called *The B.O.W.S.*, published in 1945, recounting the story of the tour from beginning to end. A collaboration of the two women but written in the first person from Margalo Gillmore's point of view, the book is as moving and funny today as it was then and supplied much of the information for the telegraphic summary of the tour that follows.

After Caserta, Bagnoli; billeted in Naples, twenty minutes away. Kit and Guthrie celebrate their twenty-third wedding anniversary, a special one for superstitious Guthrie, since they have lived all twenty-three years at 23 Beekman Place. At Bagnoli's Receiving Hospital, the troupe's first performances, under Nancy's direction, as ward entertainers.

Kit's first plane ride across the boot of Italy from Naples to Foggia, at the mercy of a pilot so eager to make it a memorable experience for her that — among other tricks and stunts — he dangles her, and everyone else, in breathless suspense over the crater of Mount Vesuvius. Her gracious, rattled but smiling thanks to him: "It was wonderful — and so *terribly* interesting when we flew right over the equator."

Down to Bari, Lecce, then up to Rome. A special audience with the Pope for members of the cast, and a special performance of the play for civilians at ten-thirty one morning, the performance dedicated to the memory of Eleonora Duse.

Siena. Florence. Another "twenty-three" for Guthrie: the number of performances for the Fifth Army. A visit to the dark, cramped apartment where Robert Browning and Elizabeth Barrett lived. A wedding in the company: Betty Brewer (Bella Hedley) to Lt. Robert Hester, whom she met on the ship crossing the Atlantic. Of the bride's immediate family, Guthrie gives her away, Brenda Forbes is her attendant, and Kit gives the wedding supper.

A communication from General Mark Clark asks if Miss Cornell can be in Montecatini in twenty-four hours to give performances at a newly organized rest camp. Her reply is yes. After seven performances there, the company is given a citation by General Clark for excellence in performance, merit, and discipline. Presenting the plaque on stage, he says that from the start he was sure of the first two excellences, and when Miss Cornell appeared on twenty-four hours' notice with her entire troupe ready to work, he was sure of the third. Everybody authorized to wear Fifth Army shoulder patch.

Leghorn. Marseilles. Scenery, following by sea, marooned on rocks. The company transferred to the aegis of General Eisenhower, who will book them through France. Guthrie returns to the United States to fulfill professional commitments, taking home with him telephone numbers of two hundred and sixty-three three G.I.'s, with instructions to call their families and "Just tell them I'm okay." Wind changes, allowing scenery to float off rocks, as it changed on banks of Loire, allowing Joan to lead her forces on to Orléans. Performances resume.

Dijon, nine performances. Vittel, N.E. France, seven performances beginning December 23. Nancy's Christmas party revives flagging spirits. Prepared for bombing, but spared. Town eight miles distant badly hit. December 28, the Battle of the Bulge.

Versailles, January 3, 1945.

Paris. Gertrude Stein and Alice B. Toklas wish to see the play, but performances strictly limited to enlisted personnel and officers. Nancy and Gert supply Stein and Toklas with G.I. raincoats and o.d. visored caps. Poet and companion sit in box, passing as U.S. military personnel with assimilated rank of captains, wearing Fifth Army shoulder patches. No one the wiser.

Kit told she has done enough for one war, asked by top brass to relax and spend the remainder of tour of duty in Paris. She asks to be sent as close to the front as possible.

Maastrich, Holland, as close to the front as possible: twenty miles.

Heerlen, Holland, even closer: eight miles.

Rheims, where Joan the Maid crowned the Dauphin King of France, climaxing her life. Last performance of the B.O.W.S., its one hundred and fortieth, climaxing tour.

Twenty-four hours in London — the Lunts give a matinee to the sound of V-2's exploding — Clemence Dane gives a surprise party — Glasgow and the homeward voyage, January 31, 1945, aboard the U.S. Hospital Ship, the S.S. *Queen Mary*.

Gert had assured the top-ranking brass in the War Department that Miss Cornell was aware of the discomforts and hardships involved in the proposed tour and fully prepared to endure them. And yet Gert was the one to bristle at the treatment Kit received, starting at Camp Patrick Henry where she bunked with twenty other women in enlisted WAC barracks, sharing a latrine (no doors on the toilets, public showers) with two other barracks, despite the existence of two cottages next to the commanding officer's for visiting celebrities, one occupied by an Italian general while the other sat empty.

Colonel Frank McCarthy, Secretary of the War Department, General Staff, had a theatrical background, having once been press representative for George Abbott. He had told Gert that Kit would be infinitely more comfortable crossing the ocean on the S.S. *General Meigs* than on a plane for two sleepless nights. This turned out to be untrue. On board ship, Kit was once again bunked in with twelve other women in a small cabin (actually the isolation ward of the ship's hospital) without a single closet. Coast Guard officers on board lived in the most luxurious accommodations, and, as if to rub it in, Kit was invited to their quarters frequently for before-dinner refreshments.

From the start Kit, at fifty-one, accepted what she was given and did what she was told, always with her consistent attitude of "business as usual," whatever came along. On the S.S. *General Meigs* Brian Aherne and the men in the company had better quarters than the women, with a table and chairs, and each man — there were only six in the cabin — was given a locker. In fact, wherever they went there was a tendency for Brian Aherne to be given spontaneous preferential treatment because he was immediately recognized as a movie star, whereas Kit's name might have been known to some, but her face to very few. It would have been natural to resent being penalized for her single-minded dedication to the theatre, but she was as grateful — and amused — as everyone else that Aherne's status as a movie star (and Brenda's, since she had appeared recently in *Mrs. Miniver*) sometimes resulted in special treats for the others.

By the middle of the tour, however, her popularity had spread from one army installation to the next and she was famous in Italy. Under the headline "Actress in Hot Water," the *New York Times* reported:

ROME, Dec. 4 (U.P.) — Katharine Cornell . . . rated number one of the "bathtub circuit", proving a bigger draw than fourteen generals, a king, seven Italian counts and a Sardinian acrobat.

The bathtub circuit — in local, heatless parlance — is the vital hot-water artery in Rome's swank Grand Hotel, where one's importance is measured by the amount and temperature of hot water allowed to circulate. With the acuteness of the current fuel shortage, the hotel fires the boiler only when the staff deems one of its guests a very important person.

Thus Miss Cornell rates number one on the hot parade, with the hotel permitting the circulation of hot water both morning and afternoon for a solid week. Naturally, the hotel's other patrons are grateful to her, as are Rome's theatregoers for her performance in *The Barretts of Wimpole Street*.

Miss Cornell's only serious challengers to date have been Gen. George C. Marshall, United States Army Chief of Staff, and Prime Minister Winston Churchill.

The G.I. dysentery caught up with the troupe as early as Lecce, and the actors were laid low at such a rate and were doubling up for each other in performance so frequently that Guthrie said soon they would have to call the play *The Barrett of Wimpole Street*, and the Barrett left standing would be Elizabeth and the actress who played her, whose well-known hypochondria at home sometimes inspired her associates to say she had "never known a well day." Every day was a well day for her up through Italy to Marseilles, where the scenery was lost and performances had to be delayed. First they tried giving the play without scenery, props, or costumes in the hospital at Aix. As Margalo Gillmore remembers it in *The B.O.W.S.*, "It was an odd performance, all of us in our olive drab uniforms, Elizabeth Barrett reclining in shirt and army blouse instead of trailing gown, drinking porter from a lily cup instead of a silver tankard, holding a piece of kleenex in lieu of a lacy handkerchief." It didn't work, and frustrated, feeling they had disappointed the men in the audience "with cages covering the stumps of their missing feet," Kit at last succumbed and "felt so ill that they persuaded her to stay in the hospital." Apparently her sinus had been acting up for some time (as had everybody's), for an operation was found necessary. The minute the errant scenery extricated itself from the rocks and blew into port, she came out of the hospital to resume her place on the stage couch, dabbing her brow with a lacy handkerchief, drinking porter from a silver tankard.

The opening of the G.I. tour in Santa Maria, fifteen miles north of Naples, in August 1944 was a vindication of Kit's personal vision for the theatre, and a vindication of her faith in the people who go to the theatre.

When the Army Special Service Division back in the United States had reasoned with her not to take *The Barretts of Wimpole Street* overseas, to take any play *but*, her answer had been that if she was going to entertain the soldiers, she must take them her very best, and her very best was *The Barretts of Wimpole Street*. Her answer was unanswerable, except with the truth, which no one was about to utter, that the Special Service Division did not want her to take her best, they wanted her second best, her tenth best, which would be good enough for the G.I.'s overseas because that was all they were capable of understanding. From the start her audience was depicted for her as the army brass saw their own men — boorish, mindless, rude, tasteless, ignorant, insensitive, interested only in sex, the coarser and more vulgar the better. Kit's smiling contradiction was greeted with a respectful shrug, as if she were digging her own grave.

Once overseas, before the performances began, the army became protective and tried to prepare her, or help her prepare herself, for the onslaught, which they assured her was coming. To begin with, she had better send someone out before the curtain to explain what a play was and how it differed from a movie, for the poor dumb G.I. did not know. The system of acts had better be gone into carefully, otherwise he would leave when the curtain came down on the first act, not having the sense to realize he had seen only a third of the play.

Next — no matter how patient the audience had been at Mitchell Field (which was, after all, close to New York City and more so-phisticated than Italy) — no G.I. audience, tired, strained, homesick, fearful, brought in truckloads from the front or about to be sent there, would sit through three hours of anything (barring naked women), let alone three hours of talk from dead poets. Since it was imperative that the play be cut drastically, she had better begin with the love scenes. Cut them altogether, if possible, because the actors would certainly never be able to get through them for the jeers and catcalls and general mayhem that would result. The audience might even throw things. To kiss on the stage was to commit suicide.

The catechism was long, offered matter-of-factly without prejudice or malice in a genuine effort to be helpful. Kit smiled and refused to act on it, and the rest of the cast stood with her, despite some misgivings. Brian Aherne was sure that Browning, in his sideburns and tight pants, would be taken for "an old pansy" and treated accordingly; McKay Morris, having been told the G.I.'s took their make-believe villains as seriously as the real ones at the front, made nervous jokes about wearing a bulletproof vest. As the theatre filled for the first performance, Margalo Gillmore recalls Kit visiting "each dressing room, separating herself from her own nerves to give us a share of her strength, which we clung to like a talisman."

In Guthrie's own words, when he acted on the stage Kit "shook like an aspen leaf," but it was undoubtedly fortunate that when the curtain went up, they had to play the first scene together, if only because it gave Kit something to worry about besides the audience's mood. But more than that, it was not a performance in which the fine points of acting would be rated, but where the power to communicate would be tested, and it stands to reason that their almost telepathic theatrical response to each other, refined over the years, gave them a combined assurance.

But five minutes into the play Guthrie, as Dr. Chambers, trying to prescribe some sort of change that will get his patient away from her dismal surroundings, out of the chill English winters and damp English springs, suggests that the place for her is Italy. What followed was a moment of stage crisis far more critical to the play and the performance than Raymond Massey's amnesia in *The Doctor's Dilemma*. The mere suggestion that Italy was the place for anyone, man, woman, or beast, was greeted with an explosion of laughter, hooting, yelling, and stamping that went beyond hilarity to the edge of hysteria. For the McClintics on the stage it was a moment of indoctrination that went beyond any they had been given at Camp Patrick Henry, a moment for which their basic training at the American Academy of Dramatic Art and the Jessie Bonstelle Stock Company left them completely unprepared. If there was a single moment of truth, this was it, the moment in which it would be decided if Kit was right about *The Barretts of Wimpole Street* or the army brass were right about their own men. In *The B.O.W.S.* Margalo Gillmore tells what happened next: "It was true, then, we thought, they would go on laughing and never stop and the Barretts would go under a tidal wave of derision. But we were wrong. Kit and Guthrie were holding the laugh, just as if they had heard it a hundred times, not showing any alarm, not even seeming to wait for it, but handling it, controlling it, ready to take over at the first sign of its getting out of hand. It rose and fell and before it could rise again, Kit spoke." In her next line she had to state that Italy was her "heavenly dream," but she held off any further demonstration, by now with authority as well as understanding, and as the laughter stopped, the scene went on. Perhaps she made them believe that Italy, even wartime Italy — being there with them — was indeed her heavenly dream.

They were not out of danger yet. For a time a battle was waged for the soul of the play, the heart of the audience, and the nerves — if not the bodies — of the actors. Flush's entrance in Brenda's arms was greeted with yips and yaps and arfs and barks; when the Barrett brothers kissed Ba on their entrance, there was lascivious smacking of lips and isolated cries of "Pass it around!"; on his stern, white-faced appearance McKay Morris drew heckles, hisses, and a lone inquiry, "Who does he think he is, a top sergeant?" But by then the hecklers were shushing each other, and when the intermission came they sat quietly in their seats — without being told — waiting for the second act.

Robert Browning — pansy pants and all — drew a solid round of applause on his exit, and at the end of the second act Margalo writes: "Kit had a shining light in her. With that strange sixth sense of the actor that functions unexplainably in complete independence of lines spoken and emotions projected, she had been aware of the gradual change out front from a dubious indifference to the complete absorption of interest. At first they had hung back, keeping themselves separate from us, a little self-consciously, a little defiantly, and then line by line, scene by scene, she had felt them relax and respond and give themselves up to the play and the story, till at last they were that magic indivisible thing, an audience.

" 'We must never forget this, never,' said Kit. 'We've seen an audience born.' "

At the curtain call, "We stood before what seemed to be a solid wall of applause. And we were happy and grateful and achingly humble. Gert turned up the house lights and there was nothing but khaki from floor to ceiling. Stamping, cheering, whistling khaki — and something like a great wave of affection came surging over us, and we sent back our hearts in return."

When the mail started catching up with them, the cards, V-letters, and scrawls on Red Cross stationery became almost monotonous in their repetition of thanks for the show itself, "the most nerve-soothing remedy for a weary G.I.," and for having brought "yearned-for femininity" and reminded them, unlike other U.S.O. shows, "that a woman is not all leg." A master sergeant thanks her for "the awakening of something that he felt had died with the passing of routine military life in the foreign service." A warrant officer in the Royal Australian Air Force sends her the wing off his uniform, a mascot that has flown with him in thirty missions. A corporal from Baltimore can't get over the fact that "you spoke to me, not in the stereotyped words one is usually greeted with, but with a sincere down-to-earthness which made me feel I belonged. Then you insisted that you should thank me for the privilege of appearing before me."

But the letters, continuing to arrive long after the tour ended, were not always from soldiers themselves. Wives in the United States who had never seen Katharine Cornell, and had perhaps not even heard of her before, wrote that their husbands had written "the first smiling letter in a year" after seeing *The Barretts of Wimpole Street*. Parents who hadn't heard from sons in eighteen months or two years wrote to thank her, for after seeing the play, which was like a letter from home, the sons had written home themselves. Teachers wrote, forwarding letters they had received from former students. Fellow actors, playing in U.S.O. tours of *Petticoat Fever* and *What a Life!* in the South Pacific, wrote to say that G.I.'s passing through brought news halfway around the world of *The Barretts of Wimpole Street*. It was the most astonishing, incongruous, and yet somehow inevitable success of her career.

VIII

Cornell (1945-1974)

28

A Nice Lady
from Buffalo (1945-1960)

In April 1946 Katharine Cornell revived *Candida* for the fifth time, and continuing the impressive line of young actors whose careers were enhanced — and advanced — by playing Marchbanks for her, Orson Welles and Burgess Meredith were followed, now, by Marlon Brando. The season before he had played a fifteen-year-old Norwegian boy in John van Druten's family comedy *I Remember Mama;* then he had made a startling impression in Maxwell Anderson's *Truckline Café.* Eighteen months after *Candida* he would play Stanley Kowalski in Tennessee Williams's *A Streetcar Named Desire,* and the postwar revolution in American drama would be explosively launched.

Audiences of the Depression years had responded deeply to Katharine Cornell's exalted romanticism. Her expansive, all-embracing gestures and the broad clarity of her features seemed to ennoble existence. But after World War II, audiences did not need romantic exaltation, nor did they believe in it. A growing interest in the science of the mind erupted into a new psychological approach to drama that Lynda Towle Moss, in her doctoral dissertation on Katharine Cornell, calls "psychological realism." Arthur Miller and Tennessee Williams were its chief playwrights, and Marlon Brando its most influential actor.

That Brando was also a student of the Stanislavski method of acting as espoused by the Actors' Studio is incidental, since it seems to have become the feeling that all good actors of whatever period have always used the "method" in one form or another, whether they admit it — or even know it — or not. Simply by the integrity of his talent and the force of his personality, Brando epitomized the mid-twentieth-century psychological realism — "naturalism" may be a better word — while Katharine Cornell was the ultimate of all that was good and lasting in earlier romanticism. Their appearance together on the same stage in *Candida* — he a little early, she a little late — had historical significance that with the perspective of time can be marveled at. For twenty-four performances in April 1946, the stage of the Cort Theatre provided not only a haven where Marchbanks could read his sonnets aloud to his beloved Candida, but a meeting ground as well for the theatre that was passing and the theatre that was yet to come.

Candida was received as enthusiastically as ever, although Kit's 1943 production for the American Theatre Wing was still regarded as definitive, and for all the excitement generated by her latest March-banks, the critics generally agreed that "Burgess Meredith's performance as the love-sick young poet is not equaled by that of Marlon Brando."

Vernon Rice opened his review by saying, "Judging from the reception given Katharine Cornell yesterday afternoon at the Cort, the actress-manager need not worry about finding suitable plays season after season. It will be all right with her vast following if she just sets up shop with *Candida* and acts in it forever." It was charmingly put, but extravagant. Already the changing audience was beginning to carp at the play and, more surprisingly, at the character of Candida herself. To the majority of critics and ticket-holders she was still "a lovely and understanding wife" and "paragon of feminine virtues," but to a few odd dissidents she had suddenly become "a vicious little trifler" and "a rather vain hussy." Most revealing of the new psychological interpretation of character and motivation was the reviewer who saw in Candida "a bored housewife tired of her humorless, sanctimonious Socialist husband and eager to have a discreet affair with a poet." He seems to be writing about some other play and certainly some other character; he might even be offering a postwar psychological analysis of Masha in *The Three Sisters*. Prewar ideals were not always up to — or down to — postwar standards.

The warmth and loyal affection of Kit's personal reception by the critics was touched with autumn tones: "There is nothing to be said about Cornell's Candida, except, like rare wine, her performance becomes more rich and more mellow with the passing of time." Also with the passing of time, it will be noted in this quote, critics who had once been pleased to bow to "Miss Cornell's" Candida, now felt — after the great leveling war — that a nod to "Cornell's" Candida was carrying the amenities far enough.

To accompany his agreement permitting her to produce the play once again, Shaw enclosed his card with the message: "He is devilish old (90) but still gratified that you have not done with the old play yet." But she was now thirty-five years older than Marchbanks instead of the prescribed fifteen, thirty-one years older than Marlon Brando, twenty years older than Candida herself, and she could not "set up shop and act in it forever." Her fifth revival of "the old play" would be her last.

And Vernon Rice notwithstanding, she did have to "worry about finding suitable plays season after season," although not just at first. Back from overseas in the spring of 1945, she took her G.I. *Barretts* to Boston for one week, breaking all records for legitimate drama at the Boston Opera House. Then the troupe came to New York for eleven weeks (to give the actors a chance to make decent salaries after the months overseas). So unlimited was her local popularity that one morning's *New York Times* carried a full-page ad for a Fifth Avenue department store which read, in its entirety: "Dear Mr. Barrett, Your charming daughter might never have left Wimpole Street if you'd done over her room with treasures from the Going-Gone Shop at Lord & Taylor."

It is a paradox that her subsequent trouble finding new roles can be defined by the way she successfully played Elizabeth Barrett: externalizing the woman's nature, her soul, her being, as she was revealed to the world in her poetry. The stage pictures were uniformly beautiful, the voice soothing and fluid, the speech rhythmic, the cadence majestic, the hands graceful and outstretched, reaching from sofa to chair back, from chair back to table, and from table to window drape as Elizabeth fought to rise out of weakness into strength. Suffering was only there to be conquered; debilitating illness was a theatrical illusion.

To be effective — in fact to be acceptable — in the new drama of psychological realism, the values would almost have to be reversed. Kit's Elizabeth Barrett was a poet who happened to be ill; she would have to become a sick woman who happened to write verse. The concern would not be with externalizing her inner nature, but with internalizing its outer manifestation: her illness. Psychosomatic disorders were unheard of in Elizabeth Barrett's time and were not considered proper material for drama when *The Barretts of Wimpole Street* was written (although Besier managed to imply a great deal). But after World War II a dramatized portrait of Elizabeth could not help but become a study in what a layman can only call "psychosomatic pathology," closing in on the character rather than opening her out, entrapping rather than freeing, eliminating soul rather than discovering it.

In one such two-character television dramatization of the Barrett-Browning courtship, Elizabeth was not simply fragile, as Kit had been; she was emaciated, wasted, ugly in sickness, thin and cranky of voice, so sallow and desiccated that the healthy, hearty, booming Browning's persistent love for her became a morbid obsession, sick itself, and rather sinister. It is worth noting that the dialogue was pieced together entirely from their love letters and poems which, in this new context, became no more than symptomatic outpourings. It was a stunning evocation, and as a theatre piece far more fascinating today than the romantic Victorian legend that Kit portrayed, but there is no way of knowing which is nearer to the truth of the story. One came earlier, one came later, which is about all that can be said. They represented different kinds of theatre and different kinds of thinking.

Katharine Cornell would have found such an interpretation of Elizabeth Barrett impossible to play and repellent to watch. In a cover story on her fiftieth birthday (actually her fifty-fifth) in February 1948, *Newsweek* said, "Because her most intense need is for approval, it is beyond her art to play characters who antagonize or repel her audience," which in itself was a postwar psychological discovery, the need to be "well liked" that in a few years Arthur Miller would work up into Willy Loman's theme song. Katharine Cornell felt it was her responsibility as a star to please the audience and contribute something to their sense of well-being, which is not at all the same as an "intense need for approval." It was not "beyond her art to play characters who antagonize or repel her audience," she simply thought it would be grossly unfair to them. What was beyond her art was to play a character she herself found repellent or antagonistic, and if she had to do so, it meant altering the nature of the character — twisting it around in her mind to make it her own. Thus she was never able to remember that Iris March had Napier Harpenden's illegitimate baby in the penultimate act of *The Green Hat* — because she disapproved.

In her pre-Broadway tryout of *Antony and Cleopatra* in the fall of 1947, a group of high-school girls waited for her at the stage door of the Hanna Theatre in Cleveland, and one of them said, "Cleopatra really was a wicked woman, wasn't she?" Kit stopped in her graceful tracks, and forsaking the customary star-to-fan amenities, delivered to the group of astonished girls a fifteen-minute lecture, citing lines from the play to prove that Cleopatra died for love. Love carried the day when *Antony and Cleopatra* opened triumphantly on November 26, 1947, at the Martin Beck Theatre, but around the corner at the Ethel Barrymore, loveless, repellent, antagonistic Blanche DuBois was carrying the decade and begetting a whole generation of anti-heroines that Katharine Cornell could never play.

Had her talent been more flexible, perhaps she could have bridged the decades and adapted her craft to the changing postwar tastes. Helen Hayes has been equally affecting as a Booth Tarkington wren in the 1920s, a Maxwell Anderson queen in the 1930s, a Tennessee Williams belle in the 1950s, and a survivor of Hollywood's disaster movies in the 1970s. She has also been permitted to grow old with ease and self-possession, as has Ruth Gordon. The characters Kit played — could play — so beautifully seem to have been frozen at a certain age — in the prime of life — as if Juliet and Joan, no matter how long they lived, could never have grown older than Linda Esterbrook and Candida Morell. In 1957, when it was becoming increasingly difficult for her to find suitable parts, there was talk of at last making her film debut as Candida. There had been talk once before, early in the war, when Gabriel Pascal had made successful movies of *Pygmalion* and *Major Barbara* — with Shaw graciously informing American audiences on film, "You are sending us your old battleships, and we are sending you my old plays" — but the war had intervened and nothing came of the idea. Nothing came of it again in 1957, which must be considered a blessing, for she was sixty-four, which the cameras would have dutifully recorded.

Helen Hayes and Ruth Gordon were, even as young women, character actresses, while Kit — and in this instance, perhaps, she can be grouped with Lynn Fontanne, Ina Claire, Jane Cowl, and even Tallulah Bankhead — was a leading woman. Before World War II the leading woman in the theatre was just that: the one you looked at on the stage, the prime mover of a play's action, the principal character with straight, strong emotions, good or bad, undiluted by crotchets, removed from mere eccentricities, beset by limitations, to be sure, which were, however, straightforward and clear, forging the action and resolving conflicts by her ability to make decisions, etc. After the war — in the new psychological realism — leading women's roles were more and more written as, and acted by, character women. In the 1920s and 1930s, Helen Hayes was not a leading woman, she acted leading women as characters, and after the war she simply fell into step with the new younger actresses — Jessica Tandy, Shirley Booth, Uta Hagen, Kim Stanley, Maureen Stapleton, Julie Harris, and Geraldine Page. Kit could not do that — any more than Ethel Barrymore could. Like Ethel Barrymore she was and remained to the end a leading woman... grown old.

Perhaps as a breed the leading woman was disappearing from life, too, but it is certain that she was being squeezed out of modern American drama.

———

Happily, Kit did not know that and sailed into the postwar years with all flags flying.

While in Paris with the G.I. *Barretts* she had seen Jean Anouilh's version of the *Antigone* of Sophocles, which had been a success even during the occupation. It was a modern application of the Greek legend with Antigone symbolizing the Free French, and Creon, representing the forces of fascism, was written with such rational urbanity that the Nazis were flattered beyond caring that he was the villain of the piece and allowed the play to run. With Cedric Hardwicke as Creon, Kit brought an English version by Lewis Galantiere to the Cort Theatre in February 1946. The austere production, with the men in white tie and the women in long classic robes, was hailed and respected, even by theatre intellectuals, whom Kit did not always reach, the ones who believed in turning an art form into a platform. At the other extreme, her new friend Helen Keller came backstage after a performance and said, "This play is a parable of humanity. It has no time or space." The press said of Kit, "If the world and the theatre had more courageous spirits like her, our cumulative dreams would be greater, our thoughts, nobler."

*Katharine Cornell (far left) in Antigone, 1946. Sir Cedric Hardwicke
is seated at center.*

While waiting for new parts in new plays, she took *Candida* out of storage and alternated it with *Antigone,* using as many of the same actors as possible. Wesley Addy was Morell, and Cedric Hardwicke made a marvelously raunchy Burgess. Mildred Natwick and Marlon Brando were recruited from outside.

When *Candida* went back to the warehouse, *The Barretts* came out again. With the thought that the play hadn't been seen west of the Hudson in more than a decade, it was taken on an eight-week tour to the West Coast with Wilfred Lawson as the definitive Edward Moulton-Barrett. On the afternoon when Kit finally admitted that because of his drinking he lacked the one quality she considered essential to every great actor, discipline, and reluctantly forbade him to go on, Guthrie might just have been waiting for the chance to go on in his stead, which he did, wearing the costume of the smallest Barrett brother, while the rest of the cast took turns gawking through the brass peephole incredulously at his blustering performance. Cedric Hardwicke, who always traveled without luggage — buying whatever he needed wherever he stopped — and was therefore always ready to pick up and go on a moment's notice, flew up from Los Angeles in time for the evening performance, coolly usurping the play with the identical performance he had given with Gwen Ffrangcon-Davies in the original London production, despite the fact that he was now playing with different actors sixteen years later. He was a master of theatrical legerdemain, so impressing an audience — if not intimidating them — with the perfection of his speech that they felt too middle class and ashamed to admit they couldn't understand half of what he said. But he saved the play that day and stayed on to finish the tour. Octavius Barrett was played by Anthony Randall, who later shortened his first name to Tony; Anne Jackson was Bella Hedley, and Maureen Stapleton played Wilson. On June 7, 1947, in San Francisco, Kit played Elizabeth Barrett for the one thousandth time.

Perhaps it was providential that still no suitable part could be found in a new play, for it forced Kit to fulfill her long dream — or Guthrie's, or Ray Henderson's — of playing Shakespeare's Cleopatra. Her Mark Antony was Godfrey Tearle from England (when he was knighted a few years later she sent him a cable that read, in its entirety, "Dear Sir!"), and old friends in the cast included Kent Smith, David Orrick, David J. Stewart, and Anthony Randall, with Maureen Stapleton as

Katharine Cornell as Cleopatra, 1947. (Philippe Halsman)

Iras. Newcomers to the Cornell family included Eli Wallach, Joseph Wiseman, Douglas Watson, Charles Nolte, and Charlton Heston.

Up to his old tricks, Guthrie rescued Lenore Ulric — David Belasco's *Lulu Belle* out of *Tiger Rose* by way of *Kiki* — from obscurity to play Charmian. As small as the part was, it was beyond her talents at that late, sad stage of her life, and the blunt Buffalo critics said so, infuriating Guthrie into the vehement stand that he would close the play before he would "destroy that old woman by firing her!" Instead, he called her to Kit's hotel suite and apologized to her, claiming he was to blame for her bad reviews because the costumes he had made her wear had turned her into a figure of ridicule, and he promised to have Valentina design a whole new wardrobe for her. It was an incredible rationale but the best he could think of on the spur of the moment, and the aging actress, wanting to believe it, did so and felt better, especially when she got her new costumes, although her reviews continued to be, at best, polite. She had never stopped working, but in the lesser ranks of Hollywood, and she was confused to be back in such exalted company, in a top-drawer production, with her own billing. She was quite upset one day to be invited to a luncheon at the Astor Hotel by General Foods. Since the McClintics had been overseas entertaining the troops and knew more about military circles than she did, she wondered if Gert could find out who General Foods was and if she should accept his invitation. Without cracking a smile, Gert recognized one of those big and rather demeaning commercial enterprises where the guest list is conned from current newspaper columns, and promised to write to the general himself, personally, to get Miss Ulric off the hook. At the Nixon Theatre in Pittsburgh, Charlton Heston came to the theatre early to practice his leap onto the stage to interrupt Cleopatra's suicide and heard a quiet sobbing from a backstage corner. Approaching softly, he saw Miss Ulric kneeling before a worn poster on the brick wall, a lifesize representation of herself as *Kiki* twenty-five years earlier. It is astonishing that as disoriented as she was and as outmoded as her talents were, "that old woman," as Guthrie called her, was just one year older than Kit. She spent her last years in a state mental hospital where visitors were warned not to bring up the past because it disturbed her.

Of all Shakespeare's plays, *Antony and Cleopatra* is one of the most difficult to perform and one of the most consistent failures. It can be reasoned that at fifty-four Kit's timing was perfect, since Shakespeare had written Cleopatra as a woman of mature years (historically she was thirty-nine when she died), and she had always been played by actresses intent on being youthful. There were problems with her concept. The script required Antony to enter carrying Cleopatra in his arms. Since Kit was never diminutive and he was sixty-three, there were those who found the spectacle difficult to accept as romantic revelation.

The two most recent productions had been Jane Cowl's in 1924 and Tallulah Bankhead's in 1937 (when each was thirty-four, twenty years younger than Kit), and the doleful memory of both hung over the company during the rehearsal period of five weeks — two extra weeks having been granted by Actors Equity because the play was so difficult and the production so large — and a seven-week tryout tour. John Mason Brown's review of Bankhead had not been forgotten: "Tallulah Bankhead barged down the Nile last night as Cleopatra — and sank." A few hours before the New York opening Kit could have been found on the stage measuring the number of steps in different directions required to come out even in a particularly complicated scene, concentrating on the task at hand, muttering under her breath, ". . . barged, one, two, down the Nile, three, four, and turn, five, six, and *sank*, seven, eight, *indeed!*" And Guthrie, meanwhile, in his battered lucky hat, with his two day's growth of beard, was grabbing a bite to eat and a drink at Sardi's. Teetering out, he was stopped by a concerned Jane Cowl at another table asking in a rather funereal voice, "How is it going, Guthrie?" When he sputtered and stammered that the tour had gone as well as could be expected and it looked like a good show, she lifted a graceful hand to stop him, closing her eyes in silent commiseration, opening them again to pin him with her sympathetic stare. "You don't have to say any more, Guthrie. Remember, I have done this play. And I have never felt sorrier for two people in my life than I do for you and Kit tonight."

With such sincere well-wishers it would have been a shame not to succeed, and succeed they did beyond all expectations. Ward Morehouse began his review, "The dauntless Katharine Cornell's *Antony and Cleopatra* has beauty and power and grandeur and I do not hesitate to proclaim it one of the finest achievements of her career." Robert Garland forestalled any possible adverse criticism: "Don't let anybody tell you it isn't the most exciting theatrical event of this or any other season!" Partisans felt so strongly that when a paralyzing blizzard threatened to shut down the city and all its transportation facilities, a New Jersey couple walked through the Lincoln Tunnel, not to forfeit their chance to see *Antony and Cleopatra*. Miss Cornell felt that if the audience could get to the theatre thus, so could the actors, and they all did, frustrating their understudies who had hoped the heavy snow would increase their chances of going on in the lead roles.

Sixteen weeks in New York and a nine-week tour of four major cities added up to a total of two hundred and fifty-one performances, the longest run the play has ever enjoyed in its history.

Apparently the only way she would find a new play was to commission one, and since she did not seem suited to modern roles and current themes, perhaps it was wise — and certainly courageous — to go against popular taste completely, back to the Spain of Philip II, and have the Irish writer Kate O'Brien dramatize her own historical novel, *For One Sweet Grape*. Eventually called *That Lady*, the play was a full-blooded, swashbuckling romance, replete with crafty cardinals, highborn villains, handsome heroes, assorted heroic emotions, and, as one critic put it, "other literary bric-a-brac." "That lady" was Ana de Mendoza y de Gómez, beloved of Philip, who refused to marry her because it would afford no political advantage. But unable to let her love another, when he discovers her secret passion for Antonio Pérez he walls her up in a room in her own house, condemning her to eternal darkness. As a girl of fourteen, Ana had fought a duel for the honor of Castille with a page in her father's house and lost an eye, enabling Kit to wear a glamorous eye patch in addition to the ornate hair arrangement, mantillas, and wide skirts of the period. Rolf Gerard made his American debut with spectacular sets and costumes; Henry Daniell was a cold-blooded Philip; Marian Seldes, a new and ardent member of the Cornell family, played Ana's loyal daughter; and Torin Thatcher was Ana's passionate secret lover Pérez who in their final parting, as the windows are about to be shuttered, kisses her good-bye — on her eye patch. The critics did not take kindly to such carrying-on.

In 1951 she was invited to the drama and opera festival at Central City, Colorado, for three weeks of "summer fun" playing Ethel Barrymore's 1926 role in Somerset Maugham's civilized comedy *The Constant Wife*. With Brian Aherne, Grace George, John Emery, and Gertrude Musgrove in the cast, the production was so successful that the McClintics brought it to New York the following December where they were credited with bringing "grace to a ragged season." Not only that, at the end of seventeen weeks in New York, a four-week tour of eastern cities, and a thirty-one week crisscross-country tour the following season, *The Constant Wife* grossed more money than any other production in the twenty-nine-year life of C. & M.C. Productions: $1,484,673 — $200,000 more than the original 1931 production of *The Barretts of Wimpole Street* and $400,000 more than *No Time for Comedy*, its closest runners-up. (It must be remembered, however, that ticket prices were higher in 1951 than in 1931, so the play was not necessarily seen by more people, and the dollar was worth less in 1951, so the gross may not have been commensurately more.)

At last, in 1953, a suitable role in a modern new play, *The Prescott Proposals* by Howard Lindsay and Russel Crouse. She played a United States delegate to the United Nations, a woman not unlike Eleanor Roosevelt, and not unlike Katharine Cornell, either, in her concern for world peace and goodwill. In the guise of dignified melodrama (death, intrigue, old love and blackmail among the delegates), the play posed a wholesome if simplistic theme, that "there is something basically decent in people of all nations," and with Felix Aylmer and Lorne Greene to support her, Brooks Atkinson said Miss Cornell "bucks things up all over town."

In Christopher Fry's verse drama *The Dark Is Light Enough*, 1955, Kit found a role so suited to her bearing, beauty, and personality that it might have been written for her (had it not been written for Edith Evans). The Countess Rosmarin Ostenburg, maintaining her Austrian country house near the Hungarian border during the revolution of 1848, "believes in the final grace of tolerance and compassion," which were the subjects of the play. The perfectly formed dialogue, the rich Oliver Messel settings, and the nature of the action, dealing with pity, cowardice, bravery, and love, seemed to suggest that the Countess was actually God, and as Kit descended a grand staircase onto the stage, having been up since dawn when, "by the confusing light of one lantern I harnessed the horses, poor angels, with my own insufficient hands," the audience, critics, and ushers were willing to embrace the suggestion, while at the same time she inspired one review to be headlined, "An Earthier Kit." On an older, more stately level, it was the same combination of marble and common clay that had gone into her Juliet. Playing a woman who, like herself, was "a foe of cruelty, hatred, destruction and all that would destroy decency and graciousness," "a neutralist or a third force," she handled problems of craft that had once plagued her — ornate verse cadences and epigrammatic wit — with what Wolcott Gibbs, in *The New Yorker*, called "almost supernatural poise." Repaying an old debt of gratitude, Tyrone Power returned from Hollywood to play the young deserter given asylum by the countess, who ends by offering her his love which she, now dying, rejects with the austere words, "Whosoever negligence it is, I never loved you."

Another Fry play in 1958, *The Firstborn*, gave an account of Moses' determination to free his people from Egypt. Actually written in 1948, it was offered as a salute to the new state of Israel on its tenth anniversary. Kit played Pharaoh's sister who had rescued Moses from the river; Anthony Quayle played Moses, with a supporting cast that included Torin Thatcher and Mildred Natwick; Leonard Bernstein, recently appointed musical director of the New York Philharmonic, wrote two songs for the production, which was designed by Boris Aronson. Under the sponsorship of the American-Israeli Committee, the production was taken to Tel Aviv for Israel's anniversary celebration, performing there between July 3 and July 10, 1958.

Nobody planned it that way, it was simply the circular form imposed by nature and time that the final production of her career should have been written — at least in part — by George Bernard Shaw, whose *Candida* had been such a send-off back at the beginning. It was not a play, but rather a theatrical presentation, a reading of the letters between Shaw and Mrs. Patrick Campbell, arranged by Jerome Kilty into dramatic dialogues and scenes. Called *Dear Liar*, the "comedy of letters" arrived at the Billy Rose Theatre (called The National when Kit last played there in *The Constant Wife*) on March 17, 1960. It was fitting that the character of Bernard Shaw should be her last vis-à-vis on any stage, and that he should be played by Brian Aherne — her Browning, her Tarquin, her Mercutio, her Warwick, and her John Middleton (the constant wife's inconstant husband).

But most fitting of all — or perhaps only the most predictable — New York was simply the last stand in one of the longest tours of her career, twenty-seven weeks. Since the trains not only did not stop, but for the most part no longer even passed through most of her favorite old stands, let alone the new ones she was eager to include, this time she literally took to the road in a luxurious pea-green landcruiser, and whereas she had once delighted in poring over timetables and train schedules from New York to San Francisco, or air routes and flying times from Lecce to Rheims, she now plotted road maps and tabulated the mileage from Phoenix, Arizona, to Greensboro, North Carolina; from Shreveport, Louisiana, to Granville, Ohio; to Winnetka, Illinois, to Manhattan, Kansas, to Vancouver, British Columbia; to Burlington, Vermont, and Clemson, North Carolina, and Florence, Mississippi, and Huntington, West Virginia, and all points between for sixty-six stands, or sixty-seven counting New York — appropriately and coincidentally, one stand for each year she had been alive.

———

It leaves one breathless simply to summarize the last fifteen post-war, postprime years of her career: a timely reinterpretation of a classic Greek theme by a modern intellectual; a Shakespearean revival; a swashbuckling period romance; a twentieth-century comedy revival; a contemporary melodrama; two verse plays, one historical, one biblical; a staged reading of literary love letters; eight new productions representing English, Irish, French, and American fictional, poetic, and philosophical writing, introducing two European giants, Jean Anouilh and Christopher Fry, to American audiences for the first time; all productions taken on the road for as long as audiences would come to see them, and depending on the varying length of the tours, offered at one- or at most two-year intervals — except for a three-year gap from 1955 to 1958 while she recuperated from the operation on her lung to rid her (unsuccessfully) of the trigger cough that had plagued her from Juliet's death through Cleopatra's to the Countess Rosmarin's.

The honors never ceased, culminating in the medal for good speech on the stage awarded by the American Academy of Arts and Letters and her citation as Woman of the Year by the American Friends of the Hebrew University, both in 1959. Her only unrealized ambition of the 1950s — rivaling her desire to play Rebecca West in the 1930s — was to play Florence Nightingale in a film version of Cecil Wood-ham-Smith's biography. She was offered other movie roles constantly, most notably the Mother Superior in *The Nun's Story*, and lest it be said in the final analysis that she was afraid to tackle a new medium, it should be noted that she made two successful expeditions into the difficult medium of live television. In 1955 she brought *The Barretts of Wimpole Street* to N.B.C.'s *Producers' Showcase*, with Anthony Quayle as Browning and Henry Daniell as Edward Moulton-Barrett; in 1958 on N.B.C.'s *Hallmark Hall of Fame* she appeared with Charles

Boyer and Bradford Dillman in Robert E. Sherwood's *There Shall Be No Night.* In neither experience did Kit — nor her advisers, protectors, and friends — realize that it was not customary for the entire hard-bitten camera crew of a live television show to break into spontaneous applause the minute they were off the air; she thought everyone was given this gracious reception. In each production, she reached an audience of twenty-eight million people, fourteen times more than saw her Elizabeth Barrett in all her many stage incarnations over a period of twenty-five years.

There was enough industry, energy, dedication and accomplishment in her glimmering years to brighten the meridian of many another actress; and more variety, more diversity, and a broader scope than the entire repertoire of some considered to be more versatile. Had she not already performed Elizabeth Barrett, Juliet, and Joan, her Antigone, her Cleopatra, and especially her Countess Rosmarin would have been of sufficient stature to serve as climax, peak, and zenith of her career. The dark was indeed light enough.

Nevertheless, the trouble began early, in fact immediately, with *Antigone.* With the kind of critical reception that ten years before would have insured a full season's run, the box office receipts were so low that in the sixth week it was necessary — in an ostensible and publicized gesture to repertory — to take old reliable, ever-popular *Candida* out of storage and alternate it five performances to *Antigone*'s three to make the weekly ends meet. When even the combination showed signs of sagging into the red, she took to the road where her attraction was as great as ever, and after five weeks between the East Coast and Chicago, the books were balanced and she was able to close both plays without a loss.

Of her twenty-nine productions as actress-manager, *Antony and Cleopatra* was the most expensive and the first to require outside backing. Despite its artistic success and record run, it could not hang on long enough to earn back its production cost, not even from audiences of old friends who had been loyal for more than a generation, while around the corner, it will be remembered, Blanche DuBois, relying "on the kindness of strangers," was making everybody rich on her way to the mental hospital. In the middle of the run, Tony Randall left *Antony and Cleopatra* for another job, but went back after a few weeks to visit Miss Cornell. He was surprised to find that she had two dressing rooms, one for the business of dressing, the other on the stage level for the business of receiving visitors after the performance. She served him bourbon, undoubtedly because it was Guthrie's drink, and seated him happily. "Sometimes," she grinned, "I sit here and nobody comes!"

After that, every production for the rest of her career — except for *The Constant Wife* — was a financial failure. Part of the blame — but only part of it — can be laid to bad plays, whether they had suitable roles or not. *That Lady* was weighty and novelistic; putting it on a stage did not make it a play. Her grandeur, far from redeeming the melodramatics of *The Prescott Proposals*, only pointed up their ordinariness. *The Firstborn*'s poetry was as pretentious and dull as Maxwell Anderson's in *The Wingless Victory*. But audiences had not stayed away from *The Wingless Victory*. It is true they had refused to patronize the unworthy dramatics of *Lucrece* and *Flowers of the Forest* early in her producing years, but *Lovers and Friends*, at her height, was given the worst critical reception of any play she ever produced, and yet it was her fourth largest money-maker. And why wouldn't audiences accept *The Dark Is Light Enough*? Before World War II, they even went to the bad plays; after World War II they even stayed away from the good ones.

There was always a strong presumption among Katharine Cornell's detractors that her career was manufactured; that only with her family's wealth was she able to sustain thirty years of producing and acting in what were considered noncommercial plays — in other words, plays she wanted to do. Since other actors and actresses had to survive at the whim and mercy of crass, commercial, hostile managements, it seemed impossible — or at least unfair — that anyone could not only survive but thrive by doggedly sticking to personal standards of integrity. The answer could not possibly be the triumph of quality; it had to be an unlimited supply of unrestricted money.

It is to refute such suppositions, to show with random figures that they are not only untrue but unjust, that financial matters have periodically been referred to in this history. Katharine Cornell was able to survive the twelve years after *Antony and Cleopatra* for four reasons: first, her financial affairs, starting with the first profits from *The Barretts of Wimpole Street* in 1931, had benefited from the expert supervision of Stanton Griffis, Conger Goodyear, and Gertrude Macy; second, the net profit of *The Constant Wife*, close to one hundred and fifty thousand dollars, provided a cushion for the productions that came after; third, having accepted outside backing for *Antony and Cleopatra*, she realized that in order to continue she would have to surrender enough self-sufficiency to accept further outside backing and even co-producing arrangements with other managers (Leland Hayward for *The Prescott Proposals*, Roger L. Stevens for *The Dark Is Light Enough* and *The Firstborn*, and S. Hurok for *Dear Liar*); and fourth, she never lost her audience outside New York where she always managed to break even and often recouped losses sustained on Broadway.

Her detractors suggested that she never lost her popularity on tour because audiences outside New York were behind the times, less sophisticated, slower to catch on to the exciting new drama of psychological realism. Starting with *The Green Hat* she had never stopped working to win the respect and affection of those audiences, and if they were less sophisticated than New Yorkers, it was in their sense of loyalty to one who had never let them down. On her last tour of all, *Dear Liar* was still breaking house records; at the Sombrero Theatre in Phoenix approximately a thousand potential patrons had to be turned away.

With no tangible profits after *The Constant Wife* and all backlog dissipated, at the end of the 1950s C. & M.C. had nothing left. Even audiences on the road were thinning out. *Dear Liar* broke the house record in Phoenix and other places, but when the tour ended, there was a fifty-five-hundred-dollar deficit. It was time to stop.

After World War II the theatre was changing, and so was she. When she was in her sixties, *Life* Magazine ran an article entitled *Ageless Beauties*, not necessarily comparing but synthesizing the qualities of Edith Sitwell, Georgia O'Keeffe, Isak Dinesen (the Baroness Blixen), and Katharine Cornell. Under a stunning Philippe Halsman photograph of Katharine Cornell's profile as Cleopatra aligned with the head of Nefertiti, the text commented, "she exudes an eternal, semi-tragic air and a provocative ripeness that have nothing at all to do with the latest fashions." To those who were aging with her, perhaps, she did not grow old. But to those who came in on her career after 1946, she was never young.

Her beauty had never been conventional; nor had it always been apparent to everyone; now Asian, now Indian, now Negroid, Shaw had summed it up on first sight, "from the cradle of the human race."

Her features broadened where they had been too broad to begin with, and while at the age of forty she had played a glowing, youthful, graying Juliet, Guthrie now insisted that she dye her hair, which only drew attention to it. She began to fight the battle of weight and developed a strange, loping walk on stage, as if her balance were not very exact, and it came across as a mannerism, like her clasped-and-unclasped hands. Her loveliness did not increase, nor did it fade into nothingness, but while it had once been gratefully accepted and taken for granted, its irregularity now evoked odd distortions in the eyes of the beholders, such as the cast in her eye that Brendan Gill asserts, in his book *Here at The New Yorker*, caused a long-running dispute between Harold Ross, the editor, and Wolcott Gibbs, the drama critic, over a drawing by Al Frueh, the artist. Did she or did she not have a cast in her eye? If she did, no one close to her ever noticed it, and it never showed up in any photograph.

In the late 1950s she went to Kenyon College to accept an honorary doctorate where her great-great-grandfather, David Bates Douglass, had been president over a hundred years before. In a postceremony photograph, she wears what appears to be a navy blue dress with white polka dots and a dignified V-neckline, a single strand of pearls, and dark pumps. Her hair is slightly mussed from the mortarboard she wore at the ceremony. Her academic gown is over her arm, her mortarboard in her hand. She has been propped against a stone memorial to David Bates Douglass and told to smile, and she smiles — broadly. One looks at the photograph and asks if this is the most beautiful Juliet of the twentieth century — is this the smiling Joan who led Dunois and his fellow soldiers in the siege of Orléans? And the answer comes back: no — it's just an awfully nice lady from Buffalo.

———

In retrospect it can be said that her loyal audiences, even in New York, never actually deserted her — just as friends were unable to part from her in life — they simply grew older and thinned out; if they stopped going to see her plays, it was because they stopped going to the theatre altogether. And after World War II, she never managed to capture the hearts and stimulate the minds of the new young audience coming up. Iris March in *The Green Hat* had something powerful to say about the mid-1920s woman, and she said it directly *to* the mid-1920s woman — the college girl up from Bryn Mawr on an allowance, the schoolteacher budgeting so much a month for culture, the shop girls who pooled their money and went to shows in a bunch, and assorted wives and mistresses, rich and poor. When Kit slouched in the doorway, white-faced with a slashing red mouth, smiling a smile that bespoke all living sorrow back to Eden, and in a low liquid voice announced, "Boy died for purity," she was speaking to and for every young woman in the audience. At her prime, men were her most ardent admirers, but women chose the plays men went to.

It is more than interesting, it is significant that her only postwar success, *The Constant Wife*, originally ran in New York in 1926, while she was touring *The Green Hat*. Coming straight from the period of her first great success, it was her last great success. But the young women of 1951, the smart young models, the executive secretaries, and the airlines reservations agents lured to New York with the promise of careers — daughters and nieces, perhaps, of 1926 Bryn Mawr graduates, schoolteachers, and shop girls — recalled their mothers back in Milwaukee, Minneapolis, and Denver remembering Katharine Cornell and went off with great anticipation to the National Theatre, where they watched a pleasant, middle-aged woman pretend to go off for a weekend with a lover — which they, like Brooks Atkinson, thought she would have too much sense to do — shrugged, mystified, and came away wondering what all the fuss had ever been about.

And they never went back to see her again.

Brooks Atkinson was not the only critic to become more critical. At a party after the closing of *Antony and Cleopatra* in Chicago, she laughed with everyone else at a cast take-off on herself and the production called *The Wanton the Critics Were Wantin'*. But after *That Lady* opened, for the first time in her career she talked back to the critics in an article headlined *Cornell Says Critics Look But Do Not Listen*, castigating them for not hearing plays with their "heart ear."

When Tony Randall became not only a fine actor but a popular television personality in the 1950s, he once ran into Miss Cornell at a performance in the old Metropolitan Opera House. During an intermission, she took his arm and they promenaded. She was between plays, heavier than anyone liked to see her, with her face grown wide like an Indian's, and she walked unrecognized, while he was pointed to with smiles and stares of recognition. He was pleased to have his old mentor see that he was so well known, but it was making him uncomfortable that she was not known at all, when she squeezed his arm and whispered, "Isn't it fun?" It is one of the few indications she ever gave that she fully appreciated the joy of being in the limelight, and it was typical that she only indulged the vanity when it was past, and then only to put someone else at ease.

She was gratified when Tyrone Power, whom she had also helped at the beginning of his career, came back from Hollywood to play opposite her in *The Dark Is Light Enough*, but it was one of the few gestures she ever made to commercialism, and it was a mistake. *The Prescott Proposals* had been such a financial disaster that Leland Hayward had even refused to send it on the road, and Kit and Guthrie were hoping that with the Fry play Tyrone Power's name would help them at the box office. He had returned to the theatre before and made a good showing in a summer revival of *Liliom* and with Judith Anderson and Raymond Massey in a staged reading of Benét's *John Brown's Body*, so they further hoped that his talent had matured to the point of being able to handle the convolutions of modern verse drama. They were wrong on both counts. In fact, it was a tribute to their highmindedness that they were so inept at being commercial. With forty-one movies to his credit, Tyrone Power had apparently worn out his welcome with the public, for his popularity, sadly, was no greater than hers, and the play would have had more panache had his role been acted by his understudy, Christopher Plummer, who unfortunately did not, as yet, have a name at the box office.

One afternoon in Pittsburgh during the pre-Broadway tryout, Plummer, who characterizes himself at that time as "ribald and naughty, ready for devilment," found himself — after a night's enjoyment of Clicquot — with a covetable woman in a posh restaurant, the table laden with food, bloody marys and other sobering comestibles, with Keene Curtis, Miss Cornell's stage manager, standing over him intoning, "You not only missed understudy rehearsal which you were supposed to attend this morning, but you are now twenty minutes late for the matinee."

In slow motion Plummer called for the check and paid it, and leaving gorgeous lunch and gorgeous woman unattended in posh restaurant, followed his executioner through the streets of Pittsburgh to the theatre where Guthrie stood inside the door, so white with rage that he could only jab the air with his shaking forefinger and articulate, "Miss Kit's dressing room." Ty Power saw the doomed man pass his open door, pointed to the next dressing room and rolled his eyes heavenward.

Knocking on Miss Kit's door, he was asked to enter and found Eveline Drysdale combing Miss Kit's hair; it occurred to him that Eveline Drysdale was *always* combing Miss Kit's hair, and an admonition from an old acting teacher flashed through his mind, "It's not you that's angry, it's the prop you're holding."

It was 1947 again, with Wilfred Lawson being told he could not be permitted to go on for the matinee or any subsequent performance; it was 1934, and Orson Welles had missed the train between stands or acted up in a public restaurant; it was 1928 and *The Age of Innocence*, with Franchot Tone showing up white-faced, having malingered the night before to be his best friend's best man in Buffalo — only Chris Plummer did not need face powder to give him pallor. What had not changed in twenty-seven years was Katharine Cornell's standard of behavior and discipline in the theatre.

"We are so disappointed in you," she said. "If you can't get through this matinee, and if this ever happens again, we can't allow you to open in New York."

Her statement was so controlled, so succinctly put, that the chastened young actor almost risked asking, "Can you lend me the money to pay my bar tab?"

Instead, he went to his dressing room where his understudy poured gallons of coffee down his throat. Fortunately he didn't go on until the end of the first act, and as he stood in the wings waiting for his cue, he saw Miss Kit emerge from her dressing room and move to the edge of the stage to watch his scene. At the same time Guthrie came through from the front of the house for the same purpose. Plummer went on and somebody else, it seemed, spoke his lines, and when he came off he slunk to his dressing room, wanting nothing more than to escape from the building. He sent his understudy ahead as a lookout, but the signals got mixed and he bumped into Miss Cornell coming out of her dressing room with two dignified Pittsburgh matrons, one of whom gushed, "Aren't you Christopher Plummer? You were just wonderful!" He didn't dare look at Miss Kit, but in the confusion he managed one quick glance which she caught and without interrupting her effusive farewell to the grandames, made a quick "O.K." sign with her thumb and forefinger. He has never forgotten "that funny, outrageous signal" to let him know he was forgiven.

When he came down with hepatitis in Baltimore and had to go into the hospital, he was sure his defection would be put down to more indulgence and further dissipation, perhaps this time costing him his job, but the next morning there were the inevitable footsteps down the corridor, and "Miss Kitty was there with television sets and flowers and books."

"I *knew* there was something wrong with you," she said, "and you're not to worry, the understudy will go on the next two towns while you get well, and you *are* going to open in New York!"

Christopher Plummer says that at the time of *The Dark Is Light Enough* she "rather encouraged naughtiness and good healthy hanky-panky" to go on around her. "She made you want to do something — to try to shock her — just to see what she would do. She was in a way boss and participant — she hired people who had a sense of life. . . ." That he believes that wholeheartedly is evidence enough that she still gave back the essential quality that people brought to her. Without compromising herself or her standards, she was what you wanted her to be.

"She gave the theatre the romantic quality it should have — the dream of it was alive in her hands — the religion of it. There was a magic about the profession you were in — you should tiptoe across a stage — it wasn't just an ordinary hall, it was a *theatre!*"

For him — come psychological realism, changing critics, changing taste; come age, weight, and box office deficits; come the end of a long career — the magnetic influence was as strong as ever.

But some other young actor, just as "ribald and naughty, ready for devilment," could go to see her for the first time in *Antigone* and come away composing new lyrics to the tune of the Cornell University Alma Mater:

> *Far above the Cort The-ayter*
> *There's an awful smell;*
> *Some say it's the Cort The-ayter,*
> *Some say Kit Cornell.*

The ditty was popular, he says, "in the byways and highways of show biz," which means among his friends, and even today, looking back on all she achieved, the most he will give her is this: "She had terrific posture, and she kept her head up. She was stately, and she knew all her words."

29

"I'm the Captain!" (1945-1961)

As THE *Buffalo Courier-Express* phrased it on September 26, 1948, "Dr. Peter C. Cornell has walked from the stage of life." He had been unwell for several years, and perhaps judging all physicians by his own youthful doctoring, he seems — from his letters — to have trusted them only in numbers, although his favorite, he reports literally, with no suggestion of humor, was a Dr. Mesmer. By 1946 he was being looked after by two full-time nurses, a live-in couple to keep house for him (Olliver, the houseman-driver, even shaved him daily), and a secretary, Mildred Baker, replacing Miss Kelsey, to type letters to his daughter which invariably began: "I have been rather uncomfortable the last day or two," "Can't say I am much improved the last few days," "I had one of my rotten dizzy attacks yesterday which lasted most of the night," or, simplest of all, "I am suffering today." His well-practiced pathetic appeal comes through even in dictation, as he keeps hoping Kit will come to see her old dad, because "I know you could straighten me out in many ways." On the other hand, he doesn't want her to take time from her busy life just to come and see her old dad and sends her a check for ten dollars "to apply on some of the long distance calls. When more is necessary, let me know." He ordered his household not to tell him of anyone's death or illness, so in discreet postscripts which her employer never saw, Miss Baker rather chattily kept Kit apprised of the status of Buffalo friends and relations as they were felled, struck down, and expired.

In his 1946 letters, Dr. Cornell, with his rather artificial heartiness,

Lynn Fontanne, Laurence Olivier, Katharine Cornell, and Alfred Lunt
at a New York party of Olivier's, 1958. (United Press Photo)

is impatient with his sister Lydia's infirmities and his brother Douglas's, complaining of their complaints, and he asserts that his nephews, back from the war, had better knuckle down and make something of themselves.

On Dr. Cornell's death, John O'Shei, his longtime business partner, asked Douglas to become a director of Trico Products, and when Douglas died in 1953, the long-lived O'Shei, sentimentally clinging to the Cornell family, asked young Doug to take his father's place. Doug served for several years, but he was little more than a figurehead, and when he resigned, all interest in or control of the company went out of the family, although funds from it provided the basis of the Peter C. Cornell Foundation.

To follow the family through to death and distribution of property: Lydia died in 1958, leaving her Cobourg house (where Kit and Guthrie had been married) to her sister-in-law Gwendolyn. Through all vicissitudes, Kit remained a kind of clearing station for family feelings, since they all wrote to her the thoughts about one another that they couldn't actually share with one another. She never stopped doing things for them, and even saw to it that Aunt Lydia had a television set so that she could see her niece's two appearances on the new medium. (At the same time Kit went so far as to install a set in the original small living room at Chip Chop, which Margalo Gillmore immediately christened the Depravity Room.) When Kit couldn't be there for Uncle Douglas's funeral because she was touring in *The Constant Wife* on the West Coast, Guthrie went in her place and on the night before the service regaled the widow with tales of Mrs. Fiske and Ethel Barrymore.

After her father's death, Kit saw to it that his oldest and steadiest girl friend received a small legacy which, she said, he had privately commissioned her to pass on. The eighty-three-year-old philanderer had done no such thing and didn't even know his daughter knew about his girl friends. The newspapers publicized the fact that Kit inherited three hundred thousand dollars outright and the lifetime income from a trust, and she was besieged with letters from strangers seeking backing for business ventures or to purchase farms, a minister wanting to start a new church, an asthmatic old woman wanting to get her song poems on the airwaves ("When you haven't got a nickel in your jeans and all your hopes have faded with your dreams"), and one forthright woman who simply wanted money "to get some things I need." Gert, anticipating Kit's propensity for putting her own money into Guthrie's independent theatrical enterprises, immediately applied the cash inheritance to paying for the house Kit had decided to build at Sneden's Landing. Being dynamited out of the Palisades, the house would be called, in honor of the late doctor's durability, Peter Rock.

Before she died, Mrs. Tonetti left instructions that if Gert Macy wanted to buy property at Sneden's Landing, she could, and Gert acquired over four acres. Eric Gugler designed and built a spacious French-style house for her, officially called Rive Gauche, using French doors and windows from the former New York residence of financier Thomas Fortune Ryan. In 1949 Gert moved from New York City to the banks of the Hudson, taking into her new establishment a five-year-old French child whose indigent family Kit and other members of the *Barretts* troupe had aided during the G.I. tour. Named Alex (by Gert), the child's father was tubercular and no longer able to provide for him, so after the war the mother agreed to have him adopted and brought up in the United States. He lived with Gert until he was ten years old, when his parents did a sudden about-face and demanded his return to France.

As a young woman in Buffalo, Kit, admiring Anna Glenny's stand-up sealskin collar, had gone out and bought one just like it, unwittingly embarrassing her friend whenever they met publicly. It was a trait everyone had to learn to forgive, because she never lost it. She certainly did not envy Gert the responsibility of a five-year-old French child. When the request for adoption first came, it was directed to her personally, and she said that the last thing she needed — or wanted — was a child. And although she was always kind to Alex, she thought Gert was showing off. But she did envy Gert her house and decided that the time had come for her to have one of her own, designed by Eric Gugler, overlooking the Hudson.

It was to be simple on the outside and all comfort on the inside, and for the center Gugler bought a barn on Long Island, had it taken down piece by piece and set up again in the middle of the seven acres Kit found on a rocky cliff. With its twenty-foot-high walls and pitched roof, the barn became a forty-five- by thirty-one-foot drawing room. Then the house began to grow, first with an entrance hall, a library, a kitchen, and several terraces on the ground level. A three-room upstairs suite was constructed at one end, and then enough rock was blasted out to make another suite, which became Kit's, running along the same side of the house as the drawing room, but below it, with its own terrace, overhanging the river.

The "simple" house took several years to build and eventually included sixteen rooms, or thereabouts. They were at such odd levels and of such indiscriminate sizes that it was difficult to count them. At one point the expenses were mounting so fast that even Kit grew cautious, and Gert called a halt to all construction until it was economically feasible to continue. There were two main reasons why the house took so long to build — and cost so much.

First, Gugler refused to dynamite a big hole and then fill it in with house. Instead, he insisted that the Palisades rock be drilled out a little bit at a time, just enough to fit each angle, each level, each corner of the house as it was needed. The rock had to be forced to accommodate the house — not the other way around.

Second, the plans kept changing, and the plans kept changing because Guthrie became interested. At first he would have nothing to do with the new house. Twenty-three Beekman Place was fine for him. He holed in there and said he would never move to Peter Rock. But when it was made clear to him that they would not be able to afford both places, and that sooner or later — probably sooner — they would have to sell 23 Beekman Place, he became interested and gradually took over the construction of the new house, changing his mind, adding elegances, chandeliers, gold ceilings, a circular staircase from the ground floor down to Kit's quarters, great subterranean storage basements for his trunks and theatre memorabilia, in his excitement almost forgetting to tack on — some place — the monk's cell that would be his own Spartan bedroom. It was a repetition of the building of Chip Chop. If Kit minded having him take over, again, what she had started, she never let on . . .

It may have been what she was hoping for.

If Guthrie had difficulty adapting to the postwar theatre, he summed it up himself to Albert McCleery, one of television's best directors in the 1950s, whose first job in the theatre had been as a spear carrier in Kit's *Romeo and Juliet*. In a rather heated discussion of the new kind of arena staging that the young directors were beginning to experiment with after the war, the theatre-in-the-round that would eventually develop into the curtainless thrust stages of the 1960s and 1970s, Guthrie said, "It's really very simple. When I was seventeen, I fell in love with a red plush curtain. And that's the kind of theatre I love most and will want to work with forever."

After the war, he started off briskly in step with the times, directing *You Touched Me*, an early play by Tennessee Williams (who claimed to be writing *Summer and Smoke* for Kit, but it never worked out that way). With Edmund Gwenn as the star, Guthrie directed Montgomery Clift in one of his first adult roles, as he would soon direct Marlon Brando, and he followed *Antigone* and *Candida* with a highly praised revival of *The Playboy of the Western World*, with Burgess Meredith, Mildred Natwick, Julie Harris, and Maureen Stapleton in the cast. Between assignments, he found time to go abroad, at the request of the Army, to serve on the staff of the Biarritz-American University, training G.I.'s in production techniques and at the same time directing them in actual productions.

McCleery and actor-director Richard Whorf walked into Sonny's Bar in Biarritz late one night and saw Guthrie on a corner settee with his feet hunched up on a small coffee table, holding forth to about ten G.I.'s, all of them wrapped in overcoats and blankets against the coldest November France had known in years. Guthrie, on what must have been his tenth cognac, didn't seem to notice the cold as he held the young men spellbound with stories of Mrs. Patrick Campbell, Shaw, Winthrop Ames, and, of course, Katharine Cornell. Whorf surveyed the scene for a moment and said, "There sits a happy man. He's got a captive audience that has never heard any of his stories — aren't they lucky to hear them all at once." Of the one hundred and seventy-eight G.I.'s who attended courses at the Biarritz University, fifteen years later thirty-nine of them were professionally engaged in television, movies, or the theatre, a percentage that most established, prestigious theatre schools in the United States have never been able to boast. With a kind of superstitious prescience, Guthrie felt he was contributing to the future.

But he may not have been the happy man that he seemed.

In December 1950, between *That Lady* and *The Constant Wife*, Kit's production of *Captain Carvallo* by an English actor-playwright, Dennis Cannon, opened in Buffalo. With a cast that included Cedric Hardwicke and Nigel Bruce (Basil Rathbone's Dr. Watson in the movies), it was a kind of *Chocolate Soldier* comedy set "in the kitchen of a farmhouse in disputed territory." There is no way of knowing what there was in the play that attracted Kit, except that it gave her a chance to wear the kind of beautifully embroidered Bavarian dirndl she had worn with so much enjoyment at Haus Hirth. Guthrie may have been drawn to the play by the fact that Laurence Olivier had produced it in London.

The action required Kit to do a great deal of cooking on stage, and she took lessons at the Cordon Bleu so that she would manipulate the pots and pans correctly, but it didn't help. With Diana Wynyard still playing it successfully in London, *Captain Carvallo*, directed by Guthrie, in the tradition of *Herod and Mariamne* and *Rose Burke*, was the third production in Katharine Cornell's career to close out of town.

After the opening-night performance in Buffalo, Guthrie blew up completely. It was not new for him to do so, but whereas Kit had always made a superhuman effort to cover up his outbreaks (some say she was afraid of them), to smooth them over, to pretend they hadn't happened — to drop her curtain — in late years she had taken to meeting them head on, and members of various companies recall that the two of them even had open squabbles in rehearsal.

Sometimes it was necessary, in Kit's wish to protect other actors. Back as far as the opening of *The Doctor's Dilemma*, David Orrick, the assistant stage manager, had been told by Guthrie to pass on the order of curtain calls to the cast. He assumed — mistakenly — that Guthrie himself had already spoken to Kit and Ray Massey, and when the curtain came down, everyone knew what to do but the stars, who came running off the stage in a panic asking, "What do we do?" When the sloppy, erratic calls were finally over, the backstage door from the auditorium literally exploded open and Guthrie, his arms raised threateningly, burst like a maniac onto the stage roaring, "Where is he? I'll kill him!" With all the dignified first-nighters in their black ties and evening gowns filing in full of congratulations, Kit had to throw herself in front of David Orrick, shouting dramatically, "No, Guthrie! It wasn't David's fault!" (It was typical, of course, that she, who had been the most damaged of all, protected him; what is significant is that she lied to do it.)

No one will ever know what caused the big blow-up after the opening of *Captain Carvallo* in Buffalo. Perhaps Guthrie was drinking too much. An acquaintance who knew him for many years asserts that at about that time he was being shadowed constantly by a male attendant of a muscular and Germanic mien. But Gert Macy denies the allegation, and if Guthrie had such a legitimate shortcoming, she would honestly not deny it; in fact it is fairly safe to say she would be the first to point it out.

Whatever devil possessed him that night was apparently more undeniable than usual, for a witness remembers that Kit immediately cleared the room and shut herself in with Guthrie, alone, for the rest of the night. The same witness, who knew them both for many years, says that after that time Guthrie "just gave up."

When told that, Gert's response is to ask, "Gave up what?"

That Lady's troubles started out of town, too, in Toronto, where a reviewer wrote, "The new play at the Royal Alexander is a slow boat to 16th century Spain, in spite of praiseworthy efforts by skipper Katharine Cornell." The play did make it to New York, where things only got worse. A few days after the opening, with the reviews still filtering in, a young actor (and member of the company) called for Kit at 23 Beekman Place to walk with her to the theatre. He could hardly keep pace as she set off across town at a brisk clip, smiling and nodding to passersby. One imagines her whistling, but even if she wasn't, she was in a buoyant, whistling mood, chatting happily, relating amusing post-opening comments and happenings.

Finally, her young escort caught his breath long enough to interrupt her stream of good cheer to ask, "Miss Kit, how can you do it? This huge production — unfavorable reviews — jobs at stake — everyone downhearted — and you go on as if everything were perfectly fine! — how can you do it?"

"I'm the captain!" she smiled, not breaking stride.

There are those who say that after the opening of *Captain Carvallo* in Buffalo when Guthrie gave up, she became the captain in earnest and made all decisions from then on. She may have made them always, obliquely, indirectly, but now she made them openly. The protected became the protector.

Gert Macy claims not to have noticed anything different.

———

Kit could be grateful for Guthrie's interest in Peter Rock, even at the expense of her own, because it provided an occupation for his mind and an outlet for his energies. Busyness became very important. In the spring of 1951, just after the *Captain Carvallo* fiasco, Kit and Guthrie sailed for Spain with Conger Goodyear and his new wife, Zadie Bliss. Kit's letters are a catalogue of busyness: Embassy luncheons with Stanton Griffis (at that time American ambassador to Spain), motor trips with Frank McCarthy and Rupert Allen (the agent), cocktails with Cecil Beaton and Margaret Case, bullfights, religious festivals involving countless, detailed fiacre rides from church to church, and the names, one after the other — Pepy Weisberger (Arnold's father), Dr. Marañón (who had written two books on Antonio Pérez, Ana de Mendoza y de Gómez's lover), Phyllis Tucker (widow of Nion Tucker, owner of the *San Francisco Chronicle*), Nick Biddle, Señor del Camino, Angie Duke, the Gerald Murphys, etc. Really important business is carried on by cable, such as arrangements for mating her dachshund Cleo with Hope Williams's Porgy. Concern is expressed for the health of "my Illo." (Kit held him when he was put to sleep later that year. He was buried under the juniper tree outside the front door of Chip Chop, prompting Margalo Gillmore to hope that Illo and Laura Elliot were compatible since they were certainly stuck with each other for all eternity.) But through all the busyness, every tenth and sometimes every fifth line reads, "Guthrie seems really fine," or "There have been moments when I thought it might be too much for Guth," or "G. seems extremely well on the whole." His welfare is her preoccupation, his reactions a leitmotif. "I'm exhausted, but he wants to do it all," she writes, and keeps up with him.

Later in the 1950s when Kenyon College wanted to confer upon her an honorary degree, she did not want to accept because such excursions were a drain and this one would have disrupted other plans. But someone at Kenyon had the wisdom to approach her again, this time offering a degree not only to her but to Guthrie as well, and she accepted at once because Guthrie wanted to — he had never been given an honorary degree.

There were times when he moaned (never publicly, where he always spoke respectfully and lovingly of "Miss Cornell") that he couldn't produce and direct all the plays he wanted to because he constantly had to adjust his schedule to hers. Everyone close to her was entitled to such periodic dissatisfaction, because being close to her was demanding, but it was not in any way, as they all realized in the long run, confining. Gert managed to continue her producing career after the war, presenting three flops on Broadway and finally (in association with Walter Starcke) one success, *I Am a Camera*, John van Druten's dramatization of Christopher Isherwood's Berlin stories, the play that would one day form the basis for the musical *Cabaret*. Julie Harris was Gert's Sally Bowles. She also presented Martha Graham and her dance troupe on Broadway for five seasons and managed her European tour in 1954. All of which Kit urged her to do, and none of which interfered with the performance of her duties for Katharine Cornell. Guthrie himself went on after *Captain Carvallo*, to prestigious independent assignments, in the fall of 1951 taking a production of *Medea*, with Judith Anderson, to the Berlin Arts Festival under the auspices of the American National Theatre and Academy.

But it cannot have lightened his spirits or strengthened his sense of security that by co-producing *The Prescott Proposals* with Leland Hayward, he was forced to surrender the directing assignment to Howard Lindsay, co-author of the play (for whom, paradoxically, Guthrie had directed *Life with Mother*). On only one other occasion in thirty-five years had Kit worked with another director, Auriol Lee in the production of *Flowers of the Forest*, and even then, because Miss Lee was not well, Guthrie had always been on hand to participate extensively in the staging of the play.

This was not to be the case with robust Howard Lindsay, and *The Prescott Proposals* must have been a sad and difficult time for both McClintics, although they knew concessions had to be made. There came a point in rehearsals when Lindsay made it clear to Kit that there was no place in this play for her usual mannerisms, and she was requested, politely and respectfully, to give them up, in other words to change her way of acting. That night she wept as she was being driven back to Sneden's Landing, and the next day she smilingly and firmly informed Lindsay that since she had been engaged knowingly by responsible men, she assumed they had engaged her for her own special quality. She was too old now to change that quality, just because they had changed their minds.

Nor was Guthrie permitted to direct Kit's two television appearances, although his lack of experience in the medium made it understandable. And here, if Kit had to manage without Guthrie, she fared well with directors who were indeed delighted to have the Cornell quality — George Shaefer for *There Shall Be No Night* and Vincent J. Donehue for *The Barretts of Wimpole Street*. Donehue originally came from a town in upstate New York where he was first bitten by the theatre bug watching touring Katharine Cornell companies arrive and depart. He had turned up once before to ease Kit's life, in Vittel, France, just before the Battle of the Bulge, when he appeared suddenly out of the bitter cold, an unknown soldier, bearing firewood. Guthrie attended the television rehearsals, which, except for the frightening peculiarities of the medium, were reasonably happy times. The younger members of the cast were taken aback when the great Katharine Cornell chose to stay in the rehearsal hall while everybody else went to lunch, and the writer who did the television adaptation of *The Barretts* cherishes the thank-you note which eventually reached her addressed with utmost simplicity in Miss Cornell's illegible scrawl, "Ellen Violett, National Broadcasting Company, New York."

For all his low moments, Guthrie's resiliency was never clearer than in the buoyant mood of his autobiography, *Me and Kit*, but a line at the beginning, concerning the title, is worth noting: "My distinguished editor, Edward Weeks, suggested we call it *Kit and I*, I dare say secretly hoping the other name would boost the tome's box-office appeal . . . but as this story begins with me, I decided to take first billing and possibly keep the box-office appeal as well."

It is also worth noting that the book's jubilant publication in the fall of 1955 coincided with Kit's entrance into the New England Deaconess Hospital for her long-delayed chest surgery. From Spain in 1951 she had written, "I'm exhausted, but he wants to do it all," and she had kept up with him. Perhaps as time went on, exhaustion was revealing itself in seemingly unrelated and unexpected ways.

For years the McClintics and the Lunts had had a tacit agreement to keep each other posted of their plans in order to avoid overlapping or duplication. The Lunts had played *There Shall Be No Night* in New York and London all through the war — they were the only ones to have played it — and it was identified with them. In the mid-1950s they, like Kit, were becoming interested in the new medium of television, and the Sherwood play would have been a logical one for them to be considering doing when Kit suddenly, unexpectedly, without a word to them, did it on the *Hallmark Hall of Fame*. It may seem unimportant, but to appreciate the magnitude of the oversight one only has to imagine Guthrie's reaction — with Kit distracted from her own reaction by the violence of his — had the Lunts suddenly burst forth in *The Barretts of Wimpole Street*. In one so fastidious in her attention to theatre protocol and tradition, it was an inexplicable lapse.

An actor who played in *The Dark Is Light Enough* that same year recalls that "she was a lesson in remoteness, a lesson she herself had learned well and knew how to practice." Maybe she was not remote so much as she was tired, or exhausted — to use her own word — in the sense that she was working on by habit, rather than reason. To keep going consumed all vitality, with none left over to realize that the Lunts had been slighted. Distractions had to be shut out because they wasted dwindling time and energy; her curtain had to be lowered even on her contemporaries, if necessary — and not always arbitrarily, sometimes with excellent cause.

While she was touring *The Constant Wife* (with Robert Flemyng in Brian Aherne's role), one of the great comediennes of the past gave a party for her. As she was being greeted on arrival, Kit expressed the gracious opinion that her part in the play might be better acted by her hostess, who demurred, laughed her famous comedy laugh and said all the proper things, assuring Kit she was divine in the part. But as Kit moved on, the hostess turned her witty mischievous eyes on the rest of the guests and gave a broad comedy wink. When Ethel Barrymore was asked if she minded Katharine Cornell playing her old role in *The Constant Wife,* she said she would rather watch a ball game.

The actor who found her remote in *The Dark Is Light Enough* goes on to say, "But she knew everything that was going on, down to the smallest detail." Maybe she knew all that was being said about her, too, from her most esteemed colleagues down to the roisterers chanting, "Far above the Cort The-ayter. . . ." She may have reached a point where she was happier not knowing any of it and shut it all out.

That she was truly weary by the time she embarked on *Dear Liar* there can be no doubt. Guthrie had directed the two Fry plays, but by the late 1950s she agreed to let *Dear Liar* be directed by its author — the arranger of the letters — Jerome Kilty. Guthrie retained an active interest, however, as associate producer with S. Hurok.

Like all those who acted with her or served her in one capacity or another, Francis Robinson never really stopped ministering to her, but *Antony and Cleopatra* was the last production which he guided officially as press representative. From then on he devoted himself to his most consuming interest, the opera, and by the late 1950s had become assistant manager of the Metropolitan.

One day during rehearsals for *Dear Liar* Kit walked down to the old Metropolitan Opera House on Thirty-ninth Street, across from the site of the Empire Theatre, by then torn down, where she had played *Casanova*, *The Age of Innocence*, *Dishonored Lady*, *The Barretts of Wimpole Street*, *The Wingless Victory*, and *Candida*. Hatless, glove-less, in a loose summer dress, she sat in Francis Robinson's office and asked if she had to go on, was there any way she could get out of it? He said no, which was apparently what she had come to be told, to be reminded of her dedication to responsibility, because she went back to rehearsal and, when the time came, set out willingly on that last long, grueling tour.

On the West Coast, the actress known for the beauty of her voice went through periods when she lost it completely, and others when she could barely get through a performance. Known for her distinctive movement on the stage, there were times when the audience would have sworn she was losing her balance.

The New York reviews greeted the presentation as "pure gold," and Walter Kerr observed that "Katharine Cornell, unruffled in red velvet, moves like a benign and loving autocrat," but for theatregoers who through the years had fought for seats to see her at the Empire, the Martin Beck, and the Ethel Barrymore, it was a saddening experi-ence at the Billy Rose, where we sat huddled in small groups or in iso-lated melancholy in an auditorium meant to accommodate eleven hun-dred and sixty-eight people.

Only with the perspective of time and an overall view of her career does the true sadness of that last performance come clear, her own true discomfort. It was in reality a simple reading of the Shaw-Campbell letters, involving the simplest of props, two lecterns and a sofa. The curtain rose on an empty stage. Brian Aherne entered, to ap-plause, announced that he was Brian Aherne, held out his hand, and Kit entered. The first words out of her mouth were "I'm Katharine Cornell." The two actors remained themselves throughout the perfor-mance. Neither the script nor the director asked that they act or be-come Bernard Shaw and Stella Campbell.

A study of her career, the parts she played and the way she played them, leads to the conclusion that the way to make her most awkward on a stage was to make her be herself. Thus, she could not make a simple curtain speech, even when it had been written beforehand, or deliver an acceptable acceptance speech when presented with the Chi Omega Woman of the Year Award at the White House.

Her detractors said she was always Katharine Cornell on the

Last production: in costume as Mrs. Patrick Campbell in
Dear Liar, *1959. (Cecil Beaton, Condé Nast)*

stage, and in a way they were right since she submerged herself in all the parts she played, starting back in the Jessie Bonstelle stock days, permitting only facets of herself to surface in this role, other facets in that, allowing dark corners to be explored that she never exposed between roles as she too smilingly, too conscientiously, too dutifully, too even-temperedly, too modestly went about her life. She was none of her roles, and yet she was all of them. To understand her, one has to put them all together into one being, and then step back, squint the eyes, and look at them from a great distance — to see her Sydney Fairfield in her Madeleine Cary, her Madeleine Cary in her Juliet, her Juliet in her Countess Rosmarin. She was indeed herself on the stage, but in fragments, twisting each part to make it her own.

But once it was her own, it still had another name, a character's name for her to hide behind. She could come out on a stage and say "I'm Linda Esterbrook" and make you believe it, although she was only being herself. But there was something hang-dog in her way of saying "I'm Katharine Cornell," as if she were not at all sure any audience would accept such an outrageous improbability — and what is more, she wouldn't blame them if they didn't.

This became even clearer within *Dear Liar* itself. At one point she had to play a short scene — in cockney — as Eliza Doolittle in *Pygmalion*. Eliza may have been one of Mrs. Campbell's greatest roles, but it was a role that was never meant to be played by Katharine Cornell. It did not suit her talent, her style, her manner, her bearing, or her voice. And yet in *Dear Liar*, as gingerly as she approached it — siding with the audience, as if to say "You and I both know I can't get away with this, but I'll give it an amusing try!" — it was one of the high points of her performance, a moment when those of us watching felt some of the old excitement, simply because she was being allowed to act. She was being able to fulfill her original reason for going onto the stage: to become herself by not being Katharine Cornell.

To his dying day Guthrie carried his English penny in his shoe. He would only have his hair cut on Mondays or Wednesdays. An astrologer once told him he would die by drowning. At the start, Kit had tried to talk him out of his superstitions by poking holes in them. Once she sent her pertinent personal data to Evangeline Adams for analysis, signing her name K. Cornell and using a plain business envelope. When her detailed horoscope came back, the first sentence read, "You should have been circumcised." Since even this did not dampen Guthrie's belief, eventually it was easier for her to acquiesce and indulge his lifelong fear of water.

When the time came, in 1961, it was cancer of the kidney that took him. Many years before, on a trip to Russia, he had been alarmed by signs of blood in his urine, but for ten years after that he had experienced the best of health. He even recovered fully from a slight stroke suffered in his office.

But then came more blood, pain in the bladder, severe loss of weight, and by April 1961 he was seriously ill. After his death Kit said she had known from the start that he had cancer and would die, which may only have been hindsight, but on the other hand may have been her sometimes uncanny wisdom. She never betrayed the thought openly to another person, not even to Guthrie's doctor, lowering her curtain and simply getting on with the business at hand, which was to make his last days as pleasant as possible.

In only two ways did she indicate that she knew all along he was dying. During a period he spent in St. Luke's Hospital, when she could not be with him every moment, she asked that no one bring him a newspaper containing news of the death of a friend. She may have gotten the idea from her father.

When she took him home to his cell-like room amid the glories of Peter Rock, perhaps she suddenly realized that he had spent most of his adult life in a world of women, her close women friends, not all of whom found him compatible, pressing in and sometimes vying with him for Kit's attention. Her women friends were asked not to come to Peter Rock. On his last day, however, as if sensing it would be his last day, she asked if there were any of his own women friends he would like to see — Lillian Gish, whom he adored; or Hope Williams, one of his oldest friends, and a most beloved bridge partner; Marian Seldes, Jean Dixon, Margalo. But he said he would like to see Gert. Gert says he only said it to please Kit. When Gert came, he had nothing special to say, except that he was tired, so tired that he could not even lift his arm. He wondered if Kit was telling the doctors the right things. Kit had left them alone.

He had lived through their fortieth wedding anniversary on September 8, 1961, but in the late hours of Saturday, October 28, or rather the early hours of Sunday, October 29, he suffered a lung hemorrhage and died. His attendants did not awaken Kit until they had made him clean and peaceful to look at. Superstitious friends nodded sagely when they heard the news: as predicted, he had drowned — in his own blood.

Just as she had made all Kit's practical arrangements since 1928, Gert arranged for Guthrie's funeral. It was not to flout his love of grandeur, pomp, and embellishment but in adherence to her own principles of death with dignity that she ordered for him the most inexpensive cremation possible. She gave Kit the kind of service Kit wanted for Guthrie, in the simple Palisades Presbyterian Church, with lots of flowers. They had to put folding chairs on the lawn and pipe the service out on a public address system to accommodate all the mourners who seemed to flood in from nowhere by the busload. His ashes were strewn across the lawn at Peter Rock. Kit was moved beyond words — while everyone else was merely surprised — to learn that in his secretive squirrelish way he had saved up one hundred thousand dollars to leave to her. She saw to it that Estelle Winwood, very old and living frugally in Hollywood, received a legacy which, she said, Guthrie had privately commissioned her to pass on.

Guthrie had always been fond of quoting lines from the plays he directed, one of his favorites being Dubedat's credo in *The Doctor's Dilemma*: "I believe in Michelangelo, Velásquez and Rembrandt; in the might of design, the mystery of color, and redemption of all things by Beauty everlasting." Inscribing a photograph requested by Francis Robinson at the time of that production, Guthrie paraphrased Dubedat's credo to make it his own: "I believe in Will Shakespeare, Bernard Shaw, and Katharine Cornell; in the stimulus of a good play, the power of direction, and the magic of the theatre."

A week after his death, Robinson pointed out in a tribute in the Sunday papers that Guthrie, facing his own last agony, might have repeated — without paraphrase — the lines that lead up to Dubedat's credo: "I know that in an accidental sort of way, struggling through the unreal part of my life, I haven't always been able to live up to my ideal. But in my own real world I have never done anything wrong, never denied my faith. . . . I've fought the good fight."

There were six hundred letters after Guthrie's death. Gert Macy believes the large number was a tribute to Kit, rather than to Guthrie. It may be true, for when death comes, our concerns are rightly with the living. But the love and admiration for him are there, no matter whom the letters are addressed to. Helen Hayes wrote, "He was one of the dazzling personalities and talents of our bright world. Aren't you grateful to have been loved by him?" May Sarton, the writer, quoted V. Sackville West quoting Homer: "There is nothing more potent or better than this: when a man and a woman, sharing the same ideas about life, keep house together. It is a thing which causes pain to their enemies and pleasure to their friends. But only they themselves know what it really means." The truth seems to be that the letters were about both of them — written to both of them.

Guthrie always sent Kit a special message on the opening night of each play, containing a quote from the play itself which had special meaning for her, for him, or for the two of them together. The quotes usually involved the word love. He might have sent "There's beggary in the love that can be reckon'd" on the opening of *Antony and Cleopatra*. Very few of these messages have survived because they were so personal and of the moment. Those that have survived are too obscure to be understood. "She brings back the moment! Always!" from an unidentified play. "You bring your light with you, lady!" supposedly on the opening of *The Wingless Victory*, but it doesn't sound anything like Maxwell Anderson.

Had Kit, in turn, tried to find a line from one of her plays to illuminate the forty years she "kept house" with Guthrie, she might have selected this one, spoken by the Countess Rosmarin in the final moments of *The Dark Is Light Enough*:

> At the one place of experience
> Where we're most at mercy, and where
> The decision will alter us to the end of our days,
> Our destination is fixed;
> We're elected into love.

30

Finishing Out
the Week (1961-1974)

AT CHRISTMAS, two months after Guthrie's death, Kit wrote from Garmisch: "My heart gets very heavy at times. I miss Guthrie and the thought of Guthrie more than I ever thought I could — forty years of companionship goes very deep into one's being."

Kit and Nancy Hamilton were staying with Johanna Hirth. Walther had died after the war, and the American Army of Occupation had used Haus Hirth until the mid-1950s. When they departed, Johanna sold the pension (it is still operated as a country hotel) and retired nearby to Kleines Haus Hirth, a retreat Walther had built many years before. Kit wrote, "Johanna is really crippled with arthritis — her back and her knees, but she keeps moving and walking her dogs."

While at Garmisch, Kit and Nancy went to Munich several days for the opera — "it gives the house here a rest" — and then were driven to Lausanne, via Lucerne, to visit Noël Coward and the Brian Ahernes. In January 1962, Kit wrote from the Beau Rivage Hotel, where she and Aunt Lydia had stayed in 1911: "I don't feel myself yet — very little appetite or real interest . . . but now I must get back and get started on a new life without Guthrie. He has invaded every fiber of me for years — deeply deeply."

Life without Guthrie did not include a return to the stage. Even though C. & M.C. had ceased to function as a producing organization (it would be liquidated in 1963), Kit could have continued acting for other managements as long as she wanted to. But with Guthrie gone, there was no point. There was no announcement of an official retirement; she simply never went back to work after *Dear Liar*, except non-professionally. At last she was able to find the fun of it again, narrating a film about Martha's Vineyard, produced by Nancy Hamilton, and once singing a duet with Mary Martin, for friends, of "Tie a Yellow Ribbon 'Round the Old Oak Tree."

For forty years Kit had often quoted a speech written by Clemence Dane and spoken by aging Queen Elizabeth to young Will Shakespeare. Now, it might have been Katharine Cornell herself speaking at the end of her career, summing up her life and times in the theatre:

> *We climb, not because we will,*
> *Because we must. There is no virtue in it;*
> *But some pride.*

Friends knew that without Guthrie, Kit's need for companionship would be greater than ever before. They were anxious to help, and willing, but the established patterns of their own lives would make it difficult. Even Gert Macy, while she never ceased to be Kit's manager and general representative, was more and more involved with ANTA, the Martha Graham Foundation, and various councils on the arts.

Judith Anderson says that Kit led a charmed life, and Laura Elliot noted Kit's talent for attracting people she needed. Perhaps they were talking about the same thing. After Guthrie's death, the charm held. From Switzerland Kit wrote, "Nan has been a joy and strength. Packing and repacking and trying to keep me straight." Not without sacrifice, Nancy Hamilton continued to be a joy and strength for the rest of Kit's life.

Without Guthrie's presence, Peter Rock and Chip Chop became unwieldy and desolate for Kit to live in and too remote for Nancy's active interests. Peter Rock was not easy to sell because it had been so disproportionately expensive to build, with a design and arrangement suitable to the McClintics and very few others. As large as it was, it didn't even have a dining room, let alone a swimming pool or a tennis court. It had to be rented for several years when Kit and Nancy moved into the city. In the late 1960s it was sold to Rebekah Harkness, who added a pool and next to it a mirror-lined Pompeian red building with white marble columns, her own private ballet studio.

Kit bought a house on East Fifty-first Street in Manhattan, just around the corner from 23 Beekman Place where she and Guthrie had started. Nancy gave a house-restoration party with the guests in dark suits and long dresses sipping champagne amid the plasterers' scaffoldings. With Brian Aherne next door and Margalo Gillmore down the street, that stretch of East Fifty-first Street became known as Wimpole Street to knowledgeable neighbors with long memories.

At the Vineyard, Nancy created attractive living quarters out of the barn that had been the center of Kit's victory garden in World War II. The cement floor was taken up, and a cellar was built beneath it for a furnace. An abandoned lighthouse was moved onto the property and attached, with the upper section converted into a bedroom. A few hundred yards inland, The Barn, as it was officially named, was sheltered, snug, and less exposed to the elements than Chip Chop. When Kit was persuaded to sell Chip Chop and move into The Barn, Nancy added a bedroom for her, quarters for a live-in couple, guest rooms, and eventually, when Kit's health worsened, a room for a nurse. A swimming pool was also added and at one time, when Nancy felt Kit needed more exercise, a putting green.

Kit seems to have had no regrets at leaving the houses she and Guthrie had built. All her life she was fond of saying, with her inevitable smile, "I refuse to let anyone take away my good nature," and the rule applied to circumstances as well as changing ways of life, even in old age. Such strong emotional discipline may have been the very quality that made her existence seem charmed. She was as enthusiastic about her new homes as she had been about the old, and in making the transitions had no qualms about letting her friends choose gifts for themselves from among the relics in both Peter Rock and Chip Chop.

But she refused to part with the frayed, overstuffed chair from Guthrie's stage set for *The Dover Road*.

———

Helen Hayes said she never drew an easy breath when she wasn't working, and she didn't understand how Kit could retire. Kit countered that she had never drawn an easy breath while she *was* working and slipped into idleness as if it were her natural state. It was good to forget about diets, to wear clothes "that don't hurt," to play solitaire, to read and walk on the beach with the dogs. If she had been left to herself, she might have receded too deeply into the lassitude of her youth, but Nancy was so energetic and active by example, as Guthrie had been, that Kit was not given the chance. She worked at her hobbies, especially her marquetry, and even when her health failed she never gave up such activities as her chairmanship of Plays for Living, a service organization dedicated to the use of drama for the alleviation of human problems.

Nor did she ever lose the interest she and Guthrie had shared in new talent. When Stanley Murphy, a young Vineyard artist from Minneapolis, tried to support his wife and children by painting island homes on commission from their owners, Nancy brought his work to Kit's attention, and she commissioned him to paint Chip Chop. When the painting was delivered after months of painstaking work, Kit was so pleased and grateful that she sent the artist a telegram, then wrote a letter, also telephoned, and wept. She insisted on paying him twice the fee he had asked, reasoning that Chip Chop was really two houses thrown together.

With funds from the Peter C. Cornell Foundation, Kit restored the three-hundred-year-old Association Hall near Vineyard Haven that served as the Tisbury Town Hall, and Stanley Murphy was commissioned to paint the murals decorating the walls of the auditorium — today known as the Katharine Cornell Theatre. She became known to all the islanders, most of whom called her "Katharine," and she was so at ease in her charmed retirement that she even enjoyed her own celebrity, reacting with spontaneous delight and more than a little showmanship to the sudden attention paid to her in public places. When she died, the front page of the *Vineyard Gazette* carried a snapshot of her taken by Nancy Hamilton, sitting on Gertrude Macy's deck, looking over her shoulder, waving her hat —

The editor's caption read, "Always in greeting, never in farewell."

***

It was only a year or so after Guthrie's death that she began to experience spells of breathlessness. At times she could not walk across a room without gasping. Paul Dudley White, the heart specialist, came from Boston to Martha's Vineyard to see her. After an examination, he had private conversations with her lasting several hours each. His conclusion was that she was suffering from old-fashioned heart failure. With digitalis and care, he said, she could live normally for many years.

With care, she even traveled. In 1969 she took a group — Nancy, Brenda, Merrill Shepard (Brenda's husband), Stanley Gilkey, and several Vineyard friends — on a boat trip through the French canals, a trip she enjoyed especially because it was her own idea, a plan she conceived and followed through herself. Before coming home, she paid what would be her last visit to Johanna Hirth, but in December was not well enough to participate in Noël Coward's seventieth birthday celebration in London.

Her own eightieth birthday in 1973 came as a surprise, since almost everybody believed her to be only seventy-five. She fretted about the age deception that had been practiced since 1928 and was pleased to acknowledge the truth. The birthday was celebrated with Nancy Hamilton and Gert Macy in Naples, Florida, where there were visits from the Lunts, Brenda Forbes, Margalo Gillmore, Hope Williams, Anne Gugler, Bill and Lois Katzenbach (he restored Association Hall for her), and Kit's cousin Douglas Cornell and his wife.

For a special birthday gift, Nancy spent months preparing a tape of birthday greetings, with the well-wishers ranging from Sybil Thorndike, Laurence Olivier, John Gielgud, Joyce Carey, and Ralph Richardson to neighbors and tradespeople at Sneden's Landing and Martha's Vineyard. Ina Claire, when asked to contribute, could not believe that Kit was eighty. When informed that Kit had indeed been born in 1893, Miss Claire reportedly gasped, "But that's the year *I* was born! — does that mean *I* am eighty?" Ruth Gordon and Garson Kanin (they were married in Washington, D.C., during the tryout run of *The Three Sisters*) taped a dramatic sketch they wrote for the occasion. Ruth March, teaching at a girls' school in Pasadena and rehearsing a student production of the musical comedy *Of Thee I Sing*, had her pupils sing one of the Gershwin songs with special "Happy Birthday to Kit" lyrics, which Nancy used to open the tape.

A press report stated that the birthday tape runs seven and a half hours, and those who have heard it in its entirety say its value is in the cumulative effect of so many people — great and small, articulate and inarticulate — trying to express what Katharine Cornell meant to them. It is to be hoped that one day the tape will be shared, just as it is to be hoped that Nancy Hamilton, with her perception, wit, and gifts as a writer, will one day share her memories of Katharine Cornell. Of all those close to Kit, she was closest after World War II, especially during the last reflective, summing-up years after Guthrie's death, and she cannot help but have observations and insights into her friend's entire life that contradict the conjectures and impressions of others. It is only by juxtaposing all views that the vastness of Katharine Cornell's nature — and therefore her art — can eventually, effectually be transmitted and understood.

After the eightieth birthday celebration, Kit had to return to New York for a brief stay at Presbyterian Hospital.

In February 1974, on the occasion of her acceptance of ANTA's national artist award, she clowned by putting the gold medal to her eye like a monocle. But recalling Noël Coward's last visit to her before his death, she revealed her own weariness: "... he was very ill, and we had that feeling of illness together. He came in the door and took off his coat and said, 'I'm going to walk to Kit,' and he came, shuffling, to me."

The *New York Times* said that she then added, quietly, "All actors fall by the wayside, but I go on."

In April, at a gathering of the most distinguished names in theatre, the Katharine Cornell–Guthrie McClintic Room was dedicated at the New York Public Library's Theatre Collection at Lincoln Center. Brooks Atkinson and Martha Graham spoke, and Lillian Gish exhibited a biography of Katharine Cornell written in Russian by a Leningrad writer, Igor Stupnikov, who had — surprisingly — been able to gather all his material from sources within the Soviet Union.

A week before the ceremony, Martha Graham went shopping and brought back a new dress for Kit to wear — as she had once magically created Juliet's nightdress for the Buffalo opening of *Romeo and Juliet* — but at the last minute Kit was not sufficiently recovered from an attack of the flu to attend. Later that night, after the ceremony, she listened for a few moments to a tape recording of the speeches of praise, reminiscence, and congratulation, but she asked that it be shut off.

Early in June, at her request, a private hospital plane took her to Martha's Vineyard, where she was settled into her room at The Barn, its broad windows looking out to Aunt Rhoda's Pond, with Lake Tashmoo beyond. She was able to be taken driving several times. She was lucid until her last few days when she seemed to think her father was expected for dinner. She died at three o'clock on Sunday morning, June 12, 1974. The cause of death was pneumonia. Nancy Hamilton was with her. She called Gert Macy at Sneden's Landing, who called Francis Robinson with the news. On Monday morning the *New York Times* carried Katharine Cornell's photograph on the front page, wearing the Mainbocher gown from *Rose Burke*.

A few days later Nancy Hamilton arranged what she called a "walk-through" in the Association Hall near Vineyard Haven. A color photograph of Katharine Cornell, smiling and squinting in a slicker, walking into the wind on the beach near Chip Chop, was projected onto a movie screen in the hall she restored in 1971. It rained for the walk-through as it had rained for so many of her opening nights. As the bells tolled, islanders, friends, and strangers from as far as California entered to mingle for a few moments and exchange greetings and memories. As the *Vineyard Gazette* reported the afternoon, "Conversation was punctuated by recordings of Miss Cornell reading, primarily from the narration of *This Is Our Island*, the film written by Nancy Hamilton — selections from poems and plays as well — and gentle music of French impressionists. When Miss Cornell's voice would suddenly fill the hall, all talk would stop and her friends would freeze, some glancing quickly at the portrait, some looking unconsciously upward."

Her ashes were buried in the old cemetery behind Association Hall, with a white marble bench marking the place.

What is there to say about the extraordinary coincidence that Kit and Guthrie both died shortly after midnight on a Saturday night? Ruth Gordon said at the time it was because, like all truly great theatre people, they first had to "finish out the week."

———

Mildred Natwick says that to call her "Kit" was like calling the Ocean "Osh."

But Martha Graham says Kit is a gallant name.

Acknowledgments

SINCE IT HAS BEEN MY HABIT in libraries, both public and private, and bookstores, both retail and remaindered, to scan the indexes of all theatre histories, memoirs, and biographies for "Cornell, Katharine" and then digest the material on the spot, it is impossible to remember, let alone list, the published source of every bit of random information, opinion, and speculation found in these chapters. But the following books have been constant, invaluable sources:

I Wanted to Be an Actress by Katharine Cornell as told to Ruth Woodbury Sedgwick; *Me and Kit* by Guthrie McClintic; *Broadway* and *Broadway Scrapbook* by Brooks Atkinson; *Broadway in Review* and *Dramatis Personae* by John Mason Brown; *The B.O.W.S.* by Margalo Gillmore and Patricia Collinge; *A Proper Job* by Brian Aherne; *Curtain Going Up* by Gladys Malvern; *The Man Who Lived Twice* by Eric Wollencott Barnes; *People in a Diary* by S. N. Behrman; *Present Indicative* by Noël Coward; *The Passionate Playgoer* by George Oppenheimer; *The Player* by Lillian Ross and Helen Ross; *Laurence Olivier* by John Cottrell; *Life among the Playwrights* by John F. Wharton; *Here at The New Yorker* by Brendan Gill; *Immortal Shadows* by Stark Young; *Curtain Time* by Lloyd Morris; *Fanfare* by Richard Maney; *Show Biz* by Abel Greene and Joe Laurie, Jr.; *Smart Aleck* by Howard Teichman; *Myself among Others* and *My Side* by Ruth Gordon; *Miss Tallulah Bankhead* by Lee Israel; *Come My Boys* by Norman Hackett; and the entire *Burns Mantle Best Plays* series.

I give special thanks to Lynda Towle Moss for her cogent synthesis of facts and figures in "A Historical Study of Katharine Cornell as an Actress-Manager, 1931–1960," A Dissertation Presented to the Faculty of the Graduate School, University of Southern California, in Partial Fulfillment of the Requirements for the Degree of Doctor of Philosophy, June 1974.

For helping me to plow through sixty years of press clippings, magazine articles, correspondence, promptbooks, press releases, citations, budget plans, tour arrangements, photographs, and fan mail at the Katharine Cornell–Guthrie McClintic Room in the Lincoln Center Library of the Performing Arts, I am greatly indebted to Paul Myers, Curator of the Theatre Collection of the New York Public Library, and his efficient, congenial, interested staff: Rod Bladel, Dorothy Swerdlove, Don Fowle, Maxwell Silverman, and Monty Arnold.

Everyone who ever knew Katharine Cornell or only met her, worked with her or, it seems, only saw her in a play is not only willing but eager to tell about it. It was my hope and intention to get around to them all, but time and geography prevented me. My apology to the many I missed, and my thanks to the following, some of whose contributions were of the spirit and therefore intangible, others of whom gave hours of their time to correspondence and conversation, sharing scrapbooks, memories and letters:

Dame Judith Anderson, Michael J. Arlen, Brian Aherne, Walter Abel, Katherine Wilson Addinsell; Charles A. Baker, Melvin Bernhardt, Frederick Bradlee; S. Douglas Cornell, Joyce Carey, Julian Claff, Jane Cecil, Robert A. Carter; Mildred Dunnock, Anna Glenny Dunbar, Evelyn Diges; Lynn Fontanne, Robert Flemyng, Brenda Forbes, Charles Forsythe, Ruth March French, Sidney Fields; Martha Graham, Lillian Gish, Margalo Gillmore, Ann Tonetti Gugler, Stanley Gilkey, Jack Gage, William H. Gurney, Thomas B. Greenslade, Albertine (Mrs. Bryant) Glenny, John Gerstad; Nancy Hamilton, Charlton Heston, Maurice Hill, the late Johanna Hirth; George Jenkins; Mildred Oppenheimer Knopf; the late Alfred Lunt; Raymond Massey, Stanley Murphy, Delbert Mann, Edwine N. Mitchell, David Orrick McDearmon, Martin and Katherine Manulis, James and Kittie Michael; Mildred Natwick, Ralph and Barbara Nelson; Christopher Plummer, Helene Pons, Hilda (Mrs. Roderick) Potter; Francis Robinson, Tony Randall, William Roehrick, Sarah L. Rowe; Natalie Schafer, Marian Seldes, Kent Smith, Margot Stevenson, Edward Streeter, Wayne Simpson, Elizabeth Suppes; Peter Turgeon, Thomas Turgeon; Richard Zeisler.

I am particularly indebted to Charles and Patty McCallum for the days they spent at Garmisch-Partenkirchen on my behalf, talking with Frau Hirth.

My appreciation of William Abrahams's enormous contribution is implicit in the fact that, respectful of his authority, I think of him more as my friend than my editor.

My deepest gratitude is reserved, of course, for Gertrude Macy. I met Katharine Cornell only once, in 1943 at the Shubert Theatre in Boston where she was playing Masha in *The Three Sisters*. I was a private in the Army Air Corps, studying meteorology at M.I.T., and I presented myself backstage toward the end of a Saturday night performance hoping that Miss Cornell, whom I knew to be a compassionate woman, would be moved by my uniform to speak to me. I still have the letter I wrote to my parents the next day recounting the experience of being taken in hand by this Miss Macy who rather brusquely informed me that I had picked a very bad night and then, perhaps noting the expression on my face, continued:

"Miss Cornell has about ten friends in the audience who will come dashing back here the minute the performance is over. But I'll tell you what we'll do. I'll grab her as she comes off the stage, and if you'll stand here I'll direct her over to you before they have a chance to get at her. How's that?"

That was fine with me, and it has been fine with me over thirty years later to have her directing me once again, still telling me where to stand, this time figuratively, in order to catch Miss Cornell. It has all seemed predestined, and yet it will always be a source of wonder to me that of all the writers she could have chosen, Miss Macy chose me to be the first to write the life of Katharine Cornell. For three years she has shared with me the vast resources of her meticulous private files and the abundant riches of her retentive memory; she has been scrupulously fair in her evaluation of herself and the other characters in the tales she has told me and, more important, in allowing me my own interpretation of those tales; she has tolerated my flights of imagination; she has advised me, led me, bullied me, fed me, at times housed me, and at all times been my strongest support and most stimulating companion. In paying my lifelong debt of gratitude to Miss Cornell, I have willingly incurred another to Miss Macy.

TAD MOSEL

Index

Abe Lincoln in Illinois, 424, 441
Abel, Marietta Bitter, 404
Abel, Walter, 99, 113–114, 116, 209, 404, 408–409, 427
Actors' Club, 204
Actors' Studio, 471
Actors' Theatre, 179–180, 183, 249
Adams, Evangeline, 509
Adams, Franklin P., 164
Adams, Maude, 33, 37–38, 67, 105, 260–261
Addy, Wesley, 478
Adler, Luther, 315
Age of Innocence, The, 218, 222, 224, 228, 233
Ah, Wilderness!, 340
Aherne, Brian, 261, 263, 265, 298, 308, 311, 323, 351, 354, 365–366, 368, 371, 431, 452, 462, 482, 484, 507, 513, 515; as Robert Browning in *The Barretts of Wimpole Street*, 272, 361, 456, 458, 465
L'Aiglon, 33
Akins, Zoe, 52; *The Old Maid*, 402–403
Albanesi, Meggie, 134–136, 139, 144
Alcott, Louisa May: *Little Women*, 44, 49, 67, 90–98, 367
Alice in Wonderland, 28
Alien Corn, 22, 304, 311–313, 315, 317, 321
Allen, Rupert, 503
Allen, Viola, 34
American National Theater and Academy (ANTA), 16, 504, 518
American Theatre Wing, 445, 456–457
Ames, Winthrop (W.A.), 68, 107–110, 116, 121, 131, 134–135, 148, 150, 162, 168, 248, 324
Anderson, John, 310, 374
Anderson, Judith, 348, 402–403, 447, 450–452, 491, 504, 514
Anderson, Maxwell, 403–404; *Both Your Houses*, 403; *Elizabeth the Queen*, 403; *High Tor*, 404; *Mary of Scotland*, 340, 399, 403; *Saturday's Children*, 210, 249, 403; *The Star-Wagon*, 404; *Truckline Café*, 471; *Valley Forge*, 403; *The Wingless Victory*, 183, 375, 404–409, 487; *Winterset*, 403–404
Andreyev, Leonid: *The Life of Man*, 67
Anglin, Margaret, 105
Ann's Adventure, 90
Anouilh, Jean, 485; *Antigone*, 476, 478, 486
Antigone, 476, 478, 486
Antony and Cleopatra, 152–153, 475, 478, 480–483, 486, 488
Archer, William: *The Green Goddess*, 121, 147
Arlen, Michael: *The Green Hat*, 13, 175, 191, 193–210, 212, 241, 283, 362, 453, 475, 489–490
Arliss, George, 36, 121, 147, 150
Armstrong, Dr. A. Joseph, 334
Aronson, Boris, 484
Art and Mrs. Bottle, 264
Ashley, Arthur, 85
Ashton, Winifred. See Dane, Clemence
At 9:45, 90
Atkinson, Brooks, 33, 34, 37, 51–52, 53, 90, 169, 240, 274, 435, 483, 490, 518
Attwater, Alan, 265, 423, 433
Atwill, Lionel, 171, 176, 183
Aumont, Jean Pierre, 444
Autumn Crocus, 431
Awake and Sing, 403
Aylmer, Felix, 483

Bainter, Fay, 218
Baker, George Pierce, 53, 67
Baker, Mildred, 495
Band Box Theatre, New York, 52
Band Wagon, The, 377
Bankhead, Tallulah, 129, 130–131, 145, 148, 194, 204, 225, 249, 278, 280, 382, 456, 475, 481; in *The Green Hat*, 199–201

Barbara Frietchie, 33
Barker, Dr., 286, 296
Barker, Margaret, 264, 452
Barnes, Howard, 399
Barnes, Margaret Ayer, 233, 247; The Age of Innocence, 218, 222, 224, 228, 233; Dishonored Lady, 233–234, 236–240, 246–247, 252, 260–261
Barnes, Maude, 127–128, 144
Barnes, William, 127–128, 132, 144
Barretts of Wimpole Street, The, 7, 240, 247, 253, 257, 259–266, 268–277, 279, 281, 284, 287, 292–296, 298–300, 318, 321, 324–325, 327–331, 348, 359, 361, 384, 387, 401, 431, 473–474, 478, 483; Army tour of, 456–458, 460–467; on television: 485, 504
Barrie, James M.: A Kiss for Cinderella, 67; The Little Minister, 33; What Every Woman Knows, 398
Barry, Philip, 260, 403; Tomorrow and Tomorrow, 257, 269
Barrymore, Ethel, 34, 105, 233, 245, 288, 348, 399, 476, 482, 506
Barrymore, John, 118, 147, 325, 402
Barrymore, Lionel, 260
Bates, Blanche, 104, 181, 209, 249
Beach, Lewis, 209; The Square Peg, 166
Beaton, Cecil, 503
Becky Sharp, 33
Beecher, Janet, 109, 143, 146
Behrman, S. N., 379, 407, 426–429, 436; Biography, 424; Brief Moment, 293, 306; End of Summer, 340, 408, 424; No Time for Comedy, 424, 426–436, 483
Belasco, David, 33, 67, 75, 176–177, 195, 306, 480
Belasco Theatre, New York, 176, 178, 293, 306, 312, 322
Bel Geddes, Norman, 403
Bell, Archie, 270
Belloc-Lowndes, Mrs., 247
Belmont, Eleanor Robson. See Robson, Eleanor
Ben-Hur, 33
Benchley, Robert, 197–198
Benét, Stephen Vincent: John Brown's Body, 491
Bennett, Arnold, 107
Bennett, Constance, 299
Bennett, Richard, 403
Bergen, Edgar, 456
Bergere, Ouida. See Rathbone, Ouida Bergere
Bergner, Elisabeth, 365
Bernhardt, Sarah, 33–34, 40, 117, 278–279
Bernstein, Henry, 443; Rose Burke, 443–445, 455
Bernstein, Leonard, 484
Bertha the Sewing Machine Girl, 162
Besier, Rudolf, 281, 283, 290, 299, 348, 375; The Barretts of Wimpole Street, see under title
Beverly of Graustark, 315
Bijou Theatre, New York, 148, 151

Bill of Divorcement, A, 134–135, 138–139, 140–146, 156, 158, 160
Billy Rose Theatre, New York, 484, 507
Biography, 424
Bird, Richard, 183, 220
Bitter, Marietta. See Abel, Marietta Bitter
Bjornsen, Miss, 287
Blind Alleys, 70
Blinn, Holbrook, 180
Bliss, Zadie. See Goodyear, Zadie Bliss
Blithe Spirit, 458
Bocher, Main, 444, 519
Bogart, Humphrey, 210
Bonanova, Fortunio, 239
Bonstelle, Jessie, 38–39, 49, 67, 71–72, 74–79, 91–93, 95, 97–98, 114, 116–118, 120, 133, 166, 356
Booth, Shirley, 476
Booth Theatre, New York, 147
Boston Opera House, 473
Both Your Houses, 403
Boyer, Charles, 485–486
Brady, Alice, 49
Brady, William A., 49, 67, 77–79, 84, 86, 90, 98–99
Brady, William A., Jr., 166
Braithwaite, Lillian, 134, 262–263
Bramson, Karen: Tiger Cats, 176–179
Brando, Marlon, 471–474, 478
Brandon, Dorothy: The Outsider, 171, 173–175
Braslau, Sophie, 252
Brewer, Betty, 460
Brief Moment, 293, 306
Briggs, Dr. Horace, 19–20
Broadhurst Theatre, New York, 212
Brooklyn Academy of Music, 326
Brooks, Mary, 211
Brooks, Ruth, 211
Broun, Heywood, 67, 145
Brown, John Mason, 354, 367, 369, 397, 407, 424, 435, 481
Browning, Robert: "On the Balcony," 40
Bruce, Nigel, 500
Buckler, John, 295
Bülow, Baron von, 11–12
Burke, Billie, 105
Burr, Anne, 455
Bushido, 66
Busley, Jessie, 315
Byron, Arthur, 371, 402

C. & M. C. Productions, Inc., 253–254, 271, 359, 401, 427, 483, 488, 513
Cabaret, 504
Caesar and Cleopatra, 183
Cagney, James, 416–417
Cahill, Lily, 313
Campbell, Mrs. Patrick, 293, 307, 338, 484, 507, 509
Candida, 7, 179–187, 322, 324–326, 348, 408, 445, 471–473, 478, 486

Cannon, Dennis: *Captain Carvallo*, 500
Captain Carvallo, 500
Carey, Joyce, 92–93, 264–265, 286, 307–308, 323, 452, 517
Carnegie, Hattie, 237
Carter, Mrs. Leslie, 33, 104, 176, 205, 338
Casanova, 169–170
Case, Margaret, 503
Cass Theatre, Detroit, 372
Cavalcade, 263
Chaplin, Charlie, 299
Chatterton, Arthur, 372
Chatterton, Ruth, 115, 246, 260, 299
Cheating Cheaters, 73
Chekhov, Anton: *The Three Sisters*, 447, 449–453, 457, 472
Cherry, Charles, 148
Children's Hour, The, 403
Church Mouse, The, 293
Churchill, Winston, 463
Ciannelli, Eduardo, 371
Civic Opera House, Chicago, 299
Civic Repertory, 260, 361
Civilian Clothes, 117, 119–120
Claire, Ina, 272, 278, 340, 424, 426, 475, 517
Clark, Mark, 460–461
Clift, Montgomery, 500
Closser, Louise. *See* Hale, Louise Closser
Cohan, George M., 340
Cohan Theatre. *See* George M. Cohan Theatre, New York
Collinge, Patricia, 460
Colton, John: *The Shanghai Gesture*, 205
Comedy Theatre, New York, 53, 65
Compagnie des Quinze, La, 307
Constant Wife, The, 240, 431, 482–483, 487, 490, 506
Cooper, Gladys, 260, 427
Coquelin, 33
Corbin, John, 69
Cornell, Alice Gardner Plimpton (mother), 7–9, 11–12, 14–15, 19, 21–22, 24, 28–29, 30–31, 43–44, 50, 55, 182, 200, 306
Cornell, Douglas, 4, 6, 27, 32, 50, 138, 155, 244, 497
Cornell, Douglas, Jr., 30, 155, 205, 497, 517
Cornell, Gwendolyn, 50, 138, 155, 497
Cornell, John, 155, 205
Cornell, Katharine: awards, 16, 400–401, 485, 518; baptism, 16; birth, 7, 12; birth date changed, 49–50; death, 518–519; handwriting, 16; marriage, 136–137; nicknamed Kit, 19; at Oaksmere, 47, 51–52, 55–57; physical appearance, 13, 18, 41, 151–152, 279, 488–489; physical dexterity, 22–23, 35; portrait by Speicher, 186; pregnancy and abortion, 155–158; relationship with father, 30, 46–48, 276; relationship with Guthrie, 153–155, 249–250, 383, 386–387, 503; relationship with mother, 29–30, 44, 55, 182; at St. Margaret's School, 29–31, 36; with Jessie Bonstelle Company, 71–77, 90, 114; with Washington Square Players, 65–70; as

writer, 35–36, 40, 57; *I Wanted to Be an Actress*, 28, 72, 78, 419–420
ROLES PLAYED: Alexander the Great, 51; Ana de Mendoza y de Gómez, 482; Antigone, 476, 478; Candida Morell, 179–187, 195, 398, 445, 471–473; Cleopatra, 398, 478, 480–482; Crystaletta Eysicle, 31; Diane, 118–119; Dora, 76; Eileen Baxter-Jones, 129–131, 135–136; Eliza Doolittle, 509; Elizabeth Barrett, 257, 259, 268–277, 284–285, 292, 294–300, 318, 473–474, 478; Ellen Olenska, 222, 224, 230–232; Elsa Brandt, 304, 311–313, 317, 321; Grace Palmer, 73–74; Henriette, 169–170; Iris March, 13, 191, 193–210, 489–490; Jennifer Dubedat, 439, 441–442; Jo March, 91–98; Saint Joan, 371–372, 374–375, 378–379, 393–394, 399; Juliet, 23, 121–122, 321; 324–326, 341, 349, 352–359; Lalage Sturdee, 171, 173–175; Laura Pennington, 165; Leslie Crosbie, 215; Linda Esterbrook, 424, 426–429, 431–432, 434–436; Lucrece, 310–311, 321; Madeleine Cary, 233–234, 236–240; Malvolio, 53; Marcelle, 84–85; Mary Fitton, 162–165, 356; Masha, 447, 450, 453; Mis' Cary Ellsworth, 70; Mr. Kris Kringle, 31; Mrs. Frank Darrel, 70; Naomi, 362–364; Napoleon, 53; Oparre, 404–409; Rebecca West (projected), 319–321; Rose Burke, 443–445, 455; Countess Rosmarin Ostenburg, 483–484; Shirley Pride, 170; Shusai, 66–67; Signora Vanucci, 75; Suzanne Chaumont, 176–178; Sydney Fairfield, 142–143, 146, 156–157
PLAYS IN WHICH KC APPEARED: *The Age of Innocence*, 222, 224, 230–232; *Alice in Wonderland*, 28; *Alien Corn*, 22, 304, 311–313, 317, 321; *Ann's Adventure*, 90; *Antigone*, 476, 478; *Antony and Cleopatra*, 478, 480–482; *The Barretts of Wimpole Street*, 240, 268–277, 284–285, 292, 294–300, 318, 384, 456–458, 460–467, 473–474, 478, (television production) 485–486; *A Bill of Divorcement*, 157, 160; *Blind Alleys*, 70; *Bushido*, 66–67; *Candida*, 179–187, 445, 471–473, 478; *Captain Carvallo*, 500–501; *Casanova*, 169–170; *Cheating Cheaters*, 73–74; *Civilian Clothes*, 117; *The Constant Wife*, 240, 482–483, 506; *Daddy-Long-Legs*, 115; *The Dark Is Light Enough*, 483–484; *Dear Liar*, 506–507, 509; *The Death of Tintagiles*, 70; *Dishonored Lady*, 233–234, 236–240; *The Doctor's Dilemma*, 439, 441–442; *The Enchanted Cottage*, 165–166; *Fanny's First Play*, 76; *The Firstborn*, 484; *Flowers of the Forest*, 362–364; *The Green Hat*, 191, 193–210, 489–490; *Heaven*, 117–119; *Herod and Mariamne*, 420–424; *The Hidden Treasure*, 35; *The Letter*, 214–217; *The Life of Man*, 67; *Little Women*, 91–98; *Lombardi, Ltd.*, 116; *Lovers and Friends*, 455; *Lucrece*, 310–311, 321; *Man of Destiny*, 53; *The Man Outside*, 76; *The Man Who Came Back*, 79–80; *Neighbors*, 70; *Nice People*,

129–131, 135–136; *No Time for Comedy*, 426–429, 431–432, 434–436; *On the Balcony*, 40; *The Outsider*, 171, 173–175; *Pals First*, 76; *Plots and Playwrights*, 67–68; *The Prescott Proposals*, 483, 504; *Romance*, 75; *Romeo and Juliet*, 152, 324–326, 341, 349, 352–359; *Rose Burke*, 443–445, 455; *Rosmersholm* (projected), 319–321; *Saint Joan*, 371–372, 374–375, 378–379, 393–394, 399; *Seven Chances*, 75; *Stage Door Canteen* (film), 456; *That Lady*, 482; *There Shall Be No Night* (television production), 486; *The Three Sisters*, 447, 450–453; *Tiger Cats*, 176–179; *Too Many Husbands*, 116; *Twelfth Night*, 53; *The Way Things Happen*, 170–171; *Will Shakespeare*, 162–165, 356; *The Wingless Victory*, 183, 404–409; *Yum Chapab*, 70

Cornell, Lydia Hadfield (grandmother), 5–6, 19

Cornell, Lydia Hadfield (aunt), 3, 5–7, 15, 27–28, 32, 50, 120, 136–137, 205, 244, 358, 497

Cornell, Peter (cousin), 155

Cornell, Peter Cortelyou (father), 4, 6–8, 12–16, 24, 30, 32–34, 55, 74, 133, 137–138, 200, 207, 242–244, 288, 358, 420; relationship with KC, 14, 19–22, 25, 30, 43–47, 133, 137, 242, 253–254, 276; theater interests of, 27–28, 33–35, 71; death, 495

Cornell, Colonel S. Douglas, 4–6, 15–16, 27–28, 32, 400

Cornell, Samuel Douglas. *See* Cornell, Colonel S. Douglas

Cornell, Samuel Garretson, 4

Cornell, Sarah Bates Douglass, 4

Cort Theatre, New York, 472, 476

Cossart, Ernest, 183, 445

Coulouris, George, 372

Coward, Noël, 129–130, 144, 207, 408, 428, 513, 517–518; *Cavalcade*, 263; *Easy Virtue*, 264, 382; *Fallen Angels*, 218; *Private Lives*, 428; *Tonight at 8:30*, 408; *The Vortex*, 191

Cowl, Jane, 233, 264–265, 324–325, 340, 348, 355, 382, 475, 481

Craig's Wife, 181

Crawford, Joan, 247, 298

Criminal at Large, 305, 307, 384

Cromwell, John, 79

Crothers, Rachel, 128–130; *Everyday*, 148; *Nice People*, 128–131, 135–136

Crouse, Russel: *The Prescott Proposals* (with Lindsay), 483, 487–488, 491, 504

Cukor, George, 389–390, 392

Curran Theatre, San Francisco, 444

Curtis, Keene, 491

Curtis, Margaret, 441

Daddy-Long-Legs, 115

Dale, Alan, 145, 150

Daly, Augustin, 90, 180–181

Dane, Clemence, 163, 175, 219, 307, 340–341, 461, 514; *A Bill of Divorcement*, 134–135, 138–139, 140–146, 156, 158, 160; *Herod and*

Mariamne, 420–424, 433, 455; *The Way Things Happen*, 170–171; *Will Shakespeare*, 162–165, 356

Daniell, Henry, 432, 455, 482, 485

Dark Is Light Enough, The, 483–484, 487–488, 491, 512

Dark Tower, The, 323

David Copperfield (film), 361

Davies, Marion, 281

Davis, Ann, 171

Davis, Donald: *Ethan Frome*, 402

Davis, Owen: *Jezebel*, 326

Dead End, 403

Dean, Basil, 139, 142–143

Dear Liar, 484, 488, 506–507, 509

Death of Tintagiles, The, 70

De Cordoba, Pedro, 183, 308

De Forest, Marian, 44; *Little Women*, 44, 49, 67, 90–98, 367

De Kruif, Paul: *Yellow Jack* (with Howard), 338

Derwent, Clarence, 441

Deside under the Elms, 183

Digges, Dudley, 181, 445

Dillingham, Charles, 135–136, 139, 142, 145–146

Dillman, Bradford, 485

Dinesen, Isak, 488

Dishonored Lady, 233–234, 236–240, 246–247, 252, 260–261

Distant Drums, 293, 307

Divided by Three, 348

Divorcons, 104

Dixon, Jean, 510

Doctor's Dilemma, The, 320, 439, 441–442, 444, 501, 511

Doll Master, The (projected), 195

Doll's House, A, 319, 450

Donehue, Vincent J., 504

Donnelly, Dorothy, 181

Donovan, Bill, 40

Double Door, 377

Douglas, Kirk, 449

Douglass, David Bates, 4–5, 400–401, 489

Douglass, Sarah Bates. *See* Cornell, Sarah Bates Douglass

Dover Road, The, 131, 133–134, 148–151, 160

Drake, Alfred, 424

Dressler, Eric, 447, 449

Drew, John, 27, 34, 105

Drysdale, Arthur, 204

Drysdale, Eveline, 153, 204, 209, 227, 239, 289, 325, 327, 408, 444, 451, 492

Dunlop, Dr., 410

Dunnock, Mildred, 421–422, 424

Duse, Eleonora, 410, 460

Dyrenforth, James, 85, 87, 89–90

Eagels, Jeanne, 175, 194–196, 212

Eames, Clare, 181, 183, 261–262, 409

Earp, Shelton, 370

Easiest Way, The, 83

Easy Virtue, 264, 382

Eckert, Jules: *The Man Who Came Back*, 79, 83–86, 98
Einstein, Albert, 338
Eisenhower, Dwight D., 461
Electra, The, 293
Elizabeth the Queen, 403
Ellicott, Andrew, 4
Ellicott, Joseph, 4
Elliot, Laura, 66, 82, 144, 150, 217, 269, 279, 289, 436, 454, 503, 514
Elliott, Maxine, 36–37
Emery, John, 295, 351, 482
Empire Theatre, New York, 37, 105, 170, 186, 222, 233, 262, 268, 271–272, 277, 284, 293, 322, 407, 417, 507
Enchanted Cottage, The, 165–166, 184
End of Summer, 340, 408, 424
English Theatre, Indianapolis, 428
Enright, Florence, 53, 66
Erlanger, Abraham Lincoln, 34
Erlanger Theatre, Buffalo, 244, 325
Ernst, Morris, 316
Ervine, St. John, 118, 224; *John Ferguson*, 168
Escape from the Harem, 103
Escape Me Never, 365
Ethan Frome, 402
Ethel Barrymore Theatre, New York, 322, 430, 451, 475
Evans, Edith, 177, 351, 357, 452, 483
Evans, Maurice, 366, 368–369, 371–372, 402
Everyday, 148

Faber, Leslie, 93, 142
Fairbanks, Douglas, Sr., 298
Fairbanks, Douglas, Jr., 298
Fallen Angels, 218
Fanny's First Play, 76
Fata Morgana, 212, 260
Faversham, Julie Opp, 69
Faversham, William, 34, 69–70, 104, 288, 377
Félines, Les, 176
Ferguson, Elsie, 260
Ffrangcon-Davies, Gwen, 262, 367, 478
Fields, William, 433
Fighting Hope, The, 104
First Lady, 340
Firstborn, The, 484, 487–488
Fiske, Mrs., 33–34, 260, 319–320
Fitch, Clyde, 107; *Barbara Frietchie*, 33; *The House of Mirth*, 222; *Sappho*, 33
Flagstad, Kirsten, 370–371, 437
Flemyng, Robert, 427–428, 431, 506
Fletcher, Bramwell, 441
Flowers of the Forest, 348, 361–365, 367–368, 487, 504
Flush, 266, 272, 277, 294, 298, 330, 340, 374–375
Fontanne, Lynn, 67, 76, 340, 355, 375, 424, 426, 447, 456, 475
For Whom the Bell Tolls (film), 280
Forbes, Brenda, 260–261, 265–266, 269–270, 286, 308, 323, 346, 357, 362, 414, 437, 445, 452, 457, 460, 462, 517

Forbes, Ralph, 299, 441
Ford, Harriet: *In the Next Room*, 171
Forrest, Sam, 130
Forty-eighth Street Theatre, New York, 183
Forty-ninth Street Theatre, New York, 173
Freedman, Harold, 427
Frohman, Charles, 34, 37, 105
Frohman, Daniel, 90
Frueh, Al, 489
Fry, Christopher, 485; *The Dark Is Light Enough*, 483–484, 487–488, 491, 512; *The Firstborn*, 484, 487–488

Gabriel, Gilbert W., 406
Galantiere, Lewis: *Antigone*, 476
Gale, Zona: *Neighbors*, 70
Garbo, Greta, 203–204, 240, 362
Garland, Robert, 178, 481
Garrick Theatre, Detroit, 71, 76, 114, 196
Gate Theatre, Dublin, 324
Gates, Nancy, 348
Gaynor, Janet, 119
George, Grace, 77–79, 90, 92, 104, 482
George M. Cohan Theatre, New York, 143, 146
George Washington Slept Here, 453
Gerard, Rolf, 482
Gerecke, Miss, 211, 213
Gershwin, George, 206–207
Gibbs, Wolcott, 484, 489
Gielgud, John, 402, 517
Gilbert, Douglas, 419
Gilkey, Stanley, 224–225, 228, 237, 251, 257, 261, 306, 359, 368, 387, 392, 424, 453, 517
Gill, Brendan, 489
Gillette, William, 105
Gillmore, Frank, 90, 147
Gillmore, Margalo, 147, 169, 198, 205, 249, 264, 286, 315, 323, 339–340, 362, 427, 452, 456–457, 460, 463, 465–466, 497, 503, 510, 515, 517
Girl of the Golden West, The, 169
Gish, Lillian, 402, 417, 510, 518
Glass, Rose, 104
Glenny, Anna, 40–41, 43
Glenny, Bryant, 40–41, 43, 45, 115
Golden, John, 118–119
Gone with the Wind (film), 429
Good Earth, The (film), 280
Goodman, Benny, 456
Goodman, Edward, 52–53, 57–58, 65–66, 71
Goodner, Carol, 455
Goodyear, A. Conger, 43, 185–186, 253–254, 260, 272, 281, 289, 292, 302, 306–307, 315, 366, 389,' 400–401, 442–443, 487, 503
Goodyear, Zadie Bliss, 503
Gordon, Ruth, 181, 205, 210, 249, 293, 319, 402–403, 447, 450–452, 475, 517, 519
Graham, Martha, 324–325, 380, 504, 518–519
Granville-Barker, 180
Green Bay Tree, The, 428
Green Goddess, The, 121, 147

Green Hat, The, 13, 175, 191, 193–210, 212, 241, 283, 362, 453, 475, 489–490
Greene, Lorne, 483
Greenwich Village Theatre, New York, 147
Greenwood, Charlotte, 67
Griffis, Stanton, 219, 253–254, 260, 272, 281, 289, 292, 315–316, 401, 426–427, 487, 503
Gringo, 166
Group Theatre, 264, 361
Guardsman, The, 183
Gugler, Anne Tonetti, 209–210, 212–213, 217, 220, 284, 376, 413, 517
Gugler, Eric, 413, 498–499
Gwenn, Edmund, 447, 450–451, 457, 500

Haddon, Noel, 80, 98
Hadfield, Lydia. *See* Cornell, Lydia Hadfield
Hagen, Uta, 476
Hale, Louise Closser, 180
Halliday, John, 220
Halsman, Philippe, 488
Hamer, Gerald, 183
Hamilton, Nancy, 371, 423–424, 437–438, 457, 460–461, 513–519
Hamlet, 402
Hammond, Percy, 199, 312
Hampden, Walter, 322
Hanna Theatre, Cleveland, 270, 475
Hanson, Charles, 50
Harcourt, Cyril, 69
Harding, Ann, 196, 198
Hardwicke, Cedric, 262, 476, 478, 500
Harkness, Rebekah, 514
Harp of Life, The, 67, 107
Harris, Jed, 264
Harris, Julie, 476, 500, 504
Harris, Robert, 408
Harris, Sam, 130
Harris, William, Jr., 171
Harshman, Harold, 104
Hart, Moss, 434; *George Washington Slept Here* (with Kaufman), 453
Hayes, Helen, 145, 183, 278, 281, 340, 375, 397–399, 475–476, 512, 515
Hays, Will, 247
Hayward, Leland, 488, 491, 504
Heartbreak House, 169, 320
Heaven, 117–118
Hebbel, Friedrich: *Herod and Mariamne*, 420–424, 433, 455
Hecht, Ben: *Twentieth Century* (with Mac-Arthur), 118
Helburn, Theresa, 52–53, 80
Hellman, Lillian: *The Children's Hour*, 403
Helmore, Tom, 431
Henderson, Ray, 70–71, 82, 292, 298–299, 312–313, 329, 331, 334, 346, 359, 365–366, 374, 377, 420, 433, 436–437, 478; developing Cornell image, 288–291, 295, 318, 324–325, 348, 394; repertory tour plan, 321–323, 358; world tour plan, 412, 416; death, 417
Hepburn, Katharine, 264, 340, 437
Her Soldier Boy, 63

Herne, Chrystal, 181
Herod and Mariamne, 420–424, 433, 455
Hesse-Darmstadt family, 304, 418
Hester, Robert, 460
Heston, Charlton, 152–153, 480
High Tor, 404
Hirth, Johanna, 301–306, 317, 348–351, 376, 415, 418, 513, 517
Hirth, Walther, 300–303, 305, 349, 513
Hokinson, Helen E., 58
Home Again, 78
Hoover, Mrs. Herbert, 277–278
Hopkins, Harry, 450
Hopkins, Louise Macy (Louie), 211, 213, 237–238, 249, 449–450
Hopper, Hedda, 348
House of Mirth, The, 222
Housman, Laurence: *Victoria Regina*, 375, 399
Howard, Claire, 409
Howard, Esther, 88–89, 207
Howard, Leslie, 196–197, 402, 452
Howard, Sidney, 170; *Alien Corn*, 22, 304, 311–313, 315, 317, 321; *The Silver Cord*, 261; *They Knew What They Wanted*, 183, 382; *Yellow Jack*, 338
Howell, Maude, 323
Hoysradt, John, 323, 333, 335
Hoyt, John. *See* Hoysradt, John
H.T.P. *See* Parker, H. T.
Hull, Henry, 84–85, 106, 148
Humbolt/Humbert, Ada, 129, 135–1'6
Humphreys, Cecil, 441
Hunter, Glenn, 217–218
Hurok, S., 488, 506
Hush, 109
Hutton, Ina Ray, 456
Hyde, Susie, 217–220

I Am a Camera, 504
I Remember Mama, 471
Ibsen, Henrik: *A Doll's House*, 319, 450; *Rosmersholm*, 319–320, 348–349, 381
Idiot's Delight, 340, 375, 404
In the Next Room, 171
Insull, Samuel, 299–300
Irwin, Helen, 225
Isherwood, Christopher, 504

Jack o' Jingles, 95
Jackson, Anne, 478
James, Gee Gee, 427
Jameson, Lois, 372
Jane Eyre, 340
Jealousy, 217, 220
Jerome, Helen: *Pride and Prejudice*, 437
Jezebel, 326
John Brown's Body, 491
John Ferguson, 168
Johns, Alice, 323
Johnson, Moffat, 362
Jones, Mrs. Cadwalader, 222
Jones, Emma, 111, 132, 167, 210, 212, 226–227, 315

Jones, Ernest, 297
Jones, Robert Edmond, 52, 69, 181, 308
Jubilee, 377
Julius Caesar, 402–403

Kane, Whitford, 441
Kanin, Garson, 517
Katharine Cornell Foundation, 401–402
Katharine Cornell Theatre, Martha's Vineyard, 516
Katzenbach, Bill, 517
Katzenbach, Lois, 517
Kaufman, Beatrice: Divided by Three, 348
Kaufman, George S.: The Dark Tower (with Woollcott), 323; George Washington Slept Here (with Hart), 453
Kaye, A. P., 323, 408
Kaye, Danny, 453
Keeler, Jane, 40
Keen, Malcolm, 134
Keith-Johnston, Colin, 441
Keller, Helen, 437, 476
Kelly, Gene, 424
Kelly, George: Craig's Wife, 181
Kendall, Messmore, 215
Kerr, Walter, 507
Kiki, 480
Kilty, Jerome, 506; Dear Liar, 484, 488, 506–507, 509
Kimball, Jeannette, 119
King, Dennis, 447, 450–451
King, Samuel Arthur, 227–228
Kingsley, Sidney: Dead End, 403
Kiss for Cinderella, A, 67
Klaw Theatre, New York, 129, 131
Kleiber, Ruth, 301–302
Klinge, Joanna, 293, 325, 327
Knopf, Christopher, 424
Knopf, Mildred Oppenheimer, 159, 207, 209, 415, 424
Knox, Alexander, 447
Koiransky, Alexander, 449
Korff, Arnold, 231
Kortner, Fritz, 420–422
Kruger, Otto, 162, 165

Lady in the Dark, 434
Lake, The, 264
Langner, Lawrence, 52, 77, 80
Larrimore, Francine, 129, 306
Last of Mrs. Cheyney, The, 281
Latham, Fred, 135–136, 139
Laughton, Charles, 281
Lawrence, Gertrude, 408, 424, 428, 434
Lawson, Wilfred, 431, 478
Lederer, Francis, 431–432
Lee, Auriol, 363, 504
Leech, Margaret: Divided by Three, 348
Le Gallienne, Eva, 260, 322, 361
Leigh, Vivien, 429–431
Lenihan, Winifred, 90, 149, 162, 170
Let's Face It, 453
Letter, The, 214–217, 383
Letty Lynton, 247

Lewis, Morgan: One for the Money, 423–424
Life of Man, The, 67
Life with Father, 293
Life with Mother, 504
Liliom, 491
Lindsay, Howard, 504; The Prescott Proposals (with Crouse), 483, 487–488, 491, 504
Litell, Robert, 272
Little Minister, The, 33
Little Theatre, New York, 107, 109
Little Women, 44, 49, 67, 90–98, 367
Litvinov, Maxim, 450
Lockridge, Richard, 357
Loew's Seventh Avenue Theatre, New York, 80
Lois Theatre, Seattle, 104
Lombard, Carole, 118
Lombardi, Ltd., 116, 426
Loraine, Robert, 177–178, 308
Lord, Pauline, 293, 402
Lovers and Friends, 455, 487
Lucrece, 307–308, 310–311, 321, 401, 437, 443, 487
Lulu Belle, 176
Lunt, Alfred, 183, 340, 375, 424, 447, 456, 461, 505–506, 517
Lyceum Theatre, New York, 170

McAllister, Lon, 456
Macauley, Rose, 64
MacArthur, Charles: Twentieth Century (with Hecht), 118
McCarthy, Frank, 462, 503
McCarthy, Lillah, 439
McCleery, Albert, 499
McClintic, Edgar Daggs, 100–102, 104–105, 133
McClintic, Ella Florence, 100–101, 104, 133
McClintic, Guthrie, 98, 100–112, 121, 127–128, 131–134, 144, 146, 152, 181, 203, 210, 213, 217, 226–227, 247–248, 257, 259, 305, 382–385, 387, 403–404, 500; relationship with Katharine Cornell, 68, 80–82, 99, 114–115, 119, 122–123, 137, 151, 160, 350; Me and Kit, 505; as actor, 106, 116–117, 218, 220, 457, 465, 478; death, 510–512
AS DIRECTOR AND/OR PRODUCER: directing Katharine Cornell, 114, 118, 171, 238, 269, 356, 404–406; technique as director, 116, 149, 253, 248–249, 268, 323–324, 366, 385; The Age of Innocence, 218; Alien Corn, 313; The Barretts of Wimpole Street, 259–260, 262–266, 268–272, 292; Brief Moment, 306–370; Candida, 326; Captain Carvallo, 501; Criminal at Large, 305; Dear Liar, 506; Dishonored Lady, 233; Distant Drums, 307; Divided by Three, 348; The Doctor's Dilemma, 441; the Dover Road, 131, 133, 148–151; Ethan Frome, 402; Fallen Angels, 218; Flowers of the Forest, 363; The Green Hat, 196; Gringo, 166; Hamlet, 402; Herod and Mariamne, 420–423; In the Next Room, 171; Jealousy, 220; Jezebel, 326; Medea,

504; *Mrs. Partridge Presents*, 181; *No Time for Comedy*, 426–427; *The Old Maid*, 402–403; *Once a Sinner*, 261; *The Playboy of the Western World*, 500; *Romeo and Juliet*, 324, 345–346, 351–359, 369; *Saint Joan*, 366, 371–372, 377; *The Shanghai Gesture*, 205; *The Square Peg*, 166; *The Three Sisters*, 447, 449, 452; *The Trial of Mary Dugan*, 261; *The Truth about Blayds*, 307; *The Way Things Happen*, 171; *The Wingless Victory*, 404–406; *Winterset*, 403; *Yellow Jack*, 338; *You Touched Me*, 500
McClintic, Mary Mathews, 100
McDermott, William, 270
McGowan, Kenneth, 145–146
McIntosh, Henry F., 230
MacLiammoir, Michael, 324
McMein, Neysa, 415
Macready, George, 323, 351
Macy, Gertrude (Gert), 225, 231, 246, 257, 264, 304–305, 327, 359, 368, 409, 413, 461, 498, 503–504
    RELATIONSHIP WITH KC: first association, 211–213, 216–217, 227–228; traveling, 218–219, 348; secretarial responsibilities, 220–221, 224, 242, 380, 419; as protector, 278, 286, 296; financial responsibilities, 315–316, 443, 487; and Guthrie McClintic, 248–252, 510–511; and Jimmy Vincent, 387–392; in *Dishonored Lady*, 252; and *The Barretts of Wimpole Street*, 266, 268, 292, 457; and *Herod and Mariamne*, 421–424; stage manager, 237, 271, 323; with C. & M.C. Productions, Inc., 253–254, 461
Macy, Louise. *See* Hopkins, Louise Macy (Louie)
Macy, Mary Lloyd (Min), 211, 249
Madden, Doris, 313
Maddern, Merle, 323
Maeterlinck, Maurice, 52
Mainbocher. *See* Bocher, Main
Majestic Theatre, Brooklyn, 85, 205
Majestic Theatre, Buffalo, 34
Major Barbara, 475
Man of Destiny, 53
Man Outside, The, 76
Man Who Came Back, The, 79, 83–86, 98
Maney, Richard, 433
Manhattan Company, 260
Manners, J. Hartley, 106; *The Harp of Life*, 67, 107; *Peg o' My Heart*, 67, 107
Mansfield, Richard, 33
Mantle, Burns, 67–68, 145–146, 183, 354, 374
March, Frederic, 281
March, Ruth, 353, 370–372, 375–376, 414, 421, 517
Margo, 403, 432
Marlowe, Julia, 33, 36–37, 278, 324–325, 355
Marshall, George C., 463
Martin, Mary, 514
Martin Beck Theatre, New York, 58, 322, 346, 354, 372, 375, 475
Mary of Scotland, 340, 399, 403

Massey, Edward: *Plots and Playwrights*, 67–68.
Massey, Raymond, 54, 70–71, 402, 424, 441–443, 445, 452, 455, 491, 501
Mathews, George, 100
Maugham, W. Somerset: *The Constant Wife*, 240, 431, 482–483, 487, 490, 506; *The Letter*, 214–217, 383; *Rain*, 212; *Too Many Husbands*, 112, 116
May, Ailleen, 103, 106
Medea, 504
Menken, Helen, 119, 402
Menuhin, Yehudi, 456
Meredith, Burgess, 361–364, 367, 403–404, 445, 447, 452, 471–472, 500
Merrill, Flora, 277
Merrill, Mrs., 47, 50–51, 54, 57
Messel, Oliver, 483
Metropolitan Theatre, Seattle, 329–330
Mielziner, Jo, 262, 269, 346, 351–352, 369, 377–378, 403, 405
Miller, Arthur, 471, 474
Miller, Gilbert, 170, 175, 218–219, 233, 253
Miller, Marilyn, 207
Miller, Dr. Sidney, 296–297
Milne, A. A.: *The Dover Road*, 131, 133–134, 148–151, 160; *The Truth about Blayds*, 307
Misalliance, 377
Modjeska, 33, 355
Moeller, Philip, 52, 80
Moissi, Alexander, 421
Molnár, Ferenc: *The Guardsman*, 183
Moore Theatre, Seattle, 104
Morehouse, Ward, 216, 481
Morgan, Alma, 115, 131
Morgan, Frank, 85, 99, 115–116, 119
Morris, McKay, 447, 457, 465–466
Moss, Lynda Towle, 275, 471
Mrs. Miniver (film), 462
Mrs. Partridge Presents, 181, 209
Murphy, Stanley, 516
Musgrove, Gertrude, 447, 482
Music Master, The, 67
Musset, Alfred de, 52

Nagel, Conrad, 85
Nash, Mary, 84, 98
Nathan, George Jean, 191, 455
National Theatre, New York, 408, 490
National Theatre, Washington, 445, 447
Natwick, Mildred, 408, 445, 452, 478, 484, 500, 519
Nazimova, Madame, 37
Neighborhood Playhouse, New York, 52, 368
Neighbors, 70
Neilson, Adelaide, 318, 324, 355
Nelson, Zell, 331
Nethersole, Olga, 33
New Faces, 437
New Theatre, London, 95
Nice People, 128–131, 135–136
Nicholson, Sidney, 97
Nielson, Jimmy, 153

Nixon Theatre, Pittsburgh, 480
Nizer, Louis B., 247
No Time for Comedy, 424, 426–436, 483
Nolte, Charles, 480
Noon, William, 457
Nordoff, Paul, 324, 349
Nun's Story, The (film), 485

Oberon, Merle, 456
Obey, André, 443; *Lucrece*, 307–308, 310–311, 321, 401, 437, 443, 487
O'Brian, John Lord, 28
O'Brien, Kate: *That Lady*, 482, 487, 502
Odets, Clifford, 403, 449; *Awake and Sing*, 403
Oenslager, Donald, 444
O'Keeffe, Georgia, 488
Old Country, The, 69–70
Old Maid, The, 402–403
Oliver Twist, 106
Olivier, Laurence, 414–415, 427–431, 452, 501, 517
Olson, Moroni, 351
Omar Khayyam, 238
Once a Sinner, 261
One for the Money, 423–424
O'Neill, Eugene, 52, 404; *Ah, Wilderness!*, 340; *Desire under the Elms*, 183; *Strange Interlude*, 214, 281; *The Straw*, 147
O'Neill, James, 34
Opp, Julie. *See* Faversham, Julie Opp
Oppenheimer, Mildred. *See* Knopf, Mildred Oppenheimer
Orrick, David, 372, 393, 432, 450, 478, 501
O'Shei, John, 243, 497
Outsider, The, 171, 173–175

Paddelford, Lawrence, 296, 299
Page, Geraldine, 476
Pals First, 76
Park, Anne, 63–64, 66, 70, 77, 82
Parker, Dorothy, 275–276, 318, 367
Parker, H. T., 174, 318, 324, 355
Pascal, Gabriel, 475
Paxinou, Katina, 280
Peary, Robert E., 30
Peck, Gregory, 447
Peg o' My Heart, 67, 107
Pemberton, Mrs. Brock, 283
Perry, Antoinette, 456
Perry, Elaine, 457
Petrified Forest, The, 403
Petticoat Fever, 467
Phelps, William Lyon, 295
Pickett, Hugh, 329
Pickford, Mary, 298
Pierce, George "Empire", 271, 277, 294
Pierce, Jo, 35
Pinero, Sir Arthur Wing: *The Enchanted Cottage*, 165–166, 184
Platt, George Foster, 108–109
Playboy of the Western World, The, 500
Playhouse, London, 260

Playhouse Theatre, New York, 77–78, 84, 99, 293
Plays for Living, 516
Playwrights' Producing Company, 424, 426–427, 433
Pleadwell, Theodora, 410
Pleasure Man, 234
Plimpton, Alice Gardner. *See* Cornell, Alice Gardner Plimpton (mother)
Plimpton, George Davis, 9
Plimpton, Lucy, 14, 63–64, 70, 77, 80, 115
Plimpton, Mary Augusta Tifft, 9, 14, 19, 24
Plots and Playwrights, 67–68
Plummer, Christopher, 491–493
Poli's Theatre, Washington, 224
Pollock, Allan, 135–136, 139, 142, 144, 146
Pollock, Arthur, 367
Porter, Cole, 453–454
Post Road, 377
Power, Tyrone, Jr., 367–369, 371, 484, 491–492
Powers, Tom, 447
Preetorius, Emil, 301
Prescott Proposals, The, 483, 487–488, 491, 504
Pride and Prejudice, 437
Private Lives, 428
Provincetown Playhouse, New York, 52
Pygmalion, 475, 509

Quayle, Anthony, 484–485
Quo Vadis?, 33

Rain, 212
Rainer, Luise, 280
Rambeau, Marjorie, 73
Randall, Anthony (Tony), 478, 486, 490
Rathbone, Basil, 323, 327, 334–335, 346, 349, 354, 361, 366, 369, 381
Rathbone, Ouida Bergere, 325, 335
Reed, Florence, 205, 367, 421
Reed, Walter, 338
Reilly sisters, 359
Reinhardt, Max, 248
Rennie, James, 313, 348
Reunion in Vienna, 340
Rice, Vernon, 472
Richard II, 402
Richardson, Ralph, 366, 517
Riley, James Whitcomb, 78–79
Ritter, Richard, 380
Robinson, Francis, 433, 444, 506–507, 511
Robson, Eleanor, 144; *In the Next Room*, 171
Roehrick, William, 370, 372
Roland, Gilbert, 299
Romance, 75
Romberg, Sigmund: *Her Soldier Boy*, 63
Romeo and Juliet, 152, 324–326, 345–346, 348–349, 351–359, 366, 368–369, 387, 402
Roosevelt, Eleanor, 17, 399–400, 450, 483
Rose Burke, 443, 445, 455
Rosmersholm, 319–320, 348–349, 381
Ross, Harold, 489
Ross, Robert, 457

Rostand, Edmond: L'Aiglon, 33
Ruined Lady (Ann's Adventure), 90
Rumann, Siegfried, 315
Ryman's Auditorium, Nashville, 332

Saint Joan, 169–170, 365–366, 368, 371–372, 374–375, 377–379, 393, 399
Santelli, Georges, 369
Sappho, 33
Sarton, May, 512
Saturday's Children, 210, 249, 403
Scarlet Sister Mary, 288
Schafer, Natalie, 47, 51–52
Schenk, Joe, 299
Seawell, David, 17
Sedgwick, Ruth Woodbury, 411, 419
Seldes, Marian, 362, 482, 510
Selwyn Theatre, Chicago, 197
Selznick, David, 429
Seven Chances, 75
Seventh Heaven (Heaven), 119, 431
Shaefer, George, 504
Shakespeare, William, 402; Antony and Cleopatra, 152–153, 475, 478, 480–482, 486, 488; Hamlet, 402; Julius Caesar, 402–403; The Rape of Lucrece, 307; Richard II, 402; Romeo and Juliet, 152, 324–326, 345–346, 348–349, 351–359, 366, 368–369, 387, 402; Twelfth Night, 52
Shanghai Gesture, The, 205
Shaw, George Bernard, 184, 187, 276, 290, 366, 377, 439, 442, 445, 473, 475, 484, 507; Caesar and Cleopatra, 183; Candida, 7, 179–187, 322, 324–326, 348, 408, 445, 471–473, 478, 486; The Doctor's Dilemma, 320, 439, 441–442, 444, 501, 511; Heartbreak House, 168–169, 320; Major Barbara, 475; Man of Destiny, 53; Misalliance, 377; Pygmalion, 475, 509; Saint Joan, 169–170, 365–366, 368, 371–372, 374–375, 377–379, 393, 399
Shea, Al, 293
Shearer, Norma, 281, 298, 387–389
Sheldon, Edward (Ned), 232–233, 236, 247; Dishonored Lady, 233–234, 236–240, 246–247, 252, 260–261; Romance, 75, 232
Shepard, Merrill, 517
Sherlock Holmes, 33
Sherman, Dr. DeWitt H., 3, 6
Sherman, Lowell, 169, 175, 437
Sherwood, Robert E., 424, 426; Abe Lincoln in Illinois, 424, 441; Idiot's Delight, 340, 375, 404; The Petrified Forest, 403; There Shall Be No Night, 486, 504–505
Shubert, J. J., 34
Shubert, Lee, 34
Shubert, Sam, 34
Shubert Theatre, New York, 445
Shubert-Majestic Theatre, Providence, 84
Shubert Teck Theatre, Buffalo, 224
Sillman, Leonard, 437
Sills, Milton, 90
Silver Cord, The, 261

Simonson, Lee, 80
Simpson, Wayne, 219, 226–227, 257, 286, 289, 315
Sitwell, Edith, 488
Skinner, Cornelia Otis, 162
Skinner, Otis, 36
Smith, Dodie: Autumn Crocus, 431; Lovers and Friends, 455, 487
Smith, Kent, 369, 372, 394, 408, 421, 478
So Long, Letty, 67
Sombrero Theatre, Phoenix, 488
Sophocles: Antigone, 476, 478, 486
Sothern, E. H., 36, 104, 324–325
Speicher, Eugene, 186
Spong, Hilda, 181
Sprague, Karl, 43–45
Spring Meeting, 427
Square Peg, The, 166
Squaw Man, The, 104
Stage Door Canteen (film), 456
Stair, Ed, 97, 133, 409
Stanley, Kim, 205, 476
Stapleton, Maureen, 476, 478, 500
Star Theatre, Buffalo, 33–35, 37, 39, 71
Star-Wagon, The, 404
Starcke, Walter, 504
Starr, Frances, 83, 169
Stein, Gertrude, 461
Stern, G. B., 219
Stevens, Ashton, 197
Stevens, Emily, 212
Stevens, Roger L., 488
Stevenson, Margot, 327, 336–337, 357
Stewart, David J., 478
Stewart, James, 338, 348
Stewart, Katherine, 245–247
Stolen by Gypsies, 107
Strange, Michael, 147
Strange Interlude, 214, 281
Straw, The, 147
Streetcar Named Desire, A, 471
Streeter, Edward, 42
Strong, Austin, 118–119; Heaven, 117–118
Stuart, Emma, 285
Stuart, Kathleen, 285
Stupnikov, Igor, 518
Successful Calamity, A, 110
Sullivan, Margaret ("Sully"), 322
Summer and Smoke, 500
Sunny, 207

Talmadge, Norma, 299
Tandy, Jessica, 476
Tarkington, Booth: The Wren, 145
Taylor, Charles A., 103
Taylor, Deems, 170, 206, 308
Taylor, Laurette, 67, 103, 106–107, 169
Tearle, Godfrey, 478
Terry, Ellen, 182, 324
Thalberg, Irving, 278, 281, 298, 372, 387–388
That Lady, 482, 487, 502
Thatcher, Torin, 482, 484
Theatre Guild, The, 77, 80, 168, 183

There Shall Be No Night, 486, 504–505
Thesiger, Ernest, 366
They Knew What They Wanted, 183, 382
Third Avenue Theatre, Seattle, 103–104
Thomas, A. E., 142
Thompson, Dorothy, 420
Thompson, Woodman, 324, 345
Thorndike, Sybil, 366–367, 517
Three Sisters, The, 447, 449–453, 457, 472
Tifft, Eugene Gay, 319
Tifft, George Washington, 9
Tifft, Mary Augusta. *See* Plimpton, Mary Augusta Tifft
Tiger Cats, 176–179
Times Square Theatre, New York, 146
Toklas, Alice B., 461
Tomorrow and Tomorrow, 257, 269
Tone, Franchot, 228–229
Tonetti, Anne. *See* Gugler, Anne Tonetti
Tonetti, Lydia, 376, 413
Tonetti, Marie, 217, 284–285, 498
Tonight at 8:30, 408
Too Many Husbands, 112, 116
Toscanini, Arturo, 310
Treadwell, Sophie: *Gringo*, 166
Trial of Mary Dugan, The, 261
Trilby, 149–150
Truckline Café, 471
Truth about Blayds, The, 307
Tucker, Sophie, 453
Tulane Theatre, New Orleans, 333
Twelfth Night, 52
Twentieth Century, 118

Ulric, Lenore, 176, 480
Urmy, Linda, 424
Urmy, Mildred Dunnock. *See* Dunnock, Mildred

Valentina, 170, 429, 449, 480
Valley Forge, 403
van Druten, John: *Flowers of the Forest*, 348, 361–365, 367–368, 487, 504; *I Am a Camera*, 504; *I Remember Mama*, 471
Van Vechten, Carl, 145
Verneuil, Louis: *Jealousy*, 217, 220
Victoria Regina, 375, 399
Vincent, Dr. George, 349
Vincent, Jimmy, 219, 228–229, 330, 353, 382–385, 387–392
Violett, Ellen, 505
Vivian, David, 372
Voight, Frederick, 271
Vortex, The, 191

Waldron, Charles, 261, 308, 323, 335–336, 346, 352, 367, 371, 452
Walker, Laura, 84–85
Wallach, Eli, 480
Walter, Eugene: *The Easiest Way*, 83
Walters, Letha, 120
Wardlaw, Lillian, 142

Warfield, David, 67, 315
Warner, H. B., 148
Warrior's Husband, The, 437
Washington Square Players, 52–53, 65–70, 77, 80, 168
Watson, Douglas, 480
Watson, Lucile, 148
Watts, Richard, Jr., 240, 397
Way Down East, 33
Way Things Happen, The, 170–171
Webb, Clifton, 207, 220
Webb, Mabel, 220
Weeks, Edward, 505
Weill, Kurt, 434
Welles, Orson, 324, 335–337, 346, 351–353, 402, 471
Wertheim, Maurice, 80
West, Mae, 210, 234
Westley, Helen, 66, 80
Wharton, Edith: *The Age of Innocence*, 218, 222, 224, 228, 233; *Ethan Frome*, 402; *The House of Mirth*, 222; *The Old Maid*, 402–403
What a Life!, 467
What Every Woman Knows, 398
What Price Glory?, 183
White, Paul Dudley, 516
Whorf, Richard, 500
Why Marry?, 110
Wilder, Thornton, 307, 319, 324
Will Shakespeare, 162–165, 356
Williams, Emlyn, 305
Williams, Hope, 510, 517
Williams, Hugh, 362
Williams, John, 427
Williams, Tennessee: *A Streetcar Named Desire*, 471; *Summer and Smoke*, 500; *You Touched Me*, 500
Wilson, Francis, 179
Wilson, John Flemyng: *The Man Who Came Back*, 79, 83–86, 98
Wilson, Katherine (Kay), 348
Winchell, Walter, 224, 236
Wingless Victory, The, 183, 375, 404–409, 487
Winterset, 403–404
Winwood, Estelle, 109–112, 116, 122, 127, 218, 511
Wiseman, Joseph, 480
Wolcott, Frances M., 68–70, 82, 128, 133, 144, 161, 224–225, 288
Woman of Affairs, A (film of *The Green Hat*), 203–204, 362
Wood, Peggy, 169, 185
Woodham-Smith, Cecil, 485
Woods, Al, 162, 170, 195–196, 205, 217, 260
Woolf, Virginia, 277
Woollcott, Alexander, 145–146, 150–151, 166, 169, 181, 194, 232, 272–273, 293, 301, 306, 324, 331, 337, 391, 431, 449; *The Dark Tower* (with Kaufman), 323
Worthington, William, 322
Wren, The, 145
Wright, Grace Latimer: *Blind Alleys*, 70

Wright, Haidee, 162
Wuthering Heights (film), 428
Wycherly, Margaret, 181
Wylie, I. A. R., 414
Wyndham, Olive, 99, 109, 121
Wynn, Keenan, 424
Wynyard, Diana, 501

Yellow Jack, 338
You Touched Me, 500
Young, Stark, 178, 236, 357, 406–407
Yum Chapab, 70
Yurka, Blanche, 308, 311, 357

Zaza, 33, 104